Lecture Notes in Artificial Inte

T0238102

Edited by J. G. Carbonell and J. Siekmann

Subseries of Lecture Notes in Computer Science

Takashi Washio   Akito Sakurai
Katsuto Nakajima   Hideaki Takeda
Satoshi Tojo   Makoto Yokoo (Eds.)

New Frontiers in Artificial Intelligence

Joint JSAI 2005 Workshop Post-Proceedings

 Springer

Series Editors

Jaime G. Carbonell, Carnegie Mellon University, Pittsburgh, PA, USA
Jörg Siekmann, University of Saarland, Saarbrücken, Germany

Volume Editors

Takashi Washio
Osaka University, Inst. of Scientific and Indust. Research (ISIR), Osaka, Japan
E-mail: washio@ar.sanken.osaka-u.ac.jp

Akito Sakurai
Keio University, Kanagawa, Japan
E-mail: sakurai@ae.keio.ac.jp

Katsuto Nakajima
Tokyo Denki University, Tokyo, Japan
E-mail: nakajima@im.dendai.ac.jp

Hideaki Takeda
National Institute of Informatics, Tokyo, Japan
E-mail: takeda@nii.ac.jp

Satoshi Tojo
Japan Advanced Institute of Science and Technology, Ishikawa, Japan
E-mail: tojo@jaist.ac.jp

Makoto Yokoo
Kyushuu University, Fukuoka, Japan
E-mail: yokoo@is.kyushu-u.ac.jp

Library of Congress Control Number: 2006927428

CR Subject Classification (1998): I.2, H.2.8, H.3, F.1, H.4, H.5.2, I.5, J.1, J.3, K.4.3

LNCS Sublibrary: SL 7 – Artificial Intelligence

ISSN   0302-9743
ISBN-10   3-540-35470-0 Springer Berlin Heidelberg New York
ISBN-13   978-3-540-35470-3 Springer Berlin Heidelberg New York

Springer is a part of Springer Science+Business Media

springer.com

© Springer-Verlag Berlin Heidelberg 2006
Printed in Germany

Typesetting: Camera-ready by author, data conversion by Scientific Publishing Services, Chennai, India
Printed on acid-free paper   SPIN: 11780496   06/3142   5 4 3 2 1 0

Preface

Intelligent information technology has significantly progressed along with the rapid growth of computer communication networks in the last decade. The research in this domain became highly active under the worldwide growing environment providing the objective study issues. The research situation in Japan is no exception in this trend. An enormous number of studies in intelligent information technology are presented every year in Japanese domestic conferences associated with this field. Many of them are outstanding in terms of the technical originality, quality and significance. The annual conference of JSAI (Japan Society for Artificial Intelligence) is one of the key and representative domestic meetings in the field of intelligent information technology. In particular, award papers in this conference have an excellent quality in international standards. The annual conference of JSAI also organizes co-located international workshops to provide excellent study reports for worldwide researchers.

The objectives of this book are to present the award papers from the 19th annual conference of JSAI 2005 and the selected papers from the five co-located international workshops and to promote the study exchange among worldwide researchers. Five papers received awards among more than 200 presentations in the conference, and 40 papers were selected from the workshops of Logic and Engineering of Natural Language Semantics 2005 (LENLS 2005), Learning with Logics and Logics for Learning (LLLL 2005), Agent Network Dynamics and Intelligence (ANDI 2005), Conversational Informatics (CI 2005) and Risk Management Systems with Intelligent Data Analysis (RMSIDA 2005).

The award papers in the 19th annual conference of JSAI 2005 were selected from all presentations covering the wide fields of artificial intelligence through the processes of candidate recommendations, detailed open discussions and voting by Program Committee members of the conference. LENLS 2005 workshop was organized with the aim of bringing together researchers working on information structure and/or dynamic semantics, and of advancing the understanding of information structure and the development of dynamic semantics for natural language. LLLL 2005 workshop was held so as to bring together researchers who are interested in both the areas of machine learning and computational logic to have intensive discussions on various relations between the two and making their interchange more active. ANDI 2005 aimed at the investigation of network structures of agents, network structures made by agents and network structures and phenomena made by the agents' rational behavior. CI 2005 was to bring together researchers and practitioners from various backgrounds and projects to collect, process and utilize conversations as knowledge contents under recent advancement of media processing, ubiquitous computing and artificial intelligence technologies. RMSIDA 2005 was held with the goal of bringing together researchers working on advanced intelligent data analysis and practitioners working on risk analysis/management systems in real fields.

We believe this book will introduce excellent AI studies in Japan to the world and contribute to the growth of the worldwide community of AI researchers.

March 2006   Takashi Washio
Primary Volume Editor
JSAI 2005

Organization and Editorial Board

The award papers were selected by the Program Committee of the annual conference of JSAI (Japan Society for Artificial Intelligence) 2005. The paper selection of each co-located international workshop was made by the Program Committee of the respective workshop. Based on the decisions of the paper awards and the paper selections, each chapter was edited by the Program Chairs of the 19th annual conference of JSAI 2005 and the co-located international workshops. The entire contents and structure of the book were managed and edited by the volume editors.

Volume Editors

Primary Volume Editor: Takashi Washio (Osaka University, Japan)
Akito Sakurai (Keio University, Japan)
Katsuto Nakajima (Tokyo Denki University, Japan)
Hideaki Takeda (National Institute of Informatics, Japan)
Satoshi Tojo (Japan Advanced Institute of Science and Technology, Japan)
Makoto Yokoo (Kyushu University, Japan)

Chapter Editors (Program Chairs)

Award Paper Chapter:	Satoshi Tojo (Japan Advanced Institute of Science and Technology, Japan)
LENLS 2005 Chapter:	Norihiro Ogata (Osaka University)
	Katsuhiko Yabushita (Naruto University of Education)
LLLL 2005 Chapter:	Akihiro Yamamoto (Kyoto University)
	Kouichi Hirata (Kyushu Institute of Technology)
ANDI 2005 Chapter:	Satoshi Kurihara (Osaka University, Japan)
	Kiyoshi Izumi (National Institute of Advanced Industrial Science and Technology, Japan)
CI 2005 Chapter:	Yasuyuki Sumi (Kyoto University, Japan)
	Toyoaki Nishida (Kyoto University, Japan)
RMSIDA 2005 Chapter:	Takahira Yamaguchi (Keio University, Japan)

Table of Contents

Part III   Learning with Logics and Logics for Learning

Part IV   Agent Network Dynamics and Intelligence

Part V   Conversational Informatics

Part VI   Risk Management Systems with Intelligent Data Analysis

Part I

Awarded Papers

Overview of Awarded Papers:
The 19th Annual Conference of JSAI

Satoshi Tojo

Japan Advanced Institute of Science and Technology
1-1 Asahidai, Nomi, Ishikawa 923-1292, Japan
tojo@jaist.ac.jp

In this chapter, we introduce five awarded papers, selected from the 19th annual conference of JSAI (Japan Society for Artificial Intelligence) 2005. These five papers are truly excellent, for they were selected out of over 290 papers, the rate of which was less than 2%, voted by the total number of approximately seventy reviewers. As has been often mentioned, the research of artificial intelligence branches to many fields; among them, we could observe such tendency that empirical methods were rather prevalent compared with theoretical issues. However, we contend that the following five papers were both sound in theory and practical in feasibility. We show the synopses of the five papers, adding short comments for the award for each.

S. Hirano et al. presented a clustering method which could construct interpretable clusters from a dissimilarity matrix, that might include subjectively defined dissimilarities. The authors have shown experimental results on the synthetic, numerical data-sets, in which this method could produce good clusters even when the proximity of the objects did satisfy the triangular inequality. The authors applied this method to chronic hepatitis data-set, and showed that this method could absorb local disturbance in the proximity matrix and produce interpretable clusters. Thus, this method exceeds conventional ones in efficiency.

T. Kitamura et al. aimed at promoting knowledge sharing about functionality of artifacts among engineers, which tended to be implicit in practice. In order to provide a conceptual viewpoint for modeling and a controlled vocabulary, the authors have developed an ontological framework of functional knowledge. This framework has been successfully deployed in a manufacturing company. As an application of the ontologies, the authors proposed a metadata schema based on the functional ontologies for functional annotation in the Semantic Web. The paper was appreciated in that the method would contribute to the further development of engineering ontology.

K. Saito et al. presented a computational approach to support creating contents by recording and reusing the conversational contents as the reusable nuggets. The authors introduced the concept of the conversation quantization, a technique of approximating a continuous flow of conversation by a series of conversation quanta that represent points of the discourse, and showed that such conversation quanta were reusable as the conversational contents. The authors showed that the method

T. Washio et al. (Eds.): JSAI 2005 Workshops, LNAI 4012, pp. 3–4, 2006.

resolve several problems which had been regarded to be difficult by the conventional question-answering systems.

Y. Hayashi et al. presented an examination of learning contents design from knowledge level and symbol level viewpoints. This study was intended to develop a foundation for the sharing and reuse of the intelligent educational systems (IES) on a global platform. This approach would allow the sharing and reuse of academic and technical expertise in the field of IES study on a common platform. We expect that the approach would contribute to the further development of IESs.

M. Yokoo et al. considered a coalition formation of automated negotiation among self-interested agents. In order for coalitions to be stable, a key issue was the distribution of the gains from cooperation. In this paper, the authors demonstrated how the preceding solutions were vulnerable to various kinds of manipulations in open anonymous environments such as the Internet. To address these threats, the authors introduced a new solution concept called the anonymity-proof core. This method can be regarded to be influential because it can be applied to micro-economy, game theory, and other cooperative games.

I, on behalf of the program committee of JSAI 2005, would like to thank all the chairmen, discussants, and attentive audience who contributed to select these awarded papers.

On Constructing Clusters from Non-Euclidean Dissimilarity Matrix by Using Rough Clustering

Shoji Hirano and Shusaku Tsumoto

Department of Medical Informatics,
Shimane University School of Medicine
89-1 Enya-cho, Izumo, Shimane 693-8501, Japan
hirano@ieee.org, tsumoto@computer.org
http://www.med.shimane-u.ac.jp/med_info/{hirano, tsumoto}/

Abstract. In this paper, we present a clustering method which can construct interpretable clusters from a dissimilarity matrix containing relatively or subjectively defined dissimilarities. Experimental results on the synthetic, numerical datasets demonstrated that this method could produce good clusters even when the proximity of the objects did satisfy the triangular inequality. Results on chronic hepatitis dataset also demonstrated that this method could absorb local disturbance in the proximity matrix and produce interpretable clusters containing time series that have similar patterns.

1   Introduction

Clustering is a process of grouping objects based on the predefined (dis-)similarity measure and grouping criteria. A lot of approaches, for example, k-means, EM algorithms and BIRCH, have been proposed in the literature [1] and are widely and successfully used for exploratory analysis of the real-world data.

Generally, clustering methods employ the following procedure in order to deal with numerical data: (1) compute the dissimilarity of objects using the pre-defined measure such as Euclidean distance. (2) derive feature values that represent the global property of the group of objects such as centroid and variance. (3) derive the best partition or groups of objects that maximizes both inter-cluster homogeneity and between-clusters isolation.

However, it becomes difficult to form appropriate clusters if we can use only the dissimilarity matrix as intrinsic information and cannot refer to the raw data values. This is because the lack of attribute-value information may induce the difficulty in computing the global properties of groups such as centroids. Additionally, the choice of global coherence/isolation measures is limited if the dissimilarity is defined as a subjective or relative measure, because such a measure may not satisfy the triangular inequality for any triplets of objects. Although conventional hierarchical clusterings are known to be able to deal with relative or subjective measures, they involve other problems such as erosion or expansion of data space by intermediate objects between large clusters and the results are dependent on the orders of object handling [2].

T. Washio et al. (Eds.): JSAI 2005 Workshops, LNAI 4012, pp. 5–16, 2006.

In this paper, we present an indiscernibility-based clustering method called rough clustering. The main benefit of this method is that it can be applied to proximity measures that do not satisfy the triangular inequality. Additionally, it may be used with a proximity matrix – thus it does not require direct access to the original data values. In the experiments, we will demonstrate the usefulness of this method on synthetic data set and medical dataset.

2 Method

2.1 Preliminaries

Here we introduce some basic definitions on rough sets that are relevant to this paper. Let $U \neq \phi$ be a universe of discourse and X be a subset of U. An equivalence relation R classifies U into a set of subsets $U/R = \{X_1, X_2, ..., X_n\}$, in which all of the following conditions are satisfied: $(1) X_i \subseteq U, X_i \neq \phi$ for any i, $(2) X_i \cap X_j = \phi$ for any $i, j, i \neq j$, $(3) \cup_{i=1,2,...,n} X_i = U$. Any subset X_i is called a category and represents an equivalence class of R. A category in R containing an object $x \in U$ is denoted by $[x]_R$. Objects x_i and x_j in U are *indiscernible on* R if $(x_i, x_j) \in P$ where $P \in U/R$. For a family of equivalence relations $\mathbf{P} \subseteq \mathbf{R}$, an indiscernibility relation over $\mathbf{P}$ is defined as the intersection of individual relations $Q \in \mathbf{P}$. Note that in the following sections we use the term 'category' instead of 'cluster'.

2.2 Overview

Our method is based on iterative refinement of N binary classifications, where N denotes the number of objects. First, an equivalence relation, that classifies all the other objects into two classes, is assigned to each of N objects by referring to the relative proximity. Next, for each pair of objects, the number of binary classifications in which the pair is included in the same class is counted. This number is termed the indiscernibility degree. If the indiscernibility degree of a pair is larger than a user-defined threshold value, the equivalence relations may be modified so that all of the equivalence relations commonly classify the pair into the same class. This process is repeated until class assignment becomes stable. Consequently, we may obtain the clustering result that follows a given level of granularity, without using geometric measures.

There are two parameters that control the behavior of this clustering method: the threshold value T_h for refinement of equivalence relations and the number N_r of iteration of refinement. As shown in the experiments, N_r can be determined automatically, because the equivalence relations will be stable after several cycles of refinement. The refinement process can be terminated when no candidates for refinement appear.

2.3 Assignment of Initial Equivalence Relations

When dissimilarity is defined relatively, the only information available for object x_i is the dissimilarity of x_i to other objects, for example to x_j, $d(x_i, x_j)$. This is because the dissimilarities for other pairs of objects, namely $d(x_j, x_k)$, $x_j, x_k \neq x_i$, are determined independently of x_i. Therefore, we independently assign an initial equivalence relation to each object and evaluate the relative dissimilarity observed from the corresponding object.

Let $U = \{x_1, x_2, ..., x_N\}$ be the set of objects we are interested in. An equivalence relation R_i for object x_i is defined by

$$U/R_i = \{P_i,\ U - P_i\}, \tag{1}$$

where

$$P_i = \{x_j |\ d(x_i, x_j) \leq Th_{di}\},\ \ \forall x_j \in U. \tag{2}$$

$d(x_i, x_j)$ denotes dissimilarity between objects x_i and x_j, and Th_{di} denotes an upper threshold value of dissimilarity for object x_i. The equivalence relation, R_i classifies U into two categories: P_i, which contains objects similar to x_i and $U - P_i$, which contains objects dissimilar to x_i. When $d(x_i, x_j)$ is smaller than Th_{di}, object x_j is considered to be indiscernible to x_i. U/R_i can be alternatively written as $U/R_i = \{\{[x_i]_{R_i}\}, \{\overline{[x_i]_{R_i}}\}\}$, where $[x_i]_{R_i} \cap \overline{[x_i]_{R_i}} = \phi$ and $[x_i]_{R_i} \cup \overline{[x_i]_{R_i}} = U$ hold.

Methods for constructing initial equivalence relations, including the choice of dissimilarity measure, is arbitrary under the condition that it has the ability of performing binary classification of U. For example, one can simply use Euclidean distance and k-means with cluster number 2, if it is appropriate based on the property of the data. We have introduced a method for constructing initial equivalence relations based on the denseness of the objects in [3]; however, one may use another approach for this purpose.

2.4 Refinement of Initial Equivalence Relations

Suppose we are interested in two objects, x_i and x_j. In indiscernibility-based classification, they are classified into different categories regardless of other relations, if there is at least one equivalence relation that has an ability to discern them. In other words, the two objects are classified into the same category only when all of the equivalence relations commonly regard them as indiscernible objects. This strict property is not acceptable in clustering because it will generate many meaningless small categories, especially when global associations between the equivalence relations are not taken into account. We consider that objects should be classified into the same category when most of, but not necessarily all of, the equivalence relations commonly regard the objects as indiscernible. In the second stage, we perform global optimization of initial equivalence relations so that they produce adequately coarse classification to the objects. The global similarity of objects is represented by a newly introduced measure, the *indiscernibility degree*. Our method takes a threshold value of the indiscernibility degree as an input and associates it with the user-defined granularity of the categories. Given the threshold value, we iteratively refine the initial equivalence relations in order to produce categories that meet the given level of granularity.

Now let us assume $U = \{x_1, x_2, x_3, x_4, x_5\}$ and classifications of U by $\mathbf{R} = \{R_1, R_2, R_3, R_4, R_5\}$ is given as follows.

$$U/R_1 = \{\{x_1, x_2, x_3\}, \{x_4, x_5\}\},$$
$$U/R_2 = \{\{x_1, x_2, x_3\}, \{x_4, x_5\}\},$$
$$U/R_3 = \{\{x_2, x_3, x_4\}, \{x_1, x_5\}\},$$
$$U/R_4 = \{\{x_1, x_2, x_3, x_4\}, \{x_5\}\},$$
$$U/R_5 = \{\{x_4, x_5\}, \{x_1, x_2, x_3\}\}. \tag{3}$$

This example contains three types of equivalence relations: $R_1 (= R_2 = R_5)$, R_3 and R_4. Since each of them classifies U slightly differently, classification of U by the family of equivalence relations $\mathbf{R}$, $U/\mathbf{R}$, contains four very small, almost independent categories.

$$U/\mathbf{R} = \{\{x_1\}, \{x_2, x_3\}, \{x_4\}, \{x_5\}\}. \tag{4}$$

In the following we present a method to reduce the variety of equivalence relations and to obtain coarser categories.

First, we define an *indiscernibility degree*, $\gamma(x_i, x_j)$, for two objects x_i and x_j as follows.

$$\gamma(x_i, x_j) = \frac{\sum_{k=1}^{|U|} \delta_k^{indis}(x_i, x_j)}{\sum_{k=1}^{|U|} \delta_k^{indis}(x_i, x_j) + \sum_{k=1}^{|U|} \delta_k^{dis}(x_i, x_j)}, \tag{5}$$

where

$$\delta_k^{indis}(x_i, x_j) = \begin{cases} 1, \text{if } (x_i \in [x_k]_{R_k} \wedge x_j \in [x_k]_{R_k}) \\ 0, \text{otherwise.} \end{cases} \tag{6}$$

and

$$\delta_k^{dis}(x_i, x_j) = \begin{cases} 1, \text{if } (x_i \in [x_k]_{R_k} \wedge x_j \notin [x_k]_{R_k}) \text{ or} \\ \quad \text{if } (x_i \notin [x_k]_{R_k} \wedge x_j \in [x_k]_{R_k}) \\ 0, \text{otherwise.} \end{cases} \tag{7}$$

Equation (6) shows that $\delta_k^{indis}(x_i, x_j)$ takes 1 only when the equivalence relation R_k regards both x_i and x_j as indiscernible objects, under the condition that both of them are in the same equivalence class as x_k. Equation (7) shows that $\delta_k^{dis}(x_i, x_j)$ takes 1 only when R_k regards x_i and x_j as discernible objects, under the condition that either of them is in the same class as x_k. By summing $\delta_k^{indis}(x_i, x_j)$ and $\delta_k^{dis}(x_i, x_j)$ for all $k(1 \leq k \leq |U|)$ as in Equation (5), we obtain the percentage of equivalence relations that regard x_i and x_j as indiscernible objects. Note that in Equation (6), we excluded the case when x_i and x_j are indiscernible but not in the same class as x_k. This is to exclude the case where R_k does not significantly put weight on discerning x_i and x_j. As mentioned in Section 2.3, P_k for R_k is determined by focusing on similar objects rather than dissimilar objects. This means that when both of x_i and x_j are highly dissimilar to x_k, their dissimilarity is not significant for x_k, when determining the dissimilarity threshold Th_{dk}. Thus we only count the number of equivalence relations that certainly evaluate the dissimilarity of x_i and x_j.

For example, the indiscernibility degree $\gamma(x_1, x_2)$ of objects x_1 and x_2 in the above case is calculated as follows.

$$\gamma(x_1, x_2) = \frac{\sum_{k=1}^{5} \delta_k^{indis}(x_1, x_2)}{\sum_{k=1}^{5} \delta_k^{indis}(x_1, x_2) + \sum_{k=1}^{5} \delta_k^{dis}(x_1, x_2)}$$

$$= \frac{1 + 1 + 0 + 1 + 0}{(1 + 1 + 0 + 1 + 0) + (0 + 0 + 1 + 0 + 0)} = \frac{3}{4}. \tag{8}$$

Let us explain this example with the calculation of the numerator $(1+1+0+1+0)$. The first value 1 is for $\delta_1^{indis}(x_1, x_2)$. Since x_1 and x_2 are in the same class of R_1 and obviously, they are in the same class to x_1, $\delta_1^{indis}(x_1, x_2) = 1$ holds. The second value is for $\delta_2^{indis}(x_1, x_2)$, and analogously, it becomes 1. The third value is for $\delta_3^{indis}(x_1, x_2)$. Since x_1 and x_2 are in the different classes of R_3, it becomes 0. The fourth value is for $\delta_4^{indis}(x_1, x_2)$ and it obviously, becomes 1. The last value is for $\delta_5^{indis}(x_1, x_2)$. Although x_1 and x_2 are in the same class of R_5, their class is different to that of x_5. Thus $\delta_5^{indis}(x_1, x_2)$ returns 0.

Indiscernibility degrees for all of the other pairs in U are tabulated in Table 1. Note that the indiscernibility degree of object x_i to itself, $\gamma(x_i, x_i)$, will always be 1.

Table 1. Degree γ for objects in Eq. (3)

	x_1	x_2	x_3	x_4	x_5
x_1	3/3	3/4	3/4	1/5	0/4
x_2		4/4	4/4	2/5	0/5
x_3			4/4	2/5	0/5
x_4				3/3	1/3
x_5					1/1

Table 2. Degree γ after the first refinement

	x_1	x_2	x_3	x_4	x_5
x_1	3/3	3/4	3/4	2/4	1/5
x_2		4/4	4/4	3/4	0/5
x_3			4/4	3/4	0/5
x_4				3/3	1/5
x_5					1/1

Table 3. Degree γ after the second refinement

	x_1	x_2	x_3	x_4	x_5
x_1	4/4	4/4	4/4	4/4	0/5
x_2		4/4	4/4	4/4	0/5
x_3			4/4	4/4	0/5
x_4				4/4	0/5
x_5					1/1

From its definition, a large $\gamma(x_i, x_j)$ represents that x_i and x_j are commonly regarded as indiscernible objects by the large number of the equivalence relations. Therefore, if an equivalence relation R_l discerns the objects that have high γ value, we consider that it represents excessively fine classification knowledge and refine it according to the following procedure (note that R_l is rewritten as R_i below for the purpose of generalization).

Let $R_i \in \mathbf{R}$ be an initial equivalence relation on U. A refined equivalence relation $R'_i \in \mathbf{R}'$ of R_i is defined as

$$U/R'_i = \{P'_i, \ U - P'_i\}, \tag{9}$$

where P'_i denotes a set of objects represented by

$$P'_i = \{x_j | \gamma(x_i, x_j) \geq T_h\}, \quad \forall x_j \in U. \tag{10}$$

and T_h denotes the lower threshold value of the indiscernibility degree above, in which x_i and x_j are regarded as indiscernible objects. It represents that when $\gamma(x_i, x_j)$ is larger than T_h, R_i is modified to include x_j into the class of x_i.

Suppose we are given $Th = 3/5$ for the case in Equation (3). For R_1 we obtain the refined relation R_1' as

$$U/R_1' = \{\{x_1, x_2, x_3\}, \{x_4, x_5\}\}, \tag{11}$$

because, according to Table 1, $\gamma(x_1, x_1) = 1 \geq T_h = 3/5$, $\gamma(x_1, x_2) = 3/4 \geq 3/5$, $\gamma(x_1, x_3) = 3/4 \geq 3/5$, $\gamma(x_1, x_4) = 1/5 \leq 3/5$, $\gamma(x_1, x_5) = 0/5 \leq 3/5$ hold. In the same way, the rest of the refined equivalence relations are obtained as follows.

$$\begin{aligned}
U/R_2' &= \{\{x_1, x_2, x_3\}, \{x_4, x_5\}\}, \\
U/R_3' &= \{\{x_1, x_2, x_3\}, \{x_4, x_5\}\}, \\
U/R_4' &= \{\{x_4\}, \{x_1, x_2, x_3, x_5\}\}, \\
U/R_5' &= \{\{x_5\}, \{x_1, x_2, x_3, x_4\}\}.
\end{aligned} \tag{12}$$

Then we obtain classification of U by the refined family of equivalence relations $\mathbf{R}'$ as follows.

$$U/\mathbf{R}' = \{\{x_1, x_2, x_3\}, \{x_4\}, \{x_5\}\}. \tag{13}$$

In the above example, R_3, R_4 and R_5 are modified so that they include similar objects into the equivalence class of x_3, x_4 and x_5, respectively. Three types of the equivalence relations remain, however, the categories become coarser than those in Equation (4) by the refinement.

2.5   Iterative Refinement of Equivalence Relations

It should be noted that the state of the indiscernibility degrees could also be changed after refinement of the equivalence relations, since the degrees are re-calculated using the refined family of equivalence relations $\mathbf{R}'$.

Suppose we are given another threshold value $T_h = 2/5$ for the case in Equation (3). According to Table 1, we obtain $\mathbf{R}'$ after the first refinement, as follows.

$$\begin{aligned}
U/R_1' &= \{\{x_1, x_2, x_3\}, \{x_4, x_5\}\}, \\
U/R_2' &= \{\{x_1, x_2, x_3, x_4\}, \{x_5\}\}, \\
U/R_3' &= \{\{x_1, x_2, x_3, x_4\}, \{x_5\}\}, \\
U/R_4' &= \{\{x_2, x_3, x_4\}, \{x_1, x_5\}\}, \\
U/R_5' &= \{\{x_5\}, \{x_1, x_2, x_3, x_4\}\}.
\end{aligned} \tag{14}$$

Hence

$$U/\mathbf{R}' = \{\{x_1\}, \{x_2, x_3\}, \{x_4\}, \{x_5\}\}. \tag{15}$$

The categories in $U/\mathbf{R}'$ are exactly the same as those in Equation (4). However, the state of the indiscernibility degrees are not the same because the equivalence relations in $\mathbf{R}'$ are different from those in $\mathbf{R}$. Table 2 summarizes the indiscernibility degrees, recalculated using $\mathbf{R}'$. In Table 2, it can be observed that the indiscernibility degrees of some pairs of objects, for example $\gamma(x_1, x_4)$, increased after the refinement, and now they exceed the threshold $th = 2/5$. Thus we perform refinement of equivalence relations again using the same T_h and the recalculated γ. Then we obtain

$$
\begin{aligned}
U/R_1' &= \{\{x_1, x_2, x_3, x_4\}, \{x_5\}\}, \\
U/R_2' &= \{\{x_1, x_2, x_3, x_4\}, \{x_5\}\}, \\
U/R_3' &= \{\{x_1, x_2, x_3, x_4\}, \{x_5\}\}, \\
U/R_4' &= \{\{x_1, x_2, x_3, x_4\}, \{x_5\}\}, \\
U/R_5' &= \{\{x_5\}, \{x_1, x_2, x_3, x_4\}\}.
\end{aligned}
\tag{16}
$$

Hence

$$
U/\mathbf{R}' = \{\{x_1, x_2, x_3, x_4\}, \{x_5\}\}. \tag{17}
$$

After the second refinement, the number of the equivalence relations in $\mathbf{R}'$ is reduced from 3 to 2, and the number of categories is also reduced from 4 to 2. We further update the state of the indiscernibility degrees according to the equivalence relations after the second refinement. The results are shown in Table 3. Since no new pairs, whose indiscernibility degree exceeds the given threshold appear, refinement process may be halted and the stable categories may be obtained, as in Equation (17).

As shown in this example, refinement of the equivalence relations may change the indiscernibility degree of objects. Thus we iterate the refinement process using the same T_h until the categories become stable. Note that each refinement process is performed using the previously 'refined' set of equivalence relations.

3   Experimental Results

We firstly applied the proposed method to artificial datasets and evaluated its clustering ability. Note that we used numerical data, but clustered them without using any type of geometric measures. Next we applied the method to a real medical dataset.

3.1   Effects of Iterative Refinement

We first examined the effects of refinement of the initial equivalence relations. A two-dimensional numerical dataset was artificially created using Neyman-Scott method [4]. The number of seed points was set to 5. Each of the five clusters contained approximately 100 objects, and a total of 491 objects were included in the data. We evaluated validity of the clustering result based on the following measure:

$$
\text{Validity } v_{\mathbf{R}}(C) = \min\left(\frac{|X_{\mathbf{R}} \cap C|}{|X_{\mathbf{R}}|}, \frac{|X_{\mathbf{R}} \cap C|}{|C|} \right),
$$

where $X_{\mathbf{R}}$ and C denote the clusters obtained by the proposed method and the expected clusters, respectively. The threshold value for refinement T_h was set to 0.2, meaning that if two objects were commonly regarded as indiscernible by

20% of objects in the data, all the equivalence relations were modified to regard them as indiscernible objects.

Without refinement, the method produced 461 small clusters. Validity of the result was 0.011, which was the smallest value assigned to this dataset. This was because the small size of the clusters produced very low coverage, namely, amount of overlap between the generated clusters and their corresponding expected clusters was very small compared with the size of the expected clusters.

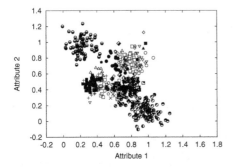

Fig. 1. Clusters after 4th refinement

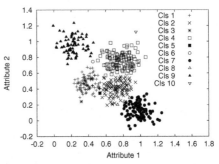

Fig. 2. Clusters after 6th refinement

By performing refinement one time, the number of clusters was reduced to 429, improving validity to 0.013. As the refinement proceeds, the small clusters merged as shown in Figures 1 and 2. Validity of the results continued to increase. Finally, clusters became stable at the 6th refinement, where 10 clusters were formed as shown in Figure 2. Validity of the clusters was 0.927. One can observe that a few small clusters, for example, clusters 5 and 6, were formed between the large clusters. These objects were classified into independent clusters because of the competition of the large clusters containing almost the same populations. Aside from this, the results revealed that the proposed method automatically produced good clusters that have high correspondence to the original ones.

3.2   Capability of Handling Relative Proximity

In order to validate the method's capability of handling relative proximity, we performed clustering experiments with another dataset. The data was originally generated on the two-dimensional Euclidean space likewise the previous dataset; however, in this case we randomly modified distances between data points in order to make the induced proximity matrix not fully satisfy the triangular inequality.

The dataset was prepared as follows. First, we created a two-dimensional data set by using the Neyman-Scott method [4]. The number of seed points was set to three, and a total of 310 points were included in the dataset. Next, we calculated the Euclidean distances between the data points and constructed a 310×310 proximity matrix. Then we randomly selected some elements of the proximity matrix and mutated them to zero. The ratio of elements to be mutated was set to 10%, 20%, 30%, 40%, and 50%. For each of these mutation ratio, we created 10 proximity matrices in order to include enough randomness. Consequently, we obtained a total of 50 proximity matrices.

We took each of the proximity matrices as an input and performed clustering of the dataset. Parameters used in the proposed method were manually determined to $\sigma = 15.0$ and $T_h = 0.3$. Additionally, we employed average-linkage and complete-linkage agglomerative hierarchical clustering methods (for short, AL-AHC and CL-AHC respectively) [2] for the purpose of comparison. Note that we partly disregarded the original data values and took the mutated proximity matrix as input of the clustering methods. Therefore, we did not employ clustering methods that require direct access to the data value.

Table 4. Comparison of the clustering results

Mutation Ratio[%]	0	10	20	30	40	50
AL-AHC	0.990	0.688±0.011	0.670±0.011	0.660±0.011	0.633±0.013	0.633±0.018
CL-AHC	0.990	0.874±0.076	0.792±0.093	0.760±0.095	0.707±0.098	0.729±0.082
Our method	0.981	0.980±0.002	0.979±0.003	0.980±0.003	0.977±0.003	0.966±0.040

We evaluated validity of the clustering results using the same measures as in the previous case. Table 4 shows the comparison results. The first row of the table represents the ratio of mutation. For example, 30 represents 30% of the elements in the proximity matrix were mutated to zero. The next three rows contain the validity obtained by AL-AHC, CL-AHC and the proposed method, respectively. Except for the cases in zero mutation ratio, validity is represented in the form of 'mean ± standard deviation', summarized from the 10 randomly mutated proximity matrices.

Without any mutation, the proximity matrix exactly corresponded to the one obtained by using the Euclidean distance. Therefore, both of AL-AHC and CL-AHC could produce high validity over 0.99. The proposed method also produced the high validity over 0.98. However, when mutation had occurred, the validity of clusters obtained by AL-AHC and CL-AHC largely reduced to 0.688 and 0.874, respectively. They kept decreasing moderately following the increase of mutation. The primary reason for inducing decrease of the validity was considered as follows. When the distance between two objects was forced to be mutated into zero, it brought a kind of local warp to the proximity of the objects. Thus the two objects could become candidates of the first linkage. If the two objects were originally belonged to the different clusters, these clusters were merged at an early stage of the merging process. Since both of AL-AHC and CL-AHC do not allow inverse of the cluster hierarchy, these clusters would never be separated. Consequently, inappropriately bridged clusters were obtained as shown in Figures 3 and 4.

On the contrary, the proposed method produced high validity even when the mutation ratio approached to 50%. In this method, effects of a mutation was very limited. The two concerning objects would consider themselves as indiscernible objects, however, the majority of other objects never change their classification. Although the categories obtained by the initial equivalence relations could be distorted, they could be globally adjusted through iterative refinement of the equivalence relations. Consequently, good clusters were obtained as shown in Figure 5. This demonstrates the capability of the method for handling locally distorted proximity matrix that do not satisfy the triangular inequality.

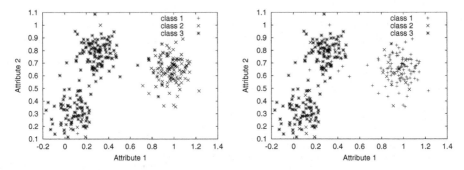

Fig. 3. Clustering results by AL-AHC. Ratio of mutation was 40%. Linkage was terminated when three clusters were formed.

Fig. 4. Clustering results by CL-AHC. Ratio of mutation was 40%. Linkage was terminated when three clusters were formed.

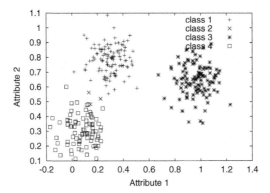

Fig. 5. Clustering results by the proposed method. Ratio of mutation was 40%. Iteration terminated at the fourth cycle.

3.3   Application to Medical Data

In order to evaluate the usefulness of the proposed method on real-world data, we applied it to a medical dataset. The dataset contained sequences of ALT values for 196 cases (Type C, with Interferon therapy) selected from the chronic hepatitis dataset [5]. The goal was to obtain interesting groups of cases that take similar temporal courses.

For calculating the dissimilarity between time series, we employed the modified multiscale matching [6]. This method compares two time series by partly changing observation scales. The resultant dissimilarity has the following characteristics: (1) comparison scales can be different for different pairs of time series; therefore, the dissimilarity should be dealt as relative dissimilarity that may not satisfy the triangular inequality for some triplet of the time series. (2) dissimilarity does not have direct relation to the original data values. (3) matching may fail due to, for example, the limitation in the variety of available scales. Consequently, the dissimilarity matrix has the similar characteristics as the artificial dataset shown previously.

The dissimilarity matrix contained 1,235,780 triplets. Out of them, 229,746 (=18.6%) did not satisfy the triangular inequality. This matrix was inputted respectively to AL-AHC and rough clustering. Figure 6 shows a dendrogram

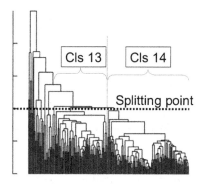

Fig. 6. Dendrogram obtained for 196 sequences obtained by AL-AHC

obtained by AL-AHC. With the aid of visual assessment of the grouped cases, we manually determined the splitting point on the dendrogram as shown in Figure 6. A total of 14 clusters were generated. Table 5 shows the cluster constitution (clusters are sorted according to the number of cases). One can see that there are two major clusters, 14 and 13, which are also shown in Figure 6. Table 6 shows the cluster constitution obtained by rough clustering. Similarly to AL-AHC, two large clusters, 5 and 1, were formed.

Figure 7 shows examples of the clustered sequences. The left of the Figure is sequences in cluster 14 generated by AL-AHC, and the right is sequences in cluster 1 generated by RC. Both clusters contained sequences for which ALT values were high at early phase and became low at late phase (seemed to be cured cases). However, AL-AHC included other types of sequences, as indicated by arrows, which show increasing trends at late phase. On the contrary, RC could exclude such cases and construct more coherent clusters.

Table 5. Cluster constitution (AL-AHC). NC=14. $N < 2$ omitted.

Cluster	14	13	11	9	8	12	10	4	7
Cases	99	64	7	6	4	4	3	2	2

Table 6. Cluster constitution (RC). NC=23. $N < 2$ omitted.

Cluster	5	1	2	8	11	7	10	12
Cases	87	77	5	3	3	2	2	2

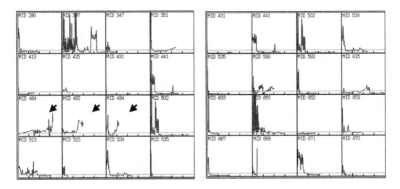

Fig. 7. Example of clustered sequences. Left: AL-AHC cluster 14, Right: RC cluster 1

4   Conclusions

In this paper, we have presented an indiscernibility-based clustering method called rough clustering, and demonstrated its ability of handling relative dissimilarity on both synthetic and medical data sets. The results showed that the method could generate good clusters even if the dissimilarity matrix locally violates the triangular inequality. Currently, the method requires the computational complexity about $O(n^3)$, due to the high cost for calculating the indiscernibility degrees. It remains as future work to reduce the complexity and find efficient implementation.

Acknowledgment

This work was supported in part by the Grant-in-Aid for Scientific Research on Priority Area (No. 13131208) by MEXT, Japan.

References

1. Berkhin, P.: Survey of clustering data mining techniques. Accrue Software Research Paper. URL: http://www.accrue.com/products/researchpapers.html (2002)
2. Everitt, B. S., Landau, S., Leese, M.: Cluster Analysis Fourth Edition. Arnold Publishers (2001)
3. Hirano, S., Tsumoto, S.: An indiscernibility-based clustering method with iterative refinement of equivalence relations. Journal of Advanced Computational Intelligence and Intelligent Informatics **7** (2003) 169–177
4. Neyman, J., Scott, E. L.: Statistical approach to problems of cosmology. Journal of the Royal Statistical Society, Series B20 (1958) 1–43
5. URL: http://lisp.vse.cz/challenge/
6. Hirano, S., Tsumoto, S.: Clustering time-series medical databases based on the improved multiscale matching. Lecture Notes in Artificial Intelligence **3488** (2005) 612–621

Towards Ontologies of Functionality and Semantic Annotation for Technical Knowledge Management

Yoshinobu Kitamura, Naoya Washio, Yusuke Koji, and Riichiro Mizoguchi

The Institute of Scientific and Industrial Research, Osaka University
8-1, Mihogaka, Ibaraki, Osaka, Japan
{kita, washio, koji, miz}@ei.sanken.osaka-u.ac.jp
http://www.ei.sanken.osaka-u.ac.jp/

Abstract. This research aims at promoting sharing of knowledge about functionality of artifacts among engineers, which tends to be implicit in practice. In order to provide a conceptual viewpoint for modeling and a controlled vocabulary, we have developed an ontological framework of functional knowledge. This framework has been successfully deployed in a manufacturing company. This paper firstly discusses an ontological definition of the concept of function from a device-centered viewpoint. Then, other types of function are discussed in order to place our definition in the related concepts in the literature. Next, as an application of the ontologies, we propose a metadata schema based on the functional ontologies for functional annotation in the Semantic Web. The functional metadata annotated to technical documents show designers intentions behind the documents and contribute to efficient retrieval of the documents. Moreover, task-oriented transformation and interoperability with other schemata can be realized based on the ontologies.

1 Introduction

The recent situation in engineering requires effective sharing of product knowledge among engineers. As well as data-level knowledge such as design drawings, geometry data in CAD systems and values of physical quantities, knowledge about functionality is very important to be shared. Intuitively, a function of a product explains what users can get using it (effects or utility of the artifact). A function of a component embedded in a system explains how it contributes to achieving the system's whole-function in so-called function structure (i.e., "how things work"). Such functional knowledge shows a part of designer's intention of artifacts (so-called design rationale (DR)) [2,16,26].

Nevertheless, in the current practical situation, such knowledge tends to be implicit behind the data-level knowledge. Even if such knowledge is explicitly described, it scatters around documents in natural language in an ad hoc manner. Its retrieval relies mainly on keyword-based search. Then, few such technical documents have been efficiently reused. For example, one might describe "to weld metals" as a function of a welding machine in a "verb+noun" style in Value Engineering [20]. However, "to weld metals" implies both the metals are joined and their parts are fused. From the viewpoint of functionality in manufacturing, joining is only the goal the designer intends to attain ("what to achieve"), while the fusion operation can be regarded as a

T. Washio et al. (Eds.): JSAI 2005 Workshops, LNAI 4012, pp. 17–28, 2006.

characteristic of "how to achieve that goal". In fact, the same goal, say, "to join", can be achieved in different ways (e.g., using nuts & bolts) without fusion. If a function of the welding machine is described as "to join", the commonality between two facilities can be found and then a search engine can find them. This issue, that is, distinguishing "what to achieve" from "how to achieve", is not a terminological but ontological.

The goal of this research is to add semantic annotation of functional knowledge based on an ontology for such technical documents in the Semantic Web. A functional annotation for a document shows functionality of a device mentioned in the document, what components achieve it and/or how to achieve it (function structure). It shows designer's intention behind the design drawings or semantic information for natural language documents. The semantic information enables us to search (and integrate) documents using a controlled vocabulary and relationship among concepts. A metadata schema for functional knowledge is designed to provide fundamental concepts such as function and entity, properties (relations) among functions and controlled vocabulary for generic functions. The fundamental concepts help knowledge authors to describe annotation consistently, and especially to distinguish "what to achieve" from "how to achieve". On the other hand, the controlled vocabulary provides a systematized set of generic verbs representing functionality of devices.

Although much research has been conducted on the representation of function in Artificial Intelligence [2,4,8,17,25], engineering design [5,6,18,21] and Value Engineering [20], there is no common definition of the concept of function itself [2,6,26] and semantic constraints are not enough for deriving effective guidelines for consistent annotation. The authors have established an ontological modeling framework for functional knowledge [9-12]. This framework includes an ontology of device and function as conceptual viewpoint and a functional concept ontology as a controlled vocabulary. This framework has been successfully deployed in a manufacturing company in Japan for sharing functional knowledge [11]. These ontologies form a basis of the metadata schema.

This paper discusses an ontological definition of function and its application to a metadata schema in the Semantic Web. Section 2 presents the ontologies about functions, which are defined on the basis of the concept of "role" in Ontological Engineering. It gives more detailed definitions to our previous definition in [9,10]. Section 3 discusses on other types of function in order to place our definition in the functional world in the literature. On the basis of the ontologies in Section 2, Section 4 proposes a metadata schema for functional annotation. The discussion in Section 3 contributes to realization of interoperability with other terminologies (i.e., schemata) for generic functions. Then, related work is discussed followed by some concluding remarks.

2   Ontological Definition of Functionality

Figure 1 shows a portion of ontological definitions of function-related concepts in our ontology editor of an environment for building/using ontology named Hozo [15]. Concepts are represented as frames (denoted by nodes in Fig. 1) with slots (right-angled link) and the *is-a* relations among concepts (straight link with "is-a"). Concepts are categorized into the wholeness concepts composed of part concepts and the relation concepts between the concepts. A wholeness concept has slots of part concepts (*part-of* relation denoted by right-angled link with "p/o") and slots of attributes ("a/o"). A relation concept has slots of participant concepts (*participate-in* relation. denoted by "p/i") and the attribute-slots.

The key concept of our definition of functionality is the "role" concept in Ontological Engineering. Intuitively, a role is something that can be played by an entity in a context. Precisely, in [23], a role is the secondness concept which is dependent on a pattern of relationship. In [19], a role is anti-rigid (i.e., contingent (non-essential) property for identity), dynamic (temporary and multiple), and founded (i.e., extrinsic property defined with external concept). Similar to these definitions, by role we mean here such a concept that an entity plays in a specific context and cannot be defined without mentioning external concepts [15]. We distinguish role (something to be played) from role-holder (something playing (holding) a specific role). For example, a man (class constraint for role) can play "husband role" (role concept) in a "marriage" relation (role context), who is called "husband" (role holder). Using Hozo, the marriage relation has two slots with *participate-in* relation, one of which is defined as a husband role with a man as a class constraint. It is defined also in the "married couple" which is a wholeness concept corresponding to the "marriage relation".

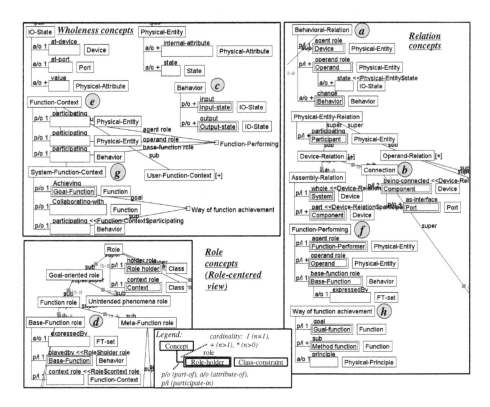

Fig. 1. A portion of an ontology of device-centered behavior and function in Hozo

As a basis of modeling of functionality, we adopt the device-centered view and then define the concepts of *device* and *behavior* (italics are defined terms). The *device* concept is defined as a role-holder in *behavioral-relation* between two *physical-entities* (Fig. 1 (a)). One of them plays the *agent* role, which is called *device*. It operates on the other entity (*operand* which is another role-holder) and changes its *physical-attributes*. Each *device* is connected to each other through its input and output *ports* (Fig. 1 (b)). The *operand* is something flows through the *device* and is affected by the *device*. The *operand* role can be played by fluid, energy, motion, force, or information. It has *IO-States*, which represents values of *physical-attributes* at a *port* of a *device*. The pairs of *IO-States* at *input ports* of a *device* and those at *output ports* of the same *device* are defined as *behavior* (Fig. 1 (c)). It represents objective (i.e., independent of the context) conceptualization of its input-output relation as a black box. Note that such a *behavior* of a *device* is founded [19], since a *behavior* of a *device* affects an *operand* and causes its temporal changes.

Such a device-oriented view comes from system dynamics theory and German systematic design approach [21], which is called a device ontology. We extended them by redefining the concepts of *behavior, conduit,* and *medium* [10]. We categorized the meanings of behavior into four types (from B0 to B3), one of which, called *B1-behaviour*, corresponds to the definition of *behavior* mentioned above.

In comparison with *behavior, function* is related to intention of a designer or a user (i.e., teleological). According to the definition of role in [19] and ontological consideration in [12], a function is a role. Firstly, a function is anti-rigid [19] and context-dependent (dynamic), because a function of a specific device can be changed without losing the device's identity. For example, a heat exchanger can be used as a heater or a radiator. The behavior is the same in any context, that is, a heat flows from the warmer fluid to the cooler fluid. The functions of the heater and the radiator can be "to give heat" and "to remove heat", respectively. This difference of functions is dependent on the embedded system, i.e., a context. Moreover, a function of a system can be recognized according to a user's goal (e.g., a chair can be used as a ladder or a hammer). A function can be performed by different components. A component can perform multiple functions simultaneously. Secondly, a function is founded [19] as *behavior* does. For example, the definition of the removing-heat function of a radiator refers to the decrease of temperature of the warmer fluid (i.e., external entity) as input and output.

Thus, a (base-)*function* is defined as a role concept which is played by a *behavior* under a *function-context* (Fig. 1 (d)). In the *function-context*, there is a *function-performing* relation among two *physical entities* and a *behavior* (Fig. 1 (e)). In the relation, a *behavior* plays a *base-function* role, which is called a *base-function* role holder (Fig. 1 (f)). A *device* which performs the *behavior* plays a *function-performer role* in the context. For example, the heat-exchange *behavior* plays the removing-heat *function* role and then a heat exchanger plays the *function-performer* role of removing-heat as a radiator.

The *function-context* represents teleological goals to be achieved by the *function*. A function-context of a function of a component in a system (called *System-Function-Context*, Fig. 1 (g)) can be determined by a goal function and method (sibling) functions, which are defined in *way of function achievement* relation (Fig. 1 (h)). It means that the *goal function* can be achieved by a sequence of functions as *method-functions*. This is similar to the function decomposition in the German-style systematic design methodology [21], whole-part relation [17], and "degree of complexity" [6]. However, the basis of the function-achievement such as a physical principle is explicated as a *way-of-function-achievement*. It forms a function decomposition tree, which represents how to achieve a goal function by components as a designer's intention.

These definitions give more detailed definitions of our definition in previous papers [9,10], that is, a function as a teleological interpretation of a B1-behavior under a goal. The "interpretation" is defined as interpretation of a role of a behavior in a function context as a "goal". The teleological interpretation of behavior to function can be described using functional toppings (FTs), which are primitives of additional information to behaviors, that is, Obj-Focus, O-Focus, P-Focus and Necessity [9]. They represent information about such an operand that the designer intends to change (focus of intention). Obj-Focus specifies its kind such as substance or energy. O-Focus specifies the type of its physical attributes to change (such as temperature and phase). P-Focus specifies ports and represents focus on a flow of operand or medium. Necessity specifies the necessity of operands in the context.

We developed an ontology of generic functions (called functional concept ontology) [9], which are sub-classes of the *function* class (its portion will be shown in Fig. 3). For example, an energy function, "to shift energy", is defined by the axioms inherited from the super-concept plus the following three axioms; (1) P-Focus on an inlet port and an outlet port, (2) Energy in the focused outlet port is made from energy in the focused inlet port, and (3) Mediums of the focused energies are different. "To take", a subtype of the *shifting* function in the *is-a* hierarchy, is defined with an additional FT, P-Focus on the port of energy provider. Likewise, "to remove" is defined as that of the *taking* function with an additional FT, the energy taken is unnecessary as Necessity FT. On the other hand, "to give" concept can be define as P-Focus on another medium-flow receiving heat (heat destination). Such functional toppings show the difference between these two functional interpretations of the heat exchanger mentioned above.

3   Other Kinds of Function

The definition of the concept of function in Section 2 is done strictly from the device-centered viewpoint, which is intended to prescribe guidelines to functional modeling. Other types of function, however, still remain to be investigated. In order to place our definition of function in other definitions of functions, this section discusses rather descriptive definitions of other kinds of function as shown in Fig. 2 on the basis of the discussion in [12]. They represent viewpoints (or context) for human's perception of a function. Thus, a device can achieve some functions in different categories simultaneously. Note that Fig. 2 shows an *is-a* hierarchy only for readability, because some distinctions are independent from each other.

Firstly, the function discussed in Section 2 represents changes of entities (behaviors) within the system boundary (here we call *device function*). On the other hand, an *environmental function* includes changes outside of the system boundary, especially, those related to users or user actions. For example, an electric fan performs moving-air function as a device function and cooling function for human body as an environmental function, where the cool-down effect by wind is on human body and thus outside of the system boundary. This cooling environmental function means physical changes of the system (called *physical environmental function*), while an *interpretational function* sets up one of necessary conditions of human's cognitive interpretation. For example, a clock has "to rotate hands (in the specific and constant rate)" as a

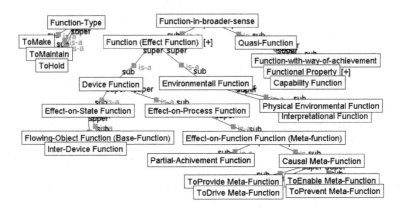

Fig. 2. Descriptive categories of function

device function and "to inform time" as an *interpretational function*, which requires human's cognitive interpretation.

Chandrasekaran and Josephson discuss a similar kind of function called environment function as effect on environment (the surrounding world of the device) [2]. Some researchers distinguish purpose from function (e.g., [17]), where the purpose represents human-intended goal in the similar sense to this *environmental function* or *interpretational function*. Hubuka distinguishes the purpose function as effects from the technical function as internal structure [6]. The situated FBS framework treats change of requirements [4]. In our collaborative work with the Delft University of Technology, we are extending our framework to include user actions as well [27].

Secondly, the *base-function* discussed in Section 2 refers to temporal changes of physical attributes of objects which flow through the device (called *flowing object function* here). It can be generalized into *effect-on-state function* which means temporal changes of physical attributes. The *effect-on-state function* has another kind, that is, *inter-device function* which refers to changes of another device (called B-3 behavior in [10]). Its example is a rod's function "to push cam". The cam is another device, which is not considered as objects flowing through the rod.

On the other hand, the *effect-on-process function* represents effect on a process or its changes. Behavior as basis of function can be regarded as a kind of a process. Thus, as a subtype of the *effect-on-process function*, *effect-on-function function* (we can call *meta-function*) represents a role of a function for another function. It includes *partial-achievement function* and *causal-meta function*. The former is performed by a method function for a goal function in the *is-achieved-by* relation. The latter represents a role for another method function and is called a meta-function in [9].

Thirdly, the function-types are additional descriptors for the functions discussed thus far. They represent causal patterns of achievement for goals of each function of a component such as ToMake and ToMaintain (we redefined the ones in [8]) [9].

Fourthly, we recognize the following three kinds of *quasi-functions*. Although the authors do not consider them as kinds of function, it is found that a *quasi-function* is confused with a function. Firstly, a *function-with-way-of-achievement* implies a specific way of function achievement as well as a function. Its examples include washing, shearing, adhering (e.g., glue adheres A to B) as well as welding mentioned in Introduction. Because meaning of this type of function is impure, we regard this *quasi-function*. Secondly, a *functional property* represents that an artifact (usually material) has a specific attribute-value which directly causes functionality. This is found in material science domain where a material whose function is dependent on its electronic, optical or magnetic property is called functional material. For example, if an electrical conductivity of a material is high (i.e., it has high conductivity property), the material can perform the "to transmit electricity" function. There is direct relationship between the high-conductivity property and the transmitting function. Lastly, a *capability function* represents that an entity can perform an activity which is not effect on others. For example, people say that "a human has walking function".

4 *Funnotation* Metadata Schema for the Semantic Web

In the semantic web context, our ontology can be used as a metadata schema for engineering documents as shown in Fig. 3. It enables us to describe metadata representing functionality of engineering devices mentioned in documents. Such metadata can be regarded as "content descriptors" like keywords or "logical structure" of "content representation" like a summary or an abstract in terms of categorization in [3]. By the logical structure, we here mean the relationship among functions such as functional decomposition. Functional metadata explicates the design rationale underlying design documents such as design drawing.

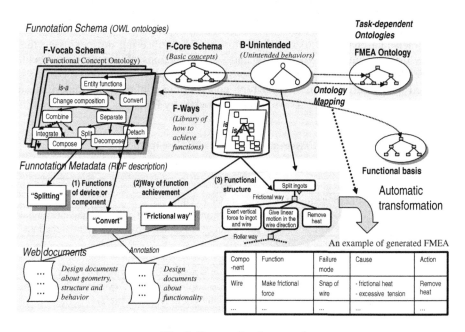

Fig. 3. *Funnotation* framework

The proposed metadata schema, called *Funnotation* Schema hereafter, has been built intended to annotate web resources about artifacts from the functional aspects. The schema consists of layers (sub-schemata), that is, F-Core, B-Unintended, F-Vocab and F-Ways schemata as shown in Fig. 3. The schema is represented in OWL [29]. F-Core schema defines fundamental concepts based on the functional ontology discussed in Section 2. Some of OWL classes and properties in F-Core are shown in Table 1. For example, the *agent* property denotes that an *entity* can perform *function* as an agent. The *part_function* property is used for representation of functional decomposition trees. Verbs such as *"convey"* and *"separate"* are defined in F-Vocab schema as sub-classes of the class of *function*. Those terms come from the functional concept ontology discussed in Section 2. F-Ways schema defines generic function-achievement ways, which are generalized from the concrete ways of function achievement in the function decomposition trees. The definition of each way of function-achievement is composed of the principle on which the achievement is based, the goal function and sub-functions which collectively constitute the way of function achievement.

The *Funnotation* schema enables users to represent functional metadata (called *Funnotation* metadata) with RDF [30] which include (1)Functions of the device/component/part of interest, (2)Function-achievement ways used, (3)Function decomposition trees representing the functional structure of the device, and (4)Generic function decomposition trees including alternative ways of function achievement. While (3) and (4) correspond to a full model of the functional structure, (1) and (2) to "indexing" information (content descriptors) representing some portion of the full model. Figure 4 shows an example of functional metadata for an explanation of a wire saw. It shows which represent that the wire saw is an instance of the *device* (*Funnotation:device*) and that it performs an instance of the *splitting function* (*Funnotation:split_entity*) as shown in the *Funnotation:has_function* property (which is the inverse property of the *Funnotaion:agent* property).

Such metadata enable us to search documents of engineering devices using their functions using a common vocabulary and *is-a* hierarchies of functional concepts. Here, the discrimination between functions and ways plays an important role. As mentioned in the introduction, usually both concepts are confused and thus it causes failure of search by functions. As well as the metadata by functions, secondly, one can

Table 1. Classes and properties of F-Core (portion)

Class			
entity	Physical entity		
function	Interpretation of behavior under a goal		
way	Way of function achievement: conceptualization of the principle essential to the achievement of the parent (goal) function by the sub(part)-functions		
Property			
Name	Domain	Range	
agent	*function*	*entity*	*Function* is achieved (performed) by the *entity*
part_function	*function*	*function*	*Function* in the Domain (Subject) is decomposed into that in Range (Object)
possible_way	*function*	*way*	*Function* can be achieved by the *way*
Method_ function	*way*	*function*	*Way* contains *function* as sub(part)-functions to achieve the goal (whole) function

Document (adapted from http://www.fine-yasunaga.co.jp/english/home/wiresaw/index.htm)

What is Wire Saw?......A wire (a piano wire of φ0.08 to 0.16mm) is wound around several hundred times along the groove of guide roller. Free abrasive grains (a mixture of grains and cutting oils) are applied to the wire while it keeps running. The abrasive grains rolled on the wire work to enable cutting of a processing object into several hundred slices at one time. It is mostly used to cut electronic materials.

Functional metadata

```
<funnotation:device rdf:about="http://ex.org/ex1.html#wire-saw">
 <funnotation:has_function>
  <funnotation:split_entity rdf:about="http://ex.org/ex1.html#cut">
   <funnotation:selected_way rdf:about="http://ex.org/ex1.html#grains">
    <funnotation:fricitional_way/></funnotation:selected_way>
  </funnotation:split_entity></funnotation:has_function>
</funnotation:device>
```

Fig. 4. Examples of metadata for a document of a wire-saw

describe ways of function achievement used in the device. In fact, Fig. 4 shows that the instance of *funnotation:frictional_way* is linked to the *split_entity function* instance via *selected_way* property to demonstrate the wire saw achieves its main function using *frictional_way*. Thanks to our functional ontologies, a user can search functions and ways separately.

Furthermore, by adding metadata about sub-functions to the metadata shown in Fig. 4, one can describe a function decomposition tree of a device as metadata of a document about the device. Many design documents describe only results of design activities without design rationale. The functional decomposition tree as metadata gives a part of the design rationale of devices described in the document. For few documents describing functional structures, the functional decomposition tree gives a kind of a summary or an abstract of the document.

Such functional metadata can play a crucial role in knowledge sharing among engineers in practice. In fact, in the deployment of our ontological framework in a manufacturing company [11], the functional modeling framework helps engineers share designer's intentions in engineering teams for design review and patent application as knowledge media. Moreover, it contributes to solving engineering tasks such as trouble-shooting and redesign [11]. Although the deployment has been done in a conventional client-server system, the same effect can be expected for that of the Semantic Web version.

Furthermore, the metadata can be automatically transformed into the form user's (engineer's) task requires according to the ontology mapping. In the current implementation, a knowledge transformation system can generates FMEA (Failure Mode and Effects Analysis) sheets for reliability analysis by transforming an extended functional model [13] as shown in Fig. 3. The transformation is done by referring to the ontology mapping knowledge between ontologies of the both knowledge models: the extended function model and the FMEA model. The *Funnotation* schema has a layer named B-Unintended (Unintended behavior layer) whose role is to represent phenomena/behavior unintended by designers rather than function intended by them.

Moreover, concerning the functional terms, the system will be able to allow users to use other vocabulary of generic functions such as Generally-Valid Functions [21] and the functional basis [5]. In order to realize interoperability between our ontology and such a terminology, the discussion on the concept of function in broader sense in

Section 3 plays a crucial role. In fact, the functional basis [5] includes *interpretational functions* in terms of the descriptive categories of function in Section 3. Using such conceptual categories of functions, we are currently developing an ontological mapping between our functional concept ontology and the functional basis. It enables us to integrate functional annotations based on different ontologies.

5 Related Work

We defined a function as a role of a behavior. In the literature, similar concepts are discussed. Chandrasekaran and Josephson use the concept of role as natural (without human's intention) effects on environment (e.g., the role of cloud is to give rain) and define function as "role+intention" [2]. In EPISTLE Framework, the concept of facility is defined as a functional thing, capability to perform a function and a service [28]. The layered structure of our ontologies is similar to the PhysSys ontology [27]. It, however, has no ontology for functions from the teleological viewpoint. Some generic function sets with *is-a* hierarchy have been proposed such as generally-valid functions [21], "degree of abstraction" of functions [6] and the functional basis [5]. We define rich generic functions with clear operational relationship with objective behaviors. Similarly to the way of function achievement, a feature of function decomposition can also be found as a "means" in [18]. We defined *is-a* relations between generic ways of function achievement, and investigated how to organize them.

A functional modeling framework for the Semantic Web has been proposed in [14]. It is based on the functional basis [5] and is represented in the description logic (DL) for repository reasoning tasks. Our ontological work aims at providing comprehensive prescriptive guidelines for knowledge modeling (annotation) rather than the reasoning task. For example, our ontology provides the concept of "way of function achievement" as a key concept for capturing the functional structures of artifacts. The framework in [14] provides not such a concept but a representation schema in DL.

The generic tasks and the generic methods (PSMs) for problem-solving task research (e.g.,[51]) are similar to our generic functions and generic ways of function achievement for engineering domain knowledge, respectively. We conceptualize the principle behind the sequence of activities (called method in both researches) as the way of function achievement. It helps us organize them in *is-a* hierarchies. Moreover, we distinguish function at the teleological level from behaviors at the objective level. Behavior of artifacts is a kind of "process" by which we intuitively mean a sequence of state changes over time. We concentrate on physical process which represents temporal changes of physical quantities. On generic "process", extensive research has been done elsewhere such as work in [7,23].

TRIZ (TIPS) theory provides some patterns (or strategies) for inventions based on the contradiction between two physical quantities [24]. We did not concentrate on design strategies but on modelling schema. TRIZ theory also concentrates on physical principles (effects), although we established a clear relationship between physical principles and functional structures.

6 Concluding Remarks

Ontological consideration on functionality of artifact and its application in the Semantic Web have been discussed. The role of ontologies is to provide semantic constraints to capture the target world consistently and controlled vocabulary for representation. The ontologies have been applied to modelling manufacturing machines, engineering plants, engineering products and manufacturing processes. The models have taken into account changes in thermal energy, flow rate, and ingredients of fluids, force and motion of operands. The current functional concept ontology can describe simple mechanical products, although it does not cover static force balancing and complex mechanical phenomena based on the shape. The modelling framework currently cannot cope with the human's mental process, body movements (so-called therblig in Industrial Engineering), business processes, or software processes.

Acknowledgements. The authors would like to thank Kouji Kozaki, Munehiko Sasajima, Eiichi Sunagawa and Shinya Tarumi for their contributions to this work. Special thanks go to Dr. Masayoshi Fuse, Mr. Masakazu Kashiwase, Mr. Shuji Shinoki and the engineers in the Plant and Production Systems Engineering Division of Sumitomo Electric Industries, Ltd. for their cooperation with the deployment.

References

1. Borst, P., Akkermans, H., Top, J.: Engineering Ontologies. Int. J. of Human-Computer Studies 46 (1997) 365-406
2. Chandrasekaran, B., Josephson, J. R.: Function in Device Representation. Engineering with Computers 16 (2000) 162-177
3. Euzenat, J.: Eight Questions about Semantic Web Annotations. IEEE Intelligent Systems March/April (2002) 55-62
4. Gero, J.S., Kannengiesser, U.: The Situated Function-Behaviour-Structure Framework. In Proc. of Artificial Intelligence in Design '02 (2002) 89-104
5. Hirtz, J., Stone, R. B., McAdams, D.A., Szykman, S., Wood, K.L.: A Functional Basis for Engineering Design: Reconciling and Evolving Previous Efforts. Research in Engineering Design 13 (2002) 65-82
6. Hubka, V., Eder, W.E.: Functions Revisited. In Proc. of the 13th International Conference on Engineering Design (ICED 01) (2001), CD-ROM
7. ISO TC184/SC4/JWG8, Process Specification Language, http://www.tc184-sc4.org/ SC4_Open/ SC4_Work_Products_Documents/PSL_(18629)/ (2003)
8. Keuneke, A.M.: A Device Representation: the Significance of Functional Knowledge. IEEE Expert 24 (1991) 22-25
9. Kitamura, Y., Sano, T., Namba, K., Mizoguchi, R.: A Functional Concept Ontology and Its Application to Automatic Identification of Functional Structures. Advanced Engineering Informatics 16 (2002) 145-163
10. Kitamura, Y, Mizoguchi, R.: Ontology-based Systematization of Functional Knowledge. Journal of Engineering Design 15(4) (2004) 327-351
11. Kitamura, Y., Kashiwase, M. Fuse, M., Mizoguchi, R.: Deployment of an Ontological Framework of Functional Design Knowledge. Advanced Engineering Informatics 18 (2004) 115-127
12. Kitamura, Y., Koji, Y., Mizoguchi, R.: An Ontological Model of Device Function and Its Deployment for Engineering Knowledge Sharing. In Proc. of the First Workshop FOMI 2005 - Formal Ontologies Meet Industry (2005) CD-ROM
13. Koji, Y., Kitamura, Y., Mizoguchi, R., Ontology-based Transformation from an Extended Functional Model to FMEA. In Proc. of the 15th Int. Conf. on Engineering Design (ICED 05) (2005) 264.81

14. Kopena, J. B., Regli, W. C.: Functional Modeling of Engineering Designs for the Semantic Web, IEEE Data Engineering Bulletin, IEEE Computer Society, 26(4) (2003) 55-62
15. Kozaki, K., Kitamura, Y., Ikeda, M., Mizoguchi, R., Hozo: An Environment for Building/Using Ontologies Based on a Fundamental Consideration of "Role" and "Relationship". In Proc. of the 13th Int. Conf. on Knowledge Engineering and Knowledge Management (EKAW 2002) (2002) 213-218
16. Lee, J. Design Rationale Systems: Understanding the Issues. IEEE Expert 12(3) (1997) 78-85
17. Lind, M.: Modeling Goals and Functions of Complex Industrial Plants. Applied Artificial Intelligence 8 (1994) 259-283
18. Malmqvist J. Improved Function-Means Trees by Inclusion of Design History Information. Journal of Engineering Design 8(2) (1997) 107-117
19. Masolo, C., Vieu, L., Bottazzi, E., Catenacci, C., Ferrario, R., Gengami, A., and Guarino, N.: Social Roles and their Descriptions. In Proc. of the 9th Int'l Conf. on the Principles of Knowledge Representation and Reasoning (KR2004) (2004) 267–277
20. Miles, L.D.: Techniques of Value Analysis and Engineering. McGraw-hill (1961)
21. Pahl, G., Beitz, W.: Engineering Design - a Systematic Approach. The Design Council (1988)
22. Schreiber, G., et al.: Knowledge Engineering and Management - The Common-KADS Methodology, The MIT Press, Cambridge, MA (2000)
23. Sowa, J. F.: Top-level Ontological Categories, Int. J. of Human-Computer Studies 43(5-6) (1995) 669–685
24. Sushkov, V.V., Mars, N.J.I., Wognum, P.M.: Introduction to TIPS: a Theory for Creative Design. Artificial Intelligence in Engineering 9(3) (1995) 177-189.
25. Umeda, Y., Ishii, M., Yoshioka, M., Shimomura, Y., Tomiyama, T.: Supporting conceptual design based on the function-behavior-state modeler. Artificial Intelligence for Engineering Design, Analysis and Manufacturing 10 (1996) 275-288
26. Umeda, Y., Tomiyama, T.: Functional Reasoning in Design. IEEE Expert (1997) 42-48
27. van der Vegte, W.F., Kitamura, Y., Koji, Y., Mizoguchi, R.: Coping with Unintended Behavior of Users and Products: Ontological Modeling of Product Functionality and Use, In Proc. of CIE 2004: ASME 2004 Design Engineering Technical Conferences and Computers in Engineering Conference (2004) DETC2004-57720
28. West, M.: Some Industrial Experiences in the Development and Use of Ontologies. EKAW 2004 Workshop on Core Ontologies in Ontology Engineering (2004) 1-14
29. W3C: OWL Web Ontology Language Reference, http://www.w3.org/TR/owl-ref/ (2004)
30. W3C: Resource Description Framework (RDF): Concepts and Abstract Syntax, http://www.w3.org/TR/rdf-concepts/ (2004)

Support for Content Creation Using Conversation Quanta

Ken Saito, Hidekazu Kubota, Yasuyuki Sumi, and Toyoaki Nishida

Graduate School of Informatics, Kyoto University,
Yoshida-Honmachi, Sakyo-ku,
Kyoto 606-8501, Japan
saitoh@ii.ist.i.kyoto-u.ac.jp
http://www.ii.ist.i.kyoto-u.ac.jp/

Abstract. In this study, we present a computational approach to support content creation by recording and reusing the conversational contents as reusable nuggets. We introduce the concept of the conversation quantization - a technique for approximating a continuous flow of conversation by a series of conversation quanta that correspond to the points in a discourse. We describe the creation of contents using conversation quanta. To realize the concept of conversation quanta, we attempt to manually extract conversation quanta from the videos of some meetings and create the conversational contents. As a result, we have confirmed that conversation quanta can be reused as conversational contents such as conversational agents and presentation contents. Further, we have obtained valuable insights into the nature of conversation quanta.

1 Introduction

A conversation is the primary method for creating and sharing knowledge in many aspects such as education, planning, decision-making, or even a coffee klatch. In this study, a novel concept for reusing the contents extracted from past conversations is described. The reuse of past contents is indispensable for a constructive discussion. In conversational situations, people record and reuse the content by using text proceedings that include only verbal information or video proceedings that are difficult to divide into reusable nuggets. Our aim is to construct a content pile by capturing the important and more reusable content of a conversation that also includes nonverbal information such as conversational rhythms, facial expressions, and gestures.

Nishida [1] proposed a computational approach to understand and augment the conversational knowledge process; this process is a collective activity for knowledge creation, management, and application where conversational communications are used as the primary means of interaction among the participating agents. The key to achieve this is conversation quantization - a technique for approximating a continuous flow of conversation by a series of conversation quanta that represent the points in a discourse. Previous studies on conversation quantization surveyed by Nishida include the application of conversation quanta in

T. Washio et al. (Eds.): JSAI 2005 Workshops, LNAI 4012, pp. 29–40, 2006.
© Springer-Verlag Berlin Heidelberg 2006

knowledge circulation, embodied conversational agents, virtual immersive environments, spatial content management, and automated conversation capture; these studies have immensely contributed to knowledge circulation by using manual extraction of conversation quanta.

In this study, we adopt conversation quanta for supporting content creation. We have experimentally performed the manual extraction of conversation quanta from practical conversational situations and reused them to investigate their nature and reusability. In the simulation, we have created two types of contents: One is a conversational agent called virtualized ego [2]. The virtualized ego can talk on behalf of an actual person by using the contents of her/his past statements. The other is a presentation content that includes nonverbal information.

2   Conversation Quantization

Conversation quantization is a technique for approximating a continuous flow of conversation by a series of objects called conversation quanta, each of which represents a point in the discourse. We define a conversation quantum as an entity that contains a minimal amount of contextual information. In other words, each conversation quantum makes a minimal sense even though it may be presented in an inappropriate context. The granularity and size of conversation quanta essentially depend on the context and background knowledge of the observer.

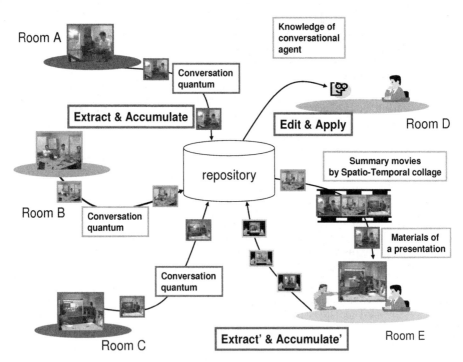

Fig. 1. Concept of conversation quantization

2.1   Framework of Conversation Quantization

Conceptually, the framework of conversation quantization consists of extraction, accumulation, editing, and the application of conversation quanta (Fig.1). The extraction of conversation quanta is performed by identifying and encoding the coherent segments of interactions in a conversational situation. The extracted conversation quanta are accumulated in a repository, edited whenever necessary, and applied to other conversational situations. The application of conversation quanta, for example, involves an embodied conversational agent and presentation content, and movie summaries by using a spatio-temporal collage. The research subjects with regard to the conversation quantum for realizing conversation quantization are given as follows:

1. The nature of conversation quanta
2. Method to use conversation quanta
3. Method to extract conversation quanta

In this study, we have manually extracted conversation quanta to analyze subjects 1 and 2 by reusing them.

2.2   Concept of Conversation Quanta

Conversation quanta are the reusable nuggets of conversational contents extracted from conversational situations. Conversation quanta are continuously accumulated and reused as the parts that constitute a conversation system. The conversation system creates various conversations by restructuring and rearranging the conversation quanta, and supports the conversations in which users participate.

The implementation of conversation quantization depends on the data structure that represents the conversation quanta. Plain video clips can be used for the representation; however, the efficiency in retrieving and processing would be fairly limited and a high cost would be incurred in retrieving, editing, and applying the conversation quanta. Alternatively, a deep semantic representation using logical formulas or case frames would not be suitable due to the cost and the limited capability for representing nonverbal information. It is reasonable to assume that conversation quantization can be implemented using the annotated video of a conversation and the annotated images that are used and acquired from a conversational situation.

3   Analysis of Conversation Quanta

In this study, we manually simulated conversation quantization in order to investigate the nature of conversation quanta in a real situation. Firstly, we selected a conversation using slides. The concept of conversation quanta is realized in the following manner:

1. Setting up a practical conversational situation
2. Capturing the conversation by using video cameras

3. Manually extracting the conversation quanta from the video stream by hand
4. Repeating steps 1-3 for different situations
5. Creating a new video content by combining the conversation quanta gathered from the recorded conversations

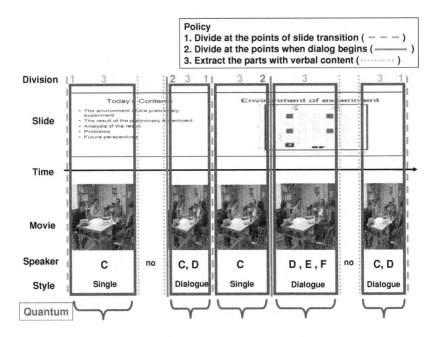

Fig. 2. Model for extracting conversation quanta

We obtained two types of videos: One video comprised the conversations of two authors (video A), and the other comprised that of four people (including one of the authors) (video B). Video A consists a recording of three meetings between two of the authors - a master's course student (subject A) and a researcher (subject B). Each meeting was held in a different place and at different times. Each of them communicated using PowerPoint slides on a mobile PC (equipped with a web camera and a microphone), which was used to capture their voices, facial expressions, and contextual information. Thus, we obtained a three and a half hour video containing the conversations between subjects A and B. In their conversation, the presentation style and discussion style were equally distributed, and their topics were concerned with conversation quantization - its history, problems, approaches, systems, and so on. Video B contains the recording of one meeting. This meeting comprised four people, in which one of the authors participated. In this meeting, a doctoral student from our laboratory presented his studies using PowerPoint slides. This meeting, 75 min in duration, was captured using a digital video camera. In this conversation, the ratio of the presentational style to discussion style was about 1:5. Therefore, we recorded a meeting video with a total duration of five hours. Further, we manually divided these videos and extracted the conversation quanta based on the following policy (Fig.2):

1. Divide at the points of slide transition
2. Divide at the points when a dialogue begins
3. Extract the parts with verbal content

First, the video is divided at the time point of slide transition (Fig.2, division 1) because we observed that speeches are almost coherent in a slide. The second division point (Fig.2, division 2) is the start of a dialogue. We suppose that a video clip from the start of a dialogue to the end of a slide is a conversation quantum; this forms the dialogue style. According to the third policy, we extracted the parts with verbal content. In other words, we excluded the parts with more than four seconds of silence from these videos. Fig.2 shows five conversation quanta; each quantum is enclosed within lines. In this simulation, a conversation quantum comprises movie clips and slides.

As a result, we obtained 252 conversation quanta (average time of 70 s). Table 1 shows the number of conversation quanta.

Table 1. Conversation quanta obtained from the five-hour video

Video	Time (min)	Number of quanta
A-1	45	76
A-2	135	91
A-3	45	20
B	75	65

In the following, we will empirically analyze the nature of conversation quanta by creating new conversational contents using these conversation quanta.

3.1 Analysis 1: Simulation of a Virtualized-Ego System

We have simulated a virtualized-ego system based on these conversation quanta. A virtualized-ego is an interactive virtual character with an autobiographical memory of an actual person. It is important that we aim to create a conversational agent that can talk about informal knowledge such as personal experience. The virtualized ego is expected to decrease the time-related, spatial, and social constraints of a conversation. We arranged the conversation quanta of subject A on the assumption that the system represents subject A and converses with a user. Fig.3 shows an overview of our simulation. First, a user comes in front of a system screen where the face of subject A is displayed. Here, the system talks on behalf of subject A when the user enquires about his interest (greeting). The system responds by arranging the past conversation quanta related to the

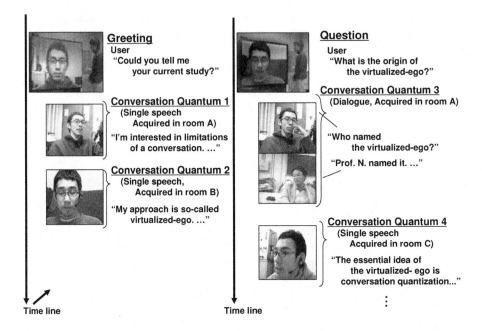

Fig. 3. Simulation of a conversational video content using conversation quanta

user's interest (conversation quantum 1 and conversation quantum 2). While the system is talking, the user can ask any question (question). Consequently, the system can respond by searching an answering conversation quantum (conversation quantum 3) and continuing to talk (conversation quantum 4). We have obtained some valuable insights into conversation quanta from the simulation and the abovementioned analysis. Firstly, the conversation quanta, which depend on the context, are reusable in the situation where the user is familiar with the original situations of the conversation quanta. In Fig.3, quantum 1, quantum 2, and quantum 4 were obtained from different rooms. Thus, we can create new conversational content from the past conversation quanta obtained from different situations. The background knowledge of the user is vital when searching the conversation quanta that are suitable for a user. However, the conversation shown in the left-hand side of Fig.3 can be complemented by the user because he is a colleague of the speakers displayed on the screen. Secondly, a dialogue-style quantum comprising speedy Q&A pairs and jokes is interesting. These quanta exhibit good instances of conversation such as conversational rhythms, presence, and dynamics. In addition, from the viewpoint of virtualized ego, a quantum that contains individual experiences and knowledge is interesting as well.

3.2 Analysis 2: Creation of a New Presentation Content

We have created a new presentation content using the conversation quanta. We used Sustainable Knowledge Globe (SKG) [3] as the software for the presentation. The SKG system is used to spatially manage and display the conversation quanta. Fig.4 (a) shows the SKG in which conversation quanta extracted from videos A and B are arranged. A conversation quantum comprised a slide with a corresponding movie clip (Fig.4 (b)). We created new presentation contents for the software agent (Fig.5 (a)) by reusing these contents. The conversation quanta of the recently created slides are connected to and placed near these slides (Fig.5 (b)). A presenter can easily refer to the conversation quanta connected to the corresponding slides.

Fig. 4. SKG image in which the conversation quanta arearranged: The left image (Fig.4 (a)) shows the SKG overview. The right image (Fig.4 (b)) shows a conversation quantum represented as a slide with the corresponding movie clip.

Fig. 5. New presentation content: The left image (Fig.5 (a)) shows an overview of the new presentation. The right image (Fig.5 (b)) shows the arrangement of conversation quanta near the new slides.

Fig.6 shows a simulation of the presentation contents shown in Fig.5. In situation A, a presenter refers to conversation quantum (a); a participant then comments on the conversation quantum. Conversation quantum (b) is extracted from situation A. In another presentation situation (situation B), the presenter refers to the conversation quanta that involves conversation quantum (b) extracted from situation A. The subjects related to the conversation quanta, which are reused in the presentation, increase due to the repeated presentation capture and subsequent conversation quanta extraction. We obtained a valuable insight by simulating the presentation using conversation quanta. The reusable conversation quanta, which can be reused as effective presentation materials, have the following information:

1. Non-verbal representation of participants such as gestures, facial expressions, etc.
2. Group setting or synchronized behavior of people
3. Conversational rhythms such as rapid conversations, jokes, etc.
4. Real-world objects observed by the participants, knowledge of operating instruments, DIY, etc.
5. Personal memories such as subjective opinions, experiences, etc.

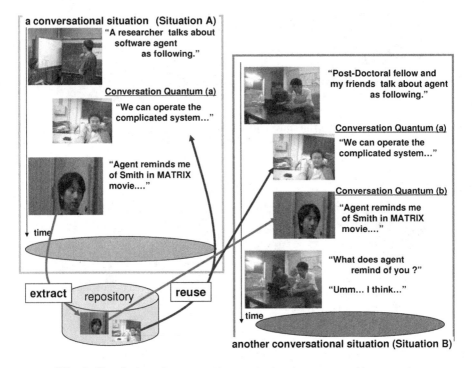

Fig. 6. Simulation of presentation content using conversation quanta

We can easily make good and interesting conversations by reusing the conversation quanta involving some of this information. Firstly, conversation quanta are useful in communicating nonverbal information. We can easily communicate the nonverbal representation of participants, such as gestures and facial expressions, by displaying the conversation quanta involving them; this is because we hardly reenact the gestures of other people (Fig.7 (a)) or verbalize facial expressions. The conversation in a group setting and synchronized behaviors tend to be important because of the interactions and considerations within the group members who share the same atmosphere; however, this behavior seldom occurs when a member is alone. We can explain these effectively by reusing the conversation quanta. Fig.7 (b) shows an example of synchronized behavior where the subjects simultaneously perform the same gesture.

Subsequently, the conversation quanta involving conversational rhythm are useful for sharing the conversational presence and atmosphere. It is difficult to elaborate on conversational rhythm, presence, and atmosphere. For example, even if a speaker indulged in a speedy conversation, the listeners would not be able to comprehend the degree of its speed. Moreover, we can seldom reuse jokes because they depend on the context, such as conversational rhythm, presence, and atmosphere. We can easily understand and share a previous conversation rhythm, presence, and atmosphere by showing the conversation quanta.

Fig. 7. Conversation quanta reused as effective presentation material: The left image (Fig.7 (a)) shows a gesture and the right image (Fig.7 (b)) shows an example of synchronized behavior

Furthermore, the conversation quanta involving real-world objects observed by the participants are useful to intuitively explain and understand the objects in a visual manner. It is difficult for a speaker to elaborate on his knowledge of operating instruments. On the other hand, it is difficult for listeners to understand the description of an unknown object. A speaker can easily explain about the objects, while the listeners would intuitively and visually understand them by reusing the conversation quanta.

Finally, the conversation quanta involving personal memory, such as subjective opinions and individual experiences, are useful for making a conversational agent called virtualized ego. We can effectively communicate the characteristic conversation atmosphere of a person even in their absence by referring to the conversation quanta.

4   Discussion

In the previous sections, we have discussed the nature of conversation quanta with regard to virtualized ego and presentation contents, and confirmed that conversation quanta can be reused as conversational agents and presentation contents during conversational situations. It is easy to create these conversational contents by editing and reorganizing the conversation quanta; however, the conversation quanta are extracted based on the following policy: divide movies at the time point of slide transition and the start of a dialogue, and extract the part with verbal content. However, much of the content is still redundant or insufficient since the policy is simple. It is necessary to adopt an extraction method for extracting a large amount of human actions in conversational situations in order to obtain more detailed conversation quanta. Sumi et al. [4] proposed a ubiquitous sensor room that can extract conversation quanta from a real world conversation. They implemented a smart room environment in which conversational activities and human actions could be recorded by environment and wearable sensors.

The more repeatedly we reuse the conversation quanta at conversational situations, the more is the increase in the amount of new conversation quanta, which are related to the original conversation quanta. The creation of content would be easier if many conversation quanta are used. Conversely, content creation becomes difficult when the amount of conversation quanta increases. In that case, we have to implement the retrieve and delete system of conversation quanta.

Additionally, from these two analyses, we have obtained some valuable insights about conversation quanta. The virtualized ego, which is generated from conversation quanta that depend on the context, can be comprehended by the user who shares that context. Although it is usually difficult to understand the virtualized ego, observers can understand it by sharing the context of the conversation quanta. For example, a community member could easily complement a fragmented conversation between members of the same community. This supposition was confirmed by Hirata [5] for the fragments of text conversation and by Kubota [2] for the fragments of voice conversation. In this study, we confirmed the abovementioned result on video conversation fragments, although it seemed difficult to quantize these fragments on account of the discontinuity in the spatial context of the video, such as a sudden change in the background and clothes. With regard to these problems, which are peculiar to videos, we concluded that a sudden change in the direction of a speaker's face prevents an observer from understanding the contents, although a change in the background and clothes are mostly unnoticed. For example, a speaker's face changes its direction when conversation quantum 3 is changed to conversation quantum 4, as shown in Fig.3; this prevents an observer from understanding the contents. The conversation quanta comprising the nonverbal representation of participants, group settings and the synchronized behaviors of people, conversational rhythms, real-world objects observed by participants, and personal memory play an important and interesting role in the reuse of conversation quanta. We concluded that conversation quanta involving this information are reusable and contribute in making an effective conversation. Another big concern is the automatic capture of conversation quanta. In addition to the works described thus far in this study, there are a number of other interesting works. Minoh and Kakusho [6] developed a robust method for automatically recognizing communicative events in a real class room by integrating audio and visual information processing. Rutkowski [7] studied a method for monitoring and estimating the efficiency of interpersonal communication based on the recorded audio and video content by computing the correlation between the activities of the sender and responses of the receiver. Kurohashi and Shibata [8] integrated the robust natural language-processing techniques and computer vision to automatically annotate videos with a closed caption. Our research is based on a casual conversation in any situation; hence, it is very difficult to automatically understand the discourse structure, especially the correspondence structure when the indication word in the video is omitted. We aim to make the conversation quantization feasible by supporting humans to understand the topics in a video in the loop of conversation quantization, such as the Q&A system of EgoChat .

5   Conclusion

In this study, we have presented a computational approach for supporting content creation by recording and reusing the ideas generated in conversations as reusable nuggets. We have introduced the concept of conversation quantization - a technique for approximating a continuous flow of conversation by a series of conversation quanta that represent the points in a discourse. We confirmed that conversation quanta can be reused as conversational contents such as conversational agents known as virtualized-ego and presentation contents. Further, we obtained valuable insights into the nature of conversation quanta by manually extracting them from practical situations and creating the contents by reusing them.

References

1. Toyoaki Nishida: Conversation Quantization for Conversational Knowledge Process. Special Invited Talk, S.Bhalla (Ed.): DNIS2005 (Fourth International Workshop on Databases in Networked Information Systems), LNCS 3433, Springer (2005) 15-33
2. Hidekazu Kubota, Toyoaki Nishida, Tomoko Koda: Exchanging Tacit Community Knowledge by Talking-virtualized-egos. Fourth International Conference on Autonomous Agents (Agents 2000, Barcelona, Catalonia, Spain. June3 - June 7) (2000) 285-292
3. Kubota, H., Sumi, Y., Nishida, T. : Sustainable Knowledge Globe: A System for Supporting Content-oriented Conversation. In Proceedings of AISB 2005 Symposium for Conversational Informatics for Supporting Social Intelligence & Interaction (2005) 80-86
4. Y.Sumi, K.Mase, C.Mueller, S.Iwasawa, S.Ito, M. Takahashi, K.Kumagai, Y.Otaka: Collage of Video and Sound for Raising the Awareness of Situated Conversations. In Proceedings of International Workshop on Intelligent Media Technology for Communicative Intelligence (IMTCI2004) (2004) 167-172
5. Takashi Hirata, Hidekazu Kubota, and Toyoaki Nishida: Talking virtualized egos for dynamic knowledge interaction. In Toyoaki Nishida, editor, Dynamic Knowledge Interaction, chapter 6, CRC press (2000) 183-222

6. Michihiko Minoh, Satoshi Nishiguchi: Environmental Media - In the Case of Lecture Archiving System. In Proceedings of Int. Conf. Knowledge-Based Intelligent Information & Engineering Systems (KES2003) (2003) Vol.2 1070-1076
7. T.M. Rutkowski, S. Seki, Y. Yamakata, K. Kakusho, M. Minoh: Toward the Human Communication Efficiency Monitoring from Captured Audio and Video Media in Real Environment. In Proceedings of Int. Conf. Knowledge-Based Intelligent Information & Engineering Systems (KES2003) (2003) Vol.2 1093-1100
8. T. Shibata, D. Kawahara, M. Okamoto, S. Kurohashi, T. Nishida: Structural Analysis of instruction Utterances. In Proceedings of Int. Conf. Knowledge-Based Intelligent Information & Engineering Systems (KES2003) (2003) 1054-1061
9. Hidekazu Kubota, Jaewon Hur, Toyoaki Nishida: Agent-based Content Management System. In Proceedings of the 3rd Workshop on Social Intelligence Design (SID2004), CTIT Proceedings (2004) 77-84

Knowledge Level Design Support for Adaptive Learning Contents: Ontological Consideration of Knowledge Level Structure of SCORM2004 Contents

Yusuke Hayashi and Mitsuru Ikeda

School of Knowledge Science,
Japan Advanced Institute of Science and Technology
{yusuke, ikeda}@jaist.ac.jp

Abstract. This paper presents an examination of learning contents design from knowledge level and symbol level viewpoints. This study is intended to develop a foundation for the sharing and reuse of IESs on a global platform. The basis of the platform was chosen as SCORM2004, which is rapidly becoming a de facto standard. On that platform, we intend to construct an environment for authors to clarify the pedagogical meaning of learning contents based on an ontology for IESs. This approach will allow the sharing and reuse of academic and technical expertise in the field of IES study on a common platform.

1   Introduction

In the research area of authoring tools of instructional systems, we have aimed at a paradigm shift from "story-board representations of instructional material to a more powerful knowledge-based representation" [5]. Storyboard representation realizes adaptive instruction on a branched presentation structure. The salient benefit of knowledge-based representation is the realization of highly adaptive instruction with integrated knowledge bases of learning domains, teaching strategies and learner models.

However, building such knowledge bases still entails extremely high cost. Many efforts have been undertaken in the Intelligent Educational System (IES) study community to devise solutions to these issues. This paper examines an approach to the following issues from the viewpoint of AI research.

The Knowledge Level concept by Newell [9] is valuable for designing intelligent systems. The concept is comprehensive consideration for intelligent systems, but this paper simply explains the following from the perspective of this study.

The Knowledge Level is a level of description of the knowledge of intelligent systems and the symbol level is one that produces intelligent behavior based on a knowledge-level description. The system is designed as a harmonious balance between the knowledge level and the symbol level if an intelligent system has high quality.

T. Washio et al. (Eds.): JSAI 2005 Workshops, LNAI 4012, pp. 41–52, 2006.

Issues we discuss in this paper include the following:

- How does a platform of IESs support construction of good-quality knowledge?
- What is "suitability" of a mechanism that generates intelligent behavior based on that knowledge?

This study particularly notes the viewpoint of ontological engineering [8, 3, 13] and the viewpoint of scalability and interoperability, which are provided by a standard for learning contents. These viewpoints are important to answer the above questions.

Most studies of IESs have sought to analyze task knowledge for learning support and to implement it as a knowledge model. Ontological engineering is widely thought to be useful to systematize the results of the studies. The purpose of ontological engineering for IES studies is to generalize and systematize components of learning support knowledge, for example, "When, to which learner, what does the system provide based on which strategy?" This study subsumes that to support describing learning support knowledge with the system of components contribute to constructing good-quality knowledge. The authors' study about ontology-aware authoring tools is advanced based on the research hypothesis [11, 10].

Turning now to the issue of "suitability", intelligent behaviors considered in IES studies include various degrees of complexity: from relatively simple behaviors to complex ones. We must consider plenty of indexes of "suitability" of intelligent behavior generated at the symbol level if we consider that suitability corresponds to the overall degree of complexity. For example, to construct a qualitative simulation-based intelligent training system for a large scale plant, one must consider a qualitative reasoning engine as a symbol level, and consider suitability including the reasoning speed and precision.

To address an index of suitability, we must consider some sort of scale for depth, which is fineness of reasoning for learning support, and a scale for scope, which is coverage of learning that the support applies to. Generally speaking, the depth is greatest when the scope is small, but the depth is shallow when the scope is large.

This study is intended to cover the "large" scope symbol level with "shallow" intelligent behavior to develop the quality of knowledge level and to organize knowledge for learning support. For these reasons, this study establishes scalability and interoperability of intelligent behavior as the index of suitability. Scalable technology combined suitably with knowledge level has not been introduced into research and development of IESs if we look at existing intelligent learning platforms from this point of view.

This study notes The Sharable Content Object Reference Model (SCORM) 2004 [1] as a candidate for a suitable symbol-level platform. SCORM2004 captures the wide attention of the e-learning field as a next-generation e-learning platform. Especially, sequencing and navigation specification, which is a part of SCORM 2004, is expected to offer the potential for symbol-level generating intelligent behavior for learning support [4].

To sum up the main points we have been discussing, this study is intended to realize systematization of knowledge for intelligent learning support on a scalable symbol-level platform to share and reuse the knowledge. Concretely speaking, the purposes are:

– Setting a description level for high-quality learning support knowledge,
– Building a support tool for authoring learning contents, and
– Establishing an SCORM2004-confirming implementation level generating "suitable" intelligent behavior.

In the remainder of this paper, we explore some of these issues: analysis of SCORM2004 from the viewpoint of IES study in Chapter 2, reconsideration of knowledge level and symbol level in Chapter 3. Finally, we propose an SCORM2004-confirming ontology-aware authoring tool in Chapter 4.

2   SCORM2004 as a Symbol Level for Learning Contents

2.1   SCORM2004

SCORM2004 is a standard for learning contents organized by the Advanced Distributed Learning Initiative (ADL). It aims to ensure interoperability and reusability of learning contents. One of the characteristic of SCORM2004 is Sequencing and Navigation specification, which is a specification for control of the behavior of learning contents. Using the specification, a learning content designer (designer) can describe the behavior of learning contents, e.g., *If the learner cannot pass the examination, then contents for review are provided for the learner, and Until the learner achieves the objective, contents for explanation and exercise are provided for the learner*, and so on.

In SCORM2004, the basic structure of learning content is a tree structure called an "Activity tree". A node is called an "Activity", which expresses the learning experience that a learner has in the contents. Only a leaf node contains learning material that is provided to learners. The material is called "Sharable Content Object (SCO)". An intermediate node expresses abstract learning activities. A learning management system (LMS) delivers SCOs to a learner while traversing an activity tree from the root according to pertinent rules.

Figure 1 shows an example of an activity tree. This content starts from "Pretest of brief of AI". The learner will learn the "details of AI" if a learner passes the pretest. If not, the learner will learn a "brief of AI" before learning the "details of AI". This control is implemented according to the sequencing rule (preConditionRule1).

A leaf node collects information about learning, for example, duration and score. Tracked data in the activity are aggregated to the parent activity when an activity is finished. The information is recorded as a "Local objective" and a "Global shared objective". A local objective allows only the related activity to access its own values, but a global shared objective permits more than one activity to access the value.

The general form of usage of a global shared objective is shown in Fig. 2. The global shared objective records the result of activity A and transfers it to activity B. For example, in Fig. 1, a global shared objective is used between "Pretest Brief of AI" and "Explanation Brief of AI". In this case, a learner's response recorded in "Pretest Brief of AI" is transferred to "Explanation Brief of AI" for PreconditionRule1.

Of course, such an adaptive preorder page-turner is only one way to use sequencing and navigation specifications. Specifications have such greater potential for realizing various types of sequencing depending on the way to describe rules and the meaning of nodes and the tree structure.

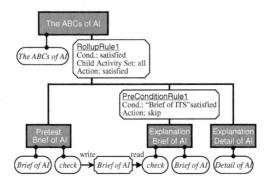

Fig. 1. An example of an adaptive preorder page-turner structure

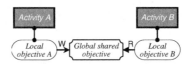

Fig. 2. General form of usage of a global shared objective

2.2 Lessons Learned from IES Studies

Educational support systems based on artificial intelligence technology are IESs. The salient characteristic of IES is its architecture, which comprises three components: domain knowledge, learner model and teaching strategy. The domain knowledge is knowledge that learners learn. The learner model is a model of a learner's understanding. The teaching strategy is a knowledge description about how to teach. The IESs determine the instruction for learners by selecting a teaching strategy based on the learner model and domain knowledge.

A typical example of such decision-making system is apparent in the study of MENO-Tutor by Woolf [14]. In MENO-Tutor, knowledge of instructional control is described in an Augmented Transition Network (ATN). A network node represents a teaching strategy or an action. Its connection with other nodes allows mutual transition. Depending on control rules that refer to a learner model, instructional control is performed through transition of nodes.

In this manner, each IES has a representation of its own structure of instructional knowledge. The IES studies aim to generate learning sequences flexibly that match each learner using a sophisticated representation of knowledge and its learner model.

However, some problems remain:

I. Sharability and Reusability of knowledge-base (learning contents) are very low because research-oriented special-purpose platforms are developed independently in respective studies.
II. Building an IES remains costly because of the complex knowledge representation and the necessity of detailed description of knowledge for a small learning content.

These problems hinder research promotion and practical application of IESs. The two following issues are important to solve the problems.

A. Organizing a constructive concept (ontology) of instructional control knowledge in IESs that allows IES designers to share their knowledge.
B. Sharing IES platform to execute instructional control knowledge that is based on the ontology in communities of researchers and practitioners.

2.3   Overview of SCORM2004 from the Vantage of IES Study

As mentioned in 2.1, an activity node in SCORM2004 is fundamentally conceptualized to represent learning experiences that learners have. An activity is "What to teach" from the viewpoint of educational systems; it is "What to learn" from the learners' viewpoint. Each node represents "A material used in learning" (e.g., contents in described in a chapter, a section and a page). An activity tree represents a "Structure of materials". It is not so difficult to describe codes of Sequencing and Navigation in SCORM2004 in the case of adding a simple control structure to a simple page-turner like a textbook. Authors are required to perform the simple task of reflecting the textbook-like structure on an activity tree and are required to describe decision-making rules that conform to that structure.

In contrast, in many cases, decision-making structures of IESs are "Which teaching action is better" from the system's viewpoint; it is "Which learning action is better" from learners' viewpoint. A node represents an action and a structure represents decision-making that is associated with teaching actions (e.g., in ATN of MENO-TUTOR, "introduce", "tutor", "hack", and "complete")[1]

To produce learning contents that are highly adaptive to individual learners, learning experiences must be organized with a central focus on a knowledge-based decision-making structure of learning action. To achieve that goal, it is

---

[1] Of course, if an "action" is embedded within "what to teach" in SCORM, it might appear as "Teaching action" in IES. However, such embedding must not be valid because it would hide knowledge to select actions. This issue will be addressed in Chapter 3.

difficult, but not impossible, to reflect that structure on an activity tree. It is necessary to reflect decision-making knowledge of learning actions selection into the Sequencing and Navigation model in SCORM2004 and simplify it so that designers can describe it. This issue, that is to say, boils down to issues of A and B mentioned in the previous section.

This issue matches the "knowledge level and symbol level" that Newell proposed as the principle of intelligent systems. Issue A is a framework of description of IES knowledge that is the source of intelligent behavior of IESs. That framework is equivalent to the knowledge level. Issue B is a platform that behaves intelligently based on that knowledge. That platform is equivalent to the symbol level. The authors consider that studies of IESs will be developed and used if it is possible to build a framework of a knowledge-level description of educational control knowledge that is based on an SCORM2004 platform as a highly scalable symbol level.

3   Building a Bridge Between a Knowledge Level and a Symbol Level

3.1   An Activity Tree as a Decision-Making Tree of Teaching Action

The required model for IESs is a structure of strategic decision-making of teaching action and a structure of information collection for learner modeling. Figure 3 indicates an example of a knowledge-level model. The learning process described in the model comprises a flow of an introduction, an acquisition, an exercise, and a review. The review is performed if a learner fails to pass the exercise. Two alternative strategies are subsumed in the review. One strategy accommodates learners who have learned the topic before, but who have since forgotten it. Such learners must review it to recall points that have slipped from understanding. The other is for learners who are learning the subject for the first time. Such learners must correct some incorrect understanding.

Figure 1 indicates a structure to select what to be learned, but Fig. 3 indicates a structure to select what to do. Clarifying knowledge to select an action is the basis of IES. It is important for the following two points:

A) The system can construct teaching sequences that fit each learner's understanding status; and
B) The system can infer a learner's learning characteristics through analysis of teaching actions that are accepted by the learner.

For the reasons mentioned above, it is important to clarify structures of decision-making, which represent "How to and what to learn", and structures of information collection, which represent "How the action will affect the learner". We suggest that the knowledge-level model comprises a combination of the decision-making structure and the information collection structure.

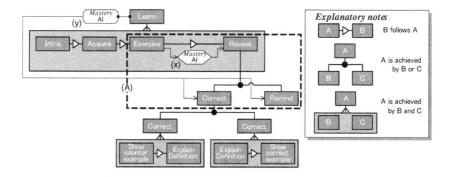

Fig. 3. An example of a decision-making model at the knowledge level

Decision-Making Structure for Selecting Teaching Action. The basic composition of the decision-making structure in IESs is a combination of an action and a content to be learned. To present some examples, the activity "Exercise AI" comprises the action "Exercise" and the content "AI"; the activity "Review AI" comprises the action "Review" and the same content. These two activities are arranged and connected by "IB: Mastery AI" in Fig. 4. This connection means that decision-making of "Review AI" is available depending on the result of "Exercise AI".

In this case, the availability of "Review AI" is determined depending on the interpretation of the learner's response in the learning process. However, that availability is sometimes determined depending on the system's understanding of a learner. Arrows from "LM: Mastery AI" to "Correct AI" and "Remind AI" show an example of the determination. "LM: Mastery AI" represents the system's understanding of a learner about "AI". Using this information, "Review AI" is performed as "Correct AI" when the learner has not learned "AI" before and is performed as "Remind AI" when the learner has learned before.

Information Collection Structure for Learner Modelling. It is important to consider the following two types of information as a learner model that justifies the decision-making of IESs:

- Hypothetical/Temporal Interpretation of a learner's behavior (IB); and
- The system's relatively stable understanding of a learner (LM).

The IB is record of a learner's behavior in a learning activity. For instance, an IB is a learner's result of a test or history of activities a learner has performed. The Learner Model (LM) represents the learner's understanding status, as inferred from that learner's prior learning history. For example, if an LM is "understand" but an IB is "not passed", the learner understands the exercise, but cannot solve it. This contradictory situation might be evidence that justifies the system's decision that the system helps to "Remind" the learner and to use prior knowledge that was gained through learning.

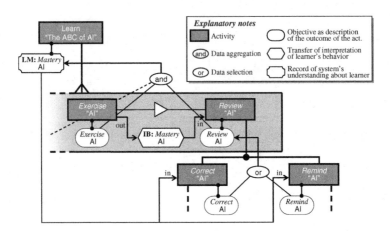

Fig. 4. Detail of the knowledge level model in terms of learner modelling

Information collection structures are those that generate IB and LM, and are represented by a connection of the upper and lower objectives. Two types of connection are defined: "And" and "Or". In the structure shown in Fig. 4, "Review AI" is achieved by either lower action: "Correct AI" and "Remind AI". Subsequently, the connection is "Or". On the other hand, the entire content of "Learn AI" consists of all the flows of lower actions. For that reason, the connection is "And".

3.2   Conversion of a Knowledge Level Model into a Symbol Level Model

Figure 5 shows the symbol-level model corresponding to the knowledge-level model shown in Fig. 4.

Decision-making structures can be described in an activity tree and sequencing rules. In Fig. 4 "Exercise AI" and "Review AI" are described as child activities of "Learn AI". The condition that "Review AI" is made available is described as PreConditionRule1.

Information collection structures are describable using roll-up rules. "Learn AI" must aggregate information of all child activities; thereby, the roll-up rule1 has value "all" in the child activity set. Both kinds of learner information mentioned in 3.1 (IB and LB) can be described in a global shared objective, but their functionality is different. The value of "IB: Mastery AI" is referred only by "Review AI". The value of "LM: Mastery AI" is used by the system as a component of the learner model.

This study introduces a concept of a pattern for connecting a knowledge-level model and a symbol-level model. The following are basic patterns for decision-making and information collection patterns listed below.

(a) Alternative pattern: pattern for selecting an activity
(b) Process division pattern: pattern for dividing a process
(c) Content division pattern: pattern for dividing content

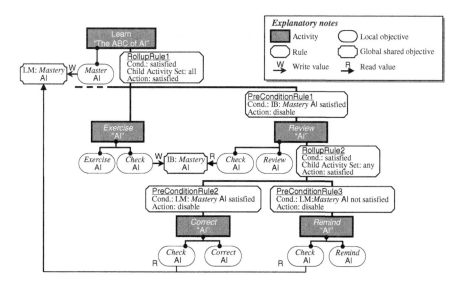

Fig. 5. A symbol level model

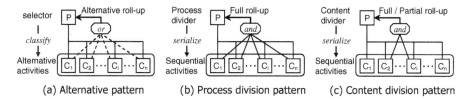

(a) Alternative pattern   (b) Process division pattern   (c) Content division pattern

Fig. 6. Patterns for designing an activity tree

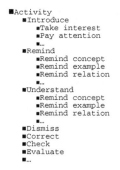

Fig. 7. Patterns for designing an activity tree

These patterns are shown in Fig. 6. Alternative patterns are used to select activities depending on the learner's status (IB or LM). The process division pattern and content division pattern are used to carry out activities serially. Each activity is put into shape by the IES ontology (shown partially in Fig. 7), which is developed in our preliminary work in [8, 10]. A combination of these patterns allows designers to construct a flexible decision-making model for various learning contents.

Pedagogical meaning of these patterns suggests a way to roll-up from lower activities. Recalling basic decision-making and information collection patterns, in the case of (a), only one activity is carried out. For that reason, that activity is used in roll-up. In contrast, in the cases of (c) and (d), the activity consists of its child activities; thereby, all or any of the child activities are used in roll-up.

4   Toward Knowledge-Level Authoring Support

As mentioned in the previous chapter, learning content that is produced considering the knowledge level has a complex structure, even if its scale is not large. In addition, designers are required to maintain consistency not only at the symbol level, but also at the knowledge level. It is difficult to manage these tasks using only human resources.

Obstacles involving production costs and knowledge description have been pointed out since the early stages of IES study. Authoring tools are expected to solve those problems; many researchers have applied their efforts to studies of authoring tools [7].

One example is REDEEM [2], an authoring tool that offers simple operation along with user-friendly interface with terms that are familiar to teachers. With their own pedagogical knowledge, teachers (not researchers) can easily use REDEEM to build IESs. However, knowledge described by authors is thought by many to be shallow because of the simplified user interface. It is important to retain the balance between simplicity of interfaces and depth of knowledge.

Through this study, we have developed an IES authoring tool that conforms to SCORM2004 based on *i*Designer [10]. The latter is an intelligent authoring tool, not for IES "knowledge based" representations, but for CAI "story-board" representations. The salient characteristic of *i*Designer is its ontology awareness [11]. Based on the ontology for CAI design, *i*Designer helps authors intelligently depending on the authors' design intentions.

The authoring tool proposed in this paper incorporates standard awareness, in addition to ontology awareness, for high scalability. These two types of awareness allow the authoring tool to maintain consistency from the author's design intention on the knowledge level through its implementation on the symbol level.

Figure 8 depicts an image of interfaces of the authoring tool. The main interface is the content editor (Fig. 8(A)), which shows a structure for decision-making and information collection. Values of nodes are set on the window in Fig. 8(B). While setting the values, authors can refer to items to be selected using the windows shown in Figs. 8(C) and 8(D).

The panel of Fig. 8(B) shows a setting of the activity "Correct", which is the node that is darkened in the window of Fig. 8(A). This activity is divisible to two child activities, "Show counter example" and "Explain definition", based on the content division pattern. The activities are selected from the window of Fig. 8(C), which presents a hierarchy of ontology from left to right.

Objects of the activities are described in common concepts, for example "Example", and "Rule", in definitions of activity concepts. The objects are arranged by items in learning item networks shown in window Fig. 8(D). Each activity defines restrictions on the object. For example, "Example" should be an instance of the target concept or its lower concept. Consequently, "Example" portrays "Mt. Fuji" as an instance of the concept "Dormant Volcano".

Such descriptions at the knowledge level are converted to a symbol-level model based on the patterns. The output is learning content that conforms to SCORM2004.

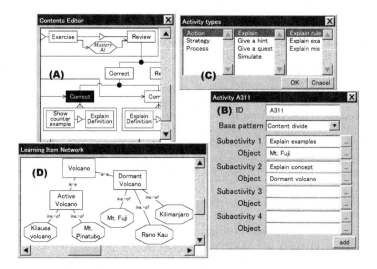

Fig. 8. Interfaces of the authoring tool (imaginary)

5   Conclusions

This paper presented an exploration of learning content design with knowledge-level representation on top of the SCORM2004 platform as a symbol-level architecture of IES decision-making structure. This approach facilitates the sharing and reuse of academic and technical expertise in the field of IES study on a common platform. Such a platform will facilitate development of SCORM into a next-generation standard specification for more adaptive and intelligent contents. Some problems remain, including organizing concepts related to educational activities, accumulating principles or empirical knowledge of construction of activities, and coordination between the knowledge level and symbol level, and others, nevertheless, an ontological engineering approach can facilitate their solution.

References

1. ADLNet: Sharable Content Object Reference Model: SCORM2004 2nd Ed., `http:/www.adlnet.org/`, (2004)
2. Ainsworth, S., Major, N. Grimshaw, S. Hayes, M., Underwood, J., Williams, B., Wood, D.: Simple Intelligent Tutoring Systems from Usable Tools, Authoring Tools for Advanced Technology Learning Environments (2003) 205-232
3. Aroyo, L., Dicheva, D., Cristea, A.: Ontological Support for Web Courseware Authoring, Proc. of ITSf02 (2002), 270-280
4. Aroyo, L., Pokraev, S., Brussee, R.: Preparing SCORM for the Semantic Web, Proc. of CoopIS/DOA/ODBASE 2003 (2003) 621-634
5. Murray, T.: Authoring Knowledge Based Tutors: Tools for Content, Instructional Strategy, Student Model, and Interface Design, J. of the Learning Sciences **7**(1) (1998) 5-64
6. Murray, T.: Authoring Intelligent Tutoring Systems: Analysis of the state of the art, Int. J. of AI and Education **10**(1) (1999) 98-129
7. Murray, T., Blessing, S. Ainsworth, S. (eds.): Authoring Tools for Advanced Technology Learning Environments, Kluwer Academic Publishers, the Netherlands (2003)
8. Mizoguchi, R., Bourdeau, J.: Using Ontological Engineering to Overcome AI-ED Problems, Int. J. of Artificial Intelligence in Education **11**(2) (2000) 107-121
9. Newell, A.: The Knowledge Level, Artificial Intelligence **18** (1982) 87-27
10. Hayashi, Y., Ikeda, M., Mizoguchi, R.: A Design Environment to Articulate Design Intention of Learning Contents, International Journal of Continuing Engineering Education and Life Long Learning **14**(3) (2004) 276-296
11. Ikeda, M., Seta, K. Mizoguchi, R.: Task Ontology Makes it Easier to Use Authoring Tools, Proc. of Intl. Joint Conf. on Artificial Intelligence (IJCAI97) (1997) 23-29
12. Ikeda, M., Hayashi, Y., Jin, L., Chen, W., Bourdeau, J., Seta K., Mizoguchi R.: Ontology more than a Shared Vocabulary, Proc. of AIED99 Workshop on Ontologies for Intelligent Educational Systems (1999) 1-10
13. Ullrich, C.: An instructional component for dynamic course generation and delivery, Proc. of Berliner XML Tag 2003 (2003) 467-473
14. Woolf, B.P., McDonald, D.D.: Building a computer tutor: design issues IEEE Computer **17**(9) (1984) 61-73

A New Solution Concept for Coalitional Games in Open Anonymous Environments

Makoto Yokoo[1], Vincent Conitzer[2], Tuomas Sandholm[2],
Naoki Ohta[1], and Atsushi Iwasaki[1]

[1] Faculty of Information Science and Electrical Engineering,
Kyushu University, 6-10-1 Hakozaki, Higashi-ku,
Fukuoka, 812-8581 Japan
{yokoo, iwasaki}@is.kyushu-u.ac.jp, oota@lang.is.kyushu-u.ac.jp
[2] Computer Science Department, Carnegie Mellon University
5000 Forbes Avenue, Pittsburgh, PA 15213 USA
{conitzer, sandholm}@cs.cmu.edu

Abstract. Coalition formation is a key aspect of automated negotiation among self-interested agents. In order for coalitions to be stable, a key question that must be answered is how the gains from cooperation are to be distributed. Various solution concepts (such as the Shapley value, core, least core, and nucleolus) have been proposed. In this paper, we demonstrate how these concepts are vulnerable to various kinds of manipulations in open anonymous environments such as the Internet. These manipulations include submitting false names (one acting as many), collusion (many acting as one), and the hiding of skills. To address these threats, we introduce a new solution concept called the *anonymity-proof core*, which is robust to these manipulations. We show that the anonymity-proof core is characterized by certain simple axiomatic conditions. Furthermore, we show that by relaxing these conditions, we obtain a concept called the least anonymity-proof core, which is guaranteed to be non-empty.

1 Introduction

Coalition formation is a key capability in automated negotiation among self-interested agents. In order for coalition formation to be successful, a key question that must be answered is how the gains from cooperation are to be distributed. *Coalitional game theory* provides a number of solution concepts for this, such as the Shapley value, the core, the least core, and the nucleolus. Some of these solution concepts have already been adopted in the multi-agent systems literature [10, 4, 7, 1, 2].

Besides being of interest of the game-theory and multi-agent systems research community, the growth of the Internet and e-commerce has expanded the application areas of coalitional game theory. For example, consider a large number of companies, some subset of which could form profitable virtual organizations that can respond to larger or more diverse orders than an individual company can.

T. Washio et al. (Eds.): JSAI 2005 Workshops, LNAI 4012, pp. 53–64, 2006.
© Springer-Verlag Berlin Heidelberg 2006

Due to the advance of the Internet, forming such virtual organizations becomes much easier, but the companies must agree on how to divide the profit among themselves.

However, existing solution concepts have limitations when applied to open anonymous environments such as the Internet. In such environments, a single agent can use multiple identifiers (or *false names*), pretending to be multiple agents, and distribute its ability (skills) among these identifiers. Alternatively, multiple agents can collude and pretend to be a single agent that combines all of their skills. Furthermore, an agent might try to hide some of its skills. Finally, complex combinations of these manipulations are also possible—for example, three agents could collude and use two identifiers, distributing some of each agent's skills to each identifier, while hiding other skills.

These manipulations are virtually impossible to detect in open anonymous environments, and have thus become an issue in such environments specifically. That is also the reason why the gamut of these manipulations, in particular, false-name manipulations, has not received much research attention previously. (An important exception is the work on pseudonymous bidding in combinatorial Internet auctions. For that setting, false-name proof protocols have been developed [9].)

In this paper, we provide a range of examples that demonstrate the vulnerability of the existing coalitional solution concepts to these new types of manipulations. We then develop a new solution concept for coalitional games called the *anonymity-proof core*, which is robust to the manipulations described above. We show that the anonymity-proof core is characterized by certain axiomatic conditions (including that an agent does not have an incentive to use the manipulations mentioned above). Furthermore, we show that by relaxing some of these conditions, we obtain a concept called the *least anonymity-proof core*, which is guaranteed to be non-empty.

2   Model

Traditionally, value division in coalition formation is studied in *characteristic function games*, where each potential coalition (that is, each subset X of the agents) has a value $w(X)$ that it can obtain. This assumes that utility is transferable (for example, utility can be transferred using side payments), and that a coalition's value is independent of what non-members of the coalition do.

The characteristic function by itself does not give us sufficient information to assess what manipulations may be performed by agents in an open anonymous environment. For example, if an agent decides to use false names and to split itself into two different identifiers, then what is the new characteristic function over the new set of agent identifiers? Presumably, this depends on *how* the agent splits itself into multiple agents—but the characteristic function does not contain any information on different ways in which the agent may split itself up. Because of this, we need a more fine-grained representation of what each agent brings to the table. Instead of defining the characteristic function over agents, we define it over *skills* that the agents possess. (The word "skills" should not be interpreted too strictly—while the skills may indeed correspond to the abilities of the agents, they may also correspond to, for example, resources that the agents possess.)

Definition 1 (skills and agents). *Assume the set of all possible skills is T. Each agent i has one or multiple skills $S_i \subset T$. For simplicity, we assume each skill is unique, that is, $\forall i \neq j, S_i \cap S_j = \emptyset$ holds.*[1]

Definition 2 (characteristic function defined over skills). *A characteristic function $v : 2^T \to \Re$, where $\Re$ is the set of real numbers, assigns a value to each set of skills.*

We will denote by w the characteristic function defined *over agents*, and by v the characteristic function defined *over skills*. For a given set of agents X, let $S_X = \bigcup_{i \in X} S_i$. Then, we have $w(X) = v(S_X)$. The characteristic function over skills is a more fine-grained representation than the characteristic function over agents (the latter can be derived from the former but not vice versa). Typically, both v and w are weakly increasing: adding more skills or agents to a coalition never hurts.

We assume that the coalition and the value division (payoffs to the agents) are established as follows.

- There exists a special agent whom we will call the *mechanism designer*. The mechanism designer knows T, the set of all possible skills,[2] and v, the characteristic function defined over T.
- If agent i is interested in joining a coalition, it declares the skills it has to the mechanism designer.
- The mechanism designer determines the value division among participants.

We assume the following three types of manipulation (or any combination of them) are possible for agents.

Definition 3 (hiding skills). *If agent i has a set of skills S_i, for any $S'_i \subseteq S_i$, it can declare that it has only S'_i.*

On the other hand, we assume that an agent cannot declare it has a skill that it does not have in reality—we assume that such a lie is detectable (because the lie will be exposed once the agents in the coalition are called on to apply their skills).

Definition 4 (false names). *Agent i can use multiple identifiers and declare that each identifier has a subset of skills S_i. Since we assume each skill is unique,*

---

[1] This assumption is just for making the notation simple; even if there are two identical skills, we can set different names on them.

[2] We do not require that each skill in T is actually possessed by some agent; the only thing that is required is that every skill that an agent possesses is indeed in T. Therefore, the mechanism designer really only needs to know an upper bound on the set of skills possessed by the agents.

two different identifiers cannot declare they have the same skill. Thus, a false-name manipulation by agent i corresponds to a partition of S_i into multiple identifiers. (If the manipulation is combined with a skill-hiding manipulation, only a subset of S_i is partitioned.)

Definition 5 (collusion). *Multiple agents can collude and pretend to be a single agent. They can declare the skills of this agent to be the union of their skills (or a subset of this union, in case we combine the manipulation with a skill-hiding manipulation).*

We can combine the various manipulations to obtain more complex manipulations. We already described how to combine the latter two manipulations with a skill-hiding manipulation. As another example, an agent with skills a and b, and another agent with only skill c, can collude and submit one identifier with only skill a, and another with skills b and c. This can be seen as a combination of the latter two manipulations: 1) the first agent splits into two false names (one with skill a and one with skill b), 2) the second false name (with skill b) colludes with the agent with skill c. More generally, the following result shows that all manipulations can be seen as a combination of these three basic manipulations.

Theorem 1. *Letting S be the union of a coalition's skills, any manipulation in which this coalition submits several identifiers with non-overlapping subsets of S as their skills can be achieved by a combination of the previous three manipulations.*

We omit the proof due to space constraint.

3   Traditional Solution Concepts

So far, we have not yet discussed how the value of the coalition should be divided. In this section, we briefly review some of the traditional solution concepts for doing so. First, we review a well-known solution concept known as the *Shapley value* [6]. The Shapley value aims to distribute the gains from cooperation in a fair manner. It has many equivalent characterizations; we will review one that gives a formula in closed form for it.

Definition 6 (Shapley value). *Give an ordering o of the set of agents W in the coalition, let $X(o, i)$ be the set of agents in W that appear before i in ordering o. Then the Shapley value for agent i is defined as*

$$Sh(W, i) = \frac{1}{|W|!} \sum_o (w(X(o, i) \cup \{i\}) - w(X(o, i))).$$

The intuitive interpretation of the Shapley value is that it averages an agent's marginal value over all possible orders in which the agents may join the coalition.

Next, we show another well-known (perhaps the best known) solution concept called the *core* [3, 8].

Definition 7 (core). *Given a set of agents W, an outcome, that is, a value division $c^W = (c_1^W, c_2^W, \ldots)$ among agents is in the core if the following two conditions hold:*

1. $\forall X \subset W, \sum_{i \in X} c_i^W \geq w(X)$,
2. $\sum_{i \in W} c_i^W = w(W)$.

The first condition is called the *non-blocking* condition: if for some set of agents X, this condition does not hold, then the agents in X have an incentive to collectively deviate from the mechanism and to divide $w(X)$ among themselves. The second condition is called the *feasibility* condition: if $\sum_{i \in W} c_i^W > w(W)$, this outcome is infeasible.[3] Thus, an outcome is in the core if it is blocked by no coalition and feasible. In general, the core can be empty. Also, the core can contain a large set of outcomes.

Next, we show a solution concept called the *least* core, which can be either a relaxation or a tightening of the core. We first define the ϵ-core, which is used in the later definition.

Definition 8 (ϵ-core). *Given a set of agents W and value ϵ, an outcome $c^W = (c_1^W, c_2^W, \ldots)$ is in the ϵ-core if the following two conditions hold:*

1. $\forall X \subset W, \sum_{i \in X} c_i^W \geq w(X) - \epsilon$,
2. $\sum_{i \in W} c_i^W = w(W)$.

If $\epsilon = 0$, this definition coincides with the definition of the core. If ϵ is positive (negative), the non-blocking condition is relaxed (resp. tightened). It is obvious that for any $\epsilon < \epsilon'$, if an outcome is in the ϵ-core, it also in the ϵ'-core.

Now, we can define the least core as follows.

Definition 9 (least core). *Given a set of agents W, an outcome $c^W = (c_1^W, c_2^W, \ldots)$ is in the least core if the following two conditions hold.*

- c^W *is in the ϵ-core,*
- $\forall \epsilon' < \epsilon$, *the ϵ'-core is empty.*

The least core is non-empty for any characteristic function, but it may contain multiple outcomes. The solution concept known as *nucleolus* [5] is a refinement of the least core. It is guaranteed to be in the least core and uniquely determined for any characteristic function. Due to limited space, we omit the formal definition of the nucleolus.

4   Manipulability of Traditional Solution Concepts

4.1   Vulnerability to False Names

Example 1. Let there be three skills a, b, and c. Let all three skills be necessary, that is, let the characteristic function over skills be as follows:

---

[3] Usually, the feasibility condition is represented as $\sum_{i \in W} c_i^W \leq w(W)$. From the non-blocking condition, the equality must hold.

- $v(\{a, b, c\}) = 1$, and for any proper subset $S \subset \{a, b, c\}$, $v(S) = 0$.

Let agent 1 have skill a and let agent 2 have skills b and c. Then, the characteristic function over agents is as follows.

- $w(\{1\}) = w(\{2\}) = 0$, $w(\{1, 2\}) = 1$.

In this example, there are only two possible orderings of the agents and in each of those, the second agent in the ordering has marginal contribution 1. Therefore, the Shapley value for each agent is $1/2$. Any outcome (c_1, c_2) that satisfies $c_1 \geq 0, c_2 \geq 0$, and $c_1 + c_2 = 1$ is in the core. The least core has only one outcome, which is identical to the Shapley value. Hence, the nucleolus is identical to the Shapley value.

Example 2. Let the skills and the function v be the same as in Example 1. Let there be three agents $1, 2$, and 3 who have skills a, b, and c, respectively. Then, the characteristic function over agents is as follows.

- $w(\{1, 2, 3\}) = 1$, and for any proper subset $X \subset \{1, 2, 3\}$, $w(X) = 0$.

In this example, there are six possible orderings of the agents, and the last agent has marginal contribution 1. Therefore, the Shapley value for each agent is $1/3$. Any outcome (c_1, c_2, c_3) that satisfies $c_1 \geq 0, c_2 \geq 0, c_3 \geq 0$, and $c_1 + c_2 + c_3 = 1$ is in the core. The least core has only one outcome, which is identical to the Shapley value. Hence, the nucleolus is identical to the Shapley value.

Now, we can see that the Shapley value, the least core, and nucleolus are all vulnerable to false-name manipulations: in Example 1, agent 2 can use two identifiers 2 and 3 and split its skills over these identifiers. Then, the situation becomes identical to Example 2. Thus, agent 2 can increase the value awarded to it from $1/2$ to $2/3 = 1/3 + 1/3$ using false-names. In fact, this example proves the following result:

Theorem 2. *There exists no payoff division function that 1) equally rewards the agents that are symmetric with respect to w, 2) distributes all the value, and 3) is false-name proof.*

Proof: Assume a function satisfies 1) and 2). Then, this function should coincide with the Shapley value (or nucleolus) on both Examples 1 and 2. However, we have just shown that such a payoff division is not false-name proof. □

4.2   Vulnerability to Collusion

Example 3. Let there be three skills a, b, and c. Let the characteristic function over skills be as follows.

- $v(\{a, b\}) = v(\{a, c\}) = v(\{a, b, c\}) = 1$,
- $v(\{a\}) = v(\{b\}) = v(\{c\}) = v(\{b, c\}) = 0$.

Let there be three agents $1, 2$, and 3 with skills a, b, and c, respectively. Then, the characteristic function over agents is as follows.

- $w(\{1,2\}) = w(\{1,3\}) = w(\{1,2,3\}) = 1$,
- $w(\{1\}) = w(\{2\}) = w(\{3\}) = w(\{2,3\}) = 0$.

In this example, there are six possible orderings of the agents. The marginal contribution of agent 1 is 0 only if it is the first agent in the ordering, and 1 otherwise. Hence, the Shapley value of agent 1 is 2/3, and the Shapley value of each of agents 2 and 3 is 1/6 (if two agents are symmetric, their Shapley values must be identical). In this example, there is only one outcome in the core, namely outcome $(1, 0, 0)$. This is because if agent 2 (or 3) obtains any value, then the non-blocking condition is violated because agent 1 and agent 3 (or 2) have an incentive to deviate from the mechanism and form their own coalition. This is also the only outcome of the least core, and hence the nucleolus also gives this outcome.

Example 4. Let the skills and the function v be the same as in Example 3. Let there be two agents, and let agent 1 have skill a and let agent 2 have skills b and c. Then, the characteristic function over agents is identical to the one in Example 1.

Since the characteristic function over agents is identical to the one in Example 1, the Shapley value, the core, the least core, and nucleolus, are also identical to those for Example 1.

   Now, we can see that the Shapley value, the least core, and the nucleolus are all vulnerable to collusion: in Example 3, agent 2 and 3 can collude and pretend to be a single agent 2, who has skills b and c. Then, the situation becomes identical to Example 4. Thus, if the Shapley value is used, agent 2 and 3 can increase the total value awarded to them from $1/3 = 1/6 + 1/6$ to $1/2$. Also, if the least core or the nucleolus is used, agent 2 and 3 can increase the total value awarded to them from 0 to $1/2$.

5   Applying the Solution Concepts to Skills

The examples from the previous section show that the characteristic function w defined over agents is too coarse-grained to represent the relative importance of agents in an open anonymous environment. In this section, we take a different approach: what if we apply the traditional solution concepts directly to the (finer-grained) characteristic function v over skills? That is, treat each submitted skill as an imaginary agent, and use the characteristic function v over these imaginary agents to compute the value division over them. Then, give each (real) agent the sum of the payoffs to the skills that it submitted. For example, in Example 1, the Shapley value, least core, and nucleolus would all give a value of 1/3 to each skill; therefore, agent 1 receives 1/3, and agent 2 (having submitted two skills) receives 2/3.

Theorem 3. *Applying any solution concept to the skills directly is robust to false names, collusion, and any combinations thereof.*

Proof: Because solution concepts applied to the skills directly are indifferent to which agent submitted which skills, changing the identifiers under which skills are submitted never changes the payoffs to those skills.   □

However, there may still be incentives to hide skills, as we demonstrate next. Consider again Example 4. If we calculate the solution concepts over the skills directly, the payoffs to these skills (for any one of the solution concepts) are the same as the payoffs to agents in Example 3. Thus, agent 1 receives 2/3 and agent 2 receives 1/3 if we use the Shapley value applied to the skills, and agent 1 receives 1 and agent 2 receives 0 if we use the core/least core/nucleolus applied to the skills. Now, consider the following example.

Example 5. Let there be two skills a and b. Let the characteristic function over skills be as follows:

$-\ v(\{a,b\}) = 1, v(\{a\}) = v(\{b\}) = 0.$

Let agent 1 have skill a and let agent 2 have skill b.

It is easy to see that both the Shapley value and the least core/nucleolus will give 1/2 to each agent in this example. Now, we can see that the Shapley value, the least core, and the nucleolus are all vulnerable to the hiding of skills when applied directly to the skills. In Example 4, agent 2 can hide skill c. Then, the situation becomes identical to Example 5. Hence the agent 2 increases its payoff from 1/3 to 1/2 for the Shapley value, and from 0 to 1/2 for the least core/nucleolus.

6   Anonymity-Proof Core

In this section, we develop a new solution concept for our setting which we call *anonymity-proof core*. As we will show, the anonymity-proof core can be characterized by certain axiomatic conditions. Again, we assume that the only knowledge that the mechanism designer has is T, that is, the set of all possible skills, and v, that is, the characteristic function defined over T. The mechanism designer does not know the number of agents, or the skills that each agent has. The mechanism designer must define an outcome function π that decides, for all possible reports by the agents of their skills, how to divide the value generated by these skills.

We require that the outcome function π is *anonymous*, that is, the payoff to an agent does not depend on the identifiers of the agents; it depends only on the skills of the agent and the distribution of skills over other agents.

More specifically, given an agent i and a set of other agents Y, let S_i be the set of skills that agent i has, and let $SS_Y = \{S_j \mid j \in Y\}$, where S_j is the set of skills that agent j has. Then, the outcome function $\pi(S_i, SS_Y)$ takes S_i and SS_Y as arguments, and returns the payoff to agent i, when agent i declares its skills as S_i and the other agents declare their skills as SS_Y.

Let the set of agents who joined the mechanism be W, and let the profile of the skills that agents declared be $k = (k_1, k_2, \ldots)$, where k_i is the set of skills that agent i declared. Let $S_X = \bigcup_{i \in X} k_i$, that is, S_X is the union of the skills declared by a set of agents X; let $S = S_W$; and let $SS_X = \{k_i \mid i \in X\}$. Also, let $SS_{\sim i} = \{k_1, \ldots, k_{i-1}, k_{i+1}, \ldots\}$, that is, a set, each of whose elements is the set of skills corresponding to agent j $(j \neq i)$.

We now give six axiomatic conditions that the outcome function π should satisfy.

1. The outcome function π is anonymous.
2. π is never blocked by any coalition, that is, $\forall k, \forall X \subseteq W, \sum_{i \in X} \pi(k_i, SS_{\sim i}) \geq v(S_X)$ holds.
3. π is always feasible and always distributes all of the value, that is, $\forall k, \sum_{i \in W} \pi(k_i, SS_{\sim i}) = v(S)$ holds.
4. π is robust against hiding skills, that is, $\forall S', S''$, where $S'' \subseteq S'$, $\forall SS$, $\pi(S'', SS) \leq \pi(S', SS)$ holds.
5. π is robust against false-name manipulations, that is, $\forall k, \forall X \subseteq W, Y = W \setminus X, \sum_{i \in X} \pi(k_i, SS_{\sim i}) \leq \pi(S_X, SS_Y)$ holds.
6. π is robust against collusions, that is, $\forall k, \forall X \subseteq W, Y = W \setminus X,$ $\sum_{i \in X} \pi(k_i, SS_{\sim i}) \geq \pi(S_X, SS_Y)$ holds.

In order to define the anonymity-proof core, we first formally define the core for skills. For a set of skills $S = \{s_1, s_2, \ldots\}$, we define a set of core outcomes for skills $Core(S)$ as follows.

Definition 10 (core for skills). $c^S = (c_{s_1}^S, c_{s_2}^S, \ldots)$ is in $Core(S)$ if it satisfies the following two conditions.

- $\forall S' \subset S, \sum_{s_j \in S'} c_{s_j}^S \geq v(S')$,
- $\sum_{s_j \in S} c_{s_j}^S = v(S)$.

Now we are ready to define the anonymity-proof core.

Definition 11 (anonymity-proof core). We say the outcome function π_{ap} is in the anonymity-proof core if π_{ap} satisfies the following two conditions.

1. For any set of skills $S \subseteq T$, there exists a core outcome for S, that is, some $c^S = (c_{s_1}^S, c_{s_2}^S, \ldots) \in Core(S)$, such that for any skill profile $k = (k_1, k_2, \ldots,)$ with $\bigcup_i k_i = S$, $\pi_{ap}(k_i, SS_{\sim i}) = \sum_{s_j \in k_i} c_{s_j}^S$ holds.
2. $\forall S', S''$, where $S'' \subseteq S'$, $\forall SS$, $\pi_{ap}(S'', SS) \leq \pi_{ap}(S', SS)$ holds.

The first condition says that for any set of skills reported by the agents, some outcome in the core for that set of skills should be used to distribute the value. The second condition says that an agent has no incentive to hide its skills.

Example 6. Let the skills and the function v be identical to those in Example 3. Since $c^{\{a,b,c\}} = (c_a^{\{a,b,c\}}, c_b^{\{a,b,c\}}, c_c^{\{a,b,c\}}) \in Core(\{a, b, c\})$ if $c_a^{\{a,b,c\}} = 1, c_b^{\{a,b,c\}} = 0, c_c^{\{a,b,c\}} = 0$, the following outcome function is in the anonymity-proof core:

- $\pi_{ap}(\{a\}, \{\{b, \ldots\}, \ldots\}) = \pi_{ap}(\{a\}, \{\{c, \ldots\}, \ldots\}) =$
  $\pi_{ap}(\{a, b\}, \{\ldots\}) = \pi_{ap}(\{a, c\}, \{\ldots\}) = \pi_{ap}(\{a, b, c\}, \{\}) = 1,$
- $\pi_{ap} = 0$ everywhere else.

First, we show that outcome functions in the anonymity-proof core satisfy the axioms.

Theorem 4. *Any outcome function π_{ap} in the anonymity-proof core satisfies the six axioms.*

Proof: Axiom 1 holds because π_{ap} only considers which skills were reported and not by which agent they were reported. Axiom 4 holds by the second condition of the anonymity-proof core.

Also, using the first condition of the anonymity-proof core, for any set of skills $S \subseteq T$, there exists a core outcome for S, that is, some $c^S = (c^S_{s_1}, c^S_{s_2}, \ldots) \in Core(S)$, such that for any skill profile $k = (k_1, k_2, \ldots,)$ with $\bigcup_i k_i = S$, $\pi_{ap}(k_i, SS_{\sim i}) = \sum_{s_j \in k_i} c^S_{s_j}$ holds. Therefore, $\forall k$ with $\bigcup_i k_i = S$, $\forall X \subseteq W$, $\sum_{i \in X} \pi_{ap}(k_i, SS_{\sim i}) = \sum_{i \in X} \sum_{s_j \in k_i} c^S_{s_j} = \sum_{s_j \in S_X} c^S_{s_j} \geq v(S_X)$. Thus, Axiom 2 holds. Also, $\sum_{i \in W} \pi_{ap}(k_i, SS_{\sim i}) = \sum_{i \in W} \sum_{s_j \in k_i} c^S_{s_j} = \sum_{s_j \in S} c^S_{s_j} = v(S)$. Thus, Axiom 3 holds. Also, $\forall k$ with $\bigcup_i k_i = S$, $\forall X \subseteq W$, $Y = W \setminus X$, $\sum_{i \in X} \pi_{ap}(k_i, SS_{\sim i}) = \sum_{i \in X} \sum_{s_j \in k_i} c^S_{s_j} = \pi_{ap}(S_X, SS_Y)$ holds. Therefore, Axiom 5 and Axiom 6 hold. □

Next, we prove that any outcome function that satisfies the above six axioms is actually in the anonymity-proof core. To prove this, we use the following lemma.

Lemma 1. *If an outcome function π satisfies the six axioms, then for any skill profile $k = (k_1, k_2, \ldots,)$ where $\bigcup_i k_i = S$, $\pi(k_i, SS_{\sim i}) = \pi(k_i, \{S \setminus k_i\})$ holds.*

We omit the proof due to space constraint. This lemma means that the outcome of agent i is determined by k_i and $S \setminus k_i$, that is, the skills of agent i and the union of skills of other agents, i.e., how the skills in $S \setminus k_i$ are distributed among other agents does not affect the payoff to agent i.

Theorem 5. *Any outcome function π that satisfies the six axioms is in the anonymity-proof core.*

Proof: If outcome function π satisfies the six axioms, then π satisfies the second condition of the anonymity-proof core, since Axiom 4 is identical to the second condition. All that remains to show is that π also satisfies the first condition of an anonymity-proof core. For a set of skills $S = \{s_1, s_2, \ldots\}$, let us denote $SS = \{\{s_j\} \mid s_j \in S\}$. ¿From Axiom 2 and Axiom 3, considering the case where each agent has exactly one skill in S, the following two conditions hold.

- $\forall S' \subset S, \sum_{s_j \in S'} \pi(\{s_j\}, SS \setminus \{\{s_j\}\}) \geq v(S'),$
- $\sum_{s_j \in S} \pi(\{s_j\}, SS \setminus \{\{s_j\}\}) = v(S).$

These conditions are identical to the conditions in Definition 10. Therefore, if we let $c^S_{s_j} = \pi(\{s_j\}, SS \setminus \{\{s_j\}\})$, this constitutes an element of $Core(S)$. Moreover, using Lemma 1, $\pi(\{s_j\}, SS \setminus \{\{s_j\}\}) = \pi(\{s_j\}, \{S \setminus \{s_j\}\}) = c_{s_j}^S$ holds. Now, using Lemma 1, Axiom 5, and Axiom 6, for any skill profile $k = (k_1, k_2, \ldots,)$, where $\bigcup_i k_i = S$, and $SS_{\sim i} = \{k_1, k_2, \ldots, k_{i-1}, k_{i+1}, \ldots\}$, $\pi(k_i, SS_{\sim i}) = \pi(k_i, \{S \setminus k_i\}) = \sum_{s_j \in k_i} \pi(\{s_j\}, \{S \setminus \{s_j\}\}) = \sum_{s_j \in k_i} c_{s_j}^S$ holds. Thus, the first condition of the anonymity-proof core is satisfied.   □

It is clear that if for some $S \subseteq T$, $Core(S)$ is empty, then there exists no function π_{ap} in the anonymity-proof core. The following theorem shows that the inverse is not true.

Theorem 6. *Even if for all $S \subseteq T$, $Core(S)$ is non-empty, it may be the case that the anonymity-proof core is empty.*

We use a counterexample that involves four skills to prove this theorem. Also, it turns out that if there are only three skills, no counterexamples exist. (We omit the proof due to space constraint.)

As in the case of the traditional core, there are conditions on the characteristic function v, such as convexity, under which the anonymity-proof core can be guaranteed to be non-empty. We omit this section due to limited space.

7   Least Anonymity-Proof Core

We first define the ϵ-core for skills.

Definition 12 (ϵ-core for skills). *For given ϵ, $c^S = (c_{s_1}^S, c_{s_2}^S, \ldots)$ is in ϵ-Core(S) if it satisfies the following two conditions.*

- $\forall S' \subset S, \sum_{s_j \in S'} c_{s_j}^S \geq v(S') - \epsilon,$
- $\sum_{s_j \in S} c_{s_j}^S = v(S).$

By replacing $Core(S)$ to ϵ-$Core(S)$ in Definition 11, we obtain the definition of an ϵ-anonymity-proof core. An ϵ-anonymity-proof core satisfies all axioms except Axiom 2. Therefore, although a group of agents might have an incentive to deviate from the mechanism, they don't have an incentive to use other manipulations.

A least anonymity-proof core can be defined as follows.

Definition 13 (least anonymity-proof core). *We say the outcome function π_{ap} is in the least anonymity-proof core if π_{ap} satisfies the following conditions.*

- π_{ap} is in the ϵ-anonymity-proof core.
- $\forall \epsilon' < \epsilon$, the ϵ'-anonymity-proof core is empty.

The following theorem holds.

Theorem 7. *$\forall T, v$, there always exists an outcome function that is in the least anonymity-proof core.*

This theorem holds since if we set ϵ large enough, we can choose an ϵ-core so that the second condition in Definition 11 can be satisfied. We omit the detail due to space constraint.

8   Conclusions

We demonstrated that traditional solution concepts of coalitional games—namely the Shapley value, core, least core, and nucleolus—are vulnerable to various kinds of manipulations in open anonymous environments such as the Internet. Specifically, we showed that they can be vulnerable to the submission of false-name identifiers and collusion. We showed that the problems of false-name identifiers and collusion can be prevented by applying the solution concepts to the skills directly rather than to the agents, but this is still vulnerable to the hiding of skills. We then introduced a solution concept called the *anonymity-proof core*, which is robust to these manipulations. We characterized the anonymity-proof core by certain simple axioms. Also, we introduced another concept called the least anonymity-proof core, which is guaranteed to be non-empty.

References

1. Conitzer, V. and Sandholm, T.: Complexity of Determining Nonemptiness of the Core, *Proceedings of the Eighteenth International Joint Conference on Artificial Intelligence (IJCAI)*, Acapulco, Mexico (2003) 613–618
2. Conitzer, V. and Sandholm, T.: Computing Shapley values, manipulating value division schemes, and checking core membership in multi-issue domains, *Proceedings of the National Conference on Artificial Intelligence (AAAI)*, San Jose, CA, USA (2004) 219–225
3. Gillies, D.: *Some theorems on n-person games*, PhD thesis, Princeton University, Department of Mathematics (1953)
4. Ketchpel, S.: Forming Coalitions in the Face of Uncertain Rewards, *Proceedings of the National Conference on Artificial Intelligence (AAAI)*, Seattle, WA (1994) 414–419
5. Schmeidler, D.: The Nucleolus of a Characteristic Function Game, *Society for Industrial and Applied Mathematics Journal of Applied Mathematics*, Vol. 17, (1969) 1163–1170
6. Shapley, L. S.: A Value for n-Person Games, in Kuhn, H. W. and Tucker, A. W. eds., *Contributions to the Theory of Games*, volume 2 of *Annals of Mathematics Studies*, *28*, Princeton University Press (1953) 307–317
7. Shehory, O. and Kraus, S.: Methods for task allocation via agent coalition formation, *Artificial Intelligence*, Vol. 101, No. 1–2, (1998) 165–200
8. von Neumann, J. and Morgenstein, O.: *Theory of games and economic behavior*, Princeton University Press (1947)
9. Yokoo, M., Sakurai, Y., and Matsubara, S.: The Effect of False-name Bids in Combinatorial Auctions: New Fraud in Internet Auctions, *Games and Economic Behavior*, Vol. 46, No. 1, (2004) 174–188
10. Zlotkin, G. and Rosenschein, J. S.: Coalition, Cryptography and Stability: Mechanisms for Coalition Formation in Task Oriented Domains, *Proceedings of the National Conference on Artificial Intelligence (AAAI)*, Seattle, WA (1994) 432–437

Part II

Logic and Engineering of Natural Language Semantics

Overview of Logic and Engineering of Natural Language Semantics (LENLS) 2005

Katsuhiko Yabushita

Department of English, Naruto University of Education
Naruto, Tokushima, Japan 772-8502
yabuchan@naruto-u.ac.jp

LENLS 2005 was held at the Kitakyushu International Conference Center, Kitakyushu, Japan on June 13-14, 2005 as one of the international workshops collocated with the 19th Annual Conference of the Japanese Society for Artificial Intelligence (JSAI 2005). The workshop was a sequel of LENLS 2004. LENLS was founded with the intent of establishing a forum where formal studies of natural-language semantics and pragmatics are presented and promoting the discipline of studies in Japan. To our delight, the workshop has grown in terms of the number of abstract submission, the number of presentations, the quality of papers, the number of participants, and the days of meeting. The general theme of the workshop was information structure and dynamic semantics. One of the characteristics of natural languages in contrast to formal languages is the existence of plural (atomic) sentences of the same propositional content but of distinct morphosyntactic and/or phonological features, as in word order, intonation, etc. Those features and their associated interpretational functions have been studied under the rubric of INFORMATION STRUCTURE. The widely accepted view as to the interpretational functions of information structure is that the information structure of a sentence reflects the speaker's assumption about the hearer's information state as the speaker conveys some information to the hearer by the utterance of the sentence. With the view of information structure, dynamic semantics, which takes the meaning of a sentence to be a (partial) function updating information states, suggests itself for an ideal framework for a formal semantic analysis of information structure. The aim of the workshop, therefore, was to bring together researchers working on information structure and/or dynamic semantics, and to advance the understanding of information structure and the development of dynamic semantics for natural language. The current chapter comprises the revised versions of the papers presented at the workshop. Shogo Suzuki presents an analysis of too couched in Rooth's Alternative Semantics and Stalnaker's Common Ground, that better implements Kripke's observations than Van der Sandt and Geurts' analysis. Yasuo Nakayama argues that the interpretation of focus makes reference to speaker's presupposition about hearer's belief state, and presents an interpretation schema for focus in terms of Natural Representation Language (NRL), a representation language for dynamic semantics. Brian Reese argues that the interpretational features characteristic of negative polarity interrogatives but absent from the positive

T. Washio et al. (Eds.): JSAI 2005 Workshops, LNAI 4012, pp. 67–68, 2006.

counterparts are not denotational but discourse-interpretational in nature. He then proposes an analysis in terms of SDRT. Patrizia Paggio proposes an approach to information structure in a unification-based grammar of Danish. Her approach is characterized by a new interface between information structure and semantics and the integration of information structure as a dimension of phrasal and clausal grammar constructions. Kei Yoshimoto, Masahiro Kobayashi, Hiroaki Nakamura, and Yoshiki Mori takes on the long-standing problem of the construal of floating quantifiers in Japanese. In contradistinction to the predominant, syntax-based approach, they put forth an alternative approach based on real-time, incremental sentence processing and information structure and demonstrate that it is empirically more adequate. Katsuhiko Yabushita questions the plausibility of the Mapping Hypothesis for an approach to the distribution of readings on nominal-predicate sentences in Japanese. Alternatively, he advances an approach based on information-structural constraints, which is demonstrated to be more adequate conceptually as well as empirically. Yurie Hara argues for the thesis that the computation of implicatures cannot be done purely in terms of semantics and pragmatics alone without recourse to syntax. As evidence, she presents an analysis of the parallelism between contrastive topic, which induces implicature and evidential morphemes in distribution in the environments of 'because' and 'when' clauses, in which Evidential Phrase plays a crucial role. Anders Søgaard argues that anaphora resolution is not triggered by grammar but results for free, from the derivation of the preferred interpretation, which is represented as a dynamically generated, minimal model. Jinung Kim and Nicholas Asher delineate the properties of the Korean modal system by examining the modal subordination phenomenon, especially, in interaction with evidentials, discourse markers, and zero pronouns. Eric McCready formalizes the semantics and pragmatics of a Japanese 'notification' particle yo in a dynamic semantic framework, in which yo's modal interpretation is also accounted for. Norihiro Ogata proposes a fully non-representational analysis of modal subordination in a dynamic semantic framework couched in System Transition Systems making use of coalgebras. Nicholas Asher argues that the embeddability of speech acts within connectives implies a dynamic semantics for speech acts; furthermore, discourse relations are indispensable for an adequate analysis. He then proposes an analysis of speech acts in SDRT terms. Besides the presenters and the audience, the reviewers were vital participants of the workshop. Credit for reviewing goes to (in the alphabetical order): Eric McCready, Yoko Mizuta, Yasuo Nakayama, Rick Nouwen, Norihiro Ogata, Rolf Schwitter, Katsuhiko Yabushita, and Kei Yoshimoto. Last but not least, I would like to acknowledge the organizational and/or financial assistance of The Japanese Society for Artificial Intelligence, especially Professor Takashi Washio, who was the chief organizer of the international workshops, The Japan Society for the Promotion of Science, and The Tohoku University 21st Century COE (Center of Excellence) Program in Humanities "Strategic Research and Education for an Integrated Approach to Language, Brain and Computation".

A Note on Kripke's Observation*

Shogo Suzuki

University of Tokyo

Abstract. In an unpublished manuscript [1], Kripke argues against the usual view on the presupposition of *too*, according to which *too* induces a presupposition that there is an object different from the referent of the focus which satisfies the unfocused part of the sentence to which *too* applies. Rather, *too* has a presupposition that has to be anaphoric to particular objects which are parallel with the referent of the focus. Van der Sandt and Geurts try to formulate this observation in their binding theory of presupposition, which, though, fails to capture the full range of Kripke's original observation. This paper proposes a simple formulation of the observation by using Rooth's Alternative Semantics for focus and Stalnaker's ideas concerning presuppositions and context.

1 *Too*'s Presupposition

In an unpublished manuscript, 'remarks on the formulation of the presupposition projection' [1], Kripke argues against the usual view on the presupposition of *too*. According to the usual view on the presupposition of *too*, *too* in (1) triggers a presupposition that 'someone other than the boss will come' in the consequent of the conditional. With the help of theories of presupposition projection (e.g., [2] among many others), the usual view would predict that the whole conditional (1) carries the same presupposition, since the antecedent does not entail the presupposition.

(1) If Herb comes to the party, the boss$_F$ will come, too.

According to Kripke, however, the presupposition of the consequent is that 'Herb is not the boss'. Important to note is, Kripke continues, that this presupposition is dependent upon the antecedent of the conditional. Even with this one example only, we can see that the usual view on *too*'s presupposition is too weak, in that it does not explain the dependence of the presupposition in the consequent on the antecedent.

Kripke further points out a problem in cases like (2).

(2) (??) Tonight, Sam$_F$ is having dinner in New York, too.

---

* I'm very grateful to Chris Tancredi for his comments. I also appreciate the members of semantics reading group at Komaba and the audience of LENLS 2005. All errors are, of course, mine.

T. Washio et al. (Eds.): JSAI 2005 Workshops, LNAI 4012, pp. 69–76, 2006.

The presupposition of (2) predicted by the usual view is that 'someone other than Sam is having dinner in New York tonight.' This predicted presupposition is problematic, however. For this presupposition is too easy to satisfy, because we know that many people different from Sam have dinner in New York every night. Despite this triviality, the sentence is not felicitous when uttered out of the blue, contrary to what the usual view predicts.

With these examples, Kripke suggests that *too* has a presupposition that has to be anaphoric to particular objects which are in some sense parallel with the referent of the focus. Moreover, he requires that these parallel objects be either explicitly mentioned previously in the conversation, or on interlocutors' minds and known to be on interlocutors' minds, or highly prominent in some fashion, namely that they come from the *active* context.

2   Van der Sandt and Geurts' DRT Analysis

Based on Kripke's observations, van der Sandt and Geurts [3] develop an analysis for *too*'s presupposition within the framework of their 'binding theory' of presupposition (cf. [4], [5]).

Assuming their binding theory of presupposition, van der Sandt and Geurts distinguish two conditions in the presupposition of *too*. Suppose that *too* applies to the sentence $\varphi(a)$, where a is the focus that *too* associates with. One condition is a descriptive condition $\varphi(x)$,[1] in which the unfocused material of the sentence φ applies to a discourse referent x. This condition could be either bound or accommodated. The other condition is an anaphoric condition $x \neq a$. Crucially this x must be bound but not accommodated. In their formal language, the full presupposition containing them is represented as $\partial[: \varphi(x), \partial[x : x \neq a]]$.[2] Here ∂ is a mark that indicates that the following DR structure is a presupposition. The two conditions inside the main presupposition are separately and independently resolved into the context.

Let's see how this proposal works. In their theory, (2) is represented as (3).

(3) [x: Sam(x), have_dinner(x), $\partial[:$ have_dinner(y), $\partial[y: y \neq x]]]$

In order for the 1st occurrence of variable y to be resolved, it must seek an antecedent. However, since the only available discourse referent is x in the out-of-the-blue context and the resolution of y to x causes inconsistency in the context, the anaphoric condition of the presupposition can not be resolved. By assumption the anaphoric condition cannot be accommodated, an assumption incorporated into definition of *too*'s presupposition, so presupposition failure results.

Turning to the conditional example (1), its initial representation is (4).

---

[1] In a recent paper [6], they ascribe the descriptive condition involved in *too*'s presupposition to focus presupposition.

[2] In [6], the discourse referent x is introduced by the anaphoric condition, and there is no embedding relationship between the descriptive condition and the anaphoric condition.

(4) [x, y: Herb(x), boss(y), [: comes(x)] ⇒ [: comes(y), ∂[: comes(z),
    ∂[z: z ≠ y]]]]
(5) [x, y: Herb(x), boss(y), x ≠ y, [: comes(x)] ⇒ [: comes(y)]]

Following the algorithm in the binding theory of presupposition, the anaphoric
condition ∂[z: z ≠ y], which is the most embedded presupposition, is processed
first. Since x is now a possible antecedent of z, the anaphoric condition is resolved
at the global context, the descriptive condition is resolved to the antecedent of
the conditional, and the result in (5) is what we expect; the presupposition 'Herb
is not the boss' comes to the global context condition.

Van der Sandt and Geurts discuss a disjunction example, as in (6).

(6) Either the boss will stay away from the party, or John$_F$ will come, too.
(7) [x, y: boss(x), John(y),
    [: stay_away(x)] ∨ [: comes(y), ∂[: comes(z), ∂[z: z ≠ y]]]]
(8) [x, y: boss(x), John(y), x ≠ y, [: stay_away(x)] ∨ [: comes(x), comes(y)]]

The initial representation of (6) is (7). The anaphoric condition is resolved to the
global context, as above, but the descriptive condition has no possible antecedent
to which to be resolved. But this time the local accommodation of the descriptive
condition is a possible option, as in (8). Again we get the desirable result.

3   Problems in Van der Sandt and Geurts' Analysis

Although their analysis succeeds in explaining several cases involving *too*, it has
problems as well. First, their analysis predicts that once there is an antecedent
referent available, the anaphoric condition is resolved to it and the descriptive condition is accommodated, regardless of conditions that referent occurs in.
Beaver and Zeevat [7][3] clearly and correctly point this out. If uttered out of the
blue, (9) surely sounds odd.

(9) ? Jane likes Bill. Bill is having dinner in New York too. ([7])

Van der Sandt and Geurts' analysis predicts, however, that the anaphoric condition can be resolved to Jane, with the descriptive condition accommodated in
the global context. The resulting structure represents that Jane likes Bill, Bill is
different from Jane, Jane is having dinner in New York and Bill is having dinner
in New York, which is obviously a wrong prediction.

Next but more importantly, their formalism fails to explain other interesting
observations by Kripke. In the following cases (10)-(12), antecedents anaphoric
to *too*'s presupposition are split.

(10) If Herb and his wife both come to the party, the boss$_F$ will come, too.
(11) Sam will come to the party. If Herb and his wife both come,
    the boss$_F$ will come, too.
(12) If the chemists come to the party, Harry$_F$ will, too.

---

[3] They attribute this observation to Nicholas Asher.

Kripke says that (10) presupposes that neither Herb nor his wife is the boss, (11) that the boss must be distinct from all three, and (12) that Harry is not a chemist. Van der Sandt and Geurts' analysis fails to capture these presuppositions because the anaphoric condition must be resolved only once. If there are several antecedents, their analysis would wrongly permit incidental identity between focus and antecedents.[4]

4   A Proposal

In formulating the presupposition of *too*, I will employ the following three tools; Alternative Semantics developed in [8], the Focus Interpretation Principle proposed in [9], and the Common Ground (cf.[10]).

In his dissertation, Rooth develops a theory of focus in which in parallel with the ordinary semantic value of a phrase, a focus semantic value of the phrase is computed, which is a set of alternatives obtainable from the ordinary semantic value by making a substitution in the position corresponding to the focused phrase. For instance, the focus value of the sentence *Mary saw John$_F$*, with the focus accent on *John*, is the set of propositions of the form 'Mary saw x', where x ranges over the domain of individuals. In notation:

(13) $[\![\text{Mary saw John}_F]\!]^f = \{\text{saw}(m, x) \mid x \in E\}$ (E: domain of individuals)

In [9], while preserving the power of Alternative Semantics, Rooth proposes a theory in which focus sensitive constructions do not directly refer to focus semantic values. The focus sensitive expressions refer to focus semantic values indirectly via the squiggle operators. The semantics of this operator is the Focus Interpretation Principle, which is defined as follows.

$$
\begin{aligned}
&(a) \; [\![\Pi]\!]^\circ \subseteq [\![\phi]\!]^f, \\
(14) \; [\![\phi \sim \Pi]\!]^\circ = [\![\phi]\!]^\circ, \text{ provided that } &(b) \; [\![\phi]\!]^\circ \in [\![\Pi]\!]^\circ, \text{ and} \\
&(c) \; \exists \pi [\pi \neq [\![\phi]\!]^\circ \; \& \; \pi \in [\![\Pi]\!]^\circ]
\end{aligned}
$$

Here, the interpretation function superscripted by o computes ordinary semantic values of expressions. Capital Π is intended as a focus anaphoric variable.

The Common Ground, as developed by Stalnaker [10], is defined as the set of propositions that interlocutors mutually assume to be true without controversy. The concept of presupposition is formulated with respect to the Common Ground. Pragmatically, presupposition is licensed when the Common Ground contains it or the intersective closure of the Common Ground (the Context Set) entails it. Semantically, presupposition is a definedness condition with respect to the Common Ground.

More formally, let $\text{Dox}_w(s)$ and $\text{Dox}_w(h)$ be doxatic sets of speaker s and hearer h, respectively, at a given possible world w, i.e., sets of propositions that

---

[4] A reviewer correctly points out that their analysis would become improved by employing summation in standard DRT. Although I agree with this observation, the summation can combine any discourse referents, regardless of whether they satisfy *too*'s presupposition, which causes the same problem as the first one.

s and h believe at w respectively (I will omit world variables henceforth). The Common Ground is formulated as the intersection of the closures of these doxatic sets under logical consequence, namely, $CG = \{\varphi \mid \text{Dox}(s) \models \varphi\} \cap \{\varphi \mid \text{Dox}(h) \models \varphi\}$. Accordingly, I will define the incrementation of the Common Ground by a proposition φ, $CG + \varphi$, as $\{\psi \mid CG \cup \{\varphi\} \models \psi\}$.[5]

With these mechanisms, I will define *too*'s presupposition as in ((15)-(16)).

(15) $[S \sim \Pi] [[\text{too } C] \Pi]$
(16) $[\![\text{too}]\!]^\circ = \lambda C.\lambda\Pi.\lambda p : C \cap \Pi \neq \emptyset.p.$

Assuming (15) as input to semantic interpretation, (16) states that *too* takes a variable C for the Common Ground and an alternative set variable Π and gives back the sentence interpretation only if the Common Ground and the alternative set share some propositions.

Let's see how this explains data so far. Consider (1), repeated here.

(1) If Herb comes to the party, the boss$_F$ will come, too.
(17) ?* If Herb comes to the party, Herb$_F$ will come, too.

Now the local context for the consequent is the Common Ground augmented by the content of the antecedent. Thus *too* takes C + the proposition 'Herb comes to the party' as the Common Ground value, rather than C alone. The presupposition of *too* is satisfied in this case. It is important to note, however, the Focus Interpretation Principle, together with the anaphoric resolution of the alternative variable Π, assigns another presupposition, which amounts to the proposition that Herb is not the boss. Consequently, the whole conditional has the presupposition that Herb is not the boss. Notice that the present formulation by itself cannot rule out (17). This is because the focus anaphoric variable must contain the sentence interpretation as a member. To remedy this, I will assume the informativity of assertion, which is independently motivated (cf. [11]). An assertion of a proposition φ is informative with respect to Common Ground CG iff $CG + \varphi \neq CG$.

Turning to (2), one might notice that the Focus Interpretation Principle in principle cannot exclude the proposition 'there is someone other than Sam who is having dinner in New York' from the set of alternative propositions.

(2) (??) Tonight, Sam$_F$ is having dinner in New York, too.
(18) Tonight many other people are having dinner in New York, and Sam$_F$ is having dinner in New York, too.

Notice also that the Common Ground would usually contain the proposition 'someone other than Sam is having dinner in New York'. This means that the present formulation would allow infelicitous uses of *too*. Nevertheless I will assume that the set of alternative propositions usually excludes the problematic proposition in question, because it does not seem to be a plausible alternative

---

[5] The complexity of this definition might be avoided if I use the context set, rather than the Common Ground, but the present formulation enables us to simplify the following discussion, especially the formulation of *too*.

to the proposition 'Sam is having dinner in New York.' This is good because in certain situations the proposition 'someone other than Sam is having dinner in New York' is a valid alternative. In (18), the first conjunct of this sentence makes the the proposition 'someone other than Sam is having dinner in New York' a valid alternative.

Let's go to the disjunction example (6).

(6) Either the boss will stay away from the party, or John$_F$ will come, too.

As suggested (but not argued for) by Soames [12], I will assume that the local context for the second disjunct is the Common Ground + the negation of the first disjunct. This solution is very different from van der Sandt and Geurts' analysis which obtains the same effect via accommodation. Since I have defined increment in the Common Ground by a proposition φ as adding φ to the Common Ground and taking the closure of the result of this addition under logical consequence, the local context for the second disjunct now entails the proposition 'the boss will come to the party'. This last proposition satisfies the presupposition of the second disjunct, only in the case in which the boss is not John, which in turn comes to be the presupposition of the whole disjunction.

And finally, split antecedent cases.

(10) If Herb and his wife both come to the party, the boss$_F$ will come, too.
(11) Sam will come to the party. If Herb and his wife both come,
     the boss$_F$ will come, too.
(12) If the chemists come to the party, Harry$_F$ will, too.

By virtue of the definition of increment in the Common Ground, the local context for the consequent of (10) now contains two propositions 'Herb comes to the party' and 'Herb's wife comes to the party'. Hence *too*'s definition together with the Focus Interpretation Principle and informativity of assertion guarantees that the boss is neither of them.

For (11), all we have to assume is that the second conjunct of a conjunction is evaluated with respect to the Common Ground + the first conjunct. This means that the local context for the consequent now contains the following three propositions; 'Sam comes to the party', 'Herb comes to the party', and 'Herb's wife comes to the party'. The presence of these propositions warrants the distinctiveness of the boss from all the three, Sam, Herb, and Herb's wife.

Now the last example for the plural antecedent (12). Notice that the proposition 'the chemists are coming to the party' by itself does not entail any proposition of the form 'x is coming to the party' for any chemist x. This is because the proposition 'the chemists are coming to the party' alone does not specify who is a chemist and who is not. To solve this problem, we assume that domain restriction for definite descriptions and quantifiers is fixed to the evaluation world.

5 Discussion

Van der Sandt and Geurts discuss cases involving inaccessible domains, the observation of which they attribute to Zeevat [13].

(19) A: Harry may well have dinner in New York.
      B: John_F is having dinner in New York, too.

The peculiarity of this example is that *too*'s presupposition is licensed by the material within the preceding modal context, which presuppositions triggered by expressions other than *too* usually cannot access. Their explanation is that, since the descriptive condition does not introduce new discourse referents in the universe, this condition is freely resolvable even to materials within inaccessible domains. Furthermore, in [6], they take 'x is inaccessible to y' as 'if y were bound to x, we would have a defective DRS on our hands'. Here a DRS becomes defective if resolution or accommodation of presuppositions causes redundancy or inconsistency in the whole structure. With this conception of inaccessibility, they regard their explanation for this case as legitimate.

   Their analysis is, however, too indulgent with respect to resolution of the descriptive condition to inaccessible domains.

(20) ? Fred is not staying at the Ritz and Barney_F is staying there too. ([14])
(21) Sue doubts that Ed attended the meeting, but we all agree that Jill attended the meeting (?too). ([15])
(22) (Sue thinks Bob married Christie.) Does Steve think Bob (?also) married Nana_F? ([16])

Their analysis incorrectly predicts that all of these examples should be felicitous, which suggests that their definition of inaccessibility is too loose. To be fair, I have to add that in the response paper [17] they submit to this counter-argument, and suggest, following Zeevat's speculation, that not all types of inaccessible domains but only those that could be called 'veridical' (cf. [18]) inaccessible domains admit this type of resolution. Notice that my analysis correctly rules out these cases by demanding that the Common Ground must be consistent, which seems to be a reasonable restriction on context. As we have seen, however, their solution overrides context consistency and wrongly predicts these to be fine.

   As far as cases like (19) are concerned, however, my proposal apparently fares no better than van der Sandt and Geurts' approach. For the Common Ground would not include propositions embedded in inaccessible domains, even if they are veridical ones. Nor would the squiggle operator permit alternatives which do not belong to focus semantic values of a given expression. According to Chris Tancredi (p.c.), however, B in (19) commits herself to *too*'s presupposition. This suggests that there is an accommodation of *too*'s presupposition in (19). The following example supports this conjecture.

(23) A: Harry may have dinner in New York, or he may not.
      B: # John_F is having dinner in New York, too.

In (23), the intended presupposition of *too* (in this case, 'Harry is having dinner in New York') cannot be accommodated (into the global context), because such an accommodation would make the second disjunct in A's utterance uninformative. My present proposal correctly predicts this. I suspect that in Zeevat's examples, *too*'s presupposition is not resolved into an inaccessible domain, but accommodated into the global context. Van der Sandt and Geurts still incorrectly predict that B's utterance in (23) is admitted in this context. For their descriptive condition can be resolved into inaccessible domains unless this resolution makes any DRSs defective. Contrary to their expectation, the notion of veridicality does not get them out of the difficulty.

References

1. Kripke, S.: Remarks on the formulation of the projection problem. Unpublished manuscript (1990)
2. Karttunen, L., Peters, S.: Conventional implicature. In Oh, C.K., Dinneen, D.A., eds.: Syntax and Semantics 11: Presupposition. Academic Press, New York (1979) 1–56
3. van der Sandt, R., Geurts, B.: Too. In: Proceedings of the 13th Amsterdam Colloquium, University of Amsterdam (2001)
4. van der Sandt, R.: Presupposition projection as anaphora resolution. Journal of Semantics **9** (1992) 333–377
5. Geurts, B.: Presuppositions and Pronouns. Elsevier, Oxford (1999)
6. Geurts, B., van der Sandt, R.: Interpreting focus. Theoretical Linguistics **30** (2004) 1–44
7. Beaver, D., Zeevat, H.: Accommodation. In Ramchand, G., Reiss, C., eds.: The Oxford Handbook of Linguistic Interfaces. OUP, Oxford (to appear)
8. Rooth, M.: Association with Focus. Ph.D. dissertation, University of Massachusetts, Amherst (1985)
9. Rooth, M.: A theory of focus intepretation. Natural Language Semantics **1** (1992) 75–116
10. Stalnaker, R.: Context and Content. Oxford University Press, Oxford, UK (1999)
11. Büring, D.: The Meaning of Topic and Focus - The 59th Street Bridge Accent. Routledge, London (1997)
12. Soames, S.: Presupposition. In Gabbay, D., Guenthner, F., eds.: Handbook of Philosophical Logic Vol. VI. Kluwer, Dordrecht (1989) 553–616
13. Zeevat, H.: Explaining presupposition triggers. In van Deemter, K., Kibble, R., eds.: Information Sharing: Reference and Presupposition in Language Generation and Interpretation. CSLI, Stanford (2002) 61–87
14. Schwarzschild, R.: Focus interpretations: comments on Geurts and van der Sandt (2004). Theoretical Linguistics **30** (2004) 137–147
15. Kratzer, A.: Interpreting focus: Presupposed or expressive meanings? a comment on Bart Geurts and Rob van der Sandt. Theoretical Linguistics **30** (2004) 123–136
16. Büring, D.: Focus suppositions. Theoretical Linguistics **30** (2004) 65–76
17. Geurts, B., van der Sandt, R.: Interpreting focus again. Theoretical Linguistics **30** (2004) 149–161
18. Giannakidou, A.: Polarity Sensitivity as (Non) Veridical Dependency. Benjamins, Amsterdam (1998)

Focus, Presupposition, and Propositional Attitude

Yasuo Nakayama

School of Human Sciences, Osaka University
1-2 Yamada-oka, Suita, Osaka, Japan
nakayama@hus.osaka-u.ac.jp

1 Introduction

A focus in an uttered sentence is the word of greatest prosodic prominence in the sentence. Most formal frameworks of focus are based on Hamblin's theory of questions, which represents a question as the set of possible answers (cf. [2]). Contrary to these approaches, this paper proposes a formal theory of focus in which propositional attitudes of communication partners play a crucial role. The central hypothesis of this theory is the following:

S uses focus either for *information supply* or for *correction*, namely
  (a) in order to give H particular information that H would need or
  (b) in order to point out something false about H's belief.
Hence, when S uses focus,
  (a) S presupposes that H lacks particular information or
  (b) S presupposes that H believes something false.

These speaker's presuppositions can be specified by using *discourse congruence*, namely *question-answer congruence* indicates presupposition (a) and *binary contrast* indicates presupposition (b). In this paper, I will show how to describe problems related to interpretation of focus, such as *question-answer congruence*, *binary contrast*, *contrast in discourse structure*, *partial negation*, and *focal presupposition*.

In what follows, NRL (Natural Representation Language)[1] is used as a representational tool. NRL is a framework of dynamic semantics, in which dynamic correlations are represented by use of Skolem symbols. Furthermore, NRL uses comma ',' as conjunction and '{' and '}' as parentheses. For example, NRL-formula $\{F(d_1), G(d_1, d_2), \neg\{H(d_2)\}\}$ has the same truth condition as FOL-formula $\exists x_1 \exists x_2 (F(x_1) \wedge G(x_1, x_2) \wedge \neg H(x_2))$. We use the sign '$\cup$' in order to merge two NRL-formulas. For example, $\{K(d_1)\} \cup \{L(d_1)\}$ is NRL-equivalent with $\{K(d_1), L(d_1)\}$. A NRL-formula K is true in structure M, iff there exists a Skolem expansion $M*$ in which K is true, where Skolem expansion $M*$ is a structure that can be constructed from M by adding arbitrary interpretation of Skolem symbols. This use of NRL enables a dynamic treatment of focus, i.e. NRL interpretation of focus can be embedded in dynamic interpretation of a discourse. In NRL, any pronoun supplemented with an index can be used as a Skolem symbol. So, we may use $something_k$ as a Skolem symbol.

---

[1] For details of NRL, see [3].

T. Washio et al. (Eds.): JSAI 2005 Workshops, LNAI 4012, pp. 77–84, 2006.
© Springer-Verlag Berlin Heidelberg 2006

2 NRL Interpretation Schema for Focus

Let $[N]_F$ indicate the focused expression in sentence $K(N)$. NRL interpretation of $K([N]_F)$ consists of a felicitous condition and a content description.

(1) NRL Interpretation schema for focus

(A) Felicitous condition: S presupposes 1 and (2a or 2b), where
  1. H believes that $K(something_k)$.
  2a. H does not know what $something_k$ is. (information requirement)
  2b. H believes that $something_k$ is not N. (false belief)
  (In a typical NP focus: 2b. H believes that $something_k \neq N$.)

(B) Content of $K([N]_F)$: $K(something_k) \cup \{something_k$ is $N\}$.
  (In a typical NP focus: (B) Content: $K(something_k) \cup \{something_k = N\}$.)

When we substitute $[N]_F$ in $K([N]_F)$ with a variable, we obtain NRL-formula $K(x)$, which corresponds to Jackendoff's Presupp$_s$ and Rooth's *ps skeleton* (presupposition skeleton) (cf. [1] p. 245, [2] p. 288, [4]). However, NRL interpretation differs from Jackendoff's interpretation in two points. First, schema (1) uses Skolem symbols instead of variables. Second, schema (1) interprets presupposition explicitly as speaker's presupposition about hearer's belief states and not as speaker's simple presupposition. So, the speaker himself need not presuppose $K(something_k)$, when he utters $K([N]_F)$. This has a crucial consequence about focal presupposition. According to (1), S's utterance of $K([N]_F)$ is only felicitous, if S presupposes that H believes that something is K. So, this utterance triggers S's presupposition about H's existential presupposition, but not S's own existential presupposition. Hence, NRL interpretation correctly classifies an utterance of "$[Nobody]_F$ likes Kim" as a felicitous assertion (cf. section 3.6).

Schema (1A) expresses the felicitous condition for S's utterance of $K([N]_F)$:

(2) S's utterance of "$K([N]_F)$" is *felicitous* iff S presupposes 1 and (2a or 2b).

Let us apply schema (1) to two differently focused utterances, where we concentrate on the case of information supply.

(3) John introduced Bill to $[Sue]_F$.
  ps skeleton: {**John introduced Bill to** x}.
(4) John introduced $[Bill]_F$ to Sue.
  ps skeleton: {**John introduced** x **to Sue**}.

(3A) Felicitous condition: S presupposes 3-1 and 3-2a, where[2]
  3-1. H believes that **John introduced Bill to** $somebody_3$.
  3-2a. H does not know who $somebody_3$ is.
(3B) Content: {**John introduced Bill to** $somebody_3$}$\cup\{somebody_3 = $ Sue$\}$.

(4A) Felicitous condition: S presupposes 4-1 and 4-2a, where
  4-1. H believes that **John introduced** $somebody_4$ **to Sue**.
  4-2a. H does not know who $somebody_4$ is.
(4B) Content: {**John introduced** $somebody_4$ **to Sue**}$\cup\{somebody_4 = $ Bill$\}$.

---

[2] In this paper, $somebody_k$ is used as a Skolem constant that satisfies condition $\{somebody_k$ ε_{human} HUMAN$\}$, which means that $somebody_k$ is human, i.e. $somebody_k$ is an atomic part of the whole human being.

It is easy to examine that differently focused utterances of the same sentence generate different pragmatic effects. For example, in case (3), we tend to interpret that S wants to tell H who John introduced Bill to, whereas in case (4), we usually interpret that S wants to convey to H who John introduced to Sue. Here, we can see that (3) and (4) differ in ps skeleton and other differences are generated from this difference.

3   Some Applications of NRL Interpretation Schema

3.1   Question-Answer Congruence

As Kadmon (2001) points out, the focus part of a sentence is the answer to an appropriate question (cf. p. 251). This general idea can be explicated in the following way.

(5) A question-answer pair has the following form:
   A: $K(what_n)$?
   B: $K([N]_F)$.
   "$K(what_n)$?" indicates that A asks B what is a value of variable $what_n$ that satisfies $K(what_n)$. In other words, by uttering the first sentence, A conveys to B that he wants to know which interpretation of $something_k$ verifies condition $K(something_k)$. Here, $K(what_n)$ is nothing else than a ps skeleton. Thus, A's utterance causes the following B's belief:
   5-1. A believes that $K(something_k)$.
   5-2a. A does not know what $something_k$ is.

By comparing 5-1 and 5-2a with 1 and 2a in (1), we can confirm that the felicitous condition of B's utterance of $K([N]_F)$ is satisfied in (5) (see (1)). In other words, A's utterance of "$K(what_n)$?" changes B's belief state, so that the felicitous condition of B's utterance of $K([N]_F)$ becomes automatically satisfied. Here, the content of B's utterance is $\{K(something_k)\} \cup \{something_k = N\}$, which is the same as described in (1). This B's utterance will please A, because it provides A with the information that the object referred by N is the object that satisfies his original question $K(what_n)$. This consideration shows that the felicitous condition of a focus sentence coincides with that of a question-answer pair.

When two utterances of the same sentence are differently focused, corresponding questions are also different. Compare the following two examples (cf. [2] p. 251).

(6) A: Who did John introduce Bill to?
   (ps skeleton: {**John introduced Bill to** who_6}).
   B: John introduced Bill to $[Sue]_F$.
(7) A: Who did John introduce to Sue?
   (ps skeleton: {**John introduced** who_7 **to Sue**}).
   B: John introduced $[Bill]_F$ to Sue.

Thus, when we apply (1) and (5) to (6) and (7), we obtain the following felicitous conditions:

B presupposes
   6-1. A believes that **John introduced Bill to** $somebody_6$.
   6-2a. A does not know who $somebody_6$ is.

B presupposes
>   7-1. A believes that **John introduced** *somebody₇* **to Sue.**
>   7-2a. A does not know who *somebody₇* is.

Here, we can confirm that felicitous conditions of (6B) and (7B) are different. This is the reason why inappropriate question-answer pairs, such as (6A)+(7B) and (7A)+(6B), are not felicitous. For example, ps skeleton of (6A) and that of (7B) are different, whereas (6A) and (6B) have the same ps skeleton.

According to (1), contents of (6B) and (7B) can be represented as follows:

Content of (6B): {**John introduced Bill to** *somebody₆*} ∪ {*somebody₆* = Sue}.
Content of (7B): {**John introduced** *somebody₇* **to Sue**} ∪ {*somebody₇* = Bill}.

These two contents are NRL-equivalent, because they are NRL-equivalent to {John introduced Bill to Sue}. However, it makes sense to distinguish these, because they can be differently correlated with new additional information (cf. Section 3.3 and 3.4) [3].

3.2   Binary Contrast

The *question-answer congruence* is one type of discourse congruence for identifying focus. Another type of discourse congruence is *binary contrast*. It is usually used for correcting particular hearer's belief. Let me explain this by using some examples (cf. [2] p. 253).

>   (8) A: Carl likes spinach.
>   B: No, Carl likes [herring]*F*.
>   (ps skeleton: {**Carl likes** *x*}.)
>   (9) A: Miriam likes herring.
>   B: No, [Carl]*F* likes herring.
>   (ps skeleton: {*x* **likes HERRING**}).

A's utterance of (8A) and (9A) usually causes the following B's beliefs, which exactly corresponds to the felicitous condition of (8B) and (9B) respectively [4]:

8-1. A believes that **Carl likes** *something₈*.
8-2b. A believes that *something₈* = SPINACH.
9-1. A believes that *somebody₉* **likes HERRING**.
9-2b. A believes that *somebody₉* = Miriam.

Content of (8B) and that of (9B) can be described as follows:

(8B): {¬ {**Carl likes** SPINACH}} ∪{**Carl likes** *something₈*}∪{*something₈* = HERRING}.
(9B): {¬ {Miriam **likes HERRING**}} ∪{*somebody₉* **likes HERRING**}∪ {*somebody₉* = Carl}.

---

[3] So far, we have only treated examples of NP focus, but VP focus can be treated in the same way, when we accept events as entities.

[4] Here, SPINACH means the fusion of the whole spinach in the world.

8-2b and 9-2b show that B thinks that A believes something false. (8B) and (9B) are uttered in order to correct A's false belief. {**Carl likes** *something*$_8$}∪{*something*$_8$ = HERRING} and {*somebody*$_9$ **likes HERRING**}∪{*somebody*$_9$ = Carl} are NRL-equivalent. However, felicitous conditions for (8) and (9) are different. For example, 8-1 and 9-1 are different. According to 8-1, B believes that A believes that Carl likes something. But, according to 9-1, B believes that A believes that somebody likes herring.

3.3   Contrast in Discourse Structure

As Umbach (2004) mentions, the prototypical marker of the discourse relation *contrast* is the connector *but* (cf. [5] p. 167). She points out that *but* is focus-sensitive and formulates the *confirm + deny condition on but-sentences* as follows: "[...], if a *but*-sentence is an appropriate answer to a question relating to both conjuncts, one conjunct has to be a confirmation and the other one has to be a denial." (p. 168)

   In this section, I will analyse semantic effects of focus by taking *contrast* as an example.

> (10) A typical *contrast in discourse structure* has the following form:
> $K([N_1]_F)$, but not $[N_2]_F$.
> (A) Felicitous condition of S's utterance: S presupposes 10-1 and 10-2b, where
>   10-1. H believes that $K(something_k)$.
>   10-2b. H believes that $something_k = N_2$ and $something_k \neq N_1$.
> (B) Content: $\{K(something_k)\} \cup \{something_k = N_1\} \cup \{something_k \neq N_2\}$.

A contrast may generate semantic difference. See the following examples.

> (11) Sue likes $[Lee]_F$, but not $[Kim]_F$. ('Sue does not like Kim')
>   ps skeleton: {**Sue likes** *who*$_{11}$}.

> (12) $[Sue]_F$ likes Lee, but not $[Kim]_F$. ('Kim does not like Lee')
>   ps skeleton: {*who*$_{12}$ **likes Lee**}.

Applying (10) to (11) and (12), we obtain the following interpretation of contents:

> (11): {**Sue likes** *somebody*$_{11}$}∪{*somebody*$_{11}$ = Lee}∪{*somebody*$_{11}$ ≠ Kim}.
> (12): {*somebody*$_{12}$ **likes Lee**}∪{*somebody*$_{12}$ = Sue}∪{*somebody*$_{12}$ ≠ Kim}.

>From these descriptions follow immediately:

> Content of (11) implies: {**Sue likes** Lee, ¬ {**Sue likes** Kim}}.
> Content of (12) implies: {Sue **likes Lee**, ¬ {Kim **likes Lee**}}.

This shows that contents of (11) and (12) are semantically different and that this difference is generated from the difference of both ps skeletons.

3.4   Dynamic Treatment of Focus

NRL is a framework of dynamic semantics. Hence, NRL-interpretation of focus can be straightforwardly combined with a formal representation of anaphora resolutions. The following example demonstrates how to combine a NRL interpretation of focus with anaphora resolution.

(13) A nurse likes $[Lee]_F$, but not $[Kim]_F$. She hates him.
Content[5]: $\{nurse_{13}$ **likes** $somebody_{13}\}\cup\{somebody_{13} = Lee\}\cup\{somebody_{13} \neq$ $Kim\}\cup\{she_{13}$ hates $him_{13}\}\cup\{she_{13} = nurse_{13}\}\cup\{him_{13} = Kim\}$.

This NRL-formula has the same truth-condition with FOL-formula $\exists x_1(nurse(x_1) \wedge like(x_1, Lee) \wedge \neg like(x_1, Kim) \wedge hate(x_1, Kim))$. In NRL interpretation, Skolem symbols play the role of discourse referents, so that they can be used in the successive NRL-formulas. This dynamic feature distinguishes NRL interpretation of focus from other focus interpretation methods.

3.5   Partial Negation

Jackendoff (1972) points out that negation associates with focus: "often negation does not seem to apply to an entire sentence, but only to part of it" ([1] p. 254, [2] p. 259). This idea of *focus-associated partial negation* can be expressed as follows: The *focused word* indicates the content that should be *negated*. This idea can be easily integrated in NRL interpretation.

(14) NRL Interpretation schema for *partial-negation* $(K([N]_F))$
Content: $K(something_k)\cup\{something_k$ is not $N\}$.

Let us apply this schema to examples (Examples are from [2] p. 259).

(15) Maxwell didn't kill the $[judge]_F$ with a silver hammer.
ps skeleton: {**Maxwell killed** x **with a silver hammer**}.
(16) Maxwell didn't kill the judge with a $[silver]_F$ hammer.
ps skeleton: {**Maxwell killed the judge with** x, x **is a hammer**}.

Let {Maxwell killed $somebody_k$ with $something_k$, $hammer(something_k)\}$ $\cup\{judge(d_k)$, $somebody_k = d_k\}\cup\{silver(something_k)\}$ be the interpretation of "Maxwell killed the judge with a silver hammer". Then, the content of (15) and (16) can be described as follows:

(15): {Maxwell killed $somebody_{15}$ with $something_{15}$, $hammer(something_{15})\}$
$\cup\{judge(d_{15})$, $somebody_{15} \neq d_{15}\}\cup\{silver(something_{15})\}$.
(16): {Maxwell killed $somebody_{16}$ with $something_{16}$, $hammer(something_{16})\}$
$\cup\{judge(d_{16})$, $somebody_{16} = d_{16}\}\cup\{\neg\{silver(something_{16})\}\}$.

According to Kadmon (2001), this is not a truth-conditional effect (p. 259). However, he is wrong, because content of (15) and that of (16) are truth-conditionally different. As shown in (1), focus always deals with presuppositions and the existence of focal presupposition does not imply absence of truth-conditional effects.

---

[5] Here, $nurse_{13}$, she_{13}, and him_{13} are used as Skolem constants that satisfy the following conditions respectively: $\{nurse_{13} \ \varepsilon_{human}$ NURSE$\}$, $\{she_{13} \ \varepsilon_{human} \ female(HUMAN)\}$, $\{him_{13} \ \varepsilon_{human} \ male(HUMAN)\}$.

3.6 The Focal Presupposition

Focal presupposition is presupposition triggered by focus. Recently, several theses about focal presupposition have been proposed. Most of them associate it with question-answer congruence (cf. [2] p. 402f). Jackendoff (1972) asks if the focus carries an existential presupposition. He denies this, because there are examples, such as "[Nobody]$_F$ likes Bill", that show evidence against this hypothesis. Thus, he weakens this hypothesis and proposes instead that the set of individuals that satisfy ps skeleton is *under discussion*. From my point of view, the question whether the focus carries an existential presupposition is misleading. It is better to ask who makes or is supposed to make an existential presupposition, when the speaker utters a focus sentence. For presupposition is always a description of the mental states of a particular person.

We should distinguish between speaker's presupposition and hearer's one. Normally, they coincide, but this is not always the case. NRL felicitous condition for focus requires only speaker's presupposition about hearer's presupposition. It can be the case that the speaker does not accept the hearer's presupposition. The following example from Jackendoff can be understood as such one (cf. [1] p. 246, [2] p. 402).

(17) [Nobody]$_F$ likes Bill.
   ps skeleton: $\{x$ **likes Bill**$\}$.
   (A) Felicitous condition: S presupposes 17-1 and 17-2a.
       17-1. H believes that *somebody*$_{17}$ **likes Bill**.
       17-2a. H does not know who *somebody*$_{17}$ is.
   (B) Content[6]: $\{$*somebody*$_{17}$ **likes Bill**$\} \cup \{cd_{human}(somebody_{17}) = 0\}$.

In this case, S believes that H presupposes that there is a person who likes Bill, but S does not share this existential presupposition with H. The focus is used in this case, in order to correct H's belief of the existence of a person who likes Bill.

Kadmon (2001) examines Strawson's idea that a definite NP carries an existential presupposition. Kadmon's proposal is the following (cf. [2] p. 407): A definite NP carries an existential ps iff it is not part of the focus.

Let us consider, at first, an example where a definite NP is not part of the focus.[7]

(18) The king of France introduced her to [Bill]$_F$.
   ps skeleton: $\{$**The king of France introduced** *her*$_{18}$ **to** $x\}$.
   (A) Felicitous condition: S presupposes 18-0, 18-1, and 18-2a.
       18-0. $K_{18}(her_{18})$ and H believes $K_{18}(her_{18})$, where K_{18} expresses an identification condition for *her*$_{18}$.
       18-1. H believes that **the king of France introduced** *her*$_{18}$ **to** *somebody*$_{18}$.
       18-2a. H does not know who *somebody*$_{18}$ is.
   (B) Content: $\{$**The king of France introduced** *her*$_{18}$ **to** *somebody*$_{18}\} \cup$
       $\{$*somebody*$_{18}$ = Bill$\}$.

In this case, both S and H presuppose the existence of the king of France. In the next example, a definite NP appears as a part of the focus.

---

[6] Here, $cd_G(x)$ means the cardinality of G-object x. For details see [3].

[7] In examples (18) and (19), we consider only cases of information supply and ignore cases of correction. For cases of correction, NRL interpretation can be formed in the same way.

(19) She introduced him to [the king of France]$_F$.
      ps skeleton: $\{she_{19}$ **introduced** him_{19} **to** $x\}$.
(A) Felicitous condition: S presupposes 19-0, 19-1, and 19-2a.
      19-0. $K_{19a}(she_{19})$, $K_{19b}(him_{19})$, and H believes $K_{19a}(she_{19})$ and $K_{19b}(him_{19})$,
      where K_{19a} and K_{19b} express identification conditions for she_{19} and
      him_{19} respectively.
      19-1. H believes that she_{19} **introduced** him_{19} **to** $somebody_{19}$.
      19-2a. H does not know who $somebody_{19}$ is.
(B) Content: $\{she_{19}$ **introduced** him_{19} **to** $somebody_{19}\} \cup \{somebody_{19} =$ the
      king of France$\}$.

In (19), it is certain that S believes in the existence of the king of France. However, it is possible that H does not believe in the existence of the king of France. So, H can point out that there is no king of France, if H thinks so. Especially, when S knows that H believes that there is no king of France, (19) should be understood as a statement that entails an explicit claim of existence of the king of France. We can conclude from these considerations:

> H need not presuppose an existence presupposition, when a definite NP is a part of the focus.

4   Conclusion

Jackendoff (1972) has already pointed out that focus is closely related to presupposition. However, his treatment of presuppositions is too simple. In this paper, I proposed an interpretation of focus that takes speaker's presupposition about hearer's belief states into consideration, where the interpretation consists of a description of felicitous conditions and that of truth-conditional content. To formalize this interpretation, NRL is used. Because NRL is a representation language for dynamic semantics, we can smoothly combine focus interpretation with dynamic semantics.

References

1. Jackendoff, R. (1972) *Semantic Interpretation in Generative Grammar*, MIT Press.
2. Kadmon, N. (2001) *Formal Pragmatics - Semantics, Pragmatics, Presupposition, and Focus*, Blackwell.
3. Nakayama, Y. (2004) "Dynamic Interpretations and Interpreation Structures," *Proceedings of the International Workshop on Logic and Engineering of Natural Language Semantics*, pp. 25-35.
4. Rooth, M. (1985) *Association with Focus*, Ph.D. dissertation, University of Massachusetts, Amherst.
5. Umbach, C. (2004) "On the Notion of Contrast in Information Structure and Discourse Structure," *Journal of Semantics* 21, pp. 155-175.

Negative Polar Interrogatives and Bias

Brian Reese

Department of Linguistics, University of Texas at Austin
bjreese@mail.utexas.edu

Abstract. This paper develops a discourse based approach to negative polar interrogatives (NIs). NIs are subject to more contextual restrictions than their positive counterparts, a fact that has lead some researchers to assign the two types of question distinct denotations. I argue in favor of standard analyses of polar questions, on which positive and negative interrogatives are equivalent. I show a certain subclass of NIs has a complex semantic type due in part to intonational cues and which constrains their contribtion to discourse logical form.

1   Introduction

Standard accounts of questions treat the denotation of an interrogative sentence as the set of propositions consisting of its direct answers [1]. For simple polar interrogatives (PIs) like (1a), this set has just two members corresponding to simple *yes* and *no* answers, as in (2).

(1)   a.   Is Jane coming?
      b.   Isn't Jane coming?

(2)   { "Jane is coming", "Jane is not coming" }

On these accounts, negative polar interrogatives (NIs) like (1b) share with (1a) the denotation in (2).[1] The predicted equivalence is correct in that simple *yes* or *no* answers to either type of question pick out the same proposition: *no* means that Jane is not coming and *yes* that she is.

But NIs have a number of features that distinguish them from PIs. First, they require a backgrounded attitude by the speaker toward a positive answer. As a result, NIs are excluded from contexts that require neutrality. A question like *Aren't you a communist?*, for example, is inappropriate at a committee hearing, since it insinuates that the addressee is a communist. The bias is often epistemic, but this is not necessarily the case.

(3)   a.   Aren't you ashamed of yourselves?
      b.   Don't you like it?

---

[1] *Negative polar interrogative* describes questions containing an auxiliary verb with the negative inflection *n't*. This excludes interrogatives like *Is Jane not coming?*, which do not always convey the range of meanings addressed in this paper.

T. Washio et al. (Eds.): JSAI 2005 Workshops, LNAI 4012, pp. 85–92, 2006.

(3a) and (3b) convey deontic and desiderative biases respectively [2]. It appears, then, that a range of background attitudes is allowed, although by default this attitude is epistemic.

A second distinguishing feature of NIS is an ambiguity between so-called p and $\neg p$ readings [3, 4]. These readings are disambiguated by including polarity sensitive lexical items, such as *too* or *either*.

(4)   a.   Didn't Kim read the report *too*?
        b.   Didn't Kim read the report *either*?

(4a) seeks confirmation of the proposition that Kim read the report (the *outer negation* (ONI) reading [3]). (4b) checks the inference that Kim has *not* read the report (the *inner negation* (INI) reading [3]).

Finally, while both ONIs and INIs are acceptable in contexts biased against p, as in (5), only ONIs can be used in neutral contexts, as shown in (6).

(5)   a.   A: Sue can't attend the workshop, so there'll be no syntacticians.
        b.   B: Isn't Jane coming (too/either)?

(6)   a.   A: A lot of syntacticians are attending the workshop: George, Mary…
        b.   B: Isn't Jane coming (too/#either)?

On the assumption that Jane is a syntactician, (5a) biases the context toward the proposition that Jane is not coming and both ONIs and INIs are felicitous. (6a) does not bias the context in the same way and only ONIs are acceptable.

The divergent behavior of NIS relative to PIs may be semantically or pragmatically determined. The backgrounded speaker attitude has characteristics of a pragmatic phenomena, while the *outer/inner* negation distinction has characteristics of a scope ambiguity. Data presented below suggest that perhaps a combination of the two tactics is in order and that a careful consideration of the discourse function of NIS sheds light on certain aspects of their use.

2   Negative Interrogatives and VERUM

2.1   The Basics of the VERUM Approach

Romero and Han [4] provide an analysis of negative polar interrogatives that addresses the facts presented in Sect. 1. The analysis is based on the observation that NIS and questions containing the epistemic adverb *really* exhibit similar epistemic biases. They suggest that *really* and preposed negated auxiliaries introduce an operator VERUM, defined in (7), into the logical form of sentences.

(7) $[\![\text{VERUM}]\!]^{g[x/i]} = \lambda p_{\langle s,t\rangle} \lambda w.\forall w' \in \text{Epi}_x(w)[\forall w'' \in \text{Conv}_x(w')[p \in \text{CG}_{w''}]]$

$\text{Epi}_x(w)$ is the set of worlds accessible from w and compatible with x's knowledge in w. $\text{Conv}_x(w')$ is the set of worlds where the conversational goals of x in w' are met. Finally, $\text{CG}_{w''}$ is the set of propositions representing the shared beliefs of the discourse participants in w'', i.e. the common ground [5]. VERUM says of a proposition p that some agent x is certain that in all of the worlds in which the conversational goals of x are met, p is part of the common ground, a meaning Romero and Han gloss as FOR-SURE-CG$_x$ p.

Epistemic Bias. VERUM is an epistemic modal that embeds a meta-conversational modal statement. i.e., one referring to the *goals* of the discourse participants. Romero and Han restrict meta-conversational moves to situations where there is epistemic conflict or a need to ensure the Gricean Maxim of Quality. If the public commitments of the discourse participants are inconsistent, a meta-conversational move is licensed in order to resolve the epistemic conflict, implying prior commitments by the discourse participants. Alternatively, a speaker may believe or think that p but lack sufficient evidence to assert it. A VERUM question is appropriate in this context to suggest and seek confirmation of p.

Ladd's Ambiguity. Adding VERUM to the logical form of NIs leads to a simple account of Ladd's ambiguity [3]. The outer negation reading arises when negation outscopes VERUM; the inner negation reading arises when VERUM outscopes negation. The logical form and denotation of the outer negation and inner negation readings of (1b) are shown in (8) and (9) respectively.

(8) a. ⟦ [$_{CP}$ Q not [VERUM [$_{IP}$ Jane is coming]]] ⟧ $=$
     b. { FOR-SURE-CG$_x$ Jane is coming,
                          ¬FOR-SURE-CG$_x$ Jane is coming }

(9) a. ⟦ [$_{CP}$ Q VERUM [not [$_{IP}$ Jane is coming]]] ⟧ $=$
     b. { FOR-SURE-CG$_x$¬ Jane is coming,
                          ¬FOR-SURE-CG$_x$¬ Jane is coming }

ONIs on Romero and Han's analysis ask the addressee whether or not he is certain that p should be added to the common ground, where p is the descriptive content of the question. INIs made the same inquiry about $¬p$.

2.2   Evaluation of the VERUM Approach

[4] assigns distinct denotations to NIs and PIs, which are used to derive the divergent features of NIs from Sect. 1. But there is reason to maintain the equivalence of PIs and NIs, or at least to reject the specific proposal in [4].

Epistemic Bias. [4] recognizes that NIs often challenge some aspect of a previous utterance and builds this discourse function into the denotation of the question through the definition in (7). I have two concerns with this approach: (i) conversational goals are not the right level of description and (ii) one cannot rely on epistemic conflict or uncertainty to derive the bias.[2] Both points are illustrated by the example in (10).

---

[2] A related problem is that the bias of NIs is not *necessarily* epistemic, as assumed in [4]. This is already demonstrated by the examples in (3) from Sect. 1.

(10)   a.   A: Some of the regents support a tuition increase.

        b.   B: Don't all of them support an increase?

(10a) conversationally implicates that not all of the regents support a tuition increase, which (10b) intuitively challenges, but it is not a conversational goal of *A* that this implicature be added to the common ground; implicatures are pragmatic enrichments of utterances made by the addressee, not the speaker. Furthermore, the statement in (10a) is not inconsistent with either answer to (10b), short-circuiting the attempt to compute a conversational implicature corresponding to the bias in (10b).[3]

Ladd's Ambiguity. As noted in Sect. 1, the meaning of an interrogative is the set of propositions that count as direct answers [1]. The most direct answer to a polar interrogative consists of a simple *yes* or *no*. Intuitively, a simple *yes* response to the ONI in (6b) or (5b) conveys the proposition that Jane is coming, not the weaker one predicted in [4] that FOR-SURE-CG$_x$ Jane is coming. Likewise, *no* means that Jane is not coming, not the weaker statement that ¬FOR-SURE-CG$_x$ Jane is coming.

The denotation of INIs, given in (9b), is even more problematic. A simple positive answer to the INI reading of (5b) is most naturally understood as expressing the proposition that Jane is coming, not FOR-SURE-CG$_x$¬ Jane is coming, which would seem to express just the opposite. And again, a negative answer intuitively means that Jane is not coming, not ¬FOR-SURE-CG$_x$¬ Jane is coming, which is more congruent with the proposition that Jane *is* coming. It appears that the denotation in (2) more accurately reflects the interpretation of NIs than the denotations in (8b) and (9b).

3   The Discourse Contribution of NIs

This section develops an alternative analysis of the discourse contribution of NIs using Segmented Discourse Representation Theory (SDRT [6]). I introduce the basic architecture of SDRT and then discuss complex speech acts, their treatment in SDRT and how they contribute to discourse logical form. Finally, I show how the complex nature of ONIs constrains their contribution to dialog.

3.1   SDRT **Basics**

SDRT extends Discourse Representation Theory (DRT [7]) with a set of labels $\pi_1, \pi_2, \ldots, \pi_n$ for DRS-formulae and formulae for rhetorical connections between labels. Each utterance receives a unique label that must be related to previous contributions via a rhetorical relation R. Inferring a particular relation adds information to the discourse above and beyond that given by the compositional semantics of the individual clauses.

---

[3] This challenge to [4] comes down to whether or not conversational implicatures are added to the common ground. If they are, then a positive answer to (10b) *is* inconsistent with the common ground.

Syntax and Semantics. The set of well-formed SDRS-formulae includes well-formed DRS-formulae, in addition to formulae of the form $R(\pi_1, \pi_2)$, where R is a discourse relation and π_1 and π_2 are labels. The dynamic conjunction $\phi \wedge \phi'$ and negation $\neg\phi$ of SDRS-formulae are also SDRS-formulae. A discourse structure, or SDRS, is a triple $\langle A, \mathcal{F}, LAST \rangle$, where A is a set of labels, $LAST$ is a label in A for the content of the last clause added to the discourse logical form and $\mathcal{F}$ is a function from A to SDRS-formula. By convention, the formula that π labels, i.e., $\mathcal{F}(\pi)$, is written K_π. SDRSs are hierarchically structured, since $\mathcal{F}$ includes in its range SDRS-formulae which themselves contain labels.

Different discourse relations have distinct affects on the interpretation of a discourse. For example, if R is *veridical*, then $R(\alpha, \beta)$ entails K_α and K_β. *Narration* and *Result* are examples of veridical relations. If R is *divergent*, then $R(\alpha, \beta)$ entails $\neg K_\alpha$ and K_β. *Correction* and *Counterevidence* are examples of divergent relations. Divergent relations are used to deny the content or appropriateness of prior contributions and have a non-monotonic affect on SDRS update. Assume $R(\alpha, \beta)$ where R is veridical. If R' is divergent and $R'(\beta, \gamma)$, it follows that both K_β and $\neg K_\beta$. In this case, $R(\alpha, \beta)$ is replaced in the SDRS with $Dis(R)(\alpha, \beta)$ indicating R is disputed.

Complex Speech Acts. A label π may be assigned incompatible types, reflecting the fact that a single utterance can play multiple rhetorical roles in a dialog. SDRT treats indirect requests like (11a) in this way, since they have properties of both questions and requests [8]. (11a), for example, occurs with *please*, which selects for genuine requests, i.e. those expressed by the imperative mood, but not with interrogatives expressing true questions. Furthermore, indirect requests can be answered with *yes* or *no* like genuine questions.

(11)　　a.　A: Can you pass the salt, please?
　　　　b.　B: Yes. [(*uttered as B passes the salt*)]

Following [9], I assume that such copredication requires (11a) be assigned a complex type (or dot type) *question • request*, since the grammar is able to utilize either of the component types. If (11a) is labeled π, a new label π_r typed *request* is introduced to serve as the argument to *please*. Conversely, a new label π_q typed *question* serves as the argument to SDRT relations like QAP (Question-Answer Pair) introduced by (11b).

[10] argues that the sentence initial discourse markers *after all* and *yet* co-occur in specific ways with assertions. *After all* can be prefixed to an assertion, but not to a (neutral) question. Sentence initial *yet* can precede an utterance that follows an assertion, but not one that follows a (neutral) question. So any utterance occuring in the proper configuration with *after all* or *yet* makes an assertion. Similar tests exist for questions. The sentence initial discourse marker *tell me* only occurs prefixed to questions [10]. Applying these tests to ONIs suggests that they are *both* assertions and questions, as shown in (12) – (14).

(12)　　a.　A: Sue can't attend, so there'll be no syntacticians there.
　　　　b.　B: That's not true. After all, isn't Jane coming (too/#either)?

An ONI can felicitously combine with *after all*, while a INI cannot, as shown by the unacceptability of including *either* in (12b). Similarly, statements that follow an ONI can be prefixed with *yet* as shown by the sequences in (13). Statements that follow an INI cannot be prefixed with *yet*.

(13)   a.   A: Isn't Jane coming (too/#either)?
        b.   A: Yet, Mary claims there will be no syntacticians there.

This suggests that ONIs have an assertoric component associated with them, despite their interrogative syntax. Both ONIs and INIs, on the other hand, behave as questions, as shown in (14).

(14)   Tell me, isn't Jane coming (too/either)?

The fact that all NIs can be answered with *yes* or *no* is yet another clue that they do function as questions. These tests establish that ONIs are complex speech acts, typed *question • assertion* by the grammar.

3.2   A Case Study: ONIs in Dialog

The complex type assigned to ONIs like (15b) constrains the rhetorical role they play relative to preceding utterances (15a) and possible answers (15c).

(15)   a.   A: No syntacticians are attending the workshop. (π_1)
        b.   B. Isn't Jane coming? (π_2)
        c.   A: No./#Yes. (π_3)

The discussion below addresses the derivation of the assertion associated with (15b) and the discourse function of the question given the assertion.

Correction, Counterevidence and Intonation. There is a correlation between the intonational contour typical of ONIS and the use of utterances to issue corrections or denials [11]. In the case of (15b), intonation is a cue to A that B means to assert a proposition correcting π_1. This proposition and its rhetorical connection to the discourse context might be directly associated with the intonational contour, i.e., as part of an intonational lexicon [12] or intonation might simply serve as a cue to the interpreter that a correction is intended. Compositional semantics alone does not permit the inference to $Correction(\pi_1, \pi_2)$, since neither that Jane is coming nor that she is not coming entail the negation of K_{π_1}, as required in order to infer $Correction$. Following [6], I assume that B's utterance provides information from which A can infer $Correction$, i.e. it provides counterevidence to A's claim.

$Counterevidence(\alpha, \beta)$ holds in case K_β *defeasibly* entails the negation of K_α, so π_2 must convey a proposition that deafeasibly entails that at least one syntactician will attend the workshop. Two salient propositions are those in the partition yielded by the interrogative (15b). The proposition that Jane is not coming does not plausibly entail that a syntactician is coming. Assuming that Jane is a syntactician does not help matters. The same assumption in conjunction with the proposition that Jane *is* coming, however, does produce the necessary entailment, so B intends this proposition as counterevidence.

Challenges in Dialog. π_2 asserts that Jane is coming which acts as counterevidence to π_1. What is the contribution of the question assoicated with π_2? It is not a simple request for information, as B is already committed to an answer. Rather, in biased contexts ONIs challenge a previous utterance. I follow [13] in treating challenges as demands for evidence, allowing an analysis in terms of the SDRT relation *Evidence*$_Q$ shown in (16).

(16)   *Challenge*(α, β) ($\equiv$ *Evidence*$_Q(\alpha, \beta)$) iff β labels a question and any answer to β provides evidence for α.

If *Evidence*$_Q(\alpha, \beta)$ and $QAP(\beta, \gamma)$, then *Evidence*(α, γ). In other words, any answer to a challenge must provide evidence for the challenged utterance.

The complex type associated with (15b) explains the felicity of simple negative answers to challenges and the infelicity of simple positive answers, as shown in (15c). The negative answer π_3 coveys that Jane is not coming, which is inconsistent with the assertion in π_2 that Jane is coming. Consequently, in addition to $QAP(\pi_2, \pi_3)$ holding, *Correction*(π_2, π_3) is inferred. This correction necessitates a revision of the context, because the *Counterevidence* relation is put into dispute. So a negative response answers the challenge by disputing the counterevidence and providing evidence for the original assertion (as required by *Challenge*). A graphic representation of the SDRS is given in Fig. 1.

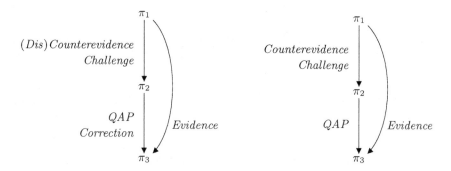

Fig. 1. SDRS of a *no* answer to (15)   **Fig. 2.** SDRS of a *yes* answer to (15)

A positive response to π_2 is infelicitous because it can not address the counterevidence. The content of the positive response is the same as that associated with B's assertion π_2. After the positive answer is given the SDRS contains as a conjunct *Counterevidence*$(\pi_1, \pi_2) \wedge$ *Evidence*(π_1, π_3), where $K_{\pi_2} \equiv K_{\pi_3}$. The proposition that Jane is coming needs to act as both evidence for and against π_1 (see Fig. 2).

This does not mean that challenges never receive positive responses, but they do require some additional content in order to be felicitous, as in (17), which attacks the implicature introduced by (15b) that Jane does syntax.

(17)   Yes, but she no longer does syntax.

Inferring *Counterevidence* requires the assumption that Jane is a syntactician. By denying this assumption, (17) puts this relation into dispute, just as the negative answer did in Fig. 1.

The analysis of NIs presented above is incomplete. Missing are (i) an account of the use of ONIs in neutral contexts and (ii) of INIs, which lack the complex type of ONIs. I leave these issues for future research. I do hope, however, that the discussion above demonstrates the promise of discourse oriented approaches to the problems posed by negative polar interrogatives.

References

1. Groenendijk, J., Stokhof, M.: Questions. In Benthem, J.v., ter Meulen, A., eds.: Handbook of Logic and Language. Elsevier, Amsterdam (1997) 1055–1124
2. Huddleston, R., Pullum, G.K.: The Cambridge Grammar of the English Language. Cambridge University Press (2002)
3. Ladd, D.R.: A first look at the semantics and pragmatics of negative questions and tag questions. In: Papers from the 17th Regional Meeting of the Chicago Linguistic Society, University of Chicago (1981) 164–171
4. Romero, M., Han, C.: On negative *yes/no* questions. Linguistics and Philosophy **27** (2004) 609–658
5. Stalnaker, R.: Assertion. In Cole, P., ed.: Syntax and Semantics. Volume 9: Pragmatics. Academic Press, New York (1978) 315–332
6. Asher, N., Lascarides, A.: Logics of Conversation. Cambridge University Press (2003)
7. Kamp, H., Reyle, U.: From Discourse to Logic. Kluwer, Dordrecht (1993)
8. Asher, N., Lascarides, A.: Indirect speech acts. Synthese **129** (2001) 183–228
9. Asher, N., Pustejovsky, J.: Word meaning and commonsense metaphysics. Available from `nasher@la.utexas.edu` (2004)
10. Sadock, J.M.: Toward a Linguistic Theory of Speech Acts. Academic Press, New York (1974)
11. Walker, M.A.: Inferring acceptance and rejection in dialog by default rules of inference. Language and Speech **39** (1996) 265–304
12. Ladd, D.R.: The Structure of Intonational Meaning: Evidence from English. Indiana University Press, Bloomington (1980)
13. Mackenzie, J.D.: Question-begging in non-cumulative systems. Journal of Philosophical Logic **8** (1979) 117–133

Representing Information Structure in a Formal Grammar of Danish*

Patrizia Paggio

Center for Sprogteknologi
University of Copenhagen
patrizia@cst.dk

Abstract. This paper presents a proposal for the integration of information structure in a unification-based grammar of Danish. Three information structure features – topic, focus and background – are defined, and it is shown how they are instantiated in a number of different grammatical constructions. Prosodic, syntactic and information structure constraints characterising the various constructions are represented as typed feature structures following Head-driven Phrase Structure Grammar (HPSG), and the constructions themselves are ordered in a type hierarchy. The proposed approach modifies and extends earlier HPSG-based accounts by i. defining a new interface between information structure and semantics, and ii. integrating information structure as a dimension of phrasal and clausal grammar constructions.

1 Introduction

In previous works [1] [2] I have described some of the peculiarities of Danish with respect to the way in which focality or topicality are expressed. The most notable features of this language in this respect are the lack of sentence accent, and the role played by word order and by syntactically marked constructions such as clefting and topicalisation. In this paper I address the issue of how information structure can be represented in a formal, unification-based grammar of the language within the framework of HPSG [3]. I propose a model in which information structure is formalised as a dimension in a hierarchy of constructions where it interacts with prosodic, syntactic and semantic properties of phrasal and clausal types.

The model is based on three well-known categories[1]. The first is the *focus*, which corresponds to the sentence elements that indicate a modification of the pragmatic information built by the overall discourse. The part of the sentence which is not in focus is the *background*, which is peripheral to the construction of the discourse, and serves the purpose of specifying or restricting the way in which the focal information must contribute to it. Finally, the third feature is the *topic*, that is the entity which the sentence expresses pertinent information about, thereby increasing the hearer's knowledge of it. Not all three categories are necessarily present in every sentence, but the focus always is. Depending

---

* This work has been funded by the Carlsberg Foundation.
[1] See e.g. [4] for an introduction to information structure.

T. Washio et al. (Eds.): JSAI 2005 Workshops, LNAI 4012, pp. 93–102, 2006.
© Springer-Verlag Berlin Heidelberg 2006

on which category is instantiated, different information structure patterns are defined, and their relation to grammatical constructions formalised in complex feature structure types.

In Sect. (2) it is clarified how the information structure of a sentence is represented, and its relation to the semantics is discussed. I argue here that my approach extends earlier HPSG-based accounts. In Sect. (3) a formal account of the four basic information structure types is given, followed in Sect. (4) by an explanation of the principles that govern the instantiation of information structure features in a syntactic derivation. In Sect. (5) an account of the interaction between information structure types and grammar constructions is provided, and finally Sect. (6) contains the conclusions.

2 Representing Information Structure

In HPSG the basic unit of linguistic representation is the sign, represented as a complex feature structure conflating all its phonological, syntactic, semantic and pragmatic properties. This representational style makes HPSG an attractive framework to capture the interaction between information structure and other aspects of the grammar. The contribution made by the various words to the information structure of a sentence is in fact represented by means of features belonging to the pragmatic description of the sign, while links between these pragmatic features and attributes pertaining to the other linguistic dimensions are ensured by structure sharing.

To represent information structure, the attribute INFOSTR is included as a value of the context (CTXT) of the sign, similarly to what proposed in [5] and [6]. Its value is a feature structure with the three attributes TOPIC, FOCUS and BG, each taking as value a list of semantic indices.

$$(1) \quad \begin{bmatrix} \text{INFOSTR} & \begin{bmatrix} \text{TOPIC (list of indices)} \\ \text{FOCUS (list of indices)} \\ \text{BG (list of indices)} \end{bmatrix} \end{bmatrix}$$

By means of the semantic indices we can let the information structure features refer to the elements that make up the semantic representation of the sentence, for which I rely on Minimal Recursion Semantics (MRS) [7] [8] [9]. In MRS, the main components of the representation are i. an unordered bag of relations, where each relation is referred to by a label and in turn refers to a number of argument variables (or indices), and ii. a number of scope assignments over pairs of relations. Furthermore, an MRS representation also contains an LTOP handle referring to the relation with the highest scope, and an instance or event INDEX introduced by the semantic head, analogous to the lambda calculus. For example, let us consider the following Danish sentence:

(2) Manden så barnet.
  Man-the saw child-the[2].
  'The man saw the child.'

---

[2] In Danish the definite article is affixed to the noun in simple NPs.

Its MRS representation may be as follows (omitting the representation of quantifiers):

$$(3) \begin{bmatrix} \text{LTOP h1} \\ \text{INDEX e2} \\ \text{RELS} \left\langle \begin{bmatrix} \_se\_v\_rel \\ \text{LBL h8} \\ \text{ARG0 e2} \\ \text{ARG1 x4} \\ \text{ARG2 x3} \end{bmatrix}, \begin{bmatrix} \_barn\_n\_rel \\ \text{LBL h5} \\ \text{ARG0 x3} \end{bmatrix}, \begin{bmatrix} \_mand\_n\_rel \\ \text{LBL h6} \\ \text{ARG0 x4} \end{bmatrix}, \begin{bmatrix} message\_m\_rel \\ \text{LBL h1} \\ \text{MARG h7} \end{bmatrix} \right\rangle \\ \text{HCONS} \left\langle \text{h7 qeq h8} \right\rangle \end{bmatrix}$$

The label (LBL) value of the *message* relation at the end of the relation list (RELS) is also the top handle (LTOP) of the sentence, whilst its argument (MARG) is equalled to the label of the relation introduced by the main verb via the *qeq* ('equality modulo quantifiers') constraint in the HCONS list. Furthermore, the verbal relation has three arguments referring to an event and to the instances associated with the relations *barn* (child) and *mand* (man), respectively.

The most obvious reading of this sentence in information structure terms is as a *topic-comment* construction, where the VP constitutes the comment to the topical subject. An alternative term well-known from the generative tradition is *wide focus*:

(4) [$_T$ Manden] [$_F$ så barnet].

On this reading, I suggest that the information structure part of the sign should look as follows:

$$(5) \begin{bmatrix} \text{INFOSTR} \begin{bmatrix} \text{TOPIC} \left\langle x4 \right\rangle \\ \text{FOCUS} \left\langle x3, e2 \right\rangle \\ \text{BG} \left\langle \right\rangle \end{bmatrix} \end{bmatrix}$$

The values of the information structure features coincide with indices in the MRS representation. The TOPIC coincides with the index associated with the subject, whilst the FOCUS is a list of two indices corresponding to the event introduced by the main verb and the instance corresponding to the object. The BG is an empty list. The possibility of referring directly to the semantic indices in the MRS relations solves a problem associated with the interpretation of wide focus present in other HPSG-based accounts of information structure[3]. The problem can be seen for instance in Engdahl's proposal [11], where VP focus is treated by letting the focus be identical with the content of the VP node. This can be contrasted with my proposal, where the individual contents

---

[3] For similar approaches see also Yoshimoto *et al* in this volume, who use MRS to represent Japanese information structure, and [10], who deals with the interaction of quantifier and focus scope in MRS.

of verb and complements are *collected* in a list of indices. Engdahl's approach is problematic because in HPSG the content of the VP cannot be distinguished from the content of the whole sentence: the HPSG semantics principle states in fact that in head-complement phrases, the content of a mother is token-identical with the content of the daughter. Therefore, if the focus is structure-shared with the VP content, it also includes the subject of the sentence, so that VP focus cannot be distinguished from S focus.

Having established the relation between the information structure features and the content expressed in the MRS representations, let us now discuss the mechanisms that account for this relationship in the grammar. In summary, three different kinds of construct are relevant and will be described below. They are i. information structure types; ii. inheritance principles; and iii. construction types.

3   Information Structure Types

Given the fact that a sentence always has a focus, whilst topic and background may not be present, we can posit four different types of information structure. They are well-known from the literature (e.g. [4]) and comparable to the reading types discussed by Yabushita (this volume). Below the same event – the fact that a known group of children have eaten icecream – is reported by means of the four possible information structures:

(6)   a.   (Hvad har børnene lavet?) [$_T$ De] [$_F$ har spist is].
          'What have the children done? They have eaten icecream.'
      b.   (Hvad har børnene spist?) [$_T$ De] [$_{BG}$ har spist] [$_F$ is].
          'What have the children eaten? They have eaten icecream.'
      c.   (Hvem har spist is?) [$_F$ Børnene] [$_{BG}$ har spist is].
          'Who has eaten icecream? The children have eaten icecream.'
      d.   (Var det sjovt?) [$_F$ Ja, børnene spiste is].
          'Was it fun? Yes, the children ate icecream.'

Working with typed feature structures gives us the possibility of structuring linguistic knowledge into type hierarchies. This applies also to the information structure types: they can be organised in a hierarchy defining the constraints that apply to each type as shown in Fig. (1) (where *ne* is an abbreviation for *nonempty*). While the most specific types are those corresponding to the examples above, the more general intermediate types also constitute valid linguistic generalisations. The topic-comment type, for example, is often used to refer to a type of information structure without specific reference to whether the comment part contains background elements.

4   Information Structure Principles

It is often assumed that the instantiation of the information structure of the main sentence is achieved by the combination of two general principles called *inheritance* and *projection*. Information structure inheritance states that the mother

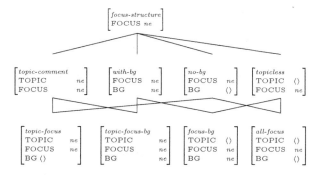

Fig. 1. Constraints on information structure types

inherits the information structure values of its daughters. Focus projection, on the other hand, predicts a wide focus structure in cases where sentence accent falls on the most oblique verbal complement. I have already noted, however, that there is no sentence accent in Danish unless the sentence displays particular emphasis or a contrastive focus, and that each non-pronominal complement or adjunct in the focus domain is accented. Therefore, it is not clear that the focus projection principle should play a role in Danish, and here I will only give a formal account of information structure inheritance.

What we need to express is the fact that for each information structure feature, the value of the mother node is a list consisting of the corresponding values of the two daughters. Engdahl and Vallduví [5] argue convincingly that such an approach, where information structure values are collected from the daughters of a node without reference to syntactic constituency, is an advantage in that it can deal with cases in which there is no direct correspondance between these different aspects of a linguistic sign, as is the case in the following Danish example:

(7) Hvor blev mine lygter af? Dem [$_F$ TOG THOMAS].
    Where disappeared my lights off? Them took Thomas.
    'Where have my bicycle lights disappeared? Thomas took them.'

Information structure inheritance is implemented in this study by means of specific inheritance principles for topic, focus and background. We show below the principle of *focus-inheritance*:

(8)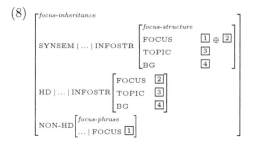

The principle states that in a binary projection where the non-head daughter is a focused constituent, the focus value of the non-head is appended to the focus value of the head daughter (which in turn may or may not be focused), and the resulting list is the FOCUS value of the mother. TOPIC and BG values are copied from head to mother node. This ensures the accumulation of focus values on the top node of the syntactic tree as well as inheritance of the other information status features.

The background and topic inheritance principles are very similar to focus inheritance: they ensure that either the background or the topic value of a non-head daughter is appended to the background value of the head, while the remaining information structure features are simply passed on from head daughter to mother. The application of all three inheritance principles is shown in Fig. (2)[4].

The figure shows the analysis of the following sentence:

(9) Hun 'ringede 'igen forleden.
     'She called again the other day.'

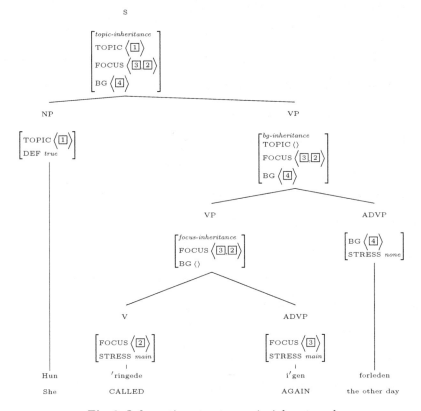

Fig. 2. Information structure principles at work

---

[4] The feature paths are simplified for the sake of space. For instance, TOPIC should be read SYNSEM|LOC|CTXT|INFOSTR|TOPIC.

In the most obvious reading, this is a topic-comment construction. The initial pronoun is the topic. Both the verb and the adverb adjacent to the verb are stressed, and therefore compatible with a focus analysis, whilst the unstressed final adverbial must be outside of the focus domain. For each binary projection, it is indicated in the feature structure type which principle has applied.

Note that the non-head daughter in a phrase to which focus inheritance applies is constrained to being a *focus* phrase, and a focus phrase has to contain an accent. Focus inheritance will therefore not apply to non-accented constituents, and a wrong assignment of background adjuncts to the focus will be avoided:

(10) * Hun [$_F$ 'ringede 'igen forleden].
      'She CALLED the other day.'

5 Construction Types

The information structure types and principles discussed so far come into play in different phrasal and clausal types to give rise to what I call information structure constructions[5].

5.1 Phrasal Constructions and Information Structure

Within HPSG, constructions are modelled in terms of phrasal types that are cross-classified along several dimensions, the two most important ones being *clausality* and *headedness* [12] [13]. Inheritance ensures that features and values of the more general types are also shared by the more specific ones. Such an approach makes it possible to define clausal as well as phrasal constructions, both of which interact with the information structure principles and types presented earlier. Fig. (3) illustrates the interaction of the head-complement (*hd-comp*) and head-adjunct (*hd-adj*) phrase types with two of the information principles.

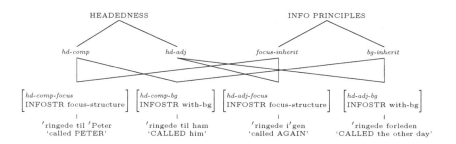

Fig. 3. Information structure of complements and adjuncts

---

[5] For the relation between information structure and grammatical constructions see i.a. [4].

The resulting types take care of information structure inheritance – whether focus or background inheritance – within the VP.

A similar cross-classification (not shown for lack of space) is posed for head-subject (*hd-subj*) and filler-head (*filler-hd*) types to ensure that information structure values are assigned at the level of the top sentence node, whether a declarative or topicalised sentence.

5.2   Clausal Constructions and Information Structure

Let us now turn to clausal constructions and see how information structure properties are realised in them. The hierarchy of Danish clausal type described in [14] is enriched so that the most specific types are cross-classified with respect to an information structure dimension. Fig. (4) shows how this approach can account for the interaction between the topic-comment information structure and two types of clausal constructions, i.e. main declarative and topicalised sentences.

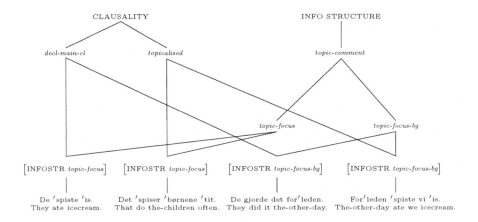

Fig. 4. Information structure in declarative main clauses

Four different specific constructions are modelled:

(11) a. [$_T$ De] [$_F$ ′spiste ′is].
        'They ate icecream.'
      b. [$_T$ Det] [$_F$ ′spiser ′børnene ′tit].
        That do the-children often.
        'The children often do that.'
      c. [$_T$ De] [$_{BG}$ gjorde det] [$_F$ for′leden].
        They did it the-other-day.
        'They did it the other day.'
      d. [$_{BG}$ For′leden] [$_F$ ′spiste] [$_T$ vi] [$_F$ ′is].
        The-other-day ate we icecream.
        'The other day they ate icecream.'

All of them are topic-comment constructions as expected. However, the topic has different grammatical functions and is placed in different positions. In the last example it is actually interposed between two focused constituents. As already mentioned, the fact that there is no direct correspondance between information structure values and syntactic constituents, is not a problem in an approach where these values are collected in lists for each of the binary projections in the syntactic tree.

Topicless constructions are modelled along the same lines by letting clausal types be cross-classified with the two topicless types *all-focus* and *focus-bg*, and specific constructions such as clefts or existential sentences can be formalised in that part of the construction hierarchy.

6   Conclusion

To sum up, in this paper I have presented a proposal for the representation of the information structure of a sentence by way of features in a typed feature structure formalism.

The interaction between information structure and grammar constructions has been formalised in a hierarchy where different phrasal and clausal types of Danish grammar are cross-classified with respect to an information structure dimension. Examples of the complex types that derive from this cross-classification are topic-comment constructions expressed as either main declarative clauses or topicalised sentences.

I plan to extend the model to include an account of syntactically marked topicless sentences such as clefts and existential sentences, and to investigate the way in which the information structure principles and types work in unbounded dependencies, of which topicalised constructions and clefts are examples.

References

1. Paggio, P.: *The Treatment of Information Structure in Machine Translation.* PhD thesis, University of Copenhagen and Centre for Language Technology (1997).
2. Paggio, P., Diderichsen, P., Elming, J.: The information structure of Danish constructions. In: *Abstracts of the third international conference on constructional grammar*, University of Provence, France (2004) 81.
3. Pollard, C., Sag, I.A.: *Head-Driven Phrase Structure Grammar.* Chicago: The University of Chicago Press (1994).
4. Lambrecht, K.: *Information Structure and Sentence Form.* Cambridge Studies in Linguistics. Cambridge: Cambridge University Press (1994).
5. Engdahl, E., Vallduví, E.: Information packaging in HPSG. In Grover, C., Vallduví, E., eds.: *Studies in HPSG.* Volume 123 of Edinburgh Working Papers in Cognitive Science. Centre for Cognitive Science, University of Edinburgh (1996) 1–32.
6. Alexopoulu, T., Kolliakou, D.: On linkhood, topicalization and clitic left dislocation. *Linguistics* **38** (2002) 193–245.
7. Copestake, A., Flickinger, D., Pollard, C., Sag, I.A.: Minimal recursion semantics: An introduction. Manuscript: available at www-csli.stanford.edu/~aac/papers/newmrs.pdf (1999).

8. Flickinger, D., Bender, E.M.: Compositional semantics in a multilingual grammar resource. In: *Proceedings of the Workshop on Ideas and Strategies for Multimodal Grammar Development*, ESSLLI (2003) 33–42.
9. Flickinger, D., Bender, E.M., Oepen, S.: *MRS in the LinGO Grammar Matrix: A Practical User's Guide*. (2003).
10. Wilcock, G.: Information structure and minimal recursion semantics. In Arppe, A., et al. ed.: *Inquiries into Words, Constraints and Contexts: Festschrift in Honour of Kimmo Koskenniemi*. CSLI Publications, Stanford (2005) 268–277.
11. Engdahl, E.: Integrating pragmatics into the grammar. In Mereu, L., ed.: *Boundaries of Morphology and Syntax*. John Benjamins: Amsterdam (1999) 175–194.
12. Sag, I.: Aspects of a theory of grammatical constructions. Lecture given at the First International Construction Grammar Conference, Berkeley (2001).
13. Ginzburg, J., Sag, I.A.: *Interrogative Investigations: Form, Meaning and Use of English Interrogatives*. CSLI Publications, University of Chicago Press (2000).
14. Neville, A., Paggio, P.: Developing a Danish grammar in the GRASP project: a construction-based approach to topology and extraction in Danish. *Electronic Notes in Theoretical Computer Science* 47 (2001).

Processing of Information Structure and Floating Quantifiers in Japanese

Kei Yoshimoto[1], Masahiro Kobayashi[2], Hiroaki Nakamura[3], and Yoshiki Mori[4]

[1] Graduate School of International Cultural Studies, Tohoku University
Kawauchi 41, Aoba-ku, Sendai 980-8576, Japan
[2] University Education Center, Tottori University
Koyama-Minami 4-101, Tottori 680-8550, Japan
[3] Department of General Subjects, Japan Coast Guard Academy
Wakaba-cho 5-1, Kure, Hiroshima 737-0832, Japan
[4] Institute of Linguistics and Literature, Tsukuba University
Tennōdai 1-1-1, Tsukuba, Ibaraki 305-8577, Japan

Abstract. Floating quantifiers (FQs) in Japanese have mainly been discussed from the perspective of syntax, which leaves some essential context-dependent aspects of the phenomena unexplained. In this paper, we approach the issue by formalizing the incremental processing of information structure in Japanese sentences by Minimal Recursion Semantics and Head-Driven Phrase Structure Grammar. The long-standing problem of asymmetry between the subject and object in terms of the quantification by a non-adjacent FQ is resolved by a self-contradictory CONTEXT specification which is obtained by expanding the MRS formalism using the information packaging theory.

1 Introduction

Floating quantifiers (FQs hereafter) in Japanese, a topic of heated discussions in the Japanese linguistics circle, have been mostly treated syntactically relying on transformational manipulations on the configurational structure. In recent years, however, contextual factors in the phenomena have been emphasized (cf. [10]). This paper proposes a surface-based approach to the issue by adopting incremental processing of sentential information including information structure. We account for the context-dependent difference in grammaticality as information structure features embedded in the Minimal Recursion Semantics (MRS; [2]).

2 Floating Quantifiers in Japanese

In Japanese, *floating* of an FQ consisting of a numeral and a classifier is allowed only from subject or object NPs. Between the two syntactic cases, however, asymmetry has been observed in terms of the hosting of an FQ (see [5], [9], [7]). An FQ floated from the subject must be adjacent to its host as in (1a) below; a sentence like (1b) in which the object intervenes between the subject and FQ is unacceptable. By contrast, the host object and the FQ can occur either next to each other or with the subject appearing between them, as in (1c) and (1d).

T. Washio et al. (Eds.): JSAI 2005 Workshops, LNAI 4012, pp. 103–110, 2006.
© Springer-Verlag Berlin Heidelberg 2006

(1) a. *Gakusei   ga   **go-nin**   hon   wo   kat-ta.*
        student   SBJ   five-CLASS$_{person}$ book   OBJ   buy-PAST
    'Five students bought books.'

   b. **Gakusei   ga   hon   wo   **go-nin**   kat-ta.*
        student   SBJ   book   OBJ   five-CLASS$_{person}$ buy-PAST
    ('Five students bought books.')

   c. Gakusei   ga   *hon   wo*   **san-satsu**   kat-ta.
        student   SBJ   book   OBJ   three-CLASS$_{book}$ buy-PAST
    'Students bought three books.'

   d. *Hon   wo*   gakusei   ga   **san-satsu**   kat-ta.
        book   OBJ   student   SBJ   three-CLASS$_{book}$ buy-PAST
    'Students bought three books.'

3   Previous Studies

Miyagawa [7] accounts for a considerable amount of linguistic data by imposing a 'mutual c-command requirement [8]' between an FQ and its host: while in (1a) both the subject NP *gakusei ga* (student-SBJ) and the FQ *go-nin* c-command each other, in (1b) the subject c-commands the FQ that is embedded in a VP but is not c-commanded by the FQ.

(1) a. $[_S [_{NP}$ *gakusei ga*$] [_{FQ}$ **go-nin**$] [_{VP}$ hon wo kat-ta$]]$
   b. *$[_S [_{NP}$ *gakusei ga*$] [_{VP} [_{NP}$ hon wo$] [_{FQ}$ **go-nin**$] [_V$ kat-ta$]]]$

The acceptability of (1c) and (1d) is also accounted for by the c-command relationship between the FQ and its host. Specifically in (1d), the FQ *san-satsu* does not directly c-command its host *hon wo*, but its trace left at the position from which the host is moved.

It is also explained within the same framework why only the subject or object of the sentence can host an FQ: Miyagawa obtains subject and object NPs by cliticizing case markers *ga* and *wo*, while other case particles combine with an NP to form a PP. In distinction from subject and object NPs, this embedding of an NP prohibits an NP from c-commanding the FQ, since there exists a node PP between the NP and FQ:

(2) *$[_S \ldots [_{PP} NP$ P$]$ **FQ** VP$]$

Furthermore, the mutual c-command requirement accounts for the distinction in acceptability which Miyagawa maintains exists between sentences with unaccusative and unergative verbs. According to Miyagawa, the subject of the former type of verb originates in the object position and is moved to the subject position by Move-α, leaving a trace standing in a mutual c-command relationship to the FQ. By contrast, unergative verbs, which do not allow quantifier floating from the subject, do not undergo the movement of the subject and are therefore not involved with a trace left behind.

Takami [10] takes an entirely new approach to the issue based on information structure. He begins his discussions by criticizing Miyagawa's mutual c-command requirement, leading to a theory with advantage over the syntactic approaches in general. He points out that there exist sentences with the same syntactic structure as (1b) above that are nevertheless acceptable:

(3) *Gakusei*   *ga*   SORE   WO   **go-nin**   katte-iki   -mashi-ta.
     student   SBJ   DEM-PRON   OBJ   five-CLASS$_{person}$ buy-go   -POL-PAST

     'Yes, this morning five students came to buy it.'

As in example (3), the ⟨NP$_{sbj}$-NP$_{obj}$-FQ⟩ construction in which the FQ quantifies the subject is appropriate if the object NP is a pronoun or another type of definitely marked NP (like *sono zasshi wo* 'that magazine-OBJ') that has already been established in the context.

Takami also cites other acceptable sentences with the same syntactic structure. When FQs are suffixed by the so-called adverbial particles (fuku-joshi) such as *dake* (only), *mo* (as many as), *shika* (only), and *tomo* (all), the sentences are also grammatical. Furthermore, he gives counterevidence against Miyagawa's claim that unergative verbs, unlike unaccusative verbs, do not have a trace left at the object position and consequently do not allow an FQ within a VP. These sentences also suggest that Miyagawa's c-command-based account of the acceptability of quantifier floating is untenable.

On the basis of the above-mentioned criticism against Miyagawa's syntactic approach, Takami [10] attempts to develop a functional account of the issue on the basis of Kuno's hypothesis that in Japanese the constituent immediately before the verb provides the newest information in the sentence [4]. He analyzes the following sentences with FQs from the information structure perspective:

(4) a. **Gakusei*   *ga*   hon   wo   **yo-nin**   kat-ta.
       student   SBJ   book   OBJ   four-CLASS$_{person}$ buy-PAST

       'The student bought a book.'

   b. *Gakusei*   *ga*   SORE/   SONO   HON   WO   **yo-nin**
       student   SBJ   DEM-PRON   DET   book   OBJ   four-CLASS$_{person}$

       kat-ta.
       buy-PAST

       'A student bought it/the book.'

According to Takami, most people feel that (4a) is an unnatural sentence, since it is hard to judge whther it is a statement on how many students bought the book or what those students bought. This is because both the FQ immediately before the verb and the indefinite object is construed as important information. On the other hand, in (4b) the object as definite NP is informationally less important and accordingly the FQ is the most important information without any competitor. Thus the sentence is appropriate.

However, from only what Takami writes it is impossible to reconstruct how these sentences are processed successfully or otherwise. Most crucial is the lack of reason for the indefinite object NP *hon wo* being interpreted as competing with the FQ for being the most important information, if, as Kuno argues, the importance depends solely on word order. To compensate for what is missing, we need to hypothesize that the object NP in a construction with a transitive verb is, even if not located immediately before the predicate, provides the newest information or focus in the sentence by default. We also propose that an FQ conveys the newest information in the sentence, and a conflict between the object NP and the FQ concerning the focus placement is the cause for unacceptable FQ sentences.

Lastly, let us point out a kind of sentence that is beyond the scope of Takami's explanation. While (1b) is unacceptable, a sentence with the same syntactic structure but with its subject being modified by an indefiniteness marking adjectival word *mishiranu* (unfamiliar) is much more acceptable. Since Takami deals with only sentences whose subject is associated with the unmarked information structure, this kind of sentence also is beyond the framework of his theory.

4   MRS/HPSG Formalization

In Section 3 we saw that to make full use of information structure brought to attention by Takami [10], asymmetric informational roles performed by the subject and object need to be introduced. However, these are not sufficient to account for the difference between (1a) and (1b) in acceptability.

What we found our theory on is an assumption shared by a great number of psycholinguistic studies (see e.g. [6]) that a sentence is processed incrementally. We develop this into a principle held throughout this paper that the interpretation on information structure of a sentence is made incrementally as the sentence is processed from left to right in real time.

On the basis of this, we put forward the three hypotheses as below:

(5) 1. An FQ provides an independent nominal meaning, which is anaphorically related with that of the host NP.
   2. The meaning of an FQ must be the focus of the sentence.
   3. A sentence with a transitive verb is given an interpretation ⟨Non-Focus (Sbj) + Focus (Obj)⟩ by default as soon as the object NP has been recognized. No later correction is possible.

By *focus* we mean the most important new information in the sentence. *Non-focus* is those constituents that are not focus. Note that non-focus includes constituents for new information except focus, particularly specific information, i.e. information known to the speaker but not to the hearer.

We account for the semantic relationship between the FQ and its host NP based on the non-transformational point of view which takes the FQ as AdvP. For this purpose, we propose a LOCAL feature FLOATING-QUANTIFIER, abbreviated as FQ, to relate the FQ to its host NP. This is lexically introduced by the FQ as shown in (6) below and discharged when the host NP is combined with the syntactic tree as illustrated in Figure 1. Complete sentences must have a void FQ value. This feature is percolated up trees similarly to the NONLOCAL features, but its application is confined within a single clause. The FQ feature prevents multiple FQs from being hosted by the same NP. The association between the FQ and its host is further constrained by the CLASSIFIER feature within ARG0 (the latter feature is called INSTANCE in the older version of MRS) which indicates the semantic category of the host NP (e.g., *book* for the classifier *satsu*, *person* for *nin*). The tree in Figure 1 illustrates how the FQ feature is introduced and discharged as sentence (1b) is processed.

We adopt as our semantic framework Minimal Recursion Semantics (MRS; [2]) that makes possible underspecified representations in terms of quantifier scope ambiguity. The most remarkable feature with MRS is its non-recursive semantic representation that allows underspecification in terms of scope. The core of the specification is given as a list value of the attribute REL(ATION)S, called LISZT in the earlier version of the theory.

The list contains *rel(ation)s*, each of which represents the semantics of a quantifier, noun, verb, etc. The specification about information structure is added to the MRS formalism following Engdahl and Vallduví [3]. The portions of sentence other than focus, i.e. link and tail, are merged into NONFO-CUS in this paper. The values of FOCUS and NONFOCUS are lists consisting of *rel(ation)s* rather than *signs* as formulated in Engdahl and Vallduví. The FOCUS and NONFOCUS values are provided by the topic of the sentence, the FQ specification, and a default interpretation of the transitive construction as proposed later.

Let us explain further how the FQ and its host are associated with each other by the introduction and discharge of the FQ feature (see also (7)). (6) is the feature specification for the FQ *san-nin* (three-CLASS$_{person}$) that is constructed by combining the specifications for the numeral *san* and classifier *nin*.

(6)
$$
\begin{bmatrix}
advp \\
\text{SYNSEM|LOC} \begin{bmatrix}
\text{FQ} \quad \boxed{1} \left\{ \begin{bmatrix}
fqed\_indef\_nom\_mrs \\
\text{KEY} \quad \boxed{2} \begin{bmatrix} nom\_rel \\ \text{ARG0} \boxed{3} [\text{CLASS } person] \end{bmatrix} \\
\text{RELS} \quad \boxed{4} \left\langle \begin{bmatrix} qt\_rel \\ \text{CARDL } three \\ \text{ARG0} \boxed{3} \end{bmatrix}, \boxed{2} \right\rangle \oplus list(rel)
\end{bmatrix} \right\} \\
\text{CONT} \qquad\qquad \boxed{1} \\
\text{CNTEXT|INF-ST|FOCUS} \boxed{4}
\end{bmatrix}
$$

The feature is percolated up the tree by the FQ Feature Principle that propagates the FQ value between the daughters and the mother. Note that this principle applies, unlike the NONLOCAL Feature Principle in HPSG, only within a single sentence. The FQ feature is bound off by the FQ Cancellation Rule shown as (7) when the host is combined with the head phrase.

(7) FQ Feature Cancellation Rule

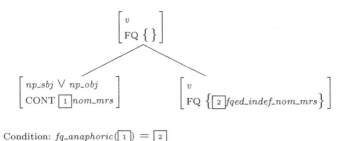

Condition: $fq\_anaphoric(\boxed{1}) = \boxed{2}$

As formulated here, the mother node's FQ value is made empty when the result obtained by applying the function *fq_anaphoric* to the CONTENT value of the complement daughter unifies with the element within the head's FQ set value. The definition for this function is given below:

(8) a. If $\boxed{1} = fqed\_indef\_nom\_mrs$,
         then $fq\_anaphoric(\boxed{1}) = \boxed{1}$;
         otherwise $= fq\_substitutional(\boxed{1})$.

    b. $fq\_substitutional([\text{KEY } \boxed{1}nom\_rel]) = \begin{bmatrix} fqed\_indef\_nom\_mrs \\ \text{KEY} \qquad copy\_rel(\boxed{1}) \end{bmatrix}$

The first half of (8a) covers typical cases in which the FQ quantifies its indefinite host NP. Then the value of the function is the same as its input. Other cases in which a whole-part relationship holds between the FQ and its definite host (e.g., when an FQ refers to a subset of the denotation of its topicalized host — see [11] for this type of FQ sentences) are dealt with by the subfunction *fq_substitutional*. This function, into which the semantic information of the host NP is fed, outputs a semantic feature structure for a quantified NP that looks like that of the host except that its semantic head is a copy of that of the host produced by the function *copy_rel*. Thus the output of *fq_substitutional* (i.e., that of *fq_anaphoric* in exceptional cases) is not semantically identical with the semantics of the host, but is a different entity of the same concept as the latter. This is the basis for establishing the semantic relationship between two NPs that refer to different denotations with the same concept, an anaphoric relationship that has traditionally been called 'substitution'.

In order to simulate an incremental, left-to-right sentence processing, we assume a kind of bottom-up, 'shift-reduce' parser (see [1]) that tries to combine lexical feature structures into larger ones, rather than words into phrase structure constituents, according to the HPSG formalism.

In the main part of the algorithm, either *Shift* or *Reduce* applies. When the *Shift* operation applies to a new input that is an object NP, if there already exists a subject within the stack, non-focus and focus are by default assigned to the subject and object, respectively, as specified in (9). This, as a default constraint, does not cover cases in which the subject and/or object are associated with

INFO-STRUCT values inconsistent with it (e.g., (3) with a definite object NP and a sentence with a new information-marked subject NP).

(9) If the new input is $\boxed{1}$:$NP_{\mathbf{wo}}$ & $L \ni \boxed{2}$:$NP_{\mathbf{ga}}$, then

$$\boxed{1} \longrightarrow \begin{bmatrix} \text{CONT|RELS} & \boxed{3} \\ \text{CONTEXT|INFO-STRUCT|FOCUS} & /\boxed{3} \end{bmatrix}$$

$$\& \ \boxed{2} \longrightarrow \begin{bmatrix} \text{CONT|RELS} & \boxed{4} \\ \text{CONTEXT|INFO-STRUCT|NONFOCUS} & /\boxed{4} \end{bmatrix}$$

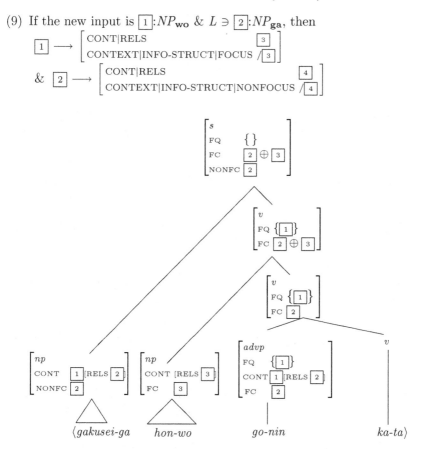

Fig. 1. Processing of Sentence (1b)

The tree diagram in Figure 1 illustrates how sentence (1b) is proved to be inappropriate by our framework. During the first two steps of sentence processing, the sequence *gakusei ga hon wo* ('student-SBJ book-OBJ') is given the default information structure 'non-focus followed by focus' by the rule in (9). When the sentence processing has been completed, the feature SYNSEM|LOC|CONTEXT|INFO-STRUCT|FOCUS contains the information corresponding to both of the object NP *hon wo*, as provided by the specification in (9), and the FQ/subject NP, *go-nin* and *gakusei ga*, deriving from the specification in (6).

On the other hand, the feature NONFOCUS is composed of a list deriving from the semantics of the subject NP, following the default constraint in (9). This information, indicated by $\boxed{2}$ in the tree diagram, occurs both within FOCUS and NONFOCUS. The contradictory processing result — the same piece of information analyzed as focus and non-focus simultaneously — explains the observation that

(1b) is an inappropriate sentence. Note that the inappropriateness does not directly correspond to a failure in unification.

5 Conclusion

We have in this paper provided a new perspective on FQs in Japanese based on real-time, incremental sentence processing and information structure. Syntactically, the FQ is analyzed without transformation or using long-distance dependency like SLASH in HPSG; the FQ and its host are matched by feature percolation within a single sentence. Semantically, the FQ is given a whole piece of information as an independent NP, and this stands in an anaphoric relation to its host. We have shown that the approach we propose covers more linguistic data than ever.

References

1. Aho, A. V., Ullman, J. D.: The Theory of Parsing, Translation, and Compiling, Vol. 1: Parsing. Prentice-Hall, Englewood Cliffs, N.J. (1972)
2. Copestake, A., Flickinger, D., Sag, I. A., Pollard, C.: Minimal Recursion Semantics: An introduction. ms., Center for the Study of Language and Information, Stanford University (1999)
3. Engdahl, E., Vallduví, E.: Information packaging in HPSG. In: C. Grover, E. Vallduví (eds.) Edinburgh Working Papers in Cognitive Science, Vol. 12: Studies in HPSG (1996) 1-31
4. Kuno, S.: Theoretical perspectives. In: J. Hinds, I. Howard (eds.) Problems in Japanese Syntax and Semantics. Kaitakusha, Tokyo (1978) 213-285
5. Kuroda, S.-Y.: What can Japanese say about government and binding? Proceedings of the Second West Coast Conference on Formal Linguistics (1983) 153-164
6. Mazuka, R., Itoh, K.: Can Japanese speakers be led down the garden path? In: R. Mazuka, N. Nagai (eds.) Japanese Sentence Processing. Lawrence Erlbaum, Hillsdale, N.J. (1995) 295-329
7. Miyagawa, S.: Structure and Case Marking in Japanese. Syntax and Semantics, Vol. 22. Academic Press, San Diego (1989)
8. Reinhart, T.: Definite NP Anaphora and C-Command Domains. Linguistic Inquiry **12:4** (1981) 605-635
9. Saito, M.: Some Asymmetries in Japanese and Their Theoretical Implications. Doctoral dissertation, Massachusetts Institute of Technology (1985)
10. Takami, K.: Nihongo no sūryōshi yūri ni tsuite: Kinōron-teki bunseki [Jō, Chū, Ge](On quantifier floating in Japanese: A functional analysis, Parts 1-3). Gengo **27:1-3** (1998) 86-95, 86-95, 98-107
11. Yoshimoto, K., Kobayashi, M.: *Floating Quantifiers* in Japanese as Non-Floating Anaphora. ms., Graduate School of International Cultural Studies, Tohoku University (2005)

An Information-Structural Analysis of the Readings for Nominal-Predicate Sentences in Japanese

Katsuhiko Yabushita

Naruto University of Education, Department of English
Naruto, Tokushima, 772-8502, Japan
yabuchan@naruto-u.ac.jp

Abstract. Japanese nominal-predicate sentences show an interesting distribution of distinct types of readings. In the literature, the so-called "Mapping Hypothesis has been considered to be a right approach to the current. However, the nature of the relation between syntactic configurations and types of the readings in question is relational, not functional as is implied by the hypothesis. In light of this, we will propose a constraint-based alternative analysis in which a syntactic configuration can be associated with more than one semantic representation as long as they conform to independently motivated information-structural constraints.

1 Introduction: The Data

[9] and [8] observed that nominal-predicate sentences in Japanese exhibit varying types of readings available depending on the following two factors among others: (i) What particle the nominal is marked with, in this case, the nominative marker *ga* or the topic marker *wa* (ii) Of what kind the predicate is, in this case, 'stage-level' or 'individual-level' ([2], [7]). The types of readings of our concern here are "neutral description," "thematic," and "exhaustive listing" in Kuno's terms. In (1), the four forms of sentences corresponding to the possible combinations of the particles and the types of predicates, and their available types of readings will be illustrated with examples.

(1)   a.   <u>NP-Nominative/Stage-Level Predicate</u>
          Meari-ga   hashitte-iru
          Mary-Nom   running
          '(Obtaining is an event/situation in which) Mary is running.' (Neutral Description Reading)
          'It is Mary who is running./MARY is running [as an answer for e.g., Who is running?].' (Exhaustive-Listing Reading)

   b.   <u>NP-Nominative/Individual-Level Predicate</u>
          Meari-ga   gakusee-desu
          Mary-Nom   student-is
          'It is Mary who is a student./MARY is a student [as an answer for e.g., Who is a student?].' (Exhaustive-Listing Reading)

   c.   <u>NP-Topic/Stage-Level Predicate</u>
          Meari-wa   hashitte-iru
          Mary-Top   running-is
          'Speaking of Mary, she is running.' (Thematic Reading)

T. Washio et al. (Eds.): JSAI 2005 Workshops, LNAI 4012, pp. 111–117, 2006.
© Springer-Verlag Berlin Heidelberg 2006

d.   <u>NP-Topic/Individual-Level Predicate</u>
Meari-wa   gakusee-desu.
Mary-Top   student-is
'Speaking of Mary, she is a student.' (Thematic Reading)

2   "Mapping Hypothesis" Approach

2.1   Diesing's "Mapping Hypothesis"

Based on German data, which we cannot review for space limitation, Diesing proposed a procedure relating the two-subject clause structure (the VP-Internal Subject Hypothesis) to the tripartite structure of logical representation ([10]) called the *Mapping Hypothesis*, which is expressed as in (2).

(2)   *Mapping Hypothesis*
Material from VP is mapped into the nuclear scope.
Material from IP is mapped into the restrictive clause.

Diesing assumed that there is a distinction between stage-level and individual-level predicates with respect to where their subject NPs can occur at LF; that is, subjects of stage-level predicates can appear either in Spec IP or in Spec VP, while those of individual-level predicates, only in Spec IP.[1] Additionally, in terms of semantic representation, or interpretation, she assumed that there is an unselective existential quantifier operating only on the nuclear scope, departing from the original Kamp-Heim version ([6], [5]) in which it operates at the text level as well. As for free variables in the restrictive clause, they are to be bound by the relevant quantifier; specifically, when there is no overt quantifier around, she proposed that they should be bound by a generic operator Gen in the sense of [15] and [4] to produce generic reading.

2.2   Uechi's Analysis

Inspired by Diesing's Mapping Hypothesis, [12] and [13] argued that indeed a direct correspondence can be attested between syntax and semantics in Japanese as well, with some modifications made to Diesing's original formulation of the hypothesis to accommodate some properties of Japanese.

Based on various pieces of syntactic and semantic evidence, which we will not review here, Uechi proposed a sentential S-Structure with three subject positions, instead of two for Japanese. With the three-subject sentence structure, he proposed the following alternative Mapping Hypothesis for Japanese. That is, TopP is mapped on to the domain of Topic (Discourse Presupposition), IP onto the domain of restrictive focus, and VP onto the domain of existential closure.

---

[1]   Diesing adopted Kratzer's account ([7]) that the distinction is due to a difference between stage-level and individual-level predicates in argument structure. Although we do not subscribe to the distinction at the syntactic level of LF, we do adopt in our analysis to be presented, Kratzer's proposal that there is a difference between the two types of predicates, which will be reviewed in Section 3.1.

The question is if Uechi's Mapping Hypothesis can explain the distribution of the readings under consideration. The general problem we have with Uechi's analysis is that it does not tell us how his semantic representations are to be interpreted in the assumed semantic framework; Kamp-Heim semantics in [12] and Büring's semantics ([1]) in [13]. It is pretty much left for the reader's intuitive understanding. In the following we will review how the example sentences in (1) would be interpreted in his analysis and point out some problems with his analysis, conceptual and empirical, irrespective of the particular semantic framework to be ultimately adopted.

First, let us start with the cases of (1c) and (1d), which are common in that the subject is marked with topic marker *wa*. It is presumed that in both cases, the subject *Meari-wa* 'Mary-Top' is mapped onto the domain of Topic and the rest of the sentence is mapped to the domain of Existential Description, resulting in the logical representations as in (3c) and (3d), respectively.

(3)   c. $\text{Top}_x[\text{MARY}(x)]\ [\text{RUNNING}(x)]$
     d. $\text{Top}_x[\text{MARY}(x)]\ [\text{STUDENT}(x)]$

Although it is not clear exactly how semantic representations of the form $\text{Top}_x[\phi(x)]$ $[\psi(x)]$ will be interpreted in Uechi's analysis as noted above, there could be a semantic framework in which (14c) and (14d) will be assigned the same type of interpretation appropriate for "thematic reading", whatever it is, for at least they have the same form.

Next, let us review (1a), whose subject is marked with nominative marker *ga* and whose predicate is stage-level. Assuming Diesing's treatment of stage-level predicates and their subject positions, i.e. the subject of a stage-level predicate can appear at either Spec VP or Spec IP, (1a) will be assigned two (S-structure) syntactic representations in which the subject appears at Spec VP and Spec IP, respectively. The corresponding semantic representations will be as in (4a) and (4a´), respectively.

(4)   a. $\exists_x[_{\text{EC}}\text{MARY}(x) \wedge \text{RUNNING}(x)]$
     a´. $\text{FOCUS}_x[\text{MARY}(x)]\ [_{\text{EC}}\text{RUNNING}(x)]$

It is time to examine if the semantic representations are really appropriate for the intended readings, i.e. the neutral-description reading that there is happening an event of Mary's running, and the exhaustive-listing reading that it is Mary who is running. Before that, a word is in order about some symbols in (4a) and (4a´), i.e. EC and FOCUS. EC indicates what Uechi referred to as the domain of existential closure, which is equivalent to the nuclear scope. He did not present a specific semantic analysis of the exhaustive-listing reading either, simply designating Spec-IP to be a "focused" position and leaving the specifics to the reader's intuitive understanding. In (4a´), FOCUS is posited for the implicitly assumed operator responsible for the exhaustive-listing reading. The operator is presumed to be something comparable to English *only*. In the following we will argue that semantic representations (4a) and (4a´) cannot be collectively coherent as the carriers of the intended readings.

First, let us review (4a´) as a semantic representation of the exhaustive-listing reading. In terms of focus structure, $[\text{MARY}(x)]$ is considered to be in focus, and $[_{\text{EC}}\text{RUNNING}(x)]$ is *not* in focus. Next, let us consider (4a) as a semantic representation for the neutral-description reading. Neutral-description sentences have been characterized as "all-focus", or "wide-focus"; thus, $[_{\text{EC}}\text{MARY}(x) \wedge \text{RUNNING}(x)]$ should be considered to be in focus. From the above considerations, it can be seen that the semantic content constituted by VP, or the domain of existential closure would have to be treated incoherently in terms of information structure—sometimes as focused and other times as non-focused. This will cast doubt on Uechi's thesis that there is a direct correspondence between (S-Structure) syntactic configurations and semantic representations (enriched with information structure).

3 Information-Structural Constraint-Based Approach

Toward the end of the preceding section we have seen some evidence that the correspondence between (S-structure) syntactic configurations and semantic representations is not so direct, or functional as suggested by the Mapping Hypothesis. In this section we will advocate the thesis that the syntax-semantics correspondence in question here is relational instead in that a syntactic representation can be associated with more than one semantic representation as long as they do not violate 'information-structural constraints'.

3.1 The Repertoire of Information-Structural Semantic Representations for the Readings

In this subsection, we will propose a repertoire of semantic representations characteristic of each reading in question, which will be collectively coherent with each other. Our semantic representations are "usual" higher-order logical λ-calculus expressions enriched with such information structures as topic structure and background-focus structure. The semantic representation for a sentence has the following schematic form (cf. [14]):

(5)   [TOPIC, <BACKGROUND, FOCUS>]

In the current analysis, each type of reading has a unique form of semantic representation characteristic of it. Before we see, a word is in order about the treatment of the distinction between stage-level and individual-level predicates. Here, following [7], we assume that stage-level predicates have an extra argument place for events besides those usually assumed in predicate logic, while individual-level predicates do not. Now let us go over the schematic form of semantic representation for each type of reading:

(6)   *Neutral-Description Reading*
        [NIL, <NIL, $\lambda x^e.P$>]

Here, NIL means that there is nothing in the place and x^e is an event variable. Thus, the characteristic of the form is that only the FOCUS part has some element, with the TOP and the BACKGROUND parts being empty, which corresponds with sentences of neutral-description reading being "all-focus", or "wide-focus". Furthermore, the element in the FOCUS part is a one-place event predicate. Thus, interpretationally, neutral description readings are analyzed as event-introducing statements.[2]

---

[2] The current semantic representation of neutral-description sentences is taken to be a formal rendition of Kuroda's descriptive characterization, i.e. "Sentences of neutral description present an objectively observable action, existence, or temporary state as a new event ([9]: 51)".

(7)   *Exhaustive-Listing Reading*
        $[\gamma, <\lambda x.\beta, \alpha>]$

Here, α is the semantic representation of the constituent that is "narrowly" focused, and will be interpreted to be the only element that has the property denoted by $\lambda x.\beta$.

(8)   *Thematic (Topical) Reading*
        $[\gamma, <\beta, \alpha>]$

Here, what is required is simply that γ is a non-NIL element. The form is compatible with that of exhaustive-listing reading, i.e. (7); that is, it is possible that the thematic and the exhaustive-listing readings are coexistent in a sentence.

3.2   Information-Structural Constraints

Next, let us propose some information-structural constraints on our current semantic representations, which are motivated independently of the distributions of the types of readings for the nominal-predicate sentences in Japanese.

(9)   C1: The semantic representation of a topic-marked constituent must be in the TOPIC part.

       This constraint is self-explanatory; it is a necessary consequence of the constituent's being topic-marked.

       C2: The semantic representation of the TOPIC part must be a semantic constituent of BACKGROUND.

       Assuming the so-called "aboutness condition" for topic phrases; that is, a sentence with a topic asserts something about the referent of the topic, it follows that the referent of the topic is in the presupposed content, i.e. the BACKGROUND part.

       C3: FOCUS cannot be empty.

       On the assumption that every sentence, or its utterance must have something to assert, it is natural to require of every semantic representation of a sentence to have a non-empty, or non-NIL element in the FOCUS part.

Now that we have proposed a form of semantic representation characteristic of each type of reading in question and some independently motivated information-structural constraints on semantic representations, let us demonstrate that the current analysis can predict the right inventory of readings for each of the four forms of sentences in question. This will be illustrated by showing that for each example in (1), there is a legitimate semantic representation of the form characteristic of each available reading, while there is no legitimate semantic representation for an unavailable reading.

3.3   The Distribution of the Readings Explained

We have proposed a form of semantic representation characteristic of each type of readings under consideration and some independently motivated information-structural constraints on (the relation between syntactic configurations and) semantic representations. We will demonstrate that the distribution of the readings of the types of sentences in question is a natural consequence of the current constraint-based characterization of the admissible semantic representations for given syntactic representations. In the following, (1a-d) will be reproduced as (10a-d). For each example, the available readings will be check-marked and followed by the associated, admissible semantic representations, while the unavailable readings will be asterisked followed by the associated, inadmissible semantic representations with the reasons provided.

(10) a.   NP-Nominative/Stage-Level Predicate
           Meari-ga   hashitte-iru
           Mary-Nom   running
     √Neutral-Description Reading, [NIL, <NIL, λe.RUNNING(MARY, e)>]
     √Exhaustive-Listing Reading, [NIL, <λx.RUNNING(x, e), MARY>].

      b.   NP-Nominative/Individual-Level Predicate
           Meari-ga   gakusee-desu
           Mary-Nom   student-is
     √Exhaustive-Listing Reading, [NIL, <λx.STUDENT(x), MARY>].
     *Neutral-Description   Reading,   *[NIL,   <NIL,   STUDENT(MARY)>];
     STUDENT(MARY) is not an event predicate.

      c.   NP-Topic/Stage-Level Predicate
           Meari-wa   hashitte-iru
           Mary-Top   running-is
     √Thematic Reading, [MARY, <MARY, λx.e.RUNNING(x, e)>].
     *Neutral-Description Reading, *[MARY, <NIL, λe.RUNNING(MARY, e)>]; a violation of Constraint C2 with the TOPIC element MARY being in FOCUS.
     *Exhaustive-Listing Reading, *[MARY, <λx.RUNNING(x, e), MARY>]; a violation of Constraint C2 with the TOPIC element MARY being in FOCUS.

      d.   NP-Topic/Individual-Level Predicate
           Meari-wa   gakusee-desu.
           Mary-Top   student-is
     √Thematic Reading, [MARY, <MARY, λx.STUDENT(x)>].
     *Neutral-Description Reading, *[MARY, <NIL, STUDENT(MARY)>]; The TOPIC is not NIL, and STUDENT(MARY) is not an event predicate.
     *Exhaustive-Listing Reading, *[MARY, <λx.STUDENT(x), MARY>]; a violation of Constraint C2 with the TOPIC element MARY being in FOCUS.

4 Conclusion

We have seen that the Mapping Hypothesis cannot adequately account for the distribution of readings over nominal-predicate sentences in Japanese because it would result in an incoherent alignment of syntactic configurations and semantic representations in terms of focus structure. We have taken the above findings to suggest the thesis that the syntax-semantics correspondence manifested by the current Japanese data should be relational, not functional as claimed by the Mapping Hypothesis. Along with the thesis, we have presented an alternative analysis, which consists of three components: (i) the specification of a semantic representation for each type of reading in question, (ii) the postulation of some independently motivated information –structural constraints, and (iii) an interpretational scheme to the effect that a given syntactic configuration can be related to more than one type of semantic representation as long as it does not violate the information-structural constraints. Then, the current constraint-based analysis has indeed been demonstrated empirically to characterize the data adequately to attest the plausibility of the thesis.

Although the current paper has succeeded in providing an adequate analysis of the syntax-semantics interface at work for the current data, it has not presented a formal semantic framework or told how the current semantic representations can or should be interpreted model-theoretically. As a matter of fact, the current schematic form of semantic representations is the one used in an existing dynamic semantic framework called "Extended File Change Semantics," which was proposed by [11] for the treatment of topic phrases and extended by [16] to incorporate background-focus structure. Therefore, the current semantic representations can be readily given model-theoretic interpretations; however, the illustration cannot but be left for another occasion because of limitation in space.

References

1. Büring, D.: *The Meaning of Topic and Focus: The 59th Street Bridge Accent*. Routledge, London (1997)
2. Carlson, G.: *Reference to Kinds in English*. Ph.D. Dissertation, UMass (1977)
3. Diesing, M.: *Indefinites*. MIT Press, Cambridge: (1992)
4. Gerstner, C., Krifka, M.: "Genericity". In: Jacobs, J. et al. (eds.): *Handbuch der Syntax*. de Cruyter, Berlin (1993) 966-978
5. Heim, I.: *The Semantics of Definite and Indefinite Noun Phrases*. Ph.D. dissertation, University of Massachusetts, Amherst (1982)
6. Kamp, H.: "A Theory of Truth and Semantic Representation". In Groenendijk, J., Janssen, T., Stokhof, M. (eds.): *Formal Methods in the Study of Language*. Mathematical Center, Amsterdam (1981) 277-321
7. Kratzer, A.: "Stage-Level and Individual-Level predicates". In Carlson, G., Pelletier, F. (eds.): *The Generic Book*. University of Chicago Press, Chicago (1995)
8. Kuno, S.: *The Structure of the Japanese Language*, Cambridge: MIT Press (1973)
9. Kuroda, S-Y.: *Generative Grammatical Studies in the Japanese Language*. Ph.D. Dissertation, MIT (1965)
10. Lewis, D.: "Adverbs of Quantification". In Keenan, E. (ed.): *Formal Semantics of Natural Language*. Cambridge University Press, Cambridge (1975) 3-15
11. Portner, P., Yabushita, K.: "The Semantics and Pragmatics of Topic Phrases". *Linguistics and Philosophy* 21 (1998) 117-157
12. Uechi, A.: "Toward Syntax-Information Mapping". *Japanese/Korean Linguistics* 5 (1996)
13. Uechi, A.: *An Interface Approach to Topic/Focus Structure*, Ph.D. Dissertation, University of British Columbia (1998)
14. Vallduví, E.: *The Informational Component*. Ph.D. Dissertation, U. of Pennsylvania (1990)
15. Wilkinson, K.: "Generic Indefinite NPs". Ms., University of Massachusetts, Amherst (1986)
16. Yabushita, K.: "Topicality in the Semantics and Pragmatics of Questions and Answers: Evidence for a File-Like Structure of Information States". In: Kruijff-Korbayová, I., Kosny, C. (eds.): *Proceedings of the 7th Workshop on the Semantics and Pragmatics of Dialogue* (2003) 147-154

Implicatures and Evidentiality of *Because* Complements at Syntax-Semantics-Pragmatics Interfaces

Yurie Hara

University of Delaware
yhara@udel.edu

1 Introduction

The Japanese contrastive marker *wa* can appear within a *because*-clause as in (1a), while it cannot appear within temporal clauses like *toki* 'when' as in (1b) and *if*-clauses (omitted for space reasons).[1]

(1)   a.   Itsumo uchi-ni   Mary-**wa**   kuru **node**   kodomo-ga
             always house-Dat Mary-CTop come because, children-Nom
             yorokob-u.
             happy-Present
             'Because Mary$_{CTop}$ always comes to our house, the children are happy.'

       b. *Itsumo uchi-ni   Mary-**wa**   kuru **toki**, keeki-o   motteku-ru.
             always house-Dat Mary-CTop come when, cake-Acc bring-Present
             'When Mary$_{CTop}$ comes to our house, she always brings a cake.'

Interestingly, the same asymmetry is found with an evidential morpheme.

(2)   a.   Kodomo-ga   kuru **souna node**,   oyatsu-o   youi-shita.
             children-Nom come Evid   because, sweets-Acc preparation-di
             'Because I heard that children are coming, I prepared sweets.'

       b. *Kodomo-ga   kuru **souna toki**, oyatsu-o   youi-shita.
             children-Nom come Evid   when, sweets-Acc preparation-did
             'When I heard that children are coming, I prepared sweets.'

This paper will analyze this parallelism of the asymmetry between *node* 'because' and *toki* 'when' in terms of the availability of Evidential Phrase in syntax, which has been proposed and investigated by Chinque [2], Speas [3] and Tenny [4]. Evidential Phrase is a syntactic manifestation of a semantics-pragmatic object, Evidentiality. This (in)compatibility of Evidential Phrases with Adjunct Clauses is further motivated by the syntax-semantics difference of Adjunct Clauses discussed by Johnston [5].

---

[1] The same asymmetry is also found in Sawada and Larson [1].

T. Washio et al. (Eds.): JSAI 2005 Workshops, LNAI 4012, pp. 118–125, 2006.
© Springer-Verlag Berlin Heidelberg 2006

2   Implicature Computation Blocked by Syntax

In [6], I argued that Japanese Contrastive Topic *wa* induces implicatures which are always attributed to some attitude-bearer x as defined in (3).[2]

(3)   CONTRASTIVE$(w)(x)(B)(T)$ (w: world variable, x: speaker or attitude-bearer, B: background, T: contrastive-marked element, C: common ground)

    a.   asserts: $B(T)(w)$

    b.   presupposes: $\exists T'[T' \in ALT_C(T)\ \&\ B(T') \Rightarrow B(T)\ \&\ B(T) \not\Rightarrow B(T')]$

    c.   implicates: $\exists w' \in \min_w[w' \in \mathrm{Dox}_x(w)] : \forall T'[T' \in ALT_C(T)\ \&\ B(T') \Rightarrow B(T)\ \&\ B(T) \not\Rightarrow B(T')][B(T')(w')=0]$

For instance, (4) is defined since there exists some stronger scalar alternative (e.g. Everyone came.) and in some worlds w' differing minimally from w and doxastically accessible to the speaker (the attitude-bearer), the stronger alternative is false ((4) implicates 'Possibly, not everyone came.').

(4)   Nanninka-wa ki-ta.
    '[Some people]$_{CTop}$ came'

In (5), *wa* can be associated to another attitude-bearer (i.e. Mary) since *wa* is embedded within an attitude predicate, hence it is ambiguous between the speaker's global implicature and Mary's local implicature. I propose that the use of *wa* introduces an operator which determines the attitude-bearer of the induced implicature (the speaker or the subject of the attitude predicate) and the contrasted proposition (the matrix or the embedded).

(5)   nanninka-**wa**   kita-to   Mary-ga   shinjite-iru
    some-people-CTop come-Comp Mary-nom believe-Prog
    'Mary believes [some people]$_{CTop}$ came.'   (ambiguous)

    a.   Local: The speaker asserts [Mary believes some people came and <u>she</u> doesn't believe everyone came]

    b.   Global: <u>The speaker</u> asserts [Mary believes some people came] and <u>the speaker</u> doesn't assert [Mary believes everyone came]

This association between the operator and the *wa*-marked item seems to be blocked in a certain syntactic configuration, adjunct island, as in (1b). In general, semantic associations, as discussed in Kratzer [9] among others for resumptive pronouns and choice function binding, are immune to islands. Hence, I propose a syntactic account, namely I speculate that the operator is originally generated locally and moves to the positions such as Speech Act Phrase or attitude predicates.

---

[2] See Nakanishi [7] and Oshima [8] for different analyses of Japanese Contrastive Topics.

Moreover, having a Contrastive within a temporal *per se* should be allowed semantically. As in (6), *wa*-marked NP can be coindexed with an argument, *pro*, within a temporal clause. Therefore, the ungrammaticality of (1b) is not due to semantic constraints but syntactic ones.

(6)   Mary$_i$-**wa**   itsumo uchi-ni   *pro$_i$* kuru **toki**, keeki-o   motteku-ru.
        Mary-CTop always house-Dat *pro* come when, cake-Acc bring-Present
        'As for Mary$_{iCTop}$, when *pro$_i$* comes to our house, she always brings a
        cake.'(Possible Implicature: As for John, he never brings anything.)

(6) is not an instance of overt movement of *Mary-wa*. As discussed in Hoji [10], the empty category e_j in (7a) is a base-generated empty pronominal (little *pro* in more recent terminology) coindexed with the *wa*-phrase, while t_j is a trace created by the movement of the object.

(7)   a.   John$_j$-wa [$_S$ Mary-ga   [$_{VP}$ e_j butta]]
             John-Top   Mary-Nom   hit
             'As for John$_j$, Mary hit him$_j$.'
        b.   John$_j$-o [$_S$ Mary-ga   [$_{VP}$ t_j butta]]
             John-Top   Mary-Nom   hit
             'John$_j$, Mary hit t_j.'   (Hoji [10];p.133)

Hoji [10] provides the following anaphor binding test to show that the sentence-initial *wa*-marked phrase is not an instance of movement. In (8a), *zibun* cannot be bound by *John*, unlike (8b).

(8)   a.   *[$_{NP}$ sono zibun$_i$ nituite-no hon   ]$_j$ -wa John$_i$-ga [$_{VP}$ e_j
                  that self   about   book   -Top John-nom
             suteta   ]
             threw-away
             'As for [that book about himself$_i$]$_j$, John$_i$ threw it$_j$ away.'
        b.   [$_S$ [$_{NP}$ sono zibun$_i$ nituite-no hon   ]$_j$ -o   [$_S$ John$_i$-ga [$_{VP}$ t_j
                  that self   about   book   -Acc   John-nom
             suteta   ]]]
             threw-away
             'That book about himself$_i$, John$_i$ threw away.'(Hoji [10];p.129,133)

This contrast proves that the sentence-initial *wa*-phrase is base-generated and coindexed with an empty pronominal which is also base-generated.

Going back to (6), *Mary-wa* is not moved out of the *when*-clause but base-generated outside; hence the implicature operator does not cross an island. On the other hand, in (1b), *Mary-wa* is generated under *when*, and the operator needs to cross an island to find its attitude-bearer.

In summary, the use of *wa* triggers implicatures which are associated to the speaker or some attitude-bearer. This association is blocked by a certain syntactic configuration, namely an adjunct island.

3   Parallelism of the Asymmetry

As noted earlier, the asymmetry between *when* and *because* with *wa* is also found with evidentials. An evidential morpheme *souna/souda* indicates that the statement is based on reported evidence. *Souna/souda* can occur within *because* ((2a)) but cannot occur within *when* ((2b)). The speculation is that whenever discourse items need to be associated to some attitude-holder, the asymmetry emerges. The same pattern is observed in other languages. For example, in English, the evidential adverb *obviously* can occur within a *because*-clause while it cannot under *when*.

(9)   a.   Mary is upset because obviously John doesn't love her.
       b.   *Mary got upset when obviously she failed the exam

Tredinnick [11] points out that sentence (10) is ambiguous. One meaning is that Mary is upset because of the fact that John doesn't love her, and the speaker comments that it is obvious that John doesn't love her. The other meaning is that Mary is upset because of the obviousness of John's lack of love for her (she might not care whether John actually loves her or not). If we switch the adjective with the adverb *obviously* as in (9a), only the former reading, namely the speaker's comment, is available. I speculate that this is because *obviously* has to be associated with the speaker's attitude such as Assert function just like Japanese *wa* is associated to an attitude-bearer.

(10)   Mary is upset because it is obvious that John doesn't love her.

Similarly, the German discourse particle *ja*, which indicates the speaker's assumption that the expressed content might be known to the addressee, can occur within a *because*-clause but not in temporal clauses.[3]

(11)   a.   Maria ist ärgerlich, weil   John sie ja nicht liebt.
             Maria is angry,   because John her JA not   love
             'Maria is angry, because John JA doesn't love her.'
       b.   *Maria wurde ärgerlich, als   sie ja die Prüfung nicht bestanden
             Maria was   angry,   when she JA the exam   not   passed
             hatte.
             have
             'Maria is angry, when she JA didn't pass the exam.'

Kratzer [12] also shows that it can be relativized to an attitude-bearer other than the speaker if it is embedded within an attitude predicate like *claim*:

(12)   Jederder Zeugen   behauptete, er habe ja mit eigenen Augen
        Each   witnesses claimed   he had JA with own   eyes
        gesehen, dass ....
        seen   that

---

[3] See Kratzer [12] for her rough definition of *ja*.

'Each of the witnesses claimed he had JA seen with his own eyes that...'
(Kratzer [12])

In summary, discourse items which need to be associated to an attitude-holder show a cross-linguistic parallelism of asymmetry among adverbial adjuncts in which they are embedded. Particularly in Japanese, both Contrastive Topics and evidential morphemes share the same pattern of the distributional asymmetry. Following Sawada and Larson [1] and Johnston [5], I will argue that the asymmetry comes from the syntactic/semantic difference between *when* and *because*; the Evidential Projections are available for *because* but not for *when*.

4   Implicatures and Evidentials

On the assumption that there exist Speech Act Phrases (Rivero, Rizzi [13],[14]) and Evidential Phrases (Cinque, Speas [2],[3]), Tenny [4] argues for the existence of an evidential argument in syntax, which refers to an individual who is "responsible for evaluating the truth of a proposition" (pp.26-27). For example, as mentioned earlier, a sentence with a *souda/souna* ending indicates that the truth value of the statement is based on reported evidence as in (13).

(13)   John-ga   sushi-o   tabeta souda.
        John-Nom sushi-Acc ate   Evid
        '(I heard that) John ate sushi.'

According to Tenny [4], this is mapped in syntax in the following way: the evidential phrase projected by *souda/souna* contains x_j, someone other than the speaker, as an invisible argument.

(14) $[_{\text{SpeechActP}}[$ the speaker$_i$ $]$ $[_{\text{EvidentialP}}$ x_j $[_{\text{Evidential'}}$ John-ga sushi-o tabeta $[_{\text{Evidential}}$ souda $]$ $]$ $]$ $]$

I equate the attitude-bearer contained within *wa* to this evidential argument. Both an evidential argument and an attitude-bearer are bearers of a point of view towards a proposition. Indeed, if an overt evidential morpheme like *souna/souda* indicates that the speaker is not the evidential argument, as in (15), the implicature induced by *wa*, 'Possibly others didn't come', is associated to the reported evidence, not to the speaker.

(15)   Kinou   John-wa   kita souda.
        yesterday John-CTop came Evid
        'Yesterday, [John]$_{CTop}$ came (I heard).'

Tenny further proposes that *node* 'because' is a head of an Evidential projection and *node* introduces two arguments: a proposition and an evidential argument.

Tenny provides different interpretation of direct experience predicates within a *because*-clause and a *when*-clause (see Tenny [4] for details). I modify Tenny's [4] analysis in a way that *because* takes an Evidential Phrase as its complement rather than itself projecting the phrase. In other words, I claim that this

Evidential Projection, which contains an evidential argument, is available in a complement of a *because*-clause, while it is not in a *when*-clause. Now, let us go back the contrast between *because* and *when* with respect to the use of *wa* and remember that the interpretation of *wa* involves the movement of the implicature operator to an attitude-holder. In the *because*-clause (1a), the implicature operator finds the local Evidential Projection as in (16).

(16)   ⋯ [$_{\text{AdjunctP}}$ [$_{\text{EvidP}}$ Op [$_{\text{EvidP}}$ [evid-arg] [$_{\text{Evid'}}$ [$_{\text{IP}}$ t Mary-wa come]]]]]
        because]   (1a)

In *when*-clauses, the operator has to target the matrix clause, which causes an adjunct island violation ((17)).

(17)   *[$_{\text{SpeechActP}}$ [speaker] [$_{\text{EvidP}}$ Op [$_{\text{EvidP}}$ ⋯ [$_{\text{AdjunctP}}$ [$_{\text{IP}}$ t Mary-wa come
        ] when]]]]   *   (1b)

In order to explain why Evidential Projection is not available for *when*, while it is for *because*, the next section will review Johnston's [5] analysis on the adjunct adverbials.

5   Semantics/Syntax of *When* and *Because*: Johnston [5]

I need to establish two points regarding the syntax of adjuncts. First, there is no Evidential Phrase under *when*. Second, there could be an Evidential Phrase under *because*.

According to Johnston, *when* combines with an open event sentence and yields a time-interval description. In this analysis of *when*, since *when* needs to apply the maximal s to the temporal runtime function f, the argument of *when* must be an open event predicate $<s,t>$, not a closed proposition t.

(18)   a.   when Marcia was at the cafe
        b.   Marcia was at the cafe $\Rightarrow \lambda e'.$**Marcia-was-at-the-cafe'**(e')
        c.   when $\Rightarrow \lambda\phi \in D_{<s,t>}\lambda i[\exists e[\text{MAX}(\phi)(e)\&i = f(e)]]$
        d.   when Marcia was at the cafe
              $\Rightarrow \lambda i[\exists e[\text{MAX}(\lambda e'.$**Marcia-was-at-the-cafe'**$(e'))(e)\&i = f(e)]]$
              (abbreviated as **when'**$_e$(**at'**(Marcia, the cafe, e)); f is the temporal
              runtime function)   (Johnston [5])

Following earlier literatures, Johnston [5] assumes that a temporal clause is always a restriction of an adverb of quantification (AoQ). When the quantification is done by an implicit existential, an episodic reading is derived as in (19a). On the other hand, (19c) is an instance of the overt adverb of quantification.

(19)   a.   Marcia wrote a letter when she was at the cafe.
        b. $\exists$[**when'**$_e$(**at'**(Marcia, the cafe, e_1))][**write'**(Marcia, a letter, e_2)]
        c.   Marcia always writes a letter when she is at the cafe.
        d. $\forall$[**when'**$_e$(**at'**(Marcia, the cafe, e_1))][**write'**(Marcia, a letter, e_2)]

On the other hand, Johnston [5] claims that *because* takes a closed event sentence and expresses a binary relation between closed event sentences. In other words, in the complement of *because*, the existential quantifier over events is not provided by *because*.

(20)   a.   Marty sold his bike because the gears broke.
        b.   **because'**$\exists e_1$[**sold'**(Marty, his bike, e_1)],$\exists e_2$[**break'**(Marty, his bike, e_2)]

Johnston [5] further argues that *because*-clause cannot be a restriction of an adverb of quantification. (21a) does not mean (21b).

(21)   a.   Jane always fixes the car because John wrecks it.
        b.   #$\forall$[**because'**$\exists e_1$[**wrecks'**(John, the car, e_1)]][**fix'**(Jane, the car, e_2)]
              # All (relevant) events caused by John's wrecking the car are ones of Jane's fixing it.

To sum, *because* takes a closed event sentence t, whereas *when* necessarily takes an open even predicate $<e,t>$. Now, how is this semantic difference manifested in syntax? In particular, how is this difference related to Evidential Projection? Since an evidential argument is a sentient being who holds evidence for judging the truth-value of an asserted proposition, Evidential Projection takes a closed event sentence (type t). One cannot hold for the evidence for the truth of an open predicate since the expression is not saturated to be a truth-condition. Given Johnston's analysis of *when*, therefore, there is no Evidential Projection under *when*. On the other hand, Johnston's analysis of *because* is compatible with the analysis in which *because* takes an Evidential Phrase as its complement. Since it is the speaker's or some attitude-bearer's reasoning that connects two conjuncts of *because*, there is a room to introduce evidentiality (point of view) in the complement of *because*.

To conclude this section, the semantic difference between *when* and *because* is that *when* takes an open event predicate and *because* takes a closed sentence. Syntactically speaking, *when* subcategorizes for an IP/TP, while *because* subcategorizes for an Evidential Projection.

6   Conclusion and Ramification of the Analysis

I have shown that implicature computation triggered by *wa* involves a syntactic operation of implicature operator movement. This movement is blocked if *wa* is embedded within a *when*-clause since it causes an adjunct island violation. *Wa* survives within an *because*-clause, since the implicature operator has a host (Evidential Projection) within the adjunct clause; hence it does not need to cross an island. The difference between *because*-clauses and *when*-clauses is represented in syntax as (un)availability of Evidential Projections.

The facts presented in this paper also have an interesting ramification regarding the connection between implicatures and evidentiality. Both concepts are previously treated within semantics-pragmatics, while recent studies have started to explore the phenomena in context of syntax-semantics-pragmatics interfaces as in Chierchia [15] for implicatures and Speas [3] and Tenny [4] for evidentiality. However, the connection between the two concepts has not been discussed in theoretical linguistics. The analysis in this paper offers several connections between the two, descriptively, semantically and syntactically. Future research on other discourse items will reveal the well-founded bond between implicatures and evidentiality in linguistic theory.

References

1. Sawada, M., Larson, R.: Presupposition & root transforms in adjunct clauses. Proceedings of NELS 34. (In press)
2. Cinque, G.: Adverbs and Functional Heads: A cross-linguistic perspective. Oxford University Press (1999)
3. Speas, M.: Evidentiality, logophoricity and the syntactic representation of pragmatic features. Lingua **114** (2004) 255–276
4. Tenny, C.: Evidentiality, experiencers, and the syntax of sentience in japanese. Carnegie-Mellon University (2004)
5. Johnston, M.: the Syntax and Semantics of Adverbial Adjuncts. PhD thesis, UCSC (1994)
6. Hara, Y.: Scope inversion and contrastive meaning by conventional implicature. University of Delaware (2004)
7. Nakanishi, K.: Prosody and inforamation structure in japanese: a case study of topic marker *wa*. In: Japanese/Korean Linguistics. Volume 10., Stanford, CA, CSLI (2001) 434–447
8. Oshima, D.Y.: Contrastive topic as a paradigmatic operator. paper presented at Workshop on Information Structure in Context (2002)
9. Kratzer, A.: The representation of focus. In von Stechow, A., Wunderlich, D., eds.: Semantics. An International Handbook of Contemporary Research. de Gruyter., Berlin (1991) 825–834
10. Hoji, H.: Logical Form Constraints and Configurational Structure in Japanese. PhD thesis, University of Washington (1985)
11. Tredinnick, V.: Modal flavor and quantificational force in free relatives with -ever. (2004)
12. Kratzer, A.: Beyond *ouch* and *oops*. how descriptive and expressive meaning interact. (1999)
13. Rivero, M.L.: Clause structure and v-movement in the languages of the balkans. Natural Language and Linguistic Theory **12** (1994) 63–120
14. Rizzi, L.: The fine structure of the left-periphery. In Haegeman, L., ed.: Elements of Grammar. Dordrecht: Kluwer (1997) 281–337
15. Chierchia, G.: Scalar implicatures, polarity phenomena, and syntax/pragmatics interface. In: Structures and Beyond. Oxford University Press (2004)

Model Generation in a Dynamic Environment*

Anders Søgaard

Center for Language Technology, University of Copenhagen
Njalsgade 80, DK-2300 Copenhagen
anders@cst.dk

Abstract. Conventionally anaphora is seen as triggered by grammar,
i.e. as a saturation requirement. In this paper, it is demonstrated how this
assumption complicates anaphora resolution considerably and instead it
is proposed to let the fly out of the bottle and reconsider grammar's
contribution to anaphora resolution.

1 Introduction

Conventional anaphora resolution techniques rely on indication of anaphoric
expressions. On some designs, anaphoric expressions introduce unresolved equations [7]or special predicates [1], while on others they are structurally different
from resolved expressions [3,12]. Our point of departure is the observation that
this kind of positive indication of anaphora is in fact redundant in most inference-
based abductive or dynamic environments. This redundancy is demonstrated in
Baumgartner and Kühn's (B&K) system [1], and indirectly in Bos' system [3]
too. The important machinery in such systems is domain minimal model search.
The domain minimal model is the model in which the most variables are assigned to the same individuals. Consequently, resolution comes for free if the
assignments are properly restricted. This is the intuition behind our approach.

The next observation is standard in the literature: Antecedents must be appropriate and accessible [7-9]. Appropriateness is secured by the generation of
consistent models, while accessibility must be ensured from other principles. In
Kamp (1981), accessibility constraints are defined on the intermediate language
of discourse representation structures and with respect to embedding. Our system is simpler in that no intermediate language is hypothesized. Accessibility is
ensured by dynamic model generation, i.e. local inferences on logical forms.

Our approach is not just an improvement of B&K (1999), it is an extension.
Introduction of discourse referents and accessibility constraints are ignored in
their paper. In this respect, our approach is reminiscent of work in discourse
representation theory (DRT) [3,7,9,12], but no unselective binding is introduced,
so the proportion problem is avoided. Objections to DRT raised in Fodor and
Sag (1982) are also met, since ambiguous indefinites are easily implemented.

A small HPSG fragment and a model generator is defined. The output of the
grammar is used to generate first order models, and the accessibility conditions
are directly implemented in the knowledge base of the model generator. The
output model is added to this base in the update algorithm's last step.

---

* Thanks to the two anonymous reviewers for their helpful comments.

T. Washio et al. (Eds.): JSAI 2005 Workshops, LNAI 4012, pp. 126–133, 2006.
© Springer-Verlag Berlin Heidelberg 2006

2 Positive Constraints on Coreference

B&K discuss the somewhat odd example in (1). Their intuition is that *the crimi-nal* refers to the gangster, by default. The resolution results from their definition of abductive explanation, their notion of (predicate-specific) minimality – which simply says that the minimal model we are interested in, is the one with the least number of instances of **anaphor**-predicates – and the semantics of anaphoric expressions.

(1) *a.* A politician chased a gangster. *b.* The criminal died.

Definition 1 (Abductive explanation). *Ω is the set of observations, Σ the background theory and Δ the abducibles. Γ is an abductive explanation iff: $\Gamma \subseteq \Delta$, $\Sigma \cup \Gamma \models \Omega$ and $\Sigma \cup \Gamma$ is satisfiable.*

(1a) adds the following to Σ, which already contains the implication that gang-sters are criminals: **politician**$(c_1) \wedge$ **gangster**$(c_2) \wedge$ **chase**(c_1, c_2). B&K offer no explanation of how indefinites introduce discourse referents; this issue is ad-dressed below. In terms of abductive reasoning, the observation that has to be explained in (1b), is that one of the discourse referents is a (dying) crimi-nal, i.e. $\Omega = \exists x_1.$**anaphor**$_1(x_1) \wedge$ **criminal**$(x_1) \wedge$ **die**(x_1). The abducibles Δ are $\{$**anaphor**$_1(c_1),$ **anaphor**$_1(c_2)\}$.[1] Since the abductive explanation must be a subset of Δ according to Definition 1, there are four candidates for such explanations: $\Gamma_1 = \{\}$, $\Gamma_3 = \{$**anaphor**$_1(c_2)\}$, $\Gamma_2 = \{$**anaphor**$_1(c_1)\}$ and $\Gamma_4 = \{$**anaphor**$_1(c_1),$ **anaphor**$_1(c_2)\}$. Γ_1 is in conflict with Definition 1, and more specifically, with $\Sigma \cup \Gamma \models \Omega$. Γ_2 and Γ_3 are both possible solutions. Γ_4 is a bad explanation, since it is not **anaphor**$_1$-minimal. B&K argue that "Γ_2 is excluded, since it does not entail with Σ the last part of the observation Ω, namely $\exists x_1.$**criminal**(x_1)." It is not clear to me what they mean, but Γ_2 can be excluded on different grounds under local minimality (Definition 2 at page 128).

$$\begin{array}{c}
\textbf{politician}(c_1) \\
\textbf{gangster}(c_2) \\
\textbf{chase}(c_1, c_2) \\
\textbf{criminal}(c_2)
\end{array}$$

$\textbf{anaphor}_1(c_1)$	$\textbf{anaphor}_1(c_2)$
$\textbf{criminal}(c_1)$	$\textbf{die}(c_2)$
$\textbf{die}(c_1)$	

Some Empirical Inadequacies. In addition to the revision of the definition of model minimality, certain other revisions are necessary to make this framework empirically adequate. B&K let definite noun phrases introduce anaphoric re-lations (presumably excluding generics, e.g. *la vecchiaia*, 'old age', and noun phrases denoting unique entities, e.g. *il sole*, 'the sun'), but this is not a viable solution in general, since definite noun phrases sometimes introduce new dis-course referents. In certain contexts, the definite noun phrase may be said to refer to an implicit discourse referent, as in (2), but this approach will run into problems when trying to explain examples such as (3,4):

---

[1] B&K write the abducibles in this way, but the **anaphor**-predicates abbreviate for-mulae, it seems, e.g. **anaphor**$_1(c_i) \wedge$ **criminal**$(c_i) \wedge$ **die**(c_i). Otherwise $\Sigma \cup \Gamma \not\models \Omega$.

(2) C'è un negozio, è la commessa ... ('there is a store, and the salesgirl ...')
(3) Ho perso l'orologio. ('I've lost my (the) watch')
(4) La signora Anna Maria è una bella donna dai capelli rossi e dai molti gioielli.
   ('AM is a beautiful lady with (the) red hair and (the) many jewels')

If the definite noun phrases in (3,4) were anaphoric expressions, the existence of a person would somehow imply the existence of watches, red hair and jewels. This is nonsensical. Only in designs with strong accommodation mechanisms (e.g. [12]) can definites be uniformly assigned anaphoric relations.

Inefficiencies. B&K employ predicate-specific minimality. If they had employed the more standard notion of local minimality, they would have been able to simplify their account considerably, since the unification of variables then comes for free. This objection also addresses new and classical DRT [8]. Consider the derivation of (1) and assume local minimality. It is now possible to ignore the abducibles. Consequently, three assignments of the variable in Ω are available:

$$\begin{array}{c} \textbf{politician}(c_1) \\ \textbf{gangster}(c_2) \\ \textbf{chase}(c_1, c_2) \\ \textbf{criminal}(c_2) \end{array}$$

$\textbf{criminal}(c_1)$	$\textbf{die}(c_2)$	$\textbf{criminal}(c_3)$
$\textbf{die}(c_1)$	.	$\textbf{die}(c_3)$

It is evident that the assignment $g(x_1) = c_2$ is the locally minimal explanation. It results in fewer relations than $g(x_1) = c_1$ and fewer individuals than $g(x_1) = c_3$. The notion of local minimality is formally defined below. In addition, B&K must also address the issue of referent-introduction. How do they analyze indefinites? On their account, nothing ensures the indefinite is not coreferential with an antecedent referential expression. Finally, B&K introduce no straightforward way of implementing accessibility constraints.

3   Preliminaries on Model Generation

Various notions of model minimality are proposed in the literature [10], but *local minimality* seems to be of interest in the context of anaphora resolution. A model is an interpretation of some utterance u, say (4), iff it satisfies $\Sigma \cup \Gamma_u$. The preferred interpretation is the locally minimal model, and the set of theories is the Cartesian product of $\{\Sigma\}$ and the set of explanations.

Definition 2 (Local minimality). *Say two theories Θ_i and Θ_j are satisfied by $\mathfrak{M}_i$ and $\mathfrak{M}_j$. $\mathfrak{M}_i$ is the locally minimal model only if $|\mathfrak{M}_i|_\iota \leq |\mathfrak{M}_j|_\iota$ (where $|.|_\iota$ assigns cardinality to structures) and vice versa. If $|\mathfrak{M}_i|_\iota = |\mathfrak{M}_j|_\iota$, then $\mathfrak{M}_i$ is the minimal model if $|\mathfrak{M}_i|_\rho \leq |\mathfrak{M}_j|_\rho$ ($|.|_\rho$ is a function that outputs the number of relations in a structure) and vice versa. The binary relation symbol $\preceq$ denotes local minimality, i.e. if $\mathfrak{M}_i$ is more locally minimal than $\mathfrak{M}_j$, $\mathfrak{M}_i \preceq \mathfrak{M}_j$.*

Consider the interpretation of (1). $\Sigma_{(1a)}$ at the time (1a) is uttered, is different from $\Sigma_{(1b)}$ at the time (1b) is uttered, since (1a) updates $\Sigma_{(1a)}$. This temporal notion of update is used to define informativity.

Definition 3 (Informativity). *In $\{u_i, u_j\}$, u_j is informative, iff $\mathfrak{M}_{u_i} \not\models u_j$.*

An informativity constraint is added to our hypothesis about preferred interpretations:

Definition 4 (Preferred interpretations). *The preferred interpretation of an utterance u_j in some discourse $\{u_1, \ldots, u_i, u_j, \ldots, u_n\}$ is $\mathfrak{M}_{u_j}$ such that:$\mathfrak{M}_{u_j} \models u_j \cup \Sigma$, $\mathfrak{M}_{u_j} \preceq \mathfrak{M}'_{u_j}$ for any model $\mathfrak{M}'_{u_j}$ such that $\mathfrak{M}'_{u_j} \models u_j \cup \Sigma$, and$\mathfrak{M}_{u_i} \not\models u_j$.*

The minimal model of (4), on this hypothesis, and relevant lexical semantics (ignoring givenness, which is introduced below, the internal complexity of the plural *molti gioielli*, and an adequate semantics of proper names), is $\mathfrak{M}_{(4)} = \{\textbf{beautiful}(a), \textbf{female}(a), \textbf{poss}(a, c_1), \textbf{hair}(c_1), \textbf{red}(c_1), \textbf{poss}(a, c_2), \textbf{jewels}(c_2)\}$.

4 Negative Constraints on Coreference

Assume Definition 4. One complexity to our account is the restriction on indefinites that in most contexts they introduce discourse referents. This question is never addressed by B&K. The exact design of the mechanism depends on how determination or *givenness* is accounted for. The conventional encoding of givenness is by lexically introduced operators, e.g. the ι-operator. Instead a scalar set of givenness predicates with set-theoretic interpretations is introduced here. Compositionally, givenness is computed at the constructional level.

Givenness. The intuition behind constructional computation of givenness is that adnominals constrain givenness rather than introduce it. The values are given in the hierarchy below, inspired by Gundel et al. (1993). They are forced down the hierarchy, as you're chased up the syntactic tree, so to say.

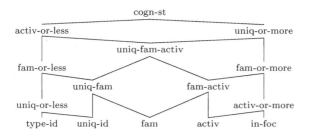

The hierarchy is used to account for light pronouns and bare singulars [2], and declension, vocatives and discourse givenness [14]. The values are subtypes of the predicate value, so they can be directly employed in logical form. The logical form of (4) is then (ignoring tense and simplifying quantification): $\textbf{type\_id}(a) \wedge \textbf{beautiful}(a) \wedge \textbf{female}(a) \wedge \exists x_1.\textbf{poss}(a, x_1) \wedge \textbf{uniq\_or\_more}(x_1) \wedge \textbf{hair}(x_1) \wedge \textbf{red}(x_1) \wedge \exists x_2.\textbf{poss}(a, x_2) \wedge \textbf{uniq\_or\_more}(x_2) \wedge \textbf{jewels}(x_2)$. As should be obvious from this, $\lambda x_1.\textbf{type\_id}(x_1)$ is the set of things given as types (in a non-technical sense), while $\lambda x_1.\textbf{uniq\_or\_more}(x_1)$ is the set of things uniquely given. A subset of $\lambda x_1.\textbf{uniq\_or\_more}(x_1)$ is e.g. the set of things in focus, which typically are referred to by pronouns. The important thing to note, however, is that, in restricted ways, objects can be referred to differently throughout a discourse. For instance, something given as a type in one utterance, may be given as a uniquely identified referent in the subsequent discourse, but not reversely.

A Constraint on Indefinites. Index givenness predicates (cf. **anaphor**-predicates in [1]). Translate the type hierarchy into a set of meaning postulates $\Pi \in \Sigma$. The constraint that indefinites introduce referents is formally stated in (A):

(A) $\neg\exists x_1.\textbf{cogn\_st}_i(x_1) \wedge \textbf{type\_id}_j(x_1)$ *where* $i < j$

Indefinites now introduce referents, since any individual is in $\lambda x_i.cogn\_st(x_i)$.

Example 1. Revisit (1). The logical form of the two utterances are, respectively, $\exists x_1.\exists x_2.\textbf{type\_id}_1(x_1) \wedge \textbf{politician}(x_1) \wedge \textbf{type\_id}_1(x_2) \wedge \textbf{gangster}(x_2) \wedge \textbf{chase}(x_1, x_2)$ and $\exists x_1.\textbf{uniq\_or\_more}_2(x_1) \wedge \textbf{criminal}(x_1) \wedge \textbf{die}(x_1)$. If Σ, soundly, conjoins $\neg\exists x_1.\textbf{chase}(x_1, x_1)$ and $\forall x_1.\textbf{gangster}(x_1) \rightarrow \textbf{criminal}(x_1)$, a tableaux equivalent to the one on page 128 is derived. Compare this to (5):

(5) *a.* A politician chased a gangster. *b.* A criminal died.

$$\textbf{politician}(c_1)$$
$$\textbf{type\_id}_1(c_1)$$
$$\textbf{gangster}(c_2)$$
$$\textbf{type\_id}_1(c_2)$$
$$\textbf{chase}(c_1, c_2)$$
$$\textbf{criminal}(c_2)$$

$\textbf{type\_id}_2(c_1)$	$\textbf{type\_id}_2(c_2)$	$\textbf{type\_id}_2(c_3)$
$\textbf{criminal}(c_1)$	$\textbf{die}(c_2)$	$\textbf{criminal}(c_3)$
$\textbf{die}(c_1)$	$*$	$\textbf{die}(c_3)$
$*$		

Now two of the assignments are suddenly inconsistent. The preferred one corresponds to our intuitions about the discourse's meaning.

Objections. On the current design, all variables are unified as long as $\Sigma \cup \Gamma$ is satisfiable, i.e. the analysis is consistent with the knowledge base, and the resulting model is minimal and informative. However, there are additional constraints on coreference, which we have not accounted for. One of these is the problem of partial accessibility. In DRT, an antecedent should be both appropriate and accessible [7-9]. Appropriateness is ensured. Accessibility is restricted by levels of embedding in discourse representation structures. Can we do something similar on our design? The problem is quantificational noun phrases, (indefinites introduced in negative and conditional contexts automatically resist coreference, since they have no representation in locally minimal models).

The simple step to implement accessibility constraints on quantificational noun phrases is to introduce a quantifier hierarchy, similar to our givenness hierarchy. Such quantifier hierarchies are independently motivated in Søgaard and Haugereid (2005), e.g. it was used to explain restrictions of measure phrases, quantifier float and agreement in the prenomial field. A constraint (B) is now added to Σ. Of course the quantifier values of individuals must be constantly updated. The flexibility of our design allows us to implement the ambiguity between referential and quantificational uses of indefinites (important in negative and conditional contexts), observed by Fodor and Sag (1982).

(B) $\neg\exists x_1.\mathbf{quant\_np}_i(x_1) \wedge \mathbf{in\_foc}_j(x_1)$ *where* $i < j$

5 Fragment

In this section, a fragment is defined for small discourses like:

(6) *a.* A man$_i$ snores. *b.* The man$_i$ sleeps.
(7) *a.* *The man$_i$ snores. *b.* A man$_i$ sleeps.
(8) *a.* *All men$_i$ snore. *b.* The man$_i$ sleeps.

Lexicon. The lexical entries are relatively simple:

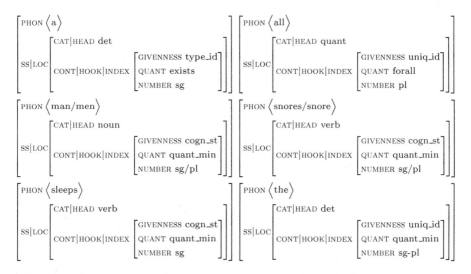

Grammar. Assume a Head Specifier Rule [11] and Minimal Recursion Semantics [4]. Then (6a) is parsed as:

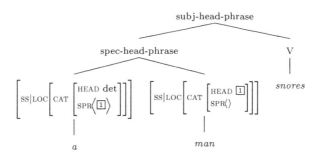

The *head-subj-phrase* inserts the quantifier, but selects the quantificational value from the index of the subject (i.e. the indices of its daughters).

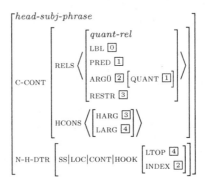

Similarly, a givenness predicate is inserted at this level. Consequently, the scoped *mrss* of (6a) and (6b) are $\exists x_1.\mathbf{man}(x_1) \wedge \mathbf{type\_id_1}(x_1) \wedge \mathbf{snore}(x_1)$ and $\exists x_2.\mathbf{man}(x_2) \wedge \mathbf{uniq\_id_2}(x_2) \wedge \mathbf{sleep}(x_2)$. In Σ, nothing prevents that $g(x_1) = g(x_2)$. Consequently, the locally minimal model satisfying (6) contains one individual, i.e. anaphora resolution is performed. Consider the output for (7): $\exists x_1.\mathbf{man}(x_1) \wedge \mathbf{uniq\_id_1}(x_1) \wedge \mathbf{snore}(x_1)$ and $\exists x_2.\mathbf{man}(x_2) \wedge \mathbf{type\_id_2}(x_2) \wedge \mathbf{sleep}(x_2)$. In this case, $g(x_1) \neq g(x_2)$, since (A) ensures that $\neg\exists x_1.\mathbf{uniq\_id_1}(x_1) \wedge \mathbf{type\_id_2}(x_1)$. This is why coreference fails in (7). This effect is ensured in (8) by number agreement, while (B) ensures it for discourses like:

(9) *a.* Each man$_i$ snores. *b.* The man$_i$ sleeps.

Grammar and Inference. Satisfiability, local minimality and informatitivity are general pragmatic constraints on discourse interpretation. Grammar encodes the constraints a constituent puts on agreement, etc., but says nothing about which elements are likely to be coreferential. Compared to Bos (2003), no account was given for presuppositional effects. It is rather predicted that presuppositional effects are extragrammatical, and that the oddness it causes to violate presuppositions is only pragmatic of nature. E.g. if (9b) is parsed in isolation, our algorithm still produces a model $\mathfrak{M}_i : \{\mathbf{man}(c_1), \mathbf{uniq\_id}(c_1), \mathbf{sleep}(c_1)\}$. If the utterance is considered odd, this is only a result of pragmatics. In our view, pragmatics should be modelled independently.

6 Conclusion

The fragment is a small grammar that outputs scoped *mrss*, which are forwarded to the inference module. The inference module is used to derive the preferred interpretation (cf. Definition 4). On related implementations, see e.g. [3,9,13]. The system introduces no intermediate structures, but consists only of a grammar and an inference module (that includes a knowledge base). Computationally, the flow is from the parser to, say, a theorem prover and a model generator. The only complication is to extract relevant information from the computed models to the knowledge base; for details, see [13]. This last step is the update function.

In processing, the system generates global models to resolve anaphora, ambiguities, etc. Bos (2003) speculates that more efficient algorithms may exploit some form of incremental model generation. It may also be useful to distinguish between local and global questions, i.e. anaphora may be resolved by local model generation. This issue is left for further research.

References

1. Baumgartner, P., Kühn, M.: Abductive coreference by model construction. In: The 1st Workshop on Inference in Computational Semantics (1999)
2. Borthen, K., Haugereid, P.: Representing referential properties of nominals. Research on Language and Computation (to appear)
3. Bos, J.: Implementing the binding and accommodation theory for anaphora resolution and presupposition projection. Comp. Ling. 29 (2003) 179–210
4. Copestake, A. et al.: Minimal recursion semantics (ms) (1999)
5. Fodor, J., Sag, I.: Referential and quantificational indefinites. Linguistics and Philosophy 5 (1982) 355–398
6. Gundel, J. et al.: Cognitive status and the form of referring expressions in discourse. Language 69 (1993) 274–307
7. Kamp, H.: A theory of truth and semantic representation. In: J. Groenendijk et al. (eds.), Formal methods in the study of language, Math. Centrum (1981) 277-322
8. Kamp, H. et al.: Discourse representation theory. In: D. Gabbay and F. Guenthner (eds.), Handbook of philosophical logic, D. Reidel (to appear)
9. Kohlhase, M.: Model generation for discourse representation theory. In: W. Horn (ed.), The 14th European Conference on Artificial Intelligence (2000) 441-445
10. Konrad, K.: Model generation for natural language interpretation and analysis, Springer (2004)
11. Pollard, C., Sag, I.: Head-driven phrase structure grammar, CSLI (1994)
12. van der Sandt, R.: Presupposition projection as anaphora resolution. Journal of Semantics 9 (1992) 333–78
13. Søgaard, A.: Update semantics for HPSG. In: H. Holmboe (ed.), Nordisk Sprogteknologi 2005, Tusculanum (2005) 167–72
14. Søgaard, A., Haugereid, P.: A computational HPSG grammar specifying the common subset of linguistic types for Danish, Norwegian and Swedish. In: H. Holmboe (ed.), Nordisk Sprogteknologi 2004, Tusculanum (2005) 247–56.

Modals and Anaphors in Korean

Jinung Kim[1] and Nicholas Asher[2]

[1] Department of Linguistics
University of Texas at Austin
borgesk@mail.utexas.edu
[2] Department of Philosophy
University of Texas at Austin
nasher@mail.utexas.edu

1   Introduction

In this paper, we investigate Korean modals such as *su isse*, *keta* and *ci*. We assume that *suisse* is an epistemic[1] possibility operator and *keta* is an epistemic necessity operator and *ci* and *keyssci* are both evidentials. Asher and McCready (2005)[2] offered an account of the discourse behavior of Japanese epistemic modal/evidential, focusing on the phenomenon of modal subordination (Roberts 1989)[11]. In this paper, too, focus on modal subordination to help analyze the Korean modal system. This article is concerned with the theory of anaphoric relations involving pronouns. Our main interest is to show that this theory amounts solely to a theory of the conditions under which pronouns and their antecedents can, must, or cannot be identified.

In section 2, we review general properties of Korean modals and evidentials. The evidential marker *ci* shows some interesting features. In section 3, we clarify that syntactic conditions can't explain the Korean zero pronouns. In section 4, we analyze modal subordination in Korean and propose that there is a tight correlation between modal operators and some discourse markers.

2   Modality and Evidentiality in Korean

2.1   Background on Korean Modality

Modality is a grammatical category which expresses the speaker's attitude towards a proposition made in his/her utterance. We will show two types of Korean modal expressions in this paper. Suffixes have a modal function. This type of modality is comparatively rare in Korean. It has two subcategories based on inflectional position. *keyss* and *te* are in non-final position of the sentence, in which *kun* and *ci* are in the sentence final.

It is well known that there is a close relation between a tense operator and a modal operator. Often classified as a future tense operator, *keyss* has been

---

[1] Epistemic modality is concerned with matters of knowledge, belief or opinion. Deontic modality is concerned with the necessity or possibility of acts performed by morally responsible agents. (Lyons 1977)[7].

T. Washio et al. (Eds.): JSAI 2005 Workshops, LNAI 4012, pp. 134–140, 2006.

extensively studied as a modal operator. As a tense operator, *keyss* gives us information about event time.

(1)   *Keyss*

    a.   nayil seul-ey pi-ka manhi o-keyss-ci.

    b.   Tomorrow Seoul-Loc rain-Nom muchcome-Fut-Evi

    c.   '(It is certain to me) it will rain a lot in Seoul tomorrow'

The suffix *ci* in (1) is an evidential marker. It only tells that the speaker obtained information relevant to the event. The event itself might have happened in the past, may be happening now, or may happen in the future. Information about the event time can be expressed by *keyss*. The interpretation of *keyss* as a tense operator is clarified when it combines with other epistemic operators or evidential markers. When it occurs without other operators, it functions as a necessity operator.

(2)   a.   Pay-ka kot ttena-keyss-ta.

    b.   Ship-Nom soon leave-MSfx-Dec.

    c.   'A ship is likely to leave soon.'

The meaning of *keyss* in (2) is prediction and it functions as a modal operator. However, it can have the meaning of volition when the sentence has a first person subject and is present tense.

(3)   a.   Nay-ka 2 si-kkaci Akhatemi kukcang-ey ka-keyss-ta.

    b.   I-Nom 2 o'clock-by Academy theater-Loc go-MSfx-Dec.

    c.   'I will go to an Academy theater by 2 o'clock'

In Korean, relative clauses have a modal function, too. However, Korean relative clauses show syntactic and semantic properties different from what English relative clauses show.

(4)   *Kesita*

    a.   na-nun sip khilo-lul 2 sikan-maney kel-ul kes-i-ta.

    b.   I-Top ten kilometer-Acc in 2 hours walk-Comp DN-Cop-Dec

    c.   '(I think) I will walk ten Kms'

As seen in (4), Korean has no words corresponding to English relative pronouns such as who, which , where, etc. In relative constructions, the head NP argument is shared by the subordinate relative clause and the main clause. NPs such as *kes* and *su* are classified as dependency nouns (DN) because they cannot occur without relative clauses. Another syntactic feature of Korean relative construction is that there is no overt gap inside of embedded clause. The combination of DN and matrix predicate introduces tense or modal function. In (4), DN *kes* and copula *i* expresses a necessity operator.

2.2   Evidentiality in Korean

Evidentials and Epistemic Modality. It has been suggested by many researchers (Palmer, 1986[9]; Faller, 2002[3]) that evidentials and epistemic modality are most closely related. It seems quite clear that one's source of information for a proposition is correlated with one's judgment of its truth. Because of this conceptual relationship, some previous studies have categorized evidentials as a subtype of epistemic modality (Palmer 1986)[9]. However, Faller (2002)[3] claims that there are sufficient grounds for distinguishing the category of evidentiality from that of epistemic modality, but that the two categories overlap. First, despite the close relationship between the two concepts, they are distinct conceptually: the indication of the speaker's source of information and the speaker's commitment to the truth of the proposition expressed conveying that information are really quite different things. Second, even though it is the case that many languages have elements that express both notions, there are clear cases of markers that only indicate one of them.

Evidential Marker: *Ci*. The linguistic elements indicating the informational source of a statement (perception, inference, or hearsay) and/or the speaker's certainty or commitment to a statement (strong or weak) are known as evidentials (Papafragou and Li 2002)[10]. Cuzco Quechua has several suffixes that mark evidentiality or the nature of the speaker's justification for making the claim. Faller(2002)[3] analyzes three suffixes in detail:

Mi: the speaker has direct (perceptual) evidence for the claim.
Si: the speaker heard the information expressed in the claim from someone else.
Cha: the speaker's background knowledge, plus inferencing, leads him to believe the information in the claim true.

We agree with Faller(2002)[3] the semantics of these particles lie at the junction of modality and evidentiality, both on the conceptual level and the language-individual level. We propose that *ci*, Korean evidential marker has a semantics similar to that of *Cha* in Cuzco Quechua. This suggestion is based on the fact that *ci* has conjectural meaning.

(5)   *Ci*
    a.   Cikum pi-ka o-ci.
    b.   Now Rain-Sub come-Pre-Evi
    c.   #' (speaker sees that it is raining) It is raining now'
    d.   #' (speaker was told that it is raining) It is raining now'
    e.   '(speaker conjectures that it is raining) It is raining now'

Ci is a suffix and the distribution of *ci* is always in sentence final position on inflectional position. On the other hand, *kyess*(a modality operator) is in non-final position of the sentence(Refer to Section 2.1.). These facts also support that evidentiality and epistemic modality are two different categories in Korean. Nam and Ko (1985)[8] has argued that there are two kinds of modality in Korean, based on their distributional positions to the sentence final verb: sentence final mood and non-final modality. The sentence final mood is related to speech act markers involving declarative, imperative, exclamatory, interrogative, promise, and permission in Korean. It is well known that the morpheme for speech act is the last one to attach to the verb after the epistemic morphemes. It is interesting that Korean evidentials and speech act markers are in the exact same position.

3 Zero Pronouns in Korean

Kratzer(1998)[4] proposed that there must be pronouns that start their syntactic life without f-features. We will refer to such pronouns as zero pronouns, and symbolize them as Ø. Zero pronouns in this sense should not be confused with unpronounced pronouns. Zero pronouns may acquire a pronunciation from a suitable antecedent at PF. In topic prominent languages like Korean and Japanese, a repeated element might be input as a zero pronoun (Lee and Byron 2004)[5]. It seems that a zero pronoun holds syntactic conditions. The contrast between (6) and (7) is explained by c-command (Lee 1999)

(6) a. Johni-i [S' Ø i Sue-lul mannassta-ko] malha-yss-ta.
     b. John-Nom [S' Ø Sue-Acc met-that] say-Pst-Dec.
     c. 'John said that (he) met Sue'(Lee 1999)[6]

(7) a. Johni-uy hyengj -i [S' Ø *i/j Sue-lul mannassta-ko] malha-yss-ta.
     b. John-Gen brother-Nom [S' Ø Sue-Acc met-that] say-Pst-Dec.
     c. 'John's brother said that (he) met Sue.'(Lee 1999)[6]

The zero pronoun in (6) refers to the matrix subject *John* as it is c-commanded by the antecedent. In (7), the zero pronoun subject is coindexed as referring to *John's brother* not *John*. This is because the genitive NP fails to c-command the zero pronoun in the embedded clause. As Lee (1999)[6] admits, however, when a zero pronoun is preceded by *Johni-uy hyeng* below, the same embedded zero subject in (8) can refer to *John* despite its failure to meet the syntactic requirement of c-command.

(8) a. John-i nwukwunka-lul cohahako issta-nun somwun-i iss-ess-ta.
     b. John-Nom someone-Acc like Prog-Comp rumor-Nom exisit-Pst-Dec.
     c. Johni-uy hyengj -i [S' Ø i/#j Sue-lul mannassta-ko] malha-yss-ta.
     d. John-Gen brother-Nom [S' Ø Sue-Acc met-that] say-Pst-Dec.
     e. 'There was a rumor that John loved someone. John's brother said that (he) met Sue.' (Lee 1999)[6]

This is a clear case in which local coherence of discourse is the prominent factor in deciding the interpretation of zero pronouns.

4 Modal Subordination in Korean

4.1 Background on Modal Subordination

Modal subordination is a phenomenon which stems from the relationships between propositions in a discourse (Roberts 1989)[11].

(9)   a.   A wolf might walk in. It would eat you first.
       b.   A wolf might walk in. # It will eat you first.

(10)   a.   A wolf must surely/ should walk in. It might eat you first.
       b.   A wolf might walk in. It might eat you first. But then it might not.

In (9), we can find some problems of anaphora theory because the indefinite noun, *wolf* under the scope of a semantic operator *might*, is available for an antecedent of a pronoun only in (9a). Discourse (9b) is infelicitous. (9b) should be interpreted as an independent assertion out of the range of the discourse(modal operator). However, though the syntactic structure of (9b) is similar with that of (9a), (9a) is felicitous.

4.2   Patterns in Korean Modal Subordination

We asked 8 Korean native speakers about coherence of discourse structures according to Modal matches. Basically, in $\square \lozenge$ pattern and $\lozenge \square$ pattern, the antecedent under the scope of a modal can be accessed to a pronoun under the scope of a modal.

(11) $\square \lozenge$
       a.   ilii-ka i sancang-ey tuleo-l ke-ta.Øi/ku nomi-i ne-lul capamek-ul su iss-e.
       b.   wolf-Nom this mountain retreat -Loc come-Comp DN-Dec. Øi/that guy-nom you-Acc eat-Comp DN exist-Dcl.
       c.   'A wolfi would come in. Iti might eat you first.'

(12) $\lozenge \square$
       a.   ilii-ka i sancang-ey tuleo-l su iss-e. (#Øi)/ku nomi-i ne-lul capamek-ul ke-ta .
       b.   wolf-Nom this mountain retreat -Loc come-Comp DN exist-Dec. Øi/that guy-nom you-Acc eat-Comp DN-Dec.
       c.   'A wolfi might come in. Iti would eat you first.'

These patterns correspond to the discourse behavior of modals in English. The use of the epistemic modal would enables the pronoun it to find its intended antecedent, the wolf is introduced under the scope of the modal in the first sentence (Asher and McCready 2005)[2].

(13)   a.   A wolfi might walk in. Iti would eat you first.
       b.   ookamii-ga kuru kamosirenai. #Øi/soitui anata-o taberu nitigainai.
       c.   wolf-Nom come might . that-guy you-Acc eat surely ((14a), (15) Asher and McCready 2005)

(13b) in Japanese is infelicitous with a covert pronoun or the pseudo-demonstrative *soitu*(Asher and McCready 2005)[2]. However, our survey shows that the access to the antecedent by the pronoun is blocked, if is substituted by '-ci', which expresses some sort of strong evidential. It follows the findings of Asher and McCready(2005)[2] concerning modal subordination in Japanese.

(14)   □Evi

   a.   ilii-ka i sancang-ey tuleo-l ke-ta. (# Øi)/ku nomi-i ne-lul capamek-
          ci.
   b.   wolf-Nom this mountain retreat -Loc come-Comp DN-Dec. Øi/that
          guy-Nom you-Acc eat-Evi.
   c.   'A wolfi would come in. It is certain that iti eats you first.'

(15)   ◊Evi

   a.   ilii-ka i sancang-ey tuleo-l su iss-e. (#Ø) i/ku nomi-i ne-lul capamek-
          ci.
   b.   wolf-Nom this mountain retreat -Loc come-Comp DN exist-Dec. Ø
          /that guy-Nom you-Acc eat-Evi.
   c.   'A wolfi might come in. Iti would eat you first.'

There is a complication in the Korean data concerning the realization of the
subject. A subject in Korean can be optionally realized on the surface. In Korean,
the use of a zero subject changes the judgments on respect to the basic modal
subordination sequences. It generally makes the result marginal compared with
the corresponding pseudo pronoun.

(16)   ◊□

   a.   ilii-ka i sancang-ey tuleo-l su iss-e. (#Øi)/ku nomi-i ne-lul capamek-
          ul ke-ta .
   b.   wolf-Nom this mountain retreat -Loc come-Comp ·DN exist-Dec. Ø
          /that guy-nom you-Acc eat-Comp DN-Dec.
   c.   'A wolfi might come in. Iti would eat you first.'(Repeated from (12))

This observation supports the claim that that Korean pronouns maintain or shift
attentional focus in the discourse structure and the occurrence of zero pronouns
in Korean should maintain the coherence of discourse structure(Lee and Byron
2004)[5]. Our goal is that we will prove some hypotheses that discourse structure
as formalized in SDRT (Asher and Lascarides 2003[1]) may affect the modal
subordination sequences.

(17)   □ DM Evi

   a.   ilii-ka i sancang-ey tuleo-l ke-ta. Kulemyen Ø i/ku nomi-i ne-lul
          capamek-ci.
   b.   wolf-Nom this mountain retreat -Loc come-Comp DN-Dec. Then Ø
          /that guy-Nom you-Acc eat-Evi.
   c.   'A wolfi would come in. Then, it is certain that iti might eat you first.'

(18)   ◊ DM Evi

   a.   ilii-ka i sancang-ey tuleo-l su iss-e. kulemyen (#Øi)/ku nomi-i ne-lul
          capamek-ci.
   b.   wolf-Nom this mountain retreat -Loc come-Comp DN exist-Dec.
          Then Ø /that guy-Nom you-Acc eat-Evi.
   c.   'A wolfi might come in. Then, it is certain that iti would eat you first.'

In (17), discourse marker(DM), *kulemyen* is inserted between two sentences in (14). However, it astonishingly improves the acceptability of them. Asher and McCready(2005)[2] found that the coherence of the modal subordination sequences in Japanese is generally improved if a discourse marker, *sosite*, is used. Similarly, in Korean we found that the discourse marker, *kulemyen* is used to connect the two modalized sentences. For instance, the use of *kulemyen* counterbalances the effect of the use of a zero pronoun restoring the basic modal subordination sequences with a zero subject in the second sentence to acceptability. However, the epistemic possibility-evidential (or inverse sequence) remains bad even when licensed by a discourse marker in (18).

5   Summary and Future Work

The relation between Evidentiality and Necessity need to be studied in future work because we only used facts about syntactic distribution to make the distinction. We need to investigate this distinction from the perspective of semantics. We also need to investigate further the properties of zero pronouns. zero pronouns in Korean affect the felicity of the modal subordination. This result shows the difference between Korean data and Japanese data in which zero pronouns in the subordinate sentences follow the same patterns as pseudo pronouns. Though clarifying the properties of zero pronouns is still a puzzle in Korean, at least, data indicates Korean zero pronouns are more sensitive to discourse relations than Japanese ones.

The primary work left in this paper is the formalization of the discourse relations in the Korean modal subordination.

References

1. Asher, N., Lascarides, A.: Logics of Conversation. Cambridge University Press (2003)
2. Asher, N., McCready, E.: Modals, emotives, and modal subordination. To appear in the proceedings of Chronos 7 (2005)
3. Faller, M.: Semantics and pragmatics of evidentials in cuzco quechua. Ph. D. Thesis, Stanford University (2002)
4. Kratzer, A.: More structural analogies between pronouns and tenses. SALT (1998)
5. Lee, S.H., Byron, D.: Semantic resolution of zero and pronoun anaphors in korean. The 5th Discourse Anaphora and Anaphora Resolution Colloquium (2004)
6. Lee, H.w.: Towards an optimal theory of referential dependency. ms (1999)
7. Lyons, J.: Semantics. Cambridge: Cambridge University Press (1977)
8. Nam, K., Ko, Y.G.: Standard Korean Grammar. Top Press (1985)
9. Palmer, F.R.: Mood and Modality. Cambridge University Press (1986)
10. Papafragou, A., P., L.: Evidential morphology and theory of mind. Proceedings from the 26th Annual Boston University Conference on Language Development (2002)
11. Roberts, C.: Modal subordination and pronominal anaphora in discourse. Linguistics and Philosophy **12** (1989) 683–721

On the Meaning of Japanese *Yo*

Eric McCready

Department of Language and Information Science
Osaka University
mccready@lang.osaka-u.ac.jp

Abstract. This paper considers the semantics and pragmatics of the Japanese particle *yo*. I argue that the meaning of *yo* is underspecified between a modal meaning and a 'strong assertion'. In addition, *yo* is associated with a presupposition for new information and a modal statement about hearer beliefs.

In this paper, I present a new analysis of the Japanese sentence-final particle *yo*. *Yo* commonly appears in spoken Japanese; an example is shown in (1).

(1)   ame-ga   futteiru yo
         rain-NOM falling   YO
         'It is raining.'

Yo is one of the class of Japanese particles known as the *sirase* 'notification' particles (cf. [10]), along with *zo* and *ze*. The *sirase* particles said to mark new information and further emphasize the sentence they appear in, in some sense making it stronger. I will take a dynamic approach to these two notions in this paper.

The paper begins with a consideration of some facts and relevant data about *yo*. I then present the formal framework I use in my analysis: a dynamic system involving sets of epistemic possibilities based on the semantics of [2]. The final part of the paper considers another use of *yo* on which it has a modal interpretation; I show that this interpretation constitutes a nonlocal dependency on other parts of the discourse, and that it can be handled compositionally by making use of underspecification at the discourse level. Finally, I show that another approach to the problem, that of assuming a null modal operator, cannot generalize to similar facts in English.

1   *Yo*: The Facts

One often hears the claim—both in the literature and from naive native speakers of Japanese—that *yo* is used in sentences that express hearer-new information. This seems to be right; (2) is odd, with *yo*, when used as a reminder, though it is fine if the hearer seems to have forgotten the meeting time. In this situation, of course, the sentence in some sense expresses hearer-new information again (though not in an absolute sense).

T. Washio et al. (Eds.): JSAI 2005 Workshops, LNAI 4012, pp. 141–148, 2006.

(2)   Kyoo no   miitingu wa   sanji kara desu (# yo)
       Today GEN meeting TOP 3:00 from COP (YO)

       'Today's meeting starts at 3:00.'   [17]

Yo can also produce a sense of insistence or pushiness. This is clearly brought
out in the following example (of an imperative); here, adding *yo* to the imperative sentence gives the feeling that the speaker is trying to force the hearer to
accept that (s)he should buy a new skirt, where the same sentence without *yo* is
much more neutral. See [11] for discussion of the declarative case, which space
considerations preclude including here.

(3)   Imperative case:

       atarasii sukaato kat-te   (yo)
       new   skirt   buy-IMP (YO)

       '(Come on,) Buy me a new skirt.'   [17]

[13] claims that *yo* has additional functions in addition to simply marking new
information. For Noda, *yo* indicates that the speaker believes that the hearer
should recognize, and accept, the propositional content of the sentence. Thus,
the content marked by *yo* must not only be new to the hearer, but also believed
by the speaker to be of importance to the hearer.

   The term *modal subordination* describes a situation in which a modalized
sentence interpreted 'in the context' set up by an earlier modal [16, 4]. Stan-
dardly, examples of this phenomenon include anaphoric pronouns in the later
context. The reason is that modal subordination was first noted in the context
of counterexamples to most theories of intersentential anaphora [7].

(4)   a.   A wolf might come in. # It eats you first.
       b.   A wolf might come in. It would eat you first.   [16]

As one can see from (4a), a modal is generally needed for modal subordination to occur. I here exclude cases of quantificational subordination (in which,
it is claimed, a quantifier can induce subordination). See [18] for details and
references.

   Given this discussion, a particularly surprising fact about *yo* is that it can
license modal subordination, even in the absence of modals in the sentence containing the anaphoric pronoun (5b). This fact is especially surprising in light
of the fact that *yo* itself is not generally interpreted as modal, as the above
examples illustrate.

(5)   a.   ookami-ga kuru kamosirenai. # ∅   anata-o taberu.
            wolf-NOM come might   ∅ you-ACC eat

            'A wolf$_i$ might come in. It$_i$ (will) eats you first.'
       b.   ookami-ga kuru kamosirenai. ∅/soitu   anata-o taberu yo.
            wolf-NOM come might   ∅/that-guy you-ACC eat   YO

            'A wolf$_i$ might come in. It$_i$ (will) eat you first, man (rough gloss).'

One might conjecture that the presence of a modal in the sentence preceding the one with the particle is enough to induce a modal flavor. But this is not the case, as shown by (6), in which *yo* serves only to provide emphasis of some sort, as in the examples I gave earlier.

(6)   John-wa   ima suupaa   ni it-tei-ru   nitigainai. soko-no
         John-TOP now supermarket to go-PROG-NPST must.   there-GEN
         sake-wa   totemo yasui n   da   yo
         alcohol-TOP very   cheap EMPH COP YO
         'John must be at the supermarket now. The liquor's very cheap there, man.'

The generalization seems in fact to be that a modal interpretation of *yo* requires a causal relation. For a modal interpretation, the second (*yo*-containing) sentence must be *weakly caused* by the first. I will return to this point below after discussing some earlier accounts of *yo*.

2   Framework

I will use the modification of the dynamic modal semantics of [2] proposed in [11]. The semantics is based on sets of epistemic possibilities, recursively defined as follows:

- Set $E_{\alpha,0} \subseteq \mathcal{P}(W \times \$)$, where $\$$ is the set of all assignment functions.
- $E_{\alpha,n+1} \subseteq \mathcal{P}(W \times \$ \times E_{\alpha,n})$
- $\mathcal{E}_\alpha \subseteq \mathcal{P}(\bigcup_{n \in \omega} E_{\alpha,n})$

The logic also has sets of deontic possibilities $\mathcal{D}_\alpha$ constructed in a similar fashion, as proposed by [11].

The dynamic contexts that form the inputs to the interpretation of formulas are 4-tuples of $\langle w, f, \mathcal{E}_\alpha, D_\alpha \rangle$ for some α. I will make use of the projection functions 1, 2, 3, 4 to pick out the world, assignment function, set of epistemic possibilities, or set of deontic possibilities for a given context in the standard way.

It is straightforward to state a semantics for contexts like these along the lines of that for dynamic predicate logic (DPL; [6]), as follows.

- $\sigma \| R t_1, \ldots, t_n \|^{\mathcal{A}} \sigma'$ iff $\sigma = \sigma' \wedge \langle \| t_1 \|^{\mathcal{A}}_{(1(\sigma),2(\sigma))} \cdots \| t_n \|^{\mathcal{A}}_{(1(\sigma),2(\sigma))} \rangle \in R^{\mathcal{A}}_{1(\sigma)}$
- $\sigma \| t_1 = t_2 \|^{\mathcal{A}} \sigma'$ iff $\sigma = \sigma' \wedge \| t_1 \|^{\mathcal{A}}_{(1(\sigma),2(\sigma))} = \| t_2 \|^{\mathcal{A}}_{(1(\sigma),2(\sigma))}$
- $\sigma \| \phi \wedge \psi \|^{\mathcal{A}} \sigma'$ iff $\sigma \| \phi \|^{\mathcal{A}} \circ \| \psi \|^{\mathcal{A}} \sigma'$
- $\sigma \| \neg \phi \|^{\mathcal{A}} \sigma')$ iff $\sigma = \sigma' \wedge \neg \exists w'', h\ \sigma \| \phi \|^{\mathcal{A}} \sigma^{\frac{1(\sigma)}{w''}, \frac{2(\sigma}{h}}$
- $\sigma \| \exists x \phi \|^{\mathcal{A}} \sigma'$ iff $\exists a \in A\ \sigma^{\frac{a}{x}} \| \phi \|^{\mathcal{A}} \sigma'$, where $\sigma^{\frac{a}{x}}$ is the result of replacing $2(\sigma)$ with $2(\sigma)^{\frac{a}{x}}$

It is less straightforward to define discourse update because of the embedded information states. Asher and McCready make use of *descendent satisfaction* along with a partial ordering on epistemic possibilities induced by a revision function. This partial ordering forms a system of spheres centered around each element σ (cf [8]). A set of such elements can also have a system of spheres $S(\epsilon) = \{\cup(S_n(\sigma)) : \sigma \in \epsilon\}$.

The revision operation $\star$ applied to φ thus picks out the (closest) set of epistemic possibilities that admits φ.

- Definition of Descendance and Satisfaction by epistemic possibilities
  - σ has a ϕ descendant σ' iff $\sigma[\phi]\sigma'$
  - $\langle \epsilon, \epsilon' \rangle \models_d \phi$ iff every $\sigma \in \epsilon$ has a ϕ descendant in ϵ'.
  - $\|\phi\| = \{\langle \sigma, \sigma' \rangle : \sigma'$ is a ϕ descendant of $\sigma\}$
  - Let $S_n(\epsilon)$ be the smallest sphere around ϵ such that elements in $S_n(\epsilon)$ have ϕ descendants. Then $\epsilon \star \|\phi\| = \{\sigma : \exists \sigma' \in S_n(\epsilon) \; \sigma$ is a ϕ descendant of $\sigma'\}$.
    $\mathcal{E} \star \|\phi\| = \{\epsilon \star \|\phi\| : \epsilon \in \mathcal{E}\}$.

Discourse update then makes use of $\star$ to filter out those possibilities that do not allow for update with φ.

- Definition of Discourse Update:
  - Let ϕ be a modal free formula. Then σ is a ϕ discourse update of σ' iff $\exists \sigma''$ such that $(\sigma'[\phi]^A \sigma'' \wedge 1(\sigma) = 1(\sigma'') \wedge 2(\sigma) = 2(\sigma'') \wedge 4(\sigma) = 4(\sigma''))$ and
    $3(\sigma) = 3(\sigma') \star \|\phi\| \wedge \forall \epsilon \in 3(\sigma) \forall \sigma''' \in \epsilon \; 2(\sigma'') =_x 2(\sigma)$ for all x free in ϕ)
  - Let ϕ be a formula of the form $might\phi$, $would\phi$ $could\varphi$, $should\varphi$ or $\phi \Rightarrow \psi$. Then σ is a ϕ discourse update of σ' iff $\sigma'[\phi]^A \sigma$

Modal operators are defined making use of $3(\sigma)$, for epistemic modalities, and $4(\sigma)$, for deontic modalities. $Might(\varphi)$ revises the set of possibilities so that φ is admitted, and $would(\varphi)$ is similar except that it requires that all possibilities already admit φ.

- $\sigma[might\phi]_A \langle 1(\sigma), 2(\sigma), \mathcal{E}' \rangle$, where $\mathcal{E}' = \{\epsilon' : \exists \epsilon \in 3(\sigma) \langle \epsilon, \epsilon' \rangle \models_d \phi\}$,
  if there is such an ϵ;
  $\sigma[might\phi]_A \emptyset$ otherwise.
- $\sigma[would\phi]_A \langle 1(\sigma), 2(\sigma), \{\epsilon' : \exists \epsilon \in 3(\sigma) \langle \epsilon, \epsilon' \rangle \models_d \phi\} \rangle$,
  if $\forall \epsilon \in 3(\sigma) \exists \epsilon^* \langle \epsilon, \epsilon^* \rangle \models_d \phi$;
  $\sigma[would\phi]_A \emptyset$ otherwise.

The deontic modalities $should$ and $could$ are similar, except that they act on the fourth element of the context tuple.

In order to analyze the effects of yo, we also need several other elements, which I will now define. These are the operators $\mathcal{B}_X$, $Sassert$, and the discourse relation Dep.

The first operator, $\mathcal{B}_X$ is an operator that lives on epistemic states. $\mathcal{B}_X \varphi$ will indicate that the individual X believes φ. I will make use of this predicate in modeling the new information and 'hearer importance' effects of yo.

– $\sigma\|\mathcal{B}_X\varphi\|\sigma'$ iff $\forall\epsilon[\epsilon \in 3(\sigma') \rightarrow \forall\psi[(believe(x,\psi) \rightarrow \wedge\epsilon \models \psi) \rightarrow \epsilon \models \varphi]]$.

The second operator, *Sassert* ('strong-assert'), is used in modeling the 'insistence' effect of *yo*. *Sassert* is a predicate that ensures that update with its complement is defined by using a downdate operation [5]. If update is already defined, just an ordinary assertion (ie standard update), but if it's not, then downdate with $\neg\varphi$ and then update with φ. Note: I ignore complications stemming from logical closure.

– $\sigma\|\text{Sassert}(\varphi)\|^a\sigma'$ iff
  - if there is an ϵ in $3(\sigma)$ such that ϵ has a φ descendent, then $\sigma\|\varphi\|\sigma'$, and
  - if there is no such ϵ, then $\sigma' = \sigma'''$, where $\sigma\| \downarrow \neg\varphi; \varphi\|\sigma'''$.

Finally, *Dep* is a discourse relation that applies to modal subordination contexts (cf. [1, 2]). *Dep* models a sort of weak causation in modal contexts. The clause $occasion_C(p,q)$ used in this definition holds just in case p weakly causes q in the sense that q cannot occur without p also holding (cf. the *weak causation* of [9]). *Dep* thus holds of two discourse segments just in case the first weakly causes the second and the first contains an epistemic modal.

– $\langle\alpha,\beta,\gamma\rangle \wedge Epist\_mod(\alpha) \wedge occasion_C(\alpha,\beta) > Dep(\alpha,\beta)$
– $occasion_C(p,q) \longleftrightarrow ((p \rightarrow \Diamond q) \wedge (\neg p \rightarrow \neg\Diamond q))$

Now we can move to the full analysis. I will begin by laying out the notion of underspecification I will use.

3   Analysis

The basic ideas of the analysis are the following. The meaning of *yo* involves a 'strong' assertion: it *forces* acceptance of its associated proposition. This accounts for the feeling of insistence associated with *yo*-marked utterances. *Yo* also asserts a belief of the speaker that the hearer *should* believe the proposition in its scope. It presupposes that new information is involved. Finally in modal subordination contexts, it is interpreted modally: its meaning is thus underspecified.

The essential notion behind underspecified semantics is that formulas can be understood as partially specified logical forms. Since I am assuming SDRT, I will make use of the SDRT approach to underspecification.[1] Since the full picture is quite complicated, I will refrain from giving all the details of this approach here, instead giving only enough background to make the picture of how discourse relations interact with the *yo* semantics clear; for the full treatment, see [1]. The basic idea is that, instead of specifying multiple complete logical forms for ambiguous expressions, one can utilize a description language over labels that tag bits of semantic content and specify certain restrictions on the relations the labels hold to one another. The end result is a single partially specified logical

---

[1] See also e.g. [15] or [3] for other realizations of the general underspecification approach.

form that, in a sense, contains within it the seeds of several distinct logical formulas. Technically, this result is achieved by making each element of a formula into a predicate over labels: each such formula has arity of one greater than the original. Thus, a formula of the form, for instance, $go(john)$ is translated into the more complex formula $R_{go}(l_j, l) \land R_{john}(l_j)$. In what follows, I will abstract away from representation of the labels when they do not play a crucial role in the semantics: thus, I will often write e.g. φ for $R_\varphi(l_\varphi)$.

Underspecification can be used even to provide multiple meanings for lexical items without resorting to oft-used devices like disjunction or defining multiple homophones. A lexical item can be stated as a relation between labels and predicates with multiple distinct realizations. Other contextual information (broadly defined; information about the meaning of other lexical items and the sorts of objects they select for, as in the *co-composition* of [14]) can then pick out one predicate or the other, effectively disambiguating the sentence. I will make use of this device in defining the *yo* semantics.

On my analysis, the meaning of *yo* is underspecified and depends on information about causal relations. In particular, I take the meaning selected for *yo* to depend crucially on the discourse relation holding between the *yo*-marked sentence and another element in the discourse structure. Specifically, if the *yo* sentence is connected to another discourse segment by *Dep*, a modal meaning for *yo* is selected.

The meaning of *yo* thus is determined by the following rules:

1. $\exists \pi' \exists R[yo_?(\varphi, l) \land R(l, \pi) \land Dep(\pi', \pi) > yo_\Diamond(\varphi, l)$
   i.e. if there is a modalized discourse segment that stands in the *Dep* relation to the segment containing *yo*, *yo* = *yo*$_\Diamond$.
2. $\exists \pi' \exists R[yo_?(\varphi, 1) \land R(l, \pi) > yo_{sassert}(\varphi, l)$
   i.e. if there is no such segment, then *yo* = *yo*$_{sassert}$.

Two additional elements of *yo*'s meaning are completely invariant, corresponding to the notions of new information and hearer relevance. The notion of new information I will capture using a presupposition about hearer beliefs. Using the $\mathcal{B}$ operator, I define a presupposition that the speaker believe the proposition *yo* applies to to be new information. The second element is an assertion that (s)he believes φ to be something the hearer should know.

The meaning of *yo* is then the following:

- Presupposition of $yo\varphi$: $\forall \epsilon \in 3(\sigma) : \langle \epsilon, \epsilon \rangle \models \mathcal{B}_S \neg \mathcal{B}_H \varphi$
  i.e. speaker believes hearer doesn't believe φ
- Semantics of *yo* $\sigma \| \mathcal{B}_S should \mathcal{B}_H \varphi \| \sigma'$
  ie. speaker believes hearer should believe φ

and
  - $\sigma \| yo_{sassert}(\varphi) \| \sigma'$ iff $\sigma \| sassert(\varphi) \| \sigma'$
  - $\sigma \| yo_\Diamond(\varphi) \| \sigma'$ iff $\sigma \| might(\varphi) \| \sigma'$

Now, how does this semantics account for the facts about *yo* discussed above? First, the fact that *yo* is used to mark new information is encoded directly in the presupposition above. On my semantics, *yo* is in part a revision operator; I argue that the effects of insistence follows from this by Gricean reasoning. One need not use a revision operator if one is confident that one's statement will be accepted. Noda's (2002) intuition that use of *yo* requires the information to be relevant to the hearer is captured by the statement that the speaker believes that the hearer should believe that information.Such a belief indicates that the speaker believes that the information has some relevance to the hearer, exactly as desired.

Null Modals. The analysis I propose, of course, is not the only possibility. Here I would like to mention another possible analysis: that *yo* is not itself modal but simply licenses a null modal in *Dep*-type contexts (suggestion due to Rajesh Bhatt). This sort of analysis would get the rest of the facts right, and also would explain why no modal interpretation arises in the presence of another modal: in such a case, there is simply no position available to add a null modal (since Japanese modals do not stack).

Null modals are known to exist in other contexts, as in Hindi, where they are licensed by habitual mood following a counterfactual conditional (example from [12]). This fact makes the proposed analysis seem both plausible and economical, since it does not introduce anything not already known to exist. But in fact, given facts from English about the similar particle (sentence-final) *man*, the underspecification analysis seems preferable. *Man* can also license modal subordination:

(7)   A wolf might come in. It will eat you first, #(man).

But here the tense/modal position in syntax is already occupied by the futurate *will*. There is no place for a null modal to 'sit'. Therefore the null modal analysis cannot go through for English. Given that a unified analysis of the two particles is desirable—and, given their similarity, I take this point to be uncontroversial— the underspecification analysis should be preferred.

References

1. Nicholas Asher and Alex Lascarides: Logics of Conversation. Cambridge University Press (2003).
2. Nicholas Asher and Eric McCready: Were, Would, Must and a Compositional Account of Counterfactuals. Paper presented at the 2004 Meeting of the Society for Exact Philosophy.
3. Johan Bos: Predicate Logic Unplugged. Proceedings of the 13th Amsterdam Colloquium (1995), 133-143.
4. Anette Frank: Context Dependence in Modal Constructions. PhD Thesis, University of Stuttgart (1997).
5. Peter Gardenfors: Knowledge in Flux. MIT Press (1988).

6. Jeroen Groenendijk and Martin Stokhof: Dynamic Montague Grammar. Papers from the Second Symposium on Logic and Language (1990).
7. Lauri Kartunnen: Discourse Referents. Syntax and Semantics 7, James McCawley (ed.), New York: Academic Press (1976).
8. David Lewis: Counterfactuals. Oxford: Basil Blackwell (1973).
9. David Lewis: Causation. Journal of Philosophy 70:17 556-567 (1973).
10. Takasi Masuoka and Yukinori Takubo: Kisoo Nihongo Bunpoo [Essential Japanese Grammar]. Tokyo: Kurosio Syuppan (1989).
11. Eric McCready: The Dynamics of Particles. PhD Thesis, University of Texas at Austin (2005).
12. Eric McCready and Brian Reese: Counterfactual Morphology and the Licensing of Modal Subordination in Hindi. Paper presented at SALA XXII (2002).
13. Harumi Noda: Syuuzoyosi no kinoo [The function of particles]. Modariti [Modality], Kurosio Syuppan (2002).
14. James Pustejovsky: The Generative Lexicon. MIT Press (1995).
15. Uwe Reyle: Dealing with Ambiguities by Underspecification. Journal of Semantics 10: 123-179 (1993).
16. Craige Roberts: Modal Subordination and Pronominal Anaphora in Discourse. Linguistics and Philosophy 12: 683-721 (1989).
17. Yuriko Suzuki Kose: Japanese Sentence-final Particles: A Pragmatic Principle Approach. PhD Thesis, University of Illinois at Urbana-Champignon (1997).
18. Linton Wang, Eric McCready and Nicholas Asher: Information Dependency in Quantificational Subordination. Where Semantics Meets Pragmatics, Klaus von Heusinger and Ken Turner, eds., Elsevier. To appear.

A Dynamic Semantics of Modal Subordination

Norihiro Ogata

Deparment of Language and Information Science, Osaka University,
1-8 Machikaneyama, Toyonaka, Osaka, Japan
ogata@lang.osaka-u.ac.jp

Abstract. This paper will propose a dynamic semantics of quantified modal logic based on the theory of *System Transition Systems*, which are abstract objects modeling "Kripke models of Kripke models" or graph rewriting systems, by exlpoiting the theory of coalgebras in order to treat *modal subordination* as a Kripke model change, which requires no ad-hoc informal treatment such as *accomodation* as in [1] or extra-ontology introduced in [2, 3].

1 Introduction

One kind of semantic problem on anaphora and modality called *modal subordination*, which is rouoghly formulated by formula

$$(\mathsf{M}\exists x\varphi(x)) \; \odot \; \mathsf{N}\psi(x)$$

where M and N denote modality, φ, ψ formulas, $\odot$ a logical connective, and $\exists x$ binds both occurrences of varibale x in φ and ψ, is investigated by [4], [1], [2], and [3] in the framework of *Discourse Representation Theory* (*DRT*), expanding their theory by adding new devices. [1] introduces a Lewsian *accomodation* and [2, 3] new higher-order ontologies of discourse referents.[1]

Both DR-theoretic treatments seem to be *ad hoc*, since both treatments basically change the above formula to formula:

$$(\mathsf{M}\exists x\varphi(x)) \odot (\mathsf{N}\forall x\varphi(x) \rightarrow \psi(x))$$

or

$$(\mathsf{M}\exists x\varphi(x)) \odot (\mathsf{N}\exists x\varphi(x) \wedge \psi(x)).$$

On the other hand, another dynamic semantics, *Dynamic Predicate Logic* (*DPL*) by [6, 7] has never treated modal subordination properly.[2] This paper will propose a dynamic semantics of modal subordination based on *system transition*

---

[1] For my detailed objection to DR-Theoretic accommodation or introductions of higher-order discourse referents proposed by [1, 2, 3], see [5].

[2] For a short survey of [6, 7, 8], see [5].

When I write this paper, [9] has proposed a dynamic predicate logic for modal subordination based on *epistemic possibilities*. Their semantics can be embedded into my semantics. We will see it the last section.

T. Washio et al. (Eds.): JSAI 2005 Workshops, LNAI 4012, pp. 149–156, 2006.

systems, which exploit the theory of *coalgebras*[3] , realize *model-change* updates which are distinguished from Veltmanian *eliminative* updates, and can treat modal subordination by model-change updates.

First I will classify modal subordination in the sense of formulas of quantified modal logic. Second I will introduce *coalgebraic* models of modal logic, a dynamic interpretation of modal logic based on the coalgebraic models, system transision systems, model-change updates, multimodal quantified modal logic for modal subordination, and reformulate the classified types of modal subordination.

2   A Classification of Modal Subordination

I classify the main examples of modal subordination into the following types in terms of formulas of quantified modal logic:

(1) A thief$_i$ might break into the house. $\left\{ \begin{array}{l} \text{\# He}_i \text{ takes the silver.} \\ \text{He}_i \text{ \textit{would} take the silver.} \end{array} \right\}$

$\Diamond \exists x \varphi(x) \wedge \Box \psi(x)$ [10]

(2) Maybe Barney owns a Honda$_i$ and $\left\{ \begin{array}{l} \text{\# He keeps it}_i \text{ hidden somewhere.} \\ \textit{Maybe} \text{ he keeps it}_i \text{ hidden somewhere.} \end{array} \right\}$

$\Diamond \exists x \varphi(x) \wedge \Diamond \psi(x)$[11]

(3) If Pedro owns a donkey$_i$, he beats it. $\left\{ \begin{array}{l} \text{\# It}_i \text{ kicks back.} \\ \text{It}_i \textit{ might} \text{ kick back.} \end{array} \right\}$

$(\exists x.\varphi(x) \Rightarrow \psi(x)) \wedge \Diamond \chi(x)$ [3]

(4) If John bought a book$_i$, he'd be home reading it by now.

$\left\{ \begin{array}{l} \text{\# It}_i \text{ is a murder mystery.} \\ \text{It}_i \textit{ would} \text{ be a murder mystery.} \end{array} \right\}$ $(\exists x.\varphi(x) \Rightarrow \psi(x)) \wedge \Box \chi(x)$ [3]

(5) If a thief$_i$ breaks into the house, he will take the silver. If, in addition, he$_i$ finds the safe, he$_i$ will try to open it.

$(\exists x.\varphi(x) \Rightarrow \psi(x)) \wedge (\varphi'(x) \Rightarrow \psi'(x))$ [3]

(6) You must find a bear$_i$. Then you may take its$_i$ picture.

$(\Box \exists x.\varphi(x)) \wedge \Diamond \psi(x)$ [10]

(7) #You may find a bear$_i$. Then you must take its$_i$ picture.

$\#(\Diamond \exists x.\varphi(x)) \wedge \Box \psi(x)$ [10]

(8) Either there's no bathroom$_i$ in this house or it$_i$'s in a funny place.

$(\neg \exists x \varphi(x)) \vee \psi(x)$ [1]

(9) I don't have a microwave oven$_i$. I wouldn't know what to do with it$_i$.[10]

$\neg \exists x \varphi(x) \wedge \neg \psi(y)$

3   A Coalgebraic Dynamic Semantics of Modal Subordination

3.1   A Revisional Dynamic Semantics Based on System Transition Systems

In dynamic semantics of [12, 8], $\Diamond$ is *eliminative*, i.e., $[\Diamond \exists x \varphi(x)] \wedge \Diamond \psi(x) \not\models \Diamond \exists x [\varphi(x) \wedge \psi]$, but not *revisional*, although modal subordination requires $\Diamond$

---

[3] For the notion and the definition of coalgebra, see [5].

functions as a model revision function, i.e., $[\Diamond \exists x \varphi(x)] \wedge \Diamond \psi(x) \models \Diamond \exists x [\varphi(x) \wedge \psi]$. I formalize revisional dynamic semantics by introducing the notion of *system transition systems* based on *coalgebra*, since system transition systems model transitions of model change. System transition systems are defined as follows:

Definition 1. *Let Γ and Δ be an endofunctor, $\langle S, \alpha \rangle$ and $\langle S', \alpha' \rangle$ Γ-coalgebras, and $s \in S$ and $s' \in S'$. A Δ, Γ-system transition system is a Δ-coalgebra $\langle \mathscr{S}, \mathscr{A} \rangle$, where $\mathscr{S}$ is a set of states, i.e., pointed Γ-coalgebras such as $\langle S, \alpha, s \rangle$ and $\langle S', \alpha', s' \rangle$.*

A Δ, Γ-system transition system is normal if Δ is the powerset functor $\mathscr{P}$ or a functor of form of $\mathscr{P}(A \times \mathcal{I}d)$ for a set A. ∎

3.2 On the Ontology of Individuals and the System of the Required Quantified Modal Logic

In (1), the term "A thief" does not denote an individual living in the actual world, but an *individual living in a virtual world*, who happens to live in the actual world. Therefore, in (1b) "He" cannot refer to the individual denoted by "A thief". This observation implies that the modality *might* or *would* presuppose possible worlds where their residents can not be identical not only with the actual world but also the other possible worlds, that is, the system of the required quantified modal logic is a systems with *world relative domains* in the sense of [13]. Systems with world relative domains satisfy the following condition:

- $\forall x \varphi$ is true at s and g iff for all $a \in D_s$, φ is true at s and $g[a/x]$ where D_s is the domain of s.

I will write this modified variable assignment $g[a/x]$ depending on the domain of s by $g[s : a/x]$.

3.3 A Dynamic Semantics of $\mathscr{L}_{Rel,Var,I}$ Based on System Transition Systems

Now we need extend the definition of dynamic interpretation of each formula φ, as follows:

Definition 2. *Let $R \in Rel(n)$ (n-ary relations; $Rel = \bigcup_{n \geq 0} Rel(n)$), $x \in Var$ (individual variables), and $i \in I$ (indicies of modalities). A formula φ of $\mathscr{L}_{Rel,Var,I}$ is defined as follows:*

$$\varphi ::= (x_1 = x_2)|R(x_1, \ldots, x_n)|\varphi_1 \wedge \varphi_2|\exists x \varphi|\forall x \varphi|\Diamond_i \varphi|\Box_i \varphi| \sim \varphi|\varphi_1 \Rightarrow \varphi_2|\varphi_1 \vee \varphi_2$$

Let $s \in S$, D_s the domain of s, $g : S \to (Var \to D)$ be a varible assignment for each set S of possible worlds, where $D = \bigcup_{s \in W} D_s$ and $W = \bigcup_i S_i$.

A Δ, Γ-system transition system $\langle \mathscr{S}, \mathscr{A} \rangle$ over W, D and $\mathscr{L}_{Rel,Var,I}$ is quantificational if it is normal and $\mathscr{S}$ consists of pointed Γ-coalgebras with a varible assignment, i.e., states, such as $\sigma = \langle S, \alpha, s, g \rangle$, for any $s \in S$, D_s is defined, and $\Gamma = \mathscr{P}(I \times \mathcal{I}d) \times \mathscr{P}(D^*)^{Rel}$, where D^* is $\bigcup_{n \geq 0} D^n$.

Let $\langle \mathscr{S}, \mathscr{A} \rangle$ be a $\mathscr{P}(\mathscr{L}_{Rel,Var,I} \times \mathcal{I}d)$, $\mathscr{P}(I \times \mathcal{I}d) \times \mathscr{P}(D^*)^{Rel}$-quantificational system transition system and $\langle S, \alpha, s, g \rangle \in \mathscr{S}$. Then the dynamic interpretation of each formula $\varphi \in \mathscr{L}_{Rel,Var,I}$ in $\langle \mathscr{S}, \mathscr{A} \rangle$, $[\![\varphi]\!] : \mathscr{S} \to \mathscr{P}(\mathscr{S})$, is defined by recursion on the formulation of φ, as follows:

1. $\langle \varphi, \sigma' \rangle \in \mathscr{A}(\sigma)$ iff $\sigma' \in [\![\varphi]\!](\sigma)$.

2. $[\![x_1 = x_2]\!](\sigma) = \begin{cases} \{\sigma\} & \text{if } g(s)(x_1) = g(s)(x_2) \\ \emptyset & \text{otherwise} \end{cases}$

3. $[\![R(x_1, \ldots, x_n)]\!](\sigma) = \begin{cases} \{\sigma\} & \text{if } \langle g(s)(x_1), \ldots, g(s)(x_n) \rangle \in \pi_2 \circ \alpha(s)(R) \\ \emptyset & \text{otherwise} \end{cases}$

4. $[\![\varphi_1 \wedge \varphi_2]\!](\sigma) = \bigcup_{\sigma' \in [\![\varphi_1]\!](\sigma)} [\![\varphi_2]\!](\sigma')$

5. $[\![\exists x \varphi]\!](\sigma) = \{[\![\varphi]\!](\sigma[g/g \circ \prod\{[u : a/x] | u \in S, a \in D_u\})$

6. $[\![\forall x \varphi]\!](\sigma) = \bigcap_{a \in D_s} [\![\varphi]\!](\sigma[g/g[s : a/x]])$

7. $[\![\Diamond_i \varphi]\!](\sigma) = \bigcup_{u \in \{u \in S | \langle i,u \rangle \in \pi_1 \circ \alpha(s)\}} ([\![\varphi]\!](\sigma[\alpha/\alpha \upharpoonright (s, g, \Diamond_i \varphi)]))[s/u]$

8. $[\![\Box_i \varphi]\!](\sigma) = \bigcap_{u \in \{u \in S | \langle i,u \rangle \in \pi_1 \circ \alpha(s)\}} ([\![\varphi]\!](\sigma))[s/u]$

9. $[\![\sim \varphi]\!](\sigma) = \begin{cases} \bigcup_{u \in \{u \in S | [\![\varphi]\!](\sigma[s/u]) \neq \emptyset\}} ([\![\varphi]\!](\sigma[u/s]))[s/u]) & \text{if } [\![\varphi]\!](\sigma) = \emptyset \\ \emptyset & \text{otherwise} \end{cases}$

10. $[\![\diamond_i \varphi]\!](\sigma) = \bigcup_{u \in \{u \in S | \langle i,u \rangle \in \pi_1 \circ \alpha(s)\}} ([\![\varphi]\!](\sigma[u/s]))[s/u]$ (the test possibility)

11. $[\![\varphi_1 \vee \varphi_2]\!](\sigma) = [\![\varphi_1]\!](\sigma) \cup \bigcup_{\sigma' \in [\![\sim \varphi_1]\!](\sigma)} [\![\varphi_2]\!](\sigma')[s/s_{\sigma'}]$ (the update disjunction)

12. $[\![\varphi_1 \Rightarrow \varphi_2]\!](\langle S, \alpha, s, g \rangle) = \bigcap_{\sigma' \in [\![\sim \varphi_1]\!](\sigma)} [\![\varphi_2]\!](\sigma')[s/s_{\sigma'}]$ (the test conditional)

where

$\alpha \upharpoonright (s, g, \Diamond_i \varphi)(u) = \begin{cases} \langle \{\langle i, v \rangle \in \pi_1 \circ \alpha(u) | [\![\varphi]\!](\sigma[v/s]) \neq \emptyset\}, \pi_2 \circ \alpha(u) \rangle & \text{if } u = s \\ \alpha(u) & \text{otherwise} \end{cases}$

and

$[\![\curvearrowright \varphi]\!](\sigma) = \begin{cases} \bigcup_{u \in \{u \in S | [\![\varphi]\!](\sigma) \neq \emptyset\}} ([\![\varphi]\!](\sigma[u/s])) & \text{if } [\![\varphi]\!](\sigma) = \emptyset \\ \emptyset & \text{otherwise} \end{cases}$ ∎

The test possibility amounts to the epistemic 'may' in $\mathscr{L}_{Rel,Var,I}$.[4]

4   A Dynamic Semantics of Modal Subordination Based on System Transition Systems

Modal subordination which is classified in section 2 is reformulated in $\mathscr{L}_{Rel,Var,I}$, where $Rel = Rel(1) \cup Rel(2) = \{P, R, S, T\} \cup \{Q\}$, as follows:

1. $\Diamond_i \exists x P(x) \wedge \Box_i R(x)$
2. $\Diamond_i \exists x P(x) \wedge \Diamond_i R(x)$
3. $(\exists x P(x) \Rightarrow R(x)) \wedge \Diamond_i T(x)$
4. $(\exists x P(x) \Rightarrow R(x)) \wedge \Box_i T(x)$
5. $(\exists x P(x) \Rightarrow R(x)) \wedge (T(x) \Rightarrow U(x))$
6. $\Box_i \exists x P(x) \wedge \diamond_i R(x)$
7. $\# \diamond_i \exists x P(x) \wedge \Box_i R(x)$
8. $(\sim \exists x P(x)) \vee R(x)$
9. $(\sim \exists x P(x)) \wedge \sim R(x)$

---

[4] On the duality among logical operators, see [5].

Let us see how the dynamic semantics of $\mathcal{L}_{Rel,Var,I}$ works on modal subordination. First let us see about 1, 2, 6, 7, 8, and 9.

Example 1. Let $P, R \in Rel(1)$ and $\sigma = \langle S, \alpha, s, g \rangle$ be the current state which is illustrated by the leftmost graph in Figure 1.
✠(The case of 1): $[\![\Diamond_i \exists x Px]\!](\sigma)$ is calculated in the way illustrated by Figure 1 (i.e., a graph transition system), i.e.,

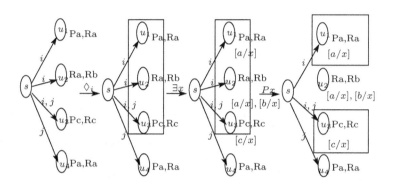

Fig. 1. The transion of σ by $\Diamond_i \exists x Px$

$[\![\Diamond_i \exists x Px]\!](\sigma) = \{\langle S, \alpha \restriction (s, g, \Diamond_i \exists x Px), s, g[u_1 : a/x][u_3 : c/x]\rangle\}$. If we define $[\![\exists x \varphi]\!]$ as the dual of $[\![\forall x \varphi]\!]$, then
$[\![\Diamond_i \exists x Px]\!](\sigma) = \{\langle S, \beta, s, g[u_1 : a/x]\rangle, \langle S, \beta, s, g[u_3 : c/x]\rangle\}$,
where $\beta = \alpha \restriction (s, g, \Diamond_i \exists x Px)$ which fails to bind the occurrence of x in $\Box_i Rx$ which checks holding of $R(x)$ at each possible world i-accessible from s, since $g[u_1 : a/x]$ fails to bind the x at u_3 and $g[u_3 : c/x]$ fails to bind the x at u_1. The successful variable assignment must be $g[u_1 : a/x][u_3 : c/x]$. On the other hand, if we keep the definiton of $[\![\exists x \varphi]\!]$ but we define $[\![\Diamond_i \varphi]\!]$ as the dual of $[\![\Box_i \varphi]\!]$, $[\![\Diamond_i \exists x Px]\!](\sigma) = \{\sigma[g/g[u_1 : a/x][u_3 : c/x]]\}$, which fails to check holding of $P(x)$ at u_2. In definition 2 of $[\![\Diamond_i \varphi]\!]$, $[\![\Diamond_i \varphi]\!]$ eliminates the i-accessibility of u_2 from s. Therefore, 1 is interpreted appropriately in definition 2.

Here let us consider another setting where $\alpha(u_1) := \langle \emptyset, \{P \mapsto \{a, b\}, R \mapsto \{b\}\}\rangle$ and the other is the same with the above setting. Then
$[\![\Diamond_i \exists x Px]\!](\sigma) = \{\langle S, \beta, s, g[u_1 : a/x][u_3 : c/x]\rangle, \langle S, \beta, s, g[u_1 : b/x][u_3 : c/x]\rangle\}$,
where $\beta = \alpha \restriction (s, g, \Diamond_i \exists x Px)$. That is, two states are generated. Then
$[\![\Box_i Rx]\!](\langle S, \beta, s, g[u_1 : a/x][u_3 : c/x]\rangle) = \emptyset$ since it fails at u_1, and
$[\![\Box_i Rx]\!](\langle S, \beta, s, g[u_1 : b/x][u_3 : c/x]\rangle) = \{\langle S, \beta, s, g[u_1 : b/x][u_3 : c/x]\rangle\}$. Therefore, $[\![\Diamond_i \exists x Px \wedge \Box_i Rx]\!](\sigma) = \{\langle S, \beta, s, g[u_1 : b/x][u_3 : c/x]\rangle\}$, i.e., it is successful at this setting.
✠(The case of 2): the situation is similar to the case of 1. The second subformula $\Diamond_i Rx$ only changes β to $(\alpha \restriction (s, g, \Diamond_i \exists x Px)) \restriction (s, g[u_1 : a/x][u_3 : c/x], \Diamond_i Rx)$. In this setting, it is equal to β.
✠(The case of 6): $[\![\Box_i \exists x Px]\!]$ fails at u_2. So, let $\pi_1 \circ \alpha(s) := \pi_1 \circ \alpha(s) \setminus \{\langle i, u_2 \rangle\}$. Then $[\![\Box_i \exists x Px]\!](\sigma) = \{\sigma[g[u_1 : a/x][u_3 : c/x]/g]\}$. This verifies $\Diamond_i Rx$ which only

checks the existence of a possible world which is i-accessible from s and where $R(x)$ holds.

✠(The case of 7): $\llbracket \Diamond_i \exists x Px \rrbracket(\sigma) = \{\sigma[g[u_1 : a/x][u_3 : c/x]/g]\}$ which falsifies $\Box_i Rx$ at u_2. Therefore, the contingency of 7 is shown.

✠(The case of 8): $\llbracket (\sim \exists x P(x)) \lor R(x) \rrbracket(\sigma)$
$= \llbracket \sim \exists x P(x) \rrbracket(\sigma) \cup \llbracket (\sim \exists x P(x)) \land R(x) \rrbracket(\sigma) = \bigcup_{u \in \{u_1, u_3, u_4\}} \{\langle S, \alpha, u, h \rangle\}[s/u] \cup \bigcup_{u \in \{u_1, u_3, u_4\}} \llbracket R(x) \rrbracket(\langle S, \alpha, u, h \rangle) = \{\sigma[u_1/s][h/g], \sigma[u_3/s][h/g], \sigma[u_4/s][h/g]\}$,
where $h = g[u_1 : a/x][u_3 : c/x][u_4 : a/x]$. The resulting variable assignment $g[u_1 : a/x][u_3 : c/x][u_4 : a/x]$ shows that $\exists x$ binds the occurence of x in $R(x)$.

✠(The case of 9): In this setting, 9 fails. So let us see 9 in another setting illustrated by figure:

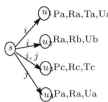

In this setting, $\llbracket (\sim \exists x P(x)) \land \sim R(x) \rrbracket(\sigma)$
$= \llbracket \sim R(x) \rrbracket(\langle S, \alpha \upharpoonright (s, g, \sim \exists x P(x)), s, g[u_1 : a/x][u_3 : c/x][u_4 : a/x] \rangle)$. Therefore, $\exists x$ binds the occurrence of x in $\sim R(x)$. ∎

Next let us see about 3, 4, and 5.

Example 2. Let $P, R, T, U \in Rel(1)$ and $\langle S, \alpha, s, g \rangle$ be the current state which is illustrated by figure

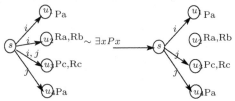

✠(The case of 3): $\llbracket (\exists x Px) \Rightarrow Rx \rrbracket(\sigma) = \bigcap_{\sigma' \in \llbracket \sim \exists x Px \rrbracket(\sigma)} \llbracket Rx \rrbracket(\sigma')[s/s_{\sigma'}]$
$= \{\langle S, \alpha, s, g[u_1 : a/x][u_3 : c/x][u_4 : a/x] \rangle\}$.
    Then $\llbracket \Diamond_i Tx \rrbracket(\langle S, \alpha, s, g[u_1 : a/x][u_3 : c/x][u_4 : a/x] \rangle)$
$= \{\langle S, \alpha \upharpoonright (s, g[u_1 : a/x][u_3 : c/x][u_4 : a/x], \Diamond_i Tx), s, g[u_1 : a/x][u_3 : c/x][u_4 : a/x] \rangle\}$. Therefore the occurence of x in $\Diamond_i Tx$ is bound by $\exists x$ in $(\exists x Px) \Rightarrow Rx$.

✠(The case of 4): $\llbracket (\exists x Px) \Rightarrow Rx \rrbracket(\sigma)$
$= \{\langle S, \alpha, s, g[u_1 : a/x][u_3 : c/x][u_4 : a/x] \rangle\}$. $\llbracket \Box_i Tx \rrbracket(\langle S, \alpha, s, g[u_1 : a/x][u_3 : c/x][u_4 : a/x] \rangle)$ fails at u_2 and u_4. Therefore, if $\langle i, u_2 \rangle, \langle i, u_2 \rangle \notin \pi_1 \circ \alpha(s)$, then $\llbracket \Box_i Tx \rrbracket(\langle S, \alpha, s, g[u_1 : a/x][u_3 : c/x][u_4 : a/x] \rangle) = \{\langle S, \alpha, s, g[u_1 : a/x][u_3 : c/x][u_4 : a/x] \rangle\}$. Anyway, since the resulting variable assignment is $g[u_1 : a/x][u_3 : c/x][u_4 : a/x]$, the occurence of x in $\Box_i Tx$ is bound by $\exists x$ in $(\exists x Px) \Rightarrow Rx$ at u_1 and u_3.

✠(The case of 5): In this setting, 5 fails. So let us consider another setting illustrated by the following figure:

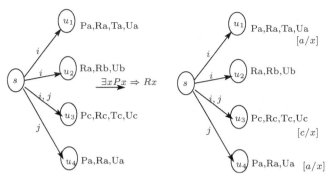

In this setting, 5 does not fails, and the output is $\{\langle S, \alpha, s, g[u_1 : a/x][u_3 : c/x][u_4 : a/x]\rangle\}$. This shows that in 5 $\exists x$ binds the occurrence of x in $Tx \Rightarrow Ux$. ∎

5 On Epistemic Possibility

[9] proposes a dynamic modal predicate logic of modal subordination, based on *epistemic possiblities*, which is roughly defined as follows: Let W be a set of possible wordls, A a set of variable assignment, D a set of individuals, $w \in W$, $f \in A$, and ϵ, ϵ' sets of epsitemic possibilities.

$\langle w, f, \mathcal{E}_\alpha \rangle$ is an epistemic possibility if $\mathcal{E}_\alpha \in \mathscr{P}(\mathscr{P}(\bigcup_{n \in \omega} E_{\alpha,n}))$, where $E_{\alpha,0} \in \mathscr{P}(\mathscr{P}(W \times A)))$ and $E_{\alpha,n+1} \in \mathscr{P}(\mathscr{P}(W \times A \times E_{\alpha,n}))$, where α is a selection function.

I show that any epistemic possibility is a system transition system state, as follows:

Proposition 1. *Any epistemic possibility* $\langle w, f, \mathcal{E}_\alpha \rangle$ *is a system transition system state.*

Proof. We can define translations T, F, and V from epistemic possibilities into system transition system states, and partial translations T', F' and V' from system transition system states into epistemic possibilities, as follows:

$T(w, g, \mathcal{E}_\alpha) = \langle W, F(w, \mathcal{E}_\alpha), w, V(g, w, \mathcal{E}_\alpha) \rangle;$

$F(w, \mathcal{E}_\alpha) \stackrel{g}{=} \bigcup_{\epsilon \in \mathcal{E}_\alpha} \{(w, u) | (u, h, \mathcal{E}_{\alpha'}) \in \epsilon\} \cup \bigcup_{(u, h, \mathcal{E}_{\alpha'}) \in \epsilon} graph(F(u, \mathcal{E}_{\alpha'}));$

$V(g, w, \mathcal{E}_\alpha) \stackrel{g}{=} \{(w, (x, g(x))) | x \in Var\} \cup \bigcup_{(u, h, \mathcal{E}_{\alpha'}) \in \epsilon \in \mathcal{E}_\alpha} graph(V(h, u, \mathcal{E}_{\alpha'}));$

$T'(W, \alpha, w, g) = \langle w, V'(g, w, \alpha), F'(\alpha, w, g) \rangle$ if $F'(\alpha, w, g)$, $V'(g, w, \alpha)$ are defined;

$F'(\alpha, w, g) = \{\{\langle u, V'(g, u, \alpha), F'(\alpha, u, g) \rangle | u \in X\} | X \in P(\alpha(w))\} \cup \bigcup_{u \in \alpha(w)}$ $\{F'(\alpha, u, g)\}$ if $F'(\alpha, u, g)$ and $V'(g, u, \alpha)$ are defined;

$V'(g, w, \alpha) \stackrel{g}{=} \{(x, g(w)(x)) | x \in Var\};$

where $X \stackrel{g}{=} Y$ iff $X = k$ such that $graph(k) = Y$ and $\bigcup P(S) = S$. Obviously, $T \circ T'$ is an identity function over epistemic possibilties if T' is defined and we select an appropriate P. □

This result shows that system transition systems are more general than epistemic possibilities.

6   Conclusion

This paper have proposed a dynamic semantics of modal subordination which is classified into nine types by exploiting the notion of coalgebras and system transition systems, which are abstract objects modeling "Kripke models of Kripke models" or graph rewriting systems, by exlpoiting the theory of coalgebras in order to treat *modal subordination* as a Kripke model change, which requires no ad-hoc informal treatment such as *accomodation* as in [1] or extra-ontology introduced in [2, 3].

References

1. Roberts, C.: Modal subordination and pronominal anaphora in discourse. Linguistics and Philosophy **12** (1989) 683–721
2. Geurts, B.: Presuppositions and Pronouns. Elsevier Science Ltd., Amsterdam (1999)
3. Frank, A.: On Context Dependence in Modal Constructions. PhD thesis, University of Stuttgart (1997)
4. Karttunen, L.: Discourse referents. In: Syntax and Semantics. Academic Press, New York (1977) 363–385
5. Ogata, N.: A dynamic semantics of modal subordination. In: Proceedings of the International Workshop of Logic and Engineering of Natural Language Semantics 2005, Tokyo, The Japanese Society of Artificial Intelligence (2005)
6. van Eijck, J., Cepparello, G.: Dynamic modal predicate logic. In Kanazawa, M., Piñón, C.J., eds.: Dynamics, Polarity, and Quantification. CSLI, Stanford (1994) 251–276
7. Groenendijk, J., Stokhof, M.: Dynamic predicate logic. Linguistics and Philosophy **14** (1991) 39–100
8. Groenendijk, J., Stokhof, M., Veltman, F.: Coreference and modality. In Lappin, ed.: The Handbook of Contemporary Semantic Theory. Cambridge University Press, Cambridge (1996) 179–213
9. Asher, N., McCready, E.: Modals and a compositional account of counterfactuals (2005)
10. Roberts, C.: Anaphora in intensional contexts. In Lappin, ed.: The Handbook of Contemporary Semantic Theory. Cambridge University Press, Cambridge (1995) 215–246
11. Kadmon, N.: Formal Pragmatics: Semantics, Pragmatics, Presupposition, and Focus. Blackwell Publishers, Malden (2001)
12. Veltman, F.C.: Defaults in update semantics. Journal of Philosophical Logic **8** (1996) 73–80
13. Garson, J.W.: Quantification in modal logic. In Gabbay, D.M., Guenthner, F., eds.: Handbook of Philosophical Logic, 2nd Edition. Volume 3. Kluwer Academic Publisher, Dordrecht (2001) 267–323

Dynamic Discourse Semantics for Embedded Speech Acts

Nicholas Asher

Departments of Philosophy and of Linguistics
The University of Texas at Austin

Abstract. This paper investigates how different speech acts can embed and interact with logical operators and quantifiers. It argues for a discourse based semantics approach to the problem.

1 Introduction

A traditional separation of pragmatics and semantics has it that speech acts are computed at the level of the entire sentence and that their illocutionary force can't be embedded under various truth conditional operators. Since speech acts other than assertions don't classically have truth values as extensions, they can't possibly combine with truth functional operators like the propositional connectives in standard logic. This much is right. But when we look at the behavior of natural language conjunctions like *and, or,* or *if..., ... then,* speech acts like directives and questions clearly embed under some of these operators. As Krifka [1] has argued in some detail, there is a lot of evidence amassed over the years that most types of speech acts do embed within conjunctions and conditionals and imperatives clearly embed under disjunctions as well. The problematic question for truth conditional semantics is then: what is the uniform account of the meaning of natural language sentential connectives that captures their behavior with interrogatives, imperatives and indicatives?

Several decades of research have shown that this question is difficult if not impossible to answer within the confines of standard truth conditional semantics. However, if the meaning of directives, questions and commissives and other speech acts is to be given dynamically, we open the way to give a uniform account of the meaning of connectives. The reason why this is so is roughly that in dynamic semantics all well-formed clauses in natural language are actions that change the input context in some way. Assertions, questions, requests and the like are all alike in this respect. But the main aim of the paper is to argue that dynamic semantics isn't by itself enough. As I've argued at length in, e.g., [2], many speech acts are relational and affect the context in a particular way over and above what their mood and other factors in their compositional semantics would indicate. This is one of the main points of of Segmented Discourse Representation Theory, or SDRT. In this paper I will use the resources of SDRT to give a uniform account of the connectives in connection with imperatives and the speech acts they convey. A fuller paper would do justice not only to imperatives

T. Washio et al. (Eds.): JSAI 2005 Workshops, LNAI 4012, pp. 157–164, 2006.

embedded under the scope of various operators and quantifiers but interrogatives as well. However space does not permit such an extended study, so I will concentrate on imperatives here.

2   A Discourse Based Semantics for Imperatives and Associated Speech Acts

There is a well known problem of alignment between clauses in the imperative mood and the speech acts they express. Sometimes imperatives yield directives and sometimes they don't. Consider the following cases.

(1)   Come home by 5pm and we will finish the shelves tonight.
(2)   Smoke a packet of cigarettes a day and you will die before you're 30.

In fact (1) is ambiguous. It could express a request, if there's falling intonation on 5pm and there's a prosodic break after that. But it can also express with a different intonation (rising intonation on 5pm with no prosodic break afterwards) a conditional. Similarly for (2), though the content of the latter makes the conditional reading much more likely.

Since the alignment problem is complex, imperatives cannot simply yield directives in the semantics. What should the semantics for imperatives be? I will propose and defend here the view that imperatives express *actions*. It is then up to the discourse glue logic to supplement the basic semantics of imperatives and to get the appropriate type of speech act in suitable discourse contexts. Thus SDRT's glue logic (see [2] for details) will interpret imperatives in certain contexts as issuing in directives, while in other contexts the actions denoted by imperatives will issue in different sorts of speech acts. Directives for their part, I will argue, have a different semantics from the basic semantics for imperatives; a directive concerns a *discourse action* with respect to the commitments of the addressee; it is part, thus, of discourse structure, like other speech acts in SDRT. Following Hamblin, most researchers have analyzed this action in terms of commitment slates. Commitment slates are a distinguished element of information states that that we use to evaluate formulas dynamically as the interpretation of discourse proceeds. Updating a discourse with a directive to do an action α amounts on those semantics to adding to the commitment slate of the addressee the action α.

Asher and Lascarides [2] extend the dynamic semantics for indicatives to a dynamic semantics for requests as action terms. These are like other formulas in dynamic semantics in that they can affect an input information context; and like formulas derived from indicatives, they operate on the basic building blocks of information states, world assignment pairs. Unlike formulas derived from indicatives, however, which never change the world the world component of an input world assignment pair, action formulas can change both the world and the assignment components. The language introduced in [2] builds on the basic idea that one can convert any formula that describes a situation into an action by an operator δ (in an analogy to the STIT operator of [3]); $\delta\phi$ denotes an action whereby ϕ is achieved. The rest of the language is a straightforward importation from propositional dynamic logic (e.g. [4])

However, if we build too much into the semantics and *identify* the meanings of natural language conjunctions with these operators, we will not be able to give a uniform account of the connectives. General clauses for conjunctions and disjunctions of imperatives look especially hopeless from this perspective. We need a pragmatics and a discourse level to get a good account of the connectives. In effect, we will turn out to need only the minimum of the action language–viz. atomic clauses and sequences. All the rest of the connections will be made through discourse relations.

2.1   Discourse Semantics for Imperativals

Imperativals do not show morphological tense features, like infinitivals. Imperativals also block the use of certain modals, which are admitted in other mood forms. Most syntacticians take this data to indicate the lack of a tense feature or a clausal head for imperatives. So if we follow standard compositional semantics for clauses of the sort given in [5], then we hypothesize that what falls under the scope of the imperatival is at least an eventuality abstract.

(3) a. Leave
     b. Imp(λe leave(x, e))

The imperative itself first of all introduces δ operator to combine with an event type to yield an action formula of the atomic sort I have outlined above. But it must also specify an operator that in the right dicourse contexts is capable of being the directive operator Dir_x. The imperative does not always issue in a directive. Right now in logical form it stands for an underspecified operator $?_x$ that will be further specified by the discourse context. Whether $?_x$ is specified to Dir_x or not will depend in what discourse contexts the imperatival clause occurs; in particular it will depend on how it is attached to other clauses and on the type of speech act the other clauses convey.

We've seen some examples already where clauses in imperatival mood doesn't yield commands—generic sentences like

(2) Smoke a packet of cigarettes a day and you will die before you're 30.

But there are many others. Consider for instance:

(4) To make onion soup, heat 10 cups of chicken or beef bouillon to a low boil. Peel and slice two pounds of yellow onions and add to the hot broth. Simmer for 30 minutes.

This recipe involves a topic *making onion soup*, which is then elaborated on by a sequence of imperatives that yield a sort of "narrative". In SDRT ([2]), imperatival clauses, just like indicative clauses, can contribute logical forms that enter into Narration relations. Each one of the imperatival clauses describes an action that is in some sense performed and is a prerequisite for the action that follows; for instance, the action of adding the onions to the *hot* broth couldn't be carried out if the action of heating the broth hadn't occurred. Thus, we naturally interpret subsequent imperatival clauses relative to the satisfaction of previous imperatival clauses in such a sequence. And each clause has an effect on the world of evaluation, transforming it via the action described. In this respect, narrative sequences of imperatival clauses and narrative sequences of indicative clauses function similarly.

Now *Narration*(π_1, π_2) entails the truth of the contents of the clauses labelled by π_1 and π_2. In other words *Narration* is a veridical rhetorical relation and obeys the following veridicality axiom of SDRT (K_α below is the logical form associated with the label α): $R(\alpha, \beta) \Rightarrow (K_\alpha; K_\beta)$. *Elaboration, Narration, Explanation, Parallel, Contrast, Background, Result, Evidence* are all veridical relations.

If *Narration* linking the imperatives in (4) is a veridical relation, the relation that links the whole narrative sequence of actions to the topic is not. That is why the actions described in the recipe are not carried out in the actual world of evaluation. The narrative sequence constituted by the clauses linked by *Narration$_p$* constitute together an elaboration of the general plan of making onion soup. The sequence forms a discourse constituent that is itself related via another discourse relation *Plan Elaboration* to the topic of the recipe, which is given by the first clause. The semantics of *Plan Elaboration* is an intensional one, and it is *not veridical*, unlike its indicative cousin, *Elaboration*. Roughly, *Plan-Elab*(π_1, π_2) says that the elaborating constituent, K_{π_2}, spells out a sequence of actions that if carried out will yield that the topic labelled K_{π_1} is satisfied. But it neither entails K_{π_1} nor K_{π_2}. Refining the view in Asher and Lascarides [2], a key clue to this relation is the use of the infinitival which is naturally interpreted as being in the antecedent of a conditional. Using our extension of dynamic semantics, the semantics for SDRT formulas involving the discourse relation *Plan-Elaboration* makes plain that no action is being carried out. And no action is directed to the addressee in (4) either. In this case the underspecified operator just resolves to an identity or truth operator that does not affect the content of the discourse. All the content is given by the discourse relations.

Another example where this happens is when imperatives attach to interrogatives.

(5)   a.   A: How does one catch the 10:20 train to London?
       b.   B: Go to the information counter and ask someone.

The imperative in (5b) is *not* to be carried out. Rather, its 'rhetorical function' is to provide sufficient information that A can compute an answer to his question (which is an adverbial of manner, given the compositional semantics of *how*-questions Asher and Lascarides 1998). The requests are to be understood as if you perform this action, your question will be answered. In SDRT, we label this relation IQAP$_r$. The meaning postulate for IQAP$_r$ is, where we assume the free variable for the subject in β to be x,

$$- \; IQAP_r(\alpha, \beta, \lambda) \wedge A : \alpha) \rightarrow (\exists \phi (\exists x (x = A; \beta) > \phi) \wedge IQAP(\alpha, \phi, \lambda))$$

For examples like (5) that exploit $IQAP_r$, it's crucial that the interpretation of the imperative not be put in terms of putting some action on a commitment slate as in [6], [7] or others. For, you're not going to get an answer to the question just by putting an action on your commitment slate; just committing yourself to a certain action doesn't guarantee that the action will get done. It's only the *doing* of the action that will give you an answer to your question—that's the intuitive meaning of the response to the question in (5b).

SDRT provides a defeasible attachment rule for imperatives when they are attached to questions:

– $IQAP_r$ rule: $(?(\alpha, \beta, \lambda) \wedge ?\alpha \wedge !\beta) > IQAP_r(\alpha, \beta\lambda)$

In this case again the underspecified operator introduced by the imperative resolves to identity.

The discourse structure changes dramatically if we change (4) just slightly:

(4')   Make onion soup! Heat 10 cups of chicken or beef bouillon to a low boil. Peel and slice two pounds of yellow onions and add to the hot broth. Simmer for 30 minutes.

The command in the "topic" position changes the semantics of the discourse as a whole. Now the discourse as a whole is a directive with a simple elaboration inside of the directive! Similarly, note the difference of the meaning of (5b) in this context from its meaning in the 'null' context, or when it is attached to an assertion of some kind as below.

(6)   a.   A: You're late.
       b.   B: Go to the information counter.

When an imperatival is given in a "null" context, which is to say that it is unattached to some other speech act, then the underspecified operator it introduces by default turns into a directive. Similarly, if it's attached to an assertion, the underspecified operator turns also into a directive.[1] I hypothesize that when an imperative occurs in a stand alone context (rule 1) or is attached to an assertion (rule 2), a rule of the glue logic takes the imperative to be a directive and attaches the imperatival with this form as a request or a directive.

– Rule 1 for Requests: $(\neg \exists \alpha ?(\alpha, \beta, \lambda) \wedge !\beta \wedge ?_u(\beta)) > (?_u = Dir_u)$
– Rule 2 for Requests: $(?(\alpha, \beta, \lambda) \wedge \neg(!\alpha) \vee ?\alpha) \wedge !\beta \wedge ?_u(\beta)) > (?_u = Dir_u)$

What this rule says is that if an imperatival doesn't form a sequence of imperatives or form an answer to a question, then defeasibly we can infer that it is a directive to some contextually specified agent u, which means roughly that the speaker intends to put the content of α on the commitment slate of the addressee.

Conditional commands are now straightforward. The conditional gives rise to a discourse relation in SDRT, Cond-Consequence, and our rule for directives yields for (7) the logical form in (7'),

---

[1] We would need to change the axiom for Plan-Elab in Asher and Lascarides 2003 to handle this. I cannot go into details here.

(7)   If you want to get an A, study hard.

(7') $\langle\{\pi_0, \pi_1, pi, \pi'\}, \pi : \text{ want an A}(u), \pi_1 : \delta(\text{ study hard}(u)) \wedge \pi' : Dir_u(\pi_1) \wedge$
$\pi_0 : \text{Cond-consequence}(\pi, \pi'))\rangle$

which corresponds to the formulation of a guarded action in the dynamic semantics, except for the fact that the semantics interprets the consequent as a directive. One might strengthen this further with the pragmatic implicature that a directive that one undertakes is normally carried out, which would simplify the consequent of the conditional to $\delta(\text{ study hard}(u))$.

Turning to conjunctions, Txurruka [8] argues that they convey some sort of coordinating discourse relation as noted by . This observation proves to be extremely important: a natural language conjunction doesn't signal a truth conditional connective in SDRT and in any case the dynamic logic doesn't have such an operation—it has the sequential update operation. The conjunction of an imperatival and an indicative clause seems to give rise to two sorts of discourse relations, Def-Consequence and something like Narration. The former corresponds to the conditional readings of sentences like (2) repeated below, while the second corresponds to

(2)   Smoke a packet of cigarettes a day and you will die before you're 30.

(8)   Go to the office, and there you'll find the files I told you about.

The former conveys a sort of generic force, but lest one think that this is a peculiar property of conjunctions involving imperatives, compare (2) with (9) which exhibits the same generic type connection between two *indicative* clauses:

(9)   a.   John walks two feet, and (normally) he's out of breath.
       b.   John has anything to drink and he goes bonkers.

Though one might argue that the generic reading of these two clauses is due to the presence of *normally*, at least some speakers find the use of the adverbial completely optional with respect to this interpretation.

Intonation, world knowledge and an analysis of cooperativity are all important in determining the generic interpretation for (2). SDRT's glue logic will infer in the presence of the requisite clues a relation of Defeasible Consequence between the two clauses, and this automatically gives us the conditional reading of such conjunctions. With (8), we have an episodic reading of the same tense sequence—and so we can conclude that the sequence by itself isn't sufficient. We also need a certain connection between the contents of the clauses, but such requirements are familiar from other SDRT examples. Some of the data by Han [9] might be additional clues for the presence of the generic reading, like the lack of negative polarity items in imperativals except in these antecedents. The same is true of the indicative clauses that are linked by the conjunction and have a generic interpretation. In any case, we see that an SDRT based account has the where with all to account for the varieties of readings when an imperative is conjoined with an assertion. In the glue logic, we will have a more specific default than the Rule 1 that will override the defeasible inference to a directive speech act.

When (8) lacks the generic reading, the first constituent is interpreted first as a directive in virtue of the SDRT rules given above. But also the action it describes is also part of a Narration sequence; it's going to the office that occasions the finding of the file folder, not the putting of the action of going to the office on one's commitment slate. How do we express that in SDRT? We want something like Narration(π_1, π_2), $\pi_1 : \delta(\text{ goes}(u, x) \land \text{ office}(x)$, $\pi_0 : Dir_u(\pi_1)$, but this results in a clash over the status of the action described in π_1. According to Narration it must be performed, but according to Dir, that's not the case. So the Maximize Discourse Coherence principle or MDC and SDRT update as defined in [2] would require that we eliminate this clash by reanalyzing the way the constituents fit together. One way of resolving the clash is to have a discourse structure in which the directive has scope over the constituent which conveys Narration(π_1, π_2). In this case, we would get the following SDRS with labels π_0, π, π_1, π_2, where

- $\pi_0 : Dir_u(\pi)$
- $pi : Narration(\pi_1, \pi_2)$
- $\pi_1 : \delta(\text{ goes}(u, x) \land \text{ office}(x)$
- $\pi_2 : (\text{ find}(u, y) \land \text{ folder}(y)$

Disjunction, unlike conjunction, gives rise typically to a particular discourse relation, Alternation. Alternation conveys a set of epistemic alternatives ([10]); a final ending intonation or rising intonation over the disjunction tells us whether the set of alternatives has been exhaustively specified or not. Suppose that the epistemic alternatives given by Alternation are understood as exhaustive. Then we can have either a simple alternation or a conditional reading. The reason for the latter is that an exhaustive alternation of epistemic possibilities has very close connections to the conditional as Gillies [11] has pointed out. The inference from (10a) to (10b) seems completely valid when the disjunction is given exhaustive intonation.

(10)   a.   Either the burglar committed the murder or the cook did it.
          b.   So if it wasn't the burglar, it was the cook.

But given this observation, the conditional reading follows immediately for (11a) repeated below.

(11)   Get out of here or I'll call the police.

when this is read with exhaustive intonation, as is natural.

3   Conclusions

There is a great deal more to be said about embeddings of speech acts. In particular one should look at quantification, which I plan to do in a longer version of this paper. But at least I hope to have shown here that a discourse based semantics can address problems about the embedding of various speech acts that stump standard semantic theories.

References

1. Krifka, M.: Embedded speech acts. Talk at the Workshop *In the Mood*, Universität Frankfurt (2002)
2. Asher, N., Lascarides, A.: Logics of Conversation. Cambridge University Press (2003)
3. Belnap, N., Horty, J., Xu, M.: Facing the Future: Agents and Choices in Our Deterministic World. Oxford University Press (2001)
4. Harel, D.: Dynamic logic. [12]
5. Asher, N.: Reference to Abstract Objects in Discourse. Kluwer Academic Publishers (1993)
6. Merin, A.: Permission sentences stand in the way of Boolean and other lattice-theoretic semantics. Journal of Semantics **9** (1992) 95–162
7. Portner, P.: The semantics of imperatives within a theory of clause types. In Watanabe, K., Young, R.B., eds.: Proceedings of Semantics and Linguistic Theory 14, Ithaca, N.Y., CLC Publications (2005)
8. Txurruka, I.: The natural language conjunction *and*. Linguistics and Philosophy **26** (2003) 255–285
9. Han, C.: The Structure and Interpretation of Imperatives: Mood and Force in Universal Grammar. PhD thesis, University of Pennsylvania (1999)
10. Zimmermann, T.E.: Free choice disjunction and epistemic possibility. Natural Language Semantics **8** (2000) 255–290
11. Gillies, A.S.: Epistemic conditionals and conditional epistemics. Noûs **38** (2004) 585–616
12. Gabbay, D., Geunthner, F., eds.: Handbook of Philosophical Logic, Vol. II. Dordrecht Reidel (1984)
13. Searle, J.R.: Speech Acts. Cambridge University Press (1969)

Part III

Learning with Logics and Logics for Learning

Workshop on Learning with Logics and Logics for Learning (LLLL)

Akihiro Yamamoto[1] and Kouichi Hirata[2]

[1] Graduate School of Informatics, Kyoto University, Japan
akihiro@i.kyoto-u.ac.jp
[2] Department of Artificial Intelligence, Kyushu Institute of Technology, Japan
hirata@ai.kyutech.ac.jp

1 The Aim and History of LLLL

Logic is a fundamental and useful representation for knowledge in Artificial Intelligence. In the area of Machine Learning, various types of computational logic, such as logic programming, first-order logic, description logic and higher-order logic, have developed by incorporating with various types of learning methodologies including identification in the limit, PAC learning, on-line learning, query learning, machine discovery and learning based on Bayesian networks. Recently, on the other hand, machine learning procedures have begun to provide semantics to logic and foundations of some procedures in mathematics.

The workshop named "Learning with Logics and Logics for Learning (LLLL)" has been planed in Japan, in order to bring together researchers who are interested in both of the areas of machine learning and computational logic, and to have intensive discussions on various relations between the two with making their interchange more active. We can draw back the root of LLLL to a Japanese workshop held in January 2002 in Sapporo. In December 2002, the special sessions for LLLL were organized in the 50th meeting of SIG-FAI (the predecessor of SIG-FPAI) of JSAI in Fukuoka.

The newest LLLL has been held on June 13 and 14, 2005 in Kitakyushu, co-located with the 19th Annual Conference of the Japanese Society for Artificial Intelligence (JSAI2005) and supported by SIG-FPAI of JSAI.

2 The Workshop

In order to hold the workshop LLLL, we first organized the program committee consisting of the 12 excellent researchers to the area in logic and/or learning, including 5 foreign researchers[1]. We also invited two speakers, Prof. Roni Khardon (Tufts University) and Prof. Luc de Raedt (The University of Freiburg).

---

[1] More information for LLLL has been available at the workshop homepage in the following URL: http://www.dumbo.ai.kyutech.ac.jp/LLLL

T. Washio et al. (Eds.): JSAI 2005 Workshops, LNAI 4012, pp. 167–168, 2006.
© Springer-Verlag Berlin Heidelberg 2006

By reviewing every submitted paper by two PC members, we have selected 13 papers for the contributed talks, which were arranged into 4 tracks in the program of LLLL[2].

1. Data mining and logic : 5 talks.
2. Foundations of logics for learning : 2 talks.
3. Computational learning related to logic : 4 talks.
4. Logical and statistical learning : 2 talks.

All talks interested the audiences very much, and each talk was given the fruitful discussion at LLLL, with two or more comments and questions.

After the workshop LLLL, by reviewing every paper (without withdrawn papers) by another PC member again, we have selected the following 6 papers to publish in the post-workshop proceedings (this volume).

For logical aspects of data minig, Minato gives a new calculator *VSOP* for the frequent pattern mining, by using *zero-suppressed BDDs* that are standard tools for logical synthesis. Satoh and Uno apply the *dualization*, which is an efficient tool for enumeration, to the problem of enumerating *minimally revised specifications* and designs the efficient algorithm to solves the problem.

As applications of inductive logic programming, Saito *et al.* provide the interesting results applying inductive logic programming system *Progol* to classifying whether or not a building is "historic" from *architectural facades*. Watanabe and Muggleton formulate a new framework to applying Plotkin's *least generalization* to learning *probabilistic logical automata for special inputs* related to an HMM.

In order to give foundations of logic for learning, Kuwabara *et al.* investigate the subsumption and the generalization, which are the important techniques of logic for learning, for *ordered clauses* as a sequence of literals and gives the computational results. Furthermore, as computataional learning related to logic, Hirowatari *et al.* study a new learning model *finite prediction* for *recursive real-valued functions*, which is one of the computable real functions recently given the logical characterization in a new computable paradigm.

Acknowledgments

We have finished the workshop LLLL successfully. We would like represent our thankfulness to the invited speakers. We are grateful for the great support that we received from the program committee members: Marta Arias, James Cussens, Susumu Hayashi, Tamás Horváth, Katsumi Inoue, Eric Martin, Taisuke Sato, Ken Satoh, Eiji Takimoto, György Turán. In particular we would express our great thankfulness to Prof. Ken Satoh, the chair of SIG-FPAI, for his encouragement and support to LLLL. We thank all speakers and all audiences attended the workshop. Finally, we are grateful for the committee of JSAI2005 for their arrangement, in particular, Prof. Takashi Washio, the organizer of the co-located international workshop of JSAI2005.

---

[2] The workshop proceedings have been published from JSAI (ISBN 4-915905-19-5 C3004).

Efficient Database Analysis Using VSOP Calculator Based on Zero-Suppressed BDDs

Shin-ichi Minato

Graduate School of Information Science and Technology,
Hokkaido University
Sapporo, 060-0814 Japan

Abstract. Manipulation of large-scale combinatorial data is one of the important fundamental technique for web information retrieval, integration, and mining. Recently, we proposed a new approach based on Zero-suppressed BDDs (Binary Decision Diagrams) for efficient database analysis. In this paper, we present *VSOP* program developed for calculating combinatorial item sets specified by symbolic expressions. Based on ZBDD techniques, VSOP can efficiently handle large-scale sum-of-products expressions with a number of item symbols. VSOP supports not only Boolean set operations but also numerical arithmetic operations based on *Valued-Sum-Of-Products* algebra, such as addition, subtraction, multiplication, division, numerical comparison, etc. VSOP will facilitate research and development for various database analysis problems.

1 Introduction

Manipulation of large-scale combinatorial data is one of the fundamental technique for web information retrieval integration, and mining[12]. In particular, frequent item set analysis is important in many tasks that try to find interesting patterns from web documents and databases, such as association rules, correlations, sequences, episodes, classifiers, and clusters. Since the introduction by Agrawal et al.[1], the frequent item set and association rule analysis have been received much attentions from many researchers, and a number of papers have been published about the new algorithms or improvements for solving such mining problems[3, 5, 14]. Recently, we proposed a new approach based on Zero-suupressed BDDs (Binary Decision Diagrams) for database analysis problems[9]. BDDs are graph-based representation of Boolean functions, now widely used in system design and verification area. Here we focus on Zero-suppressed BDDs (ZBDDs), a special type of BDDs, which are suitable for handling large-scale sets of combinations. Using ZBDDs, we can implicitly enumerate combinatorial item set data and efficiently compute set operations over the ZBDDs. In this recent work, we presented some encouraging experimental results of frequent item set mining problem for practical benchmark examples, some of which have never been generated by any other method.

In this paper, we present *VSOP* program developed for calculating combinatorial item sets specified by symbolic expressions. Based on ZBDD techniques, VSOP

T. Washio et al. (Eds.): JSAI 2005 Workshops, LNAI 4012, pp. 169–181, 2006.

can efficiently handle large-scale sum-of-products expressions with a number of item symbols. VSOP supports not only Boolean set operations but also numerical arithmetic operations based on *Valued-Sum-Of-Products* algebra, such as addition, subtraction, multiplication, division, numerical comparison, etc. VSOP will facilitate research and development for various database analysis problems. Here we show several experimental examples of using VSOP for database analysis.

2   ZBDDs and Database Analysis

2.1   BDDs and ZBDDs

BDD is a directed graph representation of the Boolean function, as illustrated in Fig. 1(a). It is derived by reducing a binary tree graph representing recursive *Shannon's expansion*, indicated in Fig. 1(b). The following reduction rules yield a *Reduced Ordered BDD (ROBDD)*, which can efficiently represent the Boolean function. (see [2] for details.)

- Delete all redundant nodes whose two edges point to the same node. (Fig. 2(a))
- Share all equivalent sub-graphs. (Fig. 2(b))

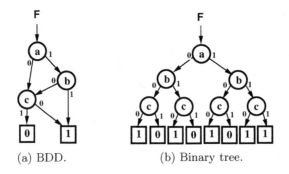

(a) BDD.   (b) Binary tree.

Fig. 1. BDD and binary tree: $F = (a \wedge b) \vee \bar{c}$

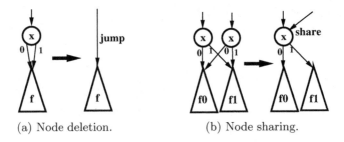

(a) Node deletion.   (b) Node sharing.

Fig. 2. Reduction rules of ordinary BDDs

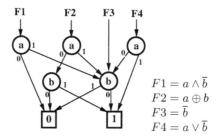

$$F1 = a \wedge \bar{b}$$
$$F2 = a \oplus b$$
$$F3 = \bar{b}$$
$$F4 = a \vee \bar{b}$$

Fig. 3. Shared multiple BDDs

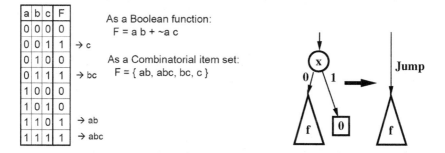

Fig. 4. Correspondence between Boolean function and set of combinations

Fig. 5. ZBDD reduction rule

ROBDDs provide canonical forms for Boolean functions when the variable order is fixed. Most research on BDDs are based on the above reduction rules. In the following sections, ROBDDs will be referred to as BDDs (or ordinary BDDs) for the sake of simplification.

As shown in Fig. 3, a set of multiple BDDs can be shared each other under the same fixed variable ordering. In this way, we can handle a number of Boolean functions simultaneously in a monolithic memory space.

Using BDDs, we can uniquely and compactly represent many practical Boolean functions including AND, OR, parity, and arithmetic adder functions. Using Bryant's algorithm[2], we can efficiently construct a BDD for the result of a binary logic operation (i.e. AND, OR, XOR), for given a pair of operand BDDs. This algorithm is based on hash table techniques, and the computation time is almost linear to the data size unless the data overflows the main memory. (see [7] for details.)

BDDs are originally developed for handling Boolean function data, however, they can also be used for implicit representation of sets of combinations. Here we call "sets of combinations" for a set of elements each of which is a combination out of n items. This data model often appears in real-life problems, such as combinations of switching devices, Boolean item sets in the database, and combinatorial sets of edges or nodes in the graph data model.

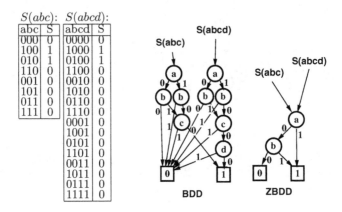

abc	S
000	0
100	1
010	1
110	0
001	0
101	0
011	0
111	0

abcd	S
0000	0
1000	1
0100	1
1100	0
0010	0
1010	0
0110	0
1110	0
0001	0
1001	0
0101	0
1101	0
0011	0
1011	0
0111	0
1111	0

Fig. 6. Example of ZBDD effect

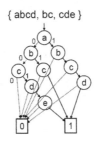

Fig. 7. Explicit representation by ZBDD

A set of combinations can be mapped into Boolean space of n input variables. If we choose any one combination of variables, a Boolean function determines whether the combination is included in the set of combinations. For example, Fig. 4 shows the truth table representing a Boolean function $ab + \bar{a}c$, but it can also be regarded as a set of combination $\{ab, abc, bc, c\}$. Such Boolean function is called *characteristic function* for the set of combinations. The set operations such as union, intersection, and difference can be performed by logic operations on characteristic functions.

By using BDDs for characteristic functions, we can manipulate sets of combinations efficiently. They can be generated and manipulated within a time roughly proportional to the BDD size. When we handle many combinations including similar patterns (sub-combinations), BDDs are greatly reduced by node sharing effect, and sometimes an exponential reduction benefit can be obtained.

Zero-suppressed BDD (ZBDD)[6, 8] is a special type of BDDs for efficient manipulation of sets of combinations. ZBDDs are based on the following special reduction rules.

- Delete all nodes whose 1-edge directly points to the 0-terminal node, and jump through to the 0-edge's destination, as shown in Fig. 5.
- Share equivalent nodes as well as ordinary BDDs.

"∅"	Returns empty set. (0-termial node)
"**1**"	Returns the set of only null-combination. (1-terminal node)
P.top	Returns the item-ID at the root node of P.
P.offset(v)	Selects the subset of combinations each of which does not include item v.
P.onset(v)	Selects the subset of combinations including item v, and then delete v from each combination.
P.change(v)	Inverts existence of v (add / delete) on each combination.
$P \cup Q$	Returns union set.
$P \cap Q$	Returns intersection set.
$P - Q$	Returns difference set. (in P but not in Q.)
P.count	Counts number of combinations.

Fig. 8. Primitive ZBDD operations

Notice that we do not delete the nodes whose two edges point to the same node, which used to be deleted by the original rule. The zero-suppressed deletion rule is asymmetric for the two edges, as we do not delete the nodes whose 0-edge points to a terminal node. It is proved that ZBDDs are also gives canonical forms as well as ordinary BDDs under a fixed variable ordering.

Here we summarise the features of ZBDDs.

- In ZBDDs, the nodes of irrelevant items (never chosen in any combination) are automatically deleted by ZBDD reduction rule. In ordinary BDDs, irrelevant nodes still remain and they may spoil the reduction benefit of sharing nodes. (An example is shown in Fig. 6.)
- ZBDDs are especially effective for representing sparse combinations. For instance, sets of combinations selecting 10 out of 1000 items can be represented by ZBDDs up to 100 times more compact than ordinary BDDs.
- Each path from the root node to the 1-terminal node corresponds to each combination in the set. Namely, the number of such paths in the ZBDD equals to the number of combinations in the set. In ordinary BDDs, this property does not always hold.
- When no equivalent nodes exist in a ZBDD, that is the worst case, the ZBDD structure explicitly stores all items in all combinations, as well as using an explicit linear linked list data structure. An example is shown in Fig. 7. Namely, (the order of) ZBDD size never exceeds the explicit representation. If more nodes are shared, the ZBDD is more compact than linear list. Ordinary BDDs have larger overhead to represent sparser combinations while ZBDDs have no such overhead.

Figure 8 shows the most of primitive operations of ZBDDs. In these operations, ∅, **1**, $P.top$ are executed in a constant time, and the others are almost linear to the size of graph. We can describe various processing on sets of combinations by composing of these primitive operations. More detailed techniques and complexity of BDD/ZBDD manipulation are discussed in the book[13].

2.2   ZBDD-Based Database Analysis

In our recent work[9], we proposed a method of handling large-scale item set data using ZBDDs. Here we consider binary item set databases, each record of which holds a combination of items, called *tuple* (or *transaction*) databases. As presented in that paper, many cases of practical item set databases have a distinctive property that the item's appearance ratio is very small. This is reasonable as considering real-life problems, for example, the number of items in a basket purchased by one customer is usually much less than all the items displayed in a shop. This observation means that we often handle very sparse combinations in many practical data mining/analysis problems, and in such cases, the ZBDD reduction rule is extremely effective. If the average appearance ratio of each item is 1%, ZBDDs may be more compact than ordinary BDDs up to 100 times. We must use ZBDDs in stead of ordinary BDDs for success in many practical data mining/analysis problems.

Here we recall the ZBDD-based method of generating histograms of item sets, which is the basic technique for data mining/analysis.

A **Tuple-histogram** is the table for counting the number of appearance of each tuple in the given database. An example is shown in Fig. 9. In the tuple-histograms, we do not consider the partial item sets in a tuple, and exactly same tuples are checked and accumulated. Since ZBDDs are representation of sets of combinations, a simple ZBDD distinguishes only existence of each tuple in the databases. In order to represent the numbers of tuple's appearances, we decompose the number into m-digits of ZBDD vector $\{F_0, F_1, \ldots, F_{m-1}\}$ to represent integers up to $(2^m - 1)$, as shown in Fig. 10. To construct a ZBDD-based tuple-histgram for given tuple database, we read a tuple data one by one from the database, and accumulate the single tuple data to the binary-coded ZBDDs.

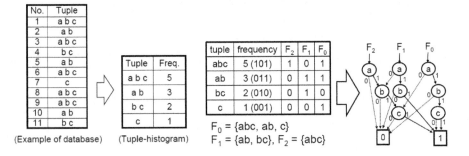

Fig. 9. Database example and tuple-histogram

Fig. 10. ZBDD vector for tuple-histogram

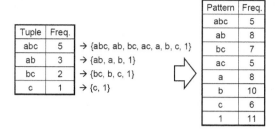

Fig. 11. Tuple-histogram and pattern-histogram

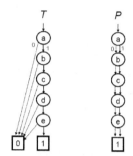

Fig. 12. ZBDDs for a tuple and all sub-patterns

Table 1. Generation of tuple-histograms

Data name	$\#T$	$total|T|$	$|ZBDD|$	Time(s)
T10I4D100K	100,000	1,010,228	552,429	43.2
chess	3,196	118,252	40,028	1.4
mushroom	8,124	186,852	8,006	1.5
pumsb	49,046	3,629,404	1,750,883	188.5
BMS-POS	515,597	3,367,020	1,350,970	895.0
BMS-WebView-1	59,602	149,639	46,148	18.3
accidents	340,183	11,500,870	3,877,333	107.0

(Pentium4, 800MHz, 512MB mem, SuSE Linux 9)

On each accumulation step, we apply a sequence of set operations which simulates a hardware algorithm of the binary full-adder logic circuit.

A **Pattern-histogram** is the table for counting the number of appearance of each *patterns*, a subset of items included in any tuple of the given database. An example is shown in Fig. 11. In general, a tuple of k items includes 2^k patterns, so generating a pattern-histogram is much harder than generating a tuple-histogram. However, using the ZBDD-based data structure, we may have more compact representation, since a number of similar patterns can be shared

Table 2. Pattern-histograms for sampling data

Data name	#T_{done}*	ratio%	|ZBDD|	Time(s)
T10I4D100K	43,395	43.40	9,968,062	1,711
chess	703	22.00	8,242,212	919
mushroom	8,124	100.00	513,762	214
pumsb	61	0.12	7,018,198	89
BMS-POS	9,837	1.90	9,679,161	266
BMS-WebView-1	17,757	29.79	9,372,436	134
accidents	133	0.04	8,394,811	223

(*) #T_{done}: Number of tuples computable in our PC.

in ZBDDs, and in some cases, this makes possible to generate complete pattern-histograms. Figure 12 shows a ZBDD for a tuple $T = abcde$ with five items and a ZBDD representing a set of all 32 patterns $P = \{1, a, b, c, d, e, ab, ac, bc, cd, abc, \ldots, abcde\}$ included in T. Clearly we can see that 2^k patterns in a k-item tuple can be represented by only k nodes of ZBDDs. As well as generating tuple-histograms, we can generate pattern-histograms by accumulating such a single ZBDD P for a set of patterns one by one. Unfortunately, ZBDDs grows larger as repeating accumulations, and eventually may overflow the memory for some large examples. It is an interesting and important point how large-scale instances we can generate pattern-histograms. Table 1 and 2 are the experimental results for some of benchmark data[4]. We can generate a complete pattern-histogram for a medium size of example. Using sampling method, we can construct partial pattern-histograms for a number of tuples in the database.

As written in [9], our method is much more efficient than one of popular previous method *FP-Tree*[5], which extracts the set of frequent patterns appearing more than α times in the database. Especially when the α is small, so many patterns are extracted and ZBDD technique is quite effective.

3   VSOP Calculator

Based on ZBDD techniques, we developed an arithmetic calculator to handle large-scale sum-of-products expressions with a number of item symbols. This program, called VSOP, is an interpreter with a lexical and syntax parser for calculating *Valued-Sum-Of-Products* expressions, and displays the results in various formats. Here we briefly present the specification of VSOP.

VSOP has a C-shell-like interface, both for interactive keyboard inputs and batch style execution from a script file. It parses the script only from left to right. Neither branches nor loop controls are supported. An execution example and the list of basic operators are shown in Figure 13 and 14.

In VSOP scripts, we can use two kind of symbols, *item symbols* and *program variables*. Item symbols, denoted by strings starting with a lower-case letter, represent the items used in the set of combinations. Program variables, starting with an upper-case letter, are used to identify the memory to which a computation

```
***** VSOP (Valued Sum-Of-Products) calculator <v0.95> *****
vsop> symbol a b c d e
vsop> F = (a + 2 b)(c + d)
vsop> print F
 a c + a d + 2 b c + 2 b d
vsop> G = (2 a - d)(c - e)
vsop> print G
 2 a c - 2 a e - c d + d e
vsop> H = F * G
vsop> print H
 4 a b c d - 4 a b c e + 4 a b c
  - 4 a b d e + a c d e - 2 a c e
  + 2 a c - a d e + 2 b c d e - 4 b c d
  + 2 b d e
vsop> print /count H
   11
vsop> print /size H
   24 (35)
vsop> print H > 0
 a b c d + a b c + a c d e + a c
  + b c d e + b d e
vsop> print H / (c e)
 - 4 a b + a d - 2 a + 2 b d
vsop> exit
```

Fig. 13. Example of VSOP execution

($expr$)	Calculate first.
$expr$.MaxVal	Maximum coefficient value in $expr$.
$expr$.Items	Set of all item symbols in $expr$.
$expr_1$ $expr_2$	Multiplication.
$expr_1$ * $expr_2$	Multiplication.
$expr_1$ / $expr_2$	Quotient of division.
$expr_1$ % $expr_2$	Reminder of division.
$expr_1$ + $expr_2$	Addition.
$expr_1$ - $expr_2$	Subtraction.
$expr_1$ == $expr_2$	Set of product terms satisfying equation.
!= < <= > >=	(Inequities similarly to ==.)
$expr_1$? $expr_2$: $expr_3$	If $expr_1$ then exp_2 else $expr_3$.

Fig. 14. Basic operators in VSOP

result to be stored temporarily. We can describe multi-level expressions by using these two type of symbols, as shown in Fig. 13. Calculation results are displayed in expressions of including item symbols only, not using program variables. VSOP allows up to 65,510 different item symbols to be used, and no limit for program variables, as long as the ZBDD nodes are handled in the main memory.

VSOP supports not only set operations but also numerical arithmetic operations based on *Valued-Sum-Of-Products* algebra, where we can handle an integer coefficient (or weight) for each product term in the expression, as used in Fig. 13. In this algebra, the addition follows the ordinary rule: $1 + 1 = 2$ and $a + a = 2\,a$. However, multiplication rule is not conventional: $2 * 2 = 4$, $a * b = a\,b$, but $a * a = a$, because we only handle combinatorial item sets, not considering higher degree of item symbols. Notice that the same algebra is also used in calculating expressions of probabilistic variables.

VSOP also supports the division operation. If the divisor is a numerical constant, the division operation calculates the integer quotient (or reminder) for each coefficient of product terms in the dividend. If the divisor is a single item symbol x, the quotient extracts all product-terms including x and then eliminate x from each terms. The reminder means all product terms not including x in the dividend. The division operation is especially useful for database analysis applications.

Numerical comparison operation is another feature of VSOP. Using equations and inequities, we can extract all product terms whose coefficients satisfy the given condition. For example, the expression (F > 0) gives all positive-valued product-terms. (F == G) extracts the combinatorial item sets such that the corresponding coefficients are the same in F and G (except zero-coefficient). These comparison operations are useful to identify frequent item patterns in the histograms.

We cannot describe all feature of VSOP due to the space limit. Detailed data structures and algorithms of VSOP calculator are written in the articles[10][11]. Lastly we mention that VSOP gives us statistical information of the computation results. For example, `print /count F` shows the number of product terms in F. These computation time is linear to ZBDD size, not depend on the number of product terms. We can check the ZBDD size by `print /size F` .

4   Database Analysis Using VSOP Calculator

Here we show a typical example of using VSOP calculator for database analysis. In the previous section, we describe the method of generating tuple- and pattern- histograms based on ZBDD manipulation. Using a VSOP script, we can easily compose of the procedure of histogram computation and applying various analysis operations to the histogram data.

We show the case of analyzing a benchmark database "mushroom"[4]. This data file consists of 8,124 tuples of combinatorial items as the following format:

```
1 3 9 13 23 25 34 36 38 40 52 54 59 63 67 76 85 86 90 93 98 107 113
2 3 9 14 23 26 34 36 39 40 52 55 59 63 67 76 85 86 90 93 99 108 114
2 4 9 15 23 27 34 36 39 41 52 55 59 63 67 76 85 86 90 93 99 108 115
. . .
```

where each line represents one tuple and each number shows the item id. To generate the tuple-histogram using VSOP, we convert the file format according to the VSOP script syntax, as follows.

```
T = 0
T = T + x1 x3 x9 x13 x23 x25 x34 x36 x38 x40 x52 x54 x59 x63 x67 \
x76 x85 x86 x90 x93 x98 x107 x113
```

```
T = T + x2 x3 x9 x14 x23 x26 x34 x36 x39 x40 x52 x55 x59 x63 x67 \
x76 x85 x86 x90 x93 x99 x108 x114
. . .
```

After executing this script for all tuples, the variable T holds the tuple-histogram of "mushroom" database.

For generating the pattern-histogram, we may prepare the following script converted from original data file.

```
P = 0
P = P + (1+x1)(1+x3)(1+x9)(1+x13)(1+x23)(1+x25)(1+x34)(1+x36) \
(1+x38)(1+x40)(1+x52)(1+x54)(1+x59)(1+x63)(1+x67)(1+x76)(1+x85) \
(1+x86)(1+x90)(1+x93)(1+x98)(1+x107)(1+x113)
P = P + (1+x2)(1+x3)(1+x9)(1+x14)(1+x23)(1+x26)(1+x34)(1+x36) \
(1+x39)(1+x40)(1+x52)(1+x55)(1+x59)(1+x63)(1+x67)(1+x76)(1+x85) \
(1+x86)(1+x90)(1+x93)(1+x99)(1+x108)(1+x114)
. . .
```

Each line represents the set of all sub-patterns contained in one tuple. After execution of this script for all tuples, the variable P holds the pattern-histogram of "mushroom" database.

Once the histogram is generated, various queries can be applied as a sequence of VSOP operations. First, we can get the number of patterns registered in the histogram. Here we show an execution example for the pattern-hinstogarm of "mushroom".

```
vsop> source "ScriptForPatternHistogram"
vsop> print /count P
 5574930438
vsop> print /size P
 513762
```

Now we can see it consists of as much as 5,574,930,438 patterns, but only 513,762 ZBDD nodes are used for the histogram. This computation time is about 4 minutes in our 800MHz Pen4 PC with 512MB memory.

Next, we can get the number of frequent patterns which appear more than 1000, 100, and 10 times in the database, respectively.

```
vsop> print /count P > 1000*(P>0)
 123278
vsop> print /count P > 100*(P>0)
 66076586
vsop> print /count P > 10*(P>0)
 1662769668
```

We can also check the number of patterns including x1 x2, and x1, x3, respectively.

```
vsop> print /count (P / x1 x2)
  0
vsop> print /count (P / x1 x3)
  359793968
```

Here we can observe that the items x1 and x2 are completely exclusive in the database, but x1 and x3 coexist in a large number of patterns. We need only a few seconds for computing such queries after generating the histogram.

Besides the above examples, more various and complicated queries can be composed by using arithmetic operations of VSOP. This interface is very flexible and highly customizable for various problems. VSOP calculator will be useful especially for the first quick analysis for given instances without developing a real full-customized solver for the problem.

5   Conclusion

In this paper, we presented *VSOP* program developed for calculating combinatorial item sets specified by symbolic expressions. Based on ZBDD techniques, VSOP can efficiently handle large-scale sum-of-products expressions with a number of item symbols. VSOP supports not only Boolean set operations but also numerical arithmetic operations based on *Valued-Sum-Of-Products* algebra, such as addition, subtraction, multiplication, division, numerical comparison, etc. We presented a typical example of using VSOP for database analysis. VSOP will facilitate research and development for various area related to combinatorial problems.

Acknowledgment

The author thanks Prof. Arimura for his technical comments. This study is partly supported by JSPS Grant-in-Aid Scientific Research on Priority Area "Informatics" (Area #006) and Scientific Research (B), 2005, 17300041.

References

1. R. Agrawal, T. Imielinski, and A. N. Swami, Mining Association rules between sets of items in large databases, In P. Buneman and S. Jajodia, editors, *Proc. of the 1993 ACM SIGMOD International Conference on Management of Data*, Vol. 22(2) of SIGMOD Record, pp. 207–216, ACM Press, 1993.
2. Bryant, R. E., Graph-based algorithms for Boolean function manipulation, IEEE Trans. Comput., C-35, 8 (1986), 677–691.
3. B. Goethals "Survey on Frequent Pattern Mining" (Pdf) Manuscript, 2003: http://www.adrem.ua.ac.be/~goethals/publications/survey.ps
4. B. Goethals, M. Javeed Zaki (Eds.), Frequent Itemset Mining Dataset Repository, Frequent Itemset Mining Implementations (FIMI'03), 2003. http://fimi.cs.helsinki.fi/data/

5. J. Han, J. Pei, Y. Yin, R. Mao, Mining Frequent Patterns without Candidate Generation: A Frequent-Pattern Tree Approach, Data Mining and Knowledge Discovery, 8(1), 53–87, 2004.
6. S. Minato: Zero-suppressed BDDs for set manipulation in combinatorial problems, In Proc. 30th ACM/IEEE Design Automation Conf. (DAC-93), (1993), 272–277.
7. S. Minato: "Binary Decision Diagrams and Applications for VLSI CAD", Kluwer Academic Publishers, November 1996.
8. S. Minato, Zero-suppressed BDDs and Their Applications, International Journal on Software Tools for Technology Transfer (STTT), Springer, Vol. 3, No. 2, pp. 156–170, May 2001.
9. S. Minato and H. Arimura, Efficient Method of Combinatorial Item Set Analysis Based on Zero-Suppressed BDDs, In Proc. of IEEE International Workshop on Challenges in Web Information Retrieval and Integration (WIRI-2005), pp. 4–11, Apr. 2005.
10. S. Minato, VSOP (Valued-Sum-Of-Products) Calculator Based on Zero-Suppressed BDDs, TCS Technical Report Series A of Division of Computer Science, Hokkaido Univ., TCS-TR-A-05-3, May 2005. http://www-alg.ist.hokudai.ac.jp/tra.html
11. S. Minato, VSOP (Valued-Sum-Of-Products) Calculator for Knowledge Processing Based on Zero-Suppressed BDDs, in "Federation over the Web", LNAI series, Springer, 2006. (to appear)
12. Ricardo Baeza-Yates, Berthier Ribiero-Neto, "Modern Information Retrieval", Addison Wesley, 1999.
13. Ingo Wegener, Branching Programs and Binary Decision Diagrams, SIAM Monographs on Discrete Mathematics and Applications 4, 2000.
14. M. J. Zaki, Scalable Algorithms for Association Mining, IEEE Trans. Knowl. Data Eng. 12(2), 372–390, 2000.

Enumerating Minimally Revised Specifications Using Dualization

Ken Satoh and Takeaki Uno

National Institute of Informatics and Sokendai
ksatoh@nii.ac.jp, uno@nii.ac.jp

Abstract. We consider the problem of enumerating minimally revised specifications in software engineering in the situation where a new specification is added to the current specification and causes a conflict. We assume that a specification is expressed as a set of ground Horn clauses which is divided into two sets T_{pst} and T_{tmp} that are the unchangeable and changeable parts of the specification, respectively. Since a minimal revision is obtained by removing a minimal set of clauses from T_{tmp} so that the remaining set is consistent, our task can be restated as enumerating maximal consistent subsets of a given set of Horn clauses. Moreover, consistency property is monotone, that is, if a set of Horn clauses is consistent then every subset of the set is also consistent. Then, we can apply our previous method of enumerating maximal frequent sets in data mining which can be used for any enumeration for maximal subsets w.r.t. a monotone property. We show that our algorithm performs a dualization only once for an enumeration of maximal subsets, and the number of consistency checks is at most $|MinI_{T_{pst}}(T_{tmp})| + |MaxC_{T_{pst}}(T_{tmp})| \cdot |T_{tmp}|$ and the necessary space is $\mathrm{O}(\Sigma_{S \in MaxC_{T_{pst}}(T_{tmp})}|S|)$ where $|MinI_{T_{pst}}(T_{tmp})|$ is the number of minimal subsets of T_{tmp} that are inconsistent with T_{pst}, and $|MaxC_{T_{pst}}(T_{tmp})|$ is the number of maximal subsets of T_{tmp} that are consistent with T_{pst}.

1 Introduction

Software evolution is one of the most important issue in software engineering. The famous report [7] states that 75% of maintenance task in software industry are activities dealing with the following issues [1].

- Changes in the software environment.
- New user requirements.

In the current network environment of computers, the above correction/updates occurs frequently and therefore the research on software evolution becomes much more important.

When we change specification, we usually do not discard the whole specification, but we keep most part of specification which is irrelevant to the change, that is, we perform a *minimal revision* of the specification. For further motivation, see our previous papers [8, 9, 10, 11]. In this paper, we consider the problem

T. Washio et al. (Eds.): JSAI 2005 Workshops, LNAI 4012, pp. 182–189, 2006.

of enumerating minimally revised specifications in the situation where a new specification is added to the current specification and causes a conflict.

Since a minimal revision is obtained by removing a minimal set of clauses from T_{tmp} so that the remaining set is consistent, our task can be restated as enumerating maximal consistent subsets of a given set of clauses. Particularly, in this paper, we focus on Horn clauses, i.e., we assume that a specification is expressed as a set of Horn clauses which is divided into two sets T_{pst} and T_{tmp} that are the unchangeable and changeable parts of the specification, respectively. By restricting the clauses to be Horn, we obtain the following advantages.

- The consistency check can be done in linear time [2].
- Horn can represent many kinds of models.

Actually, the consistency check can be done in polynomial for the other classes, but they are often more than linear time. Moreover, Horn is a good class for representing the models in the real world applications. Thus, choosing Horn is good and reasonable for the model of our problem.

We have already proposed various methods of computing a minimally revised specification [8, 9, 10, 11]. In the previous research, we concentrate on completeness and correctness of these methods, but do not consider these methods from a view point of computational complexity. In this paper, we propose another algorithm to enumerate all minimally revised specifications and analyze the new algorithm in terms of computational complexity. Thus, this paper is regarded as a reinterpretation of the results of the method in the context of software maintenance.

Consistency of specifications is monotone, that is, if a specification is consistent, then every its subset is consistent. Then, we can apply our method [12, 14] of enumerating maximal frequent itemsets in data mining. For a given transaction database and a specified number θ, an itemset E is called frequent if E is included in at least θ transactions. An itemset included in no other frequent itemset is called maximal. The problem is to enumerate all the maximal frequent itemsets from the given transaction database for a specified θ. Actually, our method is for enumerating maximal subsets with respect to a monotone property. Since the set of all frequent itemsets is monotone, we could apply our method to the problem.

The feature of our method is that the method is based on depth-first search, thus we need no memory for previously obtained solutions. This reduces both the computation time and the memory use. Moreover, the enumeration method is less redundant than the existing method in practice, that is, the number of consistency checks is small. Thus, our method can be also applied to other problems efficiently, such as finding all minimal keys in a relational database and learning monotone boolean functions as pointed out in [5].

In a part of the algorithm, we use an incremental algorithm of computing minimal hitting sets [13], in other words, *dualization* of a monotone propositional formula. This usage of a new dualization algorithm drastically reduces the space complexity compared with the algorithm proposed in [3, 5]. Specifically, we show that the number of consistency checks is at most $|MinI_{T_{pst}}(T_{tmp})| +$

$|MaxC_{T_{pst}}(T_{tmp})| \cdot |T_{tmp}|$ and the necessary space is $O(\Sigma_{S \in MaxC_{T_{pst}}(T_{tmp})}|S|)$ where $|MinI_{T_{pst}}(T_{tmp})|$ is the number of minimal subsets of T_{tmp} which are inconsistent with T_{pst} and $|MaxC_{T_{pst}}(T_{tmp})|$ is the number of maximal subsets of T_{tmp} which are consistent with T_{pst}. Moreover, we perform a dualization only once for an enumeration of maximal subsets whereas the algorithms proposed in [3, 5] execute dualization $MaxC_{T_{pst}}(T_{tmp})$ times. Unfortunately, as far as the time complexity is concerned, our algorithm is not bounded by a polynomial w.r.t. the number of maximal subsets which satisfy a monotone property and the number of minimal subsets which does not satisfy the property while the algorithms of Gunopulos et al. have the bound of a quasi-polynomial. Experiments in [12], however, show that the computation time is proportional to the product of the number of maximal subsets and the number of minimal subsets.

Note that the problem attacked in this paper is equivalent to learning monotone DNF formulas with membership queries as [3] is pointed out. So, such learning algorithms is applicable to the problem in this paper. However, as far as the space complexity is concerned, our algorithm is the best algorithm so far.

2   Minimally Revised Specification

In this section, we review a definition of minimally revised logical specification [8]. We consider a function-free language and assume the unique name axioms and domain closure axioms for a logical specification and a logical specification is represented as a set of Horn clauses. We define a persistent part of a logical specification and a temporary part of a logical specification. The temporary part can be retracted in order to maintain consistency.

Definition 1. *A logical specification T is a pair $\langle T_{pst}, T_{tmp} \rangle$ where T_{pst} and T_{tmp} are sets of Horn clauses of the form:*

$B_1 \wedge B_2 \wedge ... \wedge B_l \supset H.$

where H is an atom or $\perp$[1], and $B_1, ..., B_l$ are atoms.
    We call T_{pst} a persistent part of T and T_{tmp} a temporary part of T.

T_{pst} is a part of the current specification which cannot be changed and T_{tmp} is a part of the current specification which can be changed.
    We define a minimally revised specification based on a maximal consistent subset of the logical specification defined as follows.

Definition 2. *Let S and T be a set of function-free Horn clauses. A maximal consistent subset of S w.r.t. T is a subset S' of S such that S' is consistent with T and no proper superset of S' is consistent with T.*

Lemma 1. *Let T be a logical specification $\langle T_{pst}, T_{tmp} \rangle$. Let $\Pi_{T_{tmp}}$ be a set of ground clauses obtained by replacing all variables in each clause in T_{tmp} by every*

---

[1] $\perp$ expresses contradiction.

constant in T. Let R_{new} be a clause. A minimally revised specification *w.r.t. T and R_{new} is $\langle T_{pst} \cup \{R_{new}\}, S \rangle$ such that S is a maximal consistent subset of $\Pi_{T_{tmp}}$ w.r.t. $T_{pst} \cup \{R_{new}\}$.*

The minimally revised specification is such a specification in that ground instances of T_{tmp} which cause contradiction are minimally removed.

3   Enumerating Minimally Revised Specification

The above minimally revised specification can be computed by considering minimally revised specification of all the ground instances of the specification which can be regarded as propositional specification. Therefore, in the sequel, we only consider a propositional specification for brevity. In other words, we regards $\Pi_{T_{tmp}}$ as T_{tmp}. Moreover, we regard $T_{pst} \cup \{R_{new}\}$ as T_{pst} and consider every maximal consistent set of T_{tmp} w.r.t. the new T_{pst}. Here we assume that T_{pst} is consistent. Let $MaxC_{T_{pst}}(T_{tmp})$ be the set of all maximal consistent set of T_{tmp} w.r.t. T_{pst}. In this paper, we consider an enumeration algorithm of $MaxC_{T_{pst}}(T_{tmp})$ in the condition only consistency check is available as an oracle, and try to reduce the number of consistency checks.

For our new enumeration algorithm, we use the property of consistency called *monotonicity* meaning that, for any logical specification, if the persistent part and a subset S of temporary part is consistent, then any subset of S is also consistent with the persistent part.

Definition 3. *Let T be a logical specification $\langle T_{pst}, T_{tmp} \rangle$. Let S_1 and S_2 be any subsets of T_{tmp}. If $S_1 \subseteq S_2$ and S_2 is consistent w.r.t. T_{pst}, then S_1 is consistent w.r.t. T_{pst}.*

Enumeration methods of such sets with monotonicity using a minimal hitting set computation, or in other words, a dualization, have been proposed [3,5,12,14] and we consider an application of these methods to the task of the paper.

For our algorithm, we need the following definitions of *minimal inconsistent subset* and *minimal hitting set*.

Definition 4. *Let S and T be a set of function-free Horn clauses. A* minimal inconsistent subset *of S w.r.t. T is a subset of S, S' such that S' is inconsistent with T and there is no subset of S, S'' such that S'' is inconsistent with T and $S'' \subset S'$. (S'' is a proper subset of S'.)*

Definition 5. *Let H be a finite set and $\mathcal{H}$ be a set of some subsets of H. A* hitting set *HS of $\mathcal{H}$ is a set s.t. for every $S \in \mathcal{H}$, $S \cap HS \neq \emptyset$. A* minimal hitting set *HS of $\mathcal{H}$ is a hitting set s.t. there exists no other hitting set HS' of $\mathcal{H}$ s.t. $HS' \subset HS$ (HS' is a proper subset of HS). We denote the set of all minimal hitting sets of $\mathcal{H}$ as $MHS(\mathcal{H})$.*

Let T be a logical specification $\langle T_{pst}, T_{tmp} \rangle$. We denote the set of all minimal consistent subsets of T_{tmp} that are inconsistent with T_{pst} as $MinI_{T_{pst}}(T_{tmp})$.

Then, by interpreting the result in [6] to our task, we can show that there is a relationship between $MaxC_{T_{pst}}(T_{tmp})$ and $MinI_{T_{pst}}(T_{tmp})$ through a minimal hitting set.

Let S be a subset of T_{tmp}. We represent the complement set of S as $\overline{S}$. Let $\mathcal{S}$ be a set of sets. We represent $\{\overline{S}|S \in \mathcal{S}\}$ as $\overline{\mathcal{S}}$. We recall that $\bar{S} = T_{tmp} \setminus S$.

Proposition 1. *Let T be a logical specification $\langle T_{pst}, T_{tmp}\rangle$. $MinI_{T_{pst}}(T_{tmp}) = MHS(\overline{MaxC_{T_{pst}}(T_{tmp})})$.*

A subset S of T_{tmp} is included in a maximal consistent subset M of $MaxC_{T_{pst}}(T_{tmp})$ if and only if $S \cap \overline{M} = \emptyset$. Thus, S is inconsistent if and only if S intersects the complement of any $M \in MaxC_{T_{pst}}(T_{tmp})$, i.e., S is a hitting set. Therefore we have this proposition.

Moreover, by adapting the result in [3, 5] to our task, the following holds.

Proposition 2. *Let T be a logical specification $\langle T_{pst}, T_{tmp}\rangle$ and $Bd^+ \subseteq MaxC_{T_{pst}}(T_{tmp})$. Then, for every $S \in MHS(\overline{Bd^+})$, either $S \in MinI_{T_{pst}}(T_{tmp})$ or S is consistent with T_{pst}.*

This proposition says that S never be a non-minimal inconsistent subset. This is because that if S includes an inconsistent subset S' of a smaller size, then Bd^+ must includes a maximal consistent subset including S', contradiction.

Suppose that we find a subset of maximal consistent subsets, Bd^+. By Proposition 1, if every set in $MHS(\overline{Bd^+})$ is a minimal inconsistent subset, then we are done. Otherwise, by Proposition 2, there is some consistent set with T_{pst} in $MHS(\overline{Bd^+})$. Then, starting from such a consistent set and adding each Horn clause in T_{tmp} one by one to the consistent set, we can reach a maximal consistent subset with T_{pst}. Then, we augment Bd^+ by the newly found maximal consistent subset and continue this process. Since the number of the maximal consistent subsets is finite, we eventually enumerate $MaxC_{T_{pst}}(T_{tmp})$. This is the algorithm adapted from the one proposed in [3]. However, if we use the algorithm, it checks every set in $MHS(\overline{Bd^+})$ at every iteration step whether the set is consistent or not and so, it might make the same redundant consistency checks which have been already found to be inconsistent in the previous iteration steps. Therefore, the algorithm needs $|MaxC_{T_{pst}}(T_{tmp})|(|MinI_{T_{pst}}(T_{tmp})| + |T_{tmp}|)$ consistency checks in the worst case.

However, using the following proposition found in [12], we can enumerate maximal consistent sets without the above redundant consistency checks.

Proposition 3. *Let T be $\langle T_{pst}, T_{tmp}\rangle$ and Bd_1^+ and Bd_2^+ be subsets of $MaxC_{T_{pst}}(T_{tmp})$. If $Bd_1^+ \subseteq Bd_2^+$ then*

$$MHS(\overline{Bd_1^+}) \cap MinI_{T_{pst}}(T_{tmp}) \subseteq MHS(\overline{Bd_2^+}) \cap MinI_{T_{pst}}(T_{tmp}).$$

This proposition means that if S is a minimal inconsistent subset in $MHS(\overline{Bd_1^+})$, then S keeps being a minimal inconsistent subset by adding any newly found maximal consistent subset to Bd_1^+. A minimal hitting set S' in $MHS(\overline{Bd_1^+})$

disappears by adding new maximal consistent subset M to Bd_1^+ if and only if M includes S', and we know that M never include inconsistent subset S.

Suppose that we find a new maximal consistent S and compute $MHS(\overline{Bd^+} \cup \{S\})$. By the above Proposition 3, every minimal inconsistent subsets of $MHS(\overline{Bd^+})$ is a minimal inconsistent subset in $MHS(\overline{Bd^+} \cup \{S\})$. Therefore, once a minimal inconsistent subset is found, we do not need to check consistency of the subset again since the subset is inconsistent forever. We utilize this property and propose the algorithm in Fig. 1. The algorithm does not contain any redundant consistency check for a minimal inconsistent subset and also we do not need a space for memorizing a set of inconsistency subsets. This is realized by using the irredundant minimal hitting set computation [13]. Refer to [12, 14] for the detailed analysis.

We can show the upper bound of the number of consistency checks for the algorithm as follows. For every call of $find\_maximal\_superset(S)$, we make at most $|T_{tmp}|$ times of consistency checks and the number of calls of

---

global A set of Horn Clauses T_{pst}, T_{tmp};
global integer $bdpnum$; sets bd_0^+, bd_1^+ ....;
main()
begin
  $bdpnum := 0$;
  $construct\_bdp(0, \emptyset)$;
  output all the $bd_j^+ (0 \le j \le bdpnum)$.
end

$construct\_bdp(i, mhs)$
begin
  if $i == bdpnum$ **then goto** 1 **else goto** 2

  1. **if** mhs is inconsistent with T_{pst} **then return**;
      $bd_{bdpnum}^+ := find\_maximal\_superset(mhs)$;
      $bdpnum := bdpnum + 1$;
      /* proceed to 2 */
  2. **if** $\overline{bd_i^+} \cap mhs \ne \emptyset$ **then** $construct\_bdp(i + 1, mhs)$;
      else for every $e \in \overline{bd_i^+}$ s.t.
            $mhs \cup \{e\}$ is a minimal hitting set of $\{\overline{bd_0^+}, \overline{bd_1^+} ..., \overline{bd_i^+}\}$
        do $construct\_bdp(i + 1, mhs \cup \{e\})$;
      return;

end

$find\_maximal\_superset(S)$

  1. **for** each element e in $T_{tmp} \backslash S$ **do**
     if $S \cup \{e\}$ is consistent with T_{pst} **then** $S := S \cup \{e\}$
  2. **return** S

Fig. 1. Algorithm of enumerating maximal consistent subsets

$find\_maximal\_superset(S)$ is at most $|MaxC_{T_{pst}}(T_{tmp})|$. Also, for every minimal inconsistent subset, we make exactly one consistency check and so, the number of consistency checks for minimal inconsistent subsets is at most $|MinI_{T_{pst}}(T_{tmp})|$. Therefore, we have the following theorem.

Theorem 1. *The algorithm in Fig. 1 enumerates $MaxC_{T_{pst}}(T_{tmp})$ with at most $|MinI_{T_{pst}}(T_{tmp})| + |MaxC_{T_{pst}}(T_{tmp})| \cdot |T_{tmp}|$ consistency checks.*

Moreover, the space complexity of our algorithm is $O(\Sigma_{S \in MaxC_{T_{pst}}(T_{tmp})}|S|)$. This is because we have to store only a set of maximal consistent sets to compute every minimal hitting set of these maximal consistent sets.

In [5], Gunopulos et al. proposed a revised algorithm from the one in [3] so that the revised algorithm remembers a set of minimal inconsistent subsets and avoids redundant consistency checks by checking whether it is in the set of minimal inconsistent subsets or not before the consistency check[2]. Then, the revised algorithm has the same query complexity as our algorithm. However, if we used their revised algorithm we would still need a space for remembering not only maximal consistent sets but also inconsistent subsets and need to perform a membership check for the set.

4   Conclusion

The contributions of this work are as follows.

- We give an algorithm to enumerate all minimally revised specifications using an irredundant dualization algorithm.
- We give an analysis of complexities of the algorithm in that we show that the number of consistency checks is at most
  $|MinI_{T_{pst}}(T_{tmp})| + |MaxC_{T_{pst}}(T_{tmp})| \cdot |T_{tmp}|$ and the necessary space is
  $O(\Sigma_{S \in MaxC_{T_{pst}}(T_{tmp})}|S|)$.

As future research, we need to implement an efficient consistency check and apply this method to problems in the real domain.

Acknowledgments. This research is partly supported by Grant-in-Aid for Scientific Research Priority Area "Informatics". We would be very grateful for useful comments by anonymous referees.

References

1. Bennett, K. H., Rjlich, V. T., "Software Maintenance and Evolution: A Road Map", The Future of Software Engineering, Special Volume published in conjunction with ICSE 2000, pp. 75 – 87 (2000).
2. Dowling, W. F., Gallier, J., H., "Linear-Time Algorithms for Testing the Satisfiability of Propositional Horn Formulae", J. Log. Program. 1(3), pp. 267 – 284 (1984).

---

[2] This modification was independently proposed by Carlos Domingo [4].

3. Gunopulos, D., Khardon, R., Mannila, H. and Toivonen, H., Data mining, Hypergraph Transversals, and Machine Learning, *Proc. of PODS'97*, pp. 209 – 216 (1997).
4. Domingo, C., "Concept Learning: Theory, Applications and Related Problems", Doctoral Dissertation, Universitat Politechnica de Catalunya (1998).
5. Gunopulos, D., Khardon, R., Mannila, H., Saluja, S., Toivonen, H., Sharm, R., S., "Discovering all most specific sentences", ACM Trans. Database Syst. 28(2), pp. 140 – 174 (2003).
6. Mannila, H. and Toivonen, T., "On an Algorithm for Finding All Interesting Sentences", *Cybernetics and Systems, Vol II, The Thirteen European Meeting on Cybernetics and Systems Research*, pp. 973 – 978 (1996).
7. Lientz, B. P., and Swanson, E. B., Software Maintenance Management, Addison Wesley (1980).
8. Satoh, K., Computing Minimal Revised Logic Program by Abduction, *Proc. of the International Workshop on the Principles of Software Evolution*, pp. 177 – 182 (1998).
9. Satoh, K., "Consistency Management in Software Engineering by Abduction", Proceedings of the ICSE-2000 Workshop on Intelligent Software Engineering, pp. 90 – 99, Limerick, Ireland (2000).
10. Satoh, K., "Computing Minimal Belief Revision by Extended Logic Programming without Minimality Check", Proceedings of IJCAI-01 Workshop on Abductive Reasoning, pp. 48 – 55 (2001).
11. Satoh, K., "Computing Minimal Revised Specifications by Default Logic", Proc. of Workshop on Intelligent Technologies in Software Engineering (WITSE2003) pp. 7 – 12 (2003).
12. Satoh, K., and Uno, T., "Enumerating Maximal Frequent Sets Using Irredundant Dualization", Proc. of 6th International Conference on Discovery Science (DS2003), LNAI 2843, pp. 256 – 268 (2003)
13. Uno, T., "A Practical Fast Algorithm for Enumerating Minimal Set Coverings", *SIGAL83*, Information Processing Society of Japan, pp. 9 – 16 (in Japanese) (2002).
14. Uno, T., Satoh, K., "Detailed Description of an Algorithm for Enumeration of Maximal Frequent Sets with Irredundant Dualization", Online CEUR Workshop Proceedings of the ICDM 2003 Workshop on Frequent Itemset Mining Implementations (FIMI 2003), `http://sunsite.informatik.rwth-aachen.de/Publications/CEUR-WS//Vol-90/satoh.pdf` (2003)

Acquiring Configuration Rules of Form Elements from "Historic" Architectural Facade Employing Inductive Logic Programming

Atsushi Saito, Junzo Munemoto, and Daisuke Matsushita

Department of Architecture and Architectural Engineering, Graduate School of Engineering,
Kyoto University, C2, Kyotodaigaku-katsura, Nishikyo-ku, Kyoto, Japan
{ap.saito, munemoto, matsushi}@archi.kyoto-u.ac.jp

Abstract. A summary of application of an ILP technique to the study of architectural facades design is presented. We focused on discovering the configuration rules of form elements in the architectural facade elevations evaluated as "historic". We obtained supervisory data based on the record of Sanneizaka Preservation District for Groups of Historic Buildings archived in the Kyoto City Planning Bureau. Architectural objects were converted into simple geometric form elements based on their positional relationships. By employing Progol, an ILP application, we acquired 27 resulting sets of configuration rules.

1 Introduction

This paper reports on the application of ILP to the analysis of design in architecture. The evaluation of building facades as "historic" is very ambiguous and its mechanism is not explicit. The concept of "historic" in a facade is generally judged on the basis of the presence or absence of form elements, and the geometric interrelations among several form elements. In general, a facade is regarded as an elevated two-dimensional graphic. A facade contains many form elements of various types and shapes. These form elements are connected by geometric relations. The conventional analytical method, which greatly depends on human subjectivity, is excellent for a comprehensive evaluation of a facade but is not suitable for checking inherent rules in an objective manner. This paper presents a method of acquiring inherent rules from representative cases employing Inductive Logic Programming (ILP), a framework for machine learning. By learning based on inductive inference, rules for forming a target concept are acquired from positive cases for the target concept and negative cases against it, which are set up as logical expressions for computer processing. In looking at architectural design, acquiring configuration rules from the interrelations between form elements inherent to historic facade could be useful in obtaining a certain level of agreement about what "historic" means in this sense. The historic area under study was the Preservation District for Groups of Historic Buildings, Kyoto, Japan. When a building in this district is not regarded as "historic" by the Urban Planning Bureau of Kyoto City, the building is to be repaired or remodeled with administrative guidance based on appearance standards stipulated in law. But authorities rely on implicit knowledge as well as appearance standards, which only explains to specific examples. Therefore, we tried to acquire rules between the positive cases, facades after repair or remodeling, and the negative cases, facades before repair or remodeling.

T. Washio et al. (Eds.): JSAI 2005 Workshops, LNAI 4012, pp. 190–200, 2006.

2 Purpose and Method

The facade is substituted with a simplified planar graphic model. The purpose is to develop a method for acquiring the configuration rules of form elements inherent in "historic" facades and to describe them explicitly using logical expressions. This paper looks at the Sanneizaka Preservation District for Groups of Historic Buildings in Kyoto, Japan (hereinafter called the Sanneizaka Preservation District). We prepare positive and negative cases by creating a facade database from the results of surveys on building facades from 1999 to 2000 and from 2002 to 2003, from a report of surveys on the Sanneizaka Preservation District covering from 1994 to 1995, and from repair and remodeling records of the past 10 years (1993 to 2003) archived at the Urban Planning Bureau of Kyoto City. Through machine learning by ILP on these positive and negative cases, rules are acquired that identify a building as "historic" as determined by the authorities. The acquired rules are collated from data on "Historic buildings" in the Sanneizaka Preservation District and are compared with standards stipulated in regulations of the Sanneizaka Preservation District in order to discuss the effectiveness of the proposed method.

3 Outline of the Sanneizaka Preservation District

The Sanneizaka Preservation District was designated as a Preservation Districts for Groups of Historic buildings in June 1976[1]. In September this year, the Agency for Cultural Affairs designated the district as an Important District. In the Sanneizaka Preservation District, authorities are now giving administrative guidance on building activities[2]. In particular, "Historic buildings" are being maintained or repaired according to appearance standards stipulated in the Preservation Plan of the Sanneizaka Preservation District. "Non-historic buildings" are being maintained or remodeled according to appearance standards stipulated in a preservation plan to harmonize aesthetically with the "Historic buildings".

4 Creation of Facade Data

4.1 Field Survey

In the Sanneizaka Preservation District, a survey on building facades was conducted from June 1999 to January 2000 and an additional survey from November 2002 to March 2003. The survey subjects were "Historic buildings" and "Non-historic buildings" in the Sanneizaka Preservation District. A total of 344 buildings were

---

[1] The following regulations are related to the Sanneizaka Preservation District. The Kyoto Municipal Regulation on Preservation Districts for Groups of Historic Buildings (Enacted on June 8, 1976), the Kyoto Municipal Regulation on Ease of Building Restrictions in Preservation Districts for Groups of Historic Buildings (Enacted on April 1, 1996), the Preservation Plan for the Sanneizaka Preservation Districts for Groups of Historic Buildings (Kyoto City Notice No.69, enacted on July 1, 1976 and revised on December 20, 1995).

[2] In the Sanneizaka Preservation District, 14 building styles are defined, and are regulated by individual standards for the structures, roofs and eaves, walls, materials, and other features.

surveyed. From images of the building facades and the measured numeric data obtained by the survey, the types and coordinate data of form elements considered to represent the facade were acquired.

4.2 Targeted Information

In this paper, roofs, eaves, windows, doors, and entrances/exits are regarded as the form elements of walls. These are the major forms elements when the facade is considered as a two-dimensional graphic. The form elements are common in the Sanneizaka Preservation District and can be handled as individual common elements. Among the form element information, the subjects of this paper are narrowed down with respect to the types and locations of the form elements.

4.3 Creation of Facade Model

To create a database, a facade model is created (Fig.1). The facade of this model is segmented into the second floor roof (s_roof), second floor wall (s_wall), mezzanine wall (sh_wall), first floor roof (f_roof), and first floor wall (f_wall). Form elements of each segment are called "objects" here. For easy handling, the objects are bounded into rectangles. Each segment can be regarded as a set of objects and the set of segments is considered to form the facade elevation.

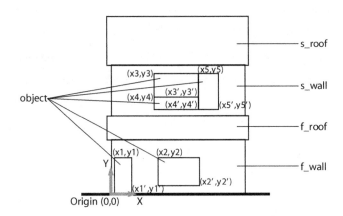

Fig. 1. Facade model

4.4 Conversion into Logical Expressions

To prepare modeled graphic information for input to ILP, the graphic coordinate data is converted into logical expressions. A module program for recognizing the geometric relations from graphic information was created and converted using Prolog[3]. Fig.2 shows the basic geometric relations contained in the graphic information.

---

[3] Prolog is a programming language developed by Alain Colmerauer on the basis of predicate logic. In this paper, one of the versions of Prolog, IF-Prolog 5.2a, was used.

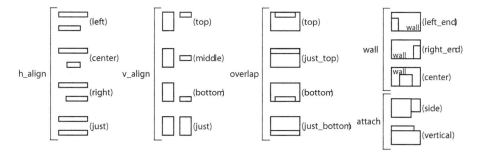

Fig. 2. Geometrical relation included in figure information

4.5 Extraction of Attributes

Attributes for the form elements, necessary for inductive inference, were extracted from the results of the aforementioned surveys on building facades, the report of surveys on Sanneizaka Preservation District from 1994 to 1995 [2], and the repair and remodeling records of the past 10 years (1993 to 2003) archived at the Urban Planning Bureau of Kyoto City.

We aimed to extract architectural terms that were already widely accepted, common to buildings in the Sanneizaka Preservation District, and that could be handled as individual elements in the district. As a result, 65 attributes of 7 classes were extracted as form elements (Fig.3).

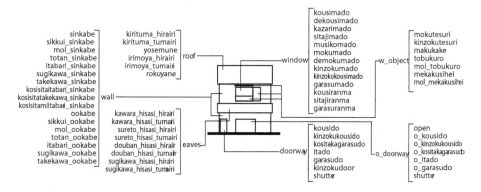

Fig. 3. Attributes extracted as architectural element

5 Employing ILP

5.1 Input Data to ILP

For inductive inference, this paper employs Progol[4], which is an ILP system. In this case, the goal for machine learning by inductive inference is to recognize a facade

---

[4] Progol is an ILP system developed by Stephen Muggleton et al. In this paper, one version of Progol, Progol 4.2.1, was used.

Case before it repairs or remodels   Case after it repairs or remodels

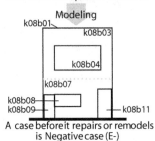

Modeling   Modeling

A case before it repairs or remodels   A case after it repairs or remodels
is Negative case (E-)   is Positive case (E+)

```
style(k08b,sounikaidate).

object(k08b01,rokuyane).

object(k08b03,mol_ookabe).

object(k08b04,kinzokumado).
part(k08b04,k08b03,ws_center).

object(k08b07,mol_ookabe).

object(k08b08,kinzokumado).
relation(k08b08,k08b09,attach,side).
relation(k08b08,k08b09,v_align,top)

object(k08b09,kinzokutobira).
part(k08b09,k08b07,wf_sideend,left).
relation(k08b09,k08b08,attach,side).
relation(k08b09,k08b08,v_align,top)

object(k08b11,kinzokutobira).
part(k08b11,k08b03,wf_sideend,right).
```

```
style(k08a,sounikaidate_hirairi).

object(k08a01,kirituma_hirairi).

object(k08a02,kawara_hisasi_hirairi).

object(k08a03,sinkabe).

object(k08a04,kousimado).
part(k08a04,k08a03,ws_center).
relation(k08a04,k08a11,h_align,right).

object(k08a07,kosisitamiitabari_sinkabe).

object(k08a08,dekousimado).
relation(k08a08,k08a09,attach,side).
relation(k08a08,k08a10,attach,side).
relation(k08a08,k08a10,v_align,bottom).

object(k08a09,kousido).
part(k08a09,k08a07,wf_sideend,left).
relation(k08a09,k08a08,attach,side).
relation(k08a09,k08a10,v_align,top).
relation(k08a09,k08a11,v_align,just).

object(k08a10,kousimado).
relation(k08a10,k08a08,attach,side).
relation(k08a10,k08a11,attach,side).
relation(k08a10,k08a08,v_align,bottom).
relation(k08a10,k08a09,v_align,top).
relation(k08a10,k08a11,v_align,top).

object(k08a11,kousido).
relation(k08a11,k08a10,attach,side).
relation(k08a11,k08a09,v_align,just).
relation(k08a11,k08a10,v_align,top).
```

Annotation
The description of the logical expression
of facade k08 was shown as an example.
The description shows the case before it
guides it by the administration and the
case after it guides it.

The configuration rules of form elements inherent in "historic" facade are extracted by employing IL P

```
:- object(A,makukake), relation(A,B,h_align,left), object(B,ka.....
:- object(A,makukake), relation(A,B,h_align,center), object(B,.....
:- relation(A,B,v_align,top), object(B,kousido), relation(B,C,.....
:- relation(A,B,wf_sideend,left), object(B,kousido), relation(.....
:- relation(A,B,ws_center,center), relation(B,C,h_align,center.....
                                    .
                                    .
```

Fig. 4. Outline chart until extracting facade rules

regarded as "historic" by the authorities. For inductive inference, positive and negative cases for the goal concept are given. Moreover, general knowledge is given as a background. Employing ILP, rules are acquired that are true in the positive cases and false in the negative cases.

The input data is obtained from the results of surveys on building facades and the report of a survey on the Sanneizaka Preservation District from 1994 to 1995 [2], as well as the repair and remodeling records of the past 10 years (1993 to 2003) archived at the Urban Planning Bureau of Kyoto City. As mentioned before, the appearance of "Historic buildings" are maintained or repaired according to guidelines of the Urban Planning Bureau of Kyoto City that also regulate the appearance of "Nonhistoric buildings" to harmonize with the surrounding views. Therefore, a facade after repair or remodeling was described as a positive case (E+) and a facade before repair or remodeling was described as a negative case (E-). By learning, facade rules are extracted from these positive and negative cases according to the administrative guidelines of the Historic Building Preservation System (Fig.4).

5.2 Description of Cases

Cases are described using a predicate "pattern" as follows:

```
Positive case (E+): pattern (ID)

Negative case (E-): -pattern (ID)
```

Detailed information about each case is described by "style" (two-place predicate), "object" (two-place predicate), "part" (four-place predicate), and "relation" (four-place predicate) as follows:

```
Appearance type: style(ID,style_type)

Element type: object(ID,object_type)

Element position: part(ID,ID,part_type,position)

Geometric relation: relation(ID,ID,relation_type,align_point)
```

The "ID" in the first and second places of the above expressions represent the ID number given to each object. A basic word giving the appearance type is assigned to "style_type" and a word representing a form element in Fig.3 is assigned to "object_type". To "part_type", "position", "relation_type", and "align_point", results acquired by the conversion method of Section 4.4 are assigned. Fig.4 shows an example of converting a facade into logical expressions.

6   Results and Discussion

6.1 Results

Machine learning produced 27 rules in total: 15 rules for a full two-storied building, 9 rules for a transformed two-storied building, and 3 rules for a semi two-storied building (Table1). The appearance rate indicates how often a rule acquired by machine learning appears in "Historic buildings" which have been preserved.

Under the administrative guidelines, in addition to the appearance standards set by the Sanneizaka Preservation District plan [10], architectural style reference drawings [11] are presented. We analyzed rules acquired for the appearance standards of the Sanneizaka Preservation District plan (hereinafter, the appearance standards) as well as for the architectural style reference drawings (hereinafter, the reference drawings). In Table 1, the symbol "Y" indicates that the acquired rule is included in the appearance standards and reference drawings, "N" means indicates the acquired rule is not included, and "Y+" indicates that more detailed information than given by the appearance standards and reference drawings is available.

Of the acquired rules, 19 rules (70.4%) conformed to the appearance standards and reference drawings. This indicates the considerable influence of the appearance standards and reference drawings given by the authorities. Of the 19 rules, 13 rules (68.4%) had more detailed information than the appearance standards and reference drawings. Further, 8 of the acquired rules (29.6%) were not included in the appearance standards or reference drawings. These results indicate that these rules may describe "historic" appearances but may not always be included explicitly in the appearance standards or reference drawings. Using the proposed method, more detailed information than that given by the appearance standards and reference drawings could be acquired.

6.2   The Facades of Full Two-Storied Buildings

For the facades of full two-storied buildings, 15 rules were acquired as follows:

Rules for the second floor: 2 (r1 and r2)

Rules for the first floor: 8 (r3, r4, r6, r8, r9, r10, r11, r12, and r14)

Rules for inter-element relations: 5 (r5, r7, r13, and r15)

The acquired rules are described below.

Rules for the Second Floor: Rules r1 (50.0%) and r2 (50.0%) indicate a feature where the form elements of the second floor wall are arranged with reference to the center. Rule r1 indicates the feature where the form elements of the second floor wall are centered. Rule r2 indicates the feature where windows in the second floor walls are side-justified with other form elements.

Rules for the First Floor: Rules r3 (39.3%) and r4 (35.7%) indicate the feature where the form elements of the first floor walls are top-justified with entrances/exits.

Rules r8 (17.9%), r9 (14.3%), r10 (14.3%), and r14 (3.6%) do not describe the first floor walls directly but are related to the features of doors and entrances/exits and are therefore related to the first floor walls. Rules r9, r10, and r14 indicate features where lattice doors are combined with related additional form elements and are centered or side-justified.

Rules r6 (28.6%), r8 (17.9%), and r11 (14.3%) indicate features where elements such as entrances/ exits and openings are centered. Rules r6 and r11 indicate features where entrances/exits and openings are arranged at the centers of walls. Rule r8 indicates the feature where openings are combined with other form elements and are centered.

Table 1. Description of positive and negative cases

Rule No.	Agreement to standards	Description of acquired rule	Pattern Diagrams of rule	Appearance rate in Historic building
r1	Y+	pattern(A):-style(A,sounikaidate), object(B,kirituma_hirairi), part(C,D,ws_center,center), relation(D,E,h_align,center)		50.0%
r2	Y+	pattern(A):-style(A,sounikaidate), object(B,kirituma_hirairi), part(C,D,ws_center,center), object(D,mokumado), relation(D,E,h_align,just)		50.0%
r3	Y+	pattern(A):-style(A,sounikaidate), object(B,kirituma_hirairi), object(C,kousido), relation(C,D,v_align,top), relation(C,E,v_align,just), relation(D,E,v_align,top)		39.3%
r4	Y+	pattern(A):-style(A,sounikaidate), object(B,kirituma_hirairi), part(C,D,wf_sideend,left), object(D,kousido), relation(D,E,v_align,top)		35.7%
r5	N	pattern(A):-style(A,sounikaidate), object(B,kirituma_hirairi), object(C,tobukuro), relation(C,D,v_align,top)		35.7%
r6	Y	pattern(A):-style(A,sounikaidate), object(B,kirituma_hirairi), part(C,D,wf_center,center), object(D,open)		28.6%
r7	Y+	pattern(A):-style(A,sounikaidate), object(B,kirituma_hirairi), object(C,mokumado), relation(C,D,v_align,bottom), object(D,mokumado), relation(C,E,h_align,just)		25.0%
r8	N	pattern(A):-style(A,sounikaidate), object(B,kirituma_hirairi), object(C,open), relation(C,D,h_align,center)		17.9%
r9	Y+	pattern(A):-style(A,sounikaidate), object(B,kirituma_hirairi), object(C,kousido), relation(C,D,h_align,just)		14.3%
r10	Y+	pattern(A):-style(A,sounikaidate), object(B,kirituma_hirairi), object(C,kousido), relation(C,D,h_align,center)		14.3%
r11	Y+	pattern(A):-style(A,sounikaidate), object(B,kirituma_hirairi), part(C,D,wf_center,center), object(D,o_garasudo)		14.3%
r12	Y+	pattern(A):-style(A,sounikaidate), object(B,kirituma_hirairi), part(C,D,wf_sideend,left), object(D,kousido), relation(D,E,h_align,just)		10.7%
r13	N	pattern(A):-style(A,sounikaidate), object(B,kirituma_hirairi), object(C,kousiranma), relation(C,D,h_align,center), object(D,makukake)		3.6%
r14	Y+	pattern(A):-style(A,sounikaidate), object(B,kirituma_hirairi), object(C,kousido), relation(C,D,v_align,top), relation(C,E,h_align,just)		3.6%
r15	N	pattern(A):-style(A,sounikaidate), object(B,kirituma_hirairi), object(C,makukake), relation(C,D,h_align,right), object(D,kazarimado)		3.6%
r16	Y	pattern(A):-style(A,henkeinikaidate), relation(B,C,h_align,left)		82.8%
r17	Y	pattern(A):-style(A,henkeinikaidate), part(B,C,ws_sideend,right)		55.1%
r18	N	pattern(A):-style(A,henkeinikaidate), object(B,douban_hisasi_hirairi)		34.5%
r19	Y+	pattern(A):-style(A,henkeinikaidate), object(B,kousido), relation(B,C,h_align,just)		34.5%
r20	N	pattern(A):-style(A,henkeinikaidate), object(B,yusemune)		31.0%
r21	Y+	pattern(A):-style(A,henkeinikaidate), part(B,C,ws_sideend,left), relation(C,D,h_align,just)		27.6%
r22	Y+	pattern(A):-style(A,henkeinikaidate), part(B,C,wf_sideend,right), relation(C,D,h_align,right)		24.1%
r23	N	pattern(A):-style(A,henkeinikaidate), part(B,C,wf_center,center)		17.2%
r24	N	pattern(A):-style(A,henkeinikaidate), object(B,douban_hisasi_hirairi), relation(B,C,h_align,center)		10.3%
r25	Y	pattern(A):-style(A,chunikaidate), object(B,kirituma_hirairi), part(C,D,ws_center,center)		45.5%
r26	Y	pattern(A):-style(A,chunikaidate), object(B,kirituma_hirairi), part(C,D,wf_sideend,left)		36.4%
r27	Y	pattern(A):-style(A,chunikaidate), object(B,kirituma_hirairi), relation(C,D,h_align,center)		36.4%

Annotation

The rule concerning full two-storied buildings is shown to rule number r1-r15, and the rule concerning transformed two-storied buildings is shown r16-r24 and even r25-r27 shows the rule concerning semi two-storied buildings.

Underline part in the description shows the description parts of information not included in the standards and the architectural style reference drawings.

Rules r4 (35.7%) and r12 (10.7%) indicate the feature where entrances/exits are arranged at the left side of the first floor walls. Rule r4 indicates the feature where entrances/exits arranged at the left side of the first floor walls are top-justified with other form elements. Rule r12 indicates the feature where lattice doors arranged on the left side of the first floor walls are side-justified with other form elements and where the lattice doors or entrances/exits are combined with related additional form elements, as described by Rules r9, r10, and r14 mentioned before.

Rules for Inter-Element Relations: Rules r5 (35.7%) and r7 (25.0%) indicate the feature where windows and window-related form elements are bottom-justified.

6.3   The Facades of Transformed Two-Storied Building

For the facades of transformed two-storied buildings, nine rules were acquired as follows:

Rules for the second floor: 2 (r17 and r21)

Rules for the first floor: 3 (r19, r22, and r23)

Rules for inter-element relations: 1 (r16)

Rules for the elements themselves: 3 (r18, r20, and r24)

The acquired rules are described below.

Rules for the Second Floor: Rules r17 (55.1%) and r21 (27.6%) indicate the feature where the form elements of the second floor walls are arranged at the sides of the walls.

Rules for the First Floor: Rule r19 (34.5%) indicates the feature where entrances/exits are side-justified with related form elements. Rule r22 (24.1%) indicates the feature where the form elements of the first floor walls are end-justified. Rule r23 (17.2%) indicates the feature where form elements are arranged at the centers of the first floor walls.

Rules for Inter-element Relations: Rule r16 (82.8%) indicates a very high appearance rate in "Historic buildings" because the rule is so simple.

Rules for the Elements Themselves: Rules r18 (34.5%), r20 (34.5%), and r24 (34.5%) give information about form elements themselves. However, these described form elements are not found either in the appearance standards or the reference drawings. Their high appearance rates in "Historic buildings" indicate that the facades of transformed second-storied buildings are not only represented by patterns stipulated in the appearance standards but also by other various patterns.

6.4   The Facades of Semi Two-Storied Buildings

For the facades of semi two-storied building, three rules were acquired as follows:

Rules for the second floor: 1 (r25)

Rules for the first floor: 1 (r26)

Rules for inter-element relations: 1 (r27)

The acquired rules are described below.

Rules r25 (45.5%), r26 (36.4%), and r27 (36.4%) appeared in "Historic buildings" at high rates and they are included in the appearance standards and reference drawings.

7 Conclusion

This paper presented a method designed to acquire the configuration rules of form elements inherent in a "historic" facade from facades modeled using simplified two-dimensional graphics, and to describe them explicitly using logical expressions. By machine learning using the repair and remodeling records archived at the Urban Planning Bureau of Kyoto City, rules inherent to facades regarded as "historic" by the authorities were acquired. Features were inferred from the acquired rules and collated with their rates of appearance in preserved "Historic buildings". The acquired rules confirm the features of facades regarded as "historic" by the authorities, and the method also proved effective for extracting implicit rules inherent in the subjects of interest. As long as the cases are prepared appropriately, the method should be useful for facade evaluation.

Acknowledgement

We would like to express our deepest gratitude to Messrs. S. Saito and S. Hashimoto at the Urban Planning Bureau of Kyoto City for providing the references used in our study.

References

1. K.Nishikawa, Y,Ikeda, Y.Takahashi: Investigation research report of maintenance plan of historical environment in Higashiyama-Yasaka district, Kyoto City urban development department, (1972)
2. N.Tani, K.Oka: Sanneizaka town survey report, Kyoto City city planning department, (1995)
3. T.Monnai: The semiotic study on townscapes, Doctoral Dissertation of the University of Tokyo, (1997)
4. Y.Aoki: Denotation system of architectural form by language -Fundamental study for architectural computer-aided design part4-, Journal of Architecture, Planning and Environmental Engineering, AIJ, No.418, (1990) 41-50
5. K.Ito, A.Yamamoto: A constructive learning algorithm which invents new predicates based on schemata and queries, Transactions of the Japanese Society for Artificial Intelligence, Vol.14, No.4, (1999) 103-112
6. H.Fujii, Y.Aoki: A logical expression of analogical reasoning related to design, Journal of Architecture and Planning, AIJ, No.574, (2003) 55-60
7. K.Chiba, H.Ohwada, F.Mizoguchi: Acquiring graphic design knowledge with inductive logic programming, Transactions of the Japanese Society for Artificial Intelligence, Vol.16, No.1, (2001) 156-163
8. N.Sugiura, S.Okazaki: Analysis of spatial composition process by inductive logic programming -Extracting peculiar rules in process of spatial composition on space montage technique-, Journal of Architecture, Planning and Environmental Engineering, AIJ, No.546, (2001) 141-148

9. D.Matsushita, J.Munemoto: A description of evaluation formulae by learning case examples with inductive inference and to sieve the alternative set, Journal of Architecture and Planning, AIJ, No.576, (2004) 31-36
10. Kyoto City city planning department: Kyoto City Preservation District for Groups of Historic Buildings ordinance, (1997)
11. Kyoto City city planning department: Architectural style reference drawing collection -Sanneizaka Preservation District for Groups of Historic Buildings-, (1977)
12. K.Furukawa, T.Ozaki, K,Ueno: Inductive Logic Programming, Kyoritsu Pub., (2001)
13. S.Muggleton: Inverse Entailment and PROGOL, New Generation Computing, 13, (1995) 245-286
14. A.Saito, J.Munemoto, D.Matsushita: A study of an acquisition method of configuration rules of form elements of facade elevations applying the inductive logic programming -A case of Sanneizaka Preservation District for Groups of Historic Buildings-, Journal of Architecture and Planning, AIJ, No.583, (2004) 187-193

Learning Stochastic Logical Automaton

Hiroaki Watanabe and Stephen Muggleton

Imperial College London, 180 Queen's Gate, London SW7 2AZ, UK
Tel.: +44 (0)20 7594 8287; Fax: +44 (0)20 7581 8024
{hw3, shm}@doc.ic.ac.uk

Abstract. This paper is concerned with algorithms for the logical generalisation of probabilistic temporal models from examples. The algorithms
combine logic and probabilistic models through inductive generalisation.
The inductive generalisation algorithms consist of three parts. The first
part describes the graphical generalisation of state transition models.
State transition models are generalised by applying state mergers. The
second part involves symbolic generalisation of logic programs which are
embedded in each states. Plotkin's LGG is used for symbolic generalisation of logic programs. The third part covers learning of parameters
using statistics derived from the input sequences. The state transitions
are unobservable in our settings. The probability distributions over the
state transitions and actions are estimated using the EM algorithm. As
an application of these algorithms, we learn chemical reaction rules from
StochSim, the stochastic software simulator of biochemical reactions.

1 Introduction

Logical Induction from temporal observations is a challenging problem since
the observations could contain uncertainties in many cases. One way to tackle
the uncertainties is to derive statistics from the observations. If we express the
statistical knowledge explicitly, we would need to combine stochastic and logical
knowledge representations.

Logic-based AI has been studying logical representations of dynamic aspects
of temporal data since McCarthy and Hayes proposed Situation Calculus [1] in
first-order logic where dynamic changing world is expressed in *time-sliced* declarative representations. In the Inductive Logic Programming (ILP) literatures,
a few studies have been reported from the time-sliced representation point of
view [5, 6].

Automata-based representations have also been studied in computer science.
One of the merits of the automata-based representations under uncertainties
would be the applicability of the well-studied statistical learning algorithms such
as EM-algorithm for Hidden Markov Models [2]. In this paper, we combine logic
and probability model from the automata-based representation point of view.
More precisely, we introduce a logical extension of stochastic non-deterministic
finite automata.

We also present its induction algorithm. Dynamic aspects of the model are
generalised by the state merging technique [10] whereas static (or symbolic)

T. Washio et al. (Eds.): JSAI 2005 Workshops, LNAI 4012, pp. 201–211, 2006.
© Springer-Verlag Berlin Heidelberg 2006

knowledge are generalised by Plotkin's LGG [12]. Regarding learning automata, inductive inferences of automata are one of the well studied area in the research of computational complexity theory. Most of the previous works are negative (that is, non polynomial time learnable) [13, 14, 15] except [16]. These previous works suggest us to introduce a relevant constraint over the hypotheses space of our inductive algorithm in order to obtain an efficiency.

The paper is organised as follows. Section2 introduces our logical automata. Section3 explains the overview of the inductive algorithms of our model. Section4 contains our initial attempt to learn chemical reaction rules from the biochemical simulator *StochSim*[9]. We discuss some related works in Section5. Discussions and future work conclude the paper in Section6.

2   Logical Automata

2.1   Definitions

Let us start from the definition of a non-deterministic finite automaton (NFA) that provides the basic idea of state transitions for our model.

Definition 1.   (NFA): *A non-deterministic finite automaton is a 5-tuple* $NFA = (S, \Sigma, T, S_0, G)$ *where S is a finite set of states, Σ is a finite alphabet, T is a transition function, S_0 is a set of initial states, and G is a set of accept states.*

We extend NFA logically next. Assume a first-order definite clausal language L is given. Let f be a definite clause in L. Then F, a finite set of clauses, is called *theory*. We represent an observation of a dynamic world as a sequence of ground theories as follows:

Definition 2.   (Logical Sequence): *logical sequence is defined as*

$$O_0 A_0 O_1 ... O_{n-1} A_{n-1} O_n$$

where O_i is the ground theory in L that describes the observed facts at time i. A_i is also the ground theory in L for the action (or input) at time i.

We call $O_i A_i O_{i+1}$ a *unit* of the logical sequence. A graphical representation of the logical sequence is shown in Fig.1.

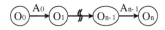

Fig. 1. A logical sequence

In a state transition system, a *state* is treated as a snapshot of the dynamic world where the state gives an *interpretation* (true or false) of each ground atom in the world.

Definition 3. (Logical State): *A logical state q is a pair (n, F) where $n \in \mathbb{N}$ is a label for a theory F in L.*

We introduce a logical edge and action as follows:

Definition 4. (Logical Edge and Action): *A logical edge is an edge between two logical states. A logical action (or input) is the set of ground theories embedded in the logical edges. All of the logical actions are denoted by $\mathcal{E}$.*

Next, we consider relations in the state transition function. In the literatures of automata theory, *equivalence relation* is usually employed between each input alphabet and the members of Σ. For example, let q and $q' = \sigma(q, a)$ be a current state and a state transition function from the state q to q' caused by the input a respectively. Now let us assume we receive an input alphabet at q. If the input *is equals to* a, the resulted state is q'. That is, we check the equivalence relation between the input alphabet and a.

In this paper, we introduce *generality relations* instead of the equality between the logical states (respectively logical edges) and the observed facts (respectively observed actions) from a logical point of view. For measuring the generality relations between theories, logical entailment would be a candidate, however, we employ the subsumption order to avoid the semi-decidability of logical entailment.

Definition 5. (Clause Subsumption): *Clause f_1 subsumes clause f_2, $f_1 \succeq f_2$, iff there exists a substitution θ such that $f_1\theta \subseteq f_2$.*

Definition 6. (Theory Subsumption [12]): *Theory F_1 subsumes theory F_2, $F_1 \succeq_T F_2$, iff $\forall C_2 \in F_2 \ \exists C_1 \in F_1 \ C_1 \succeq C_2$.*

Under the above theory subsumption order, we define the *logically special* state transition function between the logical states.

Definition 7. (Special State Transition): *For a given unit of logical sequence $O_i \ A_i \ O_{i+1}$, the state transition $q' = \sigma(q, E_i)$ between the logical states $q = (n, F)$ and $q' = (n', F')$ occurs iff $F \succeq_T O_i$, $E_i \succeq_T A_i$ and $F' \succeq_T O_{i+1}$.*

Intuitively Special State Transition accepts the unit if the unit is more *special* than the related logical states and logical edge. Here F and E_i could be viewed as the *prior* conditions, and F' as the *posterior* condition.

The scope of the first-order variables is expanded to the adjacent logical states:

Definition 8. (Scope of Variables): *For the state transition from the logical states $q = (n, F)$ to $q' = (n', F')$ by the logical action E_i, let V_F, V_E, and $V_{F'}$ be the sets of the first-order variables that appear in F, E_i, and F' respectively. Then the scope of the variables are within $V_F \cup V_E \cup V_{F'}$.*

This extension allows us to represent the relations between the first-order variables associated with the special state transition.

A Probabilistic Logical Automaton for Special inputs (PLAS) is a nondeterministic finite automaton whose states and state transitions are defined as logical states and probabilistic version of special state transitions respectively as follows:

Definition 9. (PLAS): *PLAS is a quintuplet $\langle Q, L, \sigma, I, G \rangle$ where Q is a finite set of logical states, L is a definite language, σ is a mapping defining the probabilistic special transition function, $\sigma : Q \times L \times Q \to [0,1]$, I is a mapping defining the initial probability of each state, $I : Q \to [0,1]$, and G is a mapping defining the final probability of each state, $G : Q \to [0,1]$.*

Definition 10. (Acceptance): *Let M be an PLAS such that $\langle Q, L, \sigma, I, G \rangle$, and X be a logical sequence in L. M accepts the logical sequence X if there exist a sequence of the logical states $q_0, ..., q_n$ $(q_i \in Q)$ such that: $I(q_0) = (0,1]$, $q_i = \sigma(q_{i-1}, x_i)$ for i=1,...,n, and $G(q_n) = (0,1]$. Then we call the sequence of the logical states $q_0...q_n$ an acceptance.*

The brief comparisons of Probabilistic NFA (PNFA) and PLAS are given in Table 1.

Table 1. Comparisons of PNFA and PLAS

	PNFA	**PLAS**
Language	alphabet	definite theory language
Input	word	logical sequence
Relation	equality	speciality
Acceptance	sequence of states	sequence of logical states

2.2   Semantics of Logical States

In the previous section, we introduce the first-order logical extension of NFA under the theory subsumption order. This extension would bring many benefits to graphical temporal knowledge representations since we could combine the automata-based algorithms and logical knowledge representation smoothly. Let us investigate a semantic aspect of PLAS by focusing on the generality orders. Let $\mathrm{LM}(F)$ be the least Herbrand Model of theory F. We present the following theorem in order to clarify an essential difference between propositional approach and our logical approach.

Theorem 1. *A PLAS accepts a logical sequence $O_0, A_0, ..., O_n$ such that its acceptance is $q_0...q_n$ where $q_i = (n_i, F_i)$ $(i = 0, ..., n)$, then*

$$\mathrm{LM}(O_i) \subseteq \mathrm{LM}(F_i).$$

Proof. $F \succeq_T O_i$ implies $F \models O_i$. Thus $\mathrm{LM}(O_i) \subseteq \mathrm{LM}(F)$ from the definition of the entailment relation.

Fig.2 illustrates an example of the inclusion relations between the logical states and logical sequences in PLAS such that the acceptance for the observation $O_0 A_0 O_1 A_1 O_2$ is $S_0 S_1 S_3$. Recall that the least Herbrand Model of the theory is defined by a set of ground atoms. Therefore the inclusion relations explain the semantic aspect of PLAS at the ground atom level. Note that the inclusion relations

$$\mathrm{LM}(A_j) \subseteq \mathrm{LM}(E_i)$$

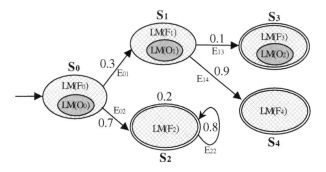

Fig. 2. Inclusion Relations in PLAS

also hold between the observed action A_j and the logical action $E_i \in \mathcal{E}$ where E_i is the logical action embedded in the logical edge between q_j and q_{j+1} of the acceptance $q_0...q_n$.

2.3   Inference in PLAS

PLAS could be applied for the probabilistic inference tasks such as *filtering, prediction, smoothing,* and *most likely explanation* [22]. However, we should recall that the inferences in PLAS would need the overheads of computing for the theory subsumption checks at each logical node and logical edge comparing with the standard inference algorithms [22]. Subsumption is decidable, however, it is an NP-complete problem [23]. Therefore the theories embedded in the logical nodes and edges must be restricted [24] for designing tractable inference algorithms.

For example of the inference tasks in PLAS, let us consider the filtering. The observations for PLAS could be partial observations as the inclusion relations show in the previous section. PLAS defines the probability distribution over *belief states* given a set of the logical sequences. In Fig.2, let us assume that the given logical sequence also has another acceptance $S_0S_2S_2$. Then the logical sequence gives

$$Pr(S3 \mid O_0A_0O_1A_1O_2) = 0.3 \times 0.1 = 0.03$$
$$Pr(S2 \mid O_0A_0O_1A_1O_2) = 0.7 \times 0.8 = 0.56.$$

3   Learning Stochastic Logical Automata

Our next interest is to learn the stochastic logical automata from observations. The above definitions indicate that PLAS could be learned by *generalising* the given inputs. Our generalisation algorithm combines logic and probabilistic models through inductive generalisation.

3.1   Setting

Given

- Positive Examples **E**: A set of Logical Sequences
- Background Knowledge **BK**: A set of ground atoms

Learn

- A PLAS that accepts **E** by the special state transitions related with **BK**.

3.2   Overview of the Algorithms

Our inductive generalisation algorithms consist of three parts. The first part describes the graphical generalisation of state transition models. Assume two logical sequences are given as positive examples (Fig.3). These sequences could be viewed as a state transition model. In our algorithm, the state transition models are generalised by applying state mergers. For example, in Fig.3 if state 2 and state 8 are merged, the new state 10 in Fig.4 is newly generated. The related transition functions are altered through the generalisation process as shown in Fig.4.

The second part involves symbolic generalisation of theories which are embedded in each states. Plotkin's LGG is used for symbolic generalisation of the theories. For example, the two theories in state 2 and state 8 (Fig.3) are generalised by LGG when the two states are merged (Fig.4).

The third part covers learning of parameters using statistics derived from the input sequences. The state transitions are unobservable in our settings. The probability distributions over the state transitions and actions are estimated using the EM algorithm. These three steps are iterated until the logical states converge to a logical state.

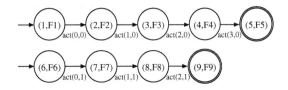

Fig. 3. Positive Examples

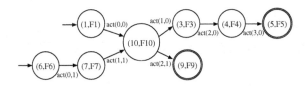

Fig. 4. Logical State Merging

4   Example

We implemented our inductive algorithm with two constraints: the depth bound for the graphical generalisation hypothesis space and the variable depth bound for LGG. In addition to the scope-extended LGG, our software has a function to invent $is(X, Y, int)$ atoms that represent $X = Y + int$ where X and Y are the variables restricted over integers.

4.1   Learning Chemical Reaction Rules from Biochemical Simulator

As an application of the system, we learn chemical reaction rules from StochSim that is a general purpose biochemical simulator in which individual molecules or molecular complexes are represented as individual software objects. Chemical reactions between the molecules occur stochastically according to probabilities derived from the given rate constants.

To run the simulator, a user needs to specify some definitions such as (1)kinds of molecules, (2)the initial numbers of molecules, and (3)possible chemical reaction rules. We assume the following simple chemical reactions in our experiment:

$$2H2 + O2 \Longleftrightarrow 2H2O$$
$$N2 + 3H2 \Longleftrightarrow 2NH3$$

After each simulation, we have a dump file that contains time-series measurements of the concentrations of the molecules. For this experiment, we modify the StochSim code to output the *one-chemical-reaction* time-series results. The following shows two artificial dump files of two simulations:

[First Run]

Time	h2o	nh3	o2	h2	n2
0	2	3	2	18	5
1	2	3	2	18	5
2	4	3	1	16	5
3	4	5	1	13	4
4	4	7	1	10	3

[Second Run]

Time	h2o	nh3	o2	h2	n2
0	2	3	2	18	5
1	2	5	2	15	4
2	4	5	1	13	4
3	6	5	0	11	4

where time units are defined as *iterations* at the one-chemical-reaction time-scale. Since the reactions occur stochastically, the concentrations do not change sometimes. For example, in the above First Run file, the initial concentration (Time 0) does not change at the next iteration (Time 1). This means that the simulator applied a chemical reaction for the molecules during the iteration, but the reaction did not happen because of its stochastic nature. During Time 1 and Time 2 in the first run, we could conclude that the reaction

$$2H2 + O2 \Longrightarrow 2H2O$$

happened, because this is only the reaction that could bring the change in our setting. The outputs are converted into two logical sequences as follows:

```
[{mol(h2o,2),mol(nh3,3),mol(o2,2),mol(h2,18),mol(n2,5)} act(0,0)
 {mol(h2o,2),mol(nh3,3),mol(o2,2),mol(h2,18),mol(n2,5)} act(1,0)
 {mol(h2o,4),mol(nh3,3),mol(o2,1),mol(h2,16),mol(n2,5)} act(2,0)
 {mol(h2o,4),mol(nh3,5),mol(o2,1),mol(h2,13),mol(n2,4)} act(3,0)
 {mol(h2o,4),mol(nh3,7),mol(o2,1),mol(h2,10),mol(n2,3)}]

[{mol(h2o,2),mol(nh3,3),mol(o2,2),mol(h2,18),mol(n2,5)} act(0,1)
 {mol(h2o,2),mol(nh3,5),mol(o2,2),mol(h2,15),mol(n2,4)} act(1,1)
 {mol(h2o,4),mol(nh3,5),mol(o2,1),mol(h2,13),mol(n2,4)} act(2,1)
 {mol(h2o,6),mol(nh3,5),mol(o2,0),mol(h2,11),mol(n2,4)}]
```

Our learning task is set as:

Given

- A set of outputs from StochSim in the form of logical sequences.

Find

- Chemical Reaction Rules happen during the simulations.

Note that learning probability distribution is omitted since the number of examples is too small in this example.

The graphical representation of the input is shown in Fig.3 where

```
F1 = {mol(h2o,2),mol(nh3,3),mol(o2,2),mol(h2,18),mol(n2,5)}
F2 = {mol(h2o,2),mol(nh3,3),mol(o2,2),mol(h2,18),mol(n2,5)}
F3 = {mol(h2o,4),mol(nh3,3),mol(o2,1),mol(h2,16),mol(n2,5)}
F4 = {mol(h2o,4),mol(nh3,5),mol(o2,1),mol(h2,13),mol(n2,4)}
F5 = {mol(h2o,4),mol(nh3,7),mol(o2,1),mol(h2,10),mol(n2,3)}
F6 = {mol(h2o,2),mol(nh3,3),mol(o2,2),mol(h2,18),mol(n2,5)}
F7 = {mol(h2o,2),mol(nh3,5),mol(o2,2),mol(h2,15),mol(n2,4)}
F8 = {mol(h2o,4),mol(nh3,5),mol(o2,1),mol(h2,13),mol(n2,4)}
F9 = {mol(h2o,6),mol(nh3,5),mol(o2,0),mol(h2,11),mol(n2,4)}.
```

Then our software starts to search the hypothesis space by applying the state merging with symbolic generalisation. Since our search space is the version space, the examples are consistent with all hypothesis learned by the software. Our program returns the state transition model shown in Fig.5 with the following is/3 atoms:

```
is(V5,V8,4), is(V3,V9,2), is(V2,V5,-3), is(V2,V8,1), is(V1,V6,-1),
is(V0,V1,-1), is(V0,V6,-2)
```

We can translate the learned rules as:

Through the reaction, the number of H2O increases by two, the number of O2 decreases by one, and the number of H2 decreases2. The number of N2 and NH3 do not change.

is(V5,V8,4), is(V3,V9,2), is(V2,V5,-3), is(V2,V8,1), is(V1,V6,-1), is(V0,V1,-1), is(V0,V6,-2)

Fig. 5. Logical State Merging: 2H2+O2 $\Longrightarrow$ 2H2O

is(V0,V7,-3), is(V1,V0,1), is(V1,V7,-2), is(V3,V9,-2), is(V4,V8,3) is(V5,V3,3), is(V5,V9,1)

Fig. 6. Logical State Merging: N2 + 3H2 $\Longrightarrow$ 2NH3

Our program also returns the model shown in Fig.6 with the following is/3 atoms:

```
is(V0,V7,-3), is(V1,V0,1), is(V1,V7,-2), is(V3,V9,-2), is(V4,V8,3)
is(V5,V3,3),  is(V5,V9,1)
```

> *Through the reaction, the number of NH3 increases by two, the number of N2 decreases by one, and the number of H2 decreases3. The number of O2 and H2O do not change.*

The system learns some additional knowledge in the form of is/3.

5   Related Works

There exist many attempts for combining first-order logic and probability [17, 18, 19, 20]. Relational extensions of Bayesian Networks have also reported including [21]. Logical Hidden Markov Model [7] and Logical Markov Decision Programs [8] are closely related to our PLAS model. Logical Decision Program could embed a set of atoms in a state. Since PLAS could put a set of definite clauses in the logical state, it would be more expressive than Logical Decision Program.

PLAS is originally designed as a graphical representation of First-order Stochastic Action Language [3] which is a first-order logical version of dynamic Bayesian networks.

Our logical automata could be viewed as a graphical version of Situation Calculus. Successor state axioms are encoded in our each conditional state transitions. Since PLAS defines probability distributions over belief states, PLAS would be suitable for representing POMDPs.

6 Discussions and Conclusions

In this paper, we propose an extension of stochastic non-deterministic finite automata. By focusing on the generality order between the logical states and the partial inputs, the semantic aspect of our models becomes clear. PLAS defines probability distributions over belief states. We also proposed the inductive learning algorithms of PLAS by combining graphical and symbolic generalisations smoothly. Parameter learning of PLAS are implemented using EM algorithm.

Regarding the complexity of the state merging technique, the size of the hypotheses space of automata is known as exponential [10, 11]. Therefore heuristic searches would be mandatory to obtain the efficiency for the state merger.

One of the advantages of first-order logic is its compact representation. In PLAS, each snapshot of dynamic worlds is captured in a definite theory. The logical state could represent multiple states under the theory subsumption order. That is, the compactness has been realised at each state level.

Our logical sequence represents temporal changes of theories, that is, we could input a series of Logic Programs (LPs) to our model. If we learn a PLAS model from the observed series of LPs, the model should capture how LPs change proceeding with time. In [4], a STRIPS-like first-order stochastic operator is proposed in order to modify LPs temporally. The operator is expressed in the form of dynamic Bayesian networks with add/delete-lists functions. The development of the translation algorithms between the operator and PLAS would be useful for the distributed executions of LPs in the Multi-Agent research.

Since our models are based on Automata, further extensions would be possible by considering the existing extensions of Automata.

Acknowledgements. The first author would like to thank Katsumi Inoue for his advice in this research. The research was supported by European Union IST programme, contract no.FP6-508861, *Application of Probabilistic Inductive Logic Programming II*. The authors are also partially supported by National Institute of Informatics (NII), Joint Research Grant no.A-5.

References

1. J. McCarthy and P. J. Hayes.: Some Philosophical Problems from the Standpoint of Artificial Intelligence. Machine Intelligence 4, pages 463–502, Edinburgh University Press, 1969.
2. L. Rabiner.: A tutorial on hidden markov models and selected applications in speech recognition. In Proceedings of the IEEE, 77, 1989.
3. First-Order Stochastic Action Language, Hiroaki Watanabe and Stephen Muggleton.: Electronic Transactions in Artificial Intelligence, 7, 2002. http://www.doc.ic.ac.uk/~hw3/doc/watanabe02FirstSAL.ps
4. Towards Belief Propagation in Shared Logic Program.: Hiroaki Watanabe and Stephen Muggleton, BN2003, Kyoto, 2003. http://www.doc.ic.ac.uk/~hw3/doc/bn2003final2.pdf
5. S. Moyle and S.H. Muggleton.: Learning programs in the event calculus. In N. Lavrac and S. Dzeroski, editors, Proceedings of the Seventh Inductive Logic Programming Workshop (ILP97), LNAI 1297, pages 205–212, Berlin, 1997. Springer-Verlag.

6. R. P. Otero.: Induction of Stable Models, in Proceedings of 11th Int. Conference on Inductive Logic Programming, ILP-01, pages 193–205, LNAI 2157, Springer, Strasbourg 2001.

7. K. Kersting, T. Raiko, and L. De Raedt.: Logical Hidden Markov Models (Extended Abstract). In J. A. Ga'mez and A. Salmero'n, editors, Proceedings of the First European Workshop on Probabilistic Graphical Models (PGM-02), pages 99–107, November 6-8, 2002, Cuenca, Spain.

8. K. Kersting, L. De Raedt.: Logical Markov Decision Programs and the Convergence of Logical TD(λ). In A. Srinivasan, R. King, and R.Camacho, editors, Proceedings of the Fourteenth International Conference on Inductive Logic Programming (ILP-2004), pages 180–197. Porto, Portugal, September 6-8, 2004.

9. Morton-Firth, C. J. (1998) Stochastic simulation of cell signalling pathways Ph. D. Thesis, University of Cambridge.

10. P. Dupont, L. Miclet and E. Vidal.: What is the search space of Regular Inference?. Lecture Notes in Artificial Intelligence, No. 862, Springer-Verlag, Grammatical Inference and Applications, pages 25–37, 1994.

11. Coste, F., and Fredouille, D.: What is the search space for the inference of non deterministic, unambiguous and deterministic automata ?. technical report INRIA RR-4907, 2003.

12. G. Plotkin.: Automatic Methods of Inductive Inference. PhD thesis, Edinburgh University, UK, 1971.

13. E. M. Gold.: Complexity of automaton identification from given data. Information and Control, 37(3): pages 302–320, 1978.

14. D. Angluin.: Negative Results for Equivalence Queries. Machine Learning, 5, pages 121–150, 1990.

15. M. Kearns and L. G. Valiant.: Cryptographic limitations on learning boolean formulae and finite automata. In Proceedings of the 21st Annual ACM Symposium on Theory of Computing, pages 433–444, New York. ACM, 1989.

16. D. Angluin.: Learning regular sets from queries and counterexamples. Information and Computation, 75: pages 87–106, 1987.

17. Joseph Y. Halpern.: An analysis of first-order logics of probability, Proceedings of IJCAI-89, 11th International Joint Conference on Artificial Intelligence, pages 1375–1381, 1989.

18. S. H. Muggleton.: Stochastic logic programs. In L. de Raedt, editor, Advances in Inductive Logic Programming, pages 254–264. IOS Press, 1996.

19. Taisuke Sato.: A statistical learning method for logic programs with distribution semantics. Proc. ICLP'95, Syounan-village, pages 715–729, 1995.

20. Kristian Kersting and Luc De Raedt. Bayesian Logic Programs. In J. Cussens and A. Frisch, editors, Proceedings of the Work-in-Progress Track at the 10th International Conference on Inductive Logic Programming, pages 138–155, 2000.

21. Friedman, N., Getoor, L., Koller, D., Pfeffer, A.: Learning probabilistic relational models. In: Proceedings of the Sixteenth International Joint Conference on Artificial Intelligence, Morgan Kaufmann Publishers Inc, pages 1300–1309, 1999.

22. Stuart Russell and Peter Norvig.: Artificial Intelligence: A Modern Approach. 2nd Edition, Prentice Hall, 2003.

23. M.R.Garey and D.S.Johnson.: Computers and Intractability: *A Guide to the Theory of NP-Completeness.* Freeman, New York, 1979.

24. J-U.Kietz and M.Lübbe.: An efficient subsumption algorithm for inductive logic programming. Proc. of the 4th International Workshop on Inductive Logic Programming (ILP-94), pages 97–105, 1994.

On Generalization and Subsumption for Ordered Clauses[*]

Megumi Kuwabara[1], Takeshi Ogawa[1,**], Kouichi Hirata[2],
and Masateru Harao[2]

[1] Graduate School of Computer Science and Systems Engineering
[2] Department of Artificial Intelligence
Kyushu Institute of Technology
Kawazu 680-4, Iizuka 820-8502, Japan
{megumik, ogawa}@dumbo.ai.kyutech.ac.jp,
{hirata, harao}@ai.kyutech.ac.jp

Abstract. In this paper, we investigate the properties of *ordered clauses* defined as a sequence of literals. First, we show that while there exists no least generalization of two ordered clauses, every minimal generalization of them has a *complete* selection to which the result applying Plotkin's algorithm is subsume-equivalent. Furthermore, we show that the number of complete selections can grow exponentially. Next, we show that the subsumption problem for ordered clauses is also NP-complete as similar as general clauses.

1 Introduction

A *clause* is one of the important forms of knowledge representation in Artificial Intelligence. Such a clause is usually defined as a *set* of literals.

It is well-known that various combinatorial problems for clauses are frequently intractable. For example, the problem of determining whether or not a clause *subsumes* another clause is NP-complete [1, 5], and the problem of determining whether or not a clause is *nonredundant* or *condensed* is coNP-complete [6]. Also the minimization problem for condensation is not polynomial-time approximable (unless NP=ZPP) [2].

The *least generalization of clauses* introduced by Plotkin [13] is one of the most important tools for Inductive Logic Programming. By using Plotkin's algorithm [13], we can find the least generalization of two clauses C and D in $O(|C||D|)$ time. However, the number of the literals in it becomes $|C||D|$ in the worst case, so it is possible to be redundant. When it is necessary to removing such redundancy, it is also hard to approximate in polynomial time as above.

---

[*] This work is partially supported by Grand-in-Aid for Scientific Research 15700137 and 16016275 from the Ministry of Education, Culture, Sports, Science and Technology, Japan.

[**] Current address: Matsushita Electric Industrial Co., Ltd.

T. Washio et al. (Eds.): JSAI 2005 Workshops, LNAI 4012, pp. 212–223, 2006.

On the other hand, nevertheless a clause is defined as a set of literals, there are many cases to deal with a clause as a sequence of literals. We call a sequence of literals an *ordered clause*, in contrast to a *general clause* as a set of literals. For example, since the computation rule [11] in SLD resolution is fixed to select left-most atom, real Prolog programs are executed as ordered clauses rather than general clauses. Also, in Inductive Logic Programming, the *determinate* clauses [4, 7, 8] are implicitly assumed to be ordered. Furthermore, van der Laag [9] has introduced *sequential clauses* and Dan Lee and De Raedt [3] have introduced *SeqLog*, both of them are similar as ordered clauses. Hence, in this paper, we investigate the properties of *ordered clauses*.

First, we discuss the generalization for ordered clauses. Unfortunately, in this paper, we show that there exists no least generalization of two or more ordered clauses. Then, instead of the least generalization, we deal with *minimal generalizations* of ordered clauses.

Note that the least generalization for general clauses is obtained by applying Plotkin's least generalization algorithm [10, 12, 13, 14] for atoms to the *selection* of them, by regarding as atoms. In this paper, we extend such a selection to a *complete* selection. Then, we show that every minimal generalization of two ordered clauses has a complete selection to which the result applying Plotkin's algorithm is subsume-equivalent. Also we show that the number of complete selections can grow exponentially. Note that such an exponential bound is just an upper bound but not a lower bound.

Next, we show that the *subsumption* problem for ordered clauses is also NP-complete, as similar as the subsumption problem for general clauses [1, 5]. Hence, the definition that a clause is a set of literals is inessential for the intractability of subsumption problem for clauses.

2   Ordered Clauses

A *term*, an *atom* and a *literal* are defined as usual. All of them are sometimes called *expressions*. For an expression E, $var(E)$ denotes the set of variables occurring in E, and $|E|$ denotes the *size* of E that is the number of symbols appearing to E.

A *substitution* is a mapping $\{t_1/x_1, \ldots, t_n/x_n\}$ from variables to terms such that t_i is a term, x_i is a variable, and $x_i \notin var(t_i)$. For a substitution $\theta = \{t_1/x_1, \ldots, t_n/x_n\}$, we call a set $\{x_1, \ldots, x_n\}$ the *domain* of θ and denote by $dom(\theta)$. We call each element t_i/x_i in θ the *binding* of θ. If $\theta = \emptyset$, we call it an *empty substitution* and denote by ε. Also a *composition* of two substitutions θ and σ are defined in a usual way [11, 12].

A substitution is called *variable-pure* if all bindings are of the forms y/x, where y is a variable $(y \neq x)$. A variable-pure substitution $\theta = \{y_1/x_1, \ldots, y_n/x_n\}$ is called a *renaming substitution* for an expression E if each x_i occurs in E and $y_1, \ldots, y_n$ are distinct variables such that each y_i is either equal to some x_j in θ or y_i does not occur in E.

A *clause* (or a *general clause* to distinguish from an *ordered clause* defined below) is defined as a *set* of literals. For clauses C and D, we say that C *subsumes*

D, denoted by $C \succeq D$ if there exists a substitution θ such that $C\theta \subseteq D$. We say that C *properly subsumes* D, denoted by $C \succ D$, if $C \succeq D$ but $D \not\succeq C$. We say that C is *subsume-equivalent* to D, denoted by $C \sim D$, if $C \succeq D$ and $D \succeq C$.

An *ordered clause*, on the other hand, is defined as a *sequence* of literals, and denoted by $[L_1, \ldots, L_m]$. An empty clause is denoted by $[\ ]$. For two ordered clauses $C = [L_1, \ldots, L_m]$ and $D = [M_1, \ldots, M_n]$, we denote the concatenation $[L_1, \ldots, L_m, M_1, \ldots, M_n]$ of C to D by $C \circ D$.

Definition 1. Let C and D be ordered clauses $[L_1, \ldots, L_m]$ and $[M_1, \ldots, M_n]$, respectively. We say that C is a *subsequence* of D, denote by $C \sqsubseteq D$, if there exists a total monotone increasing function $f : \{1, \ldots, m\} \rightarrow \{1, \ldots, n\}$ such that $L_i = M_{f(i)}$ for each i $(1 \leq i \leq m)$.

Lemma 1. *For ordered clauses C and D, if $C \sqsubseteq D$, then $C\theta \sqsubseteq D\theta$ for any substitution θ.*

Proof. Let C and D be ordered clauses $[L_1, \ldots, L_m]$ and $[M_1, \ldots, M_n]$, respectively. Since $C \sqsubseteq D$, there exists a total monotone increasing function f such that $L_i = M_{f(i)}$. Since ordered clauses are allowed to contain the duplicated elements, the results applying θ to C and D are denoted by $[L_1\theta, \ldots, L_m\theta]$ and $[M_1\theta, \ldots, M_n\theta]$, respectively, so it holds that $L_i\theta = M_{f(i)}\theta$. □

We introduce the subsumption relation $\succeq_o$ for ordered clauses, instead of the subsumption relation $\succeq$ for general clauses.

Definition 2. Let C and D be ordered clauses. We say that C *subsumes* D, denote by $C \succeq_o D$, if there exists a substitution θ such that $C\theta \sqsubseteq D$. We say that C *properly subsumes* D, denoted by $C \succ_o D$, if $C \succeq_o D$ but $D \not\succeq_o C$. We say that C is *subsume-equivalent* to D, denote by $C \sim_o D$, if $C \succeq_o D$ and $D \succeq_o C$.

Lemma 2. *For ordered clauses, $\succeq_o$ is reflexive and transitive.*

Proof. It is obvious that $C \succeq_o C$ for an ordered clause C. Suppose that $C \succeq_o D$ and $D \succeq_o E$ for ordered clauses C, D and E. Then, there exists substitutions θ and σ such that $C\theta \sqsubseteq D$ and $D\sigma \sqsubseteq E$. By Lemma 1, it holds that $C\theta\sigma \sqsubseteq D\sigma \sqsubseteq E$, so the statement holds. □

Lemma 3. *Let C and D be ordered clauses. If $C \succeq_o D$, then $C \succeq D$ as general clauses.*

Proof. If $C \succeq_o D$, then there exists a substitution θ such that $C\theta \sqsubseteq D$. Hence, it is obvious that $C\theta \subseteq D$. □

Example 1. The converse of Lemma 3 does not hold in general.
Consider the following ordered clauses C and D.

$$C = [p(x,y), p(y,x), p(z,x), p(y,z)] = [L_1, L_2, L_3, L_4],$$
$$D = [p(a,b), p(b,a), p(b,c), p(c,a)] = [M_1, M_2, M_3, M_4].$$

Then, we show that there exists no substitution θ such that $C\theta \sqsubseteq D$.

If such a θ exists, then it holds that $\{a/x, b/y\} \subseteq \theta$ from the first two literal of C, because $b/x \in \theta$ or $c/x \in \theta$ implies $C\theta \not\sqsubseteq D$. So we can construct the total monotone increasing function $f : \{1, 2, 3\} \to \{1, 2, 3, 4\}$ such that $f(1) = 1$, $f(2) = 2$ and $f(3) = 4$ satisfying that $L_i\theta = M_{f(i)}$ for each i $(1 \le i \le 3)$. However, if $f(4) = 4$, then it holds that $L_4\theta \ne M_4$. Hence, it holds that $C \not\succeq_o D$.

As general clauses, on the other hand, it is obvious that $C \succeq D$.

3 Generalization for Ordered Clauses

In this section, we discuss the generalizations of ordered clauses under $\succeq_o$. First, we show that there exists no least generalization of two ordered clauses, even if they contain the literals with just one binary predicate symbol. Next, we discuss the minimal generalizations of two ordered clauses and their number, by introducing a complete selection.

3.1 Nonexistence of the Least Generalization for Ordered Clauses

Let S be a set of general clauses. Then, G is a *generalization* of S under $\succeq$ if $G \succeq C$ for every $C \in S$. A generalization G of S under $\succeq$ is called the *least generalization* of S under $\succeq$ if $F \succeq G$ for every generalization F of S under $\succeq$.

As similar as general clauses, we can define the generalization of ordered clauses as follows.

Definition 3. Let S be a set of ordered clauses. Then, G is a *generalization* of S under $\succeq_o$ if $G \succeq_o C$ for every $C \in S$. A generalization G of S under $\succeq_o$ is called the *least generalization* of S under $\succeq_o$ if $F \succeq_o G$ for every generalization F of S under $\succeq_o$. A generalization G of S under $\succeq_o$ is called the *minimal generalization* of S under $\succeq_o$ if there exists no generalization F of S under $\succeq_o$ such that $G \succ_o F$.

In particular, if $S = \{G'\}$ and $G \succeq_o G'$, then we call G a *generalization* of G'.

Unfortunately, the following theorem claims that there exists no least generalization for ordered clauses *even if they contain the literals with just one binary predicate symbol* in general.

Theorem 1. *There exist ordered clauses C and D that have no least generalization under $\succeq_o$.*

Proof. Consider the following ordered clauses C and D.

$$C = [p(a, b), p(b, c), p(c, d), p(d, a)],$$
$$D = [p(a', b'), p(b', a')].$$

Furthermore, let E and F be the following ordered clauses.

$$E = [p(x, y), p(y, z), p(w, x)] = [L_1, L_2, L_3],$$
$$F = [p(x, y), p(z, w), p(w, x)] = [M_1, M_2, M_3].$$

Then, it holds that $E \succeq_o C$, $E \succeq_o D$, $F \succeq_o C$ and $F \succeq_o D$. So E and F are generalizations of $\{C, D\}$. Furthermore, it holds that $E \not\succeq_o F$ and $F \not\succeq_o E$, that is, E and F are incomparable w.r.t. $\succeq_o$.

Suppose that there exists an ordered clause $G = [N_1, \ldots, N_l]$ such that $E \succeq_o G$, $F \succeq_o G$, $G \succeq_o C$ and $G \succeq_o D$. Since $E \succeq_o G$ and $F \succeq_o G$, there exist substitutions θ_1 and θ_2 such that $E\theta_1 \sqsubseteq G$ and $F\theta_2 \sqsubseteq G$. Note that G contains no variables, so θ_1 and θ_2 are variable-pure.

By the existence of θ_1 such that $E\theta_1 \sqsubseteq G$, there exists a total monotone increasing function f such that $f(i) = j_i$ ($i = 1, 2, 3$ and $1 \leq j_1 \leq j_2 \leq j_3 \leq l$). In other words, it holds that $p(x, y)\theta_1 = N_{j_1}$, $p(y, z)\theta_1 = N_{j_2}$ and $p(w, x)\theta_1 = N_{j_3}$. If $j_1 = j_2$, then it holds that $N_{j_1} = N_{j_2} \sim_o p(x, x)$, which is a contradiction that $G \succeq_o C$. Furthermore, if $j_2 = j_3$, then it holds that $[p(x, y), p(y, x)] \sqsubseteq G$, which is also a contradiction that $G \succeq_o C$. Hence, it holds that $1 \leq j_1 < j_2 < j_3 \leq l$.

On the other hand, since θ_1 is variable-pure, suppose that θ_1 is not a renaming substitution for E. If θ_1 contains one of the bindings $x/y, y/x, y/z, z/y, w/x, x/w$, then it holds that $N_{j_i} \sim_o p(x, x) \in G$ for some i ($i = 1, 2, 3$), which is a contradiction that $G \succeq_o C$. If θ_1 contains one of the bindings $x/z, z/x, y/w, w/y, z/w, w/z$, then it holds that $[p(x, y), p(y, x)] \sqsubseteq G$, which is also a contradiction that $G \succeq_o C$. Hence, θ_1 is a renaming substitution for E, so we can suppose that $N_{j_1} = p(x', y')$, $N_{j_2} = p(y', z')$, and $N_{j_3} = p(w', x')$.

By the existence of θ_2 such that $E\theta_2 \sqsubseteq G$, there exists a total monotone increasing function g such that $g(i) = k_i$ ($i = 1, 2, 3$ and $1 \leq k_1 \leq k_2 \leq k_3 \leq l$). In other words, it holds that $p(x, y)\theta_2 = N_{k_1}$, $p(z, w)\theta_2 = N_{k_2}$ and $p(w, x)\theta_2 = N_{k_3}$. By using the same discussion, it holds that $1 \leq k_1 < k_2 < k_3 \leq l$, θ_2 is a renaming substitution for F, and we can suppose that $N_{k_1} = p(x'', y'')$, $N_{k_2} = p(z'', w'')$, and $N_{k_3} = p(w'', x'')$.

Consider the order of $N_{j_1}, N_{j_2}, N_{j_3}, N_{k_1}, N_{k_2}, N_{k_3}$ in G. Since $G \succeq_o C$ and $G \succeq_o D$, there exist substitutions σ_1 and σ_2 such that $G\sigma_1 \sqsubseteq C$ and $G\sigma_2 \sqsubseteq D$.

Since $G\sigma_1 \sqsubseteq C$, for j_i, it holds that $N_{j_1}\sigma_1 = p(a, b)$, $N_{j_2}\sigma_1 = p(b, c)$ and $N_{j_3}\sigma_1 = p(d, a)$. For k_i, it holds that $N_{k_1}\sigma_1 = p(a, b)$, $N_{k_2}\sigma_1 = p(c, d)$ and $N_{k_3}\sigma_1 = p(d, a)$. Thus, it holds that $j_2 < k_2$.

On the other hand, since $G\sigma_2 \sqsubseteq D$, for j_i, it holds that $N_{j_1}\sigma_2 = p(a', b')$ and $N_{j_2}\sigma_2 = N_{j_3}\sigma_2 = p(b', a')$. For k_i, it holds that $N_{k_1}\sigma_2 = N_{k_2}\sigma_2 = p(a', b')$ and $N_{k_3}\sigma_2 = p(b', a')$. Thus, it holds that $k_2 < j_2$.

Hence, we cannot construct G containing both N_{k_2} and N_{j_2}, which is a contradiction that such G exists. Therefore, there exists no least generalization of $\{C, D\}$ in general. □

3.2 Minimal Generalizations for Ordered Clauses

Theorem 1 shows that there exists no least generalization of $\{C, D\}$ under $\succeq_o$ for ordered clauses C and D. On the other hand, it is possible that there exist minimal generalizations of $\{C, D\}$ under $\succeq_o$.

Literals L and M are *compatible* if L and M have the same predicate symbol and the same sign (positive or negative). A *selection* of C and D is the sequence of pairs of compatible literals in C and D. A selection is *maximal* if all pairs of compatible literals appear in it. For a selection $S = (L_1, M_1), \ldots, (L_k, M_k)$ of C and D, we denote general clauses $\{L_1, \ldots, L_k\}$ and $\{M_1, \ldots, M_k\}$ by S^C and S^D, respectively.

Plotkin [13] has shown that the least generalization of a set S of general clauses under $\succeq$ always exists uniquely up to subsume-equivalence. Also he has designed the algorithm lgc to find the least generalization of general clauses C and D described in Figure 1. Here, since the maximal selection is determined uniquely, we apply S^C and S^D for the maximal selection S of C and D to the procedure lga in the procedure lgc, by regarding S^C and S^D as atoms.

$lgc(C, D)$ [12, 13] /* C, D: general clauses */
    $S :=$ the maximal selection of C and D;
    $lga(S^C, S^D)$;
$lga(s, t)$ [10, 12, 13, 14] /* s, t: expressions */
    if $s = f(s_1, \ldots, s_n)$ and $t = f(t_1, \ldots, t_n)$ $(n \geq 0)$ **then**
        $f(lga(s_1, t_1), \ldots, lga(s_n, t_n))$;
    else if s and t are atoms with different predicate symbols **then**
        return "There exists no generalization" and **halt**;
    else $x_{\psi(s,t)}$; /* ψ: bijection from pairs of terms to nonnegative integers */

Fig. 1. The least generalization algorithm lgc for general clauses [13]

In order to capture the properties of minimal generalizations for ordered clauses, we extend the concept of selections as follows.

Definition 4. Let C and D be ordered clauses $[L_1, \ldots, L_m]$ and $[M_1, \ldots, M_n]$, respectively.

1. A selection S of C and D is *order-preserving* if the indexes of literals in C and D are increasing in S, that is, for each $(L_i, M_j), (L_{i'}, M_{j'}) \in S$, (L_i, M_j) is antecedent to $(L_{i'}, M_{j'})$ in S if and only if $i \leq i'$ and $j \leq j'$.
2. A selection S of C and D is *total* if all literals in C and D appear in S.
3. A selection S of C and D is *complete* if S is order-preserving and total.

As similar as general clauses, for a selection $S = (L_1, M_1), \ldots, (L_k, M_k)$ of ordered clauses C and D, we also denote ordered clauses $[L_1, \ldots, L_k]$ and $[M_1, \ldots, M_k]$ by S^C and S^D, respectively. In the procedure lga, S^C and S^D are regarded as atoms.

Lemma 4. *Let C and D be ordered clauses and S a selection of C and D. If S is order-preserving, then $lga(S^C, S^D)$ is a generalization of $\{C, D\}$ under $\succeq_o$.*

Proof. Since S is order-preserving, it holds that $S^C \sqsubseteq C$ and $S^D \sqsubseteq D$. Note that $lga(S^C, S^D)$ is obtained by regarding S^C and S^D as atoms. Let θ_C and θ_D be substitutions such that $lga(S^C, S^D)\theta_C = S^C$ and $lga(S^C, S^D)\theta_D = S^D$. Then, it holds that $lga(S^C, S^D)\theta_C \sqsubseteq C$ and $lga(S^C, S^D)\theta_D \sqsubseteq D$. $\square$

Lemma 5. *Let C and D be ordered clauses. Then, an ordered clause G is a generalization of $\{C, D\}$ under $\succeq_o$ if and only if there exists an order-preserving selection S of C and D such that $G \succeq_o lga(S^C, S^D)$.*

Proof. Suppose that S is an order-preserving selection of C and D such that $G \succeq_o lga(S^C, S^D)$. By Lemma 2 and 4, it holds that $G \succeq_o C$ and $G \succeq_o D$, so G is a generalization of $\{C, D\}$ under $\succeq_o$.

Conversely, let G be a generalization of $\{C, D\}$ under $\succeq_o$. Suppose that C, D and G are of the forms $[L_1, \ldots, L_m]$, $[M_1, \ldots, M_n]$ and $[N_1, \ldots, N_l]$. Then, there exist two substitutions θ_C and θ_D and two total monotone increasing functions $f : \{1, \ldots, l\} \to \{1, \ldots, m\}$ and $g : \{1, \ldots, l\} \to \{1, \ldots, n\}$ such that $N_i\theta_C = L_{f(i)}$ and $N_i\theta_D = M_{g(i)}$ for each i ($1 \leq i \leq l$). Let S be a selection $(L_{f(1)}, M_{g(1)}), \ldots, (L_{f(l)}, M_{g(l)})$ of C and D. Since f and g are total monotone increasing functions, S is order-preserving. By the definition of lga, the following statement holds.

$$lga(S^C, S^D) = lga([L_{f(1)}, \ldots, L_{f(l)}], [M_{g(1)}, \ldots, M_{g(l)}])$$
$$= [lga(L_{f(1)}, M_{g(1)}), \ldots, lga(L_{f(l)}, M_{g(l)})].$$

Since $lga(L_{f(i)}, M_{g(i)})$ is the least generalization of $L_{f(i)}$ and $M_{g(i)}$ (as literals), there exists substitution θ_i such that $N_i\theta_i = lga(L_{f(i)}, M_{g(i)})$ for each i ($1 \leq i \leq l$). Hence, for a substitution $\theta = \theta_1 \cdots \theta_l$, it holds that $G\theta = lga(S^C, S^D)$, that is, $G \succeq_o lga(S^C, S^D)$.   □

Lemma 6. *Let C and D be ordered clauses, S a selection of C and D, and T a subsequence of S. Then, it holds that $lga(T^C, T^D) \succeq_o lga(S^C, S^D)$.*

Proof. Suppose that $S = (L_1, M_1), \ldots, (L_k, M_k)$ is a selection of C and D, and T is a subsequence of S not containing the elements $(L_{i_1}, M_{i_1}), \ldots, (L_{i_l}, M_{i_l})$ ($1 \leq i_1 < \cdots < i_l \leq k$). Then, S^C, S^D, T^C and T^D are of the following forms.

$$S^C = [L_1, \ldots, L_k],$$
$$S^D = [M_1, \ldots, M_k],$$
$$T^C = [L_1, \ldots, L_{i_1-1}, L_{i_1+1}, \ldots, L_{i_l-1}, L_{i_l+1}, \ldots, L_k],$$
$$T^D = [M_1, \ldots, M_{i_1-1}, M_{i_1+1}, \ldots, M_{i_l-1}, M_{i_l+1}, \ldots, M_k].$$

In order to represent the bijections ψ_1 and ψ_2 applied in lga, we add the subscripts ψ_1 and ψ_2 to $lga(S^C, S^D)$ and $lga(T^C, T^D)$. Then, by the definition of lga, $lga_{\psi_1}(S^C, S^D)$ and $lga_{\psi_2}(T^C, T^D)$ are of the following forms.

$$lga_{\psi_1}(S^C, S^D) = [lga_{\psi_1}(L_1, M_1), \ldots, lga_{\psi_1}(L_k, M_k)],$$
$$lga_{\psi_2}(T^C, T^D) = [lga_{\psi_2}(L_1, M_1), \ldots, lga_{\psi_2}(L_{i_1-1}, M_{i_1-1}),$$
$$lga_{\psi_2}(L_{i_1+1}, M_{i_1+1}), \ldots, lga_{\psi_2}(L_{i_l-1}, M_{i_l-1}),$$
$$lga_{\psi_2}(L_{i_l+1}, M_{i_l+1}), \ldots, lga_{\psi_2}(L_k, M_k)].$$

We can suppose that both the bijections ψ_1 and ψ_2 map the same pairs of terms in T to the same natural numbers, that is, ψ_1 is an extension of ψ_2. Then, it is obvious that $lga_{\psi_1}(L_i, M_i) = lga_{\psi_2}(L_i, M_i)$ for each i ($1 \leq i \leq k$, $i \neq i_1, \ldots, i \neq i_l$). Hence, it holds that $lga_{\psi_2}(T^C, T^D) \sqsubseteq lga_{\psi_1}(S^C, S^D)$, that is, $lga_{\psi_2}(T^C, T^D) \succeq_o lga_{\psi_1}(S^C, S^D)$.   □

If S in Lemma 6 is order-preserving, then so is T. Hence, if S is order-preserving, then both $lga(S^C, S^D)$ and $lga(T^C, T^D)$ are generalizations of $\{C, D\}$ by Lemma 5.

Theorem 2. *Let C and D be ordered clauses. For every minimal generalization G of C and D under $\succeq_o$, there exists a complete selection S of $\{C, D\}$ such that $G \sim_o lga(S^C, S^D)$.*

Proof. Let C and D be ordered clauses $[L_1, \dots, L_m]$ and $[M_1, \dots, M_n]$, respectively, and suppose that G is a minimal generalization of $\{C, D\}$ under $\succeq_o$ but there exist no complete selections of C and D satisfying the statement.

By Lemma 5 and since G is a minimal generalization of $\{C, D\}$, there exists an order-preserving selection S such that $G \sim_o lga(S^C, S^D)$. Since S is not complete but order-preserving, S is not total, so there exists either i ($1 \le i \le m$) or j ($1 \le j \le n$) such that L_i in C or M_j in D does not appear in S. Without loss of generality, we can suppose that all literals in C and D except just L_i appear in S.

Since S is order-preserving, there exist consecutive pairs (L_{i-1}, M_j) and (L_{i+1}, M_k) in S, where k is equal to either j or $j + 1$. Then, let S_1 be a selection consisting of the pairs from the first element of S to (L_{i-1}, M_j) and S_2 a selection consisting of the pairs from (L_{i+1}, M_k) to the last element of S.

Consider the selection $T = S_1, (L_i, M_j), S_2$. By the supposition, T is complete. On the other hand, it holds that $T^C = S_1^C \circ [L_i] \circ S_2^C$ and $T^D = S_1^D \circ [M_j] \circ S_2^D$. Since $S^C = S_1^C \circ S_2^C$ and $S^D = S_1^D \circ S_2^D$ and by Lemma 6, it holds that $lga(S^C, S^D) \succeq_o lga(T^C, T^D)$. Also since T is complete and by Lemma 4, $lga(T^C, T^D)$ is a generalization of $\{C, D\}$. Since G is a minimal generalization of $\{C, D\}$ and $G \sim_o lga(S^C, S^D)$, it holds that $G \sim_o lga(T^C, T^D)$, which is a contradiction. □

Example 2. The converse of Theorem 2 does not hold in general, that is, there exists a complete selection S of C and D such that $lga(S^C, S^D)$ is not a minimal generalization of $\{C, D\}$ under $\succeq_o$.

Consider the following ordered clauses C and D.

$$C = [p(a, b), p(b, b)] \quad = [L_1, L_2],$$
$$D = [p(a', a'), p(b', c')] = [M_1, M_2].$$

Furthermore, S, T and U are the following complete selections of C and D.

$$S = (L_1, M_1), (L_2, M_2),$$
$$T = (L_1, M_1), (L_1, M_2), (L_2, M_2),$$
$$U = (L_1, M_1), (L_2, M_1), (L_2, M_2).$$

Then, it holds that:

$$lga(S^C, S^D) = [p(x, y), p(z, w)] \qquad \sim_o [p(x, y)],$$
$$lga(T^C, T^D) = [p(x, y), p(y, z), p(w, z)] \sim_o [p(x, y), p(y, z)],$$
$$lga(U^C, U^D) = [p(x, y), p(y, y), p(z, w)] \sim_o [p(x, y), p(y, y)].$$

It is obvious that $lga(S^C, S^D)$, $lga(T^C, T^D)$, and $lga(U^C, U^D)$ are generalizations of $\{C, D\}$ but $lga(S^C, S^D) \succ_o lga(T^C, T^D) \succ_o lga(U^C, U^D)$, so $lga(S^C, S^D)$ and $lga(T^C, T^D)$ are not minimal generalizations of $\{C, D\}$ under $\succeq_o$.

3.3 The Number of Minimal Generalizations

In this section, we show that the number of minimal generalizations can grow exponentially. We say that a selection S of C and D is *redundant* if S contains some duplicated pair of compatible literals in C and D, and *nonredundant* if S is not redundant.

Lemma 7. Let S be a complete and redundant selection and T be a subsequence of S that is complete and nonredundant. Then, it holds that $lga(S^C, S^D) \sim_o lga(T^C, T^D)$.

Proof. It is sufficient to show the case that a complete and nonredundant selection T and a complete selection S satisfy the following conditions:

$$T^C = T_1^C \circ [L] \circ T_2^C,$$
$$T^D = T_1^D \circ [M] \circ T_2^D,$$
$$S^C = T_1^C \circ [L, L] \circ T_2^C,$$
$$S^D = T_1^D \circ [M, M] \circ T_2^D,$$

where $\#T_1^C = \#T_1^D$ and $\#T_2^C = \#T_2^D$. Then, it holds that

$$lga_{\psi_1}(T^C, T^D) = lga_{\psi_1}(T_1^C, T_1^D) \circ [lga_{\psi_1}(L, M)] \circ lga_{\psi_1}(T_2^C, T_2^D),$$
$$lga_{\psi_2}(S^C, S^D) = lga_{\psi_2}(T_1^C, T_1^D) \circ [lga_{\psi_2}(L, M), lga_{\psi_2}(L, M)] \circ lga_{\psi_2}(T_2^C, T_2^D).$$

Note that we can identify a bijection ψ_1 with a bijection ψ_2. Hence, it holds that $lga_{\psi_1}(T^C, T^D) \cong lga_{\psi_2}(S^C, S^D)$, so the statement holds. □

By Theorem 2 and Lemma 7, the number of minimal generalizations of $\{C, D\}$ is less than the number of complete and nonredundant selections of C and D. Hence, if we can enumerate all of the complete and nonredundant selections, then we can enumerate the candidate of minimal generalizations. Unfortunately, the number can grow exponentially as follows.

Suppose that C and D are ordered clauses such that $|C| = n$, $|D| = n$, and every literal in C and every literal in D are compatible. Let $F(n)$ be the number of complete and nonredundant selections of such C and D.

Theorem 3. $F(n) \geq 2^n - 1$.

Proof. Let C and D be ordered clauses $[L_1, \ldots, L_n]$ and $[M_1, \ldots, M_n]$, respectively. For the length l of a complete and nonredundant selection of C and D, it holds that $n \leq l \leq 2n-1$. Let $s_n(l)$ be the number of complete and nonredundant selections of C and D with length $n + l$. Then, it holds that $F(n) = \sum_{l=0}^{n-1} s_n(l)$.

Consider the selection with length $n + l$. First, we select repeatedly l literals in n literals $L_1, \ldots, L_n$. Then, by replacing the l literals in C with $2l$ literals in C repeatedly, we obtain the ordered clause $C' = [N_1, \ldots, N_{n+l}]$. For C', by adding literals to D as follows, we can construct the ordered clause $D' = [K_1, \ldots, K_{n+l}]$ with length $n + l$.

1. Set K_1 to M_1. Furthermore, for j such that $1 \leq j \leq n + l$ and $K_j = M_i$, if $N_j = N_{j+1}$, then we set K_{j+1} to M_{i+1}, and if $N_j \neq N_{j+1}$, then we set K_{j+1} to M_i.

2. If there exists a literal occurring in D but not in D', consider a sequence $(M_n, K_{n+l}), \ldots, (M_1, K_l)$ of pairs of literals in D and D' in this order. Then, for j such that $M_i = K_{i+l}$ and $i + 1 \leq j \leq n$, there exist literals $M_j \in D$ and $K_{j+l} \in D'$ such that $M_j \neq K_{j+l}$. Then, we set D' to $[k_1, \ldots, K_{j+l}, M_j, \ldots, M_n]$.

Consider a selection S of C' and D' from left to right. By the construction of C' and D', S is order-preserving and total, so complete. Since the selection of C' and D' constructed from the above 1 is nonredundant, so is S.

Then, for C', there exists at least one ordered clause D' such that C' and D' have a complete and nonredundant selection. Hence, it holds that $s_n(l) \geq {_nH_l}$, where $_nH_l$ denotes a repeated combination defined as $_nH_l = \binom{n + l - 1}{l}$. □

The above exponential bound is just an upper bound, but not a lower bound.

4 Intractability of Subsumption for Ordered Clauses

In this section, we show that the following subsumption problem ORDERED SUBSUMPTION for ordered clauses is also NP-complete.

ORDERED SUBSUMPTION
INSTANCE: Ordered clauses C and D.
QUESTION: Does C subsume D $(C \succeq_o D)$?

Theorem 4. *The problem* ORDERED SUBSUMPTION *is NP-complete.*

Proof. It is obvious that ORDERED SUBSUMPTION is in NP. We reduce from MONOTONE 1-IN-3 3SAT[5] to ORDERED SUBSUMPTION.

MONOTONE 1-IN-3 3SAT [5]
INSTANCE: A set X of variables and a collection S of monotone 3-clauses (i.e., clauses consisting of exactly three positive literals) over X.
QUESTION: Is there a truth assignment to X that makes exactly one literal of each clause in S true?

Let $X = \{x_1, \ldots, x_n\}$ be a set of variables and $S = \{s_1, \ldots, s_m\}$ a set of monotone 3-clauses over X. We refer s_j to $\{x_1^j, x_2^j, x_3^j\}$ for each j $(1 \leq j \leq m)$. Furthermore, let $e_1, \ldots, e_{m-1}$ be mutually distinct constant symbol.
Let c_j $(1 \leq j \leq m)$ and d be the following ordered clauses.

$$c_j = [p(x_1^j, x_2^j, x_3^j)],$$
$$d = [p(1,0,0), p(0,1,0), p(0,0,1)].$$

Furthermore, let C and D be the following ordered clauses.

$$C = c_1 \circ [q(e_1)] \circ c_2 \circ [q(e_2)] \circ \ldots \circ c_{m-1} \circ [q(e_{m-1})] \circ c_m,$$
$$D = d \circ [q(e_1)] \circ d \circ [q(e_2)] \circ \cdots \circ d \circ [q(e_{m-1})] \circ d.$$

Suppose that $(a_1, \ldots, a_n)$ is a truth assignment to X such that exactly one variable in each clause in S is true. Then, let θ be a substitution $\theta = \{a_1/x_1, \ldots, a_n/x_n\}$ and f a total monotone increasing function $f : \{1, \ldots, 2m - 1\} \rightarrow \{1, \ldots, 4m - 1\}$. Since f maps $q(e_j) \in C$ to $q(e_j) \in D$, f maps the atom $p(x_1^j, x_2^j, x_3^j)\theta$ in $c_j\theta$ to exactly one atom in the j-th d. Hence, it holds that $C\theta \sqsubseteq D$.

Conversely, suppose that $C \succeq_o D$, that is, there exists a substitution θ such that $C\theta \sqsubseteq D$. By the form of d and the existence of $q(e_j)$, a total monotone increasing function maps the atom $p(x_1^j, x_2^j, x_3^j)\theta$ in $c_j\theta$ to exactly one atom in the j-th d. Then, θ is of the form $\{a_1/x_1, \ldots, a_n/x_n\}$, where $a_i \in \{0, 1\}$ and $1 \leq i \leq n$. Let a be a truth assignment $(a_1, \ldots, a_n)$ to X. Then, a makes exactly one variable in $s_j \in S$ true for each j. $\square$

Corollary 1. *The problem* ORDERED SUBSUMPTION *is NP-complete even if one of the following statements holds.*

1. *C and D are function-free and contain* at most ternary *predicate symbols.*
2. *C and D are function-free and contain* at most binary *predicate symbols.*
3. *C and D contain* at most unary *predicate symbols.*

Proof. 1. It is straightforward from the proof of Theorem 4.
   2. In the proof of Theorem 4, replace c_j and d with the following c_j and d.

$$c_j = [p_1(x_1^j, x_2^j), p_1(x_3^j, x_1^j), p_2(x_2^j, x_3^j), p_2(x_1^j, x_2^j), p_3(x_3^j, x_1^j), p_3(x_2^j, x_3^j)],$$
$$d = [p_1(1,0), p_1(0,1), p_1(0,0), p_1(1,0)$$
$$p_2(1,0), p_2(0,1), p_2(0,0), p_2(1,0),$$
$$p_3(1,0), p_3(0,1), p_3(0,0), p_3(1,0)].$$

   3. In the proof of Theorem 4, replace every atom of the form $p(x, y, z)$ in c_j and d with $p(f(x, y, z))$. $\square$

5   Conclusion

In this paper, we have first formulated an ordered clause as a sequence of literals. Then, we have shown that there exists no least generalization in general and the number of minimal generalizations can grow exponentially. However, we can find minimal generalizations of ordered clauses by using Plotkin's algorithm *lgc* [12, 13]. Next, we have shown that the subsumption problem for ordered clauses is also NP-complete as similar as one for general clauses. This result claims that the definition that a clause is a set of literals is inessential for the intractability of subsumption problem for clauses.

It is a future work to introduce an order-preserving selection under some sense, instead of a complete selection, and discuss the generalization of it. It is also a future work to design an efficient enumeration algorithm of minimal generalizations.

As stated in Section 4, the subsumption for clauses is also intractable even if we introduce the order of literals in clauses. Such intractability is based on the fact that there exist variables occurring in two or more blocks in ordered clauses, refer to the proof of Theorem 4. It is a future work to formulate and characterize a clause to avoid to this condition, and investigate the combinatorial problems associated with the clause.

Acknowledgment

The authors would like to thank the anonymous referees in LLLL for valuable comments to revise the preliminary version of this paper. Also the authors would like to thank Prof. Katsumi Inoue and Prof. Luc De Laedt for the discussion of the related works at LLLL.

References

1. L. D. Baxter: *The complexity of unification*, Doctoral Thesis, Department of Computer Science, University of Waterloo, 1977.
2. C. Chekuri, A. Rajaraman: *Conjunctive query containment revisited*, Theoretical Computer Science **239**, 211-229, 2000.
3. S. Dan Lee, L. De Raedt: *Constraint based mining of first order sequences in SeqLog*, Database Support for Data Mining Applications, LNAI **2682**, 154–173, 2004.
4. S. Džeroski, S. Muggleton, S. Russell: *PAC-learnability of determinate logic programs*, Proc. 5th COLT, 128–135, 1992.
5. M. R. Garey, D. S. Johnson: *Computers and intractability: A guide to the theory of NP-completeness* W. H. Freeman and Company, 1979.
6. G. Gottlob, C. G. Fermüller: *Removing redundancy from a clause*, Artificial Intelligence **61**, 263–289, 1993.
7. J.-U. Kietz, S. Džeroski: *Inductive logic programming and learnability*, SIGART Bulletin **5**, 22–32, 1994.
8. J.-U. Kietz, M. Lübbe: *An efficient subsumption algorithm for inductive logic programming*, Proc. 11th ICML, 130–138, 1994.
9. P. R. J. van der Laag: *An analysis of refinement operators in inductive logic programming*, Ph.D. Thesis, Tinbergen Institute, 1995.
10. J.-L. Lassez, M. J. Maher, L. Marriot: *Unification revisited*, in J. Minker (ed.): *Foundations of deductive databases and logic programming*, Morgan-Kaufmann, 587–625, 1988
11. J. W. Lloyd: *Foundations of logic programming (2nd, extended edition)*, Springer, 1987.
12. S.-H. Nienhuys-Cheng, R. de Wolf: *Foundations of inductive logic programming*, LNAI **1228**, 1997.
13. G. D. Plotkin: *A note on inductive generalization*, Machine Intelligence **5**, 153–163, 1970.
14. J. C. Reynolds: *Transformational systems and the algebraic structure of atomic formulas*, Machine Intelligence **5**, 135–152, 1970.

Prediction of Recursive Real-Valued Functions from Finite Examples*

Eiju Hirowatari[1], Kouichi Hirata[2], and Tetsuhiro Miyahara[3]

[1] Department of Business Administration, The University of Kitakyushu Kitakyushu
802-8577, Japan
eiju@kitakyu-u.ac.jp
[2] Department of Artificial Intelligence, Kyushu Institute of Technology
Iizuka 820-8502, Japan
hirata@ai.kyutech.ac.jp
[3] Faculty of Information Sciences, Hiroshima City University
Hiroshima 731-3194, Japan
miyahara@its.hiroshima-cu.ac.jp

Abstract. In this paper, we investigate *prediction of recursive real-valued functions from finite examples* by extending the framework of inductive inference of recursive real-valued functions to be a more realistic one. First, we propose a *finite prediction machine*, which is a procedure that requests finite examples of a recursive real-valued function h and a datum of a real number x, and that outputs a datum of $h(x)$. Then, we formulate *finite prediction* of recursive real-valued functions and investigate the power of it. Furthermore, for a fixed rational closed interval I, we show that the class of all finitely predictable sets of recursive real-valued functions coincides with the class of all inferable sets of recursive real-valued functions in the limit, that is, REALFP$_I$ = REALEX$_I$.

1 Introduction

A *computable real function* [14, 16, 19], of which origin draws back into the classical work by Turing [18], is one of the computable representations of real numbers. Recently, the computable real function has been developed in a new research field of computational paradigm [4, 6] related to analysis, mathematical logic and computability. In this field, the computable real function is characterized from the logical viewpoints (*cf.*, [4, 6]).

A *recursive real-valued function* [9, 10, 11, 12], which we mainly deal with in this paper, is one of the formulations for the computable real function. The recursive real-valued function is formulated as a function that maps a sequence of closed intervals which converges to a real number to a sequence of closed intervals which converges to another real number.

* This work is partially supported by Grand-in-Aid for Scientific Research 15700137 and 16500084 from the Ministry of Education, Culture, Sports, Science and Technology, Japan.

T. Washio et al. (Eds.): JSAI 2005 Workshops, LNAI 4012, pp. 224–234, 2006.

In recursive real-valued functions, we deal with a pair $\langle p, \alpha \rangle$ of rational numbers such that p is an approximate value of x and α is its error bound, instead of a real number x which we cannot deal with directly in computers. Such a pair $\langle p, \alpha \rangle$ is called a *datum* of x. Then, an *example* of a recursive real-valued function h is formulated as a pair $\langle \langle p, \alpha \rangle, \langle q, \beta \rangle \rangle$ satisfying that there exists a real number x in the domain of h such that $\langle p, \alpha \rangle$ and $\langle q, \beta \rangle$ are data of x and $h(x)$, respectively.

Based on the above concept, *inductive inference* of recursive real-valued functions has been first introduced by Hirowatari and Arikawa [8] and developed by their co-authors [1, 9, 10, 11]. In their works, the criteria such as REALEX and REALNUM! for inductive inference of recursive real-valued functions have been formulated as extensions of EX for *identification in the limit* and NUM! for *identification by enumeration* [5], respectively, and their interaction has been widely studied (*cf.*, [3, 13]).

On the other hand, the *prediction* or *extrapolation* of recursive functions [2, 3] is to predict the n-th element of the sequence given the first $n - 1$ elements by a prediction machine. The *prediction machine* is realized as simply an algorithmic device that accepts as input a finite (possibly empty) sequence of values and may output some value and halt, or may diverge.

Note that the examples in the prediction of recursive real-valued functions is not ordered, while the examples in the prediction of recursive functions implicitly assumed to be ordered, which is a reason why the criterion NV of the prediction is named after 'next value.' Furthermore, in our previous work [12], we have formulated prediction of recursive real-valued functions as *an infinite process* and introduced the criterion REALNV as similar as NV [2, 3].

In this paper, we formulate prediction of recursive real-valued functions *from finite examples*. Hence, this work is more realistic than our previous work [12] and is considered as a bridge between our theoretical results on learning of recursive real-valued functions [1, 8, 9, 10, 11, 12] and our practical work on discovery of differential equations from numerical data [17].

First, we propose a *finite prediction machine*, which is a procedure that requests finite examples W of a recursive real-valued function h and a datum $\langle p, \alpha \rangle$ of a real number x, and that outputs a datum $\langle q, \beta \rangle$ of $h(x)$. Then, we introduce a new learning criterion REALFP for finite prediction of recursive real-valued functions and investigate the power of it in comparison with the learning criterion REALEX of recursive real-valued functions.

This paper is organized as follows. In Section 2, we review recursive real-valued functions. In Section 3, we propose a finite prediction machine and a new learning criterion REALFP for finite prediction of recursive real-valued functions. In particular, we give a sufficient condition of a recursive real-valued function that is finitely predictable. In Section 4, we discuss finite prediction of recursive real-valued functions on a fixed rational closed interval I and introduce the criterion REALFP$_I$ for finite prediction of such functions. Then, we show that REALFP$_I$ = REALEX$_I$.

2   Recursive Real-Valued Functions

In this section, we prepare some notions for a *recursive real-valued function*, which is one of the formulations for a computable real function [14, 16, 19]. Refer to papers [8, 9, 10, 11, 12] in more detail.

Let N, Q and R be the sets of all natural numbers, rational numbers and real numbers, respectively. By N^+ and Q^+ we denote the sets of all positive natural numbers and positive rational numbers, respectively. By $[a, b]$, we denote a closed interval, where $a, b \in R$ such that $a < b$. Furthermore, the length of a closed interval $[a, b]$ is defined as $b - a$.

Throughout of this paper, h is a real-valued function from S to R, where $S \subseteq R$. By $dom(h)$ we denote the domain of h, that is, $dom(h) = S$.

Definition 1. Let f and g be functions from N to Q and Q^+, respectively, and x a real number. We say that a pair $\langle f, g \rangle$ is an *approximate expression* of x if f and g satisfy the following conditions:

(1) $\lim_{n \to \infty} g(n) = 0$.
(2) $|f(n) - x| \le g(n)$ for each $n \in N$.

Note here that $f(n)$ and $g(n)$ represent an *approximate value* of x and an *error bound* of x at point n, respectively. A real number x is *recursive* if there exists an approximate expression $\langle f, g \rangle$ of x such that f and g are recursive.

In order to formulate a *recursive real-valued function*, we introduce the concepts of a *rationalized domain* and a *rationalized function*.

Definition 2. For $S \subseteq R$, a *rationalized domain* of S, denoted by RD_S, is the subset of $Q \times Q^+$ such that $RD_S = \{\langle p, \alpha \rangle \mid [p - \alpha, p + \alpha] \subseteq S\}$. For a real-valued function h, we denote $RD_{dom(h)}$ by RD_h simply.

Definition 3. Let h be a real-valued function. A *rationalized function* of h, denoted by $\mathcal{A}_h$, is a computable function from RD_h to $Q \times Q^+$ satisfying the following condition:

> For each $x \in dom(h)$, let $\langle f, g \rangle$ be an approximate expression of x. Then, there exists an approximate expression $\langle f_0, g_0 \rangle$ of $h(x)$ and it holds that $\mathcal{A}_h(\langle f(n), g(n) \rangle) = \langle f_0(n), g_0(n) \rangle$ for each $n \in N$ such that $\langle f(n), g(n) \rangle \in RD_h$.

We also call a rationalized function $\mathcal{A}_h$ of h an *algorithm which computes h*.

Definition 4. A function h is a *recursive real-valued function* if there exists a rationalized function $\mathcal{A}_h : RD_h \to Q \times Q^+$ of h, where RD_h is a rationalized domain of $dom(h)$. We demand that $\mathcal{A}_h(\langle p, \alpha \rangle)$ does not halt for all $\langle p, \alpha \rangle \notin RD_h$. Furthermore, by $\mathcal{RRVF}$ we denote *the set of all recursive real-valued functions*.

Furthermore, we introduce the criteria for inductive inference of recursive real-valued functions [9, 10, 11].

As an approximation of a real number x, we deal with a pair $\langle p, \alpha \rangle \in Q \times Q^+$ of rational numbers such that p is an approximate value of x and α is its error bound, i.e., $x \in [p - \alpha, p + \alpha]$. We call such a pair $\langle p, \alpha \rangle$ a *datum* of x.

Definition 5. An *example* of a recursive real-valued function h is a pair $\langle\langle p, \alpha\rangle,$ $\langle q, \beta\rangle\rangle$ satisfying that there exists a real number $x \in dom(h)$ such that $\langle p, \alpha\rangle$ and $\langle q, \beta\rangle$ are data of x and $h(x)$, respectively.

We can imagine an example of h as a rectangular box $[p - \alpha, p + \alpha] \times [q - \beta, q + \beta]$ such that $p, q \in Q$ and $\alpha, \beta \in Q^+$.

Definition 6. A *presentation* of a recursive real-valued function h is an infinite sequence $\sigma = w_1, w_2, \ldots$ of examples of h in which, for each real number $x \in dom(h)$ and $\zeta > 0$, there exists an example $w_k = \langle\langle p_k, \alpha_k\rangle, \langle q_k, \beta_k\rangle\rangle$ such that $x \in [p_k - \alpha_k, p_k + \alpha_k]$, $h(x) \in [q_k - \beta_k, q_k + \beta_k]$, $\alpha_k \leq \zeta$ and $\beta_k \leq \zeta$.

By $\sigma[n]$, we denote the initial segment of n examples in σ.

An *inductive inference machine* (*IIM*, for short) is a procedure that requests inputs from time to time and produces algorithms, called *conjectures*, that compute recursive real-valued functions from time to time. Let σ be a presentation of a function. For $\sigma[n] = \langle w_1, w_2, \ldots, w_n\rangle$ and an IIM $\mathcal{M}$, by $\mathcal{M}(\sigma[n])$ we denote the last conjecture of $\mathcal{M}$ after requesting examples $w_1, w_2, \ldots, w_n$ as inputs.

Definition 7. Let σ be a presentation of a function and $\{\mathcal{M}(\sigma[n])\}_{n\geq1}$ an infinite sequence of conjectures produced by an IIM $\mathcal{M}$. A sequence $\{\mathcal{M}(\sigma[n])\}_{n\geq1}$ *converges* to an algorithm $\mathcal{A}_h$ if there exists a number $n_0 \in N$ such that $\mathcal{M}(\sigma[m])$ equals $\mathcal{A}_h$ for each $m \geq n_0$.

Definition 8. Let h be a recursive real-valued function and $\mathcal{T}$ a set of recursive real-valued functions. An IIM $\mathcal{M}$ REALEX-*infers* h, denoted by $h \in$ REALEX($\mathcal{M}$), if, for each presentation σ of h, the sequence $\{\mathcal{M}(\sigma[n])\}_{n\geq1}$ converges to an algorithm that computes an extension of h.

Furthermore, an IIM $\mathcal{M}$ REALEX-*infers* $\mathcal{T}$ if $\mathcal{M}$ REALEX-infers every $h \in \mathcal{T}$, and $\mathcal{T}$ is REALEX-*inferable* if there exists an IIM that REALEX-infers $\mathcal{T}$. By REALEX, we denote *the class of all* REALEX-*inferable sets of recursive real-valued functions*.

Definition 9. Let h be a recursive real-valued function and $\mathcal{T}$ a set of recursive real-valued functions. An IIM $\mathcal{M}$ REALCONS-*infers* h, denoted by $h \in$ REALCONS($\mathcal{M}$), if it satisfies the following conditions.

1. $h \in$ REALEX($\mathcal{M}$).
2. For each presentation σ of h, conjecture $\mathcal{A}_{h_n} = \mathcal{M}(\sigma[n])$ and $\langle\langle p, \alpha\rangle, \langle q, \beta\rangle\rangle \in \sigma[n]$ such that $[p - \alpha, p + \alpha] \subseteq S$, there exists an $x \in [p - \alpha, p + \alpha]$ such that $h_n(x) \in [q - 2\beta, q + 2\beta]$, where h_n is a recursive real-valued function and $\mathcal{A}_{h_n}$ is an algorithm which computes h_n.

Furthermore, an IIM $\mathcal{M}$ REALCONS-*infers* $\mathcal{T}$ if $\mathcal{M}$ REALCONS-infers every $h \in \mathcal{T}$, and $\mathcal{T}$ is REALCONS-*inferable* if there exists an IIM that REALCONS-infers $\mathcal{T}$. By REALCONS, we denote *the class of all* REALCONS-*inferable sets of recursive real-valued functions*.

We call functions x, $-x$, $\dfrac{1}{x}$, e^x, $\log x$, $\sin x$, $\arctan x$, $x^{\frac{1}{2}}$, $\arcsin x$ and the constant functions c_r for each recursive real number r *basic functions*. Here, $\dfrac{1}{x}$ for $x = 0$, $\log x$ for each $x \leq 0$, $x^{\frac{1}{2}}$ for each $x \leq 0$, and $\arcsin x$ for each $x \in R$ such that $|x| \geq 1$ are undefined as usual. By $\mathcal{BF}$ we denote the set of all basic functions.

Definition 10. By $\mathcal{EF}$ we denote the smallest set containing $\mathcal{BF}$ and satisfying the following condition:

$$\text{If } h_1, h_2 \in \mathcal{EF}, \text{ then } h_1 + h_2, h_1 \times h_2, h_1 \circ h_2 \in \mathcal{EF}.$$

We say that a function in $\mathcal{EF}$ an *elementary function*.

We can also show that every basic function is a recursive real-valued function. Furthermore, the following theorem holds.

Theorem 1 ([8]). *Every elementary function is a recursive real-valued function.*

Hence, we can conclude that the class of recursive real-valued functions is rich enough to express the elementary functions with recursive real coefficient.

3   Finite Prediction Machine

In this section, we introduce a finite prediction machine of recursive real-valued functions.

Let $w = \langle \langle p, \alpha \rangle, \langle q, \beta \rangle \rangle$ be an example of h. Then, we can imagine an example w of h as a rectangle box $[p - \alpha, p + \alpha] \times [q - \beta, q + \beta]$. Then, a set $W = \{w_1, w_2, \ldots, w_n\}$ of such boxes is finite examples of h if each example contains a point $(x, h(x))$ on the graph of h.

A *finite prediction machine* (*FPM*, for short) is a procedure that requests finite examples of a recursive real-valued function and a datum of a real number, and that outputs a datum of a real number. For an FPM $\mathcal{P}$, finite examples W of a recursive real-valued function and a datum $\langle p, \alpha \rangle$ of a real number, by $\mathcal{P}(W, \langle p, \alpha \rangle)$, we denote the output of $\mathcal{P}$ after requesting W and $\langle p, \alpha \rangle$ as inputs. In this paper, we assume that $\mathcal{P}(W, \langle p, \alpha \rangle)$ is defined for each finite examples W of a recursive real-valued function and datum $\langle p, \alpha \rangle$ of a real number.

Definition 11. Let h be a recursive real-valued function, W finite examples of h, and $\langle p, \alpha \rangle$ a datum of a real number such that $[p - \alpha, p + \alpha] \cap dom(h) \neq \emptyset$. Then, we say that an FPM $\mathcal{P}$ *predicts* h *from* W *exactly* if the following conditions hold.

(1) $\langle \langle p, \alpha \rangle, \mathcal{P}(W, \langle p, \alpha \rangle) \rangle$ is an example of h.
(2) If $[p - \alpha, p + \alpha] \subseteq dom(h)$, then it holds that $h(x) \in [q - \beta, q + \beta]$ for each $x \in [p - \alpha, p + \alpha]$, where $\langle q, \beta \rangle = \mathcal{P}(W, \langle p, \alpha \rangle)$.
(3) For each $x \in dom(h)$ and each approximate expression $\langle f_x, g_x \rangle$ of x, there exists an approximate expression $\langle f_{h(x)}, g_{h(x)} \rangle$ of $h(x)$ satisfying that, for each $m \in N$ with $[f_x(m) - g_x(m), f_x(m) + g_x(m)] \subseteq dom(h)$, it holds that $\langle f_{h(x)}(m), g_{h(x)}(m) \rangle = \mathcal{P}(W, \langle f_x(m), g_x(m) \rangle)$.

Now consider the set T of recursive real-valued functions. It is difficult that, for a target function $h \in T$, an FPM predicts h from finite examples exactly. Then, we propose prediction from finite examples approximately which permits some error bound.

Definition 12. Let h be a recursive real-valued function, $\langle\langle p, \alpha\rangle, \langle q, \beta\rangle\rangle$ a datum of a recursive real-valued function and W finite examples of a recursive real-valued function. Then, we say that $\langle\langle p, \alpha\rangle, \langle q, \beta\rangle\rangle$ is *near to* h if there exists an $x \in [p - \alpha, p + \alpha]$ such that $h(x) \in [q - 2\beta, q + 2\beta]$. Furthermore, we say that W is *near to* h if there exists an $x \in [p - \alpha, p + \alpha]$ such that $h(x) \in [q - 2\beta, q + 2\beta]$ for each $\langle\langle p, \alpha\rangle, \langle q, \beta\rangle\rangle \in W$.

Definition 13. Let h be a recursive real-valued function, W finite examples of h, and $\langle p, \alpha\rangle$ a datum of a real number such that $[p - \alpha, p + \alpha] \cap dom(h) \neq \emptyset$. Then, we say that an FPM $\mathcal{P}$ *predicts* h *from* W *approximately* if there exists a recursive real-valued function h' such that the following conditions hold.

(1) W is near to h'.
(2) It holds that $dom(h) \subseteq dom(h')$.
(3) $\mathcal{P}$ predicts h' from W exactly.

For a target function h, by using a presentation σ of h, we introduce an FPM which finitely predicts h in the limit.

Definition 14. Let h be a recursive real-valued function. Then, we say that an FPM $\mathcal{P}$ *predicts* h *with limiting convergence* if, for each presentation σ of h, there exists a natural number $k \in N$ such that $\mathcal{P}(\sigma[n], \langle p, \alpha\rangle) = \mathcal{P}(\sigma[k], \langle p, \alpha\rangle)$ for each $n \in N$ such that $n \geq k$ and each $\langle p, \alpha\rangle \in Q \times Q^+$.

Definition 15. Let h be a recursive real-valued function. Then, we say that an FPM $\mathcal{P}$ *finitely predicts* h if the following conditions hold.

(1) $\mathcal{P}$ predicts h from W approximately, for each finite examples W of h.
(2) $\mathcal{P}$ predicts h with limiting convergence.

Also let T be a set of recursive real-valued functions. Then, we say that an FPM $\mathcal{P}$ *finitely predicts* T if $\mathcal{P}$ finitely predicts every $h \in T$, and T is *finitely predictable* if there exists an FPM that finitely predicts T. By REALFP, we denote *the class of all finitely predictable sets of recursive real-valued functions*.

Example 1. For the recursive real-valued function $e^x : R \to R$, there exists an FPM $\mathcal{P}$ which finitely predicts e^x.

e^x is a recursive real-valued function as follows: For $RD_h = Q \times Q^+$, let $\mathcal{A}_{e^x} : RD_h \to Q \times Q^+$ be a computable function defined by

$$\mathcal{A}_{e^x}(\langle p, \alpha\rangle) = \left\langle \frac{1}{2}\sum_{i=0}^{d}\frac{1}{i!}(u^i + l^i) + \frac{3^m u^{d+1}}{2(d+1)!} , \frac{1}{2}\sum_{i=0}^{d}\frac{1}{i!}(u^i - l^i) + \frac{3^m u^{d+1}}{2(d+1)!} \right\rangle,$$

where $u = p + \alpha$, $l = p - \alpha$, d is the least odd number such that $\dfrac{1}{2\alpha} \leq d$, and m is the least natural number such that $u \leq m$. Then, $\mathcal{A}_{e^x}$ is an algorithm that computes e^x described in Figure 1.

For finite examples W_{e^x} of e^x and a datum $\langle p, \alpha \rangle$ of an $x \in R$, we define that $\mathcal{P}(W_{e^x}, \langle p, \alpha \rangle) = \mathcal{A}_{e^x}(\langle p, \alpha \rangle)$. Thus, $\mathcal{P}$ finitely predicts e^x.

Algorithm: $\mathcal{A}_{e^x}(\langle p, \alpha \rangle)$
begin
  repeat
    if $\langle p, \alpha \rangle \in Q \times Q^+$ **then begin**
      $u := p + \alpha;\ \ l := p - \alpha;\ \ d := 1;\ \ m := 0;$
      while $d < \dfrac{1}{2\alpha}$ **do** $d := d + 2;$
      while $m < u$ **do** $m := m + 1;$
      output $\left\langle \dfrac{1}{2} \displaystyle\sum_{i=0}^{d} \dfrac{1}{i!}(u^i + l^i) + \dfrac{3^m u^{d+1}}{2(d+1)!}, \dfrac{1}{2} \displaystyle\sum_{i=0}^{d} \dfrac{1}{i!}(u^i - l^i) + \dfrac{3^m u^{d+1}}{2(d+1)!} \right\rangle$
    end
  forever
end.

Fig. 1. The algorithm $\mathcal{A}_{e^x}(\langle p, \alpha \rangle)$ that computes e^x

Example 2. For the set $\mathcal{T}_{e_{a,b}}$ of all recursive real-valued functions $e_{a,b}$ such that $e_{a,b}(x) = ae^x + b$ for each $a, b \in Q$, there exists an FPM $\mathcal{P}$ which finitely predicts $\mathcal{T}_{e_{a,b}}$.

Theorem 2. *For each FPM $\mathcal{P}$, there exists a recursive real-valued function that $\mathcal{P}$ cannot finitely predict.*

Proof. Consider the following function $t(x)$.

$$t(x) = \begin{cases} \left| \tan \pi \left(n - \frac{1}{2^m} - \frac{1}{2} \right) \right| & \text{if } x \in [n - \frac{1}{2^m}, n + \frac{1}{2^m}] \text{ for } n, m \in N^+ \\ & \quad \text{such that } \varphi_n(n) \text{ is defined and } \varPhi_n(n) = m, \\ \left| \tan \pi (x - \frac{1}{2}) \right| & \text{otherwise.} \end{cases}$$

Here, φ_n is a partial recursive function from N to N with an index n, and $\varPhi_n(n)$ is a step counting function for computation of $\varphi_n(n)$. Then, $t(x)$ is a recursive real-valued function.

Suppose that $\mathcal{P}$ finitely predicts $t(x)$. Then, $\mathcal{P}$ predicts $t(x)$ with limiting convergence. Let $\sigma = w_1, w_2, \ldots$ be a presentation of $t(x)$ such that $w_j = \langle \langle p_j, \alpha_j \rangle, \langle q_j, \beta_j \rangle \rangle$ for each $j \in N^+$. Then, there exists an $i \in N$ such that, for each $k \in N$ $(k \geq i)$, $\mathcal{P}(\sigma[k], \langle n, \frac{1}{2^m} \rangle) = \langle q, \beta \rangle$, where $\langle q, \beta \rangle = \mathcal{P}(\sigma[i], \langle n, \frac{1}{2^m} \rangle)$ for each $n, m \in N^+$. Thus, it holds that either $\varPhi_n(n)$ is defined and $t([n - \frac{1}{2^m}, n + \frac{1}{2^m}]) \subseteq [q - \beta, q + \beta]$ or $\varPhi_n(n)$ is not defined. If there exists a number $m \in N^+$ such that $t(n - \frac{1}{2^m}) \leq q + \beta$ and $t(n - \frac{1}{2^m}) = t(n - \frac{1}{2^{m+1}})$, then it holds that

$t([n - \frac{1}{2^m}, n + \frac{1}{2^m}]) \subseteq [q - \beta, q + \beta]$, that is, $\Phi_n(n) = m$, otherwise $\Phi_n(n)$ is not defined. Thus, we can determine whether or not $\varphi_n(n)$ is defined for each $n \in N$, which is a contradiction. Hence, $\mathcal{P}$ cannot finitely predict $t(x)$.   □

Corollary 1. $\mathcal{RRVF}$ *is not finitely predictable.*

Definition 16. Let h be a real-valued function. Then, we define the following two computable functions $Subset_h$ and $Exist_h$ from $Q \times Q^+$ to $\{0, 1\}$:

$$Subset_h(\langle p, \alpha \rangle) = \begin{cases} 1 \text{ if } [p - \alpha, p + \alpha] \subseteq dom(h), \\ 0 \text{ otherwise.} \end{cases}$$

$$Exist_h(\langle p, \alpha \rangle) = \begin{cases} 1 \text{ if } [p - \alpha, p + \alpha] \cap dom(h) \neq \emptyset, \\ 0 \text{ otherwise.} \end{cases}$$

We call the functions $Subset_h$ and $Exist_h$ a *subset function* and an *existence function* of h, respectively.

Note that, for a recursive real-valued function h, there does not always exist a subset function of h. Similarly, there does not always exist an existence function of h.

In contrast to Theorem 2, the following theorem gives a sufficient condition that a recursive real-valued function is finitely predictable.

Theorem 3. *Let h be a recursive real-valued function. If there exist both a subset function of h and an existence function of h, then there exists an FPM $\mathcal{P}$ which finitely predicts h.*

Proof. Since h is a recursive real-valued function, there exists an algorithm $\mathcal{A}_h$ that computes h. By the existence of both a subset function of h and an existence function of h, we can construct the following FPM $\mathcal{P}$:

$$\mathcal{P}(W, \langle p, \alpha \rangle) = \begin{cases} \mathcal{A}_h(\langle p, \alpha \rangle) & \text{if } [p - \alpha, p + \alpha] \subseteq dom(h), \\ \mathcal{A}_h(\mathcal{B}_h(\langle p, \alpha \rangle)) & \text{if } [p - \alpha, p + \alpha] \not\subseteq dom(h) \\ & \text{and } [p - \alpha, p + \alpha] \cap dom(h) \neq \emptyset, \\ \langle q, \beta \rangle & \text{otherwise,} \end{cases}$$

where $\langle q, \beta \rangle \in Q \times Q^+$. Note that such an algorithm $\mathcal{B}_h$ always exists and computes uniquely $\langle p_0, \alpha_0 \rangle \in Q \times Q^+$ satisfying that $[p_0 - \alpha_0, p_0 + \alpha_0] \subseteq [p - 2\alpha, p + 2\alpha] \cap dom(h)$ and $[p_0 - \alpha_0, p_0 + \alpha_0] \cap [p - \alpha, p + \alpha] \neq \emptyset$. It is obvious that $\mathcal{P}$ finitely predicts h.   □

4   Finite Prediction on a Fixed Rational Closed Interval

In this section, we investigate the finite prediction of recursive real-valued functions defined on a fixed rational closed interval I. In order to emphasize the interval I, by REALFP$_I$ we denote the class of all finitely predictable sets of recursive real-valued functions defined on I. Similarly, we define REALEX$_I$ and REALCONS$_I$. We note that REALCONS $\subsetneq$ REALEX and REALCONS$_I$ = REALEX$_I$ [9].

Theorem 4. *It holds that* $\mathrm{REALEX}_I = \mathrm{REALFP}_I$, *where* I *is a fixed rational closed interval.*

Proof. ($\subseteq$) First, we define that $I = [a, b]$. Suppose that $\mathcal{C} \in \mathrm{REALEX}_I$. Since $\mathrm{REALCONS}_I = \mathrm{REALEX}_I$, it holds that $\mathcal{C} \in \mathrm{REALCONS}_I$, that is, there exists an IIM $\mathcal{M}$ such that, for each $h \in \mathcal{C}$ and each presentation σ of $\mathcal{C}$, $\mathcal{M}$ REALCONS-infers h. There exists a natural number $n \in N$ such that, for each $l \geq n$, $\mathcal{M}(\sigma[n]) = \mathcal{M}(\sigma[l])$. Note that, without loss of generality, we can assume that, for each $m \in N$, $\mathcal{M}(\sigma[m])$ is always an algorithm of a recursive real-valued function defined on I.

For $h \in \mathcal{C}$, let W be finite examples $\{w_1, \ldots, w_s\}$ of h such that $\sigma[s] = w_1, \ldots, w_s$. Also let $\mathcal{P}$ the following FPM:

$$\mathcal{P}(W, \langle p, \alpha \rangle) = \begin{cases} \mathcal{M}(\sigma[s])(\langle p_0, \alpha_0 \rangle) & \text{if there exists a datum } \langle p_0, \alpha_0 \rangle \text{ with} \\ & [p_0 - \alpha_0, p_0 + \alpha_0] = [p - \alpha, p + \alpha] \cap I, \\ \mathcal{M}(\sigma[s])(\langle \frac{a+b}{2}, \frac{b-a}{2} \rangle) & \text{otherwise,} \end{cases}$$

where $\langle p_0, \alpha_0 \rangle \in Q \times Q^+$. Then, it holds that $\mathcal{P}$ predicts h from W approximately.

On the other hand, for each $l \geq n$ and $[p - \alpha, p + \alpha] \subseteq I$, it holds that $\mathcal{P}(\sigma[l], \langle p, \alpha \rangle) = \mathcal{M}(\sigma[l])(\langle p, \alpha \rangle) = \mathcal{M}(\sigma[l+1])(\langle p, \alpha \rangle) = \mathcal{P}(\sigma[l+1], \langle p, \alpha \rangle)$. Hence, it holds that $\mathcal{C} \in \mathrm{REALFP}_I$.

($\supseteq$) Suppose that $\mathcal{C} \in \mathrm{REALFP}_I$ and $h \in \mathcal{C}$. Then, for each presentation σ of h and $n \in N$, we can construct the following algorithm $\mathcal{A}_n$:

$$\mathcal{A}_n(\langle p, \alpha \rangle) = \begin{cases} \mathcal{P}(\sigma[n], \langle p, \alpha \rangle) & \text{if } [p - \alpha, p + \alpha] \subseteq I, \\ \text{undefined} & \text{otherwise.} \end{cases}$$

Let $I_1, I_2, \ldots$ be an enumeration of all closed intervals contained in I. Note that for each I_i, there exist $p_i \in Q$ and $\alpha_i \in Q^+$ such that $I_i = [p_i - \alpha_i, p_i + \alpha_i]$ corresponding to a datum $\langle p_i, \alpha_i \rangle$ of some real number in I. Then, let $\mathcal{M}$ be the following IIM:

$$\mathcal{M}(\sigma[1]) = \mathcal{A}_1,$$
$$\mathcal{M}(\sigma[n]) = \begin{cases} \mathcal{M}(\sigma[n-1]) & \text{if } \mathcal{M}(\sigma[n-1])(\langle p_i, \alpha_i \rangle) = \mathcal{A}_n(\langle p_i, \alpha_i \rangle) \\ & \text{for each } i \in N \text{ such that } 1 \leq i \leq n, \\ \mathcal{A}_n & \text{otherwise.} \end{cases}$$

Since $\mathcal{M}$ REALEX-infers h, it holds that $\mathcal{C} \in \mathrm{REALEX}_I$. $\square$

5   Conclusion

In this paper, we have discussed *finite prediction* of recursive real-valued functions. First, we have proposed a *finite prediction machine*, which is a procedure that requests finite examples W of a recursive real-valued function h and a datum $\langle p, \alpha \rangle$ of a real number x, and that outputs a datum $\langle q, \beta \rangle$ of $h(x)$. Then, we have introduced a new learning criterion REALFP for finite prediction of recursive real-valued functions and its variation REALFP_I, and investigated their properties. In particular, we have shown that $\mathrm{REALFP}_I = \mathrm{REALEX}_I$.

It is an important future work to compare the criterion REALFP and other criteria such as REALEX, REALNUM!, REALFIN, REALREF, REALREL, REALNV and so on [8, 9, 10, 11, 12] without a fixed closed interval. It is also a future work to compare the logical learning paradigm such as [15] with our work.

Our work as similar as *limit-computable mathematics* [7] can provide the basis of logical characterization of learning computable real functions. Hence, it is an important future work to investigate the logical aspects of recursive real-valued functions, by analyzing the relationship between our work and the recent works [4, 6].

References

1. K. Apsītis, S. Arikawa, R. Freivalds, E. Hirowatari, C. H. Smith, *On the inductive inference of recursive real-valued functions*, Theoret. Comput. Sci. **219**, 3–17, 1999.
2. J. M. Bārzdiņš, R. V. Freivalds, *On the prediction of general recursive functions*, Soviet Mathematics Doklady **13**, 1224–1228, 1972.
3. J. Case, C. Smith, *Comparison of identification criteria for machine inductive inference*, Theoret. Comput. Sci. **25**, 193–220, 1983.
4. S. B. Cooper, B. Löwe, L. Torenvliet (eds.), *New computational paradigms, Proc. 1st International Conference on Computability in Europe*, LNCS **3526**, 2005.
5. E. M. Gold, *Language identification in the limit*, Inform. Control **10**, 447–474, 1967.
6. T. Grubba, P. Hertling, H. Tsuiki, K. Weihrauch (eds.), *Proc. 2nd International Conference on Computability and Complexity in Analysis*, 2005.
7. S. Hayashi, *Mathematics based on learning*, Proc. 13th International Conference on Algorithmic Learning Theory, LNAI **2533**, 7–21, 2002.
8. E. Hirowatari, S. Arikawa, *Inferability of recursive real-valued functions*, Proc. 8th International Workshop on Algorithmic Learning Theory, LNAI **1316**, 18–31, 1997.
9. E. Hirowatari, S. Arikawa, *A comparison of identification criteria for inductive inference of recursive real-valued functions*, Theoret. Comput. Sci. **268**, 351–366, 2001.
10. E. Hirowatari, K. Hirata, T. Miyahara, S. Arikawa, *Criteria for inductive inference with mind changes and anomalies of recursive real-valued functions*, IEICE Trans. Inf. Syt. **E86-D**, 219–227, 2003.
11. E. Hirowatari, K. Hirata, T. Miyahara, S. Arikawa, *Refutability and reliability for inductive inference on recursive real-valued functions*, IPSJ Trans. Mathematical Modeling and Its Applications, **46**, 1–11, 2005.
12. E. Hirowatari, K. Hirata, T. Miyahara, S. Arikawa, *On the prediction of recursive real-valued functions*, Proc. Computability in Europe 2005, ILLC Publications, University van Amsterdam, 93-103, 2005.
13. S. Jain, D. Osherson, J. S. Royer, A. Sharma, *Systems that learn: An introduction to learning theory (2nd ed.)*, The MIT Press, 1999.
14. K. Ko. *Complexity theory of real functions*, Birkhäuser, 1991.
15. E. Martin, A. Sharma, F. Stephan, *On ordinal VC-dimension and some notions of complexity*, Proc. 14th International Workshop on Algorithmic Learning Theory, LNAI **2842**, 54–68, 2003.

16. M. B. Pour-El, J. I. Richards, *Computability in analysis and physics*, Springer-Verlag, 1988.
17. K. Niijima, H. Uchida, E. Hirowatari, S. Arikawa, *Discovery of differential equations from numerical data*, Proc. 1st International Conference on Discovery Science, LNAI **1532**, 364–374, 1998.
18. A. M. Turing, *On computable numbers, with the application to the Entscheidungsproblem*, Proc. London Mathematical Society **42**, 230–265, 1936.
19. K. Weihrauch, *Computable analysis – An introduction*, Springer-Verlag, 2000.

Part IV

Agent Network Dynamics and Intelligence

Agent Network Dynamics and Intelligence (ANDI 2005)

Satoshi Kurihara[1] and Kiyoshi Izumi[2]

[1] Osaka University, 8-1, Mihogaoka, Ibaraki, Osaka, 567-0047 Japan
kurihara@sanken.osaka-u.ac.jp
[2] National Institute of Advanced Industrial Science and Technology (AIST), AIST
Tsukuba Central 2, 1-1-1 Umezono, Tsukuba,Ibaraki, 305-8568 Japan
kiyoshi@ni.aist.go.jp

Scope of Workshop

Recently, the study of intelligence emerged from the behavior of many simple agents, such as collective intelligence, group intelligence, and Swarm-made architecture, become popular. A network structure made by the agents plays an important role in these research areas.

On the other hand, recent studies have revealed that various networks made by human beings, the most intelligent subsistence, have a scale-free structure. This has suggested that some kind of network structures, such as scale-free network and small-world network, are desirable to the emergence of behavior or intelligence.

In multi-agent coordination problems, even if each the agent's structure is homogeneous, the scale-free structures (for example, the structure of the Internet and link structure of WWW) created by the agents' rational behavior may generate intelligence and/or intelligent cooperation.

This workshop aims at the investigation of "network structures of agents", "network structure made by agents", and "network structure and phenomena made by the agents' rational behavior". And it focuses on "the intelligence from the viewpoint of a network structure", and "the intelligence emerged from the network."

Topic

- Scale-free network
- Small world
- Collective intelligence
- Collective learning
- Multi-agent network system
- Swarm-made architecture
- Web dynamics
- Web intelligence and web science
- Social intelligence
- Complex systems

T. Washio et al. (Eds.): JSAI 2005 Workshops, LNAI 4012, pp. 237–238, 2006.
© Springer-Verlag Berlin Heidelberg 2006

Committee

- Workshop chairs
  - Satoshi Kurihara (Osaka Univ.)
  - Kiyoshi Izumi (AIST)
- Program commitee
  - Eizo Akiyama (Tsukuba Univ.)
  - Kensuke Fukuda (NTT Network Innovation Labs.)
  - David Green (Monash Univ.)
  - Nobuyuki Hanaki (Columbia Univ.)
  - Takashi Hashimoto (JAIST)
  - Hidenori Kawamura (Hokkaido Univ.)
  - Koichi Kurumatani (AIST)
  - Yutaka Matsuo (AIST)
  - Akira Namatame (National Defence Academy)
  - Itsuki Noda (AIST)
  - iroshi Sato (National Defence Academy)
  - Takayuki Shiose (Kyoto Univ.)
  - Wataru Souma (ATR)
  - Keiki Takadama (Tokyo Institute of Technology)

Accepted Papers

We received 19 submissions, and after the review process 10 papers were accepted as follows:

- Toshiji Kawagoe and Shihomi Wada: A Counterexample for the Bullwhip Effect: Gaming and Multiagent Simulations
- Kosuke Ono, Takashi Hata, Toyofumi Maetani, Masateru Harao, and Kouichi Hirata: Development of a Multi-Agent Based Generic Traffic Simulator
- Syuji Miyazaki: Directed Network as a Chaotic Dynamical System
- Yuumi Kawachi and Shinichiro Yoshii: Behavior of Growing Scale-free Networks in Complex Systems
- Tadanobu Furukawa, Tomofumi Matsuzawa, Yutaka Matsuo, Koki Uchiyama, and Masayuki Takeda: Analysis of Users Relation and Reading Activity in Weblogs
- Hiromichi Kimura and Eizo Akiyama : Grand Canonical Minority Games with Variable Strategy Spaces
- Kazuhiro Kazama, Shin-ya Sato, Kensuke Fukuda, Ken-ichiro Murakami, Hiroshi Kawakami, and Osamu Katai: Evaluation of Using Human Relationships on the Web as Information Navigation Paths
- Shu-Heng Chen, Li-Cheng Sun, and Chih-Chien Wang: Network Topologies and Consumption Externality
- Tomohisa Yamashita, Kiyoshi Izumi, and Koichi Kurumatani: Information Sharing for Smooth Traffic in Road Networks
- Shinako Matsuyama, Masaaki Kunigami, and Takao Terano: Analyzing Peer to Peer Communication through Agent-Based Simulation

A Counterexample for the Bullwhip Effect: Gaming and Multiagent Simulations

Toshiji Kawagoe[1] and Shihomi Wada[2]

[1] Future University-Hakodate, Department of Complex Systems, 116-2
Kameda-Nakanocho, Hakodate, Hokkaido, 041-8655, Japan
kawagoe@fun.ac.jp
[2] Future University-Hakodate, Graduate School Systems Information Science
g3105006@fun.ac.jp

Abstract. In our experiment of a supply chain using Beer Game, to identify the cause of bullwhip effect, the number of firms in a supply chain (two or four firms), and the length of the delay in ordering and shipping between firms (one or three weeks) are controlled and compared in gaming simulations with human subjects and in the multi-agent simulations. We found a counterexample for the bullwhip effect such that inventory level of the upstream firm is not always larger than that of the downstream firm. In addition, contrary to our intuition, such counterexamples were frequently observed under the condition that (1) the number of firms in a supply chain was many, and that (2) the length of delay was rather longer.

Keywords: Supply chain, bullwhip effect, Beer Game, multiagent simulation.

1 Introduction

The bullwhip effect is the amplification of the order variability in a supply chain. Lee, Padmanabhan, and Whang [3] observes that the bullwhip effect occurs when demand orders variability in the supply chain are amplified as they moved up the supply chain. They point out that there are several causes of the bullwhip effect. As these causes are related to information sharing in a supply chain, Moyaux, Chaib-draa, and D'Amours [4][5] compare three inventory management strategies with different information sharing schemes. They find that combinations of more collaborative strategies are likely to be Nash equilibria [1]. One drawback of their study is that, due to the complexity of finding an optimal solution, they consider only a small set of strategies tractable in their study. So, the question of which factor is crucial for reducing the bullwhip effect still remains unsolved.

In our experiment of a supply chain using Beer Game, the number of firms in a supply chain (two or four firms) and the length of the delay in ordering and shipping between firms (one or three weeks) are compared in gaming simulations with human subjects and in the multi-agent simulations. To the best of our knowledge, there is no research of changing such environmental variables

T. Washio et al. (Eds.): JSAI 2005 Workshops, LNAI 4012, pp. 239–248, 2006.

to identify the cause of the bullwhip effect. In our result, we found a counterexample for the bullwhip effect in both gaming and multi-agent simulations such that inventory level of the upstream firm is not always larger than that of the downstream firm, even in the environment that the number of firms was many and the length of delay was longer.

The organization of the paper is as follows. In the next section, we explain our model of Beer Game and independent variables in our experiment. In section 3, the details of the gaming simulation with human subjects and the multi-agent simulation are presented and the results are shown. Concluding remarks are given in the final section.

2   Model

Beer game models a supply chain with several firms (the retailer, the distributor, and the factory). The game proceeds as follows (we present a three-weeks-delay case as an example, and the flow of these steps is shown in Fig. 1).

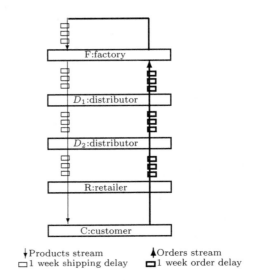

Fig. 1. Beer Game in $(D3, F4)$ Case

Step 1. In each week, each firm receives orders from the downstream firm and receives products from the upstream firm which were ordered three weeks ago. (For the retailer, orders from the customer, which follows a certain probability distribution, come every week.)

Step 2. Each firm ships products from his stock to the downstream firm if he has enough inventories to meet those orders. If not, the amount that orders minus inventories are recorded in the backorders to be shipped next week or later.

Step 3. Then each firm other than the factory makes orders to the upstream firm to fill his stock for the next week orders and to clear the backorders, if any.

Step 4. The factory starts producing new products to fill his stock for the next week orders and to clear the backorders, if any. It takes three weeks for the factory to complete producing new products.

Step 5. This ends a week. Go back to **Step 1.**

Now let us explain the following independent variables in our experiment.

$$D = \text{The length of delay in ordering and shipping}$$
$$\quad D1 \text{ A week delay case}$$
$$\quad D3 \text{ Three weeks delay case}$$
$$F = \text{The number of firms in a supply chain}$$
$$\quad F2 \text{ Two firms (the retailer and the factory)}$$
$$\quad F4 \text{ Four firms (two distributors added to F2)}$$
$$ST = \text{Strategy type}$$
$$\quad W \text{ Weighted moving average}$$
$$\quad S \text{ Standard moving average}$$
$$L = \text{The length of weeks taken for determing moving average}$$
$$\quad L3 \text{ Three weeks}$$
$$\quad L5 \text{ Five weeks}$$
$$T = \text{Time series of customer's order}$$
$$\quad T1 \text{ Pattern 1 in Moyaux et al.[5]}$$
$$\quad T2 \text{ Pattern 2 in Moyaux et al.[5]}$$
$$\quad T5 \text{ Pattern 5 in Moyaux et al.[5]}$$
$$\quad T6 \text{ Pattern 6 in Moyaux et al.[5]}$$
$$\quad TC \text{ Always 11}$$

Experimental conditions can be written with these variables, for example, as $(D3, F4, W, L5, TC)$. This means that there are four firms in a supply chain, the length of delay in ordering and shipping between firms is three weeks, each firm predicts next week orders by a weighted moving average of past five weeks orders, and the distribution of orders of customer is a constant.

In our experiment, we use another set of parameters to represent the state of each firm as follows.

$$I_t^x = \text{Firm } x\text{'s inventories in week } t$$
$$\omega_t^x = \text{The amount of demand orders which firm } x \text{ receives from the downstream firm in week } t$$
$$\Omega_t^x = \text{The amount of demand orders which firm } x \text{ states to the upstream firm in week } t$$
$$\chi_t^x = \text{The amount of products which firm } x \text{ receives from the upstream firm in week } t$$
$$S_t^x = \text{The amount of products which firm } x \text{ ships in week } t$$
$$B_t^x = \text{The amount of backorders which firm } x \text{ has in week } t$$
$$m_{t+1}^x = \text{The amount of } t+1\text{th week orders predicted by firm } x \text{ in week } t.$$

3   Experimental Results

3.1   Gaming Simulation with Human Subjects

Gaming simulations with human subjects using Beer Game were conducted at Future University-Hakodate on January 9, 2005[1]. Six undergraduate students voluntarily participated in the experiment.

In the experiment, as explained in the previous section, two independent variables, the length of delay, D1 or D3, and the number of firms, F2 or F4, were compared. In each experimental condition, they played Beer Game with six different conditions but membership of each group was changed in each condition to avoid any reputation effect. In each condition, subjects were forced to play the Beer Game at least 10 periods, then they continued to play the game unless the end of the game was determined with probability $1/6$.

At the beginning of the experiment, all firms were assigned twelve products as their initial stock and no backorder, and it is assumed that each firm has ordered and shipped four products in past every weeks, that is, for the subsequent one or three weeks, $\omega_t^x = 4$ and $S_t^x = 4$. We used three demand order distributions of the customer shown in Fig. 2. Type A is uniform distribution, type B normal distribution and type C U-shaped distribution.

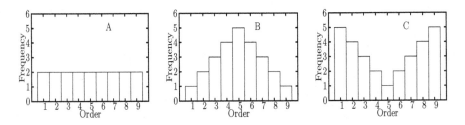

Fig. 2. Demand Order Distributions of the Customer

For 16 out of 24 cases, we could not observe the bullwhip effect in our experiment. Rather, in these 16 cases, inventory level of the upstream firm was not larger than that of the downstream firm. This is a counterexample for the bullwhip effect. This kind of a counterexample is quite clear in $(D3, F4, B)$ case shown in the left side of Fig. 3 where inventory level of the second distributor is larger than that of the first distributor, though the former is the downstream firm!

Anther counterexample is also observed in $(D1, F4, A)$ case shown in the right side of Fig. 3.

Note that both counterexamples were observed in the F4 condition. Comparing right and left side in Fig. 3, one may think that such a counterexample might be observed under the condition that there are many firms in a supply chain.

---

[1] For more details, see Kawagoe and Wada [2].

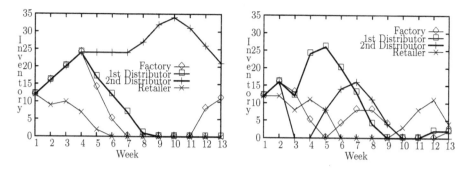

Fig. 3. A Counterexample in $(D3, F4, B)$ Case (left) and in $(D1, F4, A)$ Case (right)

To verify that conjecture, all of our experimental results are summarized in the left side of Table 1. From this table, we can see that counterexamples were observed more frequently in 1 week than in 3 weeks delay cases (11 versus 5 cases), but they were observed more frequently in four firms cases than in two firms cases (9 versus 7 cases).

Anyway, as these observation are rather counter intuitive for us, we design another series of experiment using multi-agent simulations to verify whether these findings are robust or not.

Table 1. The number of cases that counterexamples were observed

		Gaming simulation		Multi-agent simulation	
		F2	F4		F2	F4
A (Uniform)	D1	2 out of 2	2 out of 2	D1	7 out of 10	0 out of 10
	D3	1 out of 2	1 out of 2	D3	0 out of 10	10 out of 10
		F2	F4		F2	F4
B (Normal)	D1	2 out of 2	2 out of 2	D1	5 out of 10	3 out of 10
	D3	0 out of 2	1 out of 2	D3	0 out of 10	10 out of 10
		F2	F4		F2	F4
C (U-shaped)	D1	1 out of 2	2 out of 2	D1	8 out of 10	4 out of 10
	D3	1 out of 2	1 out of 2	D3	2 out of 10	10 out of 10

3.2   Multiagent Simulations

In our multi-agent simulations, the number of firm in a supply chain, F2 or F4, and the length of the delay between firms, D1 or D3, were compared. We also compared the effect of different demand order distributions of the customer and inventory strategies of each firm.

In our simulations, there is no centralized agent or meta agent controlling whole activities in a supply chain and information of the customer's orders is not shared among firms. In this sense, each firm in a supply chain is an agent and decides each inventory level in a decentralized way. A simple and deterministic inventory strategy that we adopt is as follows. After knowing orders from the downstream firm and receiving products from the upstream firm, each firm updates his stock and ships products if he has enough inventories. If not, the amount that orders minus inventories are recorded in the backorders to be shipped in later weeks. Then each firm makes orders to fill his stock to meet the next week orders and to clear the backorders, if any. The next week orders are predicted by a moving average of past orders. We used standard or weighted moving average with past three or five weeks orders for comparisons.

Thus, each firm x updates the states of inventories and backorders, and determines the amounts of products to be shipped and the amounts of demand orders according to the following algorithm **Order**.

Algorithm   Order

Input $t, x, B_t^x, I_t^x, S_t^x, \omega_t^x, \chi_t^x, \Omega_t^x$

if $\omega_t^x > I_{t-1}^x + \chi_t^x$ then
　set $S_t^x \leftarrow I_{t-1}^x + \chi_t^x$
　set $I_t^x \leftarrow 0$
　set $B_t^x \leftarrow B_{t-1}^x + \omega_t^x - (I_{t-1}^x + \chi_t^x)$
　set $\Omega_t^x \leftarrow B_t^x + m_{t+1}^x$
else
　if $B_{t-1}^x + \omega_t^x > I_{t-1}^x + \chi_t^x$ then
　　set $S_t^x \leftarrow I_{t-1}^x + \chi_t^x$
　　set $I_t^x \leftarrow 0$
　　set $B_t^x \leftarrow B_{t-1}^x + \omega_t^x - (I_{t-1}^x + \chi_t^x)$
　　set $\Omega_t^x \leftarrow B_t^x + m_{t+1}^x$
　else
　　set $S_t^x \leftarrow B_{t-1}^x + \omega_t^x$
　　set $I_t^x \leftarrow I_{t-1}^x + \chi_t^x - (B_{t-1}^x + \omega_t^x)$
　　set $B_t^x \leftarrow 0$
　　　if $I_t^x + m_{t+1}^x$ then $\Omega_t^x = 0$
　　　else $\Omega_t^x = m_{t+1}^x - I_t^x$

We also show in Fig. 4 how I_t^x, B_t^x, ω_t^x and m_t^x behave according to our algorithm **Order**. Finally, as in Moyaux et al. [5], Beer Game is repeated 50 weeks in our simulation.

Simulation with stochastic demands. In our first simulation, we tried to replicate the results observed in the gaming simulation. So we used same customer's orders distribution, A (Uniform), B (Normal) and C (U-shaped), as in the gaming simulation. In Table. 1, we show the number of cases that counterexamples were observed both in gaming and multi-agent simulations. We simply counted that a case is a counterexample if inventory level of the downstream firm exceeds that of the upstream firm. Although observations of the counterexample are widespread in our experimental conditions, a prominent difference between gaming and multi-agent simulation is that counterexamples were observed in all ten cases in $(D3, F4)$ condition in the multi-agent simulations. These results are truly counter intuitive for us because when the delay in ordering and shipping

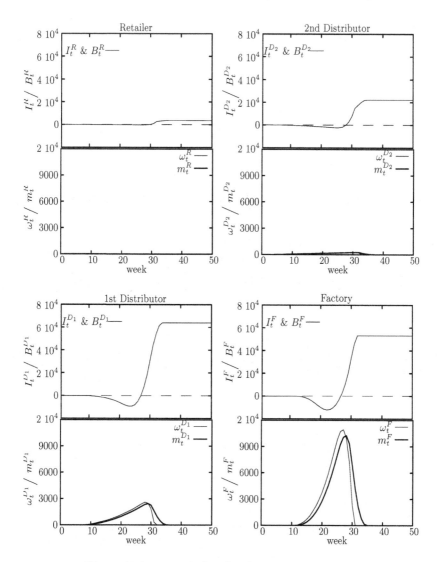

Fig. 4. Behaviors of I_t^x, B_t^x, ω_t^x and m_t^x of each firm

between firms is longer, one would expect that inventory level fluctuates more. To judge whether such counter intuitive results depend on the stochastic order distributions, we employed deterministic order distributions for comparisons in the next simulation.

Simulation with deterministic demands. In the next simulation, as for the demand order distributions, we adopt four distributions used in Moyaux et al. [5] and add a constant order distribution as a benchmark. The detail of each distribution is shown in Table 2. Note that all of these distributions are not stochastic.

Table 2. Customers Order Distributions

The Customer's Order Distribution

t	1	2	3	4	5	6	$\cdots$	48	49	50
T1	11	11	11	11	17	17	$\cdots$	17	17	17
T2	17	17	17	17	11	11	$\cdots$	11	11	11
T5	11	11	11	11	12	13	$\cdots$	55	56	57
T6	57	57	57	57	56	55	$\cdots$	13	12	11
TC	11	11	11	11	11	11	$\cdots$	11	11	11

Of 80 experimental conditions, no significant effect was observed in the factors ST, L, and T. So, from now on, we use $ST = W$, $L = 5$, and $T = TC$ as a typical case. Our results are summarized in Fig. 5. There are four panes in Fig. 5 and each pane corresponds to each combination of D and F.

Note that only for $(D3, F4)$ case, inventory level of the first distributor, $I_t^{D_1}$ exceeds that of the factory, I_t^F after $t > 32$. This is a counterexample for bullwhip effect. Of all of our data, similar counterexamples are observed only when the combinations of $(D3, F4)$ are used. However, this is rather counter intuitive because such counterexamples are observed even in the environment that the number of firms is many and length of delay is longer. So we can conclude that such a counter intuitive result does not depend on customer's orders distribution.

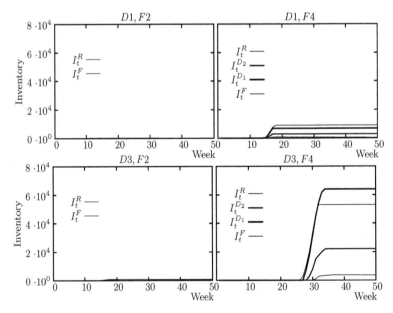

Fig. 5. Time series of inventory level of each firm in $(W, L5, TC)$ case

Although there could be many quantitative definitions of the bullwhip effect, natural one is that mean inventory level of the upstream firm is larger than that of the downstream firm. Another one is that variance of inventory level of the upstream firm is larger than that of the downstream firm. To judge our results really means a counterexample for the bullwhip effect in both quantitative senses, descriptive statistics of inventory level of each firm are given in the left side of Fig. 6.

One can easily see in Fig.6 that both mean and standard deviation (SD) of inventory level of the first distributor are larger than that of factory. So, we can say that our results really mean a counterexample for the bullwhip effect in quantitative sense.

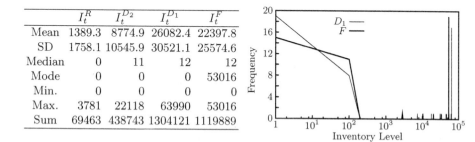

	I_t^R	$I_t^{D_2}$	$I_t^{D_1}$	I_t^F
Mean	1389.3	8774.9	26082.4	22397.8
SD	1758.1	10545.9	30521.1	25574.6
Median	0	11	12	12
Mode	0	0	0	53016
Min.	0	0	0	0
Max.	3781	22118	63990	53016
Sum	69463	438743	1304121	1119889

Fig. 6. Descriptive Statistics of Inventory Level (Left) and Frequency Distributions of inventory in $(D3, F4, W, L5, TC)$ case (Right)

In the right side of Fig. 6, we also show the frequency distribution of inventory level of the first distributor and the factory. Most frequently observed inventory level of the first distributor is 0 (19 weeks out of 50 weeks) and the next 63,900 (17 weeks out of 50 weeks). Most frequently observed inventory level of the factory is 53,000 (19 weeks out of 50 weeks) and the next is 0 (15 weeks out of 50 weeks). So, even mode of inventory level of the first distributor is less than that of the factory, as second highest frequency of inventory level of the first distributor is much higher than that of the factory, mean and SD of inventory level of the first distributor is still higher than that of the factory.

4   Conclusions

In our experiment using Beer Game, the number of firm in a supply chain (two or four firms) and the length of the delay between firms (one or three weeks) are compared in gaming simulations with human subjects and in the multi-agent simulations.

In both of our experiments, we found counterexamples for bullwhip effect such that inventory level of upstream firm is not always larger than that of downstream firm. In addition, contrary to our intuition, such counterexamples were frequently observed under the condition that (1) the number of firms in a supply chain was many (four firms), and that (2) the length of delay was rather longer (three weeks). These findings was verified both with stochastic and deterministic orders distributions.

One may criticize our results because we employ very simple inventory strategy in our simulations. It is, of course, worthwhile to run another series of experiments by introducing more sophisticated strategies. One may also feel it unrealistic that there is no capacity limit for inventory level for each firm in our experiment. Incorporating such restrictions in our environment is also worth considering in the future research.

References

1. Cachon, G. P. and S. Netessine (2003). "Game Theory in Supply Chain Analysis". In D. Simchi-Levi, S. D. Wu, and Z.-J. M. Shen, editors, *Supply Chain Analysis in the eBusiness Era*. Kluwer.
2. Kawagoe, T., S. Wada (2004). "An Experimental Evaluation of the Bullwhip Effect in A Supply Chain". The Proceedings of Third Annual Conference of the European Social Simulation Association (ESSA 2005).
3. Lee, H. L., Padmanabhan, V., Whang, S. (1997). "The Bullwhip Effect In Supply Chain," *Sloan Management Review*, **38**, 93-102.
4. Moyaux, T., Chaib-draa, B., DfAmours, S. (2004). "Experimental Study of Incentives for Collaboration in the QuebecWood Supply Game," *Management Science*, submitted.
5. Moyaux, T., Chaib-draa, B., DfAmours, S. (2004). "Multi-Agent Simulation of Collaborative Strategy In A Supply Chain," The Third International Joint Conference on Autonomos Angets and Multiagent Simulation (AAMAS 2004).

Development of a Multi-Agent Based Generic Traffic Simulator

Kosuke Ono[1], Takashi Hata[1], Toyofumi Maetani[1], Masateru Harao[2], and Kouichi Hirata[2]

[1] Graduate School of Computer Science and Systems Engineering,
Kyushu Institute of Technology, JPN
[2] Department of Artificial Intelligence, Kyushu Institute of Technology, JPN

Abstract. In this paper we develop a multi-agent based traffic simulator by considering traffic flows as emergent phenomena over two layered multi-agent systems. The first layer is composed of vehicle agents and the second layer is composed of signal agents. The system can naturally express actual road networks and can reproduce various traffic congestions induced by means of local interactions among vehicle agents. We show the system is useful for the road enhancing problem to guess the most suitable place when a new road is constructed. Further, we study a traffic control system which dissolves congestions at intersections by monitoring the traffic flow at the first layer.

1   Introduction

Recently, the traffic congestion is a big object of public concern. In order to solve this problem, a lot of efforts has been paid to the improvements such that road network systems, signal control systems, congestion information systems, car navigation systems and so on. However, it is essential for carrying out such improvements in practice to examine the effect that can be expected by the improvement beforehand and to make a best plan, since the road construction needs a vast sum of money. Currently, it has become possible to use the computer simulation for such purpose by the rapid advancement of computing ability.

It has been reported a lot of simulation systems until now. Most of them are constructed based on fluid model[1] or vehicle follow model[2]. The fluid model considers traffic flows as fluid flows and analyzes its behaviors using differential equations, and then only macroscopic properties of traffic flows can be obtained. The vehicle follow model can describe a more microscopic behavior of traffic flows by introducing the effects of interactions among vehicles into the formalization. However, vehicles are treated as homogeneous and no individualities of vehicles are not taken into consideration.

The purpose of this paper is to develop a simulator which can describe microscopic behaviors induced from individuality of vehicles such as speed, passing, action in intersections and so on, and to design signal control system by using information which is extracted from the simulation.

A cellular automaton(CA, for short) model is a new approach which looks the traffic flows as complex phenomena emerged from the mutual interactions

T. Washio et al. (Eds.): JSAI 2005 Workshops, LNAI 4012, pp. 249–260, 2006.

among vehicles, and some simulators are constructed[3, 4] baed on the CA model. The CA based simulator can also visualize the dynamics of traffics, and observe both the macroscopic and the microscopic phenomena. However, it is difficult to code many types of vehicles, signals and roads by means of local functions which are defined among neighboring cells.

A multi-agent based(MA based, for short) simulation[5, 6] is a similar method to the CA model, but can represent the various types of vehicles and environments more conveniently. For such reason, we develop a generic traffic simulator by using multi-agent model.

In the MA based traffic simulation ,we can consider the agents such as the vehicle agent, the signal agent, the road agent, the intersection agent and so on[7]. In this paper, we formalize our simulator using the vehicle agent and the signal agent.

(1) Vehicle agent: A vehicle is considered as an agent. Various types of vehicle agents can be introduced by defining the parameters such as speed, actions at intersections, passing, and so on. Their behaviors are specified by local functions.

(2) Signal agent: A signal is considered as an agent. A signal agent controls signals by monitoring the traffic flow at the first level simulation and by co-operating with the neighboring signal agents.

Until now, these vehicle models and signal models are discussed separately [9, 10]. However, these models can be integrated into a multi-layered system. We propose in this paper a two-layered MA based traffic simulator composed of vehicle agent layer and signal agent layer. Furhtermore, we realize a map system in graph style to improve the smooth road representation which are not possible by CA models.

This paper is organized as follows. In section 2, we describe the fundamental notations and definitions on multi-agent models. In section 3, we show a traffic flow simulator based on a vehicle agent model. In section 4, we discuss the signal control system based on a signal agent model. Finally, we study a generic traffic simulation system which amalgamates the vehicle agent models with the signal agent model. Section 5 is the discussion and the problems to be studied further.

2   Multi-Agent Model

An agent is anything that can be viewed as perceiving its environment through sensors and acting upon that environment through effectors. A multi-agent system is a system which is consists of a lot of agents interacting each other. Though the local interaction among agents is simple, it emerges complex phenomena as a whole. Such a system is called complex systems and a traffic flow is an example of the complex systems which is emerged from vehicle agents.

A MA based model for the urban traffic problem may be viewed as three levels. The highest level is the global urban traffic agent, executing the global planning. The middle level is composed of some traffic flow control agents, executing group planning. The lowest level consists of a lot of individual traffic

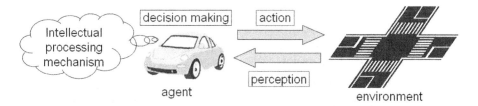

Fig. 1. Vehicle agent for traffic simulation

agents, executing individual planning. The agents used in the lowest level contain the following types:

(1) vehicle agent
(2) road agent
(3) intersection agent
(4) signal agent

Here, vehicle agents are called mobile and roads, intersections and signals are inmobile. In this paper, we discuss a simulation for the lowest level composed of a vehicle layer and a signal layer. An agent locally judges, calculates, communicates, and controls according to its environment. Here, the environment indicates the entities which exist outside of the agents and is not freely revokable by agent's intention.

One of the advantages of the MA model is to be able to express various characters of agents easily. For instance, we can implement a number of varieties of agents by using the object oriented technique. In case of the vehicle agent, the characters such as speed, passing, behaviors at intersections and so on can be easily realized by modifying a basic agent using the inheritance and overloading. By adopting this approach, we can develop a traffic simulator which is able to reproduce a more realistic traffic flow.

3   MA Based Traffic Simulator

3.1   Vehicle Agent Model

A vehicle agent can be characterized by the following factors.

- Coordinates: 2 dimensional space $Z^2 = (x, y)$.
- Velocity : integers(several kinds are set).
- Agent type : specified with bahavior rules.
- View : the scope which the vehicle agent can observe.
- Destination : coordinate(the goal of the vehicle agent).

A map is represented by a collection of cells in a lattice structured celluar space. We can draw a path by appointing its initial and end coordinates, and can set signals at any crossing positions. Each cell possesses the following informations:

- Whether it is a part of road or not.
- Which direction is the lane, when it is a road cell.
- Whether a signal exists on the cell or not.
- Whether it is a source or not.
- Whether it is a sink or not.
- Whether it is a part of a intersection or not.

Here, a source means a cell where vehicles newly appear, and a sink means a cell where vehicles disappear. These are used to represent the places such as park places, boundaries of maps. The cell has the function to observe the influence of the changes of vehicles, of the road network and signal control on the traffics.

Definition 1. A vehicle multi-agent system is a tuple $VMA= \langle A, Map \rangle$, where

1. A is a nonempty set of agents, and is denoted by $\langle ag_1, \ldots, ag_n \rangle$.
2. $Map = \langle \Gamma, Q, C \rangle$, where Γ is a finite cellular space,
   and $Q = \langle Road, Direction, Source, Sink, Intersection, Signal \rangle$, where
   (1) Road: it indicates whether a road cell or not.
   (2) Direction: it indicates the direction of road cells
   (3) Source : it indicates whether a vehicle appear at the cell or not.
   (4) Sink : it indicates whether a vehicle disappear at the cell or not.
   (5) Intersection : it indicates whether a intersection cell or not.
   (6) Signal: it indicates whether a signal exists at the cell or not.
3. C is a configuration defined by $C : \Gamma \to Q$

Definition 2. An agent is a 4-tuple $ag = \langle S, N, des, f \rangle$, where

1. S is a set of state for agent ag, where a state is a pair of current location and velocity such that $s = ((x, y), v)$.
2. N is the view of the agent ag. We denote the local configuration of ag by $Map_{|N}$.
3. des is the destination of the agent ag.
4. f is a state transition function defined by $f : S \times Map_{|N} \to S$.

3.2   Overview of the Developed MA Based Simulalor

In this section, we explain the traffic simulator which is implemented based on the formalization given in the previous section. The system consists of the following subsystems.

(1) Setting part: it sets the roads, intersections, signals and allocate vehicles on the map.
(2) State transition part: it specifies the bahavior of agents.
(3) Drawing part:it draws the configuration after every state transition.

The user interface of the system is shown in Fig.2. From control panel, we set the following parameters.

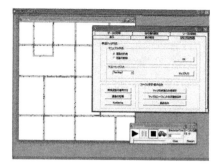

Fig. 2. MA based traffic simulator

(1) Field and cell size: set the field size and the cell size.
(2) Map: user can design any maps composed of straight lines and save the edited maps.
(3) Source: set the occurrence rate of vehicle agents.
(4) Vehicle agents: set the following parameters:
   a) types of agents,
   b) accelaration and deceleration,
   c) changing of lanes,
   d) destinations.
(5) Intersection :set the types of signals.

We can extract the following data from the trafic simulation system:

(1) The increase and decrease of the vehicle agents during an appointed period,
(2) The number of waiting agents at intersections,
(3) The average velocity of vehicle agents,
(4) The average time required to the destination,

Such data can also be displayed in the form of several kinds of graphs. Furthermore, there are 2 ways where vehicles can move from source to sink[11]. One way is to choose a route at random, and the other is to choose the shortest route under the distance

$$d = \mid (Des_x - Junc_x) \mid + \mid Des_y - Junc_y) \mid,$$

where $Des_x, Junc_y$ are the coordinates of destination and the one of the intersections. In the simulation, the rate of agents which move according to the shortest path strategy can be set.

3.3   Application: Optimal Road Enhancing

We have simulated the effects using the developed system under the alternation such as the number of lanes, traffic network, signal control system, and so on. Here, we demonstrate the optimal road enhancing problem to guess the best palace to add a new road in order to decrease the traffics of indicated region.

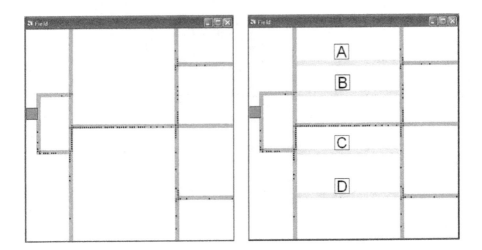

Fig. 3. Left: before enhancing. Right: after enhancing.

In Fig.3, congestion occurs in the left region. This is because there is only one road which connect the left region with the right region. We dissolve the congestion by adding a road. We assume 4 candidates of places to add roads, that is, A, B, C and D which are illustrated in Fig.3. In this experiment, we discuss which is the best place among them. We can visually observe the traffic flows by the simulation and analyze how the congestion changes according to the road extension from data gotten by the system. The result is shown in Fig.4. In this case, D is the best place to add a new road.

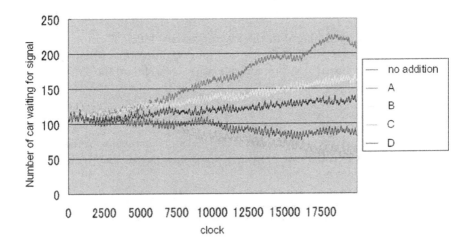

Fig. 4. The effects of road enhancement

4   MA Based Signal Control Simulator

4.1   Signal Agent Model

In this section, we discuss the problem of controling the traffic flows by adjusting the signal systems under some fixed road systems. Here, signals are considered as agents and they adjust the periods of signals by observing the traffic at intersections and by cooprerating with the other agents.

Definition 3. A signal multi-agent system is a tuple $JMA = \langle Agt, Nei \rangle$, where

1. Agt is a nonempty set of agents, and is denoted by $\langle sag_1, \ldots, sag_n \rangle$.
2. Nei is a subset of $Agt \times Agt$, and shows the adjacent relation of the agent.

Definition 4. An agent is a tuple $sag_i = \langle U, f, O \rangle$, where

1. U is a set of states of agent sag, where a state is the number of inflow.
2. f is a state transition function defined by $f : U \times U^{Nei} \to U$, where U^{Nei} is the state configuration of its neighboring signal agents.
3. O is an observation function.

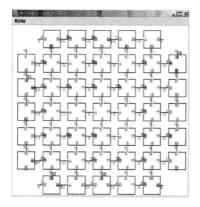

Fig. 5. Map that controls traffic style

We introduce the following types of signal agents according to the strategy to decide the mount of vehicles which can pass the intersection during a signal period:

1. Even distribution agent: this agent controls the signals by choosing one of the 3 types of signal patterns prepared beforehand.
2. Aggressive distribution agent: this agent controls the signals by observing the traffic situations of adjacent agents.
3. Learning distribution agent: this agent controls the signals by learning the optimal strategy according to the classifier system.

4.2   Experimental Results: Signal Control Problem

The signal agents are interconnected as shown in Fig.5, and the total number of vehicles which exist in this map is assumed constant. Initially, we configure vehicles so that the intersections which are congested exist at some given rate. We measure the number of turns from the initial configuration to the final configuration that its congestion is dissolved, where 1 turn is the period when all agents finish one action once. The result is shown in Fig.6. This shows the distribution of a necessary turn until congestion is dissolved. The number of the vehicles of a horizontal axis shows how many vehicles exist in the simulation space. (3200 vehicles as a whole can be allowed.)

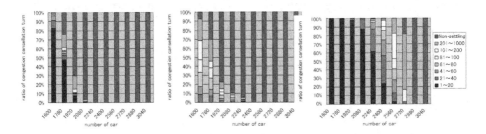

Fig. 6. Results of signal control(Left:Even Center:Lerning Right:Aggressive agent)

We can observe that the aggressive agent improves the dissolving function. On the other hand, the learning agent does not improve it as expected. The reason may be the insufficient number of rules which are used in this experiment. We should study on the learning agent model further by introducing adequate rules and a learning function.

5   Generic Traffic Simulation System

5.1   Two Layered Model

The traffic simulation system stated in Chapter 3(the vehicle agent model) and the signal control system stated in Chapter 4(signal agent model) are investigated separately. By integrating these two systems, we can expect to construct a more acculate simulator which can control traffics by reflecting the behaviors of the individual level. We are now developing a two-layered traffic simulator which integrates these two systems. The proposed system extracts information from the traffic simulator of the first layer and control the global traffic flow by using the extracted information.

Furthermore, the CA model has the defect that it can not express smooth roads like curves and is hard to realize the interactions which joins more then 5 paths. In order to express real city maps in the space, it has better to use graphical representation. Furthermore, it becomes possible to describe the natural movement of vehicles by this approach.

The following improvements are made in the two-layered system:

(1) Expression of road network: We express road networks of the first layer as graphs. A new method to express continuous curves and complex road connections is devised.
(2) Data extraction functions: Signal agents of the second layer uses the data which represent behavioral features of the first layer. We prepare several functions which efficiently compute data such as time distribution of vehicles, the degree of congestions, time variation of congestions, the size of queued vehicles and so on.
(3) Vehicle movement: Since the road networks are expressed as graphs, the local function which specifies the movement of vehicles is also improved. Especially, it is enabled to describe various speeds and accelerations. The improved system can express vehicle movements more precisely comparing to the cellular road networks.

A display of the GUI of the proposed generic traffic system is illustrated in Fig.7.

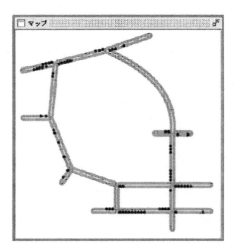

Fig. 7. GUI of the two layerd system

Most of the formalization of this system are the same to the one of Chapter 3. Here, only the main changed points are described briefly.

A road is expressed by using a Bezier line, and vehicles on the road is expressed as a queue by ordering them according to their moved distances. We can set any roads by appointing the initial position and end position, where nodes denote intersections or sinks or sources. Especially, smooth curves and intersections of more than 5 degrees can also be expressive. Thus, it becomes possible to express real road maps in the first layer. Each vehicle possesses the information on the position in a road and on the moving distance.

Definition 5. The state set of a vehicle is modified so that (b, dis, sp, ac), where

1. b shows the road which it belongs to.
2. dis shows the distance by which the vehicle moved.
3. sp is a speed of the vehicle,
4. ac is a acceleration of the vehicle.

An intersection agent or a road agent extract information that vehicles need, and vehicles act according to the information. As a result, it is possible to define a number of varieties of vehicle movements such as passing, lane change, safety drive, accelaration and so on. Especially, a simulation of a more smooth vehicle action at corners and intersection becomes possible. The other expressions of the system such as signal setting, environment and so on are the same to the system described in Section 3.

5.2 Experimental Results

We show the experimental result simulated by using the integrated model proposed in this section. The used map is the one shown in Fig.7. The target of this experiment is to optimize the global traffic flow by controlling signals of intersections.

The differences with the experiment on Chapter 4 are as follows.

(1) A vehicle agent is assumed to have intention, and acts according to it , and has a physical size.
(2) An intersection agent doesn't compulsorily specify the direction of the vehicle movement, but indirectly specifies it by controlling the time intervals of signal.

We use the following three kinds of signal controls.

(1) All the time intervals of signals are the same.
(2) If vehicles still remains in a direction when a signal(blue) ends, then the time interval of the signal(blue) of this direction is increased. If otherwise, the interval of the signal(blue) is decreased. (*)According to the increase and decrease of the signal(blue), the cycle length is also increased and decreased only the same amount.
(3) In the case of (2), the condition (*) is changed so that the cycle length is fixed. In this case, if the interval of signal(blue) decreases if the other interval of signal(blue) increases.

The performances are compared by using the number of vehicles queued at the whole signals.

In the case (1), we experimented for some different cycle length. The result is shown in Table 1. It is observed that 20 steps are suitable as the cycle length, and the number of waiting vehicles increases when it is longer or shorter than the length.

Table 1. The number of waiting vehicle at signals(Case(1))

cycle length	10	20	30	40
waiting vehicle	61.5	26.1	36.2	45.8

The result of comparison among these control methods is shown in Figure 8. A horizontal axis is the number of steps, and the vertical axis is the number of the vehicles that are waiting at signals. The case (3) gives the best result. The difference with the case (2) can be considered as follows: when cycle length is changeable, the cycle length becomes very long at crowded points.

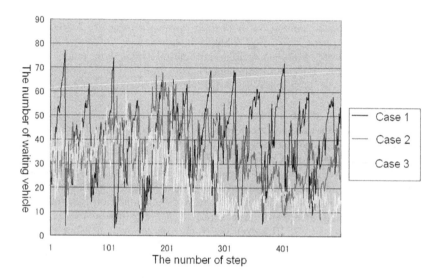

Fig. 8. Comparison among (1),(2),(3):Under fixed or changeable cycle lengths

6   Conclusion

In this paper, we developed a mult-agent based generic traffic simulator by integrating the vehicle agent system and the signal agent system. We can express complex maps in the system, and reproduce various vehicle movements such as passing, lane change, speed change and so on.

We have also shown that the proposed system is useful to the problems such as road enhancing, congestion dissolution. However, the signal control system which realize optimal flow is so complex that the essential features of the congestion cannot be made clear yet by the present simulation. We have to improve the present system so that it can simulate actual traffic flows by introducing real traffic data. Furthermore, we can reproduce various traffic flows by setting parameters moderately. How to extract essential features from the simulated data is an important problem to be studied further.

We have also discussed the signal control method under the co-operation of neighboring signal agents and the one under the reinforcement learning. In this paper no satisfactory results is obtained yet. This distributed signal control method is a problem that should be considered in addition.

The present system doesn't take the information like navigation or GPS into consideration. A simulator which fits to the future ITS should be developed further.

References

1. M. J. Lighthill, G. B. Whitham, Pric. Roy. Soc. Lond. **A**229(1955)317
2. G. F. Newell, Opr. res. **9**(1961)209.
3. Y. Kato, Road traffic simulation by cellular automata method, Artificial Intelligence Society magazine Vol15 No2, 2000(in Japanese).
4. J.Whale, L.Neubert, et al., A cellular automaton traffic flow model for online simulation of traffic, Parallel Computing 27, 2001.
5. M. Wooldridge, et al, Gerhard Weiss(ed), Multiagent Systems, pp.27–77,The MIT Press,1999.
6. Azuma. Oouchi, et al., Base and application of multiagent system -Calculation paradigm of complex systems engineering-, Coronasha, 2002(in Japanese).
7. Mingshu Li, et al., Agent-Oriented Urban Traffic Control Simulation, in 1996 IEEE Symp. on Intelligent Control, July 1996.
8. Sho, Misawa, et al., Traffic signal control by reinforced study type multi-agent, Electronic telecommunication society thesis magazine, 2000 (in Japanese).
9. Takashi Hata, et al., Development of a Traffic flow Simulation System Based on Multi-Agent Models, Hinokuni Symposium, 2005(in Japanese).
10. Toyofumi Maetani, et al., Research on traffic control system using multi-agent model, Hinokuni Symposium, 2005(in Japanese).
11. H. Koduka, Proposal and evaluation of dynamic route search technique in non-equilibrium environment, Tsukuba university master's thesis, 2002(in Japanese).

Directed Network
as a Chaotic Dynamical System

Syuji Miyazaki

Graduate School of Informatics, Kyoto University, Kyoto 606-8501, Japan
syuji@acs.i.kyoto-u.ac.jp
http://wwwfs.acs.i.kyoto-u.ac.jp/~syuji/

Abstract. A directed network such as the WWW can be represented by
a transition matrix. Comparing this matrix to a Frobenius-Perron matrix
of a chaotic piecewise-linear one-dimensional map whose domain can be
divided into Markov subintervals, we are able to relate the network structure itself to chaotic dynamics. Just like various large-deviation properties of local expansion rates (finite-time Lyapunov exponents) related
to chaotic dynamics, we can also discuss those properties of network
structure.

1 Introduction

One of the most remarkable points about deterministic chaos is the duality
consisting of irregular dynamics and fractal structure of the attractor in the
phase space. Amplifying this relation between dynamics and geometry, we will
try to construct dynamics corresponding to a directed network structure such
as the WWW. A directed network or graph can be represented by a transition
matrix. On the other hand, temporal evolution of a chaotic piecewise-linear
one-dimensional map with Markov partition can be governed by a Frobenius-
Perron matrix. Both transition matrices and Frobenius-Perron matrices belong
to a class of transition matrices sharing the same mathematical properties. The
maximum eigenvalue is equal to unity. The corresponding eigenvector is always
a real vector, and evaluates the probability density of visiting a subinterval of
the map or a site of the network, which is commercially valuable information in
the field of the WWW [1]. Relating these two matrices to each other, we are able
to represent the structure itself of the directed network as a dynamical system.
Once we relate the directed network to chaotic dynamics, several approaches to
deterministic chaos can be also applied to graph theory.

In chaotic dynamical systems, local expansion rates which evaluate an or-
bital instability fluctuate largely in time, reflecting a complex structure in the
phase space. Its average is called the Lyapunov exponent, whose positive sign
is a practical criterion of chaos. There exist numerous investigations based on
large-deviation statistics in which one considers distributions of coarse-grained
expansion rates (finite-time Lyapunov exponent) in order to extract large deviations caused by non-hyperbolicities or long correlations in the vicinity of
bifurcation points [2].

T. Washio et al. (Eds.): JSAI 2005 Workshops, LNAI 4012, pp. 261–270, 2006.

In general, statistical structure functions consisting of weighted averages, variances, and these partition functions as well as fluctuation spectra of coarse-grained dynamic variables can be obtained by processing the time series numerically. In the case of the piecewise-linear map with Markov partition, we can obtain these structure functions analytically. This is one of the reasons why we correspond a directed network to a piecewise-linear map. We herein try to apply an approach based on large-deviation statistics in the research field of chaotic dynamical systems to network analyses. What is the Lyapunov exponent of the network? What becomes of fluctuations of the network Lyapunov exponent or other coarse-grained variables?

2   One-Dimensional Map Corresponding to Directed Network

We will consider the very simple example shown in Fig.1. There exist two kinds of loops. One is a loop between node 1 and 2, the other a loop or a triangle 1, 3, 2. Let us define this adjacency matrix A, where A_{ji} is equal to unity if the node i is linked to j. If not, A_{ji} is equal to zero. Transition matrix H can be derived straightforwardly from the adjacency matrix. The element H_{ij} is equal to A_{ij} divided by the number of nonzero elements of column j. The transition matrix of the simple triangular graph mentioned before is explicitly given by the 3 by 3 matrix as

$$H = \begin{pmatrix} 0 & 1 & 0 \\ 1/2 & 0 & 1 \\ 1/2 & 0 & 0 \end{pmatrix}.$$

The maximum eigenvalue is always equal to unity. The corresponding eigenvector measures site importance in the context of the web network, which is commercially used as mentioned earlier.

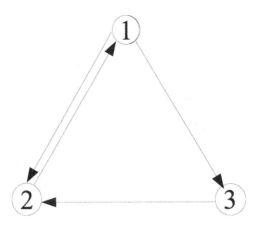

Fig. 1. Example

In the case of chaotic dynamics caused by a one-dimensional map f, the trajectory is given by iteration. Its distribution at time n, $\rho_n(x)$, is given by the average of this delta function $\langle \delta(x_n - x) \rangle$, where $\langle \cdots \rangle$ denotes the average with respect to initial points x_0. The temporal evolution of ρ is given by the following relation

$$\rho_{n+1}(x) = \int_0^1 \delta(f(y) - x)\rho_n(y)\,dy \equiv \mathcal{H}\rho_n(x).$$

This operator $\mathcal{H}$, called the Frobenius-Perron operator, is explicitly given as

$$\mathcal{H}G(x) = \sum_j \frac{G(y_j)}{|f'(y_j)|},$$

where the sum is taken over all solutions $y_j(x)$ satisfying $f(y_j) = x$.

In the case of a piecewise-linear map with Markov partition, invariant density is constant for each interval. Taking these 3 functions as a basis, we can represent the Frobenius-Perron operator as this 3 by 3 matrix. This is nothing but the transition matrix of the directed graph consisting of 3 nodes mentioned before. The map f can be chosen as

$$f(x) = \begin{cases} 2x + 1/3 & (0 \le x < 1/3), \\ x - 1/3 & (1/3 \le x \le 1), \end{cases}$$

and is shown in Fig.2.

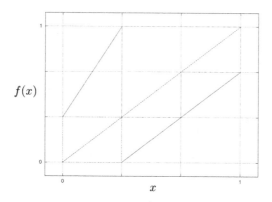

Fig. 2. One-dimensional map corresponding to the directed network shown in Fig.1

The Lyapunov exponent of the one-dimensional map is an average of the logarithm of the slope of the map with respect to its invariant density. Comparing the directed network, the map f, the matrix H, we find that the number of arrows originating from node i is equal to the slope of the interval I_i. Thus the Lyapunov exponent of the network is found to be an average of the logarithm of the number of arrows originating from each node. This exponent quantifies the complexity of link relations. Degree distribution is often used to characterize link relations. The network Lyapunov exponent and its fluctuation are also supposed to be useful in the context of the network. In this way, we can relate the network structure itself to a chaotic dynamical system, and we try to characterize the network based on an approach to deterministic chaos, namely large-deviation statistics, in other words, thermodynamical formalism.

3 Large-Deviation Statistics

Let us briefly describe large deviation statistics following the series of studies by Fujisaka and his coworkers [3, 4]. Consider a stationary time series u. The average over time interval T is given by this formula,

$$\bar{u}_T(t) = \frac{1}{T} \int_t^{t+T} u\{s\} \, ds$$

which distributes when T is finite. When T is much larger than the correlation time of u, the distribution $P_T(u)$ of coarse-grained u is assume to be an exponential form $P_T(u) \propto e^{-S(u)T}$. Here we can introduce the fluctuation spectrum $S(u)$ as

$$S(u) = -\lim_{T \to \infty} \frac{1}{T} \log P_T(u).$$

When T is comparable to the correlation time, correlation can not be ignored, so non-exponential or non-extensive statistics will be a problem, but here we do not discuss this point any further. Let q be a real parameter. We introduce the generating function M_q of T by this definition:

$$M_q(T) \equiv \langle e^{qT\bar{u}_T} \rangle = \int_{-\infty}^{\infty} P_T(u) e^{qTu} \, du.$$

We can also here assume the exponential distribution and introduce characteristic function $\phi(q)$ as

$$\phi(q) = \lim_{T \to \infty} \frac{1}{T} \log M_q(T).$$

The Legendre transform holds between fluctuation spectrum $S(u)$ and characteristic function $\phi(q)$, which is obtained from saddle-point calculations.

$$\frac{dS(u)}{du} = q, \quad \phi(q) = -S(u(q)) + qu(q).$$

In this transform a derivative $d\phi/dq$ appears, and is a weighted average of $\bar{u}_T$,

$$u(q) = \frac{d\phi(q)}{dq} = \lim_{T \to \infty} \frac{\bar{u}_T e^{qT\bar{u}_T}}{M_q(T)}$$

so we find that q is a kind of weight index. We can also introduce susceptibility $\chi(q) = \dfrac{du(q)}{dq}$ as a weighted variance. These statistical structure functions

$S(u), \phi(q), u(q), \chi(q)$ constitute the framework of statistical thermodynamics of temporal fluctuation, which characterize the static properties of chaotic dynamics. In order to consider dynamic properties, we can introduce this generalized spectrum density as a weighted average of normal spectrum density.

$$I_q(\omega) = \lim_{T \to \infty} \frac{1}{T} \times \frac{\left\langle \left| \int_0^T [u\{t+s\} - u(q)]e^{-i\omega s} ds \right|^2 \right\rangle e^{qT\bar{u}_T}}{M_q(T)}$$

Let us consider the case of a one-dimensional map. Let $u[x_n]$ be a unique function of x, which is governed by the map $x_{n+1} = f(x_n)$. The question is how to obtain statistical structure functions and generalized spectral densities of u. The answer is to solve the eigenvalue problems of a generalized Frobenius-Perron operator. As we mentioned before, the characteristic function $\phi(q)$ is given by the asymptotic form of the generating function $M_q(n)$ in the limit of $n \to \infty$ corresponding to the temporal coarse-grained quantity $\bar{u}_n = \frac{1}{n} \sum_{j=0}^{n-1} u[x_{j+m}]$, where we assume an exponential fast decay of time correlations of u. A generating function can be expressed in terms of invariant density,

$$M_q(n) = \int \rho_\infty(x) \exp \left[q \sum_{j=0}^{n-1} u[f^j(x)] \right] dx = \int \mathcal{H}_q^n \rho_\infty(x) dx,$$

where the generalized Frobenius-Perron operator $\mathcal{H}_q$ is defined and related to the original one as

$$\mathcal{H}_q G(x) = \mathcal{H}[e^{qu[x]} G(x)] = \sum_k \frac{e^{qu[y_k]} G(y_k)}{|f'(y_k)|}$$

for an arbitrary function $G(x)$ ($\mathcal{H}_0 = \mathcal{H}$). To obtain the above equation, the following relation is repeatedly used:

$$\mathcal{H} \left\{ G(x) \exp \left[q \sum_{j=0}^m u[f^j(x)] \right] \right\} = (\mathcal{H}_q G(x)) \exp \left[q \sum_{j=0}^{m-1} u[f^j(x)] \right].$$

Let $\nu_q^{(0)}$ be the maximum eigenvalue of H_q. The characteristic function is given by its logarithm as

$$\phi(q) = \log \nu_q^{(0)}.$$

The weighted average $u(q)$ and the susceptibility $\chi(q)$ are given by the first and the second derivatives of $\phi(q)$.

The generalized spectral density is as

$$I_q(\omega) = \int v_{(0)}(x)[u[x] - u(q)] \times [J_q(\omega) + J_q(-\omega) - 1] \times [u[x] - u(q)]h^{(0)}(x)dx,$$

where $J_q(\omega) = 1/\left[1 - (e^{i\omega}/\nu_q^{(0)})\mathcal{H}_q\right]$, $v_{(0)}(x)$ and $h^{(0)}(x)$ are respectively the left and right eigenfunctions corresponding to the maximum eigenvalue $\nu_q^{(0)}$ of $\mathcal{H}_q$.

The normal Frobenius-Perron operator $\mathcal{H}$ depends on the map f only. The generalized one $\mathcal{H}_q$ depends also on a dynamic variable u and determines statistical structure functions and generalized spectral densities of u. For example, in the case of local expansion rates $u[x] = \log|f'(x)|$ whose average is the Lyapunov exponent, the generalized operator is explicitly as

$$\mathcal{H}_q G(x) = \sum_k \frac{G(y_k)}{|f'(y_k)|^{1-q}}.$$

In the case of the triangular network mentioned earlier, three subintervals constitute the Markov partition, such that $\mathcal{H}_q$ can be represented by a 3×3 matrix as

$$H_q = \begin{pmatrix} 0 & 1 & 0 \\ 1/2 & 0 & 1 \\ 1/2 & 0 & 0 \end{pmatrix} \begin{pmatrix} e^{qu(I_1)} & 0 & 0 \\ 0 & e^{qu(I_2)} & 0 \\ 0 & 0 & e^{qu(I_3)} \end{pmatrix}$$

in the same way as $\mathcal{H}$.

One can choose local expansion rates (logarithmic number of arrows directed each node) $u(I_i) = \log(|f'(I_i)|)$ as a dynamic variable. One of the other choices is $u(I_i) = \delta_{ik}$, which implies that the variable is equal to unity, if the specific interval(node) k is visited. If not, it is zero. In this case, recurrence time to visit a specific interval or node is the time span between the succeeding times at which $u = 1$ is satisfied.

4   Statistical Structure Functions and Generalized Spectral Densities of Directed Network

Let us analyze the triangular directed network based on the large-deviation statistics. As a dynamic variable we choose the local expansion rates (the logarithmic number of arrows originating from each node), so that we have $u(I_1) = \log 2$, $u(I_2) = 0$, $u(I_3) = 0$, which is not essentially different from a dynamic variable $u(I_i) = \delta_{i1}$. Note that both variables have different statistics in general.

In any choice of a dynamic variable u, right and left eigenvectors corresponding to eigenvalue 1 of the aforementioned Frobenius-Perron matrix H are determined. The left eigenvector is given by $(1/3, 1/3, 1/3)$, where it is so normalized that the sum of all elements is equal to unity. Note that the element is equal to the width of the subinterval of the Markov partition. The right eigenvector gives the probability density to visit each subinterval, and is equal to $(6/5, 6/5, 3/5)$, where it is so normalized that the inner product of the right and the left eigenvectors is equal to unity.

The generalized Frobenius-Perron matrix H_q can be represented as

$$H_q = \begin{pmatrix} 0 & 1 & 0 \\ 1/2 & 0 & 1 \\ 1/2 & 0 & 0 \end{pmatrix} \begin{pmatrix} e^{q\log 2} & 0 & 0 \\ 0 & e^{q\log 1} & 0 \\ 0 & 0 & e^{q\log 1} \end{pmatrix} = \begin{pmatrix} 0 & 1 & 0 \\ 2^{q-1} & 0 & 1 \\ 2^{q-1} & 0 & 0 \end{pmatrix}.$$

The statistical structure functions $\phi(q)$, $u(q)$, $\chi(q)$, and $S(u)$ are obtained from the maximum eigenvalue of H_q and are shown in Figs. 3-6.

The weighted average $u(q)$ has two asymptotes. The upper asymptote $u(+\infty) = (\log 2 + \log 1)/2 = (\log 2)/2$ and the lower one $u(-\infty) = (\log 2 + \log 1 + \log 1)/3 = (\log 2)/3$ correspond to period-2 and period-3 loops, respectively. This can be regarded as a kind of phase transition from period-2 loop phase to period-3. The mean logarithmic number of arrows originating from each node is given by $u(0)$, which is also obtained from the right eigenvalue

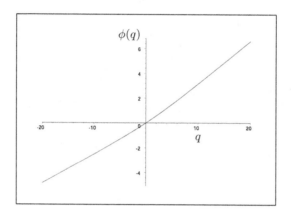

Fig. 3. Characteristic function $\phi(q)$

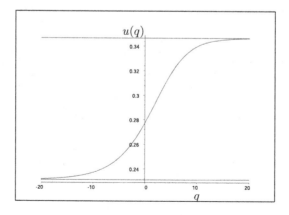

Fig. 4. Weighted average $u(q)$

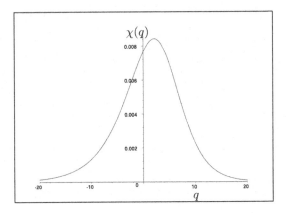

Fig. 5. Weighted variance $\chi(q)$

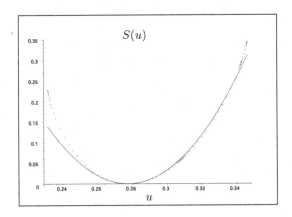

Fig. 6. Fluctuation spectrum $S(u)$ (line) and parabola indicating the central limit theorem (symbol)

(the probability density) corresponding to the eigenvalue 1 of $H = H_0$ as $\frac{1}{3} \times \frac{6}{5} \times \log 2 + \frac{1}{3} \times \frac{6}{5} \times \log 1 + \frac{1}{3} \times \frac{3}{5} \times \log 1 = \frac{2}{5} \log 2$. The average number of arrows originating from each node corresponds to $\exp(u(0))$. Its value is equal to $2^{2/5} \simeq 1.3$, which lies between 1 and 2 as expected. Period 2 and 3 trajectories are $(0,0) \rightarrow (0, 1/3 + 0) \rightarrow (1/3 + 0, 1/3 + 0) \rightarrow (1/3 + 0, 0) \rightarrow (0, 0)$ and $(1/3 - 0, 1/3 - 0) \rightarrow (1/3 - 0, 1) \rightarrow (1, 1) \rightarrow (2/3, 1) \rightarrow (2/3, 2/3) \rightarrow (2/3, 1/3 - 0) \rightarrow (1/3 - 0, 1/3 - 0)$, where $f(1/3 - 0) = 1$ and $f(1/3 + 0) = 0$. One can trace these trajectories along the grid lines shown in Fig.2.

The fluctuation spectrum $S(u)$ (the curve in Fig.6) can be defined between two values given by the asymptotes of the weighted average $0.23 \simeq (\log 2)/3 \leq u \leq (\log 2)/2 \simeq 0.35$. Expanding the spectrum around the average up to the quadratic term, we have a parabola (the symbols in Fig.6) indicating the central limit theorem. Large deviation statistics obviously do not coincide with the central limit theorem. The generalized spectral densities $I_q(\omega)$ for $q = -5, 0, 5$ are shown in Fig. 7. As q goes to $+\infty$, the density has a sharp peak at $\omega = \pi$, which corresponds to the period-2 loop. In the same way, As q goes to $-\infty$, the density has a sharp peak at $\omega = 2\pi/3$, which corresponds to the period-3 loop. There is nothing remarkable about the normal spectral density $I_0(\omega)$.

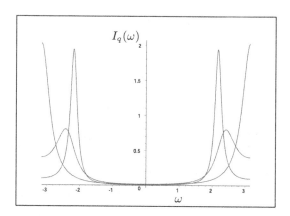

Fig. 7. Generalized spectral density $I_q(\omega)$ $(q = -5, 0, 5)$

5   Concluding Remarks

We introduced a way of relating a directed network to chaotic dynamics. Relating the directed network to a chaotic dynamical system, and applying the formalism of statistical thermodynamics to it, we can extract important loops individually and elucidate the fluctuations of arrows originating from each node.

The reason why the author insists on deterministic chaos is that chaos has a rigid skeleton of unstable periodic orbits and it determines the distribution of the coarse-grained variables concerned. Stochastic processes such as random walk or Brownian motion have no skeleton of unstable periodic orbits. The author will try to express large deviation statistics of directed networks in terms of these periodic orbits in the future.

Here we illustrated an idea which relates a directed network to chaotic dynamics using a very simple example consisting of three nodes. What becomes of more complicated networks? Dynamics corresponding to the small world are thought to need relatively short periodic orbits only. For a scale-free network, longer periodic orbits will take an important role and strongly correlated dynamics will appear. Investigation in this direction is a future problem. Furthermore, random matrix theory of normal and generalized transition matrices must play an important role.

One can choose $u(I_i) = \delta_{ik}$ $(k = 1, 2, \cdots)$ as a dynamic variable. In this case, recurrence time to visit a specific interval or node i is the time span between the succeeding times at which $u = 1$ is satisfied, as we mentioned earlier. It will be an interesting problem to analyze large-deviation statistics of recurrence times at a specific node and to relate this local information to the characteristics of the whole network such as WWW.

Acknowledgements

This study was partially supported by the 21st Century COE Program "Center of Excellence for Research and Education on Complex Functional Mechanical Systems "at Kyoto University.

References

1. L. Page, S. Brin, R. Motwani, T. Winograd, 'The PageRank Citation Ranking: Bringing Order to the Web', (1998), `http://www-db.stanford.edu/~backrub/pageranksub.ps`
2. H. Mori and Y. Kuramoto, Dissipative structures and chaos, (Springer, Berlin, 1998).
3. H. Fujisaka and M. Inoue, Prog. Theor. Phys. **77**, 1334 (1987); Phys. Rev. A **39**, 1376 (1989).
4. H. Fujisaka and H. Shibata, Prog. Theor. Phys. **85**, 187 (1991).

Behavior of Growing Scale-Free Networks in Complex Systems

Yuumi Kawachi and Shinichiro Yoshii

Hokkaido University, N14-W9, Sapporo, Hokkaido, 060-0814 Japan
`kawachi@complex.eng.hokudai.ac.jp`

Abstract. Intelligence needs connectivity and organization with some agents' intention in networks. The networks with intelligence produce some structure spontaneously. Therefore, it is important to focus on the structure in large networks like the Internet or World Wide Web that are constructed by human beings with their preferences or concepts. Especially, it has been found that even these artificial networks have scale-free structures, which are seen also in natural networks. It indicates that universal laws or phenomena exist in the properties and behaviors on scale-free networks. We investigate them from the view point of complex systems, in particular self-organization. From our proposed model and simulation experiments, it is found that growing scale-free networks have self-organized criticality. The phenomena would lead to the intelligence emerged from network structures.

1   Introduction

The term "network" has been more popular and closer than before in everyday life because of dissemination of IT such as the Internet or World Wide Web. Especially, Web pages are organized with link connectivity by human beings who are a kind of agents because they have their intentions. That is, people make web pages with their preferences or concepts and link to the other pages that they choose. It is important for network intelligence to have connectivity and organization. Although blindly connected networks have no intelligence, it is reasonable to suppose that organized networks with agents' intentions have intelligence and produce some structures spontaneously.

Structure is one of the important factors in networks. In fact, network structures attract the attention of many researchers. For example, Google search engine adopts PageRank ([1], [2]) that measures the level of importance for all Web pages. The system uses the network structures consist of Web pages and hyperlinks. Newman *et al.* [3], [4], [5] suggested the way to find community using network structures. Both examples take advantage of network structures without going through the contents of each network elements.

Intelligent systems depend on their structures and organization. Therefore, we must focus on the behavior or properties of network structures for the intelligence emerged from the network.

T. Washio et al. (Eds.): JSAI 2005 Workshops, LNAI 4012, pp. 271–279, 2006.

2   Networks in Complex Systems

In this paper, we investigate the dynamic networks which have scale-free structure from the aspect of self-organization. It is a big surprise that the Internet and World Wide Web have scale-free structure since these networks are constructed by human beings even with their intentions and seemed to be random because of their large scale and complexity. Additionally, scale-free structures are also seen in natural networks such as metabolic ones. It is likely that some universal laws or phenomena exist in scale-free networks whether they are natural or artificial. Especially, what needs to be emphasized is that not only the static structures like snapshots but also the dynamic structures are the key point in network intelligence.

Though agents in networks have some role as described above, since we would like to explore the behavior or properties on network structures, we generalize an agent as a node with fitness which indicates a sort of ability in the network or environments. It would be found that self-organized criticality emerge in growing scale-free networks because both scale-free and self-organized criticality are associated with power-law. We consider that the phenomena give a part of properties for the basis of intelligence from the viewpoint of network structures in complex systems. Self-organization means that structures of some kind appear without explicit pressures or constraints from outside the system. For complex systems, where constituent elements interact with each other, self-organization is an extremely important concept. Additionally, the interaction that emerges is more than a mere aggregation of the elements.

3   Growing Scale-Free Networks

Albert-László Barabási [6] has suggested that the formation of scale-free network needs preferential attachment. "The rich get richer" mechanism makes the property of scale-free structure related to degree distribution. This mechanism, however, does not take into consideration the fact that each node has different characteristics or properties. In the real world, nodes that form some networks are not equal. For example, all web pages on the World Wide Web are different. In this paper we propose a new model that takes into account each node's fitness, which indicates the variations in every node that is, level of importance or a kind of ability in the network like Google's PageRank. As a result of the simulation experiments, it is found that scale-free networks are formed not only by the degree of nodes, as in Barabási study, but also by the fitness for each node. Therefore we consider that node fitness generalizes nodes' degree because fitness reflect degree in more detail and we can get nondiscrete data. If initial fitness of each node is 1 and its fitness increases 1, when the node gets a new link, the model is the same as BA model [6].

3.1   Fitness Growth Model

The proposed model is the *Fitness Growth Model*. Our preferential attachment depends only on node fitness. A new node with a higher fitness has a higher

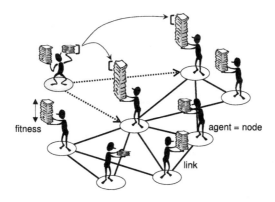

Fig. 1. Fitness Growth Model: when a new agent interacts with two other agents, their fitness increase according to the new agent's fitness. Fitness is a kind of ability that each agent has and agents are regarded as nodes in the network.

probability of acquiring links. Moreover, the node which gets a new link increases its fitness depending on a new node's fitness. The update equation for a new link and fitness are represented by Eq. (1) and Eq. (2). A new node is added to the network with two links as in the BA model [6] at one step over and over again. This idea is represented in Fig. 1. In this figure, agents are represented as nodes and they are interacted with each other through their fitness.

$$E_{t+1}(i,j) = V_t(j) \cdot \frac{f_j(t)}{\sum_m f_m(t)} \tag{1}$$

$$f_j(t+1) = f_j(t) + \alpha \cdot f_i(t) \tag{2}$$

where $E_t(i,j)$ is link existence probability between nodes i and j at time t, $V_t(j)$ is existence probability for node j at time t, $f_i(t)$ is the fitness for node i at time t and α is a positive parameter, in this paper $\alpha = 0.5$. The initial value of f is chosen from uniform distribution between 0 and 1.

Figs. 2 – 5 show the degree distribution of the growing network in this model. As we can see from these figures, the network has scale-free structure and maintains the structure during the growth. The shapes of network structures appear in Fig. 6. Therefore, it is clear that we can simulate a growing scale-free network with our fitness model. We shall analyze the spread of the network and the transition of node finesses to explain self-organized criticality phenomena. It is described further details about self-organized criticality and its models in the next section.

3.2   Self-organized Criticality

Self-organized criticality is the boundary between order and chaos where a large system, in which many elements are intricately interrelated, moves spontaneously without external control. Per Bak *et al.* [7], [8], [9] state that certain extended

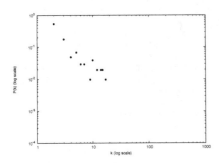

Fig. 2. Degree distribution at 100th step

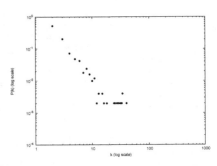

Fig. 3. Degree distribution at 500th step

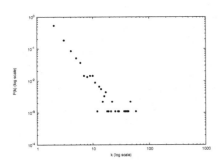

Fig. 4. Degree distribution at 900th step

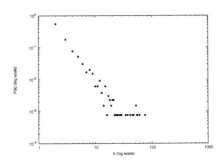

Fig. 5. Degree distribution at 1300th step

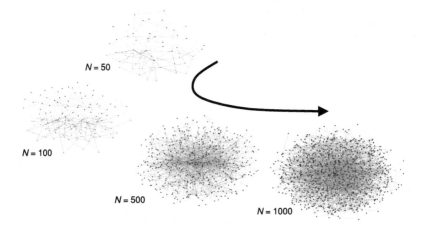

Fig. 6. Growing scale-free network with fitness growth model. N is the number of nodes.

dissipative dynamical systems naturally evolve into a critical state, with no characteristic length or time scales. That is, spatial signature is the emergence of scale-invariant structure and the temporal signature of the self-organized critical state is the presence of $1/f$ noise. The critical states system has the property in which the power-law emerges in a spatial and temporal manner. In the real world, for example, sand piles that are described below, the fractal structure of river networks, turbidities, earthquakes, starquakes, solar flares and so on have self-organized criticality.

Next, we will introduce two models for self-organized criticality phenomena. The main theoretical issues to be addressed are that these models organize themselves to the critical state, which is characterized by the power-law. Although we will show only two models, we consider that it is sufficient to explain the critical phenomena that would occur in our model.

Sand-Pile Model. When sand trickles down, a pile is formed on the ground. In the beginning, as the process continues, the pile becomes steeper. Eventually, the pile has a constant slope while there are large and small sand slides. The state in which the system maintains the structure with recurrent avalanches is self-organized criticality.

The model which expresses the forming sand pile is simulated in a two-dimensional grid $(L \times L)$. One grain of sand is dropped at the grid randomly by one step. The grid is represented by (x, y), where $1 \le x \le L$ and $1 \le y \le L$, and the number of grains which are dropped in the grid is represented by $Z(x, y)$. That is

$$z(x, y) \rightarrow z(x, y) + 1 \qquad (3)$$

Next, let us consider the avalanches of a sand pile. When the number of grains at one grid exceeds the critical value Z_{cr} $(= 3)$, in other words the number reaches four, one grain of sand is sent to each of the four neighbors. Fig. 7 shows this model.

$$Z(x, y) \rightarrow Z(x, y) - 4 \qquad (4)$$

The four neighbor sites go up by one as follows:

$$\begin{aligned} Z(x \pm 1, y) &\rightarrow Z(x \pm 1, y) + 1 \\ Z(x, y \pm 1) &\rightarrow Z(x, y \pm 1) + 1 \end{aligned} \qquad (5)$$

In this model, the number of influenced grids by one grain drop indicates the size of the avalanches. The distribution of the size of avalanches follows the power-law at the critical state. Moreover, in any grid, the power spectrum of the number of changes in $Z(x, y)$ for time steps follows $1/f$ noise. That is to say, the Sand-Pile model follows the spatial and temporal power-law.

Evolutionary Model. The basic idea for evolution is that the species with lowest fitness is inclined to disappear or mutate in environments. A simple model of evolution, which is associated with punctuated equilibrium and criticality is described in [10]. In this model, random numbers between 0 and 1 are arranged

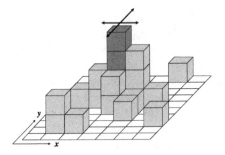

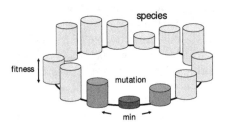

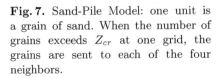

Fig. 7. Sand-Pile Model: one unit is a grain of sand. When the number of grains exceeds Z_{cr} at one grid, the grains are sent to each of the four neighbors.

Fig. 8. Evolutionary Model: a species with the lowest fitness and the two neighbors are mutated

for each species as fitness. Each of them is on the circle and interacting with its two neighbors. At every time step, the species with lowest fitness and its two neighbors mutate because of the interaction. Mutation means that each fitness of these three species is replaced by new random numbers between 0 and 1. This model is shown in Fig. 8.

Although each species' fitness fluctuates up and down, the average tends to increase to a certain value. The envelope function of the lowest fitness, defining the fitness gap, increases in a stepwise manner. Fitness gap is the difference between the lowest and that of the one higher than it. Furthermore, the size of avalanches is the length of the step while the fitness is unchanged, that is, the number of mutation. When there is a gap, a new avalanche begins.

There are avalanches of all sizes; that is to say the distribution of the size of avalanches follows the power-law. In the same manner as the Sand-Pile model, the power spectrum of the cumulative number of mutations for any species at critical state follows $1/f$ noise. The evolutionary model also follows the spatial and temporal power-law.

3.3   Model Comparison

To explain critical phenomena in our model, it is necessary to compare with other models that indicate self-organized criticality. Table 1 shows the models and conditions for the critical phenomenon. First, there exists a critical point or critical state where the system maintains equilibrium. In the case of the Sand-Pile model, it is the constant slope of the sand pile and in the case of the Evolutionary model, it is the minimum fitness in which almost all the species possess an excess. When we consider a growing scale-free network with the fitness model, structure preservation is the critical state. Even though the network is growing, it maintains the scale-free structure with the constant slope of the degree distribution graph.

Next, we must investigate whether the growing scale-free network follows the spatial and temporal power-law as described in the previous section. Par Bak

Table 1. Model comparison with self-organized criticality

	Fitness Growth Model	Sand-Pile Model	Evolutionary Model
Critical state	Constant slope of degree distribution.	Constant slope of sand pile.	Constant value of minimum fitness.
Special signature	Span distribution of maximum fitness.	Size distribution of avalanches.	Size distribution of avalanches.
Temporal signature	Transition of a node fitness.	Transition of avalanche's cumulative frequency at one site.	Transition of mutation's cumulative frequency at one species.

suggests that the size distribution of avalanches shows spatial power-law in the Sand-Pile model and Evolutionary model. The size of avalanches refers to the span of punctuated equilibrium, and during the span the elements in the system interact with each other for the equilibrium. In the case of our fitness model, the constant spans of maximum fitness represent the avalanche, because other elements are added and the network is growing during the span to maintain the structure.

In addition to spatial signature, temporal signature is the transition of any node's fitness in our model. If the power spectrum of the transition shows $1/f$ noise, it indicates the critical state. In the Sand-Pile model and Evolutionary model, temporal signatures at critical states emerge in the transition frequency at one site or species. That is, to keep the equilibrium of the whole system, the behavior of one element in the system shows temporal signature for critical states. It is considered that the signature has a characteristic power-law $1/f$ behavior.

Here we only use a model that constructs scale-free structure. What happens with the growth of a random network? With the Erdös-Rényi random model [11], even if we get the same data as scale-free network model, maximum fitness or one node's fitness, it is easily imaginable that these data would not follow any power-law. The reason why we focus on scale-free structure is that the structure is under the power-law.

On the grounds that critical states follow the spatial and temporal power-law, such as in Table 1, we conduct simulation experiments with our fitness growing network model. In the next section, some results are shown.

4   Spatial and Temporal Power-Law

As described above, Figs. 2 – 5 show the degree distribution in which a scale-free network maintains the structure during the growth. Then, the transition of maximum fitness in the whole network shown in Fig. 9. Fig. 10 is the results of the size distribution from Fig. 9. The size of one span is where the maximum

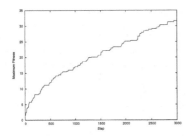

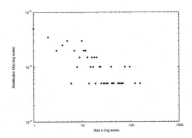

Fig. 9. The maximum fitness transition of growing scale-free network

Fig. 10. Spatial Power-Law: The distribution of the step length which is constant in Fig. 9. This graph shows approximately power-law.

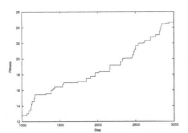

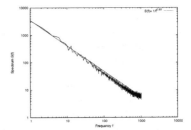

Fig. 11. Transition of a node's fitness during criticality, from step 1000 to step 3000

Fig. 12. Temporal Power-Law: Power Spectrum of Fig. 11 shows $1/f$ noise

fitness is constant between a step and the next step in the graph. The size distribution is associated with the power-law, though there has been no generic measure of how much of a power-law the network is. That is, any sizes of growth span exist. There are many short spans and some long ones. This result indicates the spatial signature at critical state.

Moreover, the transition of one node's fitness during the critical state (from step 1000 to step 3000) is shown in Fig. 11. When this transition is analyzed with Fourier analysis, we get the power spectrum as shown in Fig. 12. The power spectrum provides $1/f$ noise, which is approximated by $S(f) \sim 1/f^{0.93}$ in our simulation. Since the fitness tends to increase in Fig. 11, the transition contains many low-frequency components. The high-frequency components are caused by small changes of the fitness. $1/f$ noise is observed in some sorts of music, rhythm of the human body and so on. In other words, it is one of the natural phenomena.

From the results of spatiotemporal signature, it is found that growing scale-free networks indicate self-organized critical phenomena. One of the reasons why there exist scale-free structures in many fields in the real world is that common mechanisms that are explained by natural phenomena are at work in these networks. In this paper, we only describe the phenomena; however, it is difficult to solve that why the power-law relationship occurs. We should clarify the reasons in the future.

5 Conclusion

As consequences of simulation experiments, it is found that growing scale-free networks have self-organized criticality because of the spatial and temporal power-law. We use a simple model for growing networks; therefore, it becomes the basis of the behavior of all scale-free networks. It follows from this that some universal laws or phenomena exist in "networks" around us. These laws or phenomena would lead to the intelligence emerged from the networks which are composed of a kind of agents as nodes with fitness.

In closing, it is important to research and develop new information systems using such universal properties associated with networks. We call the approach "Hyper Net Intelligence", the idea of which is to construct information processing systems with intelligence hidden in network properties. With this approach, we aim to develop Web applications in the future.

References

1. Rajeev Motwani Lawrence Page, Sergey Brin, Terry Winograd: The pagerank citation ranking: Bringing order to the web. Technical report, Stanford Digital Library Technologies Project (1998)
2. Taher Haveliwala: Efficient Computation of PageRank. Technical Report **1999-31** (1999)
3. M. E. J. Newman, M. Girvan: Finding and evaluating community structure in networks. Phys. Rev. E **69**, 026113 (2004)
4. M. E. J. Newman: Fast algorithm for detecting community structure in networks. Phys. Rev. E **69**, 066133 (2004)
5. M. E. J. Newman, Aaron Clauset, Cristopher Moore: Finding community structure in very large networks. Phys. Rev. E **70**, 066111 (2004)
6. Albert-László Barabási: LINKED:The New Science of Networks. Perseus Publishing (2002)
7. Per Bak: How Nature Works: The Science of Self-Organized Criticality. Copernicus Books (1999)
8. Per Bak, Chao Tang, Kurt Wiesenfeld: Self-organized criticality. Phys. Rev. A **38** (1988) 364–374
9. Per Bak, Chao Tang, Kurt Wiesenfeld: Self-Organized Criticality: An Explanation of $1/f$ Noise. Phys. Rev. Lett. **59** (1987) 381–384
10. Per Bak, Kim Sneppen: Punctuated Equilibrium and Criticality in a Simple Model of Evolution. Phys. Rev. Lett. **71** (1993) 4083–4086
11. Réka Albert, Albert-László Barabási: Statistical mechanics of complex networks. Reviews of Modern Physics **74** (2002)

Analysis of User's Relation and Reading Activity in Weblogs

Tadanobu Furukawa[1], Tomofumi Matsuzawa[2], Yutaka Matsuo[3],
Koki Uchiyama[4], and Masayuki Takeda[2]

[1] Graduate School of Science and Technology, Tokyo University of Science,
2641 Yamazaki, Noda-shi, Chiba, Japan
tektf@mt.is.noda.tus.ac.jp
[2] Dept. of Information Sciences, Tokyo University of Science,
2641 Yamazaki, Noda-shi, Chiba, Japan
{t-matsu, takeda}@is.noda.tus.ac.jp
[3] National Institute of Advanced Industrial Science and Technology,
1-18-13 Sotokanda, Chiyoda-ku, Tokyo, Japan
y.matsuo@aist.go.jp
[4] hottolink, Inc.
2-11-17 Nishigotanda, Shinagawa-ku, Tokyo, Japan
uchi@hottolink.co.jp

Abstract. In a blog network, there are many relations such as comment, trackback, and so on. We consider that if the relations are related to user's reading activity, we can extract useful information from the relations for using a recommendation system. We define the strength and type as the measure for relations, and analyze the correlation between those measures and users' reading activity. We attempt to determine the relations on which users regularly read the blogs.

1 Introduction

Much information describing individuals exists on the WWW as diaries, news sites and Bulletin Board Systems (BBSs) because of the popularization of internet services. Therefore, it is difficult for users to get exactly the information they seek, so "information retrieval" or "information recommendation" services are in demand.

Recently, Weblogs (blogs) are receiving attention as a new form of a personal information transmission. Blog characteristics include: users update their contents frequently because the operations to information sending are easy to do on a web browser – basically one blog is updated by one user; it has functions called "comment" and "trackback"; and it offers the updated information in the form of an RDF Site Summary (RSS)[7]. Particularly trackback, a unique function to blog, allows interactive communication and allows the use of discussion of one chosen topic.

Blog users visit others' blogs and write comments or send trackbacks as they update their own blogs. Considering these activities, we can discover the

T. Washio et al. (Eds.): JSAI 2005 Workshops, LNAI 4012, pp. 280–290, 2006.

relationships among blogs. Actually, such relations are closely watched in business. Particularly, blogs are often read with social networking services (SNSs), which are services that record and map human relations information in recent years.

We notice the relations among blogs and analyze their effects on users' activities. First, we verify the hypothesis "whether users who visit blogs are strongly related". We prepare various relations such as Comment / Trackback, and inspect those relations that appear to be influential. Next, we clarify "whether we can distinguish blogs that users read frequently using the relations". If possible, we might build a recommendation service based on relations among blogs.

Our analyses use the database: "Doblog"[1], a blog-hosting service in Japan. Using this service, users update their blogs and perform other activities such as writing comments after they log in. Therefore, we can treat users' behavior. Doblog has a special function called "bookmark", to link to favorite blogs from one's own blog. We use it as one relation. We analyze users' activities using this data for limited users on that service.

The subsequent section explores related works. Section 3 explains the algorithms used for analysis. in Section 4, we show a concrete experiment technique. Section 5 describes analysis of the results. We conclude the paper in Section 6.

2   Related Works

Characteristics of hyperlinks on WWW were investigated in detail[1], and research of extracting useful information as webpages or web communities of a specific topic from the network structure based on hyperlinks was successful[5][6]. For example, it is known that the WWW community can be extracted as a complete bipartite subgraph comprising a hub and authority.

However, the blog network is very complex because of its unique relations such as Trackback and Comment. For that reason, we cannot easily grasp the state of information spread[3].

This paper presents analysis of this complex network and our attempt to extract useful information from it. Particularly, one strong point is that we use users' behavior as one relation.

3   Relations Between Two Blogs

We think there must be the blogs a user can access hardly by following hyperlinks but those are interesting to the user. We try to distinguish such blogs by using the relations with own blog, prepare some relations: Bookmark / Comment / Trackback. If user A, the author of blog A, makes Bookmark link to blog B in own blog, we define there is relation of Bookmark from A to B. If user A send Comment / Trackback to blog B more than once, we define there is relation of Comment / Trackback from A to B.

---

[1] ©NTT Data Corp., ©hottolink,Inc., http://www.doblog.com/ , using data of Oct. 2003 – Jul. 2004.

Herein, if user A has visited user B's blog more than once, we call it "Visiting (relation/activity)" from A to B; if user A has visited user B's blog more than 30 times, we call it "Regular Reading (relation/activity)" from A to B. The logs of user's "Visiting" are available from the Doblog database. We analyze whether correlation exists among the relations of the two blogs and Visiting / Regular Reading.

Our goal is to extract those blogs that a user wants to visit repeatedly after one access based on the relations that a user cannot access easily. Therefore, we check the two points below: (i) What relations engender Visiting behavior? (ii) What relations on Visiting relation engender Regular Reading?

Regarding the relations of blogs, we use (a) link structure using Bookmark / Comment / Trackback, (b) similarity of fields of interest.

For (a), we check the range of two hops because it seems that the most influential relation to users' activity is a two-hop relation in the relations we want to extract, i.e. indirect relations. We analyze this two-hop relation for "Strength" and "Type".

– Strength of Relation

A measure of each relational strength is represented by the number of routes that connect two blogs in two hops by one relation. For example, routes between A and B are three $(A - 1 - B/A - 2 - B/A - 4 - B)$, as shown in Fig. 1. Figure 2 shows the extent to which the rate follows the transitivity rule $(A - 1 \cap 1 - B \Rightarrow A - B)$ in these two hops. This figure reveals a positive correlation between the number of routes and the transitivity rule. For that reason, we can say that this number indicates the strength of the relations. We examine the correlation between this strength measure and Visiting / Regular Reading activity.

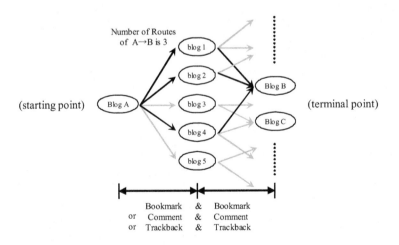

Fig. 1. Number of routes

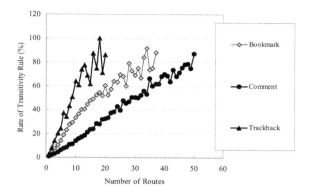

Fig. 2. Number of routes & transitivity rule

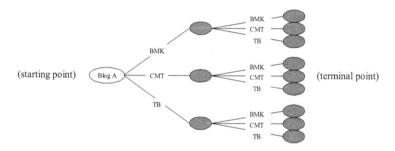

Fig. 3. 12 kinds of relations. (BMK, Bookmark; CMT, Comment; TB, Trackback)

- Type of Relation

  As Fig. 3 shows, 12 kinds of relation exist in the range of two-hop relations (gray nodes in the figure). We analyze in which relation Visiting / Regular Reading occurs readily for this 12 kinds .

With regard to (b), this uses the items[2] that users selected at the Doblog user registration. As a measure of strength among users, we use the number of identical items. We quantify the correlation between strength and Visiting / Regular Reading activity.

We analyze the above using the UserRank top 1647 blogs, 10% of all Doblog users. UserRank is calculated from monthly data of Bookmark, Comment, Trackback, and Visiting; it is a score based on how the user contributes to the network constructed. The nodes are blogs (users) and edges are relations using the spreading activation[2]. Therefore, it seems that using highly ranked blogs, i.e., blogs which have many relations to other blogs, allows more effective experiments. These are heavy users of blogs: only 1647 users' data among all data occupy 59% of Bookmark data, 64% of Comment data, and 64% of Trackback data.

---

[2] 103 items such as sports, entertainment, etc.

4   Experiment Algorithm

We conducted the following experiment to examine the Visiting / Regular Reading (we call those two activities "Reading" in this chapter) in each relation under the conditions below; we also calculate the rate. The Reading Rate is calculated using the following formula:

$$Reading\ Rate = \frac{Number\ of\ Blog\ Sets\ which\ have\ Reading\ Relation}{Number\ of\ All\ Blog\ Sets}$$

"Number of all blog sets", in the Visiting analysis, indicates the number of all blog sets of the starting and terminal points under each condition. In the Regular Reading analysis, it represents the number of the blog sets under each condition and the Visiting relation.

4.1   Regarding Strength of Relation

Number of Routes. For the two-hop relation, which consists of one Bookmark / Comment / Trackback, we calculate the Reading Rate for each number of routes.

1. One hop: Extract all blogs connected from one blog (the starting point) by one relation.
2. Two hops: Extract all blogs (the terminal point) connected from blogs in operation 1 using the same relation as operation 1, except for the starting point.
3. Check the number of routes and whether there is a Reading relation between the starting point and each terminal point.
4. For all starting points, repeat operations 1 to 3.
5. Calculate the Reading Rate according to the number of routes.

Similarity of Interests. For all two-blog sets, check the number of fields of same interests and whether they have a Reading relation. This relation does not have direction. However, considering users A and B, we found the Reading relation for $A - B$ and $B - A$. We checked about $_{1647}P_2 = 2,710,962$ sets, and calculated the Reading Rate for each number of the same fields of interest.

4.2   About Type of Relation

For all two-blog sets ($_{1647}P_2$ sets), we checked which relation among the 12 kinds of relations mentioned in the previous chapter existed, and whether they have a Reading relation (Table 1). Using each set as training data, we analyzed which relation determines the Reading activity, and constructed a decision tree using a machine learning algorithm C4.5[4]. During Visiting analysis, we analyzed the above only for the sets showing a two-hop relation because there must be a Visiting relation between one-hop relation sets.

Table 1. Form of training data for analysis of relation types (start/term, the starting/terminal point; Bmk, Bookmark; Cmt, Comment; Tb, Trackback; Rd, Regular Reading relation; Vst, Visiting relation; T, True; F, False)

2 blogs		12 Types of Relation					Vst
start	term	Bmk	Cmt	...	Tb-Cmt	Tb-Tb	(Rd)
A	B	T	F	...	F	T	T
A	C	F	T	...	F	F	F
B	C	T	T	...	T	T	T
⋮				⋮			⋮

5   Results and Analysis

This chapter explains results of the experiments explained in the previous chapter.

5.1   Strength of Relation

for Visiting Activity. The relation between the number of routes and identical fields of interest and Visiting activity is shown in Fig. 4. This figure shows that

- If the number of the routes increases, the Visiting rate rises.
- There is no correlation between the number of fields of identical interest and Visiting activity.

Regarding the former, the reason seems to be that the Bookmark / Comment / Trackback creates a hyperlink that allows a user to visit the site easily.

Regarding the latter – similarity of interest and Visiting –, we inferred the following:

- Users do not always record their interests in their own blogs. Alternatively, they do not always visit blogs that contain information that is related to their selected fields of interest.
- If not above, users have not been able to follow the blogs of interest.
- The users do not select the fields of interest carefully.

This will be argued more in the following section.

Regular Reading Activity. Figures 5 is the diagram showing the relation between strength of relation and Regular Reading activity. This figure shows that

- if the number of the routes increases, the Regular Reading rate rises.
- There is no correlation between the number of identical fields of interest and the Regular Reading rate.

The latter is supportive of the second guess of the same interest-Visiting analysis in the previous section. However, validating the users' written contents about their interests is the work of text mining, so this study ignores that analysis.

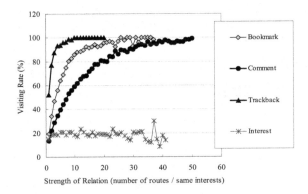

Fig. 4. Number of link routes or similarity of interest & Visiting

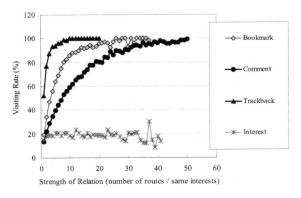

Fig. 5. Number of link routes or similarity of interest & Regular Reading (more than 30 visits)

Decision Tree. Using Figs. 4 – 5, Trackback seems to be the most influential relation for Visiting / Regular Reading activity, but we cannot determine a hierarchy among relations, because there may be more than two kinds of relations between blogs. Therefore, using these analyzed data about the strength of relation, we construct decision trees for Visiting / Regular Reading. For Visiting analysis, the training data are 568,043 sets of two blogs (starting point and terminal point) that have more than one route by any two-hop relation; for Regular Reading analysis, they are 154,549 sets of two blogs that have a Visiting relation. Each data set for machine learning consists of the number of routes of each relation and whether a Visiting / Regular Reading relation exists (Table 2). These data do not include the number of identical fields of interest because that seems to show no correlation by previous experiment.

Results are shown in Figs. 6 – 7. Figure 6 depicts the analyses of Visiting. Figure 7 is analysis of Regular Reading.

In these decision trees, the highly influential relation occupies the upper position as a node, and B / C / T represents Bookmark / Comment / Trackback.

Table 2. Form of training data for analysis of relation strength (start/term, the starting/terminal point; Bmk, Bookmark; Cmt, Comment; Tb, Trackback; Rd, Regular Reading relation; Vst, Visiting relation; T, True; F, False)

2 blogs		Number of Routes			Vst
start	term	Bmk	Cmt	Tb	(Rd)
A	B	3	3	1	T
A	C	5	6	3	T
B	C	4	2	0	F
⋮		⋮			⋮

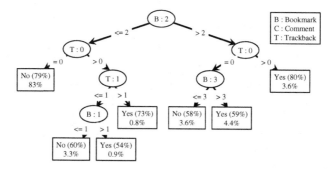

Fig. 6. Decision tree of Visiting by number of routes (568,043 training sets)

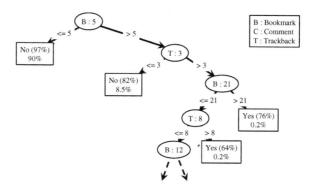

Fig. 7. Decision tree of Regular Reading by number of routes (154,549 training sets)

The left branch is a path for which there are less than the number of label routes. The right branch is a path for which there are more than the number of label routes. The leaves appear when it is classified to some extent. "Yes" and "No" represent whether the Visiting / Regular Reading relation is true or false; the values represent (right) the rate of correct distinction and (below) the percentage of classified data compared to the whole. For example, following the left part of

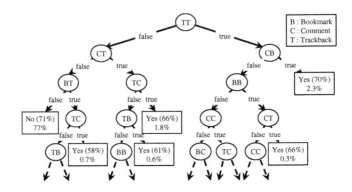

Fig. 8. Decision tree of Visiting by 19 kinds of relations (323,861 training sets)

the diagram down in Fig. 6, the rate of blog sets that have less than two routes of Bookmark and less than zero route(= no routes) of Trackback is 83%. They do not have Visiting relations with a probability if 79%. It is noteworthy that these show only the parts of the top five layers because of the space limitations of this paper.

Figure 7 shows that the most influential relation to Regular Reading activity is the number of the routes of Bookmark. Trackback follows and it is influential, in spite of its smaller number of routes. However, Trackback relation is not visible (if blog A send Trackback to blog B, there is a hyperlink of B to A, but there is not a hyperlink of A to B), so it is not clear why the two-hop Trackback routes is influential. The rate of Bookmark between two blogs which have Trackback is not very high, $2826/5192 = 54.4\%$.

On the other hand, Fig. 6 shows that the most influential relation to Visiting activity is also the number of routes of Bookmark, and the number of routes is very small(more than two). This says that users usually visit blogs by following Bookmarks. And this number is smaller than the one of Regular Reading analysis, so the probability of to visit blogs on the relations which are influential to Regular Reading activity. Because the more numerous the routes, the higher the Visiting probability according to Fig. 4. So, we cannot get relations worth recommending in this analysis.

5.2   Type of Relation

For Visiting Activity. Result showing which two-hop relation is influential on Visiting activity is Fig. 8.

The decision tree's structure is almost identical to that of the previous section. Two letter relations such as "CT" represent a two-hop relation: Comment – Trackback. The branches represent whether there is a relation (left is false, right is true).

The most influential relation to Visiting activity is the Trackback – Trackback relation, this is a similar result of Strength of Relation.

For Regular Reading Activity. Result shows the two-hop relations that are influential for Regular Reading activity is in Fig. 9.

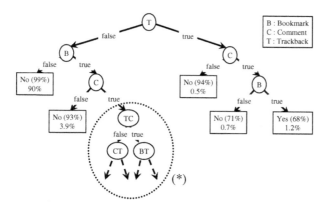

Fig. 9. Decision tree of Regular Reading by 19 kinds of relations (206,804 training sets)

The figure shows that the most influential relation for Regular Reading activity is the one-hop relation, such as Bookmark / Comment / Trackback. The sets of two blogs that have neither a Trackback nor a Bookmark relation occupy about 90% of all data and have almost no Regular Reading relation. This fact shows the large effect of one-hop relation (Users regularly read the blogs to which they have sent any Trackback / Comment or made Bookmark-link).

As the effect of one-hop relation is too big, we pay attention to only two-hop relation (the area of (*) in Fig. 9): the relations of (1) "Trackback - Comment" is true and "Bookmark - Trackback" is true and (2) "Trackback - Comment" is false and "Comment - Trackback" is true seem to be influential to Regular Reading. Now, we calculate the Visiting rate of two relations, they are not very high, (1)64% and (2)44%. So these relations may be worth recommending.

6   Conclusions

In this study, we analyzed a blog network: which blog users visit and regularly read, by exploring its unique relations. We defined the strength and type of the relations as measures and tried to elucidate the influence of those relations on the users' reading activities.

Consequently, for the Visiting activity: the two-hop Bookmark route is influential, and whether the two-hop Trackback route exists is also effective. For Regular Reading activity: in analysis of Strength we could not get useful result. However, in analysis of Type we could find the relation, that is influential for Regular Reading but user cannot surely visit. We consider that such analyses can form the basis of information recommendation.

References

1. A.Broder, R.Kumar, F.Maghoul, P.Raghavan, S.Rajagopalan, R.Stata, A.Tomkins, and J.Wiener: Graph Structure in The Web. The 9th International. World Wide Web Conference (2000)
2. A.Saad: A Multi-Agent Spreading Activation Network Model for Online Learning Objects. http://julita.usask.ca/mable/saad.pdf (2001)
3. E.Adar, L.Zhang, L.A.Adamic, and R.M.Lukose: Implicit Structure and the Dynamics of Blogspace. http://www.hpl.hp.com/research/idl/papers/blogs/ blogspace-draft.pdf (2003)
4. J.R.Quinlan, C4.5: Programs for Machine Learning, Morgan Kaufmann Publishers, Inc. (1993)
5. L.Page, S.Brin, R.Motwani, and T.Winograd: The PageRank Citation Ranking:Bringing Order to the Web. http://web.resource.org/rss/1.0/spec (1999)
6. R.Kumar, P.Raghavan, S.Rajagopalan, and A.Tomkins: Trawling the Web for Emerging Cyber-Communities. The 8th International World Wide Web Conference (2001)
7. RSS-DEV Working Group: RDF Site Summary (RSS) 1.0. http://web.resource.org/rss/1.0/spec (1999)

Grand Canonical Minority Games with Variable Strategy Spaces

Hiromichi Kimura[1,2] and Eizo Akiyama[1,3]

[1] University of Tsukuba, 1-1-1 Tennoudai, Tsukuba, Ibaraki 305-0006, Japan
[2] hkimura@sk.tsukuba.ac.jp
http://abel.sk.tsukuba.ac.jp/~kimura/index.html
[3] eizo@sk.tsukuba.ac.jp
http://infoshako.sk.tsukuba.ac.jp/~eizo/index.html

Abstract. A simplified model of an economic market is the *minority game*. In each round players choose to join one of two sides, -1 or 1. Those on the minority side at the end of a round earn a positive point. The players make decisions about the alternative based on the past data.

The aim of our paper is to investigate what occurs in a modified minority game which involves two features as follows:

- the change of the number of attendees and
- the evolution of agents' strategies.

In such a naturally extended minority game, we found that the probability density function(PDF) of price changes in our model mostly follows Gaussian function. However the PDF of price changes in real markets is known for not being Gaussian function. This result implies that we may have to modify the setteings of minority games.

1 Introduction

Statistical properties of price changes and volume changes and so on in real markets are called *stylized facts*[2][7][9]. For example, the autocorrelation function of price changes is essentially zero for all non-zero timelags in most markets. This fact is related to the *efficient market hypothesis*. In addition, the histograms of price change in most markets follow a power-law distribution, which is called a *fat tail*. Furthermore small price changes are more frequent than the prediction of Gaussian function, which is called a *high peak*. The histograms of volume change follow a high peak and a fat tail in many cases, too. The fat tail of price changes concerns markets' bubbles and crashes. Traditional economics and financial engineering have not succeeded in explaining the stylized facts well especially fat tail. For instance, a conclusion of financial engineering is that the Probability Distribution Function (PDF) of price changes is Gaussian function. This result relies on the central limit theorem.

We expect that human decision making can explain these phenomena. Such a market model, we are interested in the Minority Game (MG). B.Arthur suggested the prototype model of the MG, which is called *El Farol Bar* model[11]. And

T. Washio et al. (Eds.): JSAI 2005 Workshops, LNAI 4012, pp. 291–301, 2006.

D. Challet, M. Marsili and Robert Savi et al. developed El Farol Bar model as standard MG mathematically[1][6][8]. They made these models to understand players' inductive inference. The models can explain fluctuating prices.

However the standard MG has too simple assumptions. That is one thing all players are always supposed to participate. The volume in MGs and the like is defined as the number of participating players by Johnson, Jefferies and Hui[7]. Under this definition, the volume in the standard MG is constant. On the other hand, the volumes in real markets are not constant.

Therefore we must think that players can enter a market and exit from the market of theirs own free will. This game was named Grand Canonical MG (GCMG) by Johnson et al.[7].

Though the volume in the GCMG can vary in time, there still remain some quantitative differences between the Cumulative Distribution Functions (CDFs) of volumes and prices in the GCMG and that in real markets. As a likely explanation, it is too simple that cognitive abilities of players and adaptation mechanisms in the GCMG. Then we extended the GCMG to varying quantity of information – we call it a *memory length* – of players. Such a model which is allowed to vary strategy spaces was studied by Li, Riolo, Rick and Savit[4]. Also Lindgren suggested, not MG, the prisoner's dilemma game with variable strategy spaces[5].

The goal of our study is to compare two models based on the MG and to investigate the effect of various quantity of information used by players. So we extend the GCMG by using Lindgren's method and discuss the differences between the GCMG and our model.

Note our following results if it is easy to enter into a market:

- The fact that the autocorrelation function of price changes is essentially zero for all non-zero timelags, may be related to that players use their strategies of various memory length.
- The PDF and CDF of volume changes in our model are closer to that in a real market than that in Johnson's GCMG.
- The CDF of volume changes in our model corresponds to that in the real market when price change is small.

But our following result if it is difficult to enter into a market:

- The PDF of price changes does not emerge a high peak, not to mention a fat tail.

2   Model

In this section, we explain the GCMG and how to extend it. The explanation of Section 2.1 is common to the GCMG and our model.

2.1   Grand Canonical Minority Game

It is the minority game that is played with odd number($= N$) of heterogeneous players who choose either *buy* ($+1$) or *sell* (-1) and who win if they choose a minority group. Each player adopts the strategy whose evaluation is the best, and he or she chooses either ± 1 every time. When all the players have ended to choose, one round ends. The players have played a lot of games and learn by adopting the best strategy. We think extending this model.

The strategies in the MG (and the GCMG) are for players to decide their action based on the most recent data of M period. These data are called *histories* $\mu[t]$ and the length of these data, M, is called a memory length. So there are 2^M different histories. Each player has s strategies. The number s is called *the number of strategies*. The Table 1 is an example for the case where the number of strategies is 2 and M is 3. Indices of histories' row are information whether the players who choose 1 win (described as 1) or lose (described as 0). For instance, 000 represents that the players who have chosen -1 (sell) won most recent three times. ± 1 of strategy rows mean a player's choice whether buy or sell in the given history.

Table 1. Examples of strategies (M=3)

history	000	001	010	011	100	101	110	111
strategy 1	1	-1	-1	1	1	-1	1	-1
strategy 2	1	1	-1	-1	-1	-1	-1	1

The players have 2 strategies, then, they need to choose the best by evaluating their strategies. This evaluation of a strategy is called the *score*. If a player belongs to the minority group, he or she gets 1 point at each time step. Contrary, he or she gets -1 point when belongs to the majority. In what follows, a choice (± 1) of player i's strategy R at history $\mu[t]$ is described as $a_{i,R}^{\mu[t]}$. The sum of each players' choice $\sum_i a_i[t]$ is described as $A[t]$. A timescale over which the previous successes or failures of the predictions of strategy R are forgotten is described as T. And correspondence $sgn(x)$ is defined as follows:

$$sgn(x) = \begin{cases} 1 & (x > 0) \\ 1 \ or \ -1 \ is \ chosen \ at \ random & (x = 0) \\ -1 & (x < 0) \end{cases} .$$

We define the score of player i's strategy R at time t, $S_{i,R}[t]$, as follows:

$$S_{i,R}[t] = (1 - \frac{1}{T})S_{i,R}[t-1] - a_{i,R}^{\mu[t-1]} \ sgn(A[t]) ,$$

$$S_{i,R}[0] = 0 .$$

T equals 100 here in accordance with Johnson et al.[7].

The rules of entry and exit are as follows: The index of the strategy which has the best score is R^*. And we represent the difficulty of entry as r. It is called a *confidence level*.

- $S_{i,R^*} \leq r \Rightarrow$ *exit from the market*,
- $S_{i,R^*} > r \Rightarrow$ *entry into the market with strategy R^**.

The number of strategies is 2, the memory length is 3 and the confidence level is 4 in the GCMG formulated by Johnson et al.

Last of this section, we must think how to relate a minority game to real markets. Johnson, Jefferies and Hui[7] defined the price as follows. The price at time t is P_t and player i's choice is $a_i = \pm 1, 0$. 0 means that the player exit from the market.

$$Price\ change\ at\ time\ t \equiv log\frac{P_t}{P_{t-1}} = constant \times \sum_i a_i \,. \qquad (1)$$

That is, the price change represents the dispersion of players' choices, and if there are many players who choose buy $(+1)$, the price increases. The volume is defined as follws:

$$Volume\ at\ time\ t \equiv constant \times \sum_i |a_i|$$

In other words, the volume represents players' activity. We use these definitions unalterably in our model.

2.2   Mutations

Noe we have ended the explanation of the GCMG. Then we explain how to extend the GCMG.

Our model is based on the GCMG suggested by Johnson et al.[7]. The strategies of players in the GCMG do not mutate. However, is it unnatural that players continue to have a strategy they do not use for a long time? Players in real markets must continue to improve their strategy and think achieving better strategies.

Hence, strategies of players can mutate in our model. Memory lengths of players must become generally different from that of each other. Because it is no surprise that there are some differences among players' ways of processing the received information in real markets, since, there must be some differences among quantity of information used by players. Then the above is a natural generalization of the GCMG.

We adopted Lindgren's method[5] for our model. This method changes players' strategy gradually. It consists of three kinds of mutation as follows:

 - Point Mutation,
 - Duplication,
 - Split.

The point mutation changes a sign in a strategy (see Table 2 (a)). The memory length of the strategy does not change even if a point mutation occurs. On the other hand, when a duplication occurs (see Table 2 (b)), the memory length of the strategy increases by one. The strategy duplication attaches a copy of the strategy to itself. When a split occurs, the memory length of the strategy decreases by one (see Table 2 (c)). The split is the mutation to remove randomly

Table 2. (a)An example of the point mutation $(M = 2)$ Note that a used strategy does not change. This is the same in all mutations.   (b)An example of the duplication $(M = 2 \rightarrow M = 3)$ Note that the duplication does not change actions.   (c)An example of the split $(M = 3 \rightarrow M = 2)$.

(a)

history	00	01	10	11
used strategy	1	1	-1	1
not used strategy	-1	-1	-1	1

$\rightarrow$

00	01	10	11
1	1	-1	1
-1	-1	-1	-1

(b)

history	00	01	10	11
not used strategy	-1	-1	-1	1

$\rightarrow$

000	001	010	011	100	101	110	111
-1	-1	-1	1	-1	-1	-1	1

(c)

history	000	001	010	011	100	101	110	111
not used strategy	1	-1	-1	-1	1	1	-1	1

$\rightarrow$

00	01	10	11
1	1	-1	1

the first or second half of the strategy. In this way, the duplication and the split can change the memory length of strategies. That is, the strategy spaces are not fixed, so they are called variable strategy spaces.

Now used strategies do not change by mutation. Contrary not used strategies are under the influence of mutation. This means that used strategies remain without change and that not used strategies may mutate and evolve into better strategies. In our model, players make their strategies compete against each other and strategies continue to evolve but each player cannot see other players' evolution.

2.3   Parameters' View

We have ended the explanation of our model. This section explains the parameters to be used.

- $N = 501$ the number of players.
- $T = 100$ the timescale over which the previous results of the predictions of strategy are forgotten.
- $M = 0 \sim 13$ the maximum and minimum value of a memory length, whose initial value is 3 for all players.
- $p_1 = 0.002$ the probability that point mutations occur.
- $p_2 = 0.001$ the probability that duplications and splits occur.
- $r = -4, 4$ confidence level. the threshold to decide whether a player enters the market.
- $s = 2$ the number of strategies per an agent.

We set that the timescale T is much smaller than a timescale over which strategies change by mutations. In other words, the change of scores is faster than that of strategies by mutation. This condition is necessary for scores to bethe criterion of strategies' evaluation. The reason is that players cannot evaluate each strategy correctly if they do not forget the past scores much faster than the change of strategies by mutation. Because the players continue to count their strategies' score even if their strategies have already varied.

3   Results

We graphed various distributions of volume changes, price changes and so on in the models and in the real market. The data of the real market to be compared is Dow Jones Industrial Average (1932.10.11–2004.11.18). Dow is one of the most famous index of New York Stock Exchange(NYSE). All the data we got from our model, i.e. price and volume, are to take the statistics about 20,000 terms after 130,000 terms while players learn. PDFs and CDFs of volume changes and price changes are nealy symmetric in models and in the real market(NYSE). Then we show only positive shapes of the graphs.

We investigate the case where confidence level r is -4 and Johnson's original case where r is 4.

3.1   Autocorrelations of Price Changes

This section describes autocorrelations of price changes. Fig.1 shows autocorrelations of price changes in the cases of each models.

Fig.1 shows that the price autocorrelation comes to nearly 0 as strategies can mutate regardless of r. Then price fluctuations have no patterns, and it is difficult for players to get excess payoffs. This property, that is, the autocorrelation function of price changes is essentially zero for all non-zero timelags, is observed in most real markets.

We think the case where it is easy for players to enter into the market, i.e. r is -4. We obtain for the first time in this case, the fact that the autocorrelation function of price changes is essentially zero for all non-zero timelags, when we extended the GCMG(Johnson) with variable strategy spaces.

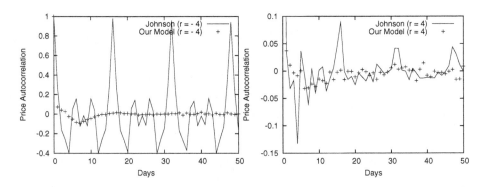

Fig. 1. Autocorrelation of price changes. The confidence levels r are -4 and 4 respectively. Note that the vertical scales of the left and the right figure are different.

3.2 Distributions of Price Changes

In this section, we discuss the distributions of price changes.

First, we consider the PDFs of price changes(see Fig.2). If $r = -4$, the PDF looks oscillatory around Gaussian function in our model. In contrast, the PDF is far from Gaussian function in the GCMG(Johnson). If $r = 4$, the PDF in our model looks closer Gaussian function than in the case of $r = -4$ in our model. In contrast, the GCMG(Johnson) makes high peak emerges.

Next, we consider the CDFs of price changes(see Fig.3). Fat tails of price changes cannot emerge in both models, the GCMG and our model. We consider it may natural that MGs cannot recreate large price changes by its nature. We explain this reason at the section 3.4.

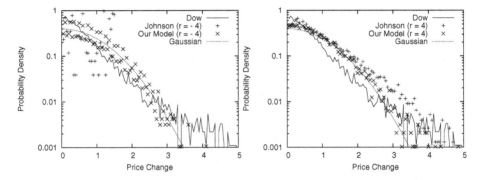

Fig. 2. The PDFs of positive price changes in real market NYSE(Dow), that in the GCMG(Johnson) and that in our model. The dotted line indicates Gaussian function. The confidence levels are -4 and 4 respectively. The horizontal axes of these graphs are normalized by the standard deviation of price changes. Except for the case of Johnson ($r = 4$), the high peak does not emerge.

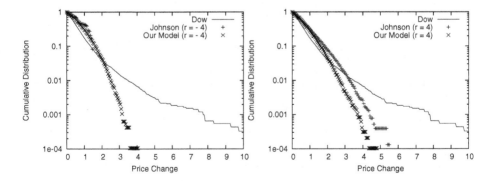

Fig. 3. The CDFs of positive price changes in real market NYSE(Dow), that in the GCMG(Johnson) and that in our model. The confidence levels are -4 and 4 respectively. The horizontal axes of these graphs are normalized by the standard deviation of price changes. We find that the fat tail dose not emerge in all the cases.

3.3 Distributions of Volume Changes

In this section, we discuss the distributions of volume changes.

First, we consider the PDFs of volume changes(see Fig.4). This parameter $r = -4$ in the GCMG(Johnson) causes that most players enter into the market. Then the standard deviation of volume change is very small. In consequence, the horizontal axis cannot be defined, so this graph cannot be described. In the case of our model, as Fig.1 shows, the autocorrelation function of price changes is essentially zero for all non-zero timelags. Players feel it difficult to do new arbitrage. That is to say, the society with variable strategy spaces is more difficult to enter into the market than the society with fixed strategy spaces. As a result, volumes in our model are far from constant. Therefore the PDFs of volume changes can be described. The PDF in our model $r = 4$ looks closer that in the real market than that in our model $r = -4$. In contrast, the PDF in the GCMG(Johnson) is completely different from Gaussian function or that in the real market.

Next, we think about the CDFs of volume changes(see Fig.5). The shape like a fat tail emerges in the case of $r = -4$ in our model. On the other hand, in the case of $r = 4$, fat tails does not emerge.

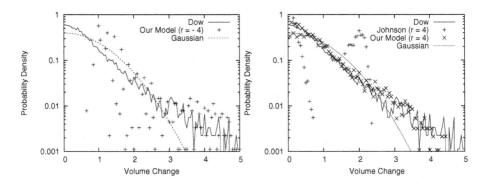

Fig. 4. The PDFs of positive volume changes in real market NYSE(Dow), that in the GCMG(Johnson) and that in our model. The dotted line indicates Gaussian function. The confidence levels are -4 and 4 respectively. The horizontal axes of these graphs are normalized by the standard deviation of volume changes. The PDFs in the case of the GCMG(Johnson) $r = -4$ cannot be described for the reason written in the body. Except for our model $r = 4$, the high peak does not emerge.

3.4 Cumulative Distributions of Volume Changes During Terms in Which Price Changes Are Small in the Real Market

Primarily MG models as real markets assume that price changes is small. If a bubble occurs in real markets, one of rational behavior of players is to keep buying assets during the bubble has continued. However such a one-sided expansion is

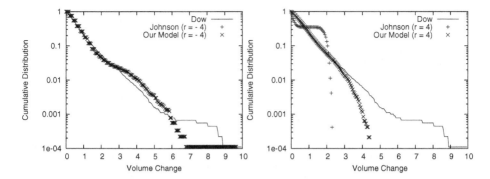

Fig. 5. The CDFs of positive volume changes in real market NYSE(Dow), that in the GCMG(Johnson) and that in our model. The confidence levels are -4 and 4 respectively. The CDFs in the case of the GCMG(Johnson) $r = -4$ cannot be described for the reason written in the body. The horizontal axes of these graphs are normalized by the standard deviation of volume changes. Our model corresponds to the real market. Especially, if $r = -4$, the volume has a large fluctuation. This looks like a fat tail.

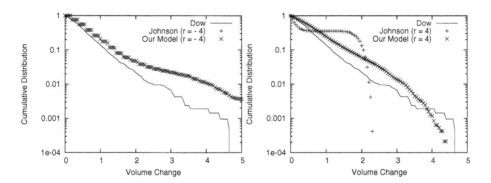

Fig. 6. The CDFs of volume changes during terms in which price changes are small in the real market. The CDFs of the models are the same at Fig.5. The horizontal axes of these graphs are normalized by the standard deviation of volume changes. The terms where price changes are small in the real market are defined as follows: The terms in which price changes are up to $2 \times$ standard deviation continue during 100 or more days. In the case of the GCMG ($r = -4$), the graph cannot be describe for the same reason at section 3.3. The graphs in the real market corresponds to that in our model remarkably.

not consistent with assumptions of an MG. We consider that, the CDFs of volume changes in MGs is easier to conform to that in real markets during terms in which price changes is small, rather than that in the real market during all terms.

Fig.6 compares the CDFs of volumes in the GCMG to that in our model and that in real market NYSE(Dow) during terms in which price changes are small. The distributions in the real market corresponds to that in our model remarkably.

4   Discussion

The goal of our study is to compare two models based on the MG and to investigate the effect of various quantity of information used by players. Details of the results are summed up in Table 3.

Table 3. The summary of our result. + means that the model makes the property emerge. − means not. r is a confidence level and means that, the larger r, the more difficult for players to enter into the market.

			GCMG	Our Model
$r = -4$	price	autocorrelation	−	+
		fat tail	−	−
		high peak	−	−
	volume	fat tail	−	+
		high peak	−	−
		CDF when price changes are small	−	+
$r = 4$	price	autocorrelation	+	+
		fat tail	−	−
		high peak	+	−
	volume	fat tail	−	−
		high peak	−	+
		CDF when price changes are small	−	+

Table 3 tells us the following three points:

First, players in real markets may use various strategies and the quantity of information (memory length). Fig.1 shows that the autocorrelations of price changes in our model are closer to that in the real market than that in the GCMG. This fact is independent of a confidence level. Thus price changes are close to be unpredictable and arbitrage becomes difficult. Players have various strategies and make up real markets, which may cause that markets have better efficiency. These phenomena are consistent with the efficient market hypothesis. Note that our model can explain the price autocorrelation naturally, in contrast financial engineering introduced the efficient market hypothesis explicitly and explained it. In sum, diversity of strategies makes efficient markets.

Second, it is understood that MGs may be able to describe markets when price changes are small. See Fig.5 and Fig.6, and compare them. The CDF of volume changes in our model corresponds to that in the real market during terms in which price changes are small, rather than that in the real market during all terms. This result is an evidence for validity of our model. At the same time, MG models including our model are insufficiency if we want to make fat tail emerge. We must invent mechanisms which can explain how to emerge fat tail.

As observed above, the price autocorrelation and the distribution of volume changes can be explained accordingly. In addition, our study may imply that entry into markets is difficult for players in real markets.

However, third, the high peak does not emerge in our model, though the GCMG makes it emerge when entry into the game is difficult and we extend the GCMG naturally. Fig. 2 shows that the PDF of our model is nearly Gaussian function when confidence level r is 4. This result is essential. Because we think that MGs are models of real markets when price changes are small. Although the high peak is the property where price changes are small, our model cannot make the high peak emerge.

So we may have to think implementing something new. For example, the relation between demand fluctuations and price changes, which is called a *market impact function*, may not be linear in real markets[3][10]. We assumes that the market impact function is linear (See equation (1)). If we think this effect, we may get better market model.

References

1. D. Challet and Y.-C. Zhang.: Emergence of Cooperation and Organization in an Evolutionary Game. Physica A, **246**, 407(1997), preprint adap-org/9708006.
2. Didier Sornette.: Why Stock Markets Crash : Critical Events in Complex Financial Systems. Princeton University Press, 2002.
3. J. Doyne Farmer, Paolo Patelli and Ilija I. Zovko: The Predictive Power of Zero Intelligence in Financial Markets. Working. Paper: Santa Fe Institue, 2003.
4. Li, Yi; Riolo, Rick and Savit, Robert.: Evolution in Minority Games II. Games with Variable Strategy Spaces. Physica A, **276**, 265–283, 2000.
5. Lindgren, K.: Evolutionary phenomena in simple dynamics. Artificial Life 2, pages 295–312. AddisonWesley, 1991.
6. M. Marsili, D. Challet and R. Zecchina.: Exact Solution of a Modified El Farol's Bar Problem: Efficiency and the Role of Market Impact. Physica A, **280**, 522, preprint cond-mat/9908480, 2000.
7. N. F. Johnson, P. Jefferies and P. Ming Hui.: Financial Market Complexity. Oxford University Press, 2003.
8. Robert Savit, Radu Manuca and Rick Riolo.: Adaptive Competition, Market Efficiency, Phase Transitions and Spin-Glasses. preprint adap-org/9712006.
9. Rosario N. Mantegna, H. Eugene Stanley.: Introduction to Econophysics: Correlations and Complexity in Finance. Cambridge University Press, 1999.
10. Vasiliki Plerou, Parameswaran Gopikrishnan, Xavier Gabaix and H. Eugene Stanley.: Quantifying stock-price response to demand fluctuations. Physical Review E **66**, 027104, 2002.
11. W. B. Arthur.: Inductive Reasoning and Bounded Rationality. American Economic Review, **84**, 406–411(1994).

Evaluation of Using Human Relationships on the Web as Information Navigation Paths

Kazuhiro Kazama[1,2], Shin-ya Sato[1], Kensuke Fukuda[1], Ken-ichiro Murakami[3], Hiroshi Kawakami[2], and Osamu Katai[2]

[1] NTT Network Innovation Laboratories,
3-9-11 Midori-cho, Musashino-shi, Tokyo 180-8585, Japan
kazama@ingrid.org
[2] Graduate School of Informatics, Kyoto University,
Yoshida-honmachi, Sakyo-ku, Kyoto 606-8501, Japan
[3] Hosei Business School of Innovation Management,
2-17-1 Fujimi, Chiyoda-ku, Tokyo 102-8160, Japan

Abstract. We investigated the use of human relationships on the web for information navigation paths. We propose a new information navigation method that uses personal names. It automatically extracts the human relationships of key people by analyzing the co-occurences of personal names on a web page from search results that are relevant to a specific topic and provides two facilities for using these relationships as information navigation paths. One is information navigation using a list of the key people and a list of related people. Another is information navigation using a network diagram of the key people. We consider human relationships on the web as new information navigation paths like hyperlinks. We analyzed the network structure of human relationships for various topics and evaluated their usefulness in order to clarify the applicable scope and improve the usefulness. The results show that human relationships are adequate shortcut networks for search results for most cases. However, if the ratio of the number of personal names to the number of web pages is too high, the relationships of the people are too tight for information navigation and our future work is to reduce the number of edges without reducing the coverage of search results. If the degree of density of human-related information in the higher ranked search results is too low, human activity is low and our method is not suitable.

1 Introduction

A huge number and large variety of documents are available to the public on the web, and the information obtained by web access has become essential to our daily lives. Currently, there are two methods for searching for information on the web: web search using a search engine and hyperlink navigation. Unfortunately, many people sometimes fail to find desired information that surely exists on the web because of the difficulty of selecting relevant search phrases or getting

T. Washio et al. (Eds.): JSAI 2005 Workshops, LNAI 4012, pp. 302–313, 2006.

too many search results. We call this the "lost in web space" problem. New technology is needed to simplify information navigation.

We propose real-world-oriented web searching that combines named entities on the web and objects in the real world automatically to assist the user's search processes. We focus on key people, who play an important role in a field. In the real world, social interactions among people occur for various reasons such as co-authoring, advising, and serving on committees. We can make use of the evidence of these interactions on the web. We have estimated the social activities of key people based on information collected from web pages. To do this, we extracted personal names from web pages included in search results and analyzed them. A personal name represents a real person. For example, an "ego search," which means searching for a person on the web by his personal name, is one common usage of search engines; it is used by many people to search for acquaintances or their activities. NEXAS//KeyPerson was our first prototype system for finding real-world entities relevant to a topic[1]. It displays a list of the key people appearing in the search results and a network diagram of their relationships. In other words, NEXAS//KeyPerson provides additional information about key people appearing in search results.

In this paper, we discuss the utilization of human relationships on the web for information navigation. Our new prototype system, called "Community Navigator," provides two facilities for using human relationships of key people as information navigation paths. One is information navigation using a list of the key people and a list of related people. Another is information navigation using the network diagram of the key people. In the real world, human relationships are useful communication paths because human relationships exhibit "small world" characteristics[2]; i.e., they provide relatively short paths among people. We thus consider human relationships on the web as new information navigation paths, like hyperlinks. However, human relationships are not useful under some circumstances. For example, the network structure of human relationships may not match the search result space obtained by a search engine. Thus, we analyzed the network structure of human relationships for various topics and evaluated their usefulness in order to clarify the applicable scope and improve their usefulness.

2 Related Work

These have been previous studies that analyzed social network structures on the web. Kautz et al.[3, 4] developed ReferralWeb, proof-of-concept version to search a social network for experts on a topic together with a chain of personal referrals from the searcher to the expert. The referral chain is extracted incrementally by searching for personal names using a web search engine. A newer version uses co-authors included in bibliography entries of leading conferences (e.g., AAAI, STOC, FOCS, and ACL) instead of co-occurences of personal names on a web page, because the results of proof-of-concept version where not so good[5]. Social-PathFinder, proposed by Ogata et al.[6] searches a social network for a collaborator with the chain of personal connections on the web. The personal connection chain is extracted incrementally by searching for e-mail addresses within the specified hop count using a web robot. These approaches incrementally obtain a partial social network, but is very slow. Because our approach obtains a social network all at once, it is fast. We can also obtain web communities that are not directly mutually related. Furthermore, our approach can derive a social network for a specific topic, not only for the vicinity of the specified person. A human network or the web space is a small world[2, 7], and each node in the network tends to have low mutual relevance with nodes a few hops away.

The Friend of a Friend (FOAF) project describes a social network on the web as metadata[8]. In FOAF, an e-mail address is considered a personal identifier, and an XML/RDF namespace is used to describe various human relationships. In our approach, although human relationships are collected automatically and widely on the web, it is difficult to extract various attributes about human relationships or to analyze the context in which they appear. It would be useful to combine the good features that each has.

3   Human Relationships on the Web

3.1   System Overview

As shown in Figure 1, in pre-processing, we create two search indices: an inverted index for full text searching and a personal name index for personal name searching.

The "Community Navigator" used for web information navigation has five parts: full text search, personal name search, data management and calculation, GUI and human relationship visualization. First, Community Navigator searches for relevant web pages base on the user's query. Next, it searches for personal names on them. It then analyze the relationships between the web pages, the web servers, and the personal names and displays the search results and human relationships. All processes are done automatically. The user can then use two interfaces: a GUI and an interactive visualizer of human relationships to investigate information on pages by using the relationships of key people as information navigation paths.

3.2   Extracting Personal Names from Web Pages

To enable searching for personal names on web pages, we extract the personal names from the pages and create an index file in advance. This personal name extraction is a kind of named entity extraction, for which there are many techniques (e.g., using linguistic rules or patterns). We use a Japanese morphological analyzer called "Mecab" to extract Japanese personal names[1]. A Japanese morphological analyzer is frequently used for Japanese information retrieval because spaces are not left between words in a Japanese text, so word separation is problematic. The additional cost of using a Japanese morphological analyzer is low.

---

[1] Mecab   is   a   high-performance   Japanese   morphological   analyzer.   See
http://chasen.org/~taku/software/mecab/.

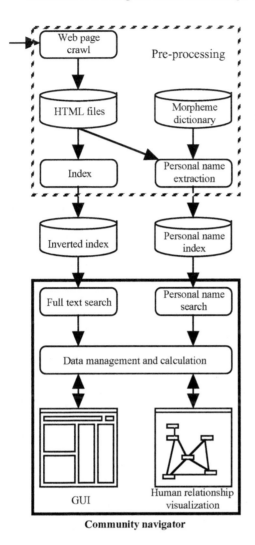

Fig. 1. System overview

This is a dictionary-centric approach, but not all personal names are registered in the dictionary. To reduce the number of extraction misses, we added many given names and family names to Mecab's morpheme dictionary, more than doubling its size. The precision is 0.935 and the recall is 0.853[1]. If a more advanced named entity extraction technique were used, precision and recall would be even better.

After deleting tags and comments from the Japanese HTML text, Mecab analyzes the text and segments it into morphemes and assigns POS (part-of-speech) tags to them. We limit personal names to

1. the set of a family name and the following given name, since that a Japanese personal name is usually written with the family name first, followed by the given name,
2. the set of a family name, any space characters, and the following given name, and
3. a special name.

A special name could be an alias or a stage name. It cannot be divided into a family name and a given name. The hiragana, katakana, and kanji writing of Japanese personal names are supported; Romanization and English personal names are not supported yet. Because our approach is basically language-independent, we could use the same approach for English personal names by using a named entity extraction technique for English. In that case, we would assume that the problem of multiple people have the same family and given name would be more serious in English than in Japanese because Japanese personal names are selected from huge Kanji characters and there are many variations of personal names.

An index that can be used to search for a personal name by document ID is created.

3.3   Searching for Web Pages

To find web pages about a specific topic, we use a query that represent the topic. For this purpose, we used the full-text search engine called "Jerky," which was used for the Japanese search engine "ODIN" from 1999 to 2002. It uses hypertext structures, anchor texts, and hyperlinks of web pages for searching, like Google does. In this type of search engine, there is a tendency for authoritative web pages to occupy the higher ranks of search results. We thus use only the top n web pages in the search results. This restriction also reduces memory usage and speeds up execution. We set n between 100 and 5,000 manually based on the appearance ratio of personal names in the search results.

When there where web pages having the same contents, such as a mirror website or a website that had moved, the one with the lower score was ignored to prevent a set of mirror pages being recognized as a web community.

3.4   Searching for Personal Names

For the top n web pages, we extract their document IDs and search for corresponding personal names from the personal name index file by document ID. We then extract the Web server host names from the URIs. These data are stored in memory as web page objects, website objects, and people objects, along with their relationships. They are used for identifying communities or for interactive browsing .

3.5   Extracting Relationships Between Key People

We extract the human relationships from the co-occurrence relationships of personal names. However, the human relationships obtained by straightforward implementation are very complicated, large-scale, and too noisy. This is a serious problem for social network analysis on the Web. To overcome it, we use the co-occurrence relationships in the narrow range of a web page and the effectiveness of people.

Co-occurrence in Narrow Range of Web Page. In our NEXAS//
KeyPerson, we extract the human relationships from the co-occurrence relationships of personal names on each web page. Because some web pages have many personal names, inadequate human relationships are often extracted. Thus, we analyze the co-occurrences in a narrow range of a web page. In our actual implementation, we save ordered personal name lists on web pages and take the personal name pairs that appear within distance d in each list as the co-occurrence relationships of the personal names.

Effectiveness. To reduce the size of the human relationship network, a centricity measure calculated from a network structure (e.g., betweenness or PageRank) is frequently used for identifying key people. However the centricity measure is not adequate under some circumstances. For example, the personal name of a website news writer may appear frequently on a specific website but rarely on other websites. If so, he or she is not a key person for the topic in question though the total number of occurrences and the co-occurence rate of his or her name is high.

To identify key people, we use the "effectiveness" centricity measure[9]. Assuming that people who are mentioned more websites are more active and famous, we define effectiveness for personal name p as

$$E(p) = |\{s|d \in s \land d \in R_{k,n} \cap D_p\}|, \qquad (1)$$

where s is the web server, d is the document, $R_{k,n}$ is the top n search results for query k, and D_p is the group of documents on which a personal name p appears. Thus, $E(p)$ is the number of web servers, have D_p in $R_{k,n}$. By deleting personal names for which E_p is less than a threshold value, T_p, we reduce the number of relationships of the key people.

3.6 Information Navigation Using Human Relationships

As mentioned, we provide two methods for information navigation using human relationships.

One method is information navigation using search result lists. As shown the example in Figure 2, the results are displayed in four lists. The upper left list displays web server information. The lower left list displays web page information. The center list displays the names of key people that appear in the search results. The right list displays the names of people related to the key people. These lists are mutually associated. Selecting the name in the center list causes selection of the related items in the other three lists. Thus, users can follow the relationships by clicking on related people in the right list.

Fig. 2. Navigation using search result lists

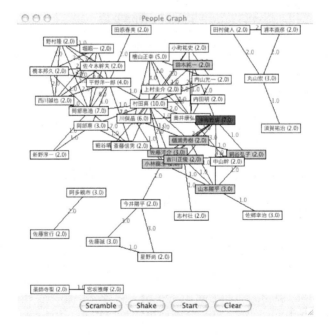

Fig. 3. Navigation using human relationship graph

The other method is information navigation using a human relationship graph. As illustrated in Figure 3, the relationships are visualized in this window and associated with the search results in the list. The darkest-colored node is the selected key person, and the dark-colored nodes are the people related to him or her. Clicking a name in the human relationship graph selects it, and the search result lists and human relationship graph are redisplayed. Thus, users can follow the relationships by clicking on a node in the relationship graph.

3.7 Quality of Human Relationships

We checked the quality of the relationships shown in Figure 3. Of the 42 nodes, three were missed in personal name extraction, and one was not a key person in the XML area. The precision of the nodes was 0.904. Of the 83 edges, six were missed in personal name extraction, one had a edge that has a node that was not a key person, and one had a edge that did not have a adequate relationship. The precision of the edges was 0.904.

Personal name extraction misses degraded quality the most. Quality degradation appeared as a string defect, such as in a given name or family name. In such cases, the relationship was adequate; the personal name was simply displayed incorrectly.

4 Evaluation

4.1 Web Data

For our prototype system, we needed to collect Japanese web pages, but it is very difficult to collect only Japanese web pages because many Japanese companies and organizations use the com or org domains instead of the jp domain. To collect mainly Japanese web pages, we collected the web pages on web servers belonging to the jp domain and also collected web pages linked from them and their anchor texts if they included Japanese characters. We collected about 52 million web pages from about 664 thousand web servers in July 2003.

4.2 Raw Human Relationships in Search Results

We analyzed the raw human relationships in the search results for a specific query. To extract them, we used $n = 1,000$ and analyzed the simple co-occurrence of personal names on the web pages of the search results without considering effectiveness. Table 1 shows the total number of search results, the occurrence of personal names (the number of personal names in the top 1,000 search results, the number of web pages or web servers on which the names appeared), and the attributes of the graphs (number of nodes, edges, and clusters) for the queries. Note that although some queries were in Japanese, we show their English translations in Table 1. The number of nodes was less than or equal to the number of names because the names that did not appear with others were not added to the graph as nodes.

Table 1. Raw human relationships extracted from top n search results

Query	Total	Names	Pages	Servers	Nodes	Edges	Clusters
lisp	19,781	53	29	18	30	27	10
wiki	13,861	103	66	33	64	316	6
perl	122,882	138	96	48	86	282	14
XML	116,965	356	283	83	251	848	34
java	465,869	364	235	112	227	876	43
information retrieval[†]	187,558	452	184	140	348	1,024	52
golf[†]	680,218	431	377	99	332	3,511	27
blog	43,786	466	358	93	369	1,283	37
soccer[†]	910,281	544	564	127	478	5,325	37
ruby	73,051	590	248	114	513	16,876	18
object oriented[†]	44,026	644	336	98	526	9,774	46
tennis[†]	406,728	790	293	140	673	7,636	55
table tennis[†]	103,709	871	511	109	785	20,189	43
baseball[†]	854,952	1,020	422	156	914	9,571	40
data mining[†]	11,215	4,630	419	194	4,577	981,200	34
artificial intelligence[†]	29,435	7,019	536	264	6.968	1,046,948	41

† Japanese query

The ratio of web pages on which personal names appeared varied with the query, but it was relatively high for most queries. This means there are many web pages related to human activities on the web, which is very important because we use only the top 1,000 search results, as determined a ranking measure based on link analysis. Although information navigation paths of human relationships do not cover all search results, they are useful for investigating human activities on the web. They are even more useful when used in combination with other named entities such as company names.

There was no clear correlation between the number of search results and the number of personal names in the top 1,000 search results. In general, the number of search results corresponds to the popularity of the specific topic represented by the query but the relationships in Table 1 are very complicated. We assert that the following properties of a topic have a strong effect on the number of personal names in the top 1,000 search results.

1. Whether interesting issues in the area involve personal information (e.g. sports news focuses people).
2. Whether activities in the area involve people (e.g. Lisp was invented in 1962, so there is little development activities at present).
3. Whether information about the topic is well documented digitally (e.g. academic activities and sports news are well documented).
4. Whether personal information and human activities are public or private (e.g., information about academic activities is generally public).

Consider, for example, the query "data mining". A large number of personal names are extracted because academic activities are numerous and dominant in this area. The ratio of the number of personal names to the number of web pages is high, meaning that human activities in this area are well documented and open to the public (e.g., papers and conference information are publicly available on the web). Furthermore, the number of edges in the human relationship graph is huge, meaning that people in this area have tight relationships.

4.3 Human Relationships Extracted by Our Method

Table 2 shows information about human relationships extracted by our method. With $d = 3$ and $T_p = 2$. In general, the number of people whose names appear on multiple websites is not so many, and the numbers of nodes, edges, and clusters are drastically smaller.

Table 2. Human relationships extracted by our method

Query	Total	Names	Pages	Servers	Nodes	Edges	Clusters
lisp	19,781	2	4	4	0	0	0
wiki	13,861	6	16	10	4	6	1
perl	122,882	17	38	21	15	22	2
XML	116,965	50	97	41	43	126	4
java	465,869	22	53	41	7	5	3
information retrieval[†]	187,558	45	60	49	33	78	3
golf[†]	680,218	81	234	52	75	482	1
blog	43,786	63	236	63	52	107	3
soccer[†]	910,281	95	471	61	93	2,080	3
ruby	73,051	102	178	75	98	1,812	3
object oriented[†]	44,026	153	149	55	148	5,196	2
tennis[†]	406,728	43	128	54	37	147	3
table tennis[†]	103,709	56	395	47	53	307	3
baseball[†]	854,952	109	305	80	107	1,197	1
data mining[†]	11,215	931	303	140	928	69,113	6
artificial intelligence[†]	29,435	1,044	437	214	1,042	92,568	3

† Japanese query

For most cases, the results show that human relationships are adequate and that there are meaningful shortcut networks for search results. The example in Figure 3 shows that human relationships are relatively sparse network for search results and that they cover most important web pages related to human activities. The human relationship space is a "small world" and the network of human relationships is scale-free. To get better human relationship graphs for information navigation on the web, we can adjust n and T_p.

However, if the ratio of the number of personal names to the number of web pages is high, the relationships of the people are too tight, there are a huge number of nodes and edges. We can reduce the number of nodes by reducing n, but the extracted human relationships are not adequate for information navigation paths because the graph structure is proximate to a complete graph and there are too many edges for the number of nodes.

If the degree of density of human-related information in the higher ranked and authoritative search results is low, such as in the results of "lisp", there is little human activity in the area. Unfortunately, our method is not suitable for information navigation in this case.

5   Conclusion

From the viewpoint of information navigation paths, we analyzed the network structure of human relationships for various topics and evaluated their usefulness in order to clarify the applicable scope and to improve their usefulness.

We found that human relationships are adequate shortcut networks for search results in most cases. However, if the degree of density of human-related information in the higher ranked search results is low, human activity is low, and our method is not suitable. If the ratio of the number of personal names to the number of web pages is too high, the relationships of the people are too tight for information navigation.

To achieve efficient information navigation in areas with tight human relationships, we need to reduce the number of edges without reducing the coverage of the search results. We will consider simultaneous use of our method with the centricity calculated from graph structures or limiting the maximum number of edges that a node can have.

Acknowledgments

We thank Masanori Harada for contributing his idea and the implementation of NEXAS. We also thank Hisao Nojima and Noriko Shingaki for their invaluable comments.

References

1. Harada, M., Sato, S., Kazama, K.: Finding authoritative people from the web. In: JCDL '04: Proceedings of the 4th ACM/IEEE-CS joint conference on Digital libraries, New York, NY, USA, ACM Press (2004) 306–313
2. Milgram, S.: The small world problem. Physiology Today **2** (1967) 60–67
3. Kautz, H., Selman, B., Shah, M.: Referral Web: combining social networks and collaborative filtering. Communications of the ACM **40** (1997) 63–65
4. Kautz, H., Selman, B., Shah, M.: The hidden web. AI Magazine **18** (1997) 27–36
5. Kautz, H., Selman, B.: Creating models of real-world communities with Referral-Web. http://www.cs.washington.edu/homes/kautz/talks/rec98talk.ppt (1998)
6. Ogata, H., Fukui, T., Yano, Y.: SocialPathFinder: Computer supported exploration of social networks on WWW. In: Advanced Research in Computers and Communications in Education. (1999) 768–771

7. Albert, R., Jeong, H., Barabási, A.L.: Diameter of the world-wide web. NATURE **401** (1999) 130–131
8. Brickley, D., Miller, L.: FOAF vocabulary specification. `http://xmlns.com/foaf/0.1/` (2004)
9. Kazama, K., Sato, S., Fukuda, K., Kawakami, H., Katai, O.: Web community discovery using personal names. In: International Workshop on Challenges in Web Information Retrieval and Integration. (2005) 116–124

Network Topologies and Consumption Externalities

Shu-Heng Chen[1], Li-Cheng Sun[1], and Chih-Chien Wang[2]

[1] AI-ECON Research Center, Department of Economics,
National Chengchi University, Taipei, Taiwan 11623
chchen@nccu.edu.tw,
lester33@mail2000.com.tw
[2] AI-ECON Research Center, Department of Computer Science,
National Chengchi University, Taipei, Taiwan 11623
g9022@cs.nccu.edu.tw

Abstract. The economic implications of network topologies are studied via a monopolist's model of market networks originally proposed by Phan, et al. (2003). By embedding the market into a larger collection of network topologies, in particular, a class of *scale-free networks*, we extend the early analysis built upon a class of *ring networks*. To facilitate the study of the impacts of network topologies upon market demand, various measures concerning social welfare (the consumer's surplus), the avalanche effect, and the hysteresis effect, are formally established. Comparisons based on these measures show that *network topologies matter*, and their implied differences will remain even when the network size becomes large.

Keywords: Scale-Free Network, Ring Networks, Network Topologies, Consumption Externality, Avalanches, Hysteresis Effect.

1 Motivation and Literature Review

The impact of social networks on economic behavior appears to have become an important issue, which has just recently been recognized by a large number of economists.[1] The efforts devoted to exploring the effects of network topologies on the resultant economic equilibria are unprecedented. Obviously, a network serves as a fundamental support for the operation of an economic system, even though its existence is sometimes only implicitly granted. The conventional neoclassical theory, which did not explicitly acknowledge the existence of networks,

---

[1] The literature can be roughly classified into two kinds. The first kind of literature regards networks as *exogenous*, and studies their economic implications. The second kind of literature treats networks as endogenously determined, and studies the formation process of networks. Given a set of cost and profit conditions, economists study the efficiency and stability of different networks, and determine the optimal or a sustainable network. See Radner (1993), Bolton and Dewatripont (1994), Jackson and Wolinsky (1996, 2003), Bala and Goyal (2000), and Goyal (2003) . Nonetheless, to the best of our knowledge, little work has been done on the interaction between network formations and their consequent performance.

T. Washio et al. (Eds.): JSAI 2005 Workshops, LNAI 4012, pp. 314–329, 2006.

seems to suggest that networks, whatever their structure may be, have no effect on resource allocation, at least, in the long run. Nevertheless, in their pioneering work on network formation, Jackson and Wolinsky (1996) proved the Pareto optimality of some well-known network topologies such as the fully-connected network and the star network. They also proved the intuition that when transaction costs are exceedingly high, there will be no network formed, i.e. these is complete independence of agents. These initial theoretical results are convincing enough for us to reconsider more generally the relationship between network topology and resource allocation.

Maybe the most natural start to establishing the link between network topologies and resource allocation, is to look at some fundamentals of economic analysis. Phan, Pajot and Nadal (2003) is a pioneering example. They use network topologies to illustrate the working of *consumption externalities* and from there to show the impact of network topologies upon market equilibrium. First, by using the case where consumers are perfectly independent (the scale of the market network is zero) as the benchmark, they find that the minimum price to win the marginal consumer (the one with the lowest willingness to pay) increases with the *scale* of the market network. In a sense, *the demand curve shifts outward.* Secondly, they also find that the emergence of *avalanches* becomes apparent when the network becomes fully-connected.[2]

Third, even though the scale of the market network remains unchanged, the demand curve still shifts outward when the market topology changes from the *regular network* to the *small-world network*. Fourth, there is also evidence that the network topology can impact the dynamic patterns (the growth or the decay) of the market when a new price is attempted.[3] Fifth, what is particularly intriguing is the hysteresis effect of the demand. With the working of the network externality, once the market is expanding to a certain level with a decreasing price, it will get stuck there and become less sensitive to the price reversal coming later. This unique feature, despite its theoretical foundation, has been well acknowledged in marketing and advertising.

Finally, maybe the most impressive part of Phan, et al.'s paper is that it provides a fully-fledged version of demand and supply analysis, which makes it feasible for market equilibrium analysis with respect to different network topologies. From there, we can see the effect of the network topology on the equilibrium price, profits, and quantity supply (penetration rate).

Despite its rich insights from exploring network topologies, Phan, et al.'s pioneering work is still largely confined to a very specific type of network typology, namely, the *ring network*.[4] A follow-up study, as they also mention, would be

---

[2] The avalanche can be understood as a phase transition with a threshold,which in our case, is a critical price. The sales can be dramatically different if the price is just a little below on above the threshold.

[3] Of course, the network topology is not their only concern. The other aspect to which they devoted a lot of space is the homogeneity of the consumers.

[4] The ring network is, however, still very useful for the purpose of tutoring. The essence of the random network, regular network, and the small-world network can easily be presented with a ring.

to consider a larger class of network topologies, even including networks which are *evolving*. In this study, we are moving in this direction. Specifically, we are considering the well-known *scale-free network*, which is probably the first kind of evolving network in the literature.[5]

2   Basic Descriptions of a Network

Following the standard notation in graph theory, one can represent a network by $G(V, E)$, where G is the name for the network in question, and V and E denote sets of *vertices* and *edges* respectively, which are the main stays of a network. $V = \{1, 2, , ...n\}$ represents all n constituents of V, and the number n also refers to the *size* of the network. In our specific application, n is the number of consumers in the market, and can, therefore, serve as a measure of the *market size*. $E = \{b_{i,j} : i, j \in V\}$ encodes the relationship between any two vertices in the net. In a special case, $b_{ij} = 1$ if there exists an edge (connection, relation) between i and j; otherwise it is zero. In this special case, $b_{ij} = b_{ji}$, implying that direction is irrelevant,which is also known as the *non-directed network*.

Given $G(V, E)$, let $d(i, j)$ be the length of the shortest path between the vertices i and j, These the mean shortest length of $G(V, E)$ is simply the mean of all $d(i, j)$,

$$L = \frac{1}{\frac{1}{2}n(n-1)} \sum_{i \geq j} d(i, j). \tag{1}$$

The definition above may be problematic if there is an isolated vertex which actually has no edge on any other vertices. So, $G(V, E)$ with isolated vertices are not considered here.

In addition to the distance measure, there are also a few density measures, and the one which is used most popularly is known as the *cluster coefficient*. Given a vertex i in a **G**, we would first like to measure how well its neighbors get connected to each other. Specifically, if j is connected to i, and k is also connected to i, is j also connected to k? Formally, we define the set of neighbors of i as

$$\vartheta_i = \{j : b_{ij} = 1, j \in G\}. \tag{2}$$

Then the cluster coefficient in terms of i is

$$C_i = \frac{\#\{(h, j) : b_{hj} = 1, h, j \in \vartheta_i, h < j\}}{\#\{j : j \in \vartheta_i\}}, \tag{3}$$

and the cluster coefficient of **G** is the average of all C_i,

$$C = \frac{1}{n} \sum_{i=1}^{n} C_i. \tag{4}$$

---

[5] The study suggested here can be further extended into two directions: first, to extend to various probabilistic combinations of random networks and scale-free networks, and second, to take into account the idea of *community*.

The size of the neighborhood ϑ_i is called the *degree* of i. Denoted by $f(k)$, the *degree distribution* of $G(V, E)$ gives the percentage of vertices of degree k. The behavior of the degree distribution has become one of the most intensively studied features of networks.

The three statistics above, *the average shortest length* (L), *the cluster coefficient* (C), and the *degree distribution* $(f(k))$ provide the basic description of a network $\mathbf{G}(\mathbf{V}, \mathbf{E})$.[6]

3   Matrix Representation of the Network Externality

The most natural way to think of a network is to consider all possible $\binom{n}{2}$ connections represented by a *matrix*, of which the geographical information can be implicit. The matrix representation also highlights the essential difference between social networks and other physical networks such as transportation networks. For the former, the geographical information is only implicit and may not even be relevant, whereas, for the latter, it is explicit and is very substantial.

Basically, space or location, those explicit geographical variables, may not be the most important variables in determining the formation of social networks. Unlike the regular ring network, agent i and agent j are connected to each other, not necessarily because their offices are just next to each other, but more because they share some common interests or attributes which connect them together. It would, therefore, leave us more freedom to form a social network if we could disentangle the *physical distance* from the *social distance*.[7]

For a market network model, we start with Phan, et al.'s (2003) set-up and will add our modification later. Phan, et al. model agents' decisions to buy as the following optimization problem:

$$\max_{\omega_i \in \{0,1\}} V_i = \max_{\omega_i \in \{0,1\}} \omega_i (H_i + \sum_{k \in \vartheta_i} J_{ik}\omega_k - p). \tag{5}$$

ω_i is an indicator for a binary decision.

$$\omega_i = \begin{cases} 1, & \textit{if agent } i \textit{ decides to buy,} \\ 0, & \textit{otherwise.} \end{cases} \tag{6}$$

---

[6] Other quantitative descriptions include.

[7] We do not intend to present a fully-fledged version of this type of social network. We just give a sketch. Consider an agent i, who is completely described by a vector of social attributes, say $x_i = (x_{1i}, x_{2i}, ..., x_{ni})$, i.e. a point on n-dimensional space. The distance between two agents i and j, $d(i, j)$ can, therefore, just be the standard Euclidean metric:
$$d(i, j) = ||x_i - x_j||.$$
An effective network of agent i, ϑ_i is determined by a $\{d(i, j) : j = 1, 2, ..., n, j \neq i, \}$. As feedback, the network therefore provides a value to agent i, i.e. the value or utility of the network, denoted by $u_i(\vartheta_i)$ At a point in time, to increase his well-being, agent i may like to change his network by modifying his attribute variables by, ϵ_i as $x_i + \epsilon_i$, is associated with the cost of making these changes, $c_i(\epsilon_i)$. The cost is subtracted from his u_i, which leaves agent i with utility $u_i(\vartheta_i) - c_i$.

What is inside the bracket is the classical linear willingness-to-pay function. H_i represents agent i's idiosyncratic utility of consuming the commodity. Written in terms of money value, it functions as the *reservation price* of agent i, i.e. his idiosyncratic willingness-to-pay for the commodity. The difference between H_i and p can be taken as the familiar *consumer's surplus* when agent i decides to buy ($\omega_i = 1$).

Now, agent i is situated in a network, and is directly connected to a collection, ϑ_i, of some other agents, called agent h, where $h \in \vartheta_i$. The network effect is captured by the parameter J_{ik}, which characterizes the influence on agent i of the decision of agent h. Clearly the larger the absolute value of J_{ih}, the larger the influence of agent h on agent j.[8] If $J_{ih} = 0$, for all $h \in \vartheta_i$, then there is no network effect on agent i; essentially, agent i makes his decision *independently*.

Consider the literature on *attention control*. If agent i's attention to the external world has an upper limit, say J, then

$$\sum_{h \in \vartheta_i} J_{ih} = J. \tag{7}$$

Furthermore, if agent i is indifferent to all his neighbors h, then J is uniformly distributed over ϑ_i, i.e.

$$J_{ih} = \frac{J}{N_{\vartheta_i}}, \quad \forall h \in \vartheta_i. \tag{8}$$

N_{ϑ_i} is the number of agents (vertices) connected to agent i. Under this setting, as the size of his neighborhood becomes larger, the influence of each individual neighbor on agent i becomes smaller.

The *external influence* of the network is demonstrated by the feature that agents are *heterogeneous* in preference, H_i.[9] However, the way to model heterogeneous preferences is not unique.[10] We shall come back to this point later.

---

[8] J_{ih} can in general be both positive and negative, while in our specific application below, we only consider the positive externality.

[9] Obviously, if all agents share the same H, there will be no need to study the network influence in this specific context, since "influence" means causality: someone will have to buy first, and someone will follow. If the agents are homogeneous in terms of preference, then from Equation (5), their decision will be perfectly homogeneous, including their timing, so that the network influence does not exist. Nevertheless, this does not mean that network topology has no effect on the market's behavior. In fact, as Phan, et al. (2003) have already shown, when agents are homogeneous in preference, then we shall have the most significant avalanche effect as well as the hysteresis effect. In fact, *it may be useful to distinguish the avalanche due to the homogeneous preference and also due to the market contagious influence of the market*

[10] For example, the *random field Ising model* is used in Phan, et al. (2003). More precisely, in their model,

$$H_i = H + \theta_i, \tag{9}$$

where θ_i follows a logistic distribution with mean 0 and $\sigma^2 = \frac{\pi^2}{3\beta^2}$.

It should be clear now that the optimization problem (5) leads to a very simple solution, namely,

$$\omega_i = \begin{cases} 1, & if \ \ H_i + \sum_{k \in \vartheta_i} J_{ik}\omega_k - p \geq 0, \\ 0, & otherwise. \end{cases} \tag{10}$$

To fully represent the network dynamics, it will be useful to extend Equation (5) as a individual decision to collective decisions as in (11).

$$\mathbf{W_{t+1}} = g(\mathbf{H} + \mathbf{J} \cdot \mathbf{B} \cdot \mathbf{W_t} - \mathbf{P}), \tag{11}$$

where

$$\mathbf{H} = \begin{bmatrix} H_1 \\ H_2 \\ \cdot \\ \cdot \\ \cdot \\ H_n \end{bmatrix}, \mathbf{J} = \begin{bmatrix} J_1 & 0 & ... & 0 \\ 0 & J_2 & ... & 0 \\ ... & ... & ... & ... \\ ... & ... & ... & ... \\ ... & ... & ... & ... \\ 0 & 0 & ... & J_n \end{bmatrix}, \mathbf{B} = \begin{bmatrix} b_{11} & b_{12} & ... & b_{1n} \\ b_{21} & b_{22} & ... & b_{2n} \\ ... & ... & ... & ... \\ ... & ... & ... & ... \\ ... & ... & ... & ... \\ b_{n1} & b_{n2} & ... & b_{nn} \end{bmatrix}, \mathbf{W_t} = \begin{bmatrix} \omega_{1,t} \\ \omega_{2,t} \\ \cdot \\ \cdot \\ \cdot \\ \omega_{n,t} \end{bmatrix}, \mathbf{P} = \begin{bmatrix} p_1 \\ p_2 \\ \cdot \\ \cdot \\ \cdot \\ p_n \end{bmatrix}.$$

The vector matrix $\mathbf{H}$ just stacks up an individual's idiosyncratic preferences H_i. The diagonal matrix $\mathbf{J}$ has the contribution from each individual i's neighbor to i as described in Equation (8). The matrix $\mathbf{B}$ is a the general representation of the network. Each entry b_{ij} represents a connection (edge) between agent i and agent j. While a great flexibility of the connection may exist, here we make two assumptions. First, either the connection exists or it does not, i.e. there is no *partial* connection, nor is there any difference in the degree of connection. Therefore,

$$b_{ij} = \begin{cases} 1, & if \ \ agent \ \ i \ \ is \ \ connected \ \ to \ \ agent \ \ j, \\ 0, & otherwise. \end{cases} \tag{12}$$

Second, we assume that the connection (edge), if it exists, is *bi-directional*. Hence

$$b_{ij} = b_{ji}. \tag{13}$$

In other words, the matrix $\mathbf{B}$ is *symmetric*. Notice that, according to Equation (8), the matrix $\mathbf{J}$ is immediately determined by the matrix $\mathbf{B}$.

For sack of illustrations, the matrix representations of a ring, star and fully-connected network with $n = 4$, denoted by $\mathbf{B_\bigcirc}$, $\mathbf{B_\star}$ and $\mathbf{B_\otimes}$, respectively, are given below from left to right:

$$\mathbf{B_\bigcirc} = \begin{bmatrix} 0 & 1 & 0 & 1 \\ 1 & 0 & 1 & 0 \\ 0 & 1 & 0 & 1 \\ 1 & 0 & 1 & 0 \end{bmatrix}, \mathbf{B_\star} = \begin{bmatrix} 0 & 1 & 1 & 1 \\ 1 & 0 & 0 & 0 \\ 1 & 0 & 0 & 0 \\ 1 & 0 & 0 & 0 \end{bmatrix}, \mathbf{B_\otimes} = \begin{bmatrix} 0 & 1 & 1 & 1 \\ 1 & 0 & 1 & 1 \\ 1 & 1 & 0 & 1 \\ 1 & 1 & 1 & 0 \end{bmatrix}.$$

With these connections, the corresponding influence matrix representations $\mathbf{J_\bigcirc}$, $\mathbf{J_\star}$, and $\mathbf{J_\otimes}$ are

$$\mathbf{J_\bigcirc} = \begin{bmatrix} J/2 & 0 & 0 & 0 \\ 0 & J/2 & 0 & 0 \\ 0 & 0 & J/2 & 0 \\ 0 & 0 & 0 & J/2 \end{bmatrix}, \mathbf{J_\star} = \begin{bmatrix} J/3 & 0 & 0 & 0 \\ 0 & J & 0 & 0 \\ 0 & 0 & J & 0 \\ 0 & 0 & 0 & J \end{bmatrix}, \mathbf{J_\otimes} = \begin{bmatrix} J/3 & 0 & 0 & 0 \\ 0 & J/3 & 0 & 0 \\ 0 & 0 & J/3 & 0 \\ 0 & 0 & 0 & J/3 \end{bmatrix}.$$

The vector $\mathbf{W_t}$ stacks up the binary decisions made by all agents in period t, with each entry described by Equation (6). To trace the dynamics of binary choices, binary decisions are now indexed by t. Initially, $\omega_{i,0} = 0$ for all $i = 1, ..., n$. The function g then drives the dynamics of $\mathbf{W_t}$ based on each agent's optimal decision (10). The vector $\mathbf{P}$ is the price charged to each individual. Notice that we have indexed this price by individual i, which indicates the possibility that the price does not have to be homogeneous among agents, considering that we want to study the effect of price discrimination under this framework. The simulation conducted in this paper, however, does assume a homogeneous price.

This matrix representation leaves us with great flexibility to deal with various network topologies. As we shall see in this paper, it helps us to deal with the scale-free network to be detailed in the next section. In addition, by varying $\mathbf{B}$, there can be other advantages. Firstly, $\mathbf{B}$ can be *asymmetric*. This is a desirable variation since social influence in general is not symmetric. Secondly, it does not have to be a binary matrix. In fact, b_{ij} can be any continuous variable between 0 and 1. This can help us to capture different degrees of connection. In sum, a continuous and asymmetric $\mathbf{B}$ provides us with an opportunity to study more complex network topologies which are beyond simple geometric representations.

4   The Scale-Free Network

The purpose of this paper is to attempt to extend Phan, et al.'s analysis from their *ring-based networks* (including small world networks) to *scale-free networks*. In this section, we shall give a brief introduction to the scale-free network.

The *scale-free network* was first proposed by Barabasi and Albert (1999), and hence is also known as the *BA model* (the Barabasi-Albert model). The BA model is based on two mechanisms: (1) networks grow incrementally, by the adding of new vertices, and (2) new vertices attach *preferentially* to vertices that are already well connected.

Let us assume that initially the network is composed of m_0 vertices, and that each is connected to m other vertices ($m < m_0$). Then, at each point in time, a number of new vertices, m_T are added to the network, each of which is again connected to m vertices of the net by the *preferential linking*. This idea of *preferential attachment* is similar to the classical *"rich get richer"* model originally proposed by Simon (1955).[11] It is implemented as follows. At time T, each of the new m_T vertices is randomly connected to a node $i \in V_T$ according to the following distribution

$$\pi_i = \frac{k_i}{\sum_{j \in V_T} k_j}, i \in V_T, \tag{14}$$

---

[11] In fact, the BA model which leads to the power-law degree distributions is an independent rediscovery of earlier work by Simon (1955) on systems with skewed distributions. It can be interpreted as an application of Simon's growth model in the context of networks, readily explaining the emergent scaling in the degree distribution.

where $V_T = \{1, 2, ..., \sum_{t=0}^{T-1} m_t\}$. That is the probability of becoming attached to a node of degree k is proportional to k, $\pi(k)$, and nodes with high degrees attracts new connections with a high probability. To avoid redundancy, the random attachment with (14) is done by sampling *without* replacement.

The scale-free networks have a power-law distribution of degree

$$f(k) \sim k^{-\lambda}, \tag{15}$$

and they have smaller L (average shortest length) and larger C (cluster coefficients), as compared to the random network.

In addition to the scale-free network, this paper also considers something in between the scale-free network and the random network, i.e. a mixture of the two. The motivation behind this device is mainly to capture some possible degree of randomness in social network formation. While the preferential attachment defines the *rationality* behind the social network formation, one should not neglect the effects of random events on the network formation. Therefore, we allow each of the incoming m_t agents (vertices)to have a probability, denoted by $1-q$, of being connected to the incumbent agents simply *randomly*, and hence a probability of q being connected to them with preferential linking. By controlling q, one can have a mixture network which is very close to the random network (e.g., $q \approx 0$), and another mixture network which is very close to the scale-free network (e.g., $q \approx 1$). It is, therefore, feasible to examine how the emergent properties may change along this spectrum. For simplicity, we shall call this the q-network. Clearly, the q-network is a random network if $q = 0$, and is a scale-free network if $q = 1$.

5   Measuring the Network Effect on Demand

It is important to know what useful observations should be seen in order to justify the non-trivial differences induced by network topologies? We notice that, if the network topology does have non-trivial effects, then the demand curve, as a summary of these changes, should naturally be the first thing to look at. As compared to the extreme case, the isolated network, the demand should shift outward when a network with some degrees of connection is introduced. However, what is not clear is which network topology should have the strongest outward shift. This question becomes more perplexing when demand curves associated with different network topologies may cross each other.

Let us define the *penetration rate* as the percentage of buyers in the market, i.e.

$$r \equiv \frac{\#\{i : w_i = 1\}}{n}. \tag{16}$$

Since each consumer buys at most one unit, $0 \leq r \leq 1$. To make the roles of the price and the network topology explicit, we write r as $r(p, \bigoplus)$, where $\bigoplus$ is the respective network topology. A network topology $\bigoplus$ is said to *uniformly dominate* other network topologies and is denoted by $\bigoplus^*$, if

$$r(p, \overset{*}{\bigoplus}) \geq r(p, \bigoplus), \forall p, \forall \bigoplus. \tag{17}$$

Since the uniformly-dominating network topology may not exist, an alternative measure is to define a *maximum price*, p_{max}, as follows:

$$p_{max} \equiv \max_{p}\{p : r(p) = 1\}. \tag{18}$$

Again, to acknowledge the influence of the network topology, p_{max} is also written as $p_{max,\oplus}$.

Instead of p_{max}, we may consider a weighted average of $r(p)$ with respect to a distribution of p, and compare the weighted averages among different network topologies:

$$\mu_p = E(p) = \int_{\underline{p}}^{\overline{p}} r(p)f_p(p)dp, \tag{19}$$

where $\underline{p}$ and $\overline{p}$ define an effective range of p, such that

$$\begin{cases} r(p, \odot) = 0, & if \ p \geq \overline{p}, \\ r(p, \odot) = 1, & if \ p \leq \underline{p}, \\ 0 < r(p, \odot) < 1, otherwise, \end{cases} \tag{20}$$

where $\odot$ denotes the isolated network. f_p is a density function of p; and when it is uniform over $[\underline{p}, \overline{p}]$, μ_p in a sense can be regarded as a *social welfare measure* if the marginal cost is zero. In this specific context, what concerns us is how the network topology impacts social welfare.

Another interesting type of behavior of the demand curve is its *jump* or *discontinuity*, known as an *avalanche*, which can be formulated as follows. The demand curve is said to demonstrate an avalanche at price p_a if

$$d_{p_a} = r(p_a - \epsilon) - r(p_a) \ is \ large. \tag{21}$$

d_{p_a} is not actually well-defined because the word "large" is not precise. Certainly, one can substantiate its content with a threshold parameter, say θ_a, and modify Equation (21) as

$$d_{p_a} = r(p_a - \epsilon) - r(p_a) > \theta_a. \tag{22}$$

The avalanche effect can then be defined as a probability A as follows:

$$A = Prob(d_{p_a} > \theta_a). \tag{23}$$

However, as we mentioned earlier (see footnote 9), the avalanche effect may have nothing to do with the network topologies, and can purely come from the homogeneous group of agents. To avoid "*spurious*" avalanches and to disentangle the effect of homogeneity from the effect of the network topology, it will be useful to maintain a great degree of heterogeneity to examine the chance of observing avalanches with respect to different topologies.

Coming to the next issue is a more subtle one in that the demand curve may not be unique and is *scenario-dependent*, an issue that is described as the *hysteresis effect* by Phan, et al. (2003). That is, the demand given the price p can depend on what happens before. Has the price before been higher or lower? This phenomenon known as the hysteresis effect arises because the demand curve, or equivalently, the penetration rate, derived by decreasing the price is different from the one derived by increasing the price.[12] Formally, hysteresis happens at price p when

$$r_u(p) > r_d(p), \tag{24}$$

where r_u and r_d refer to the penetration rates derived by moving downstream and upstream respectively. Nevertheless, with the avalanche, the hysteresis effect may occur simply because of the great homogeneity of the agents. Therefore, to see whether network topologies can have a real effect on the appearance of hysteresis, it is important to keep agents as heterogeneous as possible. The hysteresis effect of a network topology can then be measured by

$$R \equiv \int_{\underline{p}}^{\overline{p}} (r_u(p) - r_d(p)) f_p(p) dp. \tag{25}$$

$R(\oplus)$ denotes the hysteresis effect of the network topology $\oplus$.

None of the questions discussed so far may be independent of the market size n (the size of the network) or k, the degree of local interaction, It is then crucial to know the limiting behavior as well. For example, would

$$\lim_{n \to \infty} A_n = 0? \tag{26}$$

and

$$\lim_{n \to \infty} R_n = 0? \tag{27}$$

If Equations (26) and (27) are valid, then in a sense the network topology will not matter when the market becomes thick. In this spirit, we can even ask whether the demand curves associated with different network topologies will be *asymptotically equivalent*.

Similarly, we can pose the same question regarding the dimension of k, ranging from an isolated network to a full network. In addition, the asymptotic issue can be framed in time: given the same penetration rate associated with the same price, which network topology has the fastest *convergence speed* to the penetration rate?[13]

6   Experimental Designs

Experimental designs mainly concern the determination of those parametric matrices appearing in Equation (11). First, *network topologies* (Matrix **B**). To isolate the working of the network topology, it is important to always have the *isolated network* as one of the our benchmarks. Other network topologies

---

[12] This is also known as the *captive effect* in marketing.

[13] Similarly, when considering the degree of heterogeneity, we may ask: how do the network topologies work with the heterogeneity of agents? Does heterogeneity amplify or depress some of the workings of network topologies?

Table 1. Experimental Design

Basic Design	
Network Topology	Isolated, Scale-free, World Ring (Regular), q-network
Network Size (N)	1000
Idiosyncratic Preference (H_i)	$U[1,2]$
Price (p)	$[1,2]$
Incremental Size of Price	0.02
Some Details	
Degree of Regular Networks	2
Degree of Scale-free Networks	$m_0=10$, m=2
q of the q networks	0, 0.1, 0.2,...,0.9

included for comparison purposes are *random networks, regular networks (ring networks), scale-free networks,* and *mixture networks.* Once the network topology is fixed, matrix **J** in Equation (11) is determined accordingly.

Secondly, *idiosyncratic preference* or *willingness to pay, H_i.* As what has been printed it out in footnote (9), it is important to maintain a degree of heterogeneity among agents in terms of their idiosyncratic preference. Accordingly,as entities of **H**,the H_i are *uniformly* sampled from the interval $[1,2]$. With this design of **H**, the corresponding demand curve $r(p)$ is, therefore, restricted to the same interval, and is discretized with an increment of 0.02.

Once all these matrices are determined, we can have the dynamics of $\mathbf{W}_t$, which allows us to derive the demand curve r_p and other related measurements discussed in Section 5.

7   Experimental Results

7.1   Consumer's Surplus

Figure 1 is the demand curve $r(p)$ under different network topologies. The resultant demand curve is based upon 100 independent runs each with a new initialization of the matrix **H**. So, each single point along $r(p)$ is an average of 100 observations. Based on these estimated $r(p)$, we calculate the consumer's surplus. Not surprisingly, the world network and the isolated network provide the two extremes of the consumer's surplus: a maximum of 0.876 is given by the world network, whereas a minimum of 0.509 is given by the isolated network. The consumer's surplus of partially connected networks, the scale-free network and the regular network lie in between, and their differences are not that significant (0.776 vs. 0.766).

Experiment one and Figure 1 basically confirm a simple intuition that the consumer's surplus is a positive function of *degree* or *connection intensity.* The second experiment tries to explore other determinants of the consumer's surplus, particularly, the *cluster coefficient* and *average shortest length* of a network. To do

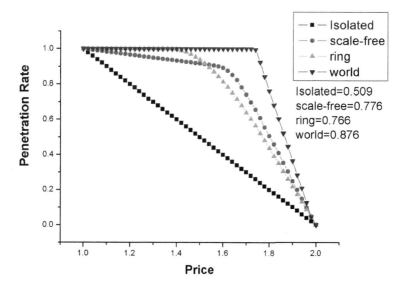

Fig. 1. Demand Curves in Various Networks

Table 2. Consumer's Surplus, Cluster Coefficient and Average Shortest Length

$CS = \alpha_0 + \alpha_1 C + \alpha_2 L$		
Regressors	coefficient	p-value
Constant	0.78019 (α_0)	0.0000
Cluster Coefficients (C)	0.52018 (α_1)	0.0041
Average Shortest Length (L)	-0.0092 (α_2)	0.1112

The R^2 of the above simple linear regression is 0.46676(R^2-adjusted=0.44625), and the mean square error is 0.00655.

so, we consider a class of q networks by controlling q from 0, 0.1,..., to 0.9, and 1. Five independent runs are conducted for each q network, and this gives us totally 55 networks.[14] The resulting consumer's surplus of these 55 networks is then regressed against two independent variables, namely, the cluster coefficient (C) and the average shortest length (L). The regression results are shown in Table 2. It can be found from Table 2, that these two variables C and L can jointly explain almost 50% of the variation in the consumer's surplus. In addition, both regression coefficients have signs consistent with our intuition: the consumer's surplus is positively related to the cluster coefficient, whereas it is adversely affected by the average shortest length.

---

[14] Only the **B** matrix is regenerated for each independent run. The **H** matrix remains unchanged for all the 55 matrices.

Table 3. Avalanche Effect

Topology/p_a	1.98	1.94	1.84	1.74	1.54
Random	0.01	0.04	0.05	0.06	0
q ($q = 0.5$)	0.07	0.05	0.11	0.03	0
Scale-free	0.06	0.06	0.04	0.09	0
World	0	0.2	0.35	0	0
Regular	0	0	0	0	0

The avalanche effect is defined in Equation 23. θ_a is set to 10%, i.e. 10% of the market capacity. $\epsilon = 0.02$.

7.2   Avalanche Effect

Network topology can matter because it can introduce critical points to market demand, which in turn cause the demand curve to no longer be continuous as conventional economics assumes. This phenomenon known as the *avalanche effect* is what we study in the third experiment. A measure of the avalanche effect is defined in Equation (23), which depends on three parameters, namely, a threshold (θ_a),the perturbation size (ϵ) and the evaluation point (p_a). Since it would be meaningless to consider small jumps when talking about "avalanches", we, therefore, set θ_a to 0.1, i.e. 10% of the market capacity, and ϵ to 0.02. In other words, if by discounting 2 cents only, one can suddenly increase sales by 10% of the market capacity, then an avalanche is detected. Finally, since H_i, uniformly distributed over the range [1,2], we choose five evaluation points of p_a from 1.98 to 1.54 (see Table 3). This is roughly the upper half of the distribution of H_i, which should be the ideal place to monitor the avalanche if there is one.

As to the network topology, except for the isolated network, all other partially-connected or fully-connected network topologies listed in Table 1 are tried in this experiment. 100 runs are conducted for each network topology. The results are shown in Table 3. From Table 3, we find that except for the regular network, avalanches unanimously exist in all four other types of network, while their structures are different in terms of the distribution of the tipping points (p_a) and the tipping frequencies (A). For example, the world network has more concentrated tipping points ($p_a = 1.94, 1.84$) and a high tipping frequency at these tipping points ($A = 0.2, 0.35$), whereas the other three network topologies have evenly distributed tipping points, although with much lower tipping frequencies.

7.3   Hysteresis Effect

The third question to address is the examination of the *hysteresis effect* as defined by Equation (25). What we do here is first derive the demand curve by running the price downstream , and then by running the price upstream. In this experiment, we consider all network topologies listed in Table (2). For the q networks, we only consider the cases $q = 0, 0.5$, and 1. 100 runs are conducted for each network topology. The result shown in Table 4 is, therefore, the average of these

Table 4. Hysteresis Effect

Topology	Downstream $(r_d(p))$	Upstream $(r_u(p))$	R
Isolated	0.510	0.510	0
World	0.876	0.889	0.013
Scale-free	0.776	0.851	0.075
Random	0.738	0.816	0.079
q $(q = 0.5)$	0.758	0.847	0.089
Regular	0.766	0.943	0.177

100 runs. Table 4, columns two and three, show the consumer's surplus associated with the $r_d(p)$ and $r_u(p)$. The fourth column of Table 4 shows the difference between the two surpluses, i.e. the measure of the hysteresis effect R. From this column, we can see that both the isolated network and the fully-connected network have very little hysteresis effect. As expected, it is identically 0 for the isolated network, and is only 0.013 for the fully-connected network. However, all partially connected networks show some degree of hysteresis. Among them, the scale-free, random and q $(q = 0.5)$ networks are close, whereas the regular network has a strong hysteresis effect.[15]

7.4 Network Size

It is interesting to know whether the property of hysteresis and avalanches obtained above is sensitive to the *size* of the network. In particular, we are interested in knowing, when the network's size becomes very large (ideally infinite), whether these two properties can still be sustained. We, therefore, simulate networks with sizes of 1000, 3000, and 5000. The results are shown in Figures 2 and 3.[16] What is shown on the left part of these two figures are the demand curve $r(p)$ associated with an isolated network and a scale-free network. By looking at these two graphs visually, we can see that the avalanche effect, characterized by the noticeable jumps in the demand curve, does not disappear as the size gets larger. Furthermore, the right part of the two figures shows the demand curve derived by running downstream and upstream. The bifurcation is clearly there with hysteresis measures of 0.0517 ($N = 3000$) and 0.0597 ($N = 5000$). Compared to the R of the scale-free network from Table 4, these two Rs become smaller, but are still quite distinct from the fully-connected network. Therefore, the asymptotic equivalence of network topologies does not hold here as far as these two properties are concerned. Generally speaking, the finding that network topology matters does not depend on network size.

---

[15] This is definitely a very interesting property of the regular network. We, however, cannot say much about the cause of it except for pointing out that it deserves further research.

[16] When the size becomes large, computation becomes very time-consuming. As a result, results based on multiple runs are not available yet. What is presented here is based on the results of a single run.

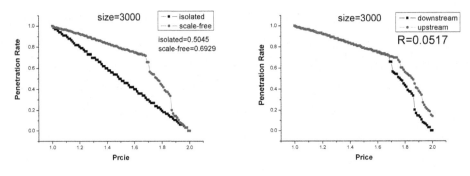

Fig. 2. Size=3000

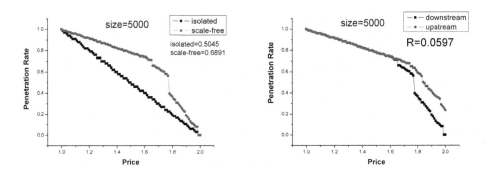

Fig. 3. Size=5000

8   Concluding Remarks

In this paper, five experiments are conducted to examine the economic implications of network topologies. To the best of our knowledge, this is probably
the first systematic and extensive study of this kind. It is extensive because six
different network topologies are considered, ranging from fully-connected and
partially-connected networks to isolated networks. Specifically, these six net-
works are world networks, ring networks, random networks, scale-free networks,
q networks, and isolated networks. By using a simple demand analysis based on
a monopolist's market, the study is also extensive in the sense that it covers the
four aspects of market behavior: the consumer's surplus, the avalanche effect,
the hysteresis effect and the size effect. Besides, it is systematic because different
measures have been developed to facilitate comparison of the market behavior
of different network topologies.

The general results are as follows. First, the network topology will impact
social welfare as conventionally described in terms of the consumer's surplus. We
have further found that it is positively affected by the cluster coefficient, whereas
it is negatively affected by the average shortest length. Second, the avalanche
effect and the hysteresis effect are observed for some network topologies, but not

others. For example, the avalanche effect does not occur in the case of the ring network (regular network), whereas it does exist for other partially- or fully-connected networks. Despite its occurrence, its extent in terms of our measure can differ among different network topologies. Finally, within our limited number of trials, it is also found that those avalanche effect and hysteresis effect will not disappear when the network size becomes larger. In other words, the asymptotic equivalence of network topologies may not be sustained and the network topology may matter to a quite general extent.

References

1. Bala, V. and S. Goyal (2000)," A Noncooperative Model of Network Formation", *Econometrica*, 68(5), pp 1181-1229.
2. Barabasi, A-L and R. Albert (1999), "Emergence of Scaling in Random Networks", *Science*, 286, pp 509-512.
3. Bolton, P., and M. Dewatripont (1994),"The Firm as a Communication Network", *Quarterly Journal of Economics*, 109(4), pp 809-839.
4. Jackson, M.O. and A. Wolinsky (1996), "A Strategic Model of Economic and Social Networks", *Journal of Economic Theory* , 71(1), pp 44-74.
5. Jackson, M.O. (2003),"A Survey of Models of Network Formation: Stability and Efficiency", In: Demange, G. and M. Wooders (Eds.), *Group Formation in Economics: Networks, Clubs, and Coalitions.* Cambridge University Press, Cambridge.
6. Goyal, S. (2003),"Learning in Networks: A Survey" Forthcoming In: G. Demange and M. Wooders(Eds.), *Group Formation in Economics: Networks, Clubs, and Coalitions*, Cambridge University Press, Cambridge.
7. Phan, D., S. Pajot , Nadal J.P. (2003) ,"The Monopolist's Market with Discrete Choices and Network Externality Revisited: Small-Worlds, Phase Transition and Avalanches in an ACE Framework", *Ninth annual meeting of the Society of Computational Economics University of Washington*, Seattle, USA, July 11-13.
8. Radner,R. (1993),"The Organization of Decentralized Information Processing", *Econometrica*, 61, pp 1109-1147.
9. Simon, H. A. (1955)," On a Class of Skew Distribution Functions", *Biometrika*, 42, pp 425-440.

Information Sharing for Smooth Traffic in Road Networks

Tomohisa Yamashita[1], Kiyoshi Izumi[1], and Koichi Kurumatani[1]

Information Technology Research Institute (ITRI)
National Institute of Advanced Industrial Science and Technology (AIST)
Sotokanda 1-18-13, Chiyoda-ku, Tokyo, Japan
tomohisa.yamashita@aist.go.jp

Abstract. With maturation of ubiquitous computing technology, it has become feasible to design new systems to improve our urban life. In this paper, we introduce a new application for car navigation in a city. Every car navigation system in operation today has the current position of the vehicle, the destination, and the currently chosen route to the destination. If vehicles in a city could share this information, they could use traffic information to globally plan semi-optimal routes for each vehicle. Thus, we propose a cooperative car navigation system with route information sharing (RIS). In the RIS system, each vehicle transmits route information (current position, destination, and route to the destination) to a route information server, which estimates future traffic congestion using this information and feeds its estimate back to each vehicle. Each vehicle uses the estimation to re-plan their route. This cycle is then repeated. Our multiagent simulation confirmed the effectiveness of the proposed RIS system. The average travel time of drivers using the RIS system is substantially shorter than the time of drivers who chose shortest distance or simple shortest time estimates. Moreover, as the number of RIS users increases, the total amount of traffic congestion in the city decreases.

1 Introduction

With maturation of ubiquitous computing technology, particularly with advances in positioning and telecommunications systems, we are now in a position to design advanced assist systems for many aspects of our lives. However, most of the research we've seen to date has focused on aspects of supporting a single person. Multiagent technology has not been tied to ubiquitous computing, except in a small number of studies [13]. We believe a mass user support system [5, 6] would have a large impact on society. The new concept would benefit not only society as a whole but would also benefit individuals. In particular, Nakashima [8] has focused on technologies that might enhance urban social life, especially transportation support systems. This paper reports on our recent multiagent simulation demonstrating the effectiveness of a new kind of car navigation system.

T. Washio et al. (Eds.): JSAI 2005 Workshops, LNAI 4012, pp. 330–339, 2006.

Many researchers have been trying to design better navigation systems, by examining the variety of traffic information available [1, 4, 9]. However, previous research efforts have revealed that individually optimizing performance with only traffic congestion information is difficult [7, 10, 12]. A navigation system recommends the route for the shortest estimated travel time based on the current state of traffic congestion. However, if other drivers, using the same information, simultaneously choose the same route, traffic would become concentrated on the new route.

Car navigation systems were originally designed as electronic enhancements of maps automatically indicating the current position of the vehicle and a route to the destination. Japan roads now support the second generation of car navigation systems connected to VICS (Vehicle Information and Communication System, http://www.vics.or.jp/english/ index.html). This new system can download traffic information and display it on the map. The system uses the information to avoid congested routes when it plans a route. What we suggest in this paper is yet another generation of car navigation systems [14]. VICS measures traffic volume with sensors located on roadsides, e.g., radar, optical, and ultrasonic vehicle detectors and CCTV (closed circuit television) cameras. The gathered information is transmitted using infrared beacon, radio wave beacon, and FM multiplex broadcasting. Each car just receives information from VICS, but does not return any.

If a car could transmit information by using a mobile phone or other short-range communication, we believe that we could design a far better navigation system. Every car navigation system in operation today has the current position of the vehicle, the destination, and the currently chosen route to the destination. If vehicles in a city could share this information, they could use traffic information to globally plan semi-optimal routes for each vehicle. Our idea is thus a cooperative car navigation system with route information sharing (RIS). In the RIS system, each vehicle transmits route information (current position, destination, and route to the destination) to a route information server, which uses this information to estimate future traffic congestion and feeds its estimate back to each vehicle. Each vehicle then uses the estimation to re-plan its route. This cycle of gathering information, estimating congestion, and planning a route is repeated many times.

The main purpose of this paper is to report the results of simulations demonstrating the validity of our idea. In particular, the simulation showed the average travel time is substantially shorter when drivers use the RIS mechanism. Moreover, as the number of RIS users increases, the total amount of traffic congestion of the city decreases.

2   Traffic Flow Model

We constructed a simple traffic flow model to examine the interdependence between traffic congestion as macro phenomena and route choice of individual drivers as micro behavior. Therefore, we did not consider the following factors:

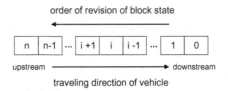

Fig. 1. Direction of vehicle movement and revision of blocks

traffic signals (e.g., stopping at red lights), waiting for oncoming cars when turning at intersections, turn lanes, multiple lanes, passing, blind allies; and U-turns in lanes, not at intersections.

Our traffic flow model designates a road between intersections as a link. It is divided into several blocks. The block length is equal to the distance that a vehicle runs at the free flow speed of V_f of the link during one simulation step. After link division, an order is assigned to each block from downstream to upstream. Concerning the block assigned to be the i-th, we define K_i as the density of block i, L_i as the length of block i, N_i as the number of the vehicles in block i, and V_i as the feasible speed of vehicles in block i. K_i is the division of N_i by L_i. In block i, V_i is revised based on Greenshield's V-K relationship as follows:

$$V_i = V_f(1 - \tfrac{K_i}{K_{jam}}), \tag{1}$$

where K_{jam} is the traffic jam density. The density signifies the minimum density that prevents vehicles in a traffic jam from moving. In our simulation, we set these coefficients as $V_f = 13.89$ and $K_{jam} = 0.14$.

The process of the flow calculation between neighboring blocks i and $i+1$ is as follows. At every step, the speed of vehicles in each block is revised according to the V-K relationship. The vehicles then move forward based on this speed. The vehicles' movement is processed from downstream to upstream, as shown in Figure 1. Depending on V_i, vehicle j can move forward. When vehicle j moves from block $i+1$ to block i, its speed changes from V_{i+1} to V_i. If K_i exceeds the jam density K_{jam}, no vehicles can move into block i from block $i+1$. After j_1 in front of vehicle j_2 moves, if j_1 is within a distance that allows j_2 to move forward at V_i, j_2 approaches j_1 to the minimum distance between them. Although j_2 has sufficient speed to advance, it must remain behind j_1. At the next step in block i, when V_i is revised based on K_i, vehicles can accelerate or slow down to V_i immediately, regardless of the speed in the last step.

3   Route Choice Mechanisms

To examine the proposed mechanism, we compared it with two other route choice mechanisms. These other mechanisms are well known and easy to understand because they seek routes minimizing the travel distance or travel time.

3.1   Shortest Distance Route

Drivers searching for the shortest distance route (SD) select a route on a map without using information on traffic congestion. That is, SD drivers simply select the shortest distance route from their respective origin to their destination, and don't consider traffic congestion at all.

3.2   Shortest Time Route

Drivers searching for the shortest time route (ST) decide a route with information on the current levels of traffic congestion. Their choice will thus vary based not only on map information, but also on congestion information on the entire network, as would be obtained from a traffic information center (e.g., a VICS Center) via vehicle equipment.

A traffic information center measures the current traffic density of all blocks, and calculates the expected travel time of each link by estimating the time spent on a link in light of the current traffic density. A traffic information center calculates expected travel time ETT_l of link l as follows.

1. Feasible speed $V_{i,l}$ on block i in l is calculated based on the V-K relationship with traffic density $K_{i,l}$.
2. Passage time $PT_{i,l}$ of block i in l is calculated based on length $L_{i,l}$ and speed $V_{i,l}$ on block i in l.
3. Expected travel time ETT_l of link l is calculated as

$$ETT_l = \Sigma^k_{0 \leq k < n} \, PT_{k,l}, \tag{2}$$

where n is the number of blocks in l.

The expected travel time is transmitted to all ST drivers at every simulation step. ST drivers search for the shortest route in terms of the expected travel times from their current position to their destination at every intersection.

3.3   Shortest Time Route with Route Information Sharing

Drivers searching for the shortest time route by using route information sharing (RIS) base their selection on information sent from a route information server. Moreover, RIS drivers transmit route information (current position, destination, and route to the destination) to the route information server. The route information server then estimates future traffic congestion levels based on this route information and transmits the estimate to the RIS drivers. The RIS drivers use the estimate to revise their route at every intersection. The route information server only provides traffic information to the RIS drivers, but does not plan the routes of drivers. Each RIS driver plans its route based on information sent from the route information server. Figure 2 shows the outline of route information sharing mechanism.

The route information sharing procedure between RIS drivers and the route information server is as follows.

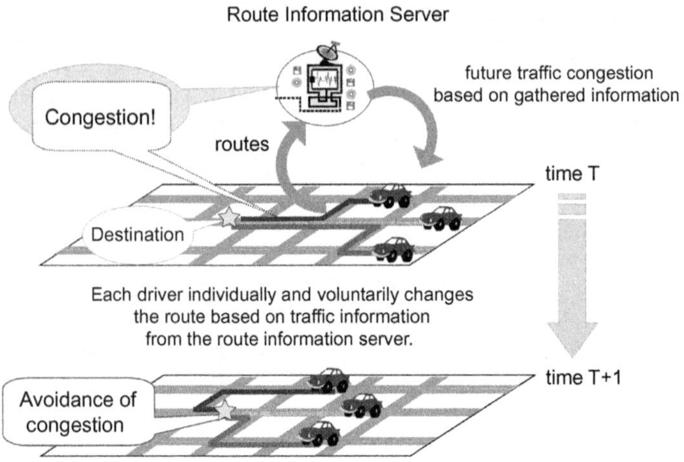

Fig. 2. Outline of route information sharing

1. RIS drivers search for the shortest route in terms of expected travel time from their origins to their destinations. They transmit their route information to the route information server.
2. The route information server collects route information from all RIS drivers, and uses it to assign a passage weight for each RIS driver to a link. The passage weight indicates the degree of accuracy with which an RIS driver will pass through the link in the future. Passage weight $PW_{j,l}$ of RIS driver j to link l is calculated as follows.
   (a) If j's route passes through p links from the current position to a destination, the links are assigned numbers in ascending order from the destination to the driver's current position.
   (b) The order of each link is divided by p, and it is regarded as the passage weight of the link. (For example, $1/p$ is assigned the link including the destination, and 1 $(=p/p)$ is assigned to the link including the current position.)
3. The route information server calculates the total passage weight of each link based on the passage weight of each link. Total passage weight means the accumulated the sum of the passage weights of all RIS drivers. Total passage weight TPW_l of link l is calculated as

$$TPW_l = \Sigma_{k \in RIS}^k PW_{k,l},$$ (3)

   where RIS is the set of RIS drivers.
4. The route information server calculates the prospective traffic volume of each link based on the total passage weight and the expected travel time. Prospective traffic volume PTV_l of link l is calculated as

Table 1. Settings of two networks

	lattice	radial and ring
Number of nodes	36	32
Number of links	60	56
Number of blocks	1,200	1,168

Table 2. Number of vehicles generated in one step

	lattice	radial and ring
N_{gen}	40, 45	30, 35

$$PTV_l = ETT_l \times (TPW_l + \alpha), \tag{4}$$

where α is a positive constant. (In our simulation, we set α to 1.0.)

5. The prospective traffic volume is transmitted from the route information server to all RIS drivers. The RIS drivers revise the shortest route in the prospective traffic volume and again transmit route information to the route information server when they reach the next intersection.
6. Processes $2 \sim 5$ are repeated.

4   Multiagent Simulation

4.1   Simulation Settings

To evaluate the RIS mechanism, we performed a multiagent simulation using the three route choice mechanisms for which the ratio of ST and RIS drivers varied from ST:RIS = 0.8:0 to ST:RIS = 0:0.8, and the ratio of the SD drivers was fixed at 0.2. This setting was based on an estimation that car navigation systems and traffic information services will be more easily accessible for many drivers in the near future. Furthermore, We evaluated the effectiveness of the RIS mechanism on two different road networks: a lattice network and a radial and ring network (see Figures 3 and 4, and also Table 1). In these road networks, all blocks in a link have the same capacity.

The origin and destination of a vehicle are assigned randomly to any block on any link. After reaching its destination, the vehicle is removed from the network. Vehicles are generated every simulation step, until the amount of vehicles reaches 25,000. Table 2 lists the numbers of vehicles generated in one step N_{gen}. N_{gen} of each network realizes a traffic situation in which roads are not vacant, yet a deadlock does not occur.

4.2   Simulation Results

We were particularly interested in the transition of the average travel time of each mechanism as the ratio of RIS drivers increased.

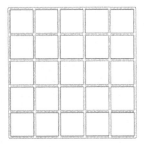

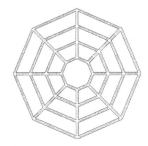

Fig. 3. Lattice network   **Fig. 4.** Radial and ring network

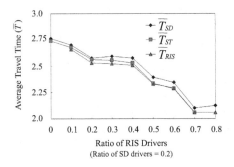

Fig. 5. Average travel time with $N_{gen} = 40$ in the lattice network

Fig. 6. Average travel time with $N_{gen} = 45$ in the lattice network

The travel time of each driver was normalized by the ideal travel time to compare the results the different road networks and different sets of vehicle origins and destinations. The ideal travel time is the time required from origin to destination when a driver passes through the shortest distance route at free flow speed. The travel time is thus defined as the ratio of the actual travel time to the ideal travel time.

Figures 5 to 8 show the simulation results averaging 30 trials. In these graphs, the horizontal axis is the ratio of RIS drivers and the vertical axis is the average travel time using each mechanism. The ratio of RIS drivers among all drivers is denoted as R_{RIS}. The average travel times of the SD, ST, and RIS drivers are denoted as $\overline{T}_{SD}$, $\overline{T}_{ST}$, and $\overline{T}_{RIS}$.

Figure 5 shows the average travel time with $N_{gen} = 40$ in the lattice network. The average travel times of the three types decreased irregularly as R_{RIS} increased. In particular, $\overline{T}_{SD}$ at $R_{RIS} = 0.2$ was longer than that at $R_{RIS} = 0.3$ as R_{RIS} increased. Similarly, $\overline{T}_{SD}$ at $R_{RIS} = 0.8$ was longer than $\overline{T}_{SD}$ at $R_{RIS} = 0.7$. The average travel times were ranked in ascending order as $\overline{T}_{SD}$, $\overline{T}_{ST}$, and $\overline{T}_{RIS}$. For $R_{RIS} = 0.5$ or more, there was only a marginal difference between $\overline{T}_{ST}$ and $\overline{T}_{RIS}$.

Figure 6 shows the average travel time with $N_{gen} = 45$ in the lattice network. The average times of all three types decreased monotonically as R_{RIS} increased,

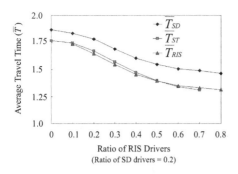
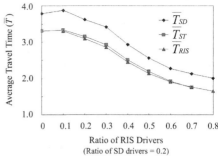

Fig. 7. Average travel time with $N_{gen} = 30$ in the radial and ring network

Fig. 8. Average travel time with $N_{gen} = 35$ in the radial and ring network

and they were always ranked in ascending order as $\overline{T}_{SD}$, $\overline{T}_{ST}$, and $\overline{T}_{RIS}$. In all cases of R_{RIS} , there was only marginal differences among them.

Figures 7 and 8 show the average travel time with $N_{gen} = 40$ and with $N_{gen} = 45$ in the radial and ring network. In both cases, the average times of all three types decreased monotonically as R_{RIS} increased and were ranked in ascending order as $\overline{T}_{SD}$, $\overline{T}_{ST}$, and $\overline{T}_{RIS}$. There was only a marginal difference between $\overline{T}_{ST}$, and $\overline{T}_{RIS}$. Only in the case with $N_{gen} = 35$ at $R_{RIS} = 0.7$ was $\overline{T}_{ST}$ longer than $\overline{T}_{RIS}$.

5   Discussion

First, we discuss the effectiveness of the RIS mechanism from the viewpoint of whether it promotes individual incentive and social acceptability. Individual incentive means an incentive by which a driver would switch from using the other navigation mechanisms to the RIS mechanism. Here it is significant that the traffic efficiency of the RIS drivers is always higher than that of drivers using the other mechanisms we simulated. Social acceptability means the acceptability of the RIS mechanism to promote its popularity. Here it is notable that as the number of RIS drivers increases, their traffic efficiency improves.

Our simulation showed that $\overline{T}_{RIS}$ was always shorter than the other average times. Therefore, of the RIS system seems to promote individual incentive in the lattice network.

In the lattice and the radial and ring networks, our method promoted social acceptability because $\overline{T}_{RIS}$ decreased monotonically as R_{RIS} increased. It follows from these results that the RIS mechanism can a realize shorter travel time than other mechanisms, and that the travel time of the RIS drivers decreases as the number of RIS drivers increases. Moreover, the results confirm the RIS mechanism's effectiveness in promoting both individual incentive and social acceptability.

Many previous researches asserted only individual incentive of their proposed traffic information system at certain diffusion rate of them. However, the effect of traffic information systems significantly depends on its diffusion rate. In our research, we introduced social acceptability as another index estimating whether an information system can spread or not. Furthermore, we examine the effect of our proposed RIS system from the point of view of social acceptability, and confirm that the RIS system satisfied social acceptability. Previous research revealed that traffic Information systems providing current congestion status doesn't satisfy social acceptability (and partly satisfy individual incentive) [7, 10, 12]. Therefore, the result that the RIS system satisfied both individual incentive and social acceptability is significantly valuable.

6   Conclusion

We proposed a cooperative car navigation system with route information sharing (RIS). For the evaluation, we constructed a simple traffic flow model using multiagent modeling. Three types of route choice were compared in a simulation: the shortest distance route (SD), the shortest time route (ST), and the shortest time route with route information sharing (RIS).

The simulations were of a lattice network and a radial and ring network. The simulation results confirmed that the RIS mechanism promoted i) drivers' individual incentive to switch to using it: the average travel time of the RIS drivers was always shorter than those of drivers using the other choice mechanisms, and ii) social acceptability: the travel time of RIS drivers became shorter as the percentage of RIS drivers increased. Moreover, the results showed that the network structure influenced the effectiveness of the RIS mechanism.

References

1. Bazzan, A., Boffo, F., Klugl, F.: Avoiding the Braess Paradox with Information Manipulation. In Proceedings of Workshop on Agents In Traffic And Transportation in Third International Joint Conference on Autonomous Agents and Multiagent Systems (ATT 2004) (2004) 1-7
2. Horiguchi, R., Kuwahara, M., Nishikawa, I.: The Model Validation of Traffic Simulation System for Urban Road Networks: 'AVENUE'. In Proceedings of the Second World Congress on Intelligent Transport Systems '95 (IV) (1995) 1977-1982
3. Inoue, M.: Current Overview of ITS in Japan. In Proceedings of the 11th World Congress on Intelligent Transport Systems (CD-ROM) (2004)
4. Klugl, F., Bazzan, A.L.C., Wahle, J.: Selection of Information Types Based on Personal Utility: A Testbed for Traffic Information Markets. In Proceedings of the Second International Joint Conference on Autonomous Agents and Multiagent systems (2003) 377-384
5. Kurumatani, K.: Mass User Support by Social Coordination Among Citizens in a Real Environment. In Multiagent for Mass User Support, LNAI 3012, Springer (2004), 1-19
6. Kurumatani, K.: Social Coordination with Architecture for Ubiquitous Agents: CONSORTS. In Proceedings of International Conference on Intelligent Agents, Web Technologies and Internet Commerce 2003 (CD-ROM) (2003)

7. Mahmassani, H. S., Jayakrishnan, R.: System Performance and User Response Under Real-Time Information in a Congested Traffic Corridor. Transportation Research 25A(5) (1991) 293-307
8. Nakashima, H.: Grounding to the Real World - Architecture for Ubiquitous Computing -. Springer LNAI 2871 Foundations of Intelligent Systems (2003) 7-11
9. Shiose, T., Onitsuka, T., Taura, T.: Effective Information Provision for Relieving Traffic Congestion. In Proceedings of the 4th International Conference on Intelligence and Multimedia Applications (2001) 138-142
10. Tanahashi, I., Kitaoka, H., Baba, M., H. Mori, H., Terada, S., Teramoto, E.: NET-STREAM, a Traffic Simulator for Large-scale Road Networks, R & D Review of Toyota CRDL, 37(2) (2002) 47-53 (in Japanese)
11. Teramoto, E., Baba, M., Mori, H., Asano, Y., Morita, H.: NETSTREAM: Traffic Simulator for Evaluating Traffic Information Systems. In Proceedings of the IEEE International Conference on Intelligent Transportation Systems '97 (CD-ROM) (1997)
12. Yoshii, T., Akahane, H., Kuwahara, M.: Impacts of the Accuracy of Traffic Information in Dynamic Route Guidance Systems. In Proceedings of The 3rd Annual World Congress on Intelligent Transport Systems (CD-ROM) (1996)
13. Workshop on Ubiquitous Agents on embedded, wearable, and mobile devices, http://autonomousagents.org/ubiagents/, July 16, 2002 University of Bologna
14. http://www.vics.or.jp/english/index.html
15. http://www.orse.or.jp/english/index.html

Analyzing Peer to Peer Communication Through Agent-Based Simulation

Shinako Matsuyama[1,3], Masaaki Kunigami[2], and Takao Terano[1]

[1] Dept. Computational Intelligence and Systems Sciences,
Tokyo Institute of Technology
4259 Nagatsuda-cho, Midori-ku, Yokohama 226-8502 Japan
Tel/Fax:+81-45-924-5583
terano@dis.titech.ac.jp
[2] Graduate School of Business Sciences, University of Tsukuba,
3-29-1, Otsuka, Bunkyo-ku, Tokyo 112-0012 Japan
Tel.:+81-3-3942-6869; Fax:+81-3-3942-6829
kunigami@gssm.otsuka.tsukuba.ac.jp
[3] Information Technologies Laboratories, Sony Corporation,
6-7-35, Kitashinagawa Shinagawa-ku, Tokyo 141-0001 Japan
Tel.:+81-3-5448-6495; Fax:+81-3-5448-6833
Shinako.Matsuyama@jp.sony.com

Abstract. This paper analyzes the characteristics of a peer-to-peer communications network through agent-based simulation. The extended BA (Balabasi and Abert) model was used as the concept model for this simulation. In developing this model, we have focused on the following two issues: (i) characteristics of agent and contents, and (ii) agent decision rules regarding sending, receiving and searching contents. The simulator processes communications among the agents and uncovers emerging social behavior. Assuming parameters of this generic scenario, the simulation results show that the network possesses scale-free and small-world properties.

1 Introduction

In recent years, the spread of mobile devices increases the opportunity for easy information exchange between people. In addition, SNS (Social Network Sites) such as Blog, Orkut, mixi, and Gree make peer-to-peer communication remarkably accessible. On the other hand, "word-of-mouth" is considered one of the most important marketing tools. Thus, for information providers, understanding the features of peer-to-peer communication would be useful. In this paper, we analyze the characteristics of information sharing peer-to-peer communication by agent simulation, and examine the characteristics of the network.

The paper is organized as follows: Section 2 yields the background and motivation for the work.; Section 3 gives an overview of the agent-based simulation system we have developed; experimental environment and the simulation results are described in Section 4; a brief discussion of the results is provided in Section 5, and the main conclusions are pointed out in Section 6.

T. Washio et al. (Eds.): JSAI 2005 Workshops, LNAI 4012, pp. 340–348, 2006.
© Springer-Verlag Berlin Heidelberg 2006

2 Backgrounds and Motivation

A number of related results regarding peer-to-peer communication have been reported in [1] and [2], for example. The virtual "word-of-mouth" system implemented on the Internet has been described and analyzed in [1]. An approach for grading exchanged information based on the relations between the persons involved in the network is proposed in [2], which includes the information-spread model. Additionally, in [3], the mechanism for information spread by the "word-of mouth" is considered through questionnaires.

On the other hand, some network characteristics, such as small-world and scale-free issues, have recently become as hot topics; similarly, certain results on related human relations in a collaborative networks of actors and of high school friends have been reported in [4] and [5].

There are few studies in this literature that cover human communication issues by experiments conducted under restricted circumstances or exclusively through the results of questionnaires, since affecting factors are numerous. For example, some information providers want to know the status of case in which the circumstances change, while alternatively others want to analyze what kind of circumstances and factors are ideal in realizing certain conditions. Therefore, it was determined that research conducted by agent-based simulation is suitable and beneficial for this kind of analysis.

3 Agent-Based Simulation of Peer-to-Peer Communication

3.1 Framework

This section describes the basic framework for the simulation and analyzes the information delivering mechanisms. The basic assignment is as follows: (i) Each "node" in the network is a person and a "network edge" corresponds to a connection between two persons; (ii) Each person is assigned to an agent related to information delivery that employs peer-to-peer communication.

Our simulation framework subsumes an extended BA (Barabasi and Albert) model; regarding this issue, it is important to note the following: in the BA model, the growth and preferential attachment are important issues with regard to power-law scaling. The preferential attachment model assumes that, should a new edge be added to a node, it should involve an additional node that already has many edges (see [5], for example). The fitness model proposed in [6] is a model that adds the concept of weight to the BA model.

Our framework originates from the following statements: In the considered peer-to-peer communication, a node related to a new edge is chosen not only by the number of edges it already involves, but by the contents to be delivered as well as by certain attributes of the node, such as preference similarities, the advantages of an edge with the node and so on. So the underlying model of peer-to-peer communication is considered as a fitness model.

On the other hand, the mutual link between people is not growing infinitely and it converges at a certain value. This can be explained as a phenomenon wherein the node makes new favorite edges, but in which some edges disappear as time passes. This mechanism corresponds to the deactivation model described in [7]. Thus, the considered peer-to-peer communication network follows a model that combines the fitness model and the deactivation model. Accordingly in our framework, we have defined the growth curve of the edges as the following;

$$\frac{dE(t)}{dt} \cong b \cdot N \cdot \left(1 - \frac{E(t)}{_N C_2}\right) - \gamma \cdot E(t) \tag{1}$$

wherein N is the number of agents, b is the rate of the performed communications by an agent per certain period (for example one day), γ is the probability of the deactivation by an agent corresponding to an edge per a day, and $E(t)$ is the total number of edges in the time instance t.

3.2 Model Components

In this subsection, we describe the main components of our agent-based simulation, which employs the framework described in the previous section. The particular framework components involved are the agents, the contents, the society, the operations and the decision rules. Also note the following: in the simulation, the subject of the communication is an agent, so a number of its characteristics should be specified. Additionally, some characteristics of the contents, which are subject to delivery, should be specified, as should the society, which defines the relations between agents. Finally, note that the simulator performs the communications between the agents during a certain period of time.

Agents. Each agent has four levels of information sharing activation rates. The relationship between each agent is determined by the definition of society described later. Each agent has a uniquely ordered identifier.

Contents. All content belongs to one respective category. We have long-term a category and a short-term category. Each agent has some categories randomly selected under a favorite contents list. According to [8], contents are categorized as either long-term or short-term for each individual. Therefore, long-term contents are randomly designated by each agent as long-term and short-term. Short-term contents disappear randomly during the simulation period. When a category disappears, a new category is created and used among agents.

Society. We have defined two societies: (i) NONE, in which nobody has known status as an initial condition (thereby entailing circumstances under which one gets to know others one by one), (ii) ALL, in which all have known status in relation to one other as an initial condition. In the society NONE, as an initial condition, agents situated side by side (neighboring agents) form a set of communication partners.

Operations. Actions of each agent consist of the following:

Send: an agent sends content to another agent

Receive: an agent receives content from another agent

Query: an agent asks other agents to introduce an agent who is familiar with the content and, in turn, asks the latter agent to send the content ([9]).

Each agent calculates an evaluation value for the received content and keeps it with the content. The content will be sent to another agent with the evaluation value. Fig.1 shows the flow of the simulation.

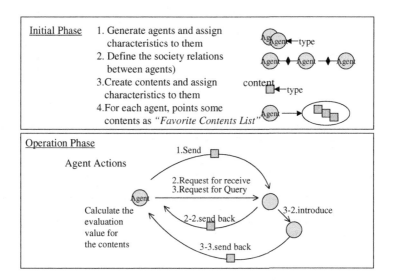

Fig. 1. Simulation Flow

Decision Making Rule. Communication between agents is expressed as sender (From), content (What), and receiver (To). In this section we define the indicators for choosing the agent to communicate with and the content to be sent/received. Although these indicators are extracted from a general situation, they are the mechanisms for generating edges in the fitness model.

We assume the following:

- Let Gk be an arbitrary content category and Ck be content in content category Gk
- $Eval_A(C)$ is the evaluation value for content C by agent A
- $Status_A(C)$ is the status (preference) of the content C of agent A
- $TrNum(Ai,Aj)$ is a communication count between agent Ai and Aj
- $Type(D)$ is an agent/content type

(1) Content selection indicator

The indicator with which agent Ai selects contents C is defined as follows:

$$I(Ai,\ C) = \{Type(C)+Eval_{Ai}(C)\} \qquad (2)$$

where $Type(C)$ is the lifetime of the content (short-term or long-term); $Eval_{Ai}(C)$ is determined by the evaluation value of the content itself and of a content sender ,

$$Eval_{Ai}(C) = Eval(C) + Eval_c(Ac) \qquad (3)$$

wherein Ac is a content sender

$Eval(C)$ increases as the time of contents sent/received increases.

$Eval_c(Ac)$ is the sum of the rate at which contents are sent, the rate at which contents are received and the number of times created contents are sent/received by the Ac in the content category.

(2) Indicator of agent selection

Fitness of agent Ai to send/receive content C to and from agent Aj is defined as follows:

$$Fitness(Ai, Aj, Ck) = |Eval_{Ai}(Gk)-Eval_{Aj}(Gk)| + Eval_{A\square}(Gk) + Status_{Ai}(Ck)$$

$$+ TrNum(Ai,Aj) + Type(Ai) + Type(Aj)\} \qquad (4)$$

wherein

- $|Eval_{Ai}(Gk)-Eval_{Aj}(Gk)|$ is the similarity of the content evaluation in the contents category Gk between two agents Ai and Aj,
- $EvalAj(Gk)$ is the parameter defining whether agent Aj is interested in the contents or not (whether the content category Gk is in the "favorite contents list" of Agent Aj or not),
- $Status_{Ai}(Ck)$ is the number of times contents Ck of agent Ai are sent/received,
- $TrNum(Ai, Aj)$ is communication (sending/receiving) amount between Agents Ai and Aj,
- $Type(Ai)$ and $Type(Aj)$ indicate whether the agent is active and whether the agent retains a number of short term contents

4   Experiments

4.1   Experimental Set Up

With "no one known" status as an initial condition (circumstances under which one gains familiarity successively, person by person), the experiment was performed with the following definitions:

Number of agents: 150/300/600/1200
Amount of communication per day: Number of agents$\times 7^1$,
Contents categories$\square 6$,
Total number of contents$\square$about 3000,
Execution days: 10 days for society NONE; 2 days for society ALL
Decision making rules: Apply the rules in section 3 with the same weight.
In this environment, considering the growth curve described in (1) in section 3.1, for 300 agents, $E(t)_{t \to \infty}$ is about 600 and b=1.0, then γ is about 0.5. Accordingly we have deactivated the edge with the probability of 0.5 per day randomly^2.

---

[1] Number of transactions against number of agents is 7, which corresponds to the number of the average sending/receiving amount of mobile phone mail, according to [10].

[2] Assuming the edges that have a strong connection will recover soon, we chose the edge to deactivate randomly.

4.2 Results

For each execution number described in 4.1, the total number of edges E(t) and clustering coefficient C, path length L which are used in small-world network[3] are shown in Table 1, Table 2 and the cumulative distribution of the number of edges with log-log scale is drawn in Fig.2, Fig.3.

Table 1. Experiment result s(C,L) – Society: NONE-

Number of Agents	Total Number of Edges (E)	Clustering Co-efficient (C)	Path Length (L)
150	303	0.24	3.2
300	637	0.26	3.4
600	1385	0.21	3.8
1200	2830	0.21	3.8

Table 2. Experiment result s(C, L) -Society: ALL-

Number of Agents	Total Number of Edges (E)	Clustering Coef-ficient(C)	Path Length(L)
150	365	0.38	2.0
300	946	0.31	2.1
600	1795	0.37	2.09
1200	3586	0.39	2.2

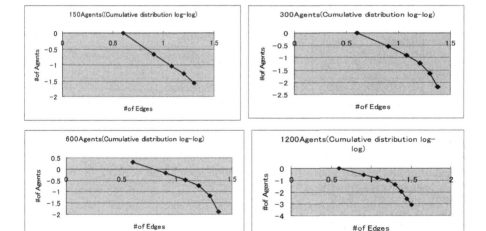

Fig. 2. Distribution of number of the edges – Society: NONE-

---

[3] We use the definition of Watts and Strogatz ([11]).

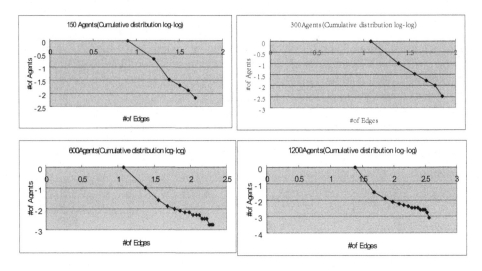

Fig. 3. Distribution of number of the edges - Society: ALL-

5 Discussions

5.1 Small-Worldness

Table2 shows the result of the experiment, of random network (which has similar edge size to those in the experiment) and the Neuron network of caenorhabditis elegans([11]), which is known as small-world network.

Table 3. Characteristics of the Links

	Random	3.9		Random	0.06
	C.elegans			C.elegans	0.28
L		2.65	C		
	Experiment (Society: NONE)	3.4		Experiment (Society: NONE)	0.26
	Experiment (Society: ALL)	2.1		Experiment (Society : ALL)	0.31

Regarding the results: compared to the random graph, the network in the experiment has closer $L(L_{rand} \sim L)$ and much larger $C(C \gg C_{rand})$ and it can be defined as a small-world network. It shows that people tend to make a "group" based on their content interests and/or tastes.

5.2 Scale-Freeness

Regarding to the characteristics of the scale-free, Fig. 2 shows that, in the range of edge 16, the probability is $P(k) \sim k^{-\alpha}$; $-1.5 < \alpha < 2.1$, and that it is clearly a scale-free network with cut-off. Fig.3 also shows that in the environment society "ALL" the network also has a scale-free property. The reason the cut off exists may be due to the fact that the total number of agents and contents categories is limited in this simulation.

5.3   Factors of the High Degree Nodes

A high percentage of the agents possessing many edges have multiple content categories in their "favorite contents list" or are "active"; both of these properties mark a significant observed trend. In this simulation, we have used 6 contents categories and have assigned some of these to the agents under "favorite contents lists" randomly. This means each agent has content categories, designated by numbers 1-6, in its favorite contents list. . Additionally, each agent has four active levels, also random, and agents that have high active level tend to communicate a great deal.

On average, about 61% of the agents have many "favorite contents lists" (5 or 6 categories) or are highly active (with activity levels rated first or second).

On the other hand, among the top 10% of agents for the number of edges, 85% of them have many "favorite contents lists" or are active.

The correlation between the number of edges and the number of content categories or active level was 0.67. The results made clear that the variety of information each agent has is an important factor, increasing the number of edges as well as their active level.Fig.4 summarizes the cause-and-effect-link for the number of edges.

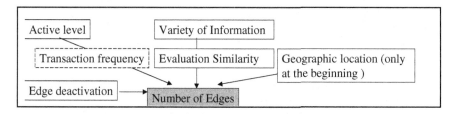

Fig. 4. Cause-and-effect link for the number of edges

5.4   Comparison with Real-World Communication

Comparing the results here with those of real-world communication, when "no one known" status was designated as an initial condition, people started talking with those nearby, those met by chance, and/or those introduced by known persons.

On the other hand, when mutual familiarity (everyone knows each other) at the outset defined status, people kept communications with those that have the same interests, although they have the capability to extend their respective loci of communication much farther.

We have conducted a survey via questionnaire to better grasp the circumstances or conditions behind real-world communication. The questions primarily focused on the number of information categories exchanged within the given group, frequency of exchange, and the number of people communicated with. According to the results, it was evident that there is a strong correlation between the amount of intriguing information categories and the amount of communication prater. Clearly, the above two simulation phenomena parallel or mesh with congruent aspects of real-world communication.

6 Conclusion and Future Work

In this paper, we have analyzed information delivery based on peer-to-peer communication employing agent-based simulation. Our results show that the network has small-world and scale-free with cutoff features.

We have used the fitness model and the deactivation model to develop an extended BA model [12]. Our experimental results show that combination of these two models can yield a network with large clustering coefficient C, small path length L, and power law.

This kind of agent simulation analysis makes it possible to examine what kind of forum (society) agents should be provided with, and what kind of contents characteristics should be distributed to certain of agents, all of which leads to development in information sharing.

As future work, using this simulator, we are planning to perform examinations by other models that can explain peer-to-peer networks such as the threshold model; an examination by parameters constructed from real-world data, and a comparative review of data obtained in the real world may also prove informative.

References

1. Y.Ito, M.Yoshida, and M.Numao, "New features of the Word-of-mouth Assisting Virtual Environment", Information Processing society of Japan Symposium No.2002-ICS-128, May. 2002 (In Japanese)
2. S.Takeuchi, et al. "Evaluation of the Information-Spread Model based on Users' Relevance", DBWS2001, Aug. 2001 (In Japanese)
3. Kokokusha, "Survey for the word of mouth", http://www.kokokusha.co.jp/service/kuchikomi.html,2005 (In Japansese)
4. L.A.N.Amaral, A.Scala, M.Barthelemy, and E.Stanley, "Classes of small-world networks", Proceedings of the National Academy of Sciences, Vol. 97, No. 21,2000
5. A.L.Barabasi,R.Albert,H.Jeong,"Mean-field theory for scale-free random networks",Physical A, 272, pp.173-187,1999
6. C.Bianconi, A.-L.Barabasi., "Competition and multiscaling in evolving networks", Europhysics Letters, 54(4), pp.436-442, 2001
7. K.Klemm, V.M.Eguiluz., "Highly clustered scale-free networks", Physical Review E,65,036123(2002)
8. J.Ishii, N.Atsumi, "Marketing in Internet society", Yuhikaku, April, 2002 (In Japanese)
9. N.S.Contractor, "IKNOW: A Tool to Assist and Study the Creation, Maintenance, and Dissolution of Knowledge Networks",LNCS 1519, pp.201-217,1998.
10. IPSe Marketing, Inc. "The third survey for the use of cellular telephone", http://www.ipse-m.com/report_csmr/report_c3/report_c3_sum.htm, 2003 (In Japanese)
11. D.J.Watts and S.H.Strongatz, "Collective dynamics of 'small-world' networks", Nature, Vol.393, pp.440-442 1998
12. Nmasuda, N.Imano, "Science of the complex networks", Sangyo-tosho, 2005 (In Japanese)

Part V

Conversational Informatics

Introduction to Conversational Informatics

Yasuyuki Sumi and Toyoaki Nishida

Graduate School of Informatics, Kyoto University,
Yoshida-Honmachi, Sakyo-ku, Kyoto 606-8501 Japan

The following six papers in this volume are selected papers from a workshop on Conversational Informatics at the 19th Annual Conference of Japanese Society for Artificial Intelligence (JSAI 2005, Kitakyushu).

The spread of the computer networks and media technologies have enabled spatially and temporally distributed people to share knowledge. The knowledge exchanged through the media, however, is basically externalized and verbalized by humans manually. Therefore, the available knowledge tends to be limited to formalized one, not tacit one.

Our daily lives are full of conversations, through which we exchange and share not only well-structured knowledge but also tacit knowledge (awareness, common sense, know-how, nebulous ideas, atmosphere, etc.) with others. Recent advancement of media processing, ubiquitous computing, and artificial intelligence technologies will become a strong infrastructure to record our daily conversations and facilitate us to access these.

The aim of the workshop was to bring together researchers and practitioners from various backgrounds and projects, having interest in the area. The workshop consisted of one invited talk by Dr. Claudio Pinhanez (IBM Research, T.J.Watson) and eleven presentations in five topic sections: Analyzing conversational structure; Conversational behaviors; Embodied conversational agents; Detecting conversational patterns; and Conversational data mining from the Network.

Conversational Informatics covers the following topics.

- Capturing and measurement of conversations
  - sensor technologies for conversation recording
  - non-verbal aspects of conversations
  - conversational scene extraction and summarization
- Content processing of conversational information
  - natural language processing for conversations
  - quantizing and generating conversations
  - conversational agents
- Analyzing conversations
  - conversation corpus
  - cognitive model for conversation understanding
  - ethnographic analysis of conversations
  - social model of knowledge exchanging by conversations

T. Washio et al. (Eds.): JSAI 2005 Workshops, LNAI 4012, pp. 351–352, 2006.
© Springer-Verlag Berlin Heidelberg 2006

The six papers published in this volume certainly give a good overview of Conversational Informatics.

In "*Probabilistic inference of gaze patterns and structure of multiparty conversations from head directions and utterances*," Kazuhiro Otsuka, Yoshinao Takemae, Junji Yamato and Hiroshi Murase proposed a method to infer structure of multiparty conversations by head directions and utterances. They evaluated their method by an experiment of group conversations by four persons.

In "*Conversational inverse information for context-based retrieval of personal experiences*," Yasuhiro Katagiri, Mayumi Bono and Noriko Suzuki also focused on structuring multiparty conversations, but dealt with more flexible situation where group party would be dynamically emerged, i.e., exhibition sites. They discussed dinamic transitions of conversational participation structure.

In "*Detecting microstructures of conversations by using physical references: Case study of poster presentations*," Ken Kumagai, Yasuyuki Sumi, Kenji Mase and Toyoaki Nishida proposed a method to detect detailed structures of conversations by associating reference gestures of speakers. They showed a system to segment conversations and associate them with referred parts of posters in the conversations between exhibitors and visitors in an exhibition site.

In "*Detection of assessment patterns in ordinary triadic conversation*," Katsuya Takanashi, Eiki Fujimoto, Yasuyuki Kono, Kazuhiro Takeuchi and Hitoshi Isahara showed a three-party conversation corpus built by the National Institute of Information and Commnications Technology, and proposed a method of analysis of turn-taking, etc.

In "*Automated gesturing for embodied agents*," Goranka Zoric, Karlo Smid and Igor Pandzic presented automatic facial gusturing of graphically embodied conversational agents. They showed a statistical model for synchronizing facial gestures with the prosody and lexical structure of uttered text.

In "*Leader qualification in managing nonprofit organization*," Naohiro Matsumura and Yoshihiro Sasaki proposed a method to analyze human relationship by e-mail archives of a group. They showed how to work their method with an example of e-mail archive among a nonprofit organization.

We hope you will find any overlap between your interests and Conversational Informatics from the six papers. If you are interested in, more detailed information of the workshop can be found at http://www.ii.ist.i.kyoto-u.ac.jp/jsai2005ws. You can find all papers presented at the workshop, related information including pointers to previous workshops sharing similar research topics.

Finally, we would like to sincerely express our thanks to the program committee members who have helped us during the preparation of the workshop and selection of papers for this volume: Prof. Koh Kakusho (Kyoto University, Japan); Dr. Hidekazu Kubota (Kyoto University, Japan); Prof. Sadao Kurohashi (The University of Tokyo, Japan); Prof. Naohiro Matsumura (Osaka University, Japan); Prof. Igor S. Pandzic (University of Zagreb, Croatia); and Prof. Helmut Prendinger (National Institute of Informatics, Japan).

Probabilistic Inference of Gaze Patterns and Structure of Multiparty Conversations from Head Directions and Utterances

Kazuhiro Otsuka[1,3], Yoshinao Takemae[2], Junji Yamato[1],
and Hiroshi Murase[3]

[1] NTT Communication Science Laboratories,
Nippon Telegraph and Telephone Corporation, Atsugi, 243-0198, Japan
{otsuka, yamato}@eye.brl.ntt.co.jp
[2] NTT Cyber Solutions Laboratories,
Nippon Telegraph and Telephone Corporation, Yokosuka, 239-0847, Japan
takemae.yoshinao@lab.ntt.co.jp
[3] Graduate School of Information Science, Nagoya University,
Nagoya, 464-8601, Japan
murase@is.nagoya-u.ac.jp

Abstract. A novel probabilistic framework is proposed for inferring gaze patterns and the structure of conversation in face-to-face multiparty communication, based on head directions and the presence/absence of utterances of participants. First, we define three classes of conversational regimes, which are characterized by the topology of the gaze pattern; we assume that they indicate the structure of the conversation, i.e. who is talking to whom. Next, the problem is formulated as joint estimation of both regime state from the gaze pattern and utterance, and the gaze pattern from head directions. We then devise a dynamic Bayesian network, called the Markov-switching model. The regime changes over time are based on Markov transitions, and controls the dynamics of the gaze patterns and utterances. Furthermore, Bayesian estimation of regime, gaze pattern, and model parameters are implemented using a Markov chain Monte Carlo method. Experiments on four-person conversations confirm accurate gaze estimation and the effectiveness of the framework toward identification of the conversation structures.

1 Introduction

Face-to-face conversation is one of the most basic forms of communication in our life and is used for conveying/sharing information, understanding others' intention/emotion, and making decisions. To enhance our communication capability beyond conversations on the spot, intense research efforts are being made to enable teleconferencing [1], archiving/summarizing meetings [2], and computer-mediated communication associated with social agents/robots [3]. To achieve such prospective applications, the automatic recognition of conversational scenes, which involve interactive human behavior both physically and psychologically,

T. Washio et al. (Eds.): JSAI 2005 Workshops, LNAI 4012, pp. 353–364, 2006.

is a basic technical goal. Our study aims to develop a novel framework for analyzing and understanding multiparty face-to-face conversation by modeling the relationship between the structure of the conversation and the nonverbal behavior that appear in it.

Automatic meeting analysis is an emerging research area, and several methods for the recognition of group actions in meeting have been proposed [4, 5]. However, so far, relatively little attention has been paid to the basic structure of conversations, known as participation roles (speaker, addressees, side-participants, etc.) [6], i.e. who is talking to whom. The identification of participation roles is a particularly important function for services such in automatic video summarization/editing and the social-participation robots that are expected. In the face-to-face setting, it has been suggested that the nonverbal behavior play important roles in the conversation, although verbal information is essential. Among various nonverbal behavior, it is widely acknowledged that gaze serves several important functions such as monitoring others, expressing one's attitudes/intentions, and regulating conversation flow [7, 8]. Based on these psychological findings, it is suggested that since people use gaze behavior as an important cue for understanding the participants' roles in a conversation, it should be possible to automatically determine roles by analyzing people's gaze [9, 10].

To analyze gaze behavior during conversations precisely and quantitatively, it is necessary to realize the automatic measurement of gaze direction in a manner that does not interfere with natural conversation. Unfortunately, the current level of eye tracking techniques fails to meet such requirements, despite recent progress [11, 12]. Instead, an approach that substitutes head direction for eye direction has been proposed [13, 14], since recent face tracking techniques make it easier to measure head direction than gaze [15]. This approach is based on the theory that a person tends to focus his/her attention on the person of interest by centering the person in his/her visual field, which results in rotation of head and/or torso, depending on the positions of other participants.

Our study unifies the above two aspects, i)the link between the structure of conversations and nonverbal behavior, and ii)gaze direction can be approximated by head direction, and formulates a framework for simultaneously solving two problems: inferring the structure of conversations from gaze pattern and utterance, and identifying gaze patterns from ambiguous head-direction measurements. To that end, first, we define three classes of conversational regimes, which can be characterized by the topology of the gaze pattern, and are assumed to indicate the structure of conversations. Next, the problem is formulated using the dynamic Bayesian network called the Markov-switching model [16]. The regime state changes over times based on Markovian transition properties, and it controls the dynamics of utterance patterns and gaze patterns, which stochastically yield head-direction measurements. Furthermore, a Bayesian estimation of the joint posterior distribution of all unknowns consisting of regime states, gaze patterns, and model parameters is implemented with the Markov chain Monte Carlo method, called the Gibbs sampler [17]. Experiments using 4-person conversation were conducted to confirm the effectiveness of the method. So far, a hidden Markov model (HMM) and its derivatives like coupled-HMM [18] have been developed for the recognition of human interaction. However, in contrast to these models, which mainly focus on direct causal relationship between visible human actions, our study tries to explore another aspect that hypothesizes a high-level process that governs how people interact within a social context.

This paper is rganized as follows. Section 2 defines the conversational regimes. Section 3 proposes the model and estimation algorithm. Section 4 shows experimental results. Finally, some discussion and our conclusion are presented in Section 5.

2   Conversation Structures and Gaze Patterns

This study aims to develop a framework for the automatic estimation of the structure of multiparty conversation from nonverbal behavior, which can be extracted from audio and visual information. As the structure of conversation, we target *participation role* such as speaker, addressees, and side-participants [6], i.e. who is talking to whom, and who is listening to whom, and the dynamics of how the structure changes over time. To that end, we hypothesize that the stream of a conversation can be segmented into a series of short periods, we call *regimes*, which satisfy two conditions: i) a specific type of nonverbal behavior is continuously present during the regime, and ii)each regime corresponds to a kind of conversation structure, and its temporal changes represent the dynamics of conversations. If such regimes could be extracted and well-defined, the structure of a conversation could be identified by observing and analyzing the sequence of nonverbal behavior. As the nonverbal behavior, we focused on the gaze patterns of participants, and found that there exist a typical topology of gaze patterns during conversations, which frequently appear and have larger temporal scales than individual gaze directions. Moreover, our experimental results suggest a strong link between gaze topology and the conversational structures such that gaze-based video editing can facilitate the viewer's understanding of recorded conversations [19]. Based on these observations, this paper hypothesizes three categories of conversation regimes according to the topologies of gaze patterns: convergence, dyad link, and divergence.

First, the regime called "convergence" corresponds to the gaze pattern in which the gazes from participants converge to one person, i.e. there is one person attracting the others' gazes more than the others, as illustrated in Figure 1(a). This regime corresponds to the conversation structure that one person talks to the others and they look at and listen to the speaker, where the person in center of gaze convergence is the speaker, and the others are the addressees. Here, we denote the regime as R_i^C, where i indicates the center person. This regime is related to past findings such "people gaze more while listening than while speaking"[8].

Second, the regime called "dyad link" corresponds to the situation that two people look at each other, i.e. mutual gaze, as illustrated in Figure 1(b). During the regime, they exchange messages and could swap their roles of speaker and addressee; the others are side-participants. This regime often appears during turn taking/giving, and is related to findings that "speakers ended an utterance with prolonged gaze to indicate that it was the turn of one listener to speak" [7, 20]. This regime is denoted as $R^{DL}_{(i,j)}$, where (i, j) represents the pair forming the dyad link.

Third, the regime called "divergence" corresponds to the gaze patterns that do not match the above two regimes, i.e. people look in different directions, as shown in Figure 1(c). In this regime, group conversation does not occur. This often occurs before a conversation starts or at a break point between topics. This regime is denoted as R^0.

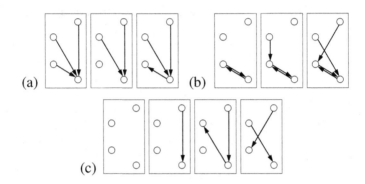

Fig. 1. Typical gaze patterns in each regime: (a)convergence, (b)dyad link, (c)divergence, in the case of 4-person conversation, (node: person, edge: gaze direction, node without outgoing edge: averted gaze)

3   Model and Estimation

3.1   Notations

This study targets N-person face-to-face conversations $(N \geq 3)$. The participants are separately seated in chairs, and no one leaves/enters during the conversation. No tools such as notes or whiteboards are used so as not to disturb the attention of the participants. Gaze direction was discretized to N exclusive states: look at the face of one of the other participants or avert from all of them. Let $X_{i,t}$ be the gaze state of person i; looking at person j if $X_{i,t} = j, (i \neq j)$ or avert if $X_{i,t} = i$, at time step t. We call the set of gaze states of all participants the gaze pattern, $\boldsymbol{X}_t = \{X_{1,t}, X_{2,t}, \cdots, X_{N,t}\}$, which takes one of N^N possible patterns. The sequence of gaze pattern is denoted by $\boldsymbol{X}_{1:T} = \{\boldsymbol{X}_1, \boldsymbol{X}_2, \cdots, \boldsymbol{X}_T\}$. Let S_t be the regime at time t; it is one of M-regimes as $S_t \in \boldsymbol{R} = \{R^C_i | i = 1 \cdots, N\} \cup \{R^{DL}_{(i,j)} | i = 1, \cdots, N, j = i+1, \cdots, N\} \cup R^0$, where $M = N + {}_NC_2 + 1$. The sequence of regimes is represented as $\boldsymbol{S}_{1:T} = \{S_1, S_2, \cdots, S_T\}$.

At each time step t, the head direction $h_{i,t}$ of each person i is observed as azimuth angle between world coordinate X and frontal direction of face, as shown in Figure 3(a). We denote the sequence of observed head directions as

$\boldsymbol{H}_{1:T} = \{H_1, \cdots, H_T\}, H_t = \{h_{1,t}, \cdots, h_{N,t}\}$. Also, state of utterance is denoted by $u_{i,t} = 1$ if person i utters and $u_{i,t} = 0$ if person i is silent, at time t; the resulting sequence is represented as $\boldsymbol{U}_{1:T} = \{U_1, \cdots, U_T\}, U_t = \{u_{1,t}, \cdots, u_{N,t}\}$.

3.2   Model Structure

To model the relationship between variables and their temporal evolution, a class of dynamic Bayesian network called the Markov-switching model is defined as shown in Figure 2. In Figure 2, nodes represent variables and edges represents dependencies between variables. This model includes regime sequence $\boldsymbol{S}_{1:T}$ and the sequence of gaze patterns $\boldsymbol{X}_{1:T}$; both of them are considered to be hidden random variables. Also, the model includes observation processes that stochastically yield both head directions with probability $P(H_t|\boldsymbol{X}_t)$ conditional to the gaze patterns, and utterance patterns with $P(U_t|S_t)$ for given regime state, at each time step t. We assume all observations at each time step are independent, and also head directions and utterances are independent.

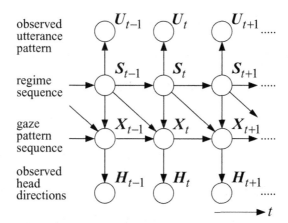

Fig. 2. Graph representation of structure of Markov-switching model

In this model, the regime dynamics is assumed to be a first order Markov process with initial probability $P(S_0 = R) = \pi_{0,R}, R \in \boldsymbol{R}$ and transition probability $P(S_t = R'|S_{t-1} = R) = \pi_{R,R'}$, which are constant over time. These model parameters are denoted as $\boldsymbol{\pi}_R = \{\pi_{R,R'}|R' \in \boldsymbol{R}\}, \boldsymbol{\Pi} = \boldsymbol{\pi}_0 \cup \{\boldsymbol{\pi}_R|R \in \boldsymbol{R}\}$. The sequence of gaze patterns $\boldsymbol{X}_{1:T}$ are stochastically generated and evolved depending on the transition probability $P(\boldsymbol{X}_t|\boldsymbol{X}_{t-1}, S_t, S_{t-1})$, conditioned on the regime states. The transition probability is defined as being propotional to the product of emission weight $g(X_{i,t}|S_t)$ and transition weight $w(X_{i,t}|X_{i,t-1}, S_{t-1})$, as written in

$$P(\boldsymbol{X}_t|\boldsymbol{X}_{t-1}, S_t, S_{t-1}) = \prod_{i=1}^{N} P(X_{i,t}|X_{i,t-1}, S_t, S_{t-1}), \qquad (1)$$

$$\propto \prod_{i=1}^{N} \left[g(X_{i,t}|S_t) \cdot w(X_{i,t}|X_{i,t-1}, S_{t-1}) \right], \qquad (2)$$

where we assume the conditional independency of gaze directions of each person for a given regime state. The emission weight $g(X_{i,t} = j|S_t = R) = \theta_{R,i,0,j}$ indicates the tendency that person i look at j during regime R, and transition weight $w(X_{i,t} = j|X_{i,t-1} = k, S_{t-1} = R) = \theta_{R,i,k,j}$ indicates the tendency of gaze changes, in which person i turn his/her gaze from k to j during regime R. Here, we denote the gaze-related model parameters as $\Theta = \{\boldsymbol{\theta}_{R,i,k}|R \in \boldsymbol{R}, i = 1, \cdots, N, k = 0, \cdots, N\}$ and $\boldsymbol{\theta}_{R,i,k} = \{\theta_{R,i,k,j}\}_{j=1}^{N}$.

Likelihood function of head direction H_t for given gaze pattern $\boldsymbol{X}_t$ is defined using Gaussian distribution so as to reflect uncertainty in head direction, as written in

$$P(H_t|\boldsymbol{X}_t) = \prod_{i=1}^{N} p(h_{i,t}|X_{i,t}), \qquad (3)$$

$$p(h_{i,t}|X_i = j) = (2\pi\sigma_{i,j}^2)^{-1/2}\exp\left[-(\mu_{i,j} - h_i)^2/(2\sigma_{i,j}^2)\right], \qquad (4)$$

where $\mu_{i,j}$, $\sigma_{i,j}^2$ are the mean and variance of the likelihood distribution when person i looks at j, respectively. Also, the independency of head directions of each person for a given gaze pattern, and the temporal invariance of these parameters are assumed. Also, the likelihood of utterance pattern is defined as $P(U_t|S_t) = \prod_{i=1}^{N} P(u_{i,t}|S_t)$, where we assume the utterance of each person at a time step occurs independently but conditional on regime state, and is generated by a Bernoulli process with utterance probability $P(u_{i,t} = 1|S_t = R) = \eta_{R,i}$.

3.3   Bayesian Estimation Via Gibbs Sampling

Based on the model proposed, the problem is to estimate the regime sequence $\boldsymbol{S}_{1:T}$, gaze pattern sequence $\boldsymbol{X}_{1:T}$, and model parameters $\varphi = \{\boldsymbol{\Pi}, \boldsymbol{\Theta}, \{\mu_{i,j}\}_{i,j}, \{\sigma_{i,j}^2\}_{i,j}, \{\eta_{R,i}\}_{R,i}\}$, from measurements $\boldsymbol{Z}_{1:T} = \{\boldsymbol{H}_{1:T}, \boldsymbol{U}_{1:T}\}$. We employ a Bayesian approach to estimate the joint posterior distribution $p(\boldsymbol{S}_{1:T}, \boldsymbol{X}_{1:T}, \varphi|\boldsymbol{Z}_{1:T})$ of all unknown variables for given measurements. In Bayesian analysis, a priori knowledge about the model is represented as the prior distributions of model parameters. To estimate the joint posterior, this study uses a Markov chain Monte Carlo method called the Gibbs sampler [17, 21], which has an advantage when dealing with complex models. The Gibbs sampler repeatedly generates random samples from the full conditional posterior distributions of each unknown variable, which constitute a Markov chain whose invariant distribution equals the desired joint posterior. The joint posterior distribution is approximated by a set of random samples after the Markov chain has converged.

This study employs natural conjugate prior distributions [22, 21]. Dirichlet distributions are used for the initial and transition probabilities of the regime state, and for emission/transition weights of gaze pattern. Priors for head-direction employ Gaussian distributions and inverse chi-squared distributions for mean and variance of its likelihood, respectively. Beta distribution is used for priors of utterance probabilities. Also, full conditional posterior distributions of each variable have the same function form as its priors. Gibbs sampling iterates a set of procedures $\mathcal{N}$ times, and in each step, each variable is sequentially replaced by a new value that is sampled from its full conditional. For example, the regime state S_t and the gaze pattern $\boldsymbol{X}_t$ are sampled from their full conditionals, respectively, as written in

$$P(S_t|\boldsymbol{S}_{1:T} \setminus S_t, \boldsymbol{X}_{1:T}, \varphi, \boldsymbol{Z}_{1:T}) \propto P(S_t|S_{t-1}) \cdot P(S_{t+1}|S_t)$$
$$\cdot P(\boldsymbol{X}_t|\boldsymbol{X}_{t-1}, S_t, S_{t-1}) \cdot P(\boldsymbol{X}_{t+1}|\boldsymbol{X}_t, S_{t+1}, S_t) \cdot P(U_t|S_t),$$
$$P(\boldsymbol{X}_t|\boldsymbol{S}_{1:T}, \boldsymbol{X}_{1:T} \setminus \boldsymbol{X}_t, \varphi, \boldsymbol{Z}_{1:T}) \propto P(\boldsymbol{X}_t|\boldsymbol{X}_{t-1}, S_t, S_{t-1})$$
$$\cdot P(\boldsymbol{X}_{t+1}|\boldsymbol{X}_t, S_{t+1}, S_t) \cdot P(H_t|\boldsymbol{X}_t).$$

After the iterations terminate, statistics are calculated from the samples $\{\boldsymbol{S}_{1:T}^{(q)}, \boldsymbol{X}_{1:T}^{(q)}, \varphi^{(q)}\}$ for iteration steps $q = \mathcal{N}'$ to $\mathcal{N}$ to ensure convergence. For regime sequence and gaze sequence, the maximum a posterior estimate is calculated as $\hat{S}_t = \arg\max_{R \in \boldsymbol{R}} \sum_{q=\mathcal{N}'}^{\mathcal{N}} \delta_R(S_t^{(q)})$, where $\delta_R(R') = 1$ if $R = R'$, otherwise $\delta_R(R') = 0$. For other variables, the minimum mean-squared error estimates are calculated as in $\hat{\mu} = (\mathcal{N} - \mathcal{N}' + 1)^{-1} \sum_{q=\mathcal{N}'}^{\mathcal{N}} \mu^{(q)}$.

4   Experiment

4.1   Recording Data and Initial Setting

Data were recorded for 4-person group conversations. The participants were four women within the same age bracket. They were instructed to have a discussion and try to reach a conclusion as a group for a given discussion topic ("*Is marriage and love same or different?*"), within five minutes. The head directions were measured at 30Hz with magnetic-based 6-DOF sensors (POLHEMUS Fastrak™), which were attached to their heads with hair bands. Figure 4(a) shows the first 3600 time steps (=2[min]) of head azimuth of each participant. Audio data were recorded with clip-on microphones attached to each participant, and utterance intervals were manually extracted using a waveform editor. Figure 4(b) shows the utterance intervals of each participant. Also, video sequences, whole shot (Figure 3(b)) and bust shots (Figure 8(a)), were recorded at 30[frame/sec]. These data were synchronized and 10000 time steps (=frames, $\simeq$ 5.6[min]) were used in the analysis. Ground truth of gaze direction at each time step was manually created by watching the video sequences.

Hyper parameters for prior distribution were set based on the following policy. The bearing angles $\Delta\phi_{i,j}$ given by the relative positions of participants, were employed as the mean values of prior distribution of head-direction likelihood (See Figure 3(a)). In regime 'convergence', the gaze-direction distribution of the speaker is set to uniform, while others look at the speaker with high probability (0.7). In regime 'dyad link', the pair look at each other with high probability (0.95), while the two others look around randomly. In regime 'divergence', people look at various directions with uniform probability.

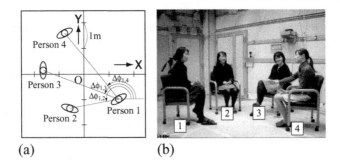

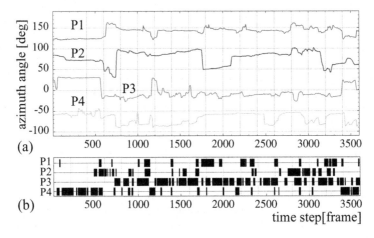

(a)   (b)

Fig. 3. Overview of scene. (a)plan view of participants' allocation, (b)whole view of participants.

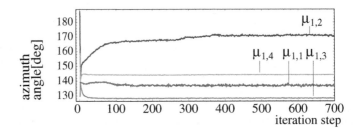

Fig. 4. Observed data for 2[min], (a)head azimuth, (b)temporal intervals with utterance, for participants

Fig. 5. Transition of $\mu_{1,1}, \mu_{1,2}, \mu_{1,3}, \mu_{1,4}$ through iteration of Gibbs sampler

4.2   Results

Estimation results were obtained after $\mathcal{N} = 700$ iterations of Gibbs sampling ($\mathcal{N}' = 500$). Figure 5, which shows the transition of the mean $\{\mu_{1,j}\}_{j=1}^{4}$ of

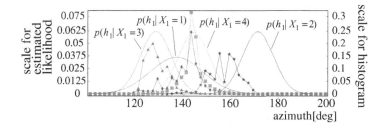

Fig. 6. Estimated likelihood function $p(h_1|X_1 = i)$ (person 1 look at person if $i \neq 1$, or avert gaze if $i = 1$), and line with symbol shows corresponding histogram, (symbol = diamond: avert, star: gaze at P2, triangle: gaze at P3, square: gaze at P4)

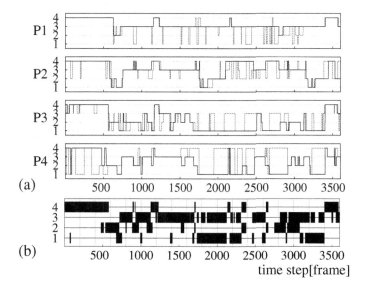

Fig. 7. Estimated sequences of (a)gaze pattern $\{X_{1,t}, X_{2,t}, X_{3,t}, X_{4,t}\}$ and (b)regime states. In (a), solid lines : estimates, dashed lines : ground truth. In (b), single band at a time slice indicates regime R_i^C (convergence), dual band at time slice indicates regime $R_{(i,j)}^{DL}$ (dyad link), and no band indicates R^0 (divergence).

head-direction likelihood distribution as a function of iteration step number, shows that convergence was achieved. Figure 7(a) shows the estimation result of gaze direction and the corresponding ground truth, illustrated for a 2[min] period. Average correct ratio of the number of frames wherein estimates and ground truth coincide, was 71.1%. Most errors were related to the 'avert' gaze status. This is because human can avert/turn their gaze from/on someone without moving their head, e.g. using a sidelong glance. Also, the cause of the error can be explained by Figure 6, which shows the estimated distributions of head-direction likelihood and histograms of head direction for separate gaze directions. In Figure 6, both distributions exhibit significant overlaps between that for averted gaze and those of the others. In addition, the average correct ratio of maximum a posteriori estimates based on the ground truth of gaze direction was 68.8%. Given that our result from 'unsupervised learning' was better than one from 'supervised learning', it is suggested that the proposed framework is an effective methodology for detecting gaze direction.

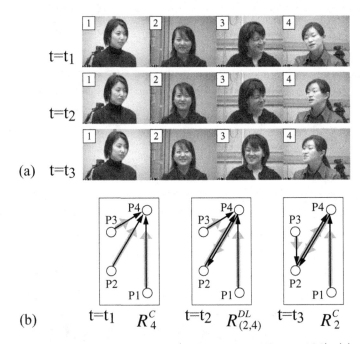

Fig. 8. An example of regime transition ($t_1 = 310, t_2 = 485, t_3 = 578$). (a)snapshot of each participant, (b)regime estimates and gaze patterns (solid arrows: estimates, wide arrows: ground truth).

Figure 8 shows an example of regime transition; $R_4^C \rightarrow R_{(2,4)}^C \rightarrow R_2^C$. Figure 8(a) shows bust-shot images of each participant and Figure 8(b) shows gaze patterns. At first ($t = 310$), person 4 talked to all others (P4: *"Even if I am not thinking of marriage, I have to think about having relations, I mean.."*) and others listen to person 4. This form of conversation was indicated by estimated regime R_4^C. Next ($t = 485$), person 2 responded to person 4 saying (P2: *"Yes, yes, yes, yes, yes"*) with nodding, and P4 looked at P2 to confirm the response from her. There was mutual gaze between person 2 and 4, which is indicated by regime estimate, dyad link $R_{(2,4)}^{DL}$. Furthermore ($t = 578$), P2 keep on speaking (P2: *"yes, in terms of ever since"*) and person 4 returned response back to P2 saying (P4: *"yes, yes"*) and then stopped speaking, which indicated that P4 was offering the floor to P2. At the same time, person 3 turned her gaze from P4 to P2, in order to watch what P2 would say. From the above results, it is confirmed that the estimated regimes seem reasonable and could be used as an indicator of conversation structure.

5   Discussion and Conclusion

A probabilistic framework based on head directions and utterances was proposed for inferring gaze patterns and the structure of conversations in face-to-face multiparty communications. To that end, we devised the Markov-switching model, whose hidden states correspond to the regime and gaze patterns. A Bayesian estimation of all unknown variables including model parameters is carried out using the Gibbs sampler. Experiments on four-person conversations confirmed the effectiveness of our framework. As the next step, it is necessary to evaluate the sequence of regime estimates by comparing them with actual events that take place during conversations. Also, we need to increase the amount of data so that it includes different people, different group size, and various actions such as locomotion and note-taking. The proposed framework can be extended to incorporate other human behavior such as head gestures like nodding and shaking, facial expressions, and prosody. Furthermore, real-time online estimation and image-based head tracking are required to develop practical applications.

References

1. Cutler, R., Rui, Y., Gupta, A., Cadiz, J., Tashev, T., He, L., Colburn, A., Zhang, Z., Liu, Z., Silverberg, S.: Distributed meetings: A meeting capture and broadcasting system. In: Proc. ACM Multimedia '02. (2002) 503–512
2. Bett, M., Gross, R., Yu, H., Zhu, X., Pan, Y., Yang, J., Waibel, A.: Multimodal meeting tracker. In: Proc. RIAO 2000: Content-Based Multimodal Inform. Access. (2000)
3. Heylen, D., Es, I.V., Nijholt, A., Dijk, B.V.: Experimenting with the gaze of a conversational agent. In: Proc. Int. CLASS Workshop on Natural Intelligent and Effective Interaction in Multimodal Dialogue Systems. (2002) 93–100
4. McCowan, I., Perez, D., Bengio, S., Lathoud, G., Barnard, M., Zhang, D.: Automatic analysis of multimodal group actions in meetings,. IEEE Trans. PAMI **27** (2005)
5. Zhang, D., Perez, D.G., Bengio, S., McCowan, I., Lathoud, G.: Modeling individual and group actions in meetings: A two-layer HMM framework. In: Proc. 2nd. IEEE Workshop on Event Mining. (2004)
6. Clark, H.H., Carlson, T.B.: Hearers and speech acts. Language **58** (1982) 332–373
7. Kendon, A.: Some functions of gaze-direction in social interaction. Acta Psychologica **26** (1967) 22–63
8. Argyle, M., Cook, M.: Gaze and Mutual Gaze. Cambridge Univ. Press (1976)
9. Jovanovic, N., Akker, R.: Towards automatic addressee identification in multi-party dialogues. In: Proc. SIGdial'04. (2004) 89–92
10. Takemae, Y., Otsuka, K., Mukawa, N.: An analysis of speakers' gaze behavior for automatic addressee identification in multiparty conversation and its application to video editing. In: Proc. of IEEE Int. Workshop on Robot and Human Interactive Communication (IEEE/RO-MAN). (2004) 581–586
11. Ohno, T., Mukawa, N.: A free-head, simple calibration, gaze tracking system that enables gaze-based interaction. In: Proc. Eye Tracking Research & Application Symposium (ETRA)'04. (2004) 115–122

12. Matsumoto, Y., Zelinsky, A.: An algorithm for real-time stereo vision implementation of head pose and gaze direction measurement. In: Proc. Int. Conf. Automatic Face and Gesture Recognition '04. (2000) 499–504
13. Stiefelhagen, R., Yang, J., Waibel, A.: Modeling focus of attention for meeting index based on multiple cues. IEEE Trans. Neural Networks 13 (2002)
14. Reidsma, D., Akker, R., Rienks, R., Poppe, R., Nijholt, A., Heylen, D., Zwiers, J.: Virtual meeting rooms: From observation to simulation. In: Proc. Social Intelli. Design '05. (2005)
15. Morency, L.P., Rahimi, A., Darrell, T.: Adaptive view-based appearance model. In: Proc. CVPR'03. (2003) 803–810
16. Kim, C.J., Nelson, C.R.: State-Space Models with Regime Switching. MIT Press (1999)
17. Gilks, W.R., Richardson, S., Spiegelhalter, D.J.: Markov Chain Monte Carlo in Practice. Chapman & Hall/CRC (1996)
18. Oliver, N.M., Rosario, B., Pentland, A.P.: A Bayesian computer vision system for modeling human interactions. IEEE Trans. PAMI 22 (2000)
19. Takemae, Y., Otsuka, K., Mukawa, N.: Impact of video editing based on participants' gaze in multiparty conversation. In: Proc. ACM CHI'04. (2004) 1333–1336
20. Novic, D.G., Hansen, B., Ward, K.: Coordinating turn-taking with gaze. In: Proc. Int. Conf. Spoken Language '96. (1996) 1888–1891
21. Chen, R., Li, T.H.: Blind restoration of linearly degraded discrete signals by Gibbs sampling. IEEE Trans. Signal Processing 43 (1995) 2410–2413
22. Bernardo, J.M., Smith, A.F.M.: Bayesian Theory. John Wiley & Sons, Ltd. (1994)

Conversational Inverse Information for Context-Based Retrieval of Personal Experiences

Yasuhiro Katagiri[1], Mayumi Bono[2], and Noriko Suzuki[2]

[1] Future University-Hakodate,
116-2 Kamedanakano-cho Hakodate Hokkaido, Japan
[2] ATR Media Information Science Laboratories,
2-2-2 Hikaridai, Keihanna Science City, Kyoto, Japan

Abstract. Recent development of capture and archival technology for experiences can serve to extend our memory and knowledge and enrich our collaboration with others. Conversation is an important facet of human experiences. We focus on the conversational participation structure as a type of inverse information associated with human socio-interactional events. Based on an analysis of the Interaction Corpus collected in the Ubiquitous Sensor Room environment, we argue that inverse information can be effectively employed in the retrieval and re-experiencing of the subjective quality of the captured events.

1 Introduction

Since Vannevar Bush's visionary conception of "Memex" machine [1], personal capture and archival of experiences have been pursued to serve for the extension and the enrichment of our memory and knowledge, both at the personal level through accumulation of information and at the collective level through collaboration among people. In this paper, inspired by the semantic notion of inverse information [2,3], we distinguish the two aspects in a capture event: captured situation and capturing situation, and argue for the significance of the second aspect of capturing situations in the retrieval and reuse, i.e., re-experiencing of the captured situations.

The captured situation is the information content of what gets captured: contents of a book, photograph, video etc. The capturing situation, on the other hand, is the environmental situation in which the capture event takes place: who is capturing what, from which direction, at what time, with what kind of intentions etc. Any capture event has these two types of situations associated with it.

Even though it is the captured situation that constitutes the bodies of memory and knowledge, the capturing situation provides people, be they original capturer or others, with valuable clues for the standpoint from which they could reflect, compare and make sense of information contents contained in the captured situation. Indexing and retrieval of experiences should incorporate information contained in capturing situations as well as those in captured situations.

T. Washio et al. (Eds.): JSAI 2005 Workshops, LNAI 4012, pp. 365–376, 2006.

We focus on the conversational participation structure [4, 5] as a type of inverse information associated with human socio-interactional events. There have been several attempts to analyze and identify social structures in conversations [6, 7]. We pursue the idea of using the social structures manifested in conversations as contextual key information to be employed in the retrieval from an archive of experience data. Based on an analysis of the Interaction Corpus collected in the Ubiquitous Sensor Room environment [8, 9], we argue that conversation participation structure information can be effectively employed in the retrieval and re-experiencing of captured data.

2   Inverse Information in Experience Capture

Suppose that Ann, Bill and Claire went to the city of Vienna to capture their travel experiences there. Ann, being an avid pianist, went for monuments, places, concert halls associated with Beethoven, Mozart and other composers. Bill, on the other hand, visited restaurants and collected photos and recipes of Vienna cuisine out of his gastronomical interests. Claire, who was an art history major, spent most of her time visiting so many museums in the city. Experiences of them are all about the city of Vienna, but captured information pieces would be quite different. Suppose further that, while they were there, Ann gave a piano concert in Musikverein. Bill and Claire purchased the tickets and went to enjoy Ann's performance. Here again, experiences are all about a particular concert that evening, but quality of their experiences could be quite different between Ann, the performer and Bill and Claire, the audience. Ann must have felt really nervous as she was keen to make the concert a success, while Bill and Claire were relaxed and just enjoyed the music. Same object, like the city of Vienna, or same event, like a concert, could turn out very different experiences depending on different interests people have, different roles people play and different attitudes and feelings people have relative to the object or to the event.

When we try to capture our experience, be it in the form of photographic images, videos, texts or web pages, we can distinguish, conceptually at least, between the captured situation, scenes, state of affairs or events about which information is extracted and stored in the form of bit sequences onto some electronic media, on the one hand, and the capturing situation in which we perform actual photo/video taking or bookmarking of a certain web page etc., on the other hand. Captured situations constitute experiential content, e.g., information on what this particular experience is about. Capturing situations, on the other hand, are about experiencers, e.g., information on how and under what circumstance they had that experience. Every experience has these two aspects associated with it. Capturing of an experience makes a bridge between these two aspects, and the outcome of the capturing, storage media produced, can carry information about both.

This is in parallel with what semanticists describe of what an utterance of a language expression does in terms of conveying both content, forward information and contextual, inverse information [2, 3]. The former concerns with events and state of affairs described by the linguistic expressions, whereas the latter concerns with circumstances under which the utterances are produced, such as who the speaker is and what attitudes and emotions the speaker has towards the events described.

The conceptual distinction between captured and capturing situations projects into a parallel distinction in the way how to index and retrieve experience data. Indexing and retrieval in terms of captured situations rely on classifications and characteristics of experience content, the objects and events involved in the experience. Indexing and retrieval in terms of capturing situations, however, could be based on classifications and characteristics of experiencers, the subjects of the experience. The two methods provide a pair of complementary views for the same experiences; the former leans toward more objective, while the latter leans toward more subjective. An official list of Vienna restaurants compiled by culinary classifications is different from a record of a Vienna restaurant tour by an opinionated gourmet.

When we review experiences of others, the vividness of experience often resides more in capturing situations rather than in captured contents. Interests and goals of the people who had the experience, their physical locations and social roles, these "background" information does the job of locating the contents of the experience, captured in the form of photographs, videos and notes, within the array of possibilities of experiencing the same contents, The capturing situations thus provide reasons and meanings for the particular form with which each specific person had the experience on them.

This is true even when we review our own past experiences. When one reflects upon her own past experiences, those characteristics of herself in the capturing situations, such as the mental and emotional states she were in, social roles she played, are often more significant than what the experiences were about in the recollection of them. In many cases, recollection of capturing situations leads to the examination of the original experience from a different perspective.

Problems we need to consider before we make full use of the inverse information on the capturing situations for indexing/retrieval of experiences are: (a) what are the possible and useful inverse information keys for experience indexing/retrieval? (b) how can those keys be extracted in the capturing process? (c) how can they be effectively utilized in the retrieval of experience data for later consumption in re-experiencing stages.

3   Conversation Participation

We focus our attention in this paper to experiences we have in conversational events. We pursue the idea of the conversation participation structure as an instance of inverse information in the case of socio-interactional experiences.

3.1   Participation Structure

To engage in a conversational interaction, people first need to establish a conversational space together with their conversational partners, or otherwise enter an existing one, before they can actually talk to each other. Conversational space formation normally proceeds by conversational partners first approaching each other to form a spatial aggregate and then exchanging eye gaze and various forms of greetings. Goffman [4] analyzed the phases of conversational interaction and defined the internal structure of conversational space as 'participation structure' or 'participation framework.' In conversation, the participants exchange their roles, such as 'Speaker' and 'Addressee,' by exchanging the right of utterance for a moment. The structure of conversation (participation structure) consists of components, e.g., participants, and their interrelationships. Both can change dynamically through the course of conversational progressions. Clark [5] proposed a hierarchical structure of participant roles. Clark defined Speaker as the agent of the illocutionary act and Addressee as the participant who is the partner of the joint action that the Speaker is projecting for them to perform. Side Participants take part in the conversation but are not currently being addressed. Other listeners are Bystanders who have no rights or responsibilities in the conversation, that is, they don't take part in it. Non-participants are non-listeners and do not belong to the conversation.

3.2   Dynamics of Participation

Clark's model of participation structure indicates a natural organization of two phases of participation: participation in the conversational space and participation in the conversation itself. We have been looking at poster presentation conversations as an instance of multi-party open member social interactional events. In a poster presentation conversation, visitors first approach the poster to hear the exhibitor's speech and to look at the poster contents in detail. This reduction of physical distance amounts to the initial participation in the conversational space, i.e., being promoted from a non-participant to a bystander participant.

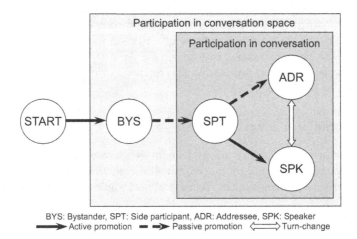

BYS: Bystander, SPT: Side participant, ADR: Addressee, SPK: Speaker
⟶ Active promotion   ⇢ Passive promotion   ⟺ Turn-change

Fig. 1. Dynamic transitions of conversational participation structure

Beyond participation in the conversational space, the participant needs to be further promoted to enter the conversation itself. The participant either takes the floor of the conversation himself/herself (i.e., being promoted to Speaker), is assigned the role of Addressee by the current Speaker (i.e., being promoted to Addressee), or is admitted to join by receiving the Speaker's gaze, namely, the recognition of his/her existence by the existing participants (i.e., being promoted to Side Participant). These are some of the possibilities explaining how participation progresses in conversation.

Figure 1 summarizes the patterns of transitions in the conversational participation structure. The process of participation in conversation is closely tied to audience design, described in Clark and Carlson [10], by the Speaker, in the sense that some of the transitions (e.g., Bystander to Side Participant and Side Participant to Addressee) need to be sanctioned by the Speaker.

4   Experience Capture for Talks in Poster Presentations

In order to empirically examine conversational participation processes from real conversation data and to investigate the possibilities of incorporating conversational participation information in experience sharing technologies, we have set up a Ubiquitous Sensor Room environment and have been collecting an Interaction Corpus, a corpus of conversational interaction data in poster presentation settings [8, 9].

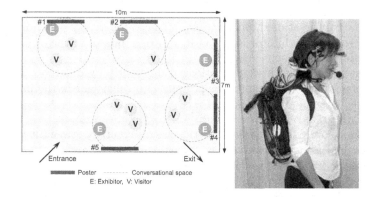

Fig. 2. (a) Ubiquitous and (b) wearable sensors for experience capture

Figure 2(a) shows a schematic layout of the Ubiquitous Sensor Room environment. It has several presentation booths, each with its own set of posters and demonstrations, where the exhibitors give poster presentations. The room has a number of cameras and sensors for recording the behaviors of both exhibitors and visitors. Two cameras are fixed to the ceiling of each booth to capture human behaviors: placement, inter-personal distance and posture. Furthermore, each participant is equipped with a headset microphone with sensors and a camera that captures speech and approximate gaze direction. The wearable sensor setup is shown in Figure 2(b).

An Interaction Corpus in this environment has been collected during the ATR Exhibitions of 2002 and 2003, when a wide variety of people from outside ATR visited poster and oral presentations and joined demonstrations. We have been examining the relationships of speech and gaze directions in the conversation by using the recorded data, which indicate patterns of interaction in the participants' verbal and non-verbal behaviors [11, 12, 13]. Based on the inspection of those participants' behaviors, conversation participation role labels were manually assigned to the conversation interactions that took place at the poster booths for Ubiquitous Sensor Room visitors who agreed to wear the wearable sensor equipments during their tour of the Room.

5   Retrieval with Participation Roles

To investigate the possibility of utilizing the conversation participation structure information in the indexing and retrieval of experiences, we examined our interaction corpus data to find pairs of contrasting video sequences that exhibit interesting apparent differences, even for the same experience contents, depending on the identities and properties of the experiencers.

We referred solely to the handcoded participation role labels and poster booth locations assigned to visitor behavior sequences in choosing our examples.

Here, we discuss three examples.

1. Talk dominance
   Same conversational event was experienced differently depending on the roles, an exhibitor and a visitor, people played in the event.
2. Interaction involvement
   Same poster booth was experienced differently by different visitors depending on their central or peripheral involvement in the interactions with the exhibitors.
3. Interest diversity
   Same room exhibits were experienced differently between a visitor who had a focused interest in a particular theme and another who had a more diverse range of interest.

These examples showcase the potential outcome of experience retrieval when inverse information keys are utilized. The conversational participation structure information in our case makes an inverse information key which classifies the capturing situations associated with the experiences visitors to the Ubiquitous Sensor Room had while walking around the poster booths and engaging in conversational interactions.

5.1   Talk Dominance

In a poster and demonstration exhibit, the exhibitor naturally assumes the dominant speaker role in presenting her materials, whereas visitors to the exhibit

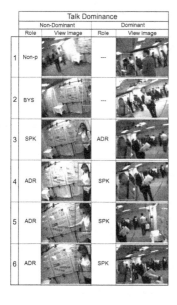

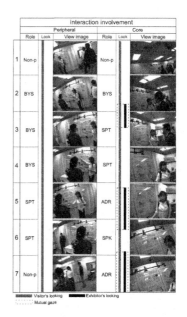

(a)Talk dominance

(b)Interaction involvement

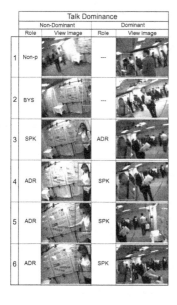

(c)Interest diversity

Fig. 3. Pairs of sequences of captured scenes displaying the differences in (a) talk dominance, (b) interaction involvement and (c) interest diversity

mostly listen in and receive the presentations. This difference in roles and its concomitant difference in speech dominance can turn out different experiences of the same conversational interaction event.

Figure 3(a) shows a pair of contrasting sequences of video captured scenes taken by the head-mounted cameras of a visitor, shown on the left column, and of the exhibitor, shown on the right column. Here, the visitor approaches the poster, asks the exhibitor for a presentation and listens in. His field of view contains only the exhibitor and her poster. In contrast, the exhibitor first looks around her surroundings waiting for interested visitors to come, receives a request from one of the visitors, focuses her attention toward him and start giving a presentation. Her field of view contains many possible visitors to her booth. She also alternates her gaze back and forth between the visitor and her poster in her presentation.

This pair of sequences also makes a typical example of perspective shift in viewing an event. When we re-use our experience by retrieving from stored experience data, the possibility of comparing different perspectives would contribute to enrich our re-experiencing both of one's own experiences and those of others.

The role difference between the exhibitor and the visitor in our data is manifested in the number of Speaker (SPK) roles they assumed in the sequences. Hence, the conversational participation roles can work as effective keys to retrieve this type of contrasting pairs of experiences.

5.2   Interaction Involvement

Our next example concerns the variety with which visitors get involved in interactions with other people, e.g., the degree with which they engage in discussions at a poster presentation booth. In visiting a poster, one might just be content with getting a grasp of its content by a brief look from a distance, or one might come to the presenter and have an intense discussion on the topic with her. These two modes of interaction turn out completely different experiences even for the same poster presentation.

Figure 3(b) shows a pair of contrasting sequences of video captured scenes taken by a visitor who only had a peripheral participation in a conversation with the exhibitor, shown on the left column, and another visitor who had a core participation at the same booth, shown on the right column. Here, both the peripheral participant and the core participant start as non-participants (Non-p) to the poster presentation. The peripheral participant approaches the poster and stays for some time. He is promoted to a Bystander (BYS) and then to a Side Participant (SPT), but is demoted to a non-participant (Non-p) and leaves without actually talking to the exhibitor. His field of view shows another visitor, who occupies a core participant role, and the exhibitor engage in a conversation, keeping him out of the core participation. In contrast, the core participant on the right column steadily steps up the ladder of conversation participation roles, from a non-participant (Non-p), a Bystander (BYS), a Side Participant (SPT) to an Addressee (ADR) and a Speaker (SPK), eventually starts exchanging talks with the presenter. His field of view captures the instant at which he gets promoted to a Side Participant (SPT) by being noticed by the presenter (scene 3). It also shows the timing at which he becomes an Addressee (ADR), when the presenter starts talking to him (scene 5).

It is clear from the example that these two types of involvement in the interaction can be characterized and classified in terms of patterns of transitions over the conversation participation roles.

5.3   Interest Diversity

Our final example looks at the contrast between focused and exploratory behaviors. People with predetermined and focused interest would restrict their behaviors only to those relevant to their interest, whereas people with diverse and indeterminate interest would wander around and take more exploratory attitudes in deciding on their behaviors.

Figure 3(c) shows contrasting sequences of video captured scenes taken by two visitors with different range of diversity in their interest. The focused interest visitor, shown on the left column, approaches and stays at one particular booth talking to the presenter there. His field of view shows that he approaches the poster booth and starts exchanging conversation with the presenter (scenes 4, 5). He stays at the booth even after another visitor comes in to talk to the presenter (scene 6). In contrast, the diverse interest visitor, shown on the right column, looks around and visits whatever poster booth he finds easy to participate in. He frequently moves to different posters and quickly shifts participation roles. His field of view shows his frequent moves across several posters and different presenters he encountered.

Both the location of conversations (poster booth) and participation role transitions characterize and classify the two contrasting behaviors in this example.

6   Recognition of Participation Structures

In order to incorporate the inverse information type keys in the retrieval of experience data, we need to develop a method to extract and identify the inverse information keys in the experience capture process. We have been developing a rule-based recognition algorithm for identifying conversation participation structures, aiming to incorporate the algorithm into experience retrieval and summarization system for our Interaction Corpus data.

Current version of the algorithm utilizes the following set of information provided from both the wearable and environmental sensors embedded in the Ubiquitous Sensor Room environment [14].

– Time a visitor has spent at a poster booth
    A visitor's head-mounted IR tracker can sense the IR signal emitted from IR markers embedded in the poster booth. The signal is decoded to identify which poster booth he is staying at and how long he has spent his time there. The algorithm judges that a visitor comes into a conversational space and gets promoted from a non-participant to

a Side Participant when he has spent certain duration of time (longer than a minute) at the corresponding poster booth.
- Occurrence of speech
  A pair of open air microphone and throat microphone in the wearable sensor equipment can detect the speech onset and offset produced by the person who is equipped with the wearable setup. The producer of speech is judged to be the Speaker, except for the very short speech segments characteristic of backchannel utterances.
- Receiving of the gaze of the speaker
  Speaker's approximate gaze direction is detected by the speaker's head mounted IR tracker. When the speaker's tracker senses IR signal emitted from an IR marker attached to the wearable setup of another person, the second person is judged to be the recipient of the speaker's gaze. The recipient of the speaker's gaze is judged to be the Addressee.

Smoothing was applied in all three cases to ignore temporary lapse caused by momentary head movements or short pausings.

Table 1. Simulated identification rates of conversation participation structures

Participant	Speaker (SPK)		
	Booth(1)	Booth(2)	Booth(3)
A	88.3 %	66.5 %	43.0 %
B	63.4 %	99.3 %	67.1 %
C	83.9 %	91.4 %	—
D	—	—	48.4 %

Participant	Addressee (ADR)		
	Booth(1)	Booth(2)	Booth(3)
A	4.4 %	97.1 %	77.5 %
B	58.2 %	23.4 %	91.1 %
C	36.5 %	40.8 %	—
D	—	—	86.8 %

Participant	Side Participant (SPT)		
	Booth(1)	Booth(2)	Booth(3)
A	31.8 %	23.8 %	41.0 %
B	56.3 %	27.2 %	25.8 %
C	72.2 %	52.3 %	63.5 %
D	52.8 %	21.5 %	14.0 %

We have tried out the algorithm on a small portion of collected sensor data in the Interaction Corpus. Unfortunately, some of the original sensor data contained relatively large errors, particularly in poster booth identification, due to the difficulties we had in adjusting IR tracker sensitivities. We first manually inspected the sensor data by matching them against video images, and adjusted them to their ideal values as needed. We then ran the algorithm on the adjusted data and checked the outcome against the manually coded conversation participation structure labels.

Table 1 shows our initial result of the recognition experiment conducted on the poster exhibit tour behaviors of four visitors. Behaviors of each of the four visitors at three poster booths were examined. The rate of correct identification of each of the participation roles: Speaker (SPK), Addressee (ADR) and Side Participant (SPT), is indicated for each subject at each poster booth. The algorithm failed to identify the participation roles, Speaker (SPK) and Addressee (ADR), in some of the cases, which are marked "—" in the table. Those cases include poster booth visits in which visitors approached the posters, but did not get involved in substantive dialogue exchange with the exhibitors. If we exclude those anomalous cases, the identification rates range from less than 20% to more than 95%. The results obtained are obviously still preliminary, but considering the simple algorithm we tested, it appears to be promising to explore further refinements.

7   Conclusions

We proposed, inspired by the semantic notion of forward and inverse information, a conceptual distinction between a captured situation and a capturing situation for an experience capture event. We then focused on the conversational participation structure as a type of inverse information associated with human socio-interactional events. We examined the conversational interaction events in the poster presentation settings recorded in the Ubiquitous Sensor Room environment, and argued for the significance of the aspect of capturing situations in the retrieval and reuse, i.e., re-experiencing of the captured situations. Our examples that juxtaposed a pair of video sequences with different capturing situations demonstrated the significance of inverse information in experience retrieval in widening one's perspectives and promoting re-interpretation of events experienced, which is the whole point of the sharing one's experiences. We are now experimenting with algorithms for automatically identifying participation structures from the sensor data obtained in the Ubiquitous Sensor Room environment. We believe that inverse information, particularly, the conversational participation structure information, makes a promising candidate for an effective and a universal inverse information key in human social and interactional experiences.

Acknowledgment

The research reported here was supported in part by the National Institute of Information and Communication Technologies of Japan.

References

1. Bush, V.: As we may think. The Atlantic Monthly **176** (1945) 101–108
2. Barwise, J., Perry, J.: Situations and Attitudes. MIT Press (1983)

3. Israel, D., Perry, J.: What is information? In Hanson, P., ed.: Information , Language and Cognition. University of British Columbia Press, Vancouver (1990)
4. Goffman, E.: Forms of talk. University of Pennsylvania Press (1981)
5. Clark, H.H.: Using language. Cambridge University Press (1996)
6. Basu, S.: Conversational Scene Analysis. PhD thesis, Massachusetts institute of Technology (2002)
7. Choudhury, T.K.: Sensing and modeling human networks. PhD thesis, Massachusetts institute of Technology (2004)
8. Hagita, N., Kogure, K., Mase, K., Sumi, Y.: Collaborative capturing of experiences with ubiquitous sensors and communication robots. In: IEEE International Conference on Robotics and Automation (IEEE ICRA). (2003)
9. Sumi, Y., Ito, S., Matsuguchi, T., Fels, S., Mase, K.: Collaborative capturing and interpretation of interactions. In Mase, K., Sumi, Y., Fels, S., eds.: Pervasive 2004 Workshop on Memory and Sharing of Experiences. (2004) 1–7
10. Clark, H.H., Carlson, T.B.: Hearers and speech acts. Language **58** (1982) 332–373
11. Bono, M., Suzuki, N., Katagiri, Y.: An analysis of participation structure in conversation based on interaction corpus of ubiquitous sensor data. In et al., M., ed.: INTERACT 03: Proceedings of the Ninth IFIP TC13 International Conference on Human-Computer Interaction, IOS Press (2003) 713–716
12. Bono, M., Suzuki, N., Katagiri, Y.: An analysis of non-verbal cues for turn-taking through observation of speaker behaviors. In: ICCS/ASCS-2003: Proceedings of the Joint International Conference on Cognitive Science (CD-ROM), Elsevier (2003)
13. Katagiri, Y., Bono, M., Suzuki, N.: Capturing conversational participation in a ubiquitous sensor environment. In Mase, K., Sumi, Y., Fels, S., eds.: Pervasive 2004 Workshop on Memory and Sharing of Experiences. (2004) 101–106
14. Bono, M., Suzuki, N., Katagiri, Y.: Identification of conversation participation procedures with Ubiquitous Sensors. Technical Report SIG-SLUD 41, Japanese Society of Artificial Intelligence (2004)

Detecting Microstructures of Conversations by Using Physical References: Case Study of Poster Presentations

Ken Kumagai[1,2], Yasuyuki Sumi[1,2], Kenji Mase[2,3], and Toyoaki Nishida[1,2]

[1] Graduate School of Informatics, Kyoto University,
Yoshida-Honmachi, Sakyo-ku, Kyoto 606-8501, Japan
[2] ATR Media Information Science Laboratories,
Seika-cho, Soraku-gun, Kyoto 619-0288, Japan
[3] Information Technology Center, Nagoya University,
Chikusa, Nagoya 464-8601, Japan

Abstract. The purpose of the work presented in this paper is reusing conversational archives for supporting knowledge circulation in the real world. So far, we have proposed a method to give structures to conversations by analyzing gaze and utterance data from an interaction corpus, which is a semi-structured set of a large amount of interaction data collected by various sensors. In this paper, we give more detailed structures to conversations by analyzing poster touch data. We devise a poster touch capturing method and investigate the correlation between poster touch and conversation structure, that is, a topic of conversation has a relation to a sub-theme in a poster that an exhibitor touched at the time when it was made. By analyzing the relation between conversations and poster touch data, we can detect the transition of topics and divide a long conversation that is composed of many topics into some microstructured conversations that are composed of a single topic or context.

1 Introduction

Conversation is one of the most powerful media for knowledge circulation because many people have excellent conversational communication skills, that is, people engage in conversations in daily life [1]. Conversation as media has potential advantages; however, we cannot make optimum use of them because conversations are too informal and unstructured to be processed by computational technologies. If knowledge in conversation is reusable, the following benefits can be derived.

- Information Retrieval: Retrieval of our favorite conversation from a large number of conversations indexed appropriately
- Editing: Creation of stories in a new situation by editing conversations extracted from various scenes
- Expression: Effective presentation of conversations by means of agents using indexes

T. Washio et al. (Eds.): JSAI 2005 Workshops, LNAI 4012, pp. 377–388, 2006.
© Springer-Verlag Berlin Heidelberg 2006

This paper aims to facilitate reusability of conversations by giving structures to interaction data collected in conversational situations. Traditionally, speech recognition researches have attempted to process conversations from the viewpoint of natural language. Since conversations can be made anywhere, there are many situations in which they do not work well. In daily life, we can often utilize such contextual data as objects or places related to our conversation, and we therefore believe that making good use of such data easily gives more detailed structures to conversations without speech recognition. For example, we often use paper documents for discussions at meetings, and our conversations have a close relation to these documents. In such cases, we can say that paper documents serve as a conversational focal point, and making good use of such contextual data enables us to give detailed structures to conversations. This paper proposes a method to make good use of contextual data in conversation scenes and give detailed structures to such conversations.

We examine conversations between exhibitors and visitors at a poster presentation, called *poster conversation* – conversation made with posters at a poster exhibition. From our preliminary analyses, exhibitors explain topics to visitors by poster touch actions; in particular, they explicitly indicate a current topic by touching a particular area of the poster. Such an action is considered as contextual data that accompanies the conversation. In this paper, we consider the utility of poster touch data as contextual data.

In the following sections, we refer to related research and explain our position (Section 2); explain how to capture poster touch data and propose a tree model (Section 3); examine these data (Section 4); test our method by conducting an experiment (Section 5); explain applications (Section 6); and present a summary and describe future works (Section 7).

2 Related Works

This paper proposes a method to give structures to conversations in particular domains. In relation to this concept, some systems extract important meeting scenes from video data, e.g., [2]. These systems extract scenes according to changes in the physical quantity of video data captured by fixed cameras. Instead of using physical data, we use contextual data as modalities accompanying conversations and then semantically extract scenes from the conversations.

Minoh, et al. [3] proposed an automatic lecture archiving system that recognizes dynamic situations in the classroom by using multimodal sensors. This system captures human activities for reuse – an aspect that is of interest to us as well. However, we deal with conversations in more casual situations, which often include physical actions such as gestures.

The Smart Courier system [4] makes good use of annotations on objects. It makes various annotations on electronic papers. The system creates user models based on keywords annotated by users and offers recommendations to others according to interests by dealing with asynchronous user annotations on the

Web. However, we use real world annotations in which exhibitors explicitly touch posters to show visitors a current topic.

There have been studies on giving structures to conversations by using nonverbal data, e.g., [5]. These studies proposed a method to give structures to conversations in face-to-face multiparty communication by using head directions and the presence/absence of the utterances of participants. Their aim was to construct models to explain the states of conversations. We, however, deal with conversations related to some objects or places and are concerned with physical references to them in conversations. In such situations, we aim to give more detailed structures to conversations by using physical references to focal points in addition to gazing and utterances.

In relation to physical references to objects in conversations, McNeil [6] characterized communicative arm gestures into several categories: iconic, metaphoric, deictic, cohesive, and beat gestures. Of these, our method is concerned with deictic gestures. Deictic gestures are pointing movements, which are typically performed with the index finger and may refer to people or spatializable things.

These pointing gestures are made when the focal content is orientation or change of orientation. In this paper, we use posters as spatializable things and give structures to conversations by using physical references to them.

In general, we believe that conversation structure has the following attributes.

1. Who talked
2. When s/he talked
3. Where s/he talked
4. What s/he talked about

Sumi, et al. [7] proposed a system that builds an interaction corpus – a semi-structured set of a large amount of interaction data collected by various sensors. In addition to cameras and microphones, they adopted an infrared ID system, which identifies persons or objects, in order to estimate the user's state of gazing at a particular person/object or of staying at a particular place. They also adopted a throat microphone that is used to detect whether the user makes an utterance.

With the interaction corpus, we can assign the attributes of 1, 2, and 3 to poster conversations but attribute 4 can only be assigned to the entire poster. In poster conversations, current topics can be chosen as sub-themes of the poster so that visitors do not always ask exhibitors the same questions. In addition, those who visit a booth at the same time are not always interested in the same topic. In order to give more detailed structures, we need more contextual data; therefore, we focus on the poster touch actions of exhibitors who explicitly show current topics when explaining a poster to visitors. A topic of conversation is related to a sub-theme of a poster that an exhibitor touched at the time when it was brought up. An analysis of the relation between conversations and poster touch data can detect the transition of conversation, and we can divide a conversation composed of many topics into smaller units that are composed of a single topic or context.

3   How to Capture Poster Touch Data and Construct a Data Model

We utilize a large touch panel display for capturing the exhibitor's poster touch data. Exhibitors provide explanations to visitors with reference to an electronic poster on a touch panel display (Fig.1), and poster touch data are accumulated when this poster is touched. Fig.2 is an example of accumulated poster touch data, represented by red dots.

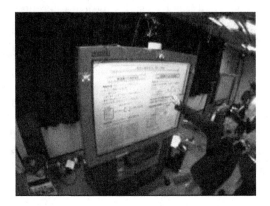

Fig. 1. Explanations with reference to an electronic poster

Fig. 2. Example of accumulated poster touch data

Next, we explain the data model for poster touch data. We suppose that posters have several topics corresponding to their layout, that is, one topic is related to one area, and an exhibitor provides an explanation by selecting one of them. Analyses of preliminary experiments revealed the following interesting case in some scenes.

An exhibitor touches more than one area within a short span of time.

In this case, exhibitors often speak about the topics of both areas that they touch alternately (Fig.3); therefore, we believe that all areas of a poster are semantically related. As one such semantic relationship, we suppose that areas of a poster are hierarchically related; therefore, we adopt a tree model for posters. In this respect, we propose the following hypothesis.

Exhibitors attempt to explain concepts that include all the topics that they explain when they alternately touch some areas.

Fig. 3. Scene of alternate touches

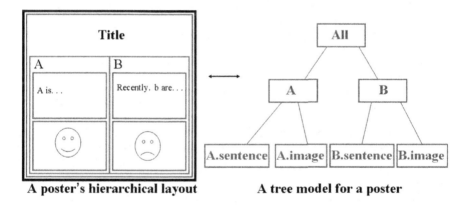

Fig. 4. Tree model based on a poster structure

We now explain these concepts with examples (Fig.4, Fig.5). The image on the left panel of Fig.4 represents a typical poster in which there are three main parts: a title, element A, and element B. Both elements A and B have areas of explanatory text and images of concepts. Based on the semantic position of each area in the poster, we can derive a tree model as the hierarchical structure of the poster layout; this is depicted on the right panel of Fig.4. In the model, sentences of element A correspond to sentence A and images of element A correspond to image A (the same is the case with element B). The title area usually corresponds to All. If sentence A has some keywords, we may be able to divide an area of sentence A into some areas of keyword A; however, this aspect requires further discussion because it is more difficult to touch smaller areas accurately.

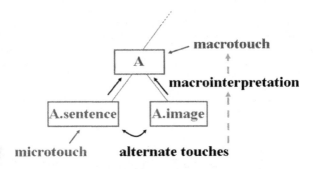

Fig. 5. *Macrointerpretation* by alternate touches

In the scene depicted in Fig.3, the exhibitor touched several areas alternately in a span of approximately thirty seconds, while continuously speaking about the topics in those areas. According to our method, we can interpret such a scene by calculating a common parent of those areas and consider the exhibitor's alternate touches on the poster as *macrotouches* in the tree model (we term this process *macrointerpretation*). Thus, using the tree model, we can deal with alternate touches as *macrotouches*, in addition to *microtouches* (Fig.5).

A network model can also be used for the structure of a poster; however, we deem the tree model to be more appropriate for the following two reasons.

- The structure of a poster is static.
- We often order information in a simple structure when we need to summarize it in a small space.

Once a poster is created, new information cannot be added to it. In other words, the structure of the poster is static. Since the network model is appropriate for a dynamic structure in which elements are added or removed, it is not very appropriate in this case. Further, a poster does not always have ample space. In order to summarize information in such a space, a simple structure should be adopted. The tree model is simpler than the network model. Due to these reasons, the tree model is more appropriate for the structure of a poster.

The process of constructing a tree model from the layout of a poster is manual. We can automatically extract segments by image processing methods. However, since we cannot construct a tree model based on semantic relations of nodes, it is advisable for exhibitors who are knowledgeable about the hierarchical structure of posters to construct the model from the poster.

4   Relation Between Conversation Topics and Poster Touch Data

In this section, we explain the relation between poster conversations and poster touch data. In general, it can be considered that an exhibitor explicitly indicates a current topic by touching a particular area of the poster; however, poster touch data does not necessarily correspond exactly to conversations of the exhibitor and the visitors.

For example, the exhibitor may chat with visitors for a period of time regardless of the poster and without touching it. Further, visitors often change topics suddenly, and an exhibitor may begin to explain with touches after visitors finish asking their questions. It could also be said that the topic of conversation may change if the conversation continues for a long time without poster touch. Therefore, the problem is how to relate conversations to poster touch data. In order to resolve this, we establish the following hypothesis.

Conversations made almost synchronously with poster touch actions are closely related to topics indicated by touch.

We now discuss concrete procedures for relating conversations to poster touch data. First, we make segments from ON-OFF data of utterance that are obtained using the Interaction Corpus system [7]. The segments have start and end times. Second, we process segments according to the following three cases.

- Case 1: If there are poster touch data pertaining to one node of a poster between the start and end of a segment, we relate the segment to it.
- Case 2: If there are some poster touch data pertaining to some nodes of a poster between the start and end of a segment, we divide the segment into sub-segments based on the time of the poster touch data. Next, we relate segments to corresponding poster touch data.
- Case 3: If there is no poster touch data between the start and end of a segment, we relate the segment to the nearest poster touch data.

Case 2 includes scenes in which an exhibitor provides an explanation. In this case, we make a segment with a long time span; however, we divide it into sub-segments with shorter time spans by using poster touch data and relate each sub-segment to corresponding poster touch data (Fig. 6: Case 2).

Case 3 includes scenes in which either the topic of the conversation changes to the one that is not related to the poster, or the topic suddenly changes from

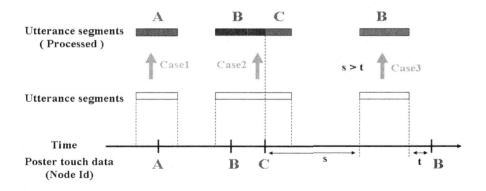

Fig. 6. Examples of processing segments

the topic C discussed for a long time to the topic B. In this case, we relate a segment to the time nearest to it (Fig. 6: Case 3); however, it is not always obvious whether we should consider both weights of "s" and "t" to be equal. Further discussion on this aspect is required.

5   Experiment and Analyses

We conducted the following experiment in order to examine our theory.

- One exhibitor and one visitor engaged in a conversation about a poster at a given time.
- Four sets were made.
- A tree model was constructed manually from the poster.

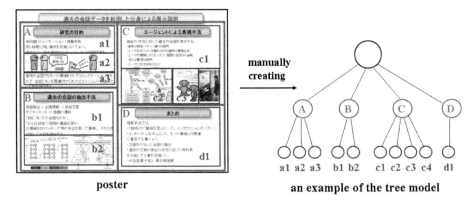

poster   an example of the tree model

Fig. 7. An example of a poster and a tree model

The poster and the tree model that we used in the experiment are shown in Fig.7. The poster has four main parts, and each part has some micro parts. We created a tree model manually according to sentences and images. This is just one example. The red parts can be divided into a larger number of parts, in which case the red nodes in the tree model would have more blue nodes. In such a case, we can distinguish one touch from another more accurately but experience difficulties in finding groups of touches having a connection. Further discussion on this ratio is required.

The three findings from the experiment are as follows.

1. New topics were often started when the area touched by the exhibitor changed and visitors began making utterances at that time.
2. Dispersion of touches differed between the situation in which the exhibitor provided explanations to visitors and that in which he engaged in discussion with them.
3. There was a connection between the touches of visitors and the beginning of a discussion on a new topic.

With regard to the first finding, the utterances of visitors had an effect on the change of the area touched by the exhibitor. The reason for this is as follows. Initially, the exhibitor was speaking while touching one area. Next, visitors asked questions or voiced some opinions, causing the exhibitor to touch another area in order to indicate his thoughts in relation to the poster. This scenario mainly occurred when the exhibitor and visitors engaged in discussion.

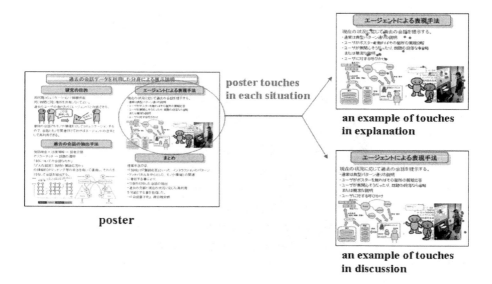

Fig. 8. An example of touches in both situations – explanation and discussion

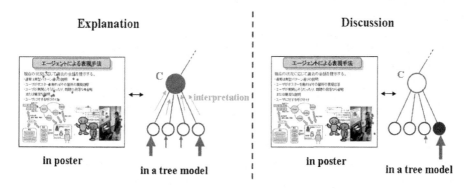

Fig. 9. Tree model with touches in both situations

While providing an explanation, the exhibitor spoke continuously and touched some areas. The visitors rarely spoke. In this case, not all of the utterance data of visitors could be used, but a typical pattern of touches was detected: the touches accompanying explanations were inclined to be dispersed in one part of the poster, while those accompanying discussions were inclined to be collected in micro areas of one part of the poster (Fig.8). This indicates that when he provided explanations, the exhibitor spoke while touching almost all of one part, but when he engaged in discussion, he touched only a few micro areas of one part because visitors often asked questions based on that part. Fig.9 shows a tree model with touches of both situations. In this case, the touches in the explanation situation were interpreted by macro interpretation as belonging to the upper node, and those in the discussion situation were interpreted as belonging to the lower node. These interpreted touch data reminded us of the change in the area that the exhibitor touched during a long time span and enabled us to detect topic transition in the explanation situation more accurately.

Fig. 10. Scene of visitor touch

Fig.10 shows a visitor touching areas of his interest and discussing the topic. We believe that poster touch data reflects the content of a conversation. It is probable that a visitor has questions about or is interested in the content related to areas that he touches; therefore, the exhibitor and the visitors will discuss it thenceforth. From this point, the actions of the visitors and the exhibitor have similar meanings, and we consider them to be almost the same. At present, we cannot distinguish between visitor and exhibitor touches. However, in the future, we may be able to do so by detecting exact information of their location against a poster.

6   Applications of Microstructured Conversational Data

We can detect the transition of topics by using poster touch data. Therefore, poster touch provides us with a topic-based index of microstructured conversational data and enables topic-based reuse of these data. We now explain applications such as recommendation of conversations based on interest, evaluation of lecture conversations, and circulation of conversational content on the Web. We utilize poster touch data in order to give detailed structures to poster conversations pertaining to scenes that an exhibitor and visitors discuss. We can obtain data of the times at which visitors stop by at each booth by using the Interaction Corpus system; however, visitors with almost the same visiting time do not always speak to the exhibitor about the same node of a tree model of a poster. We can obtain information on the nodes that the exhibitor and the visitors discuss by using poster touch data and the Interaction Corpus. Further, we can construct detailed models of visitors based on visitor interests and promote conversation reusability.

We utilize poster touch data to give detailed structures to lecture conversations that are poster conversations involving an exhibitor providing an explanation. Making segments of the utterances of an exhibitor and setting parameters that divide segments into lectures and non lectures enable us to structure an exhibitor's lecture; however, these lectures do not always have the same features. For example, there are two kinds of short lectures: one in which an exhibitor explains all topics smoothly and another in which he has to explain continuously because of frequent questioning by visitors. We can construct a detailed model based on lectures and promote conversation reusability. As an application, we could create an excellent poster conversation video by connecting the interaction parts in which the visitors asked questions about all topics and the lecture parts in which the exhibitor provided smooth explanations. Such conversations can also have Web applications. For example, visitors can select the best conversation extracted from conversations of other visitors interested in common topics, and non-visitors can select conversations of explanations by an exhibitor, interactions of an exhibitor and visitors on favorite topics, and the video of a poster conversation. In all cases, users can obtain not only the video containing the conversations they selected but also the contents by agent expression [8].

7   Conclusion and Future Works

We proposed a method to give detailed structures to poster conversations, which enables us to relate conversations to contextual data such as poster touch data without voice recognition, and facilitate conversation reusability.

The following are two topics for future study. First, we consider the poster touch action accompanying the gestures of an exhibitor and visitors when they speak in front of posters; we need to analyze these gestures in addition to the touch action. Second, we need to discover the method of evaluating microstructured conversational data on content by analyzing the times of the actions, the synchronous timing of gazing, poster touch actions, etc. By considering these factors, we may be able to give more detailed structures to conversations in discussion situations.

Acknowlegements

We are grateful to our colleagues at ATR Media Information Science Laboratories for their assistance with the experiments. Hidekazu Kubota, Yohei Kawaguchi, and Norman Lin made valuable contributions to the discussion and experiments in this paper. The research presented here was supported in part by the National Institute of Information and Communications Technology.

References

1. Nishida, T.: Conversation quantization for conversational knowledge process. Special invited talk, S. Bhalla (Ed.): DNIS 2005, LNCS 3433, Springer, pp. 15-33, 2005.
2. Chiu, P., Kapuskar, A., Reitmeier, S., Wilcox, L.: Meeting capture in a media enriched conference room. In Proceedings of CoBuild '99 (Springer LNCS1670), pp. 79-88, 1999.
3. Minoh, M.: Automatic lecture archiving system. Proceedings of the 12th International Conference on Informatics Research for Development of Knowledge Society Infrastructure (ICKS '04), 2004.
4. Ito, S., Sumi, Y., Mase, K., Kunifuji, S.: SmartCourier: Annotation management tool for research labs. Proceedings of the Sixth International Conference on Knowledge-based Intelligent Information Engineering Systems and Allied Technologies (KES 2002), pp. 827-832, IOS Press, September 2002.
5. Otsuka, K., Takemae, Y., Yamato, J., Murase, H.: Probabilistic inference of gaze patterns and structure of multiparty conversations from head directions and utterances. In Proceedings of JSAI 2005 Workshop on Conversational Informatics, pp. 7-12, 2005. http://www.ii.ist.i.kyoto-u.ac.jp/jsai05ws/
6. McNeill, D.: Hand and Mind: What Gestures Reveal about Thought. U. of Chicago Press, 1992.
7. Sumi, Y., Ito, S., Matsuguchi, T., Fels, S., Mase, K.: Collaborative capturing and interpretation of interactions. Pervasive 2004 Workshop on Memory and Sharing of Experiences, pp. 1-7, 2004. http://www.ii.ist.i.kyoto-u.ac.jp/~sumi/pervasive04/
8. Kawaguchi, Y., Sumi, Y., Nishida, T., Mase, K.: Presentation agents by reusing past conversational data in exhibition sites. IPSJ SIG Technical Reports, Vol. 2005, No. 28, pp. 225-232. (In Japanese), 2005.

Detection of Assessment Patterns in Ordinary Triadic Conversation

Katsuya Takanashi[1,2], Eiki Fujimoto[3], Yasuyuki Kono[3], Kazuhiro Takeuchi[4], and Hitoshi Isahara[4]

[1] Kyoto University, Nihonmatsu-cho, Yoshida,
Sakyo-ku, Kyoto, Japan
takanasi@ar.media.kyoto-u.ac.jp
[2] The University of Tokyo, 7-3-1 Hongou, Bunkyou-ku, Tokyo, Japan
[3] Nara Institute of Science and Technology, 8916-5 Takayama-cho,
Ikoma City, Nara, Japan
[4] National Institute of Information and Communications Technology,
3-5 Hikaridai, Seika-cho, Kyoto, Japan

Abstract. Recent interests in conversation in the field of artificial intelligence have expanded beyond the development of particular task-oriented dialogue systems toward technologies for supporting human-human communication in various circumstances. Within such communication supportive approaches, the importance of the analysis of multi-party conversation has increasingly been recognized. In accordance with these orientations, this article outlines a three-party conversation corpus built by the National Institute of Information and Communications Technology, and introduces three preliminary analyses of it that will contribute to the development of Conversational Informatics: The characteriscits of turn-taking procedure in three-person conversation; assessment sequential patterns that appeared in the data; and shared knowledge and interpersonal relationships between participants observable from the assessment sequences in triadic conversation.

1 Communication-Suppportive Approach

There are at least two main concerns of artificial intelligence regarding conversation [1].

a) **Dialogue-Systemic Approach.** In most cases, since the knowledge concerned is restricted to certain domains and tasks performed through dialogues are well defined with reference to their goal states, finite state- or frame-based approaches are dominant [16]. Further, in the field of information search, since the type of user utterance is prescribed to 'question', the trend is toward a stochastic QA approach [24]. Unlike the task-oriented dialogue system, the target of this approach is a large amount of open domain knowledge, though the concern is not the dynamic process of conversation.

---

[1] This classification, and the shift of emphasis from the former to the latter, is based on a classical proposal of Winograd [25].

T. Washio et al. (Eds.): JSAI 2005 Workshops, LNAI 4012, pp. 389–400, 2006.
© Springer-Verlag Berlin Heidelberg 2006

b) Communication-Supportive Approach. The main target is not the inter-action between human-machine, but human-human conversation. This approach subsumes computer supported co-operative work (CSCW), agent-mediated com-munication and so forth. In addition, several off-line uses are also included, such as meeting record creation, visualization and information recycling, which are major research topics in information design [22]. This article primarily pursues the communication-supportive approach.

The communication-supportive approach differs from the dialogue-systemic approach in that the target interaction is that between humans; therefore, sys-tems do not necessarily participate in the real-time process of interaction. This means that if the system participates in interaction, such interaction generally involves more than three participants. This situation is contrastive to that of the dialogue-systemic approach most of which involves only two participants: a user and a system.

2   Significance of Triadic Conversation Analysis

2.1   Multi-participant Interaction

Multiple (more than three) -participant interaction is complex in comparison with a dialogue of two participants. Goffman points out the diversity of 'hearers' and divides them into such participation roles as addressee, side-participant and overhearer [7]. Clark and Carlson characterize the complexity of participation roles in terms of 'audience design'[3]. Audience design comprises linguistic and nonverbal devices by which 1) each participant is assigned a certain participa-tory role, while at the same time 2) the utterance can be understood by all participants. The most apparent issue in 1) is the determination of the proper next speaker [2] in turn-taking [20]. In a conversation including three or more participants, there is no security or obligation for a current non-speaker to be-come the next speaker; determination of the next speaker therefore becomes an indispensable concern for participants. As for 2), though understanding by side-participants cannot be directly examined in this article, it should at least be noted that side-participants must be able to recognize themselves as not se-lected as the addressee and therefore the next speaker. Thus, multi-participant interaction is very complex, so it is crucial to observe what happens when the participant number increases from two to three.

2.2   Triadic Conversation Analysis in Japan

The importance of triadic conversation analysis has begun to be recognized in various research disciplines in Japan in recent years. Here are the following at-tempts of corpus construction, analysis and implementation:

---

[2] This article simply assumes that addressee normally becomes the next speaker, though this is not the case as lateral indirect speech acts where an intended next speaker is side-participant [3].

1. Social psychological analysis of "social skills" in triadic conversation [4] [10]: Clarifying the perceived relationships between nonverbal behaviors and expressive dimensions or impressions and rapports.
2. Social agents mediating network communication between two users and the analysis of their social influence power [9] [17].
3. Multimodal humanoid robots coping with "who to whom" problem in human-human conversation [15].
4. Building interaction corpus [23] and capturing the dynamics of participation framework [12] from ubiquitous or wearable sensor information in poster presentation environment.
5. Systematics of turn-taking and participation roles in triadic conversation [5] [6]: Fine-grained video analysis of nonverbal behaviors like gaze, gesture and body posture.

2.3   Modality Augmentation Approach is Not the Only Way

Most of the researches on triadic conversation mentioned above examine nonverbal aspects of communication and / or influences of conversation on human relationships. This tendency is understandable, given the recent dissemination of computer-mediated communication technology and several related problems in our society. One problem is the paucity of social context information [13] such as nonverbal information, which can be plentifully observed and is actually used by participants in face-to-face interaction. One obvious resolution to this problem therefore is to develop multimodal communication technologies; various methodologies have in fact been advocated in this vein. However, multimodality augmentation is not the only way to improve mediated communication. It is quite apparent that detection of participation roles via nonverbal information, such as gaze and body direction, is only a part of jobs of hearers in different participation roles [3] . Audience design of language use in multiparty conversation should also be reexamined from the perspective of communication-supportive technologies .

Thus, points we especially tried to clarify for the audience design are:

1. What kind of 'linguistic' devices enable participants to find who, or what kind of participant, should or can become a recipient or the next speaker, besides nonverbal cues like gazes? (Sect.4)
2. What kind of shared knowledge and interpersonal relationships between participants are detectable from a variety of audience designs and turn-allocation dependent on them? (Sect.5 & 6)

3   NICT Three-Party Conversation Corpus

The National Institute of Information and Communications Technology (NICT) has developed and analyzed a three-party conversation corpus. The number of

---

[3] Of course, problems of language understanding in context are deliberately escaped in most researches, presumably for the similar reasons of what Winograd [25] has negatively pointed out before.

subjects was 45 (15 triads). Each group performed two experiments and 30 sets of dialogue were recorded. The average duration required for each experiment was approximately 20 minutes.

Fig. 1. Soundproof compartment

Fig. 2. Photo task: these two figures are a) brothers, b) husband and wife for four years, or c) strangers

The speech sound was recorded via DAT and the video image of nonverbal information was via DV. Three DAT decks were utilized: Deck 1 recorded the speech of subjects A+B; D2 recorded that of B+C; and D3 recorded that of C+A on the L & R tracks, respectively. The images of the three subjects were synthesized through the 4-divider and was recorded with one DV deck. The recording by the DV was not for detailed analysis, but for overview of all sounds and images in a dialogue. Each subject entered an individual soundproof compartment to clearly record each speech on an independent track. Therefore, subjects were not placed in a face-to-face situation. We installed two small monitors according to the direction of the input sound so that the members could receive feedback as naturally as possible: A, for example, heard the voices of B and C through the L and R headphones, respectively and could see an image of B in the left monitor and of C in the right (Fig. 1). This environment is like the video telephone conference by three persons, where subjects cannot use eye contact though can obtain speech and nonverbal information. However, the timing of turn-taking seems to be smooth enough.

All subjects were university students. Each group consists of three members of the same sex (besides one group). The following four combinations were prepared: (a) subject A, B and C are friends with each other; (b) A and B are friends + A and C are friends; (c) only A and B are friends; and (d) everyone is a stranger with each other. Each group went through the two tasks consecutively. Experiment 1 was a "photo task" [1], in which subjects are seeking an answer for each of three questions like in Fig.2, on which all of them can agree. Experiment 2 was a "free topic conversation", in which subjects could use an optional topic list.

4   Characteristics of Turn-Taking in Triadic Conversation

Table 1 [4] shows a list of resources for next speaker determination that resulted from our corpus analysis. Unlike explicit devices like vocatives, tacit resources are not specified for speaker selection but have some propositional or modal contents. This means that each of them cannot be used for speaker selection in a context-independent manner, but their functions are implicit triggers for activating shared knowledge or having participants orient to local sequential organization of conversation. Therefore, it is important to clarify their nature of dependency on the context of knowledge or conversational sequences.

Table 1. Resources for speaker determination

1. Nonverbal devices: gaze, etc.
2. Linguistic devices:
   (a) Explicit: vocatives, etc.
   (b) Tacit: references to participants (personal pronouns or names, their grammatical functions are not vocatives but nominatives, possessives, etc.), choices of addressee honorific/non-honorific particles, selection of specific vocabularies (+ 3), discourse markers (+ 4), etc.
3. Use of shared knowledge: Mention to shared episodes, information requests from or giving to someone who does not know them.
4. Use of sequential organization: Second parts of adjacent pairs, continuous questions to the preceding answerer, etc.

Excerpt 1 [5]
   (C questions A and B: 'Have you decided your seminar yet?')
1 B: *A, mada desu ne.*   [→ C] 'Ah, not yet.'
   Haitte kara dayo ne. [→ A] 'Will it be determined after the new
                                academic year begins?'

Excerpt 2
1 B: *Kataku dou natta?* [→ A]   'How did Kataku go?'
2 A: *Are wa na: ichibu.* [→ B]   'It was only by some members.'
3 B: *Ah.*   'Oh.'
4 A: *Camp de sa: adana ga kettei shiten.* 'My nickname was determined
   [→ C]   during the camp.'
5 C: *Ah.*   'Oh.'

---

[4] This list is similar to that of Lerner [10], in which use of "shared knowledge" and "sequential organization" are called use of "social" and "sequential" identities, respectively.

[5] Transcriptional notation: Each line consists of four elements: Turn ID, speaker ID, utterance and English translation. = shows that the line is continuing from the prior line. : shows that the vowels are prolonged. In $_{xn}$/, / shows the starting points of overlapped speech, $_{a\text{-}c}$ means between whom they are (a: between participants A and B; b: B and C; c: C and A); and $_x$ are serial numbers in each except for a, b and c, respectively. =>and ->at the head of line points [1st Assessment] and [2nd Assessment], respectively, these terms introduced in Sect.5.

In Excerpt 1, the former half of the utterance is an answer to C's question and the latter is a confirmation to A who is B's friend and belongs to the same university and class as B. These selections of addressees are expressed by the distinction between honorific post-verbal particle "desu ne" and non-honorific "dayo ne". In Excerpt 2, the use of the word Kataku in 1B implies that it is the one sharing the episode about Kataku with B, who is selected as the next speaker. After this exchange, 4A explains this episode to C, who has no knowledge of it yet.

5   Assessment Sequences in Free Topical Conversation

From the perspective of 'Conversational Informatics' [2], the flood of information [26] is not the only problem. One of the most important characteristics of information included in conversation is the fusion of objective world knowledge and subjective information. The latter includes such 'meta-information' as distribution of knowledge among participants in regard to things, persons or events referred to in the conversation [8][11], and participants' attitudes or opinions toward them [18]. Any attempts to develop technologies of conversational informatics must struggle with how to utilize such subjective information [6]. This section proposes that sequential analysis of assessment patterns appearing in conversation can be contributory in this regard.

Though one of the urgent problems for conversational informatics is how to extract subjective information like attitudes or opinions of participants from conversational data in an effective and reliable manner, it is not easy to do this because these kinds of information are mingled tightly with objective propositional information, and often omitted from the surface forms of utterances. For instance, it could be said that "USJ is interesting" is an expression of the speaker's subjective judgment, while "USJ is in Osaka" is objective information. However, as clearly seen from the following excerpts, even "USJ is in Osaka" and "Cockroaches can fly" will not always transmit only objective information but can sometimes imply the subjective judgment or taste of speakers as well.

Excerpt 3

1 A: *USJ tte Osaka shinai desu yone?* 'Is USJ in Osaka?'
2 B: *Hai, totemo benri desuyo.*   'Yes, it is very convenient.'

Excerpt 4

1 C: *Gokiburi tte tobu yan na, yappa.* 'Cockroaches can fly, can't they?'
2 B: *Iya: kowai kowai.*   'Yeah, it is very very scary.
=: *Iya ne.*   I hate them.'
3 A: *Tobu tobu.*   'They can fly.'
4 C: *Mou sore ga kowai nen.*   'That terrifies me.'
5 A: *Kowai.*   'Terrible.'

---

[6] In addition, subjective information is important not only for anonymous users but also for participants themselves of the conversation, as in the case of recycle of information from past meeting records.

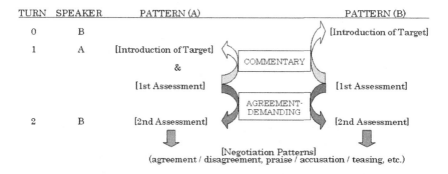

TURN	SPEAKER	PATTERN (A)		PATTERN (B)

Fig. 3. Assessment sequence schema

In general, some expressions like "The score of the test was 28 points" and "We visited a hot spring after the conference", in addition to 1A in Excerpt 3 and 1C in Excerpt 4, regularly evoke subjective or emotional responses from the recipients. In other words, it is one of the most important features of conversation data that some implicit aspects of prior utterances become overt by listeners' responses to them. This nature is properly grasped by the doctrine "responses display how the speakers understand prior utterances" proposed by conversation analysts, called "sequential analysis" [19], which appears most clearly in the formulation of adjacency pairs [21]. From this viewpoint, Pomeranz analyzed assessment sequences in conversation and found that a first assessment makes relevant the occurrence of the second assessment, expressing agreement or disagreement to the first [18]. Based on her formulation, we developed the "assessment sequence schema" (Fig.3).

A typical assessment sequence consists of four elements: [Introduction of Target], [1st Assessment], [2nd Assessment], and [Negotiation Pattern]. The procedures and notices for analysts to identify them are the following:

Agreement Demanding Relation. As mentioned above, the targeted parts are only those which include the pairs of [1st Assessment] and [2nd Assessment]. The relations between these elements are called "agreement-demanding" because the most typical relevant response to the [1st Assessment] is agreement/disagreement.

Commentary Relation. The [1st Assessment] also has "commentary" relations with things or events taken up in the [Introduction of Target]. There are two kinds of [Introduction of Target] according to where and how they are introduced into the conversation: In pattern A, the Target elements are introduced by the speaker of the [1st Assessment] in the same utterance, and in pattern B, things or events that have already been the topics of conversation are retrospectively recognized as the Target by virtue of the occurrence of a [1st Assessment], where those who introduced these things or events for the first time are not necessarily the speakers of the [1st Assessment]; these introductions can be done through several utterances of several participants. In either case, the criterion of identification is the occurrence of the [2nd Assessment].

Negotiation Pattern. There appear various kinds of [Negotiation Pattern], according to whether the [2nd Assessment] is agreement or disagreement, whether the type of attitude in the [1st Assessment] is praise, accusation or teasing, etc., and what kinds of things or events the [Introduction of Target] includes, etc. For instance, when the [2nd Assessment] is disagreement, the speaker of the [1st Assessment] often either tries to justify his or her prior judgment or modifies it in pursuit of agreement [18].

Excerpt 5: The number 6 is big

1 A:	*Doko koukou?*	'Where is your high school?'
2 C:	*Koukou? Koukou wa Edogawa-*	'High school? My high school
=:	*Higashi tte iu kore mata kore*	is called Edogawa-Higashi.
=:	$_{c1}$[*mata miner na un.*	It is not so famous, either.'
3 A:	$_{c1}$[*A sou nanya:*	'I see.'
4 C:	*Kouritsu, Kouritsu* $_{b2c2}$[:	'Public, public.'
5 B:	$_{b2}$[*He* $_{a1}$[:	'Oh.'
6 A:	$_{c2a1}$[*He:,*	'Oh:, was there anyone
=:	*K-dai kita hito otta?*	who passed K university?'
7 C:	*K-dai kita hito roku nin*	'There were six students who
=:	*kana* $_{c3}$[:	passed K university.'
=> 8 A:	$_{c3}$[*Roku nin* $_{a2}$[*mo orun?*	'Six persons is a lot.'
9 B:	$_{a2}$[*He* $_{b3}$[:	'Oh:.'
-> 10 C:	$_{b3}$[*Un, roku nin,*	'Yeah, six persons,
=:	*ooi n kana* $_{c4}$[:	is it big number?'
11 A:	$_{c4}$[*Ooi yo* $_{c5}$[:	'It is big.'
12 C:	$_{c5}$[*Nanka watashi*	'Well, I was thinking that
=:	*sukunai* $_{c6}$[*toka omottotta kedo.*	it was small.'
13 A:	$_{c6}$[*Iya, uchi atashi dake damo:n.*	'No, it was only I who passed from my high school.'

In Excerpt 5, the fact "It was six students who passed K university", counted as the [Introduction of Target], appears in lines 1-7. 8A is the [1st Assessment], in which A declares a subjective judgment that 6 is a big number. This assessment is not agreed upon by the corresponding [2nd Assessment] in 10C. Thus, the fact that six persons passed K university from a high school can be judged as either a big or small number, depending on the knowledge and experiences possessed by each of the participants. The sequence after 10C, which is engendered by this disagreement, should be regarded as the [Negotiation Pattern], in which, especially, 13A tries to justify her argument.

Of course, all implicit aspects of participants' attitudes cannot always be identified by this methodology, and it might therefore seem to be too strict to restrain our analytic focus only on the parts where both a [1st Assessment] and [2nd Assessment] do occur. However, as pointed out above, it is difficult for analysts to securely extract subjective information like participants' attitudes toward things or events, which are an integrated part of conversational information, and therefore methods to do this must successfully provide a way to identify evidence that some attitude information is really used by participants in the conversation. The sequential analysis of assessment patterns proposed above enables analysts to treat only those subjective information items that become overt ("publicized") by and for participants themselves in the particular conversational context.

6 Shared Knowledge and Interpersonal Relationships Between Participants

The combination of two kinds of analyses introduced above, the analysis of turn-taking in triadic conversation in Sect.4 and of assessment sequence patterns in Sect.5, enables us to discover shared knowledge and interpersonal relationships between participants. The excerpts for detailed analysis are those in which either speaker or recipient of the [1st Assessment] is the one who has not become either speaker or addressee (focal recipient) in the exchange immediately before the [1st Assessment]. Here, they are classified as "from or to side-participant", correspondingly.

Excerpt 6: Even though you're in the 4th grade
   (C is explaining the advantage of a part-time job in convenience store.)

1 C:	*A, nanka betsuni isshuukan ni nikai*	'It's no problem if I can work
=:	*demo ii shi, shiken kikan toka mo*	only twice a week, and it's
=:	*meccha raku nan desu yo.*	flexible too even during exams.'
2 B:	*Ah* $_{a1}$[:	'Oh:'
3 A:	$_{a1}$[*Sore wa ii desu wa* $_{c1}$[*ne.*	'That's good.'
4 C:	$_{c1}$[*Un.*	'Yeah.'
5 A:	*Kateikyoushi nante kekkou shiken no*	'In case of tutors, exam periods
=:	*jiki mo kasanatte kuru n desu* $_{c2}$[*yo.*	often come simultaneously.'
6 C:	$_{c2}$[*Hu:n.*	'Oh.'
7 A:	*Demo shiken mae ni wa ma: fudan*	'But during exams, because
=:	*okane moratte irushi, zettai*	I'm ordinarily paid a salary,
=:	*ika nai to ikkenai tte yuu* $_{c3}$[*ka*	I must be sure to go.'
8 C:	$_{c3}$[*U:n*	'Oh.'
9 A:	*Tsugi no hi gogaku ga futatsu arou*	'Even if I have two exams of
=:	$_{c4}$[*to* $_{a2}$[*mo.*	foreign language classes
		the next day.'
10 C:	$_{c4}$[*Ha* $_{b1}$[*hahaha.*	(laughter)
11 B:	$_{a2b1}$[*Hahaha hahhahha.*	(laughter)
12 A:	*Report ga arou* $_{c5}$[*tomo*	'Or even if I have a deadline
		for my report,'
13 C:	$_{c5}$[*U:*	'mhm:'
14 A:	*ikanai* $_{c6}$[*to ikenai*	'I have to go.'
15 C:	$_{c6}$[*u:*	'mhm'

16 A:	*To iu* $_{a3}$[*no ga arimasu kara ne.*	'I think so.'
17 B:	$_{a3}$[*Hahha.*	(laughter)
18 C:	*U:n*	'Oh:'
19 A:	$_{a4}$[*Kukuku*	(laughter)
=> 20 B:	$_{a4}$[*Kimi yon kaisei nanoni mada*	'You're still taking a foreign
=:	*gogaku totteru kara*	language class even though you're in the 4th grade.
=:	*da* $_{a5}$[*me nan* $_{b2}$[*desu yo,*	So, it's your own sake,'
-> 21 A:	$_{a5}$[*Hu* $_{c7}$[*hu.* $_{c8a6}$[*Kukuku.*	(laughter)
22 C:	$_{c7b2}$[*Hahaha* $_{c8}$[*haha.*	(laughter)
23 B:	$_{a6}$[*hahahahaha.*	(laughter)

Excerpt 6 illustrates the "from side-participant" type. As a response to C's argument about the advantage of the part-time job in a convenience store up to 1C, 3-9A compares it with the case of a tutor, and conversation is going on between A and C. The [1st Assessment] is 20B, noting that 1) B has not become a speaker before it, and 2) B's assessment resorts to shared knowledge between only A and B that A is taking a foreign language class despite in the 4th grade. Thus, one who issues [1st Assessment] often utilizes an existing interpersonal relationship and shared knowledge between him and the target person.

Excerpt 7: We are only new acquaintances

1 C:	*Nande ore shin-san shiri attan darou*	'How did I get acquainted with you, Ms. Shin?'
2 A:	*E?*	'Pardon?'
3 C:	*Ma, doko de ore no kao mitakke?*	'Well, where did you meet me?'
4 A:	*Hu, ichiban saisho ni atta no wa: test*	'The first time was at the Fuyou
=:	*no saishuubi no fuyou-kan ja nai?*	Pavilion on the final day of exams, wasn't it?'
5 C:	$_{c1}$[*E?*	'Really?'
6 A:	$_{c1}$[*A, chigau?*	'Oh, that's not right?'
7 C:	*Sou nano?*	'Surely?'
8 A:	*Atashi hajimete mita no wa,*	'The first time I saw you was,
=:	*a test chuu kana test*	oh it might have been during
=:	$_{c2}$[*chuu.*	the exam, during the exam.'
9 C:	$_{c2}$[*Doko nanoka wakaranakute sa.*	'I can't remember.'
10 A:	*Fuyou-kan, fuyou-* $_{c3}$[*kan*	'Fuyou Pavilion, Fuyou Pavilion.'
11 C:	$_{c3}$[*Un.*	'I see.'
12 C:	*De koe kakerarete dare daka jitsuwa*	'But actually, when I was called
=:	*wakatte nakatta*	on at that time, I couldn't find who you were.'
=> 13 A:	*So atashi tachi sugoi: tomodachi reki*	'So, we are only new
=:	*asaku* $_{c4}$[*te*	acquaintances.'
-> 14 C:	$_{c4b1}$[*Asai.*	'Recently.'
-> 15 B:	$_{b1}$[*A, sou na* $_{a1}$[*n?*	'Oh, so.'
16 A:	$_{a1}$[*shichigatsu no*	'It was at the end of July when
=:	*owari yone,* $_{a2}$[*shiriatta.*	we first met, wasn't it?'
17 B:	$_{a2}$[*A mada kotoshi nan?*	'Oh, it was this year.'

Excerpt 7 is the "to side-participant" type. Participants A and C are jointly recalling the situation of their first encounter. It does not seem that the conversation between A and C is not co-telling to B though B has not known this episode. Therefore, the [1st Assessment] in 13A turns the conversation to B in the form of resuming it. It is appropriate for A to introduce the relationship between A and C to B, because only A is an acquaintance of both B and C. Both 14C and 15B are two different kinds of [2nd Assessment] responding to 13A. 14C shows agreement from the standpoint of the one who has shared the episode with A while B in 15 shows himself as a person who hears it for the first time.

Thus, shared knowledge and interpersonal relationships between participants appear clearly in the assessment sequences in the "from and to side-participant" types.

7   Conclusion

In this article, we have insisted on the significance of analysis of triadic conversation to develop Conversational Informatics, and proposed a method of analysis of turn-taking in triadic conversation, assessment sequence patterns as the exchange and negotiation process of attitudes and opinions of participants, and shared knowledge and interpersonal relationships made explicit through assessment sequences between three participants.

Generalization of typical patterns of characteristic phenomena in conversation from the corpus is a sound phase necessary for developing various conversation supporting technologies, and is considered to consist of at least two aspects: What sort of information should be discovered from conversation data and how such information can be detected efficiently and securely. This article has focused on the significance of the target phenomenon and the fine-grained description of it. Hereafter, the efficiency and objectivity of the method are to be examined through constructing a reliable coding schema for corpus annotation and building a method for automatic extraction and utilization of the information.

References

1. Archer, D.: *How to Expand Your S.I.Q.* M. Evans and Company, Inc. (1980)
2. International Workshop on Conversational Informatics: http://www.ii.ist.i.kyoto-u.ac.jp/jsai2005ws/
3. Clark, H. H., Carlson, T. B.: Hearers and speech acts. *Language*, **58** (1982) 332–373 Also in Clark, H. H.: *Arenas of Language Use.* University of Chicago Press & Center for the Study of Language & Information (1992) 205–247
4. Daibo, I., Goto. M., Miyagi, H.: The perceived relationship between the conversation style and the nonverbal cues in a triadic conversation. *28th International Congress of Psychology (ICP2004).* (2004)
5. Den, Y.: Towards a Science of Conversation. *Technical Report of the Institute of Electronics, Information and Communication Engineers.* (2004) (in Japanese)

6. Enomoto, M.: An analysis of nonverbal behavior affecting participation-role taking. *JSAI SIG-SLUD-A301-02* (2003) 25–30 (in Japanese)
7. Goffman, E.: *Forms of Talk.* University of Pennsylvania Press (1981)
8. Heritage, J., Raymond, G.: The terms of agreement: Indexing epistemic authority and subordination in assessment sequences. *Social Psychology Quarterly,* **68** (2005) 15–38
9. Isbister, K., Nakanishi, H., Ishida, T., Nass, C.: Helper agent: Designing an assistant for human-human interaction in a virtual meeting space. *International Conference on Human Factors in Computing Systems (CHI2000).* (2000) 57–64
10. Iso, Y., Kimura, M. Sakuragi, A., Daibo, I.: The effects of nonverbal behaviors on impression formation and rapport in a triadic communication. *28th International Congress of Psychology (ICP2004).* (2004)
11. Kamio, A.: *Territory of Information.* John Benjamins (1997)
12. Katagiri, Y., Bono, M., Suzuki, N.: Conversational inverse information for context-based retrieval of person experiences. *Proceeginds of JSAI 2005 Workshop on Conversational Informatics.* (in conjunction with the 19th Anual conference of the Japanese Society for Artificial intelligence, 2005) (2005) 1–6
13. Kiesler, S., Siegel, J., McGuire, T.: Social psychological aspects of computer-mediated communication. *American Psychologist,* **39** (1984) 1123–1134
14. Lerner,G.H.: Selecting next speaker: The context -sensitive operation of a context-free organization. *Language in Society,* **32** (2003) 177–201
15. Matsusaka, Y., Tojo, T., Kobayashi, T.: Conversation robot participating in group conversation. *IEICE Transaction of Information and System,* E86-D, **1** (2003) 26–36
16. McTear, M. F.: *Spoken Dialogue Technology: Towards the Conversational User Interface.* Springer (2004)
17. Nakanishi, H., Nakazawa, S., Ishida, T., Takanashi, K., Isbister, K.: Can software agents influence human relations?: Balance theory in agent-mediated communities. *International Joint Conference on Autonomous Agents and Multiagent Systems (AAMAS2003)* (2003) 717–724
18. Pomeranz, A.: Agreeing and disagreeing with assessments: Some features of preferred / dispreferred turn shapes. In Atkinson, J. M. & Heritage, J. (eds.), *Structures of Social Action: Studies in Conversation Analysis.* Cambridge University Press (1984) 57–101
19. Psathas, G.: *Conversation Analysis: The Study of Talk-in-Interaction.* Sage Publications (1995)
20. Sacks, H., Schegloff, E. A., Jefferson, G.: A simplest systematics for organization of turn-taking for conversation. *Language,* **50(4)** (1974) 696–735
21. Schegloff, E. A.: Sequencing in conversational openings. *American Anthropologist,* **70(6)** (1968) 1075–1095
22. Shedroff, N.: Information interaction design: A unified field theory of design. In Jacobson, R. E. (ed.), *Information Design.* MIT Press (1999)
23. Sumi, Y., Ito, S., Matsuguchi, T., Fels, S., Mase, K.: Collaborative capturing and interpretation of interactions. *Proceedings of Pervasive 2004 Workshop on Memory and Sharing of Experiences.* (2004)
24. TREC-8 QA Track: http://trec.nist.gov/data/qa.html
25. Winograd, T., Flores, F.: *Understanding Computers and Cognition: A New Foundation for Design.* Ablex (1986)
26. Wurman, R. S.: *Information Anxiety 2.* Que Corporation (2000)

Automated Gesturing for Embodied Agents

Goranka Zoric[1], Karlo Smid[2], and Igor S. Pandzic[1]

[1] Department of Telecommunications,
Faculty of Electrical Engineering and Computing,
University of Zagreb,
Unska 3, HR-10000 Zagreb, Croatia
[2] Ericsson Nikola Tesla
Krapinska 45, HR-10002 Zagreb, Croatia F-91405
{Goranka.Zoric, Igor.Pandzic}@fer.hr,
karlo.smid@ericsson.com

Abstract. In this paper we present our recent results in automatic facial gesturing of graphically embodied animated agents. In one case, conversational agent is driven by speech in automatic Lip Sync process. By analyzing speech input, lip movements are determined from the speech signal. Another method provides virtual speaker capable of reading plain English text and rendering it in a form of speech accompanied by the appropriate facial gestures. Proposed statistical model for generating virtual speaker's facial gestures, can be also applied as addition to lip synchronization process in order to obtain speech driven facial gesturing. In this case statistical model will be triggered with the input speech prosody instead of lexical analysis of the input text.

1 Introduction

Conversational Agent is a graphically embodied animated agent capable of human-like behavior, most importantly talking and natural-looking facial gesturing. A human face can express lots of information, such as emotions, intention or general condition of the person. In this article, we concentrate on two ways for automatic facial animation - Lip sync and Visual Text-to-Speech (VTTS). The goal is to animate the face of a Conversational Agent in such a way that it realistically pronounces the given text. In order to appear realistic, the produced face animation should also include facial gesturing.We have achieved this in case of VTTS through statistical modeling of behavior and plan to extend this method to lip sync as well. Lip sync produces lip movements synchronized with the input speech. The most important issue in Lip Sync research is Audio to Visual mapping which consists of the speech analysis and classification in visual representatives of the speech (Fig. 1). We present a new method for mapping natural speech to lip shape animation in real time. The speech signal is classified into viseme classes using neural networks. The topology of neural networks is automatically configured using genetic algorithms.

We propose a new approach, Autonomous Speaker Agent that combines the lexical analysis of input text with the statistical model describing frequencies

T. Washio et al. (Eds.): JSAI 2005 Workshops, LNAI 4012, pp. 401–410, 2006.
© Springer-Verlag Berlin Heidelberg 2006

and amplitudes of facial gestures. Using a lexical analysis of input text to trigger the statistical model, a virtual speaker can perform gestures that are not only dynamically correct, but also correspond to the underlying text. Fig. 2 depicts training and content production processes. The Section 2 and Section 3 describe respectively automatic lip sync system and autonomous speaker agent in more details. The paper closes with a conclusion and a discussion of the future work.

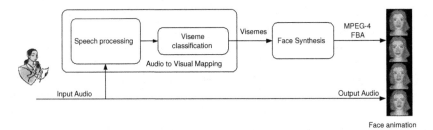

Fig. 1. Schematic view of a lip sync system

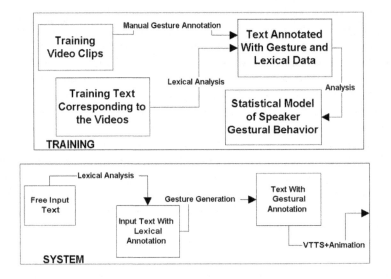

Fig. 2. Schematic view of an Autonomous Speaker Agent

2 Automatic Lip Sync

Lip synchronization is the determination of the motion of the mouth and tongue during speech [1]. To make lip synchronization possible, position of the mouth and tongue must be related to characteristics of the speech signal. There are many acoustic sounds that are visually ambiguous. Therefore, there is a many-to-one mapping between phonemes and visemes, where viseme is a visual representation of phoneme [2].

The process of automatic lip sync consists of two main parts (Fig. 1). The first one, audio to visual mapping, is key issue in bimodal speech processing. In this first phase speech input is analyzed and classified into viseme categories. In the second part, calculated visemes are used for animation of virtual character's face.

2.1   The Proposed Lip Synchronization Algorithm

Our system for automatic lip sync is suitable for real-time and offline applications. It is speaker independent and multilingual. We use visemes as the main classification target. Speech is first segmented into frames. For each frame most probable viseme is determined. Classification of speech in viseme classes is performed by neural networks. Then MPEG-4 compliant facial animation is produced. What follows is short description of the system components.

Phoneme Database. As training data, a set of phonemes is collected. For every phoneme, three different samples were recorded by nine test subjects. This gives 27 versions of each phoneme in our database. These phonemes are manually mapped onto MPEG-4 visemes, and in doing so the database is organized in 14 classes, each corresponding to one MPEG-4 viseme. On average, each viseme class is represented by 50 samples in the database.

For fine tuning of animation, phonemes specific for certain language might be added in the database.

Audio to Visual Mapping. In order to synchronize the lips of a computer generated face with the speech, speech must be first preprocessed and then classified into visemes.

The Mel-Frequency Cepstrum Coefficients (MFCC) representation of the speech is chosen as first step in preprocessing the speech.

MFCC is audio feature extraction technique which extracts parameters from speech similar to ones that are used by humans for hearing speech, while, at the same time, deemphasizes all other information.

Additionally, Fisher linear discriminant transformation (FLDT) is done on MFCC vectors to separate classes. If there is no separation between classes before FLDT, transformation will not enhance separability, whereas if there is only slight distinction between classes, the FLDT will separate them satisfactory.

In order to use MFCCs on the speech signal, frame length and the dimension of the MFCC vectors must be determined. The choice is frame length of 256 samples and 12 dimensional MFCC vector. Overlapping of the frames is used to smooth transition from frame to frame.

The phoneme database is now used as a training set in order to train NN. Every frame of the speech is classified in the correct viseme class. When correct viseme is chosen, it can be sent to animated face model.

MPEG-4 Face Animation. Face animation (FA) is supported in MPEG-4 standard [2]. MPEG-4 FA specifies a face model in its neutral state, a number of feature points (FPs) and a set of Facial Animation Parameters (FAPs). Each

FAP corresponds to a particular facial action deforming a face model in its neutral state. The first group of FAPs contains high-level parameters, visemes and expressions. Only 15 static visemes are included in the standard set.

Facial animation can be generated for any parameterized face model for speech animation if the visemes are known.

2.2 Training Neural Networks for AV Mapping Using GA

Neural networks (NNs) are widely used for mapping between the acoustic speech and the appropriate visual speech movements [4]. Many parameters, such as weights, topology, learning algorithm, training data, transfer function and others can be controlled in neural network. A major unanswered question in NN research is how best to set a series of configuration parameters so as to maximize the network's performance. As training neural network is an optimization process where the error function of a network is minimized, genetic algorithms can be used to search optimal combination of parameters.

Genetic algorithms (GA) are a method for solving optimization or search problems inspired by biological processes of inheritance, mutation, natural selection and genetic crossover. A conventional GA consists of coding of the optimization problem and set of the operators applied on the set of possible solutions [5].

GAs might be used to help design neural networks by determining [6]:

- *Weights.* Algorithms for setting the weights by learning from presented input/output examples with given fixed topology often get stuck in local minima. GAs avoid this by considering many points in the search space simultaneously.
- *Topology* (number of hidden layers, number of nodes in each layer and connectivity). Determining a good/optimal topology is even more difficult - most often, an appropriate structure is created by intuition and time consuming trial and error.
- *A suitable learning rule.*

Training NNs. In our approach, we use multilayer feedforward networks to map speech to lip movements. These kind of neural networks are widely used and operate in a way that an input layer of nodes is projected onto output layer through a number of hidden layers. Backpropagation algorithm is used as training algorithm for adjusting weights. 15 networks, each for every viseme class, is trained since phonemes that are visual ambitious, do not need to be separated.

The 12-dimensional MFCC vectors are used as inputs to networks. For each viseme class, a NN with 12 inputs, a number of hidden nodes and 1 output is trained. The number of hidden layers and the number of nodes per each layer should have been determined for each network. This is laborious and time consuming work since the training session must be run until the result is satisfactory. In order to avoid time consuming trial and error method, we introduced simple genetic algorithm to help find suitable topology for our NNs.

GA and NNs in our Approach. Since the design of neural network is optimized for a specific application, we had to find suitable network for our lip sync application. As determining a good or optimal topology is even the most difficult task in design of NN, we tried to solve this problem with GAs.

In our example, given the learning rule, we used GA for training a backpropagation feedforward network to determine near optimal network topology, including the number of hidden layers and the number of units within each layer.

We use simple genetic algorithm [7], where number of genes specify the number of hidden layers (n). Gene maximum and minimum values are defined in the range from zero to m, determining the number of nodes per layer. If a value of the single gene is set to zero, the number hidden layers is decreased, so practically it ranges from zero to n.

By using genetic algorithms, the process of designing neural network is automated. Once the problem to be solved is coded and GA parameters are determined, the whole process is automated. Although it is still a time consuming work, much time is saved since all work is done automatically by computer.

2.3   Implementation

Constructing database and creation of 15 neural networks have to be done only once. In training process, network's biases and weights are extracted and saved for later use. Together with Fisher matrix (obtained by calculating FLDT), biases and weights matrix are loaded in the application.

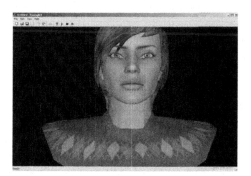

Fig. 3. GUI of our application

Fig. 3 shows GUI (Graphical User Interface) of our application. Application captures speech from the microphone and segments it into frames of 256 samples. When a frame has been captured, data is stored and calculations are performed during capturing of the next frame. These calculations consist of MFCC extraction and simulation of 15 networks. The outputs are added to outputs from the previous frame. Every fourth frame, the viseme class that has the largest sum of output values from NNs is presented on the screen [3]. It is important that calculation time does not exceed time needed for recording of a frame (in case of 16 kHz, 16 bit coding takes 16 ms).

3   Autonomous Speaker Agent

In this article our focus is on facial gestures and how they are synchronized and driven by the prosody and lexical structure of the uttered text. We distinguish three main classes of facial gestures [8]: head, eyes and eyebrows movement. Within each class we distinguish specific gestures, each characterized by their particular parameters. Table 1 shows the types of facial gestures as identified during our data analysis. We introduce symbols incorporating both a gesture type and a movement direction.

Table 1. The specification of facial gestures

Head	Nod	An abrupt swing of a head with a sim ilarly abrupt motion back. We have four nod dire ctions: up and down (ˆ), down and up (v), left and right (<) and right and left (>).
	Ove rshoot nod	Nod with an overshoot at the return, i.e. the pattern looks li ke an 'S' lying on its side (~).
	Swing	An a brupt swing of a head without a back motion. Som etimes rotation moves slowly, barely visible, back to the orig inal pose, sometimes it is followed by an abrupt m otion back after some delay. Five directions: up (u), down (d), left (I), right (R) and diagonal (diag).
	Reset	Sometimes follows swing movement. Returns head in central pos ition.
Eyes	Movement in var ious directions	The eyes are always moving. Parameters are: gaze dire ction, points of fixation, the perce ntage of eye contact over gaze avoidance, dur ation of eye contact.
	Blink	Periodic blinks keep the eyes wet. Voluntary blinks support conversational signals and punctuators.
Eyebrows	Raise	Eyebrows go up and down (ˆˆ).
	Frown	Eyebrows go down and up ( ).

3.1   Lexical Analysis of English Text

The speech analysis module [9] performs linguistic and contextual analysis of a text written in English language with the goal of enabling the nonverbal (gestures) and verbal (prosody) behaviour assignment and scheduling. Starting from plain English text, it produces an XML document annotated with tags for each word. These tags allow the distinction of the newly introduced words, words known from the previous text and punctuation marks. The input text is first phrase-parsed, because the module needs to know the morphological, syntactic and part-of-speech information. In order to get the morphologic and semantic data about words in a sentence, we have made simplified version of morphologic and semantic analyzer extending WordNet 2.0 database [10]. In order to determine the correct word type based on the output queried from the extended WordNet 2.0 database, we must pass multiple times through whole sentence and apply various English grammatical rules.

3.2   Statistical Model of Gestures

As a training set for our analysis, we used the footage showing the newscasters presenting news. We investigated three female and two male Swedish newscasters. Observing those news casting clips, we marked the starting and ending frames for every eye blink, eyebrow raise and head movement. Analyzing those frames, the speakers Mouth-Nose Separation unit (MNS0) value, facial gesture amplitude value, facial gesture type and direction were determined. In our model, the basic unit which triggers facial gestures is a word. The raw data for the complete training set was statistically processed in order to build a statistical model of speaker behaviour. A statistical model consists of a number of components, each describing the statistical properties for a particular gesture type in a specific speech context. A speech context can be an old word, a new word or a punctuator. The statistical properties for a gesture type include the probability of occurrence of particular gestures and histograms of amplitude and duration values for each gesture. Such statistics exist for each gesture type and for each speech context we treated. They are built into the decision tree (Fig. 4) that triggers gestures. The process is described in the following section. Note that, in the context of punctuators, only eyes gestures are used, because the statistics show that other gestures do not occur on punctuators.

3.3   The System

The input to the system is plain English text. It is processed by a lexical analysis which converts it into an XML format with lexical tags. The facial gesture module is the core of the system - it actually inserts appropriate gestures into

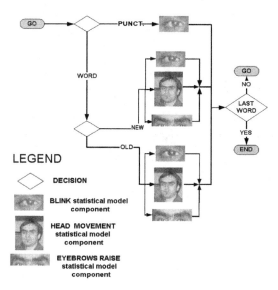

Fig. 4. Decision tree with components of the statistical model

text in the form of special bookmark tags that are read by the TTS/MPEG-4 Encoding module. While the Microsoft Speech API (SAPI) [11] Text To Speech (TTS) engine generates an audio stream, the SAPI notification mechanism is used to catch the timing of phonemes and bookmarks the containing gesture information. Based on this information, an MPEG-4 FBA bit stream is encoded with the appropriate viseme and facial gestures animation. The facial gesture module is built upon the statistical model described in the previous section. The statistical model is built into the decision tree illustrated in Fig. 4.

The first branch point classifies the current context as either a word or a punctuation mark. Our data analysis showed that only eye blink facial gesture had occurred on the punctuation marks. Therefore only the blink component of the statistical model is implemented in this context. The words could be new or old in the context of uttered text - this is the second branch point. All facial gestures occurred in both cases but with different probabilities. Because of that, in each case we have different components for facial gestures parameters.

Results. We conducted a subjective test in order to compare our proposed statistical model to simpler techniques. We synthesized facial animation on our face model using three different methods. In the first (Type 1), head and eye movements were produced playing animation sequence that was recorded by tracking movements of a real professional speaker. In the second (Type 2), we produced a facial animation using the system described in this paper. In the third (Type 3), only the character's lips were animated.

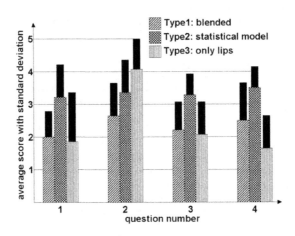

Fig. 5. Results of subjective evaluations

The three characters (Type 1, Type 2 and Type 3) were presented in random order to 29 subjects.The subjects were asked the following questions:

Q1: Did the character on the screen appear interested in (5) or indifferent (1) to you?

Q2: Did the character appear engaged (5) or distracted (1) during the conversation?

Q3: Did the personality of the character look friendly (5) or not (1)?

Q4: Did the face of the character look lively (5) or deadpan (1)?

Q5: In general, how would you describe the character?

Note that higher scores correspond to more positive attributes in a speaker. For questions 1 to 4, the score was graded on a scale of 5 to 1. Fig. 5 summarizes the average score and standard deviation (marked with a black color). From the figure, we can see that the character of type 2 was graded with the highest average grade for all questions except for the Q2. The reason for that is because type 3 character only moves its lips and its head is static. This gave the audience the impression of engagement in the presentation. According to general remarks in Q5, our character had a more natural facial gesturing and facial gestures were coarticulated to some extend. Head movements and eye blinks are related to the spoken text. However, eyebrow movements were with unnatural amplitudes and were not related to the spoken text.

4   Conclusion and Future Work

In this paper we present two methods for automatic facial gesturing of graphically embodied animated agents. One approach is an autonomous speaker agent with full facial animation produced automatically from the plain text. With statistical data that we have gathered during our work, we have confirmed some of the conclusions of other papers. We confirmed that, on average, the amplitude of a faster head nod is lesser than the amplitude of a slower nod. Furthermore, we concluded that the words, that bring something new in the utterance context, are very often accompanied by some facial gesture. An extension to Embodied Conversational Characters is a logical item for future work, adapting and extending the statistical model to include more complicated gesturing modes and speech prosody that occur in a conversation.

As well, we propose our approach for lip sync system by speech signal analysis. Speech is classified into viseme classes by neural networks and GA is used for obtaining optimal NN topology. By introducing segmentation of the speech directly into viseme classes instead of phoneme classes, computation overhead is reduced, since only visemes are used for facial animation. Automatic design of neural networks with genetic algorithms saves much time in the training process. Moreover, better results are achieved than with manual search of network configuration.

However, a face that only moves the lips, looks extremely unnatural because natural speech always involves facial gestures. Our next step will be to extend automatic lip sync system with the similar statistical model for facial gestures as proposed here in order to generate facial expressions in addition to lip movements from the speech signal. But in case of speech driven facial gesturing, statistical model will be based on the input speech prosody, instead of lexical analysis of the text.

Acknowledgment

The initial version of this lip sync system has been implemented by A. Axelsson and E. Bjrhall as part of their master thesis of Linkping University [3] and in collaboration with Visage Technologies AB, Linkping, Sweden. This work is also partly supported by Visage Technologies. Research on autonomous speaker agent is partly supported by Ericsson Nikola Tesla (ETK).

References

1. McAllister, D.F., Rodman, R.D., Bitzer, D.L., Freeman, A.S.: Lip synchronization for Animation, Proceedings of SIGGRAPH 97, Los Angeles, CA, 1997.
2. Pandic, I.S., Forchheimer, R., Editors, MPEG-4 Facial Animation - The Standard, Implementation and Applications, John Wiley & Sons Ltd, ISBN 0-470-84465-5, 2002.
3. Axelsson, A.,Björhall, E., Real time speech driven face animation, Master Thesis at The Image Coding Group, Dept. of Electrical Engineering at Linkping University, Linkping 2003.
4. Dávila, J.J., Genetic optimization of neural networks for the task of natural language processing, dissertation, New York, 1999.
5. Rojas, R., Neural networks, A Systematic Introduction, Springer-Verlag Berlin Heidelberg, 1996.
6. Jones, A.J., Genetic algorithms and their applications to the design of neural networks, Neural Computing & Applications, 1(1):32-45, 1993.
7. Black Box Genetic algorithm, http://fdtd.rice.edu/GA/
8. Pelachaud, C., Badler, N., Steedman, M., Generating Facial Expressions for Speech. Cognitive, Science, 20(1), 1-46, 1996.
9. Radman, V., Leksicka analiza teksta za automatsku proizvodnju pokreta lica, Graduate work no. 2472 on Faculty of Electrical Engineering and Computing, University of Zagreb, 2004.
10. http://www.cogsci.princeton.edu/ wn/
11. Microsoft Speech Technologies, http://www.microsoft.com/speech

Leader Qualification in Managing Nonprofit Organization

Naohiro Matsumura and Yoshihiro Sasaki

Osaka University, Osaka 560-0043, Japan
matumura@econ.osaka-u.ac.jp
http://www2.econ.osaka-u.ac.jp/~matumura/

Abstract. Qualification that a leader should satisfy in managing nonprofit organization (NPO) is revealed by integrating the analysis of questionnaire survey and E-mail archives. Questionnaire survey is applied to 104 staffs in dot-jp, a specific nonprofit organization in Japan. E-mail archives are analyzed by applying the IDM (Influence Diffusion Model) that measures the influential relationships between staffs. The results of this paper conclude that a leader should catch staffs' messages as well as throw messages to construct trust relationships. Otherwise, the leader become self-righteous, and make staffs complaint about the organization.

1 Introduction

NPO (NonProfit Organization) is an organization where staffs are engaged in social activity apart from administration and commercial business. After NPO law was established in December 1998 in Japan, specified nonprofit activities have been promoted by the Japanese government, and as a result, more NPOs have been established than before. According to the government web site, the number of authorized NPOs is increasing as follows: 1,000 NPOs in Nov. 1999, 5,000 NPOs in Oct. 2001, 10,000 NPOs in Feb. 2003, 18,000 NPOs in September 2004[1]. The boom reflects the growing needs of citizens to take part in social activities. At the same time, however, it comes to reveal the difficulty of managing NPOs. This difficulty comes from the mission of NPO, voluntarism of staffs, and the scale of organization:

- The primary mission of NPO is the public benefits, not the profitability. Changing the mission is justified in profit-driven organization if more profit is promising, whereas not in NPO.
- The commitment of citizens to NPO depends on their voluntarism, not on their obligation. Therefore, a leader can't force staffs to engage in a task against their wills.
- As the number of staffs increases, sharing mission becomes a challenge and weaken staffs' voluntarism.

---

[1] http://www.npo-homepage.go.jp/data/pref.html (In Japanese).

T. Washio et al. (Eds.): JSAI 2005 Workshops, LNAI 4012, pp. 411–419, 2006.

Much research showed that the relationships between staffs were crucial properties in an organization for making the most of human and knowledge capital [1, 2, 3]. In the ongoing project regarding NPO research [4], the aspects of capital, scale of operation, human resources, partnerships with government and organizations has been illuminated. Yet the relationship between NPO staffs is not investigated enough although it is quite relevant to sharing missions and motivating voluntarism. In this paper, we target "dot-jp"[2], an NPO established in 2000, to reveal leader qualification by integrating the analysis of questionnaire survey and E-mail archives.

The reminder of this paper proceeds as follows. In Section 2, we briefly introduce the aim, activity, and operation manner of dot-jp. We then present the questionnaire survey analysis in Section 3. In Section 4, E-mail archives are analyzed to reveal leader qualification. Conclusions and directions for future work are given in Section 5.

2   Overview of dot-jp

"dot-jp" is a specified nonprofit corporation in Japan that organizes seminars and intern programs giving university students the opportunity to participate in political activities with diet members. Through the intern program, students learn how diet members engage in political activities in their field.

The period of dot-jp's activity continues six months as a unit, and about half of staffs are renewed when new period starts. At the beginning of each period, staffs have to advertise dot-jp's activity to university students to gather them to seminars. Also, staffs have to contact with each diet member, explain about the activity of dot-jp, and ask him/her to take student(s) in as a intern program. Through the seminars being held several times, staffs fix up an intern programs to each student who is interested in the political activity of a diet member. Then, intern programs start and students experience political activities as assistants of diet members.

The headquarters of dot-jp is in Osaka, and seven branch offices are distributed all over Japan according to the areas (Branch-A, Branch-B, Branch-C, Branch-D, Branch-E, Branch-F, Branch-G [3]). Each branch office is organized by nine to twenty one staffs, and three of them are appointed one of the managers below.

- **Area Manager (AM):** AM is the person who has responsible for managing all staffs in a branch office.
- **Seminar Manager (SM):** SM is the person who has responsible for gathering students to seminars.
- **Intern Manager (IM):** IM is a person who has responsible for contacting with diet members for intern programs.

Most staffs in dot-jp are also university students, and having face-to-face meeting is difficult because of their distant residences and classes. For these

---

[2] http://www.dot-jp.or.jp/

[3] Here we use pseudo branch names instead of real branch names to keep the secrecy.

reasons, staffs mainly use E-mail to exchange information, plan and arrange events, argue and agree on matters. On-line communication over E-mail realize a virtual office, and works as the complement of actual office.

The activity for each branch office is numerically evaluated by the number of both students coming to seminars and diet members accepting intern programs. Each branch office sets goal values at an early stage of each period. The achievement of the activity for each branch office is evaluated by comparing the goals with actual results.

3   Analysis 1: Questionnaire Survey Analysis

3.1   Satisfaction of Staffs to Their Branch, AM, SM, and IM

To investigate staffs' satisfaction to their branch offices, AM, SM, and IM, we conducted questionnaire surveys to 104 staffs working on seven branch offices on March 2005, the last month of the period at the moment. In more details, the questions are as follows:

Q1. Please rate your satisfaction to the activity of your belonging branch office? (1:Satisfaction, 5:Complaint).
Q2. Please rate your satisfaction to the activity of the Area Manager in your belonging branch office? (1:Satisfaction, 5:Complaint).
Q3. Please rate your satisfaction to the activity of the Seminar Manager in your belonging branch office? (1:Satisfaction, 5:Complaint).
Q4. Please rate your satisfaction to the activity of the Intern Manager in your belonging branch office? (1:Satisfaction, 5:Complaint).
Q5. Please name up to three contributors in your belonging branch office?

The results of questionnaire surveys (Q1, Q2, Q3, and Q4) and the achievement rate for each branch office are shown in Table 1.

Table 1. Achievement percentages and averaged satisfaction for each branch office

Branch	% of Achievement	Averaged satisfaction (1:Satisfaction, 5:Complaint)			
		Branch	AM	SM	IM
Branch-A	135	1.22	1.00	1.00	1.21
Branch-B	109	1.63	1.63	1.75	2.00
Branch-C	106	3.31	3.00	1.44	1.38
Branch-D	97	2.42	1.50	3.25	2.00
Branch-E	99	3.31	3.25	2.06	3.06
Branch-F	79	3.13	2.31	2.56	1.69
Branch-G	69	3.18	1.50	2.20	1.70

The column of "% of Achievement" is measured by the following equation.

$$\% \ of \ Achievement = \frac{x}{y} \times 100 \tag{1}$$

where

x : actual number of students and diet members

y : supposed number of students and diet members

Based on the achievement percentages in Table 1, we can understand that the achievement of Branch-F and Branch-G was quite bad compared to other branch offices.

3.2   Statistical Analysis

We applied correlation analysis to the data in Table 1 to reveal the relationships between Branch, AM, SM, IM, and Achievement. The significance level for each correlation is shown in Table 2 where we can recognize that each pair of {Branch, AM} and {Branch, Achievement} has statistically significant correlation, while AM and Achievement have no significant correlations with others.

Table 2. Significance levels for correlations between Branch, AM, SM, IM, and Achievement, obtained from Table 1

	Branch	AM	SM	IM	Achievement
Branch	–	–	–	–	–
AM	**0.052**	–	–	–	–
SM	0.403	0.978	–	–	–
IM	0.457	0.238	0.408	–	–
Achievement	**0.054**	0.634	0.113	0.624	–

3.3   Discussions

Looking at Table 1 based on the discussion in Section 3.2, we realize two noteworthy points that could not be explained yet.

- Staffs in Branch-C did not satisfy the activity of Branch-C and AM although the achievement of Branch-C is high enough.
- Staffs in Branch-G satisfied the activity of AM although their achievement was law.

From the first point, we can presume that staffs' satisfaction to their AM gives strong effect on the satisfaction to their branch office much more than the achievement. And, from the second point, we can suppose that staffs evaluate the activity of their AM apart from the achievement and the satisfaction to their branch office.

To investigate these assumptions, we interviewed 10 staffs individually after questionnaire surveys, and found that the AM of Branch-C was not trusted by the staffs, whereas the AM of Branch-B won staffs' esteem. In the next section, we will reveal leader qualification by analyzing E-mail archives used in each branch office.

4 Analysis 2: E-Mail Analysis

4.1 E-Mail Archives

Staffs exchange information, plan and arrange events, argue and agree on matters on E-mail. Table 3 shows the overview of E-mail archives we analyzed in this study. From the data, we can see that thousands of E-mails were exchanged during a period.

Table 3. The number of staffs and E-mails exchanged on 14th period (October 2004 – March 2005)

Branch	Branch-A	Branch-B	Branch-C	Branch-D	Branch-E	Branch-F	Branch-G
# of staffs	21	9	16	14	16	16	12
# of emails	2297	1198	2465	2076	3258	1309	1717

4.2 Measuring Influential and Influenced Values

Let us explain the IDM (Influence Diffusion Model) [5] that we use here for analyzing the E-mail archives to measure the influential relationships between staffs. In IDM, the influence between a pair of staffs is defined as the sum of propagating terms among them via messages. Here, let a message chain be a series of messages connected by post-reply relationships, and the influence of a message x on a message y (x precedes y) in the same message chain be $i_{x \to y}$. Then, define $i_{x \to y}$ as

$$i_{x \to y} = |w_x \cap \cdots \cap w_y|, \qquad (2)$$

where w_x and w_y are the set of terms in x and y respectively, and $|w_x \cap \cdots \cap w_y|$ is the number of terms propagating from x to y via other messages. If x and y are not in the same message chain, I define $i_{x \to y}$ as 0 because the terms in x and y are used in a different context and there is no influence between them.

Based on the influence between messages, I next measure the influence of a staff p on a staff q as the total influence of p's messages on the messages of others through q's messages replying to p's messages. Let the set of p's messages be α, the set of q's messages replying to any of α be β, and the message chains starting from a message z be ξ_z. The influence from p onto q, $j_{p \to q}$, is then defined as

$$j_{p \to q} = \sum_{x \in \alpha} \sum_{z \in \beta} \sum_{y \in \xi_z} i_{x \to y}. \qquad (3)$$

The influence of p on q is regarded as q's contribution toward the spread of p's messages.

The influence of each staff is also measurable using $j_{p \to q}$. Let the influence of p to others be $I_p^{<1>}$, the influence of others to p be $I_p^{<2>}$, and the set of all staffs except p be γ. Then, $I_p^{<1>}$ and $I_p^{<2>}$ are defined as

$$I_p^{<1>} = \sum_{q \in \gamma} j_{p \to q} \tag{4}$$

$$I_p^{<2>} = \sum_{q \in \gamma} j_{q \to p}. \tag{5}$$

As an example of measuring the influence, let us use the simple message chain in Figure 1 where solid arrows show the replies to previous messages, and dotted arrows show the flows of influence. In this case, the influential value ($I^{<1>}$) and influenced value ($I^{<2>}$) of each staff is measured as shown in Table 4.

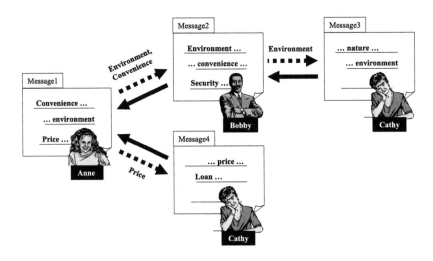

Fig. 1. A message chain of four messages sent by three individuals

Table 4. The influential/influenced values for each staff

Staff	Anne	Bobby	Cathy
$I^{<1>}$	4	1	0
$I^{<2>}$	0	3	2

By measuring influential and influence value, we can understand the roles of staffs in the communication [6]. In this study, we apply IDM to the E-mail archives for each branch office to investigate leader qualification.

4.3   Leader Qualification

At the questionnaire surveys we conducted, we also asked staffs to vote for three staff whom you thought as outstanding contributors. The number of votes shows how much the staff is evaluated. After measuring influential value ($I^{<1>}$) and influenced value ($I^{<2>}$) for every staffs, we applied correlation analysis to the data composed of Vote (the number of votes), $I^{<1>}$, and $I^{<2>}$. The significance levels for correlations between them are shown in Table 5 where each pair of $\{$Vote, $I^{<1>}\}$ and $\{I^{<1>}, I^{<2>}\}$ has statistically significant correlations.

Table 5. Significance level for correlations between Vote, $I^{<1>}$, and $I^{<2>}$

	Vote	$I^{<1>}$	$I^{<2>}$
Vote	–	–	–
$I^{<1>}$	**0.028**	–	–
$I^{<2>}$	0.165	**0.010**	–

These correlations might be the qualification a contributor must satisfy. To investigate this assumption, let us look at the ranking of Vote, $I^{<1>}$, and $I^{<2>}$. Table 6 shows the achievement of each branch office and the AMs' ranking by vote, $I^{<1>}$, and $I^{<2>}$. The results indicate that AMs having high $I^{<1>}$ and $I^{<2>}$ also obtained much votes. We can conclude that having high $I^{<1>}$ and $I^{<2>}$ is the qualification AM should satisfy.

Based on the qualification, we can interpret why the satisfaction to AM in Branch-C was low and why the satisfaction to AM in Branch-G was high. AM in Branch-C did not obtain any vote. The ranking of $I^{<1>}$ was high, but $I^{<2>}$ was quite low (14th out of 16 staffs). This means that the AM throw information to others while hardly catch any information from others. That is, the AM is considered to fail in constructing trust relationships. What is worse is that the AM believed to be a great leader. High $I^{<1>}$ might reduce awareness of such self-righteous situation. AM in Branch-G obtained the most votes, and $I^{<1>}$ and $I^{<2>}$ was ranked high as well. That is, the AM closely communicated with other staffs, and succeeded in creating trust relationships.

The trust relationships around AM can be seen from Figure 2 and 3, the graphical outputs of IDM[4], obtained from E-mail archives of Branch-A and Branch-C respectively. Figure 2 shows that the AM (depicted as p2) is involved in the communication by giving influence to five staffs and receiving influence from eight staffs. On the other hand, Figure 3 shows unequal communication where the AM (denoted as p1) gives influence to six staffs, and receive influence from only two staffs.

---

[4] The figures are composed of top eight influential staffs because of the complexity.

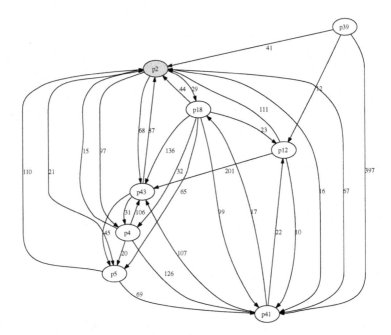

Fig. 2. Influential relationships of eight staffs on Branch-A where each node corresponds to a staff and each arrow corresponds to the flow of influence propagating through message-chain (post-reply relationships of E-mails). Gray node shows AM. Note that AM receive influence from everyone, and give influence to five staffs.

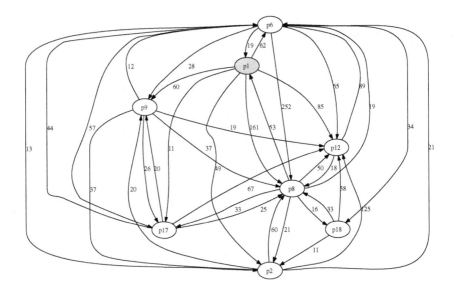

Fig. 3. Influential relationships of eight staffs on Branch-C. Note that AM shown as gray node gives influence to six staffs, whereas AM received influence from only two staffs.

Table 6. Achievement percentages and ranking of AM for each branch office

Branch	% of Achievement	Ranking of AM		
		Vote	$I^{<1>}$	$I^{<2>}$
Branch-A	135	1	1	3
Branch-B	109	2	1	4
Branch-C	106	N/A	2	14
Branch-D	97	2	1	6
Branch-E	99	4	5	4
Branch-F	79	N/A	4	8
Branch-G	69	1	2	3

5   Conclusions

The management of NPO is based on the staffs' voluntarism, however staffs often lose it and eventually leave the organization. The reason comes from staffs' unsatisfactory to the management policy of the organization. This study revealed the importance of trust relationships between staffs to maintain staffs' satisfaction and suggested the approach to construct it. All leaders are not qualified to foster trust relationships. As a future work, we will establish a guideline to create qualified leaders.

References

1. David Krackhardt and Jeffery R. Hanson: Informal Networks: The Company behind the Chart, Harvard Business Review, July-August, (1993) 104–111
2. Peter F. Drucker: Post-Capitalist Society, Harper Business, Harper Collins (1993)
3. Etienne Wenger: Communities of Practice: Learning, Meaning, and Identity. Cambridge University Press (1999)
4. OSIPP Center for Nonprofit Research & Information: NPO 2004 White Paper – The Japan Nonprofit Almanac –. http://www.osipp.osaka-u.ac.jp/npocenter/NPO2004.pdf (2004)
5. Naohiro Matsumura: Topic Diffusion in a Community, Chance Discovery, Yukio Ohsawa and Peter McBurney (Eds.), Springer, (2003) 84–97
6. Naohiro Matsumura: Collaborative Communication Strategies in Online Community, The Fourth International Workshop on Social Intelligence Design (SID2005), Stanford, March (2005)

Part VI

Risk Management Systems with Intelligent Data Analysis

Risk Management Systems with Intelligent Data Analysis – Overview

Takahira Yamaguchi

Department of Administration Engineering, Keio University
3 14 1 Hiyoshi Kohoku-ku Yokohama 223-8522 Japan
yamaguti@ae.keio.ac.jp
http://www.yamaguti.comp.ae.keio.ac.jp/

Abstract. The workshop on Risk Management Systems with Intelligent Data Analysis(RMDA2005)was held in conjunction with the 19th Annual Conference of the Japanese Society for Artificial Intelligence(JSAI2005), Kitakyushu Japan, June 2005. It was the workshop aiming to share and compare experiences on real risk analysis/management systems and to exploit the better integration of risk management systems and intelligent data analysis technologies. The workshop brought together researchers working on advanced intelligent data analysis and practitioners working on risk analysis/management systems in real fields.

1 Introduction

As we can take huge data over electrical social infrastructure, in order to manage many different kinds of risk, we should exploit a new type of risk management systems with advanced intelligent data analysis including data pre/post-processing, machine learning, data mining, XML, domain modeling, ontology engineering, semantic web and so on. The aim of the workshop – Risk Management Systems with Intelligent Data Analysis(RMDA2005)– was to bring together researchers working on such advanced intelligent data analysis and practitioners working on risk analysis/management systems in real fields.

The main topics of the workshop were all fields of risk management systems and intelligent data analysis, including the following topics :

- Risk Management Systems in the fields of Medical, Chemistry, Security, Sensor Data, Social Activities, Human Relationships, and Decision Support in Business.
- Intelligent Data Analysis Techniques such as Data Pre/post Processing, Machine Learning, Data Mining, Active Mining, XML, Domain Modeling, Ontologies, and Semantic Web.

2 Workshop Overview

All submitted papers were carefully peer reviewed by program committee members. In the workshop, we had total 9 excellent presentations in the following 3

T. Washio et al. (Eds.): JSAI 2005 Workshops, LNAI 4012, pp. 423–424, 2006.

sessions: "Risk Management and Data Mining", "Risk Management and System, Security", and "Evaluation and Analysis of Risk Management Systems".

In the first session, we had three talks concerning to data mining approaches to risk analysis/management systems. Abe et al. proposed an integrated approach of data mining environment on a medical domain. Washio et al. presented a state-of-the-art approach and the results on medical risk analysis by using data mining techniques. In the second session, we had three talks that presented practical approaches to realize risk analysis/management systems. Maeda et al. presented a novel warning support system for food safety risk management domain. In the third session, we had three talks about evaluation and analysis techniques for current and future risk analysis/management systems. Ichise et al. proposed a new structure mining method for social networks. Kobayashi et al. proposed a linguistic approach for consumer opinion mining.

We would like to thank all the authors who submitted papers to the workshop and participated in the interesting discussions at the workshop. We would also like to thank the all active program committee members for their efforts in careful reviewing of papers and supporting the success of the workshop.

3   Program Committee

Workshop Chair
> Takahira Yamaguchi(Keio University)

Program Committee (Alphabetical)
> Hidenao Abe (Shimane University)
> Naoki Fukuta (Shizuoka University)
> Mitsuru Ikeda (Japan Advanced Institute of Science and Technology)
> Satoshi Kurihara (Osaka University)
> Yuji Matsumoto (Nara Institute of Science and Technology)
> Einoshin Suzuki (Yokohama National University)
> Shusaku Tsumoto (Shimane University)
> Takashi Washio (Osaka University)
> Yoshimasa Takahashi(Toyohashi University of Technology)
> Hideaki Takeda (National Institute of Informatics)
> Katsutoshi Yada (Kansai University)
> Jerome Yen (Chinese University of Hong Kong)
> Kenichi Yoshida(University of Tsukuba)
> Ning Zhong(Maebashi Institute of Technology)

Implementing an Integrated Time-Series Data Mining Environment Based on Temporal Pattern Extraction Methods: A Case Study of an Interferon Therapy Risk Mining for Chronic Hepatitis

Hidenao Abe[1], Miho Ohsaki[2], Hideto Yokoi[3], and Takahira Yamaguchi[4]

[1] Department of Medical Informatics, Shimane University, School of Medicine
abe@med.shimane-u.ac.jp
[2] Faculty of Engineering, Doshisha University
mohsaki@mail.doshisha.ac.jp
[3] Department of Medical Informatics, Kagawa University Hospital
yokoi@med.kagawa-u.ac.jp
[4] Faculty of Science and Technology, Keio University
yamaguti@ae.keio.ac.jp

Abstract. In this paper, we present the implementation of an integrated time-series data mining environment. Time-series data mining is one of key issues to get useful knowledge from databases. With mined time-series patterns, users can aware not only positive results but also negative result called risk after their observation period. However, users often face difficulties during time-series data mining process for data preprocessing method selection/construction, mining algorithm selection, and post-processing to refine the data mining process as other data mining processes. It is needed to develop a time-series data mining environment based on systematic analysis of the process. To get more valuable rules for domain experts from a time-series data mining process, we have designed an environment which integrates time-series pattern extraction methods, rule induction methods and rule evaluation methods with active human-system interaction. After implementing this environment, we have done a case study to mine time-series rules from blood and urine biochemical test database on chronic hepatitis patients. Then a physician has evaluated and refined his hypothesis on this environment. We discuss the availability of how much support to mine interesting knowledge for an expert.

1 Introduction

In recent years, KDD (Knowledge Discovery in Databases)[5] has been known as a process to extract useful knowledge from databases. In the research field of KDD, 'Time-Series Data Mining' is one of important issues to mine useful knowledge such as patterns, rules, and structured descriptions for a domain expert. Although time-series data mining can find out useful knowledge in given

T. Washio et al. (Eds.): JSAI 2005 Workshops, LNAI 4012, pp. 425–435, 2006.

data, it is difficult to find out such knowledge without cooperation among data miner, system developers, and domain experts. Besides, EBM (Evidence Based Medicine) has been widely recognized as a new medical topic to care each patient with the conscientious, explicit and judicious use of current best evidence, integrating individual clinical expertise with the best available external clinical evidence from systematic research and the patient's unique values and circumstances. These evidences have been often found out in clinical test databases, which are stored on HIS (Hospital Information Systems). Looking at such findings, time-series rules are one kind of important medical evidences related to clinical courses of patients. However, it is difficult to find out such evidences systematically. Medical researchers need some systematic method to find out these evidences faster.

To above problems, we have developed a time-series data mining environment, which can apply medical data mining to find out medical evidences systematically, considering cooperation among data miners, system developers, and medical experts. Through a case study with a chronic hepatitis database, we have identified the procedures, which have been needed to execute time-series data mining cooperatively with active human-system interaction. With this analysis, we have developed a time-series data mining environment, integrating time-series pattern extraction, rule induction, and rule evaluation through visualization/evaluation/operation interfaces.

In this paper, we present an implementation of the integrated time-series data mining environment. Then we demonstrate the process of development of system, evaluating with a case study of time-series rule mining on chronic hepatitis dataset.

2   Related Work

Many efforts have been done to analyze time-series data at the field of pattern recognitions. Statistical methods such as autoregressive model and ARIMA (AutoRegressive Integrated Moving Average) have been developed to analyze time-series data, which have linearity, periodicity, and equalized sampling rate. As signal processing methods, Fourier transform, Wavelet[4], and fractal analysis method have been also developed to analyze such well formed time-series data. These methods based on mathematic models restrict input data, which are well sampled. However, time-series data include ill-formed data such as clinical test data of chronic disease patients, purchase data of identified customers, and financial data based on social events. To analyze these ill-formed time-series data, we take another time-series data analysis method such as DTW (Dynamic Time Wrapping)[2], time-series clustering with multiscale matching[7], and finding Motif based on PAA (Piecewise Approximation Aggregation)[8].

As the one of the methods to find out useful knowledge depended on time-series, time-series/temporal rule induction methods such as Das's framework[3] have been developed. We can extract time-series rules in which representative patterns are expressed as closes of their antecedent and consequent with this method.

IF:
courses of observation period

THEN:
course of prediction period

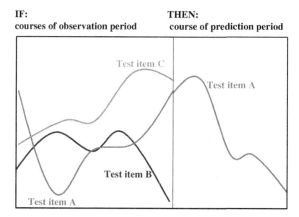

Fig. 1. Typical output if-then rule, which consists of patterns both its antecedent and its consequent

To succeed in a KDD process, human-system interaction especially need at data pre-processing and post-processing of mined result. Current time-series data mining frameworks focus on not human-system interaction but automatic processing. We introduce human-system interaction for data pre-processing and post-processing of mined result with visualization and evaluation interfaces for patterns and if-then rules based on time-series patterns.

3   An Integrated Time-Series Data Mining Environment

Our time-series data mining environment needs time-series data as input. Output rules are if-then rules, which have time-series patterns or/and ordinal closes, which are allowed to represent $A = x$, $A <= y$, and $A > z$ as their antecedent and consequent, depending on selected rule induction algorithm by a user. Fig. 1 illustrates a typical output it-then rule visualized with our time-series data mining environment.

3.1   Designing the Integrated Time-Series Data Mining Environment

Our integrated time-series data mining environment combines the following measure functional components: time-series data pre-processing, mining, post-processing for mined results, and other database operators to validate data and results of every phase. The component structure of this environment is illustrated as Fig. 2.

With this environment, we aim the following efforts for each agent:

1. Developing and improving time-series data mining procedures for system developers.
2. Collaborative data processing and rule induction for data miners.
3. Active evaluation and interaction for domain experts.

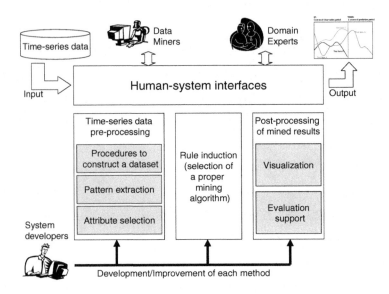

Fig. 2. The component structure of the integrated time-series data mining environment

Since we have standardized input/output data formats, data miners and domain experts can execute different algorithms/methods in each procedure seamlessly. They can execute these procedures on graphical human-system interfaces, discussing each other. Beside, system developers can connect new or improved method for any procedure separately. Only following input/output data formats, system developers can also connect a complex sub-system, which selects a proper algorithm/method to the procedure before executing it. If an algorithm/method lacks of a procedure, they are only needed to develop its wrapper to connect the procedure, because each procedure assumes plug-in modules in this environment.

3.2   Details of Time-Series Rule Mining Procedures

We analyzed our time-series data mining process based on temporal pattern extraction and rule induction methods. Fig. 3 shows the system flow, including time-series rule mining procedures to execute each data mining process.

With this analysis, we have identified procedures for time-series data mining as follows:

- Data pre-processing
  - pre-processing for data construction
  - time-series pattern extraction
  - attribute selection
- Mining
  - rule induction
- Post-processing of mined results
  - visualizing mined rule

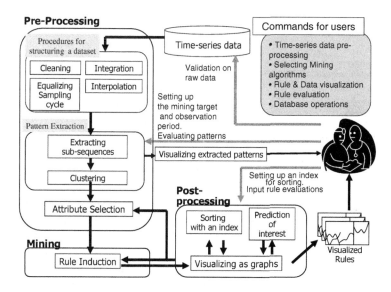

Fig. 3. A system flow view of the integrated time-series data mining environment

- rule selection
- supporting rule evaluation
- Other database procedures
  - selection with conditions
  - join

As data pre-processing procedures, pre-processing for data construction procedures include data cleaning, equalizing sampling rate, interpolation, and filtering irrelevant data. Since these procedures are almost manual procedures, they strongly depend on given time-series data and a purpose of the mining process. Time-series pattern extraction procedures include determining the period of subsequences and finding representative sequences with a clustering algorithm. We have taken our original pattern extraction method[13] for the case study described in Section 4. Attribute selection procedures are done by selecting relevant attributes manually or using attribute selection algorithms[9].

At mining phase, we should choose a proper rule induction algorithm with some criterion. There are so many rule induction algorithms such as Version Space[11], AQ15[10], C4.5 rules[15], and any other algorithm. To support this choice, we have developed a tool to construct a proper mining application based on constructive meta-learning called CAMLET[1]. However, we have taken PART[6] implemented in Weka[14] in the case study to evaluate improvement of our pattern extraction algorithm.

To validate mined rules correctly, users need readability and ease for understand about mined results. We have taken 39 objective rule evaluation indexes to select mined rules[12], visualizing and sorting them depended on user's interest. Although these two procedures are passive support from a viewpoint of the

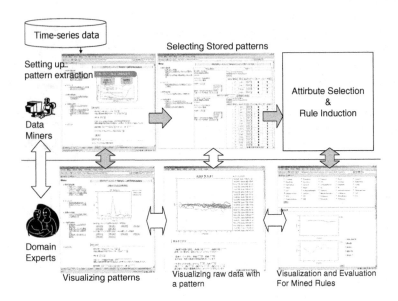

Fig. 4. Human-System interfaces of the integrated time-series data mining environment

system, we have also identified active system reaction with prediction of user evaluation based on objective rule evaluation indexes and human evaluations.

Other database procedures are used to make target data for a data mining process. Since the environment has been designed based on open architecture, these procedures have been able to develop separately. To connect each procedure, we have only defined input/output data format.

3.3 Designing Human-System Interfaces to Team Up Domain Experts, Data Miners, and System Developers for Time-Series Data Mining

We have designed user interfaces as shown in Fig. 4

Data miners are assigned setting up procedure of pattern extraction parameters and selection procedure of stored patterns to construct a dataset, interacting with domain experts. Pattern extraction setting interfaces are separated two phases. In first phase, a data miner set up basic settings such as an input time-series data set, a period for patterns, a target dataset for the purpose of the data mining process, and a clustering algorithm for pattern extraction. Then other detailed parameters such as the period for equalizing sampling rate and maximum interpolation period are set up at detailed setting phase. A data miner also set up detailed parameters of selected clustering algorithm at this phase. Besides, visualization of patterns, visualization of given raw data included selected pattern, and visualization of mined rules have been assigned for domain experts. Each visualization interface can be switched each other depended on their interest.

4   A Case Study About Interferon Therapy Risk Mining with a Chronic Hepatitis Database

To evaluate the implementation of integrated time-series data mining environment described in Section 3, we have done a case study to mine interesting rules for domain expert with this system.

In this medical KDD, we have taken a clinical test dataset from Chiba University Hospital[16], which includes clinical blood and urine test data on chronic hepatitis B and C. Their test intervals are not only daily, weekly, or monthly but also randomized intervals depended on patients statements. This dataset has approximately 1.6 million records. Each record consists of MID, test date, test item name, and test result. This dataset includes 771 patients, who have up to 20 years as his/her treatment period. We have taken IFN (interferon) therapy results of 195 patients as the target of rules, which represent as if-then classification rules. Each instance of this target data consists of MID, start date of IFN treatment, end date of it, his/her therapy result decided with GPT (ALT) values, and his/her therapy result based on virus markers. We have set up observation periods before finishing IFN therapy.

4.1   Phase1: Rousing New Hypothesis in an Expert's Mind

As the first phase of the mining process, we extract some temporal pattern of IFN therapy periods of patients from the chronic hepatitis data. We repeatedly presented extracted patterns with different observation periods, interacting with a physician in real time.

Finally, we could extract the representative patterns about albumin (ALB)[1] as shown in Fig. 5.

He noticed distinguishing patterns on ALB as shown 'pattern 1' and 'pattern 2' in Fig. 5. He validated this pattern with each sequence of patients. He said that 'pattern 0' indicates typical course while in IFN therapy period. However, the other patterns show remarkable courses based on his knowledge. Since he thought 'pattern 2' shows what patients included in this pattern had adverse reactions at the end of IFN therapy period, he interested in their treatment results. On the other hand, 'pattern 1' indicates less reaction to IFN therapy at the end of the period. He roused a hypothesis that patients, who indicate good reaction after IFN therapy, have moderate adverse reaction during IFN therapy.

4.2   Phase2: Ensuring Expert's Hypothesis

To endure the hypothesis, we have extracted patterns of 0.8 years (40 weeks) as observation period for 40 test items. After joining these patterns as attributes of the dataset, we have induced if-then rules with the dataset.

Then the patterns and rules are evaluated by the physician, visualizing patterns, rules and patient data on demand. He interested in the rule shown in Fig. 6.

---

[1] ALB is an important index to comprehend his/her status of chronic hepatitis patients.

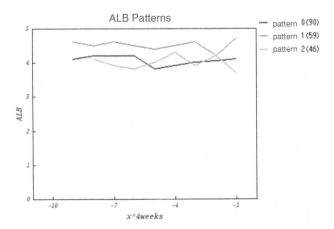

Fig. 5. Representative patterns on ALB while IFN therapy. '-1' on X axis means finishing date of IFN therapy for each patient.

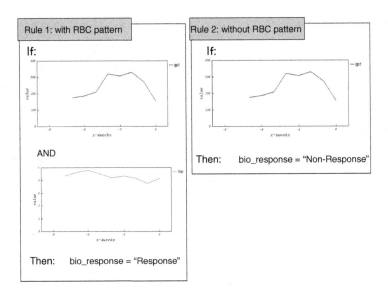

Fig. 6. Typical pair of interesting rules, having opposite class values. Only one pattern is deleted from the antecedent of the left rule.

The right hand end of each pattern means the end date of IFN therapy for the patients. The class values were labeled with GPT values after IFN therapy by the physician. "Response" means what the therapy succeeded. Besides, "Non-Response" means what his/her therapy was failed. These rules shows one of the reasons why IFN therapy success or not, representing how his/her adverse reaction related to their results.

Although the patients included in the right rule failed with of accuracy, the patients included in the left rule succeeded in IFN therapy with of accuracy. The difference is one of the patterns of RBC (Red Blood-cell Count). This pattern shows trend of anemia, which is one of typical adverse reactions (side effect) of IFN therapy. Validating row data with the graphical interface shown in Fig. 1, these patients included in this pattern would be anemia, he said.

After evaluating all of mined if-then rules, he noticed that some combination of patterns show good result after IFN therapy but other combinations of patterns show no good result. He has ensured his hypothesis with this mining result.

4.3   Improving the Pattern Extraction Independent from the Mining Process

With developing the process for IFN therapy rule mining, we have also developed pattern extraction method based on irregular sampling and quantization. Table 1 shows us numbers of experts evaluations.

Table 1. Number of evaluated rules from before and after improvement of the pattern extraction algorithm

Evaluation Labels by a Expert	Before improvement	After improvement
Very Interesting	4	15
Interesting	7	5
Fair	11	11
Difficult to Understand	4	1
TOTAL	26	32

The number of 'very interesting' increases after improving the quantization procedure. Between the two evaluations, we improved this procedure to quantize data points of each sub-sequence with non-parametric statistical measurements[14]. With this improvement of the pattern extraction procedure, we have been able to represent characteristic shapes of each sub-sequence more obviously. So, this result has been caused by one of the reasons why the improvement of pattern extraction algorithm extracts patterns, which can be suitable to his knowledge about patients' course.

5   Conclusion

We have designed and implemented a time-series data mining environment, which integrates time-series pattern extraction, rule induction, and rule evaluation with active interaction on graphical interfaces. As the result of the case study on a chronic hepatitis dataset, we have succeeded in rousing and ensuring hypothesis about IFN therapy in the mind of a medical expert. We have also developed the pattern extraction method, cooperating with the data mining process. This case study also shows the availability of this environment as a development infrastructure to develop both time-series data mining method and specific data mining process.

As the result of the case study on chronic hepatitis, this environment mines valuable time-series rules based on both data and knowledge of domain experts. With these models, we will be able to predict some medical risks such as fails of a treatment in medical domain in easier, faster and more properly.

Although we did not try to select proper algorithms for the attribute selection procedure and the mining procedure, it is also able to connect subsystems for selecting a proper attribute selection algorithm and a proper rule induction algorithm to this environment. Then we will construct time-series data mining application based on active user reactions with rule evaluation interface.

We also plan to apply this environment for other time-series data mining on other domain such as treading, customer purchasing, and so forth.

References

1. H. Abe and T. Yamaguchi, Constructive Meta-Learning with Machine Learning Method Repositories, in Proc. of the seventeenth International Conference on Industrial and Engineering Applications of Artificial Intelligence and Expert Systems. (2004) 502–511

2. D. J. Berndt and J. Clifford, Using dynamic time wrapping to find patterns in time series, in Proc. of AAAI Workshop on Knowledge Discovery in Databases. (1994) 359–370

3. G. Das, L. King-Ip, M. Heikki, G. Renganathan, and P. Smyth, Rule Discovery from Time Series, in Proc. of International Conference on Knowledge Discovery and Data Mining. (1998) 16–22

4. I. Daubechies, Ten lectures on wavelets, Society for Industrial and Applied Mathematics. (1992)

5. U. M. Fayyad, G. Piatcktsky-Shapiro, and P. Smyth, From Data Mining to Knowledge Discovery: An Overview, Advances in Knowledge Discovery and Data Mining, AAAI Press / The MIT Press, CA. (1996) 1–34

6. E. Frank, I. H. Witten, Generating accurate rule sets without global optimization, in Proc. of the Fifteenth International Conference on Machine Learning, 1998, pp.144-151.

7. S. Hirano and S. Tsumoto, Mining Similar Temporal Patterns in Long Time-Series Data and Its Application to Medicine, in Proc. of the 2002 IEEE International Conference on Data Mining, 2002, pp.219-226.

8. J. Lin, E. Keogh, S. Lonardi, and P. Patel, Finding Motifs in Time Series, in Proc. of Workshop on Temporal Data Mining, 2002, pp.53-68.

9. H. Liu and H. Motoda, Feature selection for knowledge discovery and data mining, Kluwer Academic Publishers. (1998)

10. R. Michalski, I. Mozetic, J. Hong, and N. Lavrac., The AQ15 Inductive Leaning System: An Overview and Experiments, Reports of Machine Leaning and Inference Laboratory, MLI-86-6, George Maseon University. (1986)

11. T. M. Mitchell, Generalization as Search, Artificial Intelligence. **18(2)** (1982) 203–226

12. M. Ohsaki, S. Kitaguchi, K. Okamoto, H. Yokoi, and T. Yamaguchi, Evaluation of Rule Interestingness Measures with a Clinical Dataset on Hepatitis, in Proc. of ECML/PKDD 2004, LNAI3202. (2004) 362–373
13. M.Ohsaki, H. Abe, S. Kitaguchi, S. Kume, H. Yokoi, and T. Yamaguchi, Development and Evaluation of an Integrated Time-Series KDD Environment - A Case Study of Medical KDD on Hepatitis-, Joint Workshop of Vietnamese Society of Artificial Intelligence, SIGKBS-JSAI, ICS-IPSJ and IEICE-SIGAI on Active Mining. (2004) No.23
14. M. Ohsaki, H. Abe, S. Kitaguchi, H. Yokoi, and T. Yamaguchi, Development and Evaluation of A Time-Series Pattern Extraction Method Based on Irregular Sampling and Quantization, in Proc. of the 69th workshop on knowledge base systems (SIG-KBS-A405-07). (2005) 39–43 (in Japanese)
15. J. R. Quinlan, Programs for Machine Learning, Morgan Kaufmann (1992)
16. S. Tsumoto, Hepatitis Dataset for Discovery Challenge, http://lisp.vse.cz/challenge/ecmlpkdd2002/index.html. (2002)
17. I. H. Witten and E. Frank, Data Mining: Practical Machine Learning Tools and Techniques with Java Implementations, Morgan Kaufmann, San Francisco. (2000)

Mutagenicity Risk Analysis
by Using Class Association Rules

Takashi Washio, Koutarou Nakanishi, Hiroshi Motoda[1], and Takashi Okada[2]

[1] I.S.I.R., Osaka University
washio@sanken.osaka-u.ac.jp
[2] Kwansei Gakuin University
okada-office@ksc.kwansei.ac.jp

Abstract. Mutagenicity analysis of chemical compounds is crucial for the cause investigation of our modern diseases including cancers. For the analysis, accurate and comprehensive classification of the mutagenicity is strongly needed. Especially, use of appropriate features of the chemical compounds plays a key role for the interpretability of the classification results. In this paper, a classification approach named *"Levelwise Subspace Clustering based Classification by Aggregating Emerging Patterns* (LSC-CAEP)" which is known to be accurate and provides interpretable rules is applied to a mutagenicity data set. Promising results of the analysis are shown through a demonstration.

1 Introduction

Mutagenicity is one of the important biological activities of chemical compounds for our health [1]. Mutation is a structural alteration in DNA. In most cases, such mutations harm human health. A high correlation is also observed between mutagenicity and carcinogenicity. However, the experimental identification of the mutagenicity for all compounds is very hard due to the required cost and time of the experiments. Accordingly, an analytical screening of the mutagenic chemical compounds have been attempted in the field of Structure Activity Relationship (SAR) analysis [2]. The study of SAR between chemical structures and biological activity is a well-established domain in medicinal science. However, the automated classification of the mutagenicity based on the chemical structures is still difficult due to the variety of the structure activity relationships. In recent innovation of chemical analysis technologies, the high throughput screening on the biological activity of chemical compounds became to provide the vast amount of SAR data. The introduction of data mining techniques to SAR analysis will be an efficient remedy to the difficulty of the mutagenicity classification. The extensive and detailed analysis of SAR data by some new classification technique is expected to figure out chemical substructures causing the mutagenicity and to facilitate the drug development process.

In the field of data mining, a new rule-based classification framework has been proposed recently where each classification rule relates a class of instances with

T. Washio et al. (Eds.): JSAI 2005 Workshops, LNAI 4012, pp. 436–445, 2006.

a quantitative frequent itemset appearing in the class instances. This framework called "*Levelwise Subspace Clustering based Classification by Aggregating Emerging Patterns* (LSC-CAEP)" [3] is based on both of "*Subspace Clustering* (SC)" and "*Class Association Rule* (CAR)" techniques. It is known to have significant advantages on both accuracy and interpretability of the classification results. These advantages are highly desired for the SAR analysis on the mutagenicity where the feasible relationships between the classification results and the chemical substructures must be understood by chemists.

In this paper, some related work to LSC-CAEP is described at first to clarify its features. Second, the principle of CAR mining used in LSC-CAEP is explained. Third, the principle and the algorithm to mine QFIs which are the conditional parts of CARs of LSC-CAEP are outlined. Subsequently, the performance of LSC-CAEP is demonstrated for UCI benchmark data in comparison with some major classification approaches. Finally, the mutagenicity analysis of chemical compounds by using LSC-CAEP is shown together with the discussion on the analysis result by an expert chemist.

2   Related Work

Subspace Clustering (SC) is to search numeric attribute subspaces to obtain better clusters than these in the original attribute space. An initiative study CLIQUE performs an axis-parallel grid based clustering where maximal sets of connected dense blocks are searched by greedy merging the blocks in every subspace [4]. DOC seeks dense clusters in every subspace by counting the instances in axis-parallel windows [5]. The computational complexity of the representative grid and window based SC approaches is between $O(N)$ and $O(N \log N)$ which is tractable, where N is the number of instances in data. However, they miss some clusters due to inadequate orientation, shape and size of the axis-parallel grids and windows. The recently developed SUBCLU searches density-based subspace clusters under a rigid density measure proposed by DBSCAN [6, 7]. It uses (anti-) monotonicity property for the dense clusters that the instances in a cluster in an attribute space are always included in some clusters in its subspaces. By combining this property with the Apriori algorithm, SUBCLU exhaustively derives all dense clusters in every attribute subspace. However, because it basically needs the pairwise distances among instances, its computational complexity under a well designed algorithm lies between $O(N \log N)$ and $O(N^2)$ which is often unacceptable for large data sets [8]. Another drawback of these approaches is the less interpretability, because the clusters having high dimensional and complex shapes are hardly understood.

To overcome this interpretability issue, the approaches to mine "*Quantitative Frequent Itemsets* (QFIs)" and "*Quantitative Association Rules* (QARs)" have been studied. The items including numeric interval attributes such as "$< Age : [32, 35] >$" are called "*numeric items.*" A numeric item having a unique numeric value is represented by using a point interval such as "$< NumCars : [2, 2] >$." On the other hand, the items including categorical attributes such as

"$< Married : Yes >$" are called "*categorical items.*" An itemset consists of numeric and categorical items where each attribute does not appear in more than one item in the itemset, *i.e.*, any item does not share its attribute with the other items. An itemset is a QFI if it is supported by given instances (transactions) frequently more than a threshold called minimum support *minsup*. An example QFI is "$\{< Age : [30, 39] >, < Married : Yes >, < NumCars : [2, 2] >\}$" which states "There are many persons who are in their thirties, married and has two cars." Most of studies in this field take preprocessing approaches to partition the value range of each numeric attribute into some intervals and to greedily merge the adjacent intervals [9, 10]. The conventional Basket Analysis is subsequently applied to find QFIs. Their complexity is $O(N \log N)$. QFIs and QARs are comprehensive to analyze the clusters and their inter-subspace relations. However, the discretization of the entire numeric attribute space is not optimal for local instance distribution in each subspace, and the greedy merging may miss the optimal discretization.

The recent study is extending to classification based on "*Class Association Rules (CARs)*" where the body is a QFI and the head a class value. Given a training data set D which is an attribute-value and class table or a set of class labeled transactions, let D_{cl} be a set of all instances having a class cl in D. The body of a CAR is a QFI which is supported by D_{cl} more frequently than a *minsup* threshold. The classification of an instance is made by using the CARs which bodies are included in the instance. CBA is an initiative work on this topic [11]. It seeks QFIs similarly to the above QFI mining, and subsequently CARs are searched. CMAR and CAEP are the successors to improve the performance by using multiple CARs for a classification [12, 13]. Especially the CAEP shows better performance in comparison with the conventional classifiers such as C4.5. However, these approaches have a problem on the optimality of the discretization of the entire numeric attribute space similarly to the above QAR mining approaches.

Aforementioned LSC-CAEP is an efficient remedy to overcome these difficulties. It is based on a novel Subspace Clustering (SC) technique similar to SUB-CLU which is based on a rigid density measure proposed by DBSCAN while extending the algorithm to process both numeric and categorical items. This technique enables a complete mining of QFIs while reducing the computational complexity to $O(N log N)$ by the application of the density measure to each numeric attribute axis. LSC-CAEP derives accurate and comprehensive Class Association Rules (CARs) together with QFIs consisting of categorical items and an axis-parallel and hyper-rectangular and optimum cluster in a numeric attribute subspace.

3   Principle of CAR Mining

CARs in LSC-CAEP are derived by following the principle of CAEP [13]. The training of CAEP consists of two processes. The first process is to derive all rule bodies of CARs. Let the support of an itemset a by D_{cl} be $support_{D_{cl}}(a) = |\{t \in$

$D_{cl}|a \in t\}|/|D_{cl}|$. For every cl, a set of QFIs, $LQFI(cl)$, in which every itemset a satisfies $support_{D_{cl}}(a) \geq minsup$, is derived from D_{cl}. In the original CAEP, this is done through a procedure identical to the standard Apriori algorithm whereas a SC is applied in this paper as described later. Subsequently, for every $a \in LQFI(cl)$, the following "*growth rate*" of a for a class cl is calculated. Let $\bar{D}_{cl} = D - D_{cl}$ be the opponent instances of cl.

Growth rate

If $support_{\bar{D}_{cl}}(a) \neq 0$, $growth\_rate_{\bar{D}_{cl} \rightarrow D_{cl}}(a) = \frac{support_{D_{cl}}(a)}{support_{\bar{D}_{cl}}(a)}$,

If $support_{\bar{D}_{cl}}(a) = 0$ and $support_{D_{cl}}(a) \neq 0$, $growth\_rate_{\bar{D}_{cl} \rightarrow D_{cl}}(a) = \infty$,

Otherwise $growth\_rate_{\bar{D}_{cl} \rightarrow D_{cl}}(a) = 0$.

When the growth rate a is more than a "*growth rate threshold*" $\rho(> 1)$, *i.e.*, $growth\_rate_{\bar{D}_{cl} \rightarrow D_{cl}}(a) \geq \rho$, a is selected as a rule body where its head has the class cl, *i.e.*, $a \Rightarrow cl$. The underlying principle here is to select the rule bodies having the strength to differentiate the class cl from the others. This is more advantageous than the confidence based rule selection of CBA and CMAR. Even if the rule confidence is high in D_{cl}, the rule can match many instances in $\bar{D}_{cl}$. Such rules are weak for classification.

The second process is to derive a "*base score*" of each cl which is a weighting factor on the votes for class prediction. First, a strength of a rule body a is introduced as $support_{D_{cl}}(a)/(support_{D_{cl}}(a) + support_{\bar{D}_{cl}}(a)) = growth\_rate_{\bar{D}_{cl} \rightarrow D_{cl}}(a)/(growth\_rate_{\bar{D}_{cl} \rightarrow D_{cl}}(a) + 1)$. This is because the rule strength is mainly defined by the relative difference between $support_{D_{cl}}(a)$ and $support_{\bar{D}_{cl}}(a)$. Let $LRB(cl)$ be the set of all rule bodies selected from $LQFI(cl)$ in the aforementioned process. The following "*aggregate score*" of an instance t for a class cl represents the possibility of t to be classified into cl by the rule bodies in $LRB(cl)$.

Aggregate score

$$score(t, cl) = \sum_{a \subseteq t, a \in LRB(cl)} \frac{growth\_rate(a)}{growth\_rate(a) + 1} * support_{D_{cl}}(a). \qquad (1)$$

Because the number of rule bodies in $LRB(cl)$ may not be balanced among classes, instances usually may get higher scores for some specific classes. To eliminate this bias, the base score is introduced to weight each class cl.

Base score:
$base\_score(cl)$ is the aggregate score where the number of instances having their aggregate scores less than this score is $Tail\%$ of all instances in D_{cl}.

The classification of CAEP is performed based on the CARs obtained in the training phase. It uses the results of $base\_score(cl)$, $growth\_rate(a)$ and $support_{D_{cl}}(a)$ for all classes cl and all $a \in LRB(cl)$ obtained in the training phase. Given an instance t to be classified, its aggregate score for cl, $score(t, cl)$, is computed from these results and Eq.(1). Then, it is normalized by $base\_score(cl)$ to eliminate the aforementioned bias as follows.

Normalized score

$norm\_score(t, cl) = \frac{score(t,cl)}{base\_score(cl)}$.

cl having the maximum normalized score is assigned to the class of t. Except the derivation of $LQFI(cl)$ for all cl, the computational complexity of the training and the classification is $O(N)$ where $N = |D|$, since it scans the training data only twice.

4   Mining Rule Bodies of CARs

LSC-CAEP searches QFIs of rule bodies from a data set D_{cl} where each transaction consists of numeric and categorical items. LSC-CAEP assumes that dense clusters of the transactions exist with scattered background noise in the subspace. The upper part of Fig. 1 depicts this example where every numeric item takes a point interval (unique) value in each transaction, and two dense clusters exist in a two dimensional attribute subspace $S = \{p_1, p_2\}$.

LSC-CAEP uses a definition of density similar to DBSCAN. This approach significantly reduces the possibility to miss clusters under an appropriate density threshold. LSC-CAEP uses a levelwise algorithm where it starts from the clusters in one dimensional subspaces, and joins $(k - 1)$ dimensional clusters into a candidate cluster $\hat{C}^S$ in k dimensional subspace S. While this is similar to SUBCLU, LSC-CAEP can derive clusters on both numeric and categorical items by embedding the levelwise subspace clustering into the standard Apriori algorithm. At each level, first, it derives frequent itemsets consisting of categorical items and numeric item's attributes, then second, dense clusters in S formed by the numeric attributes in the frequent itemsets are searched. The clusters supported more than a minimum support ($minsup$) in numeric and categorical attribute subspaces are exhaustively mined.

To avoid $O(N^2)$ computational complexity, LSC-CAEP does not compute the pairwise distances among transactions. Instead, it projects transactions in a candidate dense cluster $\hat{C}^S$ onto each attribute axis of the subspace S. The upper part of Fig. 1 shows a case that $\hat{C}^S$ is a $[0, 100] \times [0, 100]$ region. All maximal density-connected sets are searched in the transactions projected onto every axis p, where a density-connected set on p is such that for each transaction in the set $\pm \Delta_p$ neighborhood on p has to contain at least a minimum number of $MinPts$ transactions, and a maximal density-connected set is a density-connected set which is not contained in any other density-connected set. An intersection of the maximal density-connected sets on all axes in the subspace becomes a new $\hat{C}^S$ due to the (anti-)monotonicity of the density. In Fig. 1, the four intersections are new $\hat{C}^S$. These projection and searching maximal density-connected sets are iterated until each $\hat{C}^S$ converges to a dense cluster C^S. The two intersections containing the dense clusters in Fig. 1 are retained under this iteration and the rest pruned. In the lower part of Fig. 1, dense region of each retained intersection is further narrowed down to ensure the density within the region projected to every axis. Because the density on every axis is evaluated in a scan of sorted transactions, the complexity of this algorithm is expected to be $O(N \log N)$.

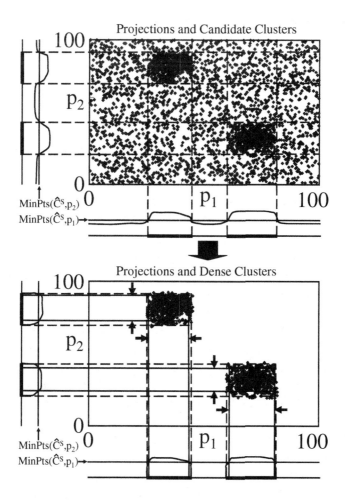

Fig. 1. Derivation of dense clusters

In the search of maximal density-connected sets on an axis, if $MinPts$ is lower than the background noise level, the projection of dense clusters may be buried in the background. If it is too high, the projection of dense clusters may be missed. Accordingly, $MinPts$ is adapted to $MinPts(\hat{C}^S, p)$ which is the expected number of transactions projected to the $\pm\Delta_p$ neighborhood on an axis p from each $\hat{C}^S$ assuming that $\hat{C}^S$ has the average density of the subspace S. $MinPts(\hat{C}^S, p)$ is always between the densities of the dense cluster and the background. In Fig. 1, $MinPts(\hat{C}^S, p)$ efficiently extracts the maximal density-connected sets reflecting the dense clusters. This adaptive density threshold further accelerates LSC-CAEP, because $MinPts(\hat{C}^S, p)$ is higher for a lower subspace dimension, and prunes more maximal density-connected sets below the noise level. In summary, LSC-CAEP takes the input parameters Δ_p (usually given by a unique relative width α_Δ over the total range of data on every axis) and $minsup$.

5   Evaluation of Classification Performance

Table 1 shows the comparison of accuracy among C4.5, CBA and LSC-CAEP in the experiments by using 23 data sets in UCI repository. The accuracies of C4.5 and CBA were evaluated through 10 fold cross validations. J48 implemented in a data mining tool, Weka [15], was used for C4.5. CBA was obtained from its authors. The default parameters are applied to C4.5 and CBA.

The optimal parameters of LSC-CAEP was determined by a grid search of the parameter combinations to minimize the average classification error of 10 fold cross validations for each data set. The parameters of LSC-CAEP are $minsup$, α_Δ, ρ and $Tail$. Mining QFIs for the rule bodies which computational complexity is $O(NlogN)$ needs the parameters of $minsup$ and α_Δ. The other part to mine the relations between the rule bodies and the rule heads by following the principle of CAEP is only $O(N)$, and takes ρ and $Tail$. Accordingly, the grid search of ρ and $Tail$ was made over their wide ranges, whereas the search on $minsup$ and α_Δ was limited to their feasible ranges based on our experience.

Table 1. Comparison of accuracies

dataset	num. of records	num. of attri-butes(numeric)	num. of classes	C4.5	CBA	LSC-CAEP	SD of LSC-CAEP
Australian	690	14(6)	2	.8608	.8538	**.8666**	.0347
Cars	392	7(6)	3	.9617	.9744	**1.0000**	0
Cleve	303	13(5)	2	.7656	.8283	**.8383**	.0422
Crx	690	15(6)	2	.8608	.8538	**.8715**	.0442
Diabetes	768	8(8)	2	.7226	**.7445**	.7229	.0681
Ecoli	336	8(7)	8	**.8422**	.7018	.7794	.0992
German	1000	20(7)	2	.7070	**.7350**	.7173	.0517
Heart	270	13(6)	2	.7666	8187	**.8222**	.0694
Hepatitis	155	19(6)	2	**.8387**	.8182	.8236	.1062
Horse	368	22(8)	2	.6933	.8236	**.8394**	.0488
Hypo	3163	25(7)	2	**.9889**	.9826	.9793	.0071
Iris	150	4(4)	3	.9600	.9467	**.9733**	.0466
Labor	57	16(8)	2	.7368	.8633	**.9500**	.1124
Led7	3200	7(0)	10	.7337	.7206	**.7400**	.0117
Lymph	148	18(2)	4	.7635		**.8157**	.1189
Nursery	12960	8(0)	5	**.9705**	.8289	.9408	.0048
Pima	768	8(8)	2	**.7382**	.7290	.7141	.0338
Sonar	208	60(60)	2	**.7884**	.7746	.6681	.1288
Tae	151	5(1)	3	**.5099**	.4717	.5067	.1470
Tic-Toc-Toe	958	9(0)	2	.8507	.9959	**1.0000**	0
waveform	5000	21(21)	3	.7664	**.7968**	.7886	.0153
Wine	178	13(13)	3	.9382	.9496	**.9833**	.0374
Zoo	101	16(0)	7	.9207	**.9709**	.9309	.0477
Average				.8123	.8264	**.8379**	.0555

The final classification accuracies of LSC-CEAP were evaluated through 10 fold cross validations over the randomly shuffled original data sets.

Table 1 indicates the top accuracies for each data set by a bold face. The bottom row shows the average accuracy of each classifier over the 23 data sets. The right most column shows the standard deviations of the accuracies of LSC-CAEP over the 10 fold cross validations. The difference between the best accuracy and the second best is smaller than the standard deviation for each data except car, nursery, tic-toc-toe. Accordingly, LSC-CAEP is not very significant in terms of the absolute difference of the accuracy from the other methods. However, the average accuracy of LSC-CAEP is higher than the other methods. Under a scoring to assign 2 points to the best method and 1 point to the second for each data, the total scores of C4.5, CBA and LSC-CAEP are 19, 18 and 32 points respectively. Moreover, LSC-CAEP took the first place for 12 data sets among 23. Under the assumption of equal accuracy of three methods, the probability of this fact which follows a binominal distribution $B(23, 1/3)$ is $_{23}C_{12}(1/3)^{12}(2/3)^{11} = 2.9\%$. Based on these observations, LSC-CAEP is concluded to outperform C4.5 and CBA.

6   Mutagenicity Risk Analysis

Data sets on the mutagenicity of 230 chemical compounds are released for a benchmark of KDD Challenge 2000 in PKDD2000 conference [16]. We applied the LSC-CAEP to a dataset called MOE.CSV which includes 2D descriptors generated using the MOE QuaSAR-Descriptors. This data contains 102 attributes which include weight, density, hydrophobicity, geometric and physical descriptors of each molecule such as diameters, surface areas, shape parameters, bond connectivity, numbers of atoms and bonds of each type, electric charge distribution parameters and van der Waals force parameters. The quantitative mutagenicity activity of each instance is discretized by an expert chemist into four class levels of Inactive, Low, Medium and High. The parameters of LSC-CAEP are set as $\alpha_\Delta = 0.1Cminsup = 0.01$, $\rho = 1.3$ and $Tail = 50\%$ according to parameter survey.

Figure 2 represents QFIs of each class on an der Waals force area and volume plain. They should have a positive correlation in physics, and this fact is clearly reflected. In addition, this result indicates that higher values of vdw.area and vdw.vol lead high mutagenicity. LSC-CAEP can easily discover this type of quantitative correlation and its association with class values among massive attributes while this has been difficult within the conventional statistics and data mining. The followings are a set of rules on the inactivity having significant aggregate scores.

$\{< logP(o/w) : [1.69, -2.63] >\} \Rightarrow Inactive$
$\{< PEOE_PC+ : [0.659, 1.11] >, < PEOE_PC- : [-1.11, -0.659] >\} \Rightarrow Inactive$
$\{< radius : [3.0, -3.0] >, < vdw.area : [127.2, 162.4] >, < vdw.vol : [152.7, -198.1] >\} \Rightarrow Inactive$

The expert chemist suggested based on these rules that LogP (hydrophobicity), vdw.area, vdw.vol, radius and PC (number of positive valence electrons) of each

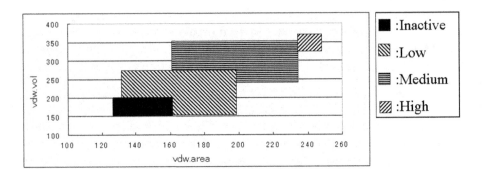

Fig. 2. QFIs of each class on vdw.area-vdw.vol plain

molecule are mutually correlated among inactive molecules, and could build a feasible assumption that hydrophobic and small molecules having less electric charge skewness have a tendency to be inactive. Based on the high rule interpretability, the risk of the mutagenicity of every chemical compound supported by chemical expertise can be predicted.

7 Conclusion

The generic high accuracy and interpretability of CARs derived by LSC-CAEP have been demonstrated through its application to the benchmark datasets of UCI and KDD2000 Challenge. Especially, its high practicality for chemical risk analysis has been demonstrated. Further study on the wide applicability of LSC-CAEP is currently underway.

Acknowledgements

This study has been supported by Grant-in-Aid for Scientific Research No.16300045 and No.17650042 of the Japan Society for the Promotion of Science (JSPS).

References

1. Debnath, A.K. et al.: Structure-Activity Relationship of Mutagenic Aromatic and Heteroaromatic Nitro compounds. J. Med. Chem. **34** (1991) 786–797
2. Klopman G.: Artificial Intelligence Approach to Structure-Activity Studies. J. Amer. Chem. Soc. **106** (1984) 7315–7321
3. Washio, T., Nakanishi, K., Motoda, H.: Deriving Class Association Rules Based on Levelwise Subspace Clustering. Proc. of PKDD2005: 9th European Conference on Principles and Practice of Knowledge Discovery in Databases. LNAI **3721** (2005) 692–700

4. Agrawal, R., Gehrke, J., Gunopulos, D., Raghavan, P.: Automatic subspace clustering of high dimensional data for data mining applications. Proc. of the 1998 ACM SIGMOD international conference on Management of data (1998) 94–105
5. Procopiuc, C.M., Jones, M., Agarwal, P.K., Murali, T.M.: A Monte Carlo algorithm for fast projective clustering. Proc. of the 2002 ACM SIGMOD international conference on Management of data. (2002) 418–427
6. Kailing, K., Kriegel, H.P., Kroger, P.: Density-Connected Subspace Clustering for High-Dimensional Data. Proc. Fourth SIAM International Conference on Data Mining (SDM'04). (2004) 246–257
7. Ester, M., Kriegel, H.P., Sander, J., Xu, X.: A density-based algorithm for discovering clusters in large spatial databases with noise. Proc. 2nd Int. Conf. on Knowledge Discovery and Data Mining. (1996) 226–231
8. Brecheisen, S., Kriegel, H.P., Pfeifle, M.: Efficient density-based clustering of complex objects. Proc. of Fourth IEEE International Conference on Data Mining (2004) 43–50
9. Srikant, R., Agrawal, R.: Mining quantitative association rules in large relational tables. Proc. of 1996 ACM SIGMOD Int. Conf. on Management of Data. (1996) 1–12
10. Wang, K., Hock, S., Tay, W., Liu, B.: Interestingness-based interval merger for numeric association rules. Proc. of 4th Int. Conf. on Knowledge Discovery and Data Mining (KDD) (1998) 121–128
11. Liu, B., Hsu, W., Ma, Y.: Integrating classification and association rule mining. Proc. of Fourth International Conference on Knowledge Discovery and Data Mining (1998)
12. Li, W., Han, J., Pei, J.: Cmar: Accurate and efficient classification based on multiple class-association rules. Proc. of First IEEE International Conference on Data Mining (2001) 369–376
13. Dong, G., Zhang, X., Wong, L., Li, J.: Caep: Classification by aggregating emerging patterns. Proc. of Second International Conference on Discovery Science, LNCS **1721** (1999) 30–42
14. Friedman, N., Geiger, D., Goldszmidt, M.: Bayesian network classifiers. Machine Learning **29** (1997) 131–163
15. Witten, I.H., Frank, E.: Data Mining: Practical Machine Learning Tools and Techniques (2nd ed.). Morgan Kaufmann (2005).
16. Okada, T.: Guide to the Mutagenicity Data Set. KDD Challenge 2000 in PKDD2000: The Fourth European Conference on Principles and Practice of Knowledge Discovery in Databases. (2000) http://www.clab.kwansei.ac.jp/mining/datasets/PAKDD2000/okd.htm

An Early Warning Support System for Food Safety Risks

Yasunobu Maeda[1], Norio Kurita[1], and Saburo Ikeda[2]

[1] Department of Systems Engineering, Shizuoka University,
3-5-1 Johoku, Hamamatsu, Shizuoka 432-8561 Japan
maeda@sys.eng.shizuoka.ac.jp
[2] Professor Emeritus, University of Tsukuba

Abstract. An early warning support system for food safety risks is developed. This system is designed for people to facilitate the detection of signs of risks from a variety of documents that are scattered in the WWW. This system comprises two parts—clearinghouse and the Risk Path Finder. The former is a database of documents related to food safety risks, which are retrieved from the WWW by using Google Web APIs. The latter visualizes the relationship between terms and documents and enables users to find the paths from sources to risk events. For this function, the system utilizes GETA, the generic engine for transposable association, and DualNAVI, a user interface for text retrieval by using GETA.

1 Introduction

Innovations in science and technology are considered to have significantly benefited society at large. On the other hand, a variety of new types of risks have emerged in modern society as well as the global environment since the late 20th century.

For example, health risks from electromagnetic fields, new types of food safety risks—such as genetically modified organisms (GMO) and bovine spongiform encephalopathy (BSE)—and biodiversity risks caused by the invasion of exotic species, which are globally proliferated by developed transportation technologies, are included in these types of risks. The manner in which our society copes with the types of risks, which are called "new emerging environmental and technological risks" [1, 2] or "systemic risks"[3], is a significant social issue.

These risks are considered to have three characteristics: complexity, uncertainty, and ambiguity[3]. Therefore, the conventional risk-based approach, in which risks are managed on the basis of the results of science-based risk assessment, is not necessarily appropriate to deal with them. On the other hand, the precaution-based approach or precautionary framework has been widely proposed as the basic principle to deal with such types of risks. The Commission of European Communities stated that "the precautionary principle covers specific circumstances where scientific evidence is insufficient, inconclusive or uncertain and there are indications through preliminary objective scientific evaluation that

T. Washio et al. (Eds.): JSAI 2005 Workshops, LNAI 4012, pp. 446–457, 2006.

there are reasonable grounds for concern that the potentially dangerous effects on the environment, human, animal or plant health may be inconsistent with the chosen level of protection"[4].

However, the precautionary approach for these risks requires the detection of their signs and the deliberation of countermeasures based on the detection. This study proposes a type of decision support information system supporting early warning for one of these risks by helping detection of signs of the risk.

The basic concept for detecting the risk sings is as follows. In "Early Risk Detection in Environmental Health" written by Wiedemann et al.[5], risks are categorized into three types: "known risks", "unclear risks", and "new risk fields." If a risk is known and can be proven by evidence, it is categorized as known risks, while those that are known but lack sufficient evidence to be proven are unclear risks. The new risk fields include those that have never been experienced or perceived by people. This study focuses on new risk fields. Wiedemann et al.[5] state that the identification of new risk fields is primarily based on qualitative methods, particularly the scenario technology. In this study, the proposed system is designed for users to facilitate the determination of causal paths from the sources to the consequences in risk scenarios.

This system comprises two subsystems: clearinghouse for food safety risks and the Risk Path Finder (Fig 1). The clearinghouse for food safety risks is a database of documents on food safety risks. It is designed for providing comprehensive knowledge about the risk events; this knowledge is required for determining the possible paths from causes to consequences. The Risk Path Finder is a tool that facilitates the determination of the relationships between causes and consequences from a pile of documents. The target users of this system are Japanese consumers who are concerned about food safety risks.

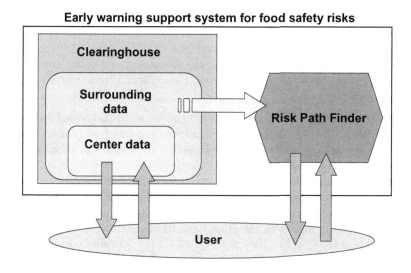

Fig. 1. System framework

With regard to food policy, early warning support systems pertaining to food production were developed from the viewpoint of food security by FAO[6] and Matsumura[7]. Wiedemann[5] proposed a framework of early warning systems for environmental health risks that involve food safety. In addition, Maeda[8] also developed a framework of this system for food safety. This paper discusses the results obtained by the implementation of this system.

2   Clearinghouse for Food Safety Risks

The subsystem of the clearinghouse for food safety risks is designed along the following lines. Firstly, the system deals with documents on food safety risks. Secondly, the target users of this system are consumers who are concerned about food safety risks. Finally, the documents stored in the clearinghouse are collected from the WWW in a semi-automatic manner. There exist two examples of the clearinghouse with regard to food safety—JIFSAN Food Safety Risk Analysis Clearinghouse[9] and UNEP CBD Biosafety Clearinghouse[10]. These systems are maintained by teams of experts in food safety, genetic engineering, systems engineering, and library science; further, the systems contain only quality documents selected by the experts themselves. However, this approach requires the participation of qualified experts and involves high costs. Hence, in this study, a less expensive method is adopted for building the clearinghouse, in which documents are collected and selected by a set of program codes of knowledge engineering tools.

The algorithm used for collecting and selecting the documents is as follows:

1. Keywords for collecting the documents are selected based on interviews with experts in food safety.
2. HTML documents are retrieved by using keywords in Google[11].
3. The retrieved documents are ranked and selected by an evaluation procedure utilizing the glossaries of technical terms in food safety risks.

Sixty-five keywords pertaining to food safety risks were selected. A set of program codes written in Perl retrieves the documents by using keywords and generates Web pages of the clearinghouse. The following procedures are carried out in the program codes:

- The retrieval of document files by using the keywords is carried out by using Google Web APIs[12]. For each keyword, the top hundred files are obtained. The file group that is obtained is referred to as "center data," which acts as the contents of the clearinghouse.
- The files that are directly or indirectly linked with the center data are extracted. For each center data file, up to 20 linked files are extracted. These files are termed "surrounding data." Both the center data and surrounding data are used as inputs to the Risk Path Finder.
- The "Importance" of the files in the center data is evaluated with regard to each keyword. In this study, the importance I of a file is defined as follows:

$$I = P_g \times D_s, \tag{1}$$

where P_g is the "Google point," which is defined as

$$P_g = 101 - R_g. \tag{2}$$

Here, R_g indicates the ranking of the file by Google Web APIs and D_s denotes the "degree of specialty" of the file, which is defined as follows:

$$D_s = n_s/l, \tag{3}$$

where n_s is the number of technical terms in food safety risks that appeared in the file and l, the length of the file. The technical terms listed in the "food safety" section of the draft of the Dictionary for Risk Analysis[13] edited by the Society for Risk Analysis Japan-Section, and the food safety glossary edited by the Food Safety Committee in the Cabinet Office, Japan[14], are used for determining n_s.

- The HTML files for representing the ranking chart of the files for each keyword are automatically generated.

3   Risk Path Finder

The design of the Risk Path Finder, which is another subsystem for detecting the signs of food safety risks, is based on the following hypothesis: people are unable to recognize the emergence of risk events if they fail to identify the paths from the causes to the consequences of these events. For exapmple, as shown in Fig. 2, there exists a path from source A to the consequence of risk event D through events B and C. If the risk managers acknowledge all these paths, problems do not arise. However, if they failed to notice path BC, although they were aware of paths AB and CD, they would estimate that the possibility of the occurrence of risk event D would below.

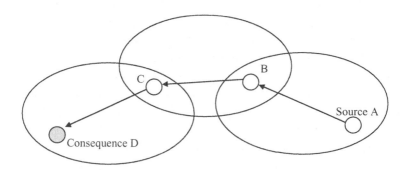

Fig. 2. Causal path of a risk event

In such a situation, if the risk managers are informed that path ABCD exists as a combination of the fragments of information of path AB, BC, and CD, it will lead to an awareness of the emerging risk.

The Risk Path Finder is designed on the basis of this concept. This system visually displays the interrelation of about 350,000 HTML files included in the center and surrounding data by using DualNAVI[15]. The Risk Path Finder is a system that facilitates in determining the path of the risk event that is hidden in a pile of documents by visualizing the interrelations of the documents.

DualNAVI is a text retrieval system designed to assist users approaching to their goals through interactions between the users and the system by simultaneously visualizing the interrelation of documents as well as that of the topics included in the documents.

Fig. 3 shows an example of DualNAVI. (This is not an image of the Risk Path Finder, but the DualNAVI BACE[16] maintained by the Human Genome Analysis Center, University of Tokyo). When a keyword is input (in this case, "risk"), documents containing this word are retrieved and listed in the left pane, while the interrelation of the terms (topic words) included in these documents is displayed as a topic-word graph in the right pane. Words appearing unusually frequently in the retrieval results are extracted as topic words. A pair of topic words is linked if they co-appear very frequently in the retrieval results. The topic words are arranged roughly in the order of their frequencies. Upper part words have relatively higher frequencies.

If a document title that appeared in the left pane is selected, the right pane changes and shows a graph of words included in the document (Fig. 4). In addition, if a word (e.g., "mutation") in the topic-word graph is clicked, the documents including the word are retrieved and the left pane displays a list of the retrieved results, while the topic-word graph in the right pane is rearranged (Fig. 5). In this manner, users can trace the interrelations of documents by understanding the interrelation of terms and documents.

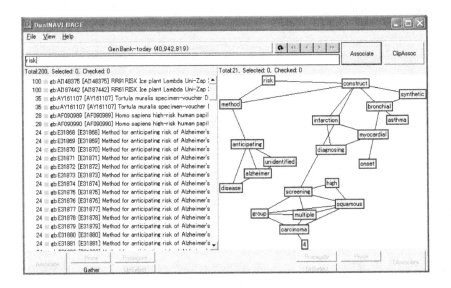

Fig. 3. DualNAVI

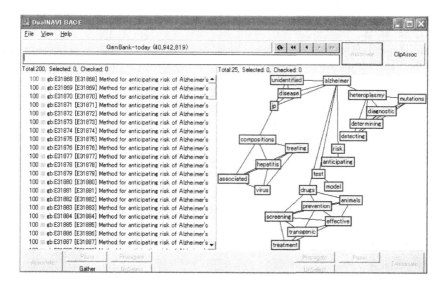

Fig. 4. Rearranged DualNAVI

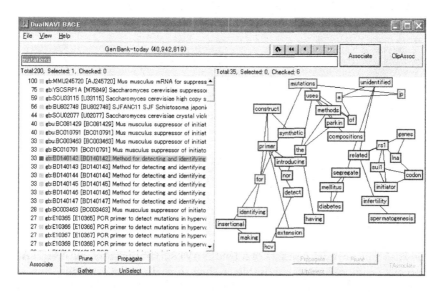

Fig. 5. DualNAVI focusing on "mutation"

4   Implementation

A prototype of the support system for detecting the signs of food safety risks was implemented. The server of this system was constructed on a machine with the following specifications:

- CPU: Intel Xeon 2.8MHz
- RAM: 1GB
- HDD: 144GB
- OS: Vine Linux 2.6

About 6,500 files were categorized by 65 keywords, and they were collected and stored in the clearinghouse based on the procedure described in Sect. 2. This system has already been installed and is operated at `http://dss.sys.eng.shizuoka.ac.jp/clh/`. Users can use the clearinghouse by a Web browser. Fig. 6 is an image of the clearinghouse.

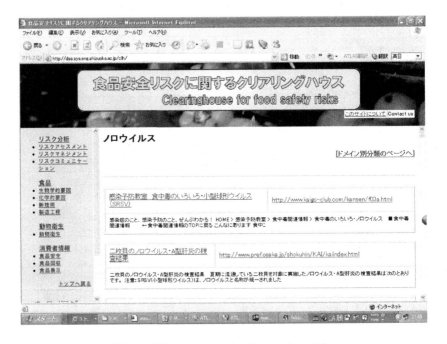

Fig. 6. Clearinghouse for food safety risks

The Risk Path Finder consists of a DualNAVI server operated with GETA[17], the generic engine for transposable association, installed on `dss.sys.eng. shizuoka.ac.jp`, and the DualNAVI clients that are operated on the user's computers. About 350,000 files with regard to food safety risks are input in GETA. The DualNAVI client is required for using the Risk Path Finder.

Fig. 7 is an image of the Risk Path Finder. In this case, the keyword "Tokubetsu Yougo Roujin Homu" (special nursing home for the elderly) is input. The URLs of HTML documents including the keyword are listed on the left pane, while the topic-word graph of these documents is displayed on the right pane. The interrelation of the terms and documents can be observed on the basis of the interactions with the system. If the word "Hoken" (hygiene) in the topic-word

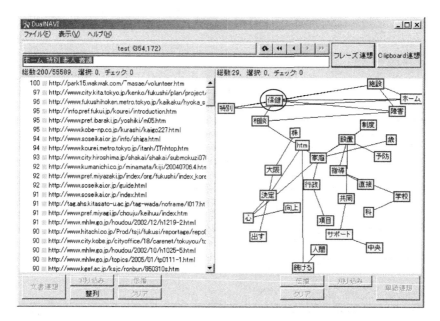

Fig. 7. Example of Risk Path Finder (1). If the word in the ellipse "Hoken" is selected, this view changes to that shown in Fig. 8.

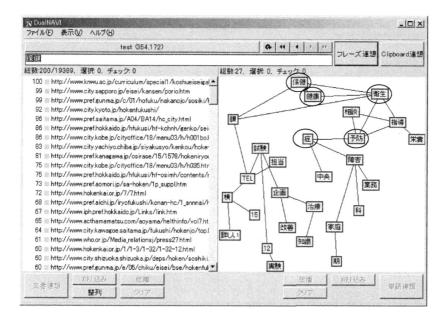

Fig. 8. Example of Risk Path Finder (2). If the words in the ellipses, "Hoken", "Kenkou", "Eisei", "Yobou" and "Shou", are selected, this view changes to that shown in Fig. 9.

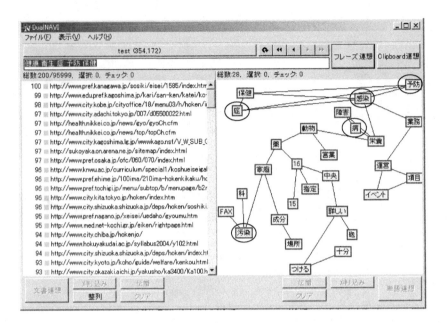

Fig. 9. Example of Risk Path Finder (3). If the words in the ellipses, "Kansen", "Shou", "Byou", and "Osen", are selected, this view changes to that shown in Fig. 10.

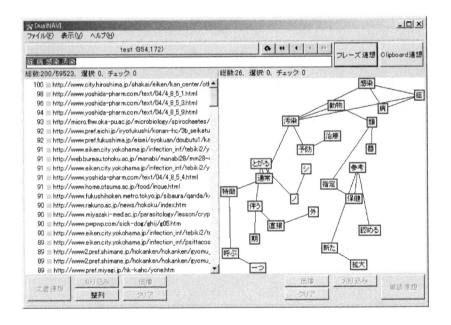

Fig. 10. Example of Risk Path Finder (4)

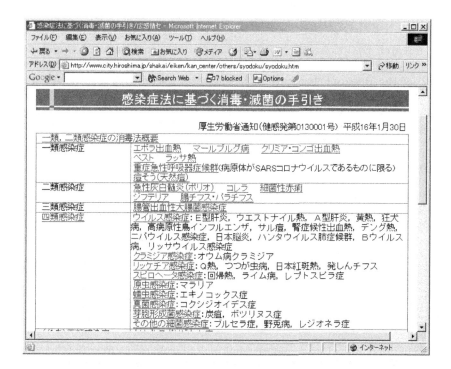

Fig. 11. Document appearing at the top of the left pane shown in Fig. 10

graph shown in Fig. 7 is selected, the graph is rearranged as shown in Fig. 8. In this manner, if the words "Hoken" (hygiene), "Kenkou" (health), "Eisei" (sanitation), "Yobou" (prevention), and "Shou" (disease) are selected as shown in Fig. 8, the window changes, as shown in Fig. 9. In addition, "Kansen" (infection), "Shou" (disease), "Byou" (illness), and "Osen" (contamination) are chosen in Fig. 9, and the view is rearranged as shown in Fig. 10. In this figure, the URL appearing on top of the left pane represents a table of infectious diseases and their countermeasures that are specified by the Infectious Disease Law (Fig. 11). This result suggests that some of the diseases listed in the table are possible causes of health risks in nursing homes. In this manner, the Risk Path Finder aids users in detecting the paths from the sources to the risk events.

5   Conclusion

An early warning support system for food safety risks was developed. A prototype system was implemented for performing field experiments in order to verify the system performance. Further, a different approach for detecting the signs of risks (for example, the chance discovery approach[18]) could be included in this system in order to improve the detection of a variety of signs or signals, possibly by developing selection criteria on the basis of rule-based or empirical approaches.

Acknowledgement

This research has been supported by the project "International Comparative Study on the Governance of New Emerging Environmental and Technological Risks" of the Research Institute of Science and Technology for Society, Japan Science and Technology Corporation. We wish to express our gratitude to Dr. Yoshiki Niwa and Dr. Mari Minowa from the Life Science Research Laboratory, Hitachi Ltd., for their cooperation in implementing DualNAVI in our system.

References

1. Ikeda, S., Kabuto, M., Kunugi, M., Maeda, Y., Mizuno, T., Nishizawa, M., Yamada, Y.: New Framework for Consumer involvement—Cases of Food/EMF/Invasive Species. Society for Risk Analysis 2004 Annual Meeting. http://birenheide.com/sra/2004AM/program/singlesession.php3?sessid=T26&order=6#6 Palm Springs, CA (2004)
2. Ikeda, S.: Risk Society and Planning Administration (Risuku Syakai To Keikaku Gyousei). Planning Administration. **27**(3) (2004) 3–11 (In Japanese)
3. Renn, O, Dressel, K., Dreyer, M., Klinke, A., Nishizawa, M., Rohrmann, B.: Systemic Risks, Report to Steering Group of the OECD Future Project on Emerging Systemic Risks. Center of Technology Assessment in Baden-Württenberg, Baden-Württenberg (2002)
4. Commission of the European Communities: Communication from the Commission on the Precautionary Principle. COM(2000) 1, European Communities, Brussels (2000)
5. Wiedemann, P., Karger, C., Clauberg, M.: Early Risk Detection in Environmental Health. Feasibility Study, Executive summary, Environmental Research Plan of the Federal Ministry for the Environment, Nature Conservation and Nuclear Safety. R+D-Project 200 61 218/09, Research Center Jülich GmbH, Jülich (2002)
6. FAO: Global Information and Early Warning System on Food and Agriculture. http://www.fao.org/giews/english/index.htm Rome (2005)
7. Matsumura, K., Gemba, K., Nakano, Y., Ichinose, T., Shibasaki, R.: Asian Early Warning System for Food. Proceedings of the 5th International Conference on Ecobalance, S5-46, Tsukuba (2002) 783–786
8. Maeda, Y., Kurita, N.: Early Warning System for New Emerging Environmental and Technological Risks. Sharing Experience of Human and Ecological Risk Assessment and Management in Asia/Pacific Region, Proceedings of International Joint Conference "Risk Assessment and Management" with SRA Japan & China/ KOSET / SETAC A/P, Seoul (2004) p.178.
9. JIFSAN: JIFSAN Food Safety Risk Analysis Clearinghouse. http://www.foodrisk.org/index.cfm College Park, MD (accessed in 2005)
10. UNEP CBD: Biosafety Clearinghouse. http://bch.biodiv.org/ Montreal, Quebec (2004)
11. Google: Google. http://www.google.com/ Mountain View, CA (2005)
12. Google: Google Web APIs (beta). http://www.google.com/apis/ Mountain View, CA (2005)
13. SRA Japan Editorial Committe for the Dictionary for Risk Analysis: SRA Japan Glossary for Risk Analysis (Nihon Risuku Kenkyu Gakkai Risuku Yougosyu Sakusei). http://www.oita-nhs.ac.jp/~risk_term/ Oita (accessed in 2005) (In Japanese)

14. Food Safety Committee: Glossary about Food Safety (Syokuhin No Anzensei Ni Kansuru Yougosyu). `http://www.fsc.go.jp/yougoshu_fsc.pdf` Food Safety Committee, Tokyo (2004)
15. Takano, A., Niwa, Y., Nishioka, S., Iwayama, M., Hisamitsu, T., Imaichi, O., Sakurai, H. : Information Access Based on Associative Calculation. Lecture Notes in Computer Science, Vol. 1963. Springer-Verlag, Berlin Heidelberg New York (2000) 187–201
16. Human Genome Center: DualNAVI (for BACE) guidance. `http://bace.hgc.jp/dn_intro/` Human Genome Center, University of Tokyo, Tokyo (accessed in 2005)
17. Takano, A., Niwa, Y.: Generic Engine for Transposable Association (GETA). `http://geta.ex.nii.ac.jp/e/index.html` National Institute of Informatics, Tokyo (accessed in 2005)
18. Chance Discovery Consortium: Chance Discovery Consortium. `http://www.chancediscovery.com/english/index.php` Chance Discovery Consortium, Suita (accessed in 2005)

Exploration of Researchers' Social Network for Discovering Communities

Ryutaro Ichise[1], Hideaki Takeda[1], and Kosuke Ueyama[2]

[1] National Institute of Informatics,
2-1-2 Hitotsubashi Chiyoda-ku, Tokyo 101-8430, Japan
{ichise, takeda}@nii.ac.jp
[2] TRIAX Inc.
4-18-2-203 Takadanobaba, Shinjyuku-ku, Tokyo 169-0075, Japan
ko@triax.jp

Abstract. The research community plays a very important role in helping researchers undertake new research topics. The authors propose a community mining system that helps to find communities of researchers by using bibliography data. The basic concept of this system is to provide interactive visualization of communities both local and global communities. We implemented this concept using actual bibliography data and present a case study using the proposed system.

1 Introduction

Our modern life has become fundamentally supported by various technical systems, ranging from traditional systems like roads and bridges to highly technological systems like nuclear power plants, all of which have been built and thus maintained with scientific and technical knowledge. Sustaining our modern life is dependent on maintenance of these systems. Accordingly, to avoid fatal failure of such systems, preserving this scientific and technical knowledge is vital.

Scientific and technical knowledge is kept explicitly by means such as published papers, but that it is not the only way. The crucial part of knowledge is kept implicitly among communities of scientists and engineers. Not only papers themselves but also communities behind the papers play an important role in keeping knowledge from generation to generation. In this paper, we discuss how research communities can be discovered from bibliographic information. In particular, we do not aim at an automatic discovery system but an interactive system with people, i.e., users can browse various types and sizes of communities.

This paper is organized as follows. In the following section, we clarify community discovery with related studies. In Section 3, we discuss the proposed design for a community mining system. In Section 4, we describe an implemented community mining system based on the design policies discussed in Section 3. In Section 5, we explain the proposed system using a number of examples. Finally, in Section 6, we discuss our conclusions and areas for future study.

T. Washio et al. (Eds.): JSAI 2005 Workshops, LNAI 4012, pp. 458–469, 2006.

2   Discovery of Research Communities

We can obtain useful and reliable information from communities. Most researchers do not include all of the techniques used in their experiments when writing a paper because some of them, such as computer coding, cannot be represented in words, such as computer coding techniques. Such techniques propagating within a local research community, however, may be useful for developing new technologies and learning about existing technologies.

To clarify existing research communities, bibliographic information is widely used. In co-citation analysis [1], all the papers that are cited in a paper make up a community for a certain research area. However, this paper-based analysis overlooks the characteristics of individual researchers. As a result, realizing that each researcher has an individual research area is difficult. On the other hand, CiteSeer [2] and Google Scholar [3] are able to handle research communities from a micro viewpoint because they handle co-author and citation information from bibliographies and use the information for individual researchers. Although these systems are good for finding micro communities, they are not suitable for finding the position of a researcher within a global research community. In the present paper, we propose a community mining system for researchers that has both local and global viewpoints. The proposed system will facilitate understa! nding of the researcher community and will advance new areas of research.

3   System Design

3.1   Relationships for Communities

The most important information for finding communities of researchers is contained in the bibliography. In scientific network research, several relationships can be obtained from this information. The relationships in the knowledge domain include co-authorship [4], citation [5] and co-citation [1]. In the present paper, we use the following three relationships in the knowledge domain to find research communities:

- co-authorship
- citation
- author citation

The relationships are shown in Figure 1. The first two relationships are well known by knowledge domain researchers. With respect to co-authorship, if we consider the researcher as a node and co-authorship as an arc, we can obtain networks of researchers. We can consider that researchers whose nodes are linked have the same research interests. With respect to citation, if we can consider the research paper as a node and citations in papers as arcs, we can obtain networks of papers. The final relationship is author citation. This relationship also represents relationships among authors. Research papers include citations of papers, as described above. This citation indicates that both papers (which have a citation relationship) are related to the same subject. In the same manner, the authors of both papers have the same research interests. In the present study, these relationships are referred to as "author citations" and are used for community mining.

Fig. 1. Three relationships in the knowledge domain

3.2 Community Mining

In this section, we describe the community mining method for the networks described in the previous section. We use a policy for community mining borrowed from the active mining approach [6]. The basic concept of active mining is to utilize interactions between the user and the computer. We separate the mining method into two steps. The first step is to automatically mine communities by computer, and the second step is to visualize the information in order to facilitate the user's understanding of it. After viewing the communities that are discovered by the computer, the user can specify a command to find more refined communities. As described above, the proposed method can facilitate the finding of communities through interactive manipulation of the mining result by computer.

Several types of indexes have been proposed for finding communities [7]. In the present study, we used the following indexes for finding communities.

1. Simple weight
2. Maximum flow
3. Closeness

The first index, simple weight, is a measure for using weight on arcs such as representing the number of co-authors. When the weight is small, the arc is considered to represent an unimportant relationship. Therefore, highly weighted arcs represent communities and thus can be used as an index for the community. The second index, max flow, is a measure that focuses on the connection between two different nodes. This index considers the weight on an arc as the thickness of a pipe and measures the connection between the two nodes. The index is able to calculate the distance between two nodes that are not directly connected. When the two nodes have a thick connection, even though they have relay nodes, the index may have a high value. This index may therefore be a good measure for finding communities. The third index, closeness, is a measure that is used to calculate the distance between two nodes. This index represents the shortest distance between the two nodes. Therefore, when the distance is small, the two nodes are considered to be in the same community.

4   Research Community Mining System

4.1   System Architecture

We implemented a community mining system using the policies presented in the previous section. The components of the system are shown in Figure 2. The system has two databases, the CiNii (Citation Information by NII) [8] database and an experimental database, and five program units. The CiNii database will be described in detail later herein.

The database generation unit in Figure 2 selects records from the CiNii database and sends them to the database management unit. MySQL [9] is used as the database management unit. If possible, the mining index discussed in Section 3.2 is then calculated by the mining index calculation unit. The components are written in Perl. Note that the entire mining index cannot be calculated at this stage because of the need for a user query. The result of the calculated index is also stored in the experimental database, which is handled by the database management unit.

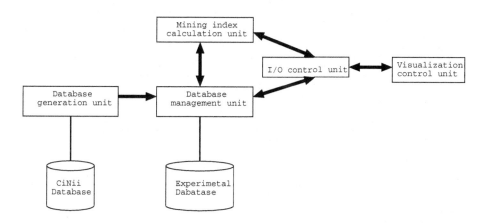

Fig. 2. System architecture

Users access the system through the visualization control unit, which is constructed using a web browser that includes Flash Player and SVG Viewer. When a user inputs data from the web browser, the data will be sent to the I/O control unit via the Internet. The I/O control unit, which is constructed by a web server including the CGI program, generates data for visualization from the user input. The components are also written in Perl. The I/O control unit calls the database management unit to retrieve data and calls the mining index calculation unit to calculate the mining index.

In the remainder of this section, the CiNii database, the preprocessing method for data, and the visualization method are discussed in detail.

4.2   Bibliography Database

The CiNii database is used to obtain bibliographic information. The database is described by approximately 320 megabytes of SGML data. The CiNii database contains bibliography entries, such as title, author, and year of publication. The number of data are listed in Table 1. The number of database records in CiNii denotes the number of records in the original database, as described in SGML format. The "Paper" and "Researcher" entries denote the number of records for papers and the number of records for researchers, respectively. The number of researchers is less than the number of papers, because one researcher can write more than one paper. The "Author" entries in Table 1 denote the number of authors for each paper. For example, the record is counted as three when three researchers write a paper corroboratively. The "Co-author" entries denote the number of combinations of authors for a paper. For example, when a paper is written by four authors, it is! counted as $_4C_2 = 6$ for the paper. The "Citation(Paper)" entries denote the number of citations of a paper. Although one paper usually cites a number of other papers, the "Citation(Paper)" entries are lower than the Paper entries because the CiNii database contains part of the citation information. The "Citation(Author)" entries denote the number of researchers who wrote cited papers, with duplication. Comparing the Paper and Researcher entries reveals that the number of researchers is less than the number of papers. In contrast, comparing the Citation(Paper) and Citation(Author) entries, the number of Citation(Author) entries is larger than the number of Citation(Paper), which implies that writers prefer citing various papers to citing several papers written by the same author. Note that the database used in the present study was created in October of 2003, so it is different from the current CiNii database.

Table 1. Number of data

	Number of records in CiNii ($\times 1,000$)	Number of records in Experimental Database ($\times 1,000$)
Paper	544	128
Researcher	224	90
Author	787	358
Co-author	1103	231
Citation(Paper)	445	36
Citation(Author)	1562	349

4.3 Preprocessing of Database

To construct the experimental database, the data discussed in the previous section was preprocessed by a database generation unit. In this process, a few attributes are selected from the CiNii database, because most of the attributes, such as ISSN number, included in the CiNii database are not useful in the present experiment. In addition, the database generation unit conducts record linkage for author records. It has heuristics for dividing author records, because the author records in the CiNii database sometimes have multiple author names in a single author field. For treating such records, the database generation unit divides long author names using special characters, such as $\star$. In addition, a number of other small record linkage techniques are also used in this stage.

After the preprocessing has been completed, the experimental database is created by the database management unit. The numbers of records for the experimental database are listed in Table 1. The experimental database contains much less data than the original CiNii database because only the bibliographies of the papers included in the CiNii database as original information were used. Although the CiNii database contains cited paper information, the information is not complete and contains several mistakes; it was therefore not used in the present experiment.

4.4 Visualization

The visualization control unit creates a visualization screen for finding communities easily. For a user to find a community, they must be able to browse the data interactively. For this purpose, we used a web browser, which includes Flash Player and SVG Viewer, as a visualization control unit. Data for this unit was provided by a web server on the Internet. The server is referred to as the I/O control unit. We used two types of visualization data provided by the I/O control unit: global visualization by SVG [10] and local visualization by Flash. Global visualization by SVG facilitates the location of macro communities by showing global relationships on the graph, whereas local visualization by Flash facilitates the location of micro communities by showing the local relationships near the individual. Both of these methods will be discussed in this section.

We first discuss graph visualization by SVG. As discussed in Section 3.1, representing the relationships between communities in the form of a graph will facilitate the finding of communities. We therefore use a graphic representation scheme by SVG, an XML format for representing graphs. The SVG file can be visualized by an SVG viewer. An example of a SVG graph visualization of relationships among researchers is shown in Figure 3. However, using such a graphical representation is not suitable for finding communities in the graph, because most of the nodes will be connected [11]. As a result, the graph could be very large and the user might not be able to find communities in the graph. To discern communities from a large graph, the system should have a function that shows the parts of the graph that may contain the desired communities. Accordingly, we herein propose interactive mining in conjunction with the indexes presented in Section 3.2. When the user specifies an index and its threshold, the system automatically divides the graph. This is very important for finding communities because it is hard to specify an index to match the purpose of the user. Although the current implementation of the mining index calculation unit calculates the three indexes presented in Section 3.2, the I/O control unit can only create an SVG graph for simple weight.

Next, we will discuss local representation by Flash. After finding a community via visualization by SVG, we must learn more about each researcher in order to refine the communities. For this purpose, users require not only a global point of view with respect to the communities, but also a local point of view that focuses on each researcher. We propose visualizing local communities, to which a specified researcher belongs, in order to facilitate the refinement of communities. Locally, a specified researcher is located at the center of a field, and related researchers are placed around the circumference of the initially specified researcher. This visualization is suitable for finding communities that are built around a researcher. Since we focused on communities of researchers, the current implementation includes only the relationships of co-author and author citation,

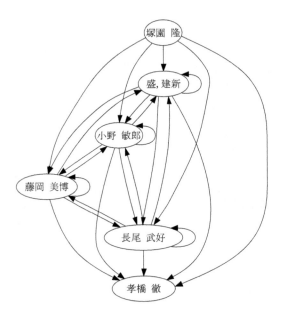

Fig. 3. An example of graph representation by SVG

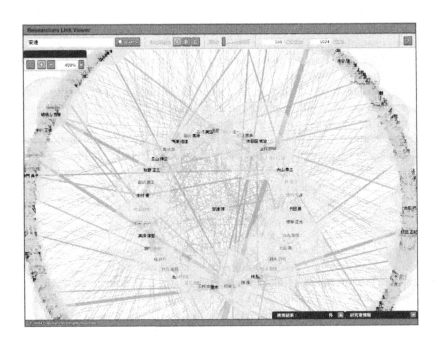

Fig. 4. An example of a local view

as discussed in Section 3.1. An example of the local point of view is shown in Figure 4. The circle in the center represents the currently specified researcher of interest. The surrounding circles represent researchers who! are related to the initially specified researcher. Finally, the outermost ring of circles represents researchers who are related to the researchers of the inner ring. The size of each circle represents the number of papers that were written by the researcher. The thickness of the line represents the strength of the relationships.

The user can also perform the following operations to find communities interactively.

- Change the researcher of focus by specifying another researcher.
- Move circles to find relationships among particular researchers.
- Change the type of relationships.
- Show the bibliography of the researcher.

4.5   Other Functions

In addition, the following basic functions for facilitating the finding of communities by the user are implemented.

- Paper search: The user can search for a paper or researcher by specifying author name or paper title. This function helps to understand the meaning within discovered communities and helps to find similar communities.
- Ranking: The user can easily find dense communities by using ranking for co-author or citation. In addition, this function also helps to show the starting point for community mining.

5   Case Study of Community Mining System

In order to demonstrate how the proposed system works, we will discuss the system using actual examples. Figure 5 illustrates the start screen of the proposed system. From this screen, any of the functions of the proposed system can be easily chosen.

From the center of the start screen, we can access the local view by Flash, as discussed in Figure 4. By clicking the center of the start screen, a search window is opened. After the user inputs the name of a researcher, whom the user wants to know more about, a visualized screen representing the local communities for that researcher is shown. For example, if we input "Takeda" (in Japanese) and choose "Hideaki Takeda" from the Takeda list, the screen shown in Figure 6 will be displayed. The list at the bottom-left corner of the screen is a list of authors. When "Hideaki Takeda" is selected from this list, a circle denoting "Hideaki Takeda" is shown in the center of the screen. The circles around "Takeda" denote researches who have co-authored papers with him. To find communities that are built around a specified researcher, the user can visualize the researchers related to a specified researcher. In addition, the system has a function for eliminating relationships that do not exceed a particular threshold specified by the user, as well as a function for changing the scale or location of circ! les in order to more clearly display the desired information. Although Figure 6 illustrates the co-author relationships, the proposed system also has the ability to show the author citation relationships in different colors. The bottom-right window shows the bibliography of the researcher at the center of the screen and is used to determine the field of the researcher.

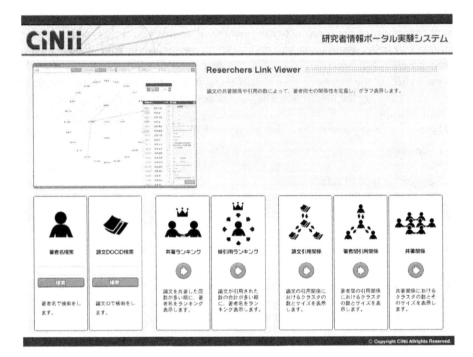

Fig. 5. Start screen of system

The two items in the box at the bottom-left, shown in Figure 5, are used for searching for authors and papers. The two items in the center are used to show rankings. These rankings include researchers with whom papers have been written and papers that are cited frequently. This function is used for obtaining knowledge for community mining.

The three items in the box at the bottom-right, shown in Figure 5, are used for visualizing the graphs for community mining. These items are used to show citation relationships, author citation relationships, and co-author relationships. Since each of these functions is similar, we will show only the case of the author citation relationships. When the user clicks the area for the author citation in Figure 5, the screen shown in Figure 7 is displayed. From this screen, the threshold of the weight of the relationships can be set. In this example, as shown on the center-left side of the screen, the weight of the relationships is set to 1. In other words, the graph is created using relationships in which the two researchers have at least one author citation relationship. As a result, we can divide the researchers into a number of communities. In this case, we can obtain, for example, a community constructed with 30,536 researchers or a community constructed with 26 researchers. The relationships between community size, number of communities and threshold are shown in Figure 8. The list of the communities is shown at the bottom in Figure 7. When the user selects a community from the list, the user can view a graph using the SVG viewer, as shown in Figure 3. If the user judges the community to be too large to understand easily, the threshold for dividing the communities can be adjusted by the user. If the threshold is increased, weak relationships

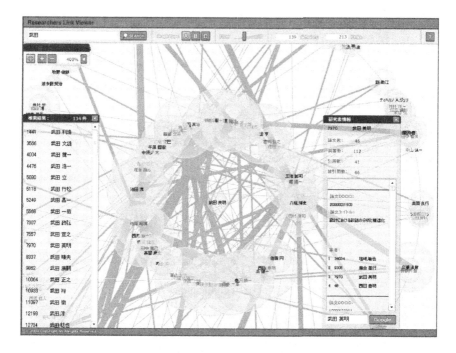

Fig. 6. Local view for searching a particular researcher

will be eliminated, and as a result the user will obtain a screen similar to that shown in Figure 7 for the threshold. In this way, the user can interactively use the system to find the desired communities.

6   Conclusions

Community mining is a method to find communities with implicit knowledge. In this paper, we propose a new approach to community mining, namely, including both a macro view of all researchers and a micro view of individual researchers. We implemented and demonstrated the proposed system. In the macro view, the systems shows clusters of networks as communities. Users can browse clusters of networks by controlling cluster size. In the micro view, users can focus on individual researchers and their neighbors and can shift from one researcher to another. The system can be accessed on the website listed in the following reference [12].

Although the proposed system is functional in its current state, a number of areas for improvement remain. First, the proposed system must be tested by actual users under actual conditions of use. We hope to receive feedback from researchers regarding our system and will make improvements based thereupon. Another area for improvement is how to assist the user with the indexes. In this study, we do not use an automatic approach for finding communities because of the variety of purpose for such a task. We intend to investigate the support of a user driven community mining system, and also to

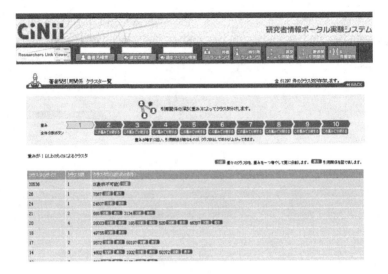

Fig. 7. List of communities

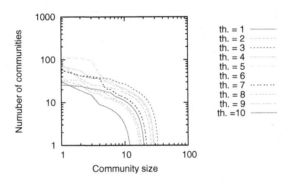

Fig. 8. Number of communities

develop a computer driven community mining system. Finally, we must investigate the seamless integration of global and local views of communities.

References

1. Small, H.: Co-citation in the scientific literature: A new measure of the relationship between two documents. Journal of the American Society of Information Science **24** (1973) 265–269
2. Scientific literature digital library (2004) http://citeseer.ist.psu.edu/.
3. Google scholar (2004) http://scholar.google.com/.
4. Newman, M.E.J.: Coauthorship networks and patterns of scientific collaboration. Proceedings of the National Academy of Sciences of the USA **101** (2004) 5200–5205
5. Garfield, E.: Citation indexes for science: A new dimension in documentation through association of ideas. Science **122** (1955) 108–111

6. Motoda, H.: Active Mining. IOS Press (2002)
7. Freeman, L.C.: Centrality in social networks: Conceptual clarification. Social Networks **1** (1979) 215–239
8. CiNii (Citation Information by NII).   National Institute of Informatics (2004) http://ci.nii.ac.jp/.
9. Mysql (2004) http://www.mysql.com/.
10. Scalable Vector Graphics (SVG) 1.1 specification.   W3C SVG Working Group (2003) http://www.w3.org/TR/SVG/.
11. Barabási, A.L.: LINKED: The New Science of Networks. Perseus Books Group (2002)
12. Ichise, R., Takeda, H.: Community mining system (2005) http://irweb.ex.nii.ac.jp/.

Opinion Mining as Extraction of Attribute-Value Relations

Nozomi Kobayashi, Ryu Iida, Kentaro Inui, and Yuji Matsumoto

Nara Institute of Science and Technology,
Takayama, Ikoma, Nara 630-0192, Japan
{nozomi-k, ryu-i, inui, matsu}@is.naist.jp

Abstract. This paper addresses the task of extracting opinions from a given document collection. Assuming that an opinion can be represented as a tuple ⟨*Subject, Attribute, Value*⟩, we propose a computational method to extract such tuples from texts. In this method, the main task is decomposed into (a) the process of extracting *Attribute-Value* pairs from a given text and (b) the process of judging whether an extracted pair expresses an opinion of the author. We apply machine-learning techniques to both subtasks. We also report on the results of our experiments and discuss future directions.

1 Introduction

For manufactures of consumer products, it is important to know users' opinions on their newly introduced products. Acquiring the sources of users' complaints and/or the product's defects at a very early stage helps to reduce the risk of widely distributing defective products and to improve marketing strategies.

Nowadays, there exist a very large number of message boards and weblog pages on the Web where users of consumer products are discussing or describing their personal opinions and evaluation of the products. This situation attracts an increasing interest in an automatic text analysis of opinions or sentiments appearing in such documents.

Previous approaches to the task of mining a large-scale document collection for opinions can be classified into two groups: the document classification approach and the information extraction approach. In the document classification approach, researchers have been exploring techniques for classifying documents according to semantic/sentiment orientation such as positive vs. negative (e.g. [1, 2, 3]). The information extraction approach, on the other hand, focuses on the task of extracting elements which constitute opinions (e.g. [4, 5, 6]).

The aim of this paper is to propose and evaluate a method for extracting opinions that represent an evaluation of a products together with the evidence from documents. To achieve this, we consider our task from the information extraction viewpoint. We term the above task **opinion extraction** in this paper.

While they can be linguistically realized in many ways, opinions on a product are in fact often expressed in the form of an attribute-value pair. An attribute represents one aspect of a subject and the value is a specific language expression that qualifies or quantifies the aspect. Given this observation, we approach our goal by reducing the task

T. Washio et al. (Eds.): JSAI 2005 Workshops, LNAI 4012, pp. 470–481, 2006.

to a general problem of extracting four-tuples ⟨*Subject, Attribute, Value, Evaluation*⟩ from a large-scale text collection. Technology for this opinion extraction task would be useful for collecting and summarizing latent opinions from the Web. A straightforward application might be generation of radar charts from collected opinions as suggested by Tateishi et al.[7].

Consider an example from the automobile domain, *I am very satisfied with the powerful engine (of a car)*. We can extract the four-tuple ⟨*CAR, engine, powerful, satisfied*⟩ from this sentence. Note that the distinction between *Value* and *Evaluation* is not easy. Many expressions used to express a *Value* can also be used to express an *Evaluation*. For example, given *I feel comfortable with the wide interior*, we may take it that *interior* is an attribute, *wide* its value and *feel comfortable* the evaluation. However, from the expression *comfortable interior*, we may regard *comfortable* as the value of the *interior*. For this reason, we do not distinguish value and evaluation, and therefore consider the task of extracting triplets ⟨*Subject, Attribute, Value*⟩. Another problem with opinion extraction is that we want to get only subjective opinions. Given this setting, the opinion extraction task can be decomposed into two subtasks: extraction of attribute-value pairs related to a product and determination of its subjectivity.

As we discuss in Section 3, an attribute and its value may not appear in a fixed expression and may be separated. In some cases, the attribute may be missing from a sentence. In this respect, finding the attribute of a value is similar to finding the missing antecedent of an anaphoric expression. In this paper, we discuss the similarities and differences between opinion extraction and anaphora resolution. Then, we apply a machine learning-based method used for anaphora resolution to the opinion extraction problem and report on our experiments conducted on a domain-restricted set of Japanese texts excerpted from review pages on the Web.

2   Related Work

In this section, we discuss previous approaches to the opinion extraction problem. In the pattern-based approach [8, 6], pre-defined extraction patterns and a list of evaluative expressions are used. These extraction patterns and the list of evaluation expressions need to be manually created. However, as is the case in information extraction, manual construction of rules may require considerable cost to provide sufficient coverage and accuracy.

Hu et al. [5] attempt to extract the attributes of target products on which customers have expressed their opinions using association mining, and to determine whether the opinions are positive or negative. Their aim is quite similar to our aim, however, our work differs from theirs in that we extract the value and its corresponding attribute at the expression level while they extract the attributes and determine their semantic orientation at the sentence level.

Taking the semantic parsing-based approach, Kanayama et al. [4] apply the idea of transfer-based machine translation to the extraction of attribute-value pairs. They regard the extraction task as translation from a text to a sentiment unit which consists of a sentiment value, a predicate, and its arguments. Their idea is to replace the translation patterns and bilingual lexicons with sentiment expression patterns and a lexicon that specifies the polarity of expressions. Their method first analyzes the predicate-argument structure of a given input sentence making use of the sentence analysis component of an existing machine translation engine, and then extracts a sentiment unit from it, if any, using the transfer component.

One important problem the semantic parsing approach encounters is that opinion expressions often appear with anaphoric expressions and ellipses, which need to be resolved to accomplish the opinion extraction task. Our investigation of an opinion-tagged Japanese corpus (described below) showed that 30% of the attribute-value pairs we found did not have a direct syntactic dependency relation within the sentence, mostly due to ellipsis. For example[1]

$\langle dezain\text{-}wa \rangle_a$ *hen-dato iwarete-iruga watashi-wa [ϕ-ga]* $\langle suki\text{-}da \rangle_v$
$\langle design \rangle_a$ *weird   be-said but   I   [it]* $\langle like \rangle_v$
(It's often said that the design is weird, but I like it.)

This type of case accounted for 46 out of 100 pairs that did not have direct dependency relations. To analyze predicate argument structure robustly, we have to solve this problem. In the next section, we discuss the similarity between the anaphora resolution task and the opinion extraction task and propose to apply to opinion extraction a method used for anaphora resolution.

3   Method for Opinion Extraction

3.1   Analogy with Anaphora Resolution

We consider the task of extracting opinion tuples $\langle Subject, Attribute, Value \rangle$ from review sites and message boards on the Web dedicated to providing and exchanging information about retail goods. On these Web pages, products are often specified clearly and so it is frequently a trivial job to extract the information for the *Subject* slot. As we show later in Section 4.6, if the product name is given, it is not difficult to detect the *Subject* according to the *Value*, even if the products are not specified in given documents. We therefore focus on the problem of extracting $\langle Attribute, Value \rangle$ pairs.

In the process of attribute-value pair identification for opinion extraction, we need to deal with the following two cases: (a) both a value and its corresponding attribute appear in the text, and (b) a value appears in the text while its attribute is missing since it is inferable form the value expression and the context. The upper half of Figure 1 illustrates these two cases in the automobile domain. In (b) of Figure 1, the writer is talking about the "speed" of the car, but the expression "speed" is not explicitly mentioned in the text. In addition, the case (b) includes the case where the writer evaluates the product itself. For example, "I'm very satisfied with my car!": in this case, a value expression "satisfied" evaluates the product as a whole, therefore a corresponding attribute does not exists.

---

[1] [ϕ-ga] is an ellipsis, which does not appear in the sentence and is called a "zero pronoun". $\langle \rangle_a$ denotes the word sequence corresponding to the Attribute. Likewise, we also use $\langle \rangle_v$ for the Value.

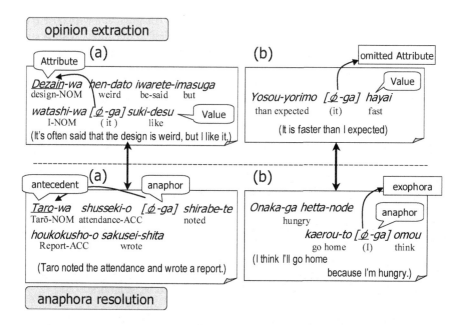

Fig. 1. Similarity between opinion extraction and anaphora resolution

For the case (a), we first identify a value expression (*like* in Figure 1) in a given text and then look for the corresponding attribute in the text. Since we also see the case (b), on the other hand, we additionally need to consider the problem of whether the corresponding attribute of the identified value expression appears in the text or not.

The structure of these problems is analogous to that of anaphora resolution; namely, there are exactly two cases in anaphora resolution that have a clear correspondence with the above two cases as illustrated in Figure 1: in (a) the noun phrase (NP) is *anaphoric*; namely, the NP's antecedent appears in the text, and in (b) the noun phrase is *non-anaphoric*. A non-anaphoric NP is either exophoric (i.e. the NP has an implicit refer-ent) or indefinite. While the figure shows Japanese examples, the similarity between anaphora resolution and opinion extraction is language independent. This analogy nat-urally leads us to think of applying existing techniques for anaphora resolution to our opinion extraction task since anaphora resolution has been studied for a considerably longer period in a wider range of disciplines as we briefly review below.

3.2 Existing Techniques for Anaphora Resolution

Computational approaches to anaphora resolution have been roughly evolving in two different but complementary directions: theory-oriented rule-based approaches and em-pirical corpus-based approaches.

In rule-based approaches [9, 10, 11], efforts have been directed to manual encoding of various linguistic cues into a set of rule based on theoretical linguistic work such as Centering Theory [12, 13] and Systemic Theory [14]. The best-achieved performance for the coreference task test set of MUC-7 [2] was around 70% precision with 60% recall, which is still far from being satisfactory for many practical applications. Worse still, a rule set tuned for a particular domain is unlikely to work equally for another domain due to domain-dependent properties of coreference patterns. Given these facts, further manual refinements of rule-based models will be prohibitively costly. Corpus-based empirical approaches, such as [15, 16, 17, 18], on the other hand, are cost effective, while having achieved a better performance than the best-performing rule-based systems for the test sets of MUC-6 and MUC-7.

As suggested by Figure 1, anaphora resolution can be decomposed into two subtasks: *anaphoricity determination* and *antecedent identification*. Anaphoricity determination is the task of judging whether a given NP is anaphoric or non-anaphoric. Recent research advances have provided several important findings as follows:

- Learning-based methods for antecedent identification can also benefit from the use of linguistic clues inspired by Centering Theory [12].
- One useful clue for anaphoricity determination is the availability of a plausible candidate for the antecedent. If an appropriate candidate for the antecedent is found in the preceding discourse context, the NP is likely to be anaphoric.

For these reasons, an anaphora resolution model performs best if it carries out the following process in the given order [19]:

1. **Antecedent identification**: Given an NP, identify the best candidate antecedent for it, and
2. **Anaphoricity determination**: Judge whether the candidate really stands for the true antecedent of the NP.

3.3 An Opinion Extraction Model Inspired by Analogy with Anaphora Resolution

As illustrated in Figure 2, an opinion extraction model derived from the aforementioned analogy with anaphora resolution as follows:

1. **Initialization:** Identify attribute and value candidates by dictionary lookup
2. **Attribute identification:** Select a value and identify the best candidate attribute corresponding to the value
3. **Pairedness determination:** Decide whether the candidate attribute stands for the real attribute of the value or not (i.e. the value has no explicit corresponding attribute in the text)
4. **Opinionhood determination:** Judge whether the obtained attribute-value pair[3] expresses an opinion or not

---

[2] The Seventh Message Understanding Conference (1998):
www.itl.nist.gov/iaui/894.02/related_projects/muc/

[3] For simplicity, we call a value both with and without an attribute uniformly by the term *attribute-value pair* unless the distinction is important.

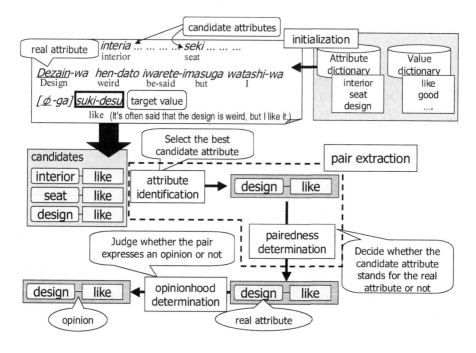

Fig. 2. Process of opinion extraction

Here, the attribute identification and pairedness determination processes respectively correspond to the antecedent identification and anaphoricity determination processes in anaphora resolution.

Note that our opinion extraction task requires an additional subtask, opinionhood determination — an attribute-value pair appearing in a text does not necessarily constitute an opinion. We elaborate on the notion of opinionhood in section Section 4.1.

From the above discussion, we can expect that the findings for anaphora resolution mentioned in Section 3.2 stated above apply to opinion extraction as well. In fact, the information about the candidate attribute is likely to be useful for pairedness determination. We therefore expect that carrying out attribute identification before pairedness determination should outperform the counterpart model which executes the two subtasks in the reversed order. The same analogy also applies to opinionhood determination; namely, we expect that opinion determination is better performed after attribute determination. Furthermore, our opinion extraction model also can be implemented in a totally machine learning-based fashion.

4   Evaluation

We conducted experiments with Japanese Web documents to empirically evaluate the performance of our opinion extraction model, focusing particularly on the validity of the analogy discussed in the previous section.

4.1 Opinionhood

In these experiments, we define an opinion as follows:

> An opinion is a description that expresses the writer's subjective evaluation of a particular product or a certain aspect of it.

By this definition, we exclude requests, factual or counter-factual descriptions and hearsay evidence from our target opinions. For example, *"The engine is powerful"* is an opinion, while a counter-factual sentence such as *"If only the engine were more powerful"* is not regarded as opinion.

4.2 Opinion-Tagged Corpus

We created an opinion-tagged Japanese corpus consisting of 288 review articles in the automobile domain (4,442 sentences). While it is not easy to judge whether an expression is a value or an attribute, we asked the annotator to identify attribute and value expressions according to their subjective judgment.

If some attributes are in a hierarchical relation with each other, we asked the annotator to choose the attribute lowest in the hierarchy as the attribute of the value. For example, in *a sound system with poor sound*, only *sound* is annotated as the attribute of the value *poor*.

The corpus contains 2,191 values with an attribute and 420 values without an attribute. Most of the attributes appear in the same sentence as their corresponding values or in the immediately preceding sentence (99% of the total number of pairs). Therefore, we extract attributes and their corresponding values from the same sentence or from the preceding sentence.

4.3 Experimental Method

As preprocessing, we analyzed the opinion-tagged corpus using the Japanese morphological analyzer *ChaSen*[4] and the Japanese dependency structure analyzer *CaboCha*[5].

We used Support Vector Machines to train the models for attribute identification, pairedness determination and opinionhood determination. We used the 2nd order polynomial kernel as the kernel function for SVMs. Evaluation was performed by 10-fold cross validation using all the data.

Dictionaries. We use dictionaries for identification of attribute and value candidates. We constructed a attribute dictionary and a value dictionary from review articles about automobiles (230,000 sentences in total) using the semi-automatic method proposed by [20]. The data used in this process was different from the opinion-tagged corpus. Furthermore, we added to the dictionaries expressions which frequently appearing in the opinion-tagged corpus. The final size of the dictionaries was 3,777 attribute expressions and 3,950 value expressions.

---

[4] http://chasen.naist.jp/
[5] http://chasen.org/~taku/software/cabocha/

Table 1. Features used in each model. AI: the attribute identification model, PD: the pairedness determination model, OD: the opinionhood determination model.

	Proc.1			Proc.2			Proc.3			Proc.4			
	AI	PD	OD	AI	PD	OD	AI	PD	OD	AI	PD	OD(A-V)	OD(V)
a	√	√	√	√	√	√	√	√	√	√	√	√	√
b	√	√		√			√	√	√	√	√	√	

Order of Model Application. To examine the effects of appropriately choosing the order of model application we mentioned in the previous section, we conducted four experiments using different orders (AI indicates attribute identification, PD indicates pairedness determination and OD indicates opinion determination):

Proc.1: OD→PD→AI, Proc.2: OD→AI→PD
Proc.3: AI→OD→PD, Proc.4: AI→PD→OD

Note that Proc.4 is our proposed ordering.

In addition to these models, we adopted a baseline model. In this model, if the candidate value and a candidate attribute are connected via a dependency relation, the candidate value is judged to have an attribute. When none of the candidate attributes have a dependency relation, the candidate value is judged not to have an attribute.

We adopted the tournament model [17] for attribute identification. This model implements a pairwise comparison (i.e. a match) between two candidates in reference to the given value treating it as a binary classification problem, and conducting a tournament which consists of a series of matches, in which the one that prevails through to the final round is declared the winner, namely, it is identified as the most likely candidate attribute. Each of the matches is conducted as a binary classification task in which one or other of the candidate wins.

The pairedness determination task and the opinionhood determination task are also binary classification tasks. In Proc.1, since pair identification is conducted before finding the best candidate attribute, we used Soon et al.'s model [15] for pairedness determination. This model picks up each possible candidate attribute for a value and determines if it is the attribute for that value. If all the candidates are determined not to be the attribute, the value is judged not to have an attribute. In Proc.4, we can use the information about whether the value has a corresponding attribute or not for opinionhood determination. We therefore create two separate models for when the value does and does not have an attribute.

Features. We extracted the following two types of features from the candidate attribute and the candidate value:

(a) surface spelling and part-of-speech of the target value expression, as well as those of its dependent phrase and those in its depended phrase(s)
(b) relation between the target value and candidate attribute (distance between them, existence of dependency, existence of a co-occurrence relation)

Table 1 summarizes which of the following types of features are used for each model. We extracted (b) if the model could use both the attribute and the value information.

Table 2. The precision and the recall for opinion extraction

procedure		value with attribute	value without attribute	attribute-value pairs
baseline	precision	60.5% (1130/1869)	10.6% (249/2340)	32.8% (1379/4209)
	recall	51.6% (1130/2191)	59.3% (249/420)	52.8% (1379/2611)
	F-measure	55.7	21.0	40.5
Proc.1	precision	47.3% (864/1828)	21.6% (86/399)	42.7% (950/2227)
	recall	39.4% (864/2191)	20.5% (86/420)	36.4% (950/2611)
	F-measure	43.0	21.0	39.3
Proc.2	precision	63.0% (1074/1706)	38.0% (198/521)	57.1% (1272/2227)
	recall	49.0% (1074/2191)	47.1% (198/420)	48.7% (1272/2611)
	F-measure	55.1	42.0	52.6
Proc.3	precision	74.9% (1277/1632)	29.1% (151/519)	63.8% (1373/2151)
	recall	55.8% (1222/2191)	36.0% (151/420)	52.6% (1373/2611)
	F-measure	64.0	32.2	57.7
Proc.4	precision	80.5% (1175/1460)	30.2% (150/497)	67.7% (1325/1957)
	recall	53.6% (1175/2191)	35.7% (150/420)	50.7% (1325/2611)
	F-measure	64.4	32.7	58.0

Existence of a co-occurrence relation is determined by reference to a predefined co-occurrence list that contains attribute-value pair information such as "height of vehicle – low". We created the list from the 230,000 sentences described in section Section 4.3 by applying the attribute and value dictionary and extracting attribute-value pairs if there is a dependency relation between the attribute and the value. The number of pairs we extracted was about 48,000.

4.4   Results

Table 2 shows the results of opinion extraction. We evaluated the results by recall and precision defined as follows (For simplicity, we substitute "A-V" for attribute-value pair):

$$Recall = \frac{\text{correctly extracted A-V opinions}}{\text{total number of A-V opinions}},$$

$$Precision = \frac{\text{correctly extracted A-V opinions}}{\text{total number of A-V opinions found by the system}}.$$

We also used the F-measure which is the harmonic mean of precision and recall:

$$F - measure = \frac{2 * recall * precision}{(recall + precision)}$$

In order to demonstrate the effectiveness of the information about the candidate attribute, we evaluated the results of pair extraction and opinionhood determination separately. Table 3 shows the results. In the pair extraction, we assume that the value is given, and evaluate how successfully attribute-value pairs are extracted.

Table 3. The result of pair extraction and opinionhood determination

	procedure	precision	recall
pair extraction	baseline (dependency)	71.1% (1385/1929)	63.2% (1385/2191)
	PD→AI	65.3% (1579/2419)	72.1% (1579/2191)
	AI→PD	76.6% (1645/2148)	75.1% (1645/2191)
	(dependency)	87.7% (1303/1486)	79.6% (1303/1637)
	(no dependency)	51.7% (342/ 662)	61.7% (342/ 554)
opinionhood determination	OD	74.0% (1554/2101)	60.2% (1554/2581)
	AI→OD	82.2% (1709/2078)	66.2% (1709/2581)

4.5 Discussions

As Table 2 shows, our proposed ordering is outperformed on the recall in Proc.3, however, the precision is higher than Proc.3 and get the best F-measure. We can also see that recall of our model outperforms the baseline model, since this method can extract pairs which are not connected via a dependency relation in the sentence. Moreover, the precision of our method also outperforms the baseline model.

In what follows, we discuss the results of pair extraction and opinionhood determination.

Pair Extraction: From Table 3, we can see that carrying out attribute identification before pairedness determination outperforms the reverse ordering by 11% better precision and 3% better recall. This result supports our expectation that knowledge of attribute information assists attribute-value pair extraction. Focusing on the rows labeled "(dependency)" and "(no dependency)" in Table 3, while 80% of the attribute-value pairs in a direct dependency relation are successfully extracted with high precision, the model achieves only 51.7% recall with 61.7% precision for the cases where an attribute and value are not in a direct dependency relation.

According to our error analysis, a major source of errors lies in the attribute identification task. In this experiment, the precision of attribute identification is 78%. A major reason for this problem was that the true attributes did not exist in our dictionary. In addition, a major cause of error in the pairedness determination stage is cases where an attribute appearing in the preceding sentence causes a false decision. We need to conduct further investigations in order to resolve these problems.

Opinionhood Determination: Table 3 also shows that carrying out attribute identification followed by opinionhood determination outperforms the reverse ordering, which supports our expectation that knowing the attribute information aids opinionhood determination.

While it produces better results, our proposed method still has room for improvement in both precision and recall. Our current error analysis has not identified particular error patterns — the types of errors are very diverse. However, we need to at least address the issue of modifying the feature set to make the model more sensitive to modality-oriented distinctions such as subjunctive and conditional expressions.

4.6 Subject Detection

As mentioned in Section 3, we have so far put aside the task of filling the *Subject* slot assuming that it is not bottle-neck problem. Here, we provide a piece of evidence for the assumption by briefly reporting on the results of another experiment.

For the experiment, we created a corpus annotated with subject-value pairs. The corpus consisted of 308 weblog articles in the automobile domain (3,037 sentences) containing 870 subject-value pairs.

We assumed that for each given article, all the subject expressions and value expressions had been properly identified. The task was to identify the subject corresponding to a given value expression. For this task, we implemented simple heuristics as follows:

1. If there are any subject expressions preceding the given value expressions, choose the one nearest to the value
2. Otherwise, choose the first one of those following the value expression

The precision was 0.92 (822/890), and the recall is 0.94 (822/870). A major error was that the heuristics could not appropriately handle opinions that exhibited a comparison between a subject and its counterpart. However, this problem was not a big deal in terms of frequency. The results suggest that the problem of identifying subject-value pairs is solvable with reasonably high precision and recall provided that subject expressions are properly identified. Subject expression identification is a subclass of named entity recognition, which has been actively studied for a decade. We are planning to incorporate state-of-the-art techniques for named entity recognition to the overall opinion mining system we are new developing.

5 Conclusion

In this paper, we have proposed a machine learning-based method for the extraction of opinions on consumer products by reducing the problem to that of extracting attribute-value pairs from texts. We have pointed out the similarity between the tasks of anaphora resolution and opinion extraction, and have applied the machine learning-based anaphora resolution method to opinion extraction. The experimental results reported in this paper show that identifying the corresponding attribute for a given value expression is effective in both pairedness determination and opinionhood determination. As the future work, we will plan to extract opinions from weblog pages which include many descriptions which are not opinions.

These findings and further investigation for opinion extraction is quite useful for risk management of manufacturing consumer products by quickly collecting users' opinions that proliferate through the internet world.

References

1. Dave, K., Lawrence, S., Pennock, D.M.: Mining the peanut gallery: opinion extraction and semantic classification of product reviews. In: Proc. of the 12th International World Wide Web Conference. (2003) 519–528

2. Pang, B., Lee, L.: A sentiment education: Sentiment analysis using subjectivity summarization based on minimum cuts. In: Proc. of the 42nd Annual Meeting of the Association for Computational Linguistics. (2004) 271–278

3. Turney, P.D.: Thumbs up or thumbs down? semantic orientation applied to unsupervised classification of reviews. In: Proc. of the 40th Annual Meeting of the Association for Computational Linguistics. (2002) 417–424

4. Kanayama, H., Nasukawa, T.: Deeper sentiment analysis using machine translation technology. In: Proceedings of the 20th International Conference on Computational Linguistics. (2004) 494–500

5. Hu, M., Liu, B.: Mining and summarizing customer reviews. In: Proc. of the Tenth International Conference on Knowledge Discovery and Data Mining. (2004) 168–177

6. Tateishi, K., Ishiguro, Y., Fukushima, T.: Opinion information retrieval from the internet. In: IPSJ SIGNL Note 144-11. (2001) 75–82 (in Japanese).

7. Tateishi, K., Fukushima, T., Kobayashi, N., Takahashi, T., Fujita, A., Inui, K., Matsumoto, Y.: Web opinion extraction and summarization based on viewpoints of products. In: IPSJ SIGNL Note 163. (2004) 1–8 (in Japanese).

8. Murano, S., Sato, S.: Automatic extraction of subjective sentences using syntactic patterns. In: Proc. of the Ninth Annual Meeting of the Association for Natural Language Processing. (2003) 67–70 (in Japanese).

9. Mitkov, R.: Factors in anaphora resolution: they are not the only things that matter. a case study ba sed on two different approaches. In: Proc. of the ACL'97/EACL'97 Workshop on Operational Factors in Practical, Robust Anaph ora Resolution. (1997)

10. Baldwin, B.: CogNIAC: A Discourse Processing Engine. PhD thesis, Department of Computer and Information Sciences, University of Pennsylvania (1995)

11. Nakaiwa, H., Shirai, S.: Anaphora resolution of japanese zero pronouns with deictic reference. In: Proceedings of the 16th International Conference on Computational Linguistics (COLING). (1996) 812–817

12. Grosz, B.J., Joshi, A.K., Weinstein, S.: Centering: A framework for modeling the local coherence of discourse. Computational Linguistics 21 (1995) 203–226

13. Kameyama, M.: A property-sharing constraint in centering. In: Proceedings of the 24th Annual Meeting of the Association for Computational Linguistics. (1986) 200–206

14. Halliday, M.A.K., Hasan, R.: Cohesion in English. English Language Series, Title No.9. Longman (1976)

15. Soon, W.M., Ng, H.T., Lim, D.C.Y.: A machine learning approach to coreference resolution of noun phrases. Computational Linguistics 27 (2001) 521–544

16. Ng, V., Cardie, C.: Improving machine learning approaches to coreference resolution. In: Proceedings of the 40th Annual Meeting of the Association for Computational Linguistics (ACL). (2002a) 104–111

17. Iida, R., Inui, K., Takamura, H., Matsumoto, Y.: Incorporating contextual cues in trainable models for coreference resolution. In: Proc. of the EACL Workshop on the Computational Treatment of Anaphora. (2003) 23–30

18. Ng, V.: Learning noun phrase anaphoricity to improve coreference resolution: Issues in representation and optimization. In: Proc. of the 42nd Annual Meeting of the Association for Computational Linguistics. (2004) 152–159

19. Iida, R., Inui, K., Matsumoto, Y., Sekine, S.: Noun phrase coreference resolution in japanese base on most likely antecedant candidates. Journal of Information Processing Society of Japan 46 (2005) (in Japanese).

20. Kobayashi, N., Inui, K., Matsumoto, Y., Tateishi, K., Fukushima, T.: Collecting evaluative expressions for opinion extraction. In: Proc. of the 1st International Joint Conference on Natural Language Processing. (2004) 584–589

Author Index

Lecture Notes in Artificial Intelligence (LNAI)

Vol. 3817: M. Faundez-Zanuy, L. Janer, A. Esposito, A. Satue-Villar, J. Roure, V. Espinosa-Duro (Eds.), Nonlinear Analyses and Algorithms for Speech Processing. XII, 380 pages. 2006.

Vol. 3814: M. Maybury, O. Stock, W. Wahlster (Eds.), Intelligent Technologies for Interactive Entertainment. XV, 342 pages. 2005.

Vol. 3809: S. Zhang, R. Jarvis (Eds.), AI 2005: Advances in Artificial Intelligence. XXVII, 1344 pages. 2005.

Vol. 3808: C. Bento, A. Cardoso, G. Dias (Eds.), Progress in Artificial Intelligence. XVIII, 704 pages. 2005.

Vol. 3802: Y. Hao, J. Liu, Y.-P. Wang, Y.-m. Cheung, H. Yin, L. Jiao, J. Ma, Y.-C. Jiao (Eds.), Computational Intelligence and Security, Part II. XLII, 1166 pages. 2005.

Vol. 3801: Y. Hao, J. Liu, Y.-P. Wang, Y.-m. Cheung, H. Yin, L. Jiao, J. Ma, Y.-C. Jiao (Eds.), Computational Intelligence and Security, Part I. XLI, 1122 pages. 2005.

Vol. 3789: A. Gelbukh, Á. de Albornoz, H. Terashima-Marín (Eds.), MICAI 2005: Advances in Artificial Intelligence. XXVI, 1198 pages. 2005.

Vol. 3782: K.-D. Althoff, A. Dengel, R. Bergmann, M. Nick, T.R. Roth-Berghofer (Eds.), Professional Knowledge Management. XXIII, 739 pages. 2005.

Vol. 3763: H. Hong, D. Wang (Eds.), Automated Deduction in Geometry. X, 213 pages. 2006.

Vol. 3755: G.J. Williams, S.J. Simoff (Eds.), Data Mining. XI, 331 pages. 2006.

Vol. 3735: A. Hoffmann, H. Motoda, T. Scheffer (Eds.), Discovery Science. XVI, 400 pages. 2005.

Vol. 3734: S. Jain, H.U. Simon, E. Tomita (Eds.), Algorithmic Learning Theory. XII, 490 pages. 2005.

Vol. 3721: A.M. Jorge, L. Torgo, P.B. Brazdil, R. Camacho, J. Gama (Eds.), Knowledge Discovery in Databases: PKDD 2005. XXIII, 719 pages. 2005.

Vol. 3720: J. Gama, R. Camacho, P.B. Brazdil, A.M. Jorge, L. Torgo (Eds.), Machine Learning: ECML 2005. XXIII, 769 pages. 2005.

Vol. 3717: B. Gramlich (Ed.), Frontiers of Combining Systems. X, 321 pages. 2005.

Vol. 3702: B. Beckert (Ed.), Automated Reasoning with Analytic Tableaux and Related Methods. XIII, 343 pages. 2005.

Vol. 3698: U. Furbach (Ed.), KI 2005: Advances in Artificial Intelligence. XIII, 409 pages. 2005.

Vol. 3690: M. Pěchouček, P. Petta, L.Z. Varga (Eds.), Multi-Agent Systems and Applications IV. XVII, 667 pages. 2005.

Vol. 3684: R. Khosla, R.J. Howlett, L.C. Jain (Eds.), Knowledge-Based Intelligent Information and Engineering Systems, Part IV. LXXIX, 933 pages. 2005.

Vol. 3683: R. Khosla, R.J. Howlett, L.C. Jain (Eds.), Knowledge-Based Intelligent Information and Engineering Systems, Part III. LXXX, 1397 pages. 2005.

Vol. 3682: R. Khosla, R.J. Howlett, L.C. Jain (Eds.), Knowledge-Based Intelligent Information and Engineering Systems, Part II. LXXIX, 1371 pages. 2005.

Vol. 3681: R. Khosla, R.J. Howlett, L.C. Jain (Eds.), Knowledge-Based Intelligent Information and Engineering Systems, Part I. LXXX, 1319 pages. 2005.

Vol. 3673: S. Bandini, S. Manzoni (Eds.), AI*IA 2005: Advances in Artificial Intelligence. XIV, 614 pages. 2005.

Vol. 3662: C. Baral, G. Greco, N. Leone, G. Terracina (Eds.), Logic Programming and Nonmonotonic Reasoning. XIII, 454 pages. 2005.

Vol. 3661: T. Panayiotopoulos, J. Gratch, R. Aylett, D. Ballin, P. Olivier, T. Rist (Eds.), Intelligent Virtual Agents. XIII, 506 pages. 2005.

Vol. 3658: V. Matoušek, P. Mautner, T. Pavelka (Eds.), Text, Speech and Dialogue. XV, 460 pages. 2005.

Vol. 3651: R. Dale, K.-F. Wong, J. Su, O.Y. Kwong (Eds.), Natural Language Processing – IJCNLP 2005. XXI, 1031 pages. 2005.

Vol. 3642: D. Ślęzak, J. Yao, J.F. Peters, W. Ziarko, X. Hu (Eds.), Rough Sets, Fuzzy Sets, Data Mining, and Granular Computing, Part II. XXIII, 738 pages. 2005.

Vol. 3641: D. Ślęzak, G. Wang, M. Szczuka, I. Düntsch, Y. Yao (Eds.), Rough Sets, Fuzzy Sets, Data Mining, and Granular Computing, Part I. XXIV, 742 pages. 2005.

Vol. 3635: J.R. Winkler, M. Niranjan, N.D. Lawrence (Eds.), Deterministic and Statistical Methods in Machine Learning. VIII, 341 pages. 2005.

Vol. 3632: R. Nieuwenhuis (Ed.), Automated Deduction – CADE-20. XIII, 459 pages. 2005.

Vol. 3630: M.S. Capcarrère, A.A. Freitas, P.J. Bentley, C.G. Johnson, J. Timmis (Eds.), Advances in Artificial Life. XIX, 949 pages. 2005.

Vol. 3626: B. Ganter, G. Stumme, R. Wille (Eds.), Formal Concept Analysis. X, 349 pages. 2005.

Vol. 3625: S. Kramer, B. Pfahringer (Eds.), Inductive Logic Programming. XIII, 427 pages. 2005.

Vol. 3620: H. Muñoz-Ávila, F. Ricci (Eds.), Case-Based Reasoning Research and Development. XV, 654 pages. 2005.

Vol. 3614: L. Wang, Y. Jin (Eds.), Fuzzy Systems and Knowledge Discovery, Part II. XLI, 1314 pages. 2005.

Vol. 3613: L. Wang, Y. Jin (Eds.), Fuzzy Systems and Knowledge Discovery, Part I. XLI, 1334 pages. 2005.

Vol. 3607: J.-D. Zucker, L. Saitta (Eds.), Abstraction, Reformulation and Approximation. XII, 376 pages. 2005.

Vol. 3601: G. Moro, S. Bergamaschi, K. Aberer (Eds.), Agents and Peer-to-Peer Computing. XII, 245 pages. 2005.

Vol. 3600: F. Wiedijk (Ed.), The Seventeen Provers of the World. XVI, 159 pages. 2006.

Vol. 3596: F. Dau, M.-L. Mugnier, G. Stumme (Eds.), Conceptual Structures: Common Semantics for Sharing Knowledge. XI, 467 pages. 2005.

Vol. 3593: V. Mařík, R. W. Brennan, M. Pěchouček (Eds.), Holonic and Multi-Agent Systems for Manufacturing. XI, 269 pages. 2005.

Vol. 3587: P. Perner, A. Imiya (Eds.), Machine Learning and Data Mining in Pattern Recognition. XVII, 695 pages. 2005.